SELECTED LETTERS
OF
Edmund Burke

SELECTED LETTERS

OF

Edmund Burke

EDITED AND WITH AN INTRODUCTION

BY

HARVEY C. MANSFIELD JR.

THE UNIVERSITY OF CHICAGO PRESS
Chicago and London

HARVEY C. MANSFIELD, JR., is professor
of government at Harvard University and
the author of *Statesmanship and Party
Government: A Study of Burke
and Bolingbroke.*

The University of Chicago Press, Chicago 60637
The University of Chicago Press, Ltd., London

LIBRARY OF CONGRESS CATALOGING IN PUBLICATION DATA

Burke, Edmund, 1729?–1797.
  Selected letters of Edmund Burke.

  Selected from The correspondence of Edmund Burke,
published by University of Chicago Press and Cambridge
University Press, from 1958 to 1978.
  Includes index.
  1. Burke, Edmund, 1729?–1797.   2. Statesmen—Great
Britain—Correspondence.   I. Mansfield, Harvey Claflin,
1932–   .   II. Title.
DA506.B9A4   1984   941.07′3′0924   83-18138
ISBN 0-226-08068-4

CONTENTS

PREFACE

THIS SELECTION from Burke's correspondence is taken from *The Correspondence of Edmund Burke*, published in ten volumes from 1958 to 1978 by the University of Chicago Press and Cambridge University Press, under the general editorship of the late Thomas W. Copeland. The special editors of the individual volumes are distinguished historical scholars, and their collected labor is a monument to modern historical scholarship. Many new letters of Burke were found; all were dated; all were properly introduced; every allusion was identified and footnoted; and many other sources were cited to confirm or to question Burke's assertions and speculations. The result is a production marvelous in detail and imposing as a whole, as if it were intended to reveal to every reader what could have been known only to an omniscient witness.

In selecting from the letters which these editors published entire, I condensed their comment and annotation and in a few instances added comment of my own. In place of their narrative history following on the flow of Burke's private pen, I have organized my selection around the grand themes of Burke's life. The result is a thematic Burke given to deliberation, reflection, and argument, rather than a contextual Burke known mainly for his whereabouts and his acquaintances. Which of the two views is closer to the true Burke cannot be decided here, but any reader who desires the full annotation of the letters selected for this volume must look in the original edition. For the notes in this volume I am indebted to the scholarship of the original editors; my labor has consisted only in erasing or appropriating theirs.

I would like to thank my research assistant, Miss J. Potts of Cleveland, Ohio, and the staff of the National Humanities Center in Research Triangle Park, North Carolina, for the help they graciously provided.

SHORT TITLES

Corr. (1958)
  The Correspondence of Edmund Burke. Edited by Thomas W. Cope-
  land. 10 vols. Chicago: University of Chicago Press; and London:
  Cambridge University Press, 1958–78.

Works (Bohn)
  The Works of Edmund Burke. 8 vols. Bohn's British Classics. London: Bohn, 1854–89.

Works (Little, Brown)
  The Works of Edmund Burke. 12 vols. Rev. ed. Boston: Little, Brown,
  1865–67.

Writings and Speeches
  The Writings and Speeches of Edmund Burke. Edited by Paul Lang-
  ford. 2 vols. to date. Oxford: Clarendon Press, 1981.

INTRODUCTION

BURKE'S THEORY OF POLITICAL PRACTICE

To INTRODUCE A selection of Burke's correspondence may seem the wrong task for the survey of his political philosophy which I propose here. Although some of his letters were written for publication, most are private; and in a private correspondence, behind the scenes, first names and small events necessarily fill our view and take precedence over the grand themes of Burke's speeches, pamphlets, and books. We tend to think that, in securing a view of the private Burke, we are getting a glimpse of the real Burke, with whom we share universal, but petty, concerns for near troubles and close kin. But Burke was a remarkable man, and while we have our eye on him backstage, we see him with his eye on the play of public issues even when his own concerns clamored to distract him. He was always busy, and his letters are not the profusions of a gossip, remarks of a wry observer, or effusions of a tormented soul, but the letters of a busy man. The Duke of Richmond once suggested, when a portrait of Burke was in question, that he be painted at work, busy "doing something."[1]

Yet, absorbed as he was, Burke looked at public issues with almost matchless penetration. Among observers of modern politics—a field which excludes no modern adult—only Tocqueville and perhaps Churchill are his rivals in seeing the meaning of events. Like Tocqueville and unlike Churchill, Burke did not enjoy the ruling view that an office of command affords. His highest office was Paymaster-General, a dignified secretaryship that was lacking in glory. Though the

[1] *Corr.* (1958), II, 238.

1

ablest in his party, prominent in debate, and influential to the point of being indispensable in the management of affairs, he never sought and was never trusted with leadership. He was indeed distrusted by the leading statesmen of his time for the very energy he used in their behalf, for his eagerness to act against dangers of which only he could see and feel the full measure, and for the passion displayed in the gorgeous rhetoric they admired. "Much to admire, and nothing to agree with,"[2] was Pitt's famous summary judgment on Burke's longer persuasions for counterrevolution against the French Revolution. And when, in 1788, it looked as though Burke's party might regain office during a regency for George III who had gone mad, Charles Fox and his confidants omitted him from a list of leading office holders: he was too heated in counsel, too passionate in his prosecution of Warren Hastings, to seem responsible to them.

In our day historians, particularly those influenced by that master of minute investigation, Sir Lewis Namier, have taken up this distrust and faulted Burke rather than his contemporaries for it. They find him pretentious, his behavior extreme, and his words exaggerated. If Burke once spoke of foolishness in the individual, wisdom in the species, they consider Burke foolish in his own time, wise only for eternity, if then. For to see deep into the roots of events, into the "cause of the present discontents," cannot but seem a sort of inflation as daily occurrences are put in a trend and seen as effects. Burke's attempts to invest the mundane with significance seem to make it lose its character as mundane, and while historians may find his eloquence thrilling, they also fear it and distrust him. Even his prescient understanding of the character, importance, and future of the French Revolution is obscured by the extreme partisanship to which his understanding compelled him. He loses credit for his foresight because he acted on it.

Yet Burke was a remarkable man because he was a remarkable thinker. One cannot confine his merit to his rhetoric and sum up his accomplishments as literary, while putting aside the substance of his thought as controversial or embarrassing. His words do not ring hollow; his flights of imagination are not empty abstractions. His marvelous literary skills do not excuse us from taking him seriously, which requires taking his thought seriously as political philosophy. Although he never wrote a treatise of political philosophy, there is ample reason for his having omitted to do this in his political philosophy itself.

[2] *Corr.* (1958), VIII, 335n.

Burke's thought in a treatise would have lost the essence of his thought, and his style was suited to its substance. Thus, we cannot read Burke's correspondence without being constantly reminded that the private Burke lives for the public stage, that the public Burke is the real Burke. But we would not know of Burke if it were not for his speeches and writings, and we would not know them if the substance of his thought were bombast. The most affecting event of Burke's private life was the death of his son Richard in 1794, three years before he himself died. His feeling, however, cannot be adequately described as a father's grief. One cannot appreciate his hopes for his son without knowing what he thought of England's great political families and how they were related, politically and constitutionally, to men of great abilities like himself, who might hope to found a great family.[3] As a rule, philosophers do not make good fathers, do not, as it were, have children: Burke was the only philosopher, as philosopher, to have a (legitimate) son, and his son died before him.

If the reader will grant a hearing for Burke's political philosophy, or for its possibility, then how does he come to grips with it? Burke is known today as the philosopher of "conservatism." But he has not yet shared much in the revival of American conservatism in the 1980s. Of the two schools of thought that have been identified in that revival, traditionalism and libertarianism, Burke is very much with the former. Although he favored the freeing of commerce wherever possible, contributed his *Thoughts and Details on Scarcity* (1795) to the new school of political economy, and was an admiring friend of Adam Smith, he so opposed unhampered individual freedom, theoretical systems of self-interest, and the influence of new property that he surrounded and enveloped the abstract free economy of political economists with the traditions of the British constitution. But of course these traditions—"establishments," Burke called them—are far from the provisions of the American constitution, and even farther, as we shall see, from the planned character of the American constitution. Such are the obstacles to Burke's influence in American politics today. A generation ago, however, Burke was discovered for American conservatism as the proponent of a theory of natural law. Hoffman and Levack's *Burke's Politics* (1949), Kirk's *The Conservative Mind* (1953), and Stanlis's *Edmund Burke and the Natural Law* (1958) brought him forward to oppose the irreligion and relativism of liberals and to provide conservatives with a theory that conceded the political advantage or ne-

[3] *Works*, II, 102; v, 135.

cessity of religion and the bearing of circumstances on morality, but
that nonetheless affirmed natural law, the will of God, as authoritative
for men.[4] Burke's frequent references to natural law, previously ig-
nored or dismissed as rhetorical, were gathered together by these
writers in a system that could be described as Thómism conservatively
modernized.

Whatever one may think of the success of this system—at the least
it was a public service to rescue Burke from the disgrace of being
mistaken for a utilitarian—it is striking that Burke was made the
purveyor of a *theory* necessary to healthy politics. If there is one re-
current theme in Burke's letters, speeches, and writings, it is his
emphasis on the moral and political evils that follow upon the intrusion
of theory into political practice. It is theory as such that he rejects;
his emphasis on the evils of intrusive theory is not balanced by a
compensating reliance on sound theory that men would need as a
guide to their politics. Sound theory, to him, would seem to be self-
denying theory. Although Burke may occasionally refer to "the pretended philosophers of the hour,"[5] thus implying the existence of
another sort, he is usually content to denounce philosophers, metaphysicians, and speculators as such without making a point of what
might seem to be the vital distinction among them. In a famous passage
in *A Letter to a Member of the National Assembly* (1791), he attacks
Rousseau—"the philosopher of vanity," "a lover of his kind but a
hater of his kindred"[6]—in terms no philosopher had flung publicly at
another, until a decline of decorum in this matter occurred in the
nineteenth century. In that place Burke distinguishes "modern philosophers," which expresses "everything that is ignoble, savage and
hard-hearted," from "the writers of sound antiquity" whom Englishmen continue to read more generally, he believes, than is now done
"on the continent." But Burke does not propose that ancient authors
be adopted, even remotely, as guides to show the way out of the crisis
into which modern philosophers have brought all mankind. Reading
them is not so much the cause as the effect of English good taste,
something that is sadly lacking "on the continent."[7] Considering Burke's

---

[4] Ross J. S. Hoffman and Paul Levack, eds., *Burke's Politics* (New York: Knopf, 1949);
Russell Kirk, *The Conservative Mind* (Chicago: Regnery, 1953); and Peter J. Stanlis, *Edmund
Burke and the Natural Law* (Ann Arbor: University of Michigan Press, 1958). On the sidelines,
sometimes seeming to nod with approval, were Leo Strauss, *Natural Right and History* (Chicago:
University of Chicago Press, 1953), pp. 294–323 on Burke; and Francis P. Canavan, *The Political
Reason of Edmund Burke* (Durham, N.C.: Duke University Press, 1960).

[5] *Works*, II, 430.

[6] *Works*, II, 535–41.

[7] See also *Works*, I, 501; and *Corr.* (1958) V, 337.

hostility to the intrusion of philosophy in politics, yet recalling too that Burke does not merely despair at the growing influence of philosophy, the problem of his political philosophy would seem to be to design a theory that never intrudes into practice. Our question in assessing it is: can theory serve solely as a watchdog against theory and never be needed as a guide?

The harms done by theory to sound practice had been under Burke's eye from the first. His first publication, *A Vindication of Natural Society* (1756), was a satire showing the absurd political consequences of Bolingbroke's theory, and in the early pamphlets on party, *Observations on a Late Publication Intituled 'The Present State of the Nation'* (1769) and *Thoughts on the Cause of the Present Discontents* (1770), he argued against the factious effects of a theoretical preference for "men of ability and virtue" over parties composed of gentlemen acting together publicly in mutual trust. In his speeches opposing British policy in America, he attacked the government's insistence on the rights of taxation and sovereignty without regard to consequence or circumstance as a speculative, legalistic reliance on "the virtue of paper government." For lawyers with their concern for rights and forms do not have regard to the actual exercise of formalities, substitute legal correctness for prudent policy, and seek to generalize in the manner of law—which is also that of theory.[8] In a speech given in 1785, Burke was already denouncing "the speculatists of our speculating age."[9] But it was in the French Revolution that the evils of speculation in politics became visible in their full extent and as a whole. Burke was surprised by the outbreak of that revolution, but he had been prepared by every major concern of his previous career in politics to identify it as a philosophical revolution, the first "*complete* revolution," a "revolution in sentiments, manners and moral opinions" that reached "even to the constitution of the human mind."[10] The French Revolution displayed and summed up all the evils of speculative politics.

These evils, as Burke sees them, may be quickly summarized.[11] First, the French revolutionaries went to the extreme of destroying the old regime and of defeating every moderate reform short of destruction because, as theorists (or inspired by theorists), they based their reasoning on the extreme case. The universality of their theory of revolution was achieved by generalizing from the extreme case when

[8] *Works*, I, 431, 453, 476; II, 7.
[9] *Works*, III, 139.
[10] *Works*, II, 352; III, 350; V, 76, 111.
[11] The following is based on Leo Strauss, *Natural Right and History*, pp. 299–311. .

revolution might be unavoidable. In the course of generalization, limited actions undertaken with great circumspection and compunction in the extreme case are transformed into wanton, irresponsible destructiveness in the universal case. The vaunted humanity of the revolutionaries is similarly affected. From concern for improving particular human beings, it is diluted to a humanitarian profession on behalf of the French people and of mankind which requires a ruthless sacrifice of natural affections. Since in the extreme case one may or must be selfish, no universal argument either for self-restraint or for helping others can be sustained, and loose morals are seen to accompany hard hearts. This humanitarianism forces men down to the level of bestiality, all the while perversely claiming to free them and even to ennoble them.

Second, theorists wrongly suppose that politics is predictable. Having stated the ends of government in universal terms, they believe that the means to these ends can be put in rules equally universal, unless they put aside the question of means altogether. But means are determined by circumstances, which are "infinite and infinitely combined . . . variable, and transient." Anyone who does not take them into consideration is "metaphysically mad."[12] Circumstances, in turn, are determined by chance, and chance always brings new situations.[13] Since universal ends are always refracted through new, unpredictable circumstances, Burke concludes: "Nothing universal can be rationally affirmed on any moral or political subject."[14]

Third, theory is simple; for the extreme and the universal case with which it is concerned is also the simple case, uncomplicated by accidents and confusions. But practice, especially political practice, is complex. It is faced with rival claims of simple justice, which it must compromise, and with claims of exceptions, which it must accommodate. And while theory is simple, it is at the same time refined. It goes beyond common experience in its attempt to exclude everything accidental. But common people cannot see beyond common experience and will distrust those who explore "the labyrinths of political theory";[15] refined policies that depend on their cooperation will fail as a result of their confusion. Theoretical men, in addition, are as such detached from whatever is their own; if they turn to themselves, it is only to their own "case," which is merely one case among others.

[12] *Works*, V, 114.
[13] *Works*, I, 312, 365; V, 153–54, 257.
[14] *Works*, III, 16.
[15] *Works*, III, 106.

That is why speculation in the theoretical sense is connected to speculation in the sense of gambling; theoretical speculation is unconscious
gambling with one's own stake.[16] But practical men are as such attached to whatever is their own; their loyalty is presupposed by their
responsibility. They cannot act without being partial to a group they
have not chosen and cannot choose; all their choosing is in a context
imposed on them by circumstance or providence. "No man examines
into the defects of his title to his paternal estate, or to his established
government."[17] The neutrality of speculators is, in political effect,
therefore, a desire to have everything their own way, regardless of the
needs of those in their own family or country who might depend on
them.

Next, theoretical questions are timeless and reversible; practical
questions are for decision here and now and cannot be reversed. Political men are bound by dangers that are imminent, that do not permit
"a long discourse, belonging to the leisure of a contemplative man."[18]
Last, the activity of speculators is essentially private, unconcerned
with or critical of common opinion; but politics rests on opinion and
must respect it. If opinion be called prejudice or superstition, Burke
does not hesitate to defend it. Prejudice contains "latent wisdom"
which is "of ready application in the emergency"; superstition must
be tolerated, "else you will deprive weak minds of a resource found
necessary to the strongest."[19]

In developing the evils of speculative or metaphysical politics, Burke
does not trouble to discriminate good speculation from bad, or to
make that difference unmistakable to his readers. He seems to mix
together the faults of the theory on which the French Revolution was
based, the theory of the rights of man set forth by Hobbes, Locke,
and Rousseau, with the necessary defects of all theory, of which previous theorists might have been aware. Burke mentions Aristotle's
objections to geometrical morality, and several times calls Aristotle to
his aid;[20] but he does not use Aristotle's fundamental investigations
into the nature of theory and practice. Except for the attack on Rousseau that we have mentioned, he does not consider the theoretical
sources of the doctrine of the rights of man; and even his attack on
Rousseau was not a theoretical consideration but expressly confined

[16] *Works*, II, 463.
[17] *Works*, II, 26, 428.
[18] *Works*, I, 323; II, 552.
[19] *Works*, II, 359, 429–30.
[20] *Works*, I, 501; see also II, 396, 454–55; V, 342; VI, 251; *Corr.* (1958), IV, 36.

to the use of Rousseau's theories by the French revolutionaries.[21] In sum, he does not offer a theoretical clarification and reconstruction which would meet the revolutionaries on their own ground. Instead, he attempts to stand on the ground and stay within the realm of political practice, insofar as possible. His writings proposing action are much richer in political wisdom—hence seemingly more "theoretical"—than those of ordinary statesmen even when reminiscing, yet they are also much more circumscribed and circumstantial than treatises which are intended to interest theorists: thus, fullsome for historians, meager for philosophers. He once said: "The operation of dangerous and delusive first principles obliges us to have recourse to the true ones"[22]—thereby admitting the necessity of such recourse, by constrast to ordinary statesmen, and declaring his reluctance, against the habit of theorists.

Yet the first principles to which Burke has recourse do not appear to be first principles. Instead of providing theoretical clarification, he asserts that direction of human affairs belongs to prudence; and instead of establishing what might be the best or legitimate state, he celebrates the genius of the British constitution. Burke's political philosophy emerges from the elaboration of these two things, prudence and the British constitution. They may not be the first, grounding principles, but they are surely the principles Burke puts forward to claim our attention before all others.

Prudence, Burke says, is "the god of this lower world," since it has "the entire dominion over every exercise of power committed into its hands."[23] Prudence is "the first of all the virtues, as well as the supreme director of them all."[24] This means, in particular, that "practical wisdom" justly supersedes "theoretic science" whenever the two come into contention.[25] The reason for the sovereignty of prudence is in the power of circumstances to alter every regularity and principle. "Circumstances (which with some gentlemen pass for nothing) give in reality to every political principle its distinguishing color and discriminating effect."[26] Burke emphasizes that the prudence he speaks of is a "moral prudence" or a "public and enlarged prudence" as opposed to selfish prudence, not to mention cleverness or cunning.[27] But he

---

[21] *Works*, II, 541.
[22] *Works*, V, 213.
[23] *Works*, II, 28.
[24] *Works*, VII, 161; see III, 16.
[25] *Works*, II, 306.
[26] *Works*, II, 282; see I, 497.
[27] *Works*, II, 29, 56; V, 218.

does not say how to be sure of the morality of prudence. If prudence is supreme, it must reign over morality; but if prudence can be either moral or selfish, it would seem to require the tutelage of morality. Aristotle, when facing this problem, was led to understand prudence as the comprehensive legislative art, and then to subordinate that to theory. Burke makes a different disposition. Instead of pursuing an inquiry into the first principles or ends of prudence, which necessarily leads beyond prudence, he distinguishes within prudence between "rules of prudence" available to ordinary statesmen and "prudence of a higher order."[28] Rules of prudence are not mathematical, universal, or ideal; but they are nonetheless rules, Burke says grandly, "formed upon the known march of the ordinary providence of God," that is, visible in human experience. But as these rules are sovereign over all theoretical rights or metaphysical first principles, so higher prudence, the prudence of prudence, can suspend the rules of prudence when necessary.[29]

This distinction within prudence, by which Burke attempts to secure the morality of prudence without subverting its sovereignty, corresponds to a distinction he draws between presumptive virtue and actual virtue: "There is no qualification for government but virtue and wisdom, actual or presumptive."[30] Presumptive virtue and wisdom are the lesser, probable virtue that can be presumed in well-bred gentlemen of prominent families born into situations of eminence where they are habituated to self-respect; to the "censorial inspection of the public eye"; to taking a "large view of the wide-spread and infinitely diversified combinations of men and affairs in a large society"; to having leisure to reflect; to meeting the wise and learned as well as rich traders; to military command; to the caution of an instructor of one's fellow citizens thus acting as a "reconciler between God and man"; and to being employed as an administrator of law and justice.[31] Actual virtue, such as Burke's own perhaps, is higher but more dubious; it must intervene when the rules of prudence fail, but it must not rule ordinarily lest society fall victim to the instability of men of ability. The idea of presumptive virtue presumes ability, not the highest but ordinarily sufficient, in men of property; at the same time it presumes at least instability, and sometimes immorality, in those who have nothing but ability, and rather than being born and

[28] *Works*, II, 284; III, 16; V, 236.
[29] *Works*, III, 81.
[30] *Works*, II, 323.
[31] *Works*, III, 85–86.

bred in an elevated condition they must rise to eminence by means
that may not be moral and should not be exemplary. No country can
reject the service of those with actual virtue, but "the road to eminence
and power, from obscure condition, ought not to be made too easy."[32]
When that road is made too easy, too many follow it, and men of
actual virtue are encouraged to display their ability rather than their
virtue, and are crowded out by new men who have cleverness and
little property, as happened in the French Revolution. Actual virtue
therefore must be kept subordinate ordinarily to presumptive virtue,
while being allowed, after due probation, the right of intervention in
an emergency, such as the French Revolution, when men of presumptive virtue are confronted with an event so astonishing that they do
not know how to react.

Thus Burke solves the problem of prudence within prudence: he
keeps moral prudence distinct from mere cleverness, yet maintains its
sovereignty over clever theorists except for occasional interventions
by higher prudence. But to sustain this solution, the presumptions of
presumptive virtue must of course hold true. They are "legitimate
presumptions, which, taken as generalities, must be admitted for actual truths."[33] But this is not enough: actual truth must be behind
what is admitted for actual truth. These presumptions are shown to
be sound in Burke's admiring, not to say worshipful, analysis of the
British constitution. The British constitution guarantees both the sovereignty and morality of prudence by sustaining the presumptions
necessary to ward off or subordinate the claims of higher virtue. The
theory of that constitution, or *in* it, is the theory that enables prudence
to remain sovereign over theory.

Burke was not the first to laugh at modern philosophers. He himself
refers to "the learned academicians of Laputa and Balnibarbi" in the
pages of Swift's *Gulliver's Travels*.[34] But when Swift had made fun of
political projectors whose inventions smack of the same inappropriate
extension of theory into practice that Burke described, Swift then did
not turn to vaunting the beauties of the British constitution. On the
contrary, he carried his satire to that hallowed ground. Of modern
political philosophers, Montesquieu is most obviously Burke's inspi-
ration in praise of the British constitution as the model of liberty
(Montesquieu's admiration of that constitution is apostrophized by
Burke in a closing passage of *An Appeal from the New to the Old Whigs*,

[32] *Works*, II, 323.
[33] *Works*, III, 86.
[34] *Works*, II, 404.

1791).[35] But Montesquieu was not so hostile to theory as Burke was, and he believed that prudence would need guidance from theory to escape from the mistaken simplicity of modern sovereignty, the inhuman ambition of religion, and the allure of ancient virtue.

Tocqueville shared Burke's opinion of the influence of theorists in the French Revolution, but the two diverge in a manner that will help introduce Burke's thoughts on the British Constitution. Tocqueville's theme, in regard to the French Revolution, was democracy; and he showed how the influence of literary men and *philosophes* fed the passion for equality that characterized the Revolution. Burke's theme was the intrusion of metaphysicians, one consequence of which was a democratic leveling that "perverts the natural order of things."[36] Yet, whereas Burke could not believe that democracy was in accord with nature and hence must be traced to a perversion by theorists, Tocqueville believed that democratic claims were at least partly natural to men, hence always available to be endorsed by theorists. This difference appears in utterly contrary judgments of the French constitution-makers of 1789: Burke calls the "constitution-mongers of 1789 . . . the wickedest and most foolish of men," and condemns them for trying vainly to make a constitution wholly anew; Tocqueville praises them for this very attempt, despite their failure.[37]

Making a constitution or founding a society was for classical political science, and, even more, for such modern thinkers as Machiavelli, Bacon, Hobbes, and Locke, the crux of politics where theory and practice met. At that point prudence, sovereign over practice, cannot be satisfied with temporary shifts and arrangements, and must extend itself to legislation embodying fundamental, comprehensive choices. Such legislation, in turn, must be guided by an art, ultimately by a theory, that elaborates the model for choice, which is the best, most choiceworthy regime. When prudence becomes comprehensive and makes its determinations for good—both for the best and permanently—then it must cooperate with theory and perhaps even subordinate itself. It is the ruling characteristic of Burke's political philosophy as well as the guiding theme of his politics to avoid the

[35] *Works*, III, 113.

[36] *Works*, II, 322.

[37] *Works*, V, 317. Alexis de Tocqueville, *L'Ancien Régime et la révolution*, ed. J. P. Mayer, 2 vols. (Paris: Gallimard, 1952), I, 72, 88, 193–201, 247; see Pierre Manent, *Tocqueville et la nature de la démocratie* (Paris: Julliard, 1982), p. 173. Tocqueville's somewhat unfair criticisms of Burke—that he did not foresee the power that would be released by the Frnech Revolution and did not appreciate that the ancient common law was being abolished (*L'Ancien Régime*, I, 80, 96)—can be traced to this difference of outlook.

ground on which theory and practice converge. Founding, which prior to Burke had been considered by all political thinkers to be the essential political act, is for him a nonevent. The making of a constitution can never be "the effect of a single instantaneous regulation."[38] It cannot happen, and it is wrong to try to make it happen.

In complete disagreement with Tocqueville, Burke does not consider that democracy is a possible regime. The people cannot rule; they are the passive element in contrast to the "active men in the state." Though the people may be led by a vicious oligarchy of some kind, it should be led by a "true natural aristocracy," by ministers who "are not only our natural rulers, but our natural guides."[39] Thus, for Burke, one cannot choose between democracy and aristocracy, nor can there be a democratic or an aristocratic age, as for Tocqueville; nature has made the many incapable of governing themselves. "A perfect democracy is . . . the most shameless thing in the world,"[40] because each person's share of responsibility is so small that he does not feel it, and because public opinion which should restrain government is in the case of democracy nothing but the people's self-approbation. Responsible government is capable of shame, perhaps more than anything else; it is defending what one has had to do rather than taking credit for what one has chosen to do. No aristocracy, any more than a democracy, can rule long or well without the sense of a power above it; the lack of this sense is what makes democracy impossible as well as shameless. Only in an attenuated sense, therefore, is any human government, even a true natural aristocracy, a kind of self-government. Government is so far from a matter of choice, of choosing a form of rule, that it is a "power out of ourselves."[41]

Fundamentally, government is not ruling; it is changing, reforming, balancing, or adjusting. Government is not nourished, as Aristotle thought, by claims to rule asserted by democrats and oligarchs in defense (and exaggeration) of their equality and inequality to others. The people do not claim to rule of their own accord; only when inflamed by a few do they believe they want to rule. And aristocrats, however natural, are bred to their eminence, which they accept rather than demand.

As far as Burke is from the Aristotelian sense of rule—government by human choice, art, and political science—he does not rush into

---

[38] *Works*, II, 554.
[39] *Works*, III, 85; V, 227.
[40] *Works*, II, 365.
[41] *Works*, II, 333.

theocracy and grasp at divine right in order to keep governments under control by shame. To make it certain that government has a human origin, Burke adopts the language of contract from modern theorists. But since government by contract might seem calculated, if not chosen, for convenience—in effect, a matter of arbitrary will or pleasure, not of judgment— he stresses the great differences between ordinary contracts "taken up for a little temporary interest" and the social contract that establishes the state. The latter contract is a "partnership in all science; a partnership in all art; a partnership in every virtue, and in all perfection."[42] And it is a contract made between the living, the dead, and those to be born—that is, a contract not in the power of the present generation but in trust for the past and the future. The past and the future, one could say, substitute for divine law to ensure that present governments govern with a sense of shame. This does not mean, again, that present governments assume responsibility for ruling on principles established by their founders. The dead are not founders; they are silent partners who have had their say and now make their point by unspoken reproach.[43] Thus, for Burke, the rights of man do not include the right to rule.[44] The right to rule would be the right to alter rule, that is, at pleasure; but the right to alter rule at pleasure is destructive of rule. Rulers must accept limitations to their rule, yet without submitting themselves to superhuman rule. To do this, they must, for the sake of future generations, accept the authority of the past without submitting to the rule of founders. The only way to do this, Burke saw, was to attenuate the meaning of rule and make the present generation equal to the past, as is necessary to a contract. He praises the British constitution to the skies, but never its founders. The old Whigs, to whom he appeals against new Whigs favorable to the French Revolution, set a good example but did not lay down principles that new Whigs must follow.[45] They made a revolution in 1688 only from dire necessity arising from unique circumstances;[46] so their conduct (Burke ignores the theory of John Locke which might interpret their conduct) does not imply, much less express, a principle of revolution available for use a century later. For Burke the essence of morality is self-restraint, not choice: "Much the strongest moral obligations are such as were never the results of our

[42] *Works*, II, 368.
[43] *Works*, II, 177–78; VI, 21.
[44] *Works*, II, 332.
[45] *Works*, III, 54–66; see I, 375; II, 293; VI, 153; *Corr.* (1958), II, 283–86.
[46] *Works*, II, 292, 299; see Harvey C. Mansfield, Jr., *The Spirit of Liberalism* (Cambridge, Mass.: Harvard University Press, 1978), pp. 82–84.

option."[47] That is why morality must be understood as it is in a contract, which cannot be broken without the consent of all parties, rather than in a founding or a revolution, where the principles of choice come to light.

The founding of a constitution relies on its form. The form of a constitution must be capable of prevailing over its material and circumstances, which are bound to change over time, by embodying the end peculiar to the constitution and making that end visible to its citizens or subjects. Hence in classical political science one sometimes sees actual governments classified by their form and imaginary governments fashioned by the improvement of the forms of actual governments, to the point where political science almost forgets the varied material of politics. For Burke, however, "the circumstances and habits of every country . . . decide upon the form of its government."[48] When circumstances change, forms change. "A state without the means of some change is without the means of its conservation."[49] Not a fixed form but precisely the contrary, "a principle of growth," preserves states. Constitutional forms are superseded by timely reforms, made in cool blood after the people feel a grievance but before they become aroused; and if such reforms are to be temperate, they must be left incomplete. "Whenever we improve, it is right to leave room for further improvement."[50] Thus even the best constitution has a principle of growth; this is its only "ruling principle . . . a power like that which some of the philosophers have called a plastic nature."[51] Although Burke has praise for Britain's ancient constitution, he thinks it "visionary" to suppose that its ancient form could have been the same as that enjoyed today;[52] the constitution is ancient today insofar as it has lasted by constant adjustment, not because its forms remain as they were in ancient times.

Accordingly, Burke maintains that "manners are of more importance than laws."[53] Laws, which are formal decisions by governments because they have been made in accordance with its forms, depend on informal manners rather than the reverse. "In all forms of government," therefore, "the people is the true legislator" since the people makes its manners. "The people are the masters"; we statesmen,

[47] *Works*, III, 76–78.
[48] *Works*, III, 36; see II, 313.
[49] *Works*, II, 295.
[50] *Works*, II, 65.
[51] *Works*, II, 440; see George Berkeley, *Alciphron*, III, 14.
[52] *Works*, VI, 294.
[53] *Works*, V, 208.

Burke says, "shape their desires into perfect form."[54] Since the people is the true legislator, not some part of the people promoting and imposing its own end, the best constitution has neither a single end nor a hierarchy of ends but the "greatest variety of ends."[55] To secure our natural rights is the "great and ultimate purpose of civil society"; therefore, "all forms whatsoever of government are only good as they are subservient to that purpose to which they are entirely subordinate."[56] *The* purpose of civil society is to secure the natural rights which we exercise diversely in the "greatest variety of ends." As the best constitution is defined by rights variously exercised, it cannot be found in the "rich treasury of the fertile framers of imaginary commonwealths";[57] it is here and now, the British constitution. The British constitution is not perfect (for example, it is not made for offensive warfare as is required against the French revolutionary state),[58] but if it were perfect it would not have a principle of growth and then would not be best.

Since the British constitution does not have a lasting form, the order it establishes is not visible in its form, as was the order of the classical regime according to Aristotle.[59] The British constitution, then, does not have a *kind* of order (democratic or oligarchic) corresponding to one of the several forms of constitutions; rather, it has order that is of no particular kind because its parts have variety and diversity. The parts represent interests that combine or oppose one another in "that action and counteraction, which, in the natural and in the political world, from the reciprocal struggle of discordant powers, draws out the harmony of the universe."[60] Discordance does not produce social contradiction, in that strange Marxist expression so familiar to us today which holds society to the standards of logic, but it yields a harmony that owes much more to the experience of living together in liberty than to thinking alike or holding certain common parinciples.[61] Such an order is complicated; indeed, one might say that it consists in complication, in never directly affirming or denying any claim of justice that would require a particular ordering of society. These claims must be compromised, but not by finding a principle that preserves

---

[54] *Works*, II, 121–22; VI, 20.
[55] *Works*, V, 254.
[56] *Works*, VI, 29.
[57] *Works*, I, 489.
[58] *Works*, V, 423–25.
[59] Aristotle, *Politics*, III, 1274b38–39, 1276b5–6.
[60] *Works*, II, 308–9; see III, 25.
[61] *Works*, II, 554.

what is true in each claim, as in the classical mixed regime. A safer, truer compromise will result from deflecting claims of right to matters of convenience, so that "the whole organization of government becomes a consideration of convenience."[62] A statement like this one certainly smacks of utilitarianism, and insofar as Burke gives priority to what is convenient in the sense of actual, useful, and effectual over what is formally correct, he may be said to have inspired "utilitarianism," a nineteenth-century doctrine that narrowed Burke's notion of convenience, and exploited it to attack the British constitution he held dear and the rule of gentlemen he thought necessary. In keeping with the growth of constitutions, "convenience" to Burke does not refer to what is truly or naturally suitable, but rather, with typical British understatement, it means "not inconvenient." Thus, the whole organization of government which must be described as "a consideration of convenience" can also be said to "balance inconveniences."[63]

Burke adopts the Machiavellian notion that every human good has its accompanying inconvenience and that, consequently, all human things are in motion,[64] but he does not agree that this motion need be violent and he does not accept the calculation of convenience that Machiavelli, and utilitarians, recommend. Although constitutions must grow, they are kept from mere fluidity and from violent change by their establishments. The "establishments" of the British constitution do the work, in Burke's thought, of the constitutional forms and formalities of which he thinks so little. They supply stability and security, slowing and directing the flow of passions and ideas while gradually establishing themselves in this task; like our "institution," establishment is a verbal noun whose substance is gathered from its process. Like the familiar use of "the Establishment" today, Burke's establishments refer to informal social classes, but they differ by being plural and in the public eye. Burke's establishments are not a conspiracy united to diminish and reduce to nothing the formal rights of a people; rather, they are the social prominences that result from the actual, necessarily unequal exercise of those rights: the Church, the monied interest, the landed nobility, the military, even the monarchy.[65] These institutions are so far from subverting liberty that they are the only means for securing it. Burke contrasts the growth of establishments in Britain over centuries, a work not of mindless adjustment

---

[62] *Works*, II, 333; see III, 109; VI, 22.
[63] *Works*, I, 500.
[64] Machiavelli, *Discourses on Livy*, I, 6.
[65] *Works*, II, 106, 363, 434.

but one that "requires the aid of more minds than one age can furnish," in which "mind must [benignly] conspire with mind," to the hasty legislators of the French Revolution, who begin their work with science, demolishing the old establishments and reducing the French people to "one homogeneous mass,"[66] and end with sheer force, replacing the old establishments with new republics, delineated mathematically, which promise anarchy but are held together in fact by speculation on confiscated wealth, by the power of Paris, and by the army. Whereas establishments keep the British constitution steady and balanced, with an "excellence in composition" that makes a "consistent whole"[67] of the varied interests of a free society because it does not impose a plan, the cementing principles of the French Republic are instruments and evidence of tyranny, because they cannot unite without revealing a bias. Burke quotes Montesquieu's praise of the "great legislators of antiquity," who knew better than to deal with men as abstract, metaphysical entities,[68] but he does not infer from the legislator's need to consult the actual human material, as did Plato and Aristotle, that no actual constitution can be a "consistent whole," that all must be partisan.

The constitution made steady by establishments is maintained by the principle of property, that is, of inherited property. Each of the establishments is a property, and Burke makes it clear, even in the example of the Church, whose high purpose is to consecrate the commonwealth and to elevate men's wills above selfishness, that the attack of the French revolutionaries was a usurpation of property.[69] Such property in social eminence survives and grows not by the reason that justified its original acquisition but by the benefits that can be seen in its present working—benefits often discernible only by the eye of wisdom and experience, since appearances are deceiving and the forms of free government are compatible with the ends of arbitrary government, and vice versa.[70] Therefore we must "venerate where we are not able presently to comprehend";[71] we must regard the constitution as an inheritance, which means (to repeat) not inherited from founders but as if it has come to us from no beginning.

Burke illustrates "the idea of inheritance" with a "philosophic analogy." Our political system, he says, "working after the pattern of

[66] *Works*, II, 439–40, 455.
[67] *Works*, II, 440.
[68] *Works*, II, 454–55.
[69] *Works*, V, 132.
[70] *Works*, I, 313; II, 397, 399.
[71] *Works*, III, 114.

nature," is "in a just correspondence and symmetry with the order of the world." He calls it "a permanent body composed of transitory parts," and he compares it to the whole of the human race, which at any given time is never old, or middle-aged, or young, but always the same, while it moves on through decay, fall, rise, and progress.[72] In this figure the constitution is likened to a body—the human race—which is a whole and has no form. It is not likened to an individual human body with a form, as certain medieval thinkers conceived it. Burke's analogy is generic rather than organic, so that we conceive that we inherit our constitution as we do our human nature, with no possibility of rejection. We can and must accept our opportunities and limitations without attempting to find the origin or the purpose of the whole. Burke settles his politics on a notion of property, rather than the reverse; but he manages to keep his politics free of the spirit of acquisition—indeed, to keep it directed against that spirit.

What does it mean to say that the idea of inheritance works by "the method of nature"? Burke said that man's nature is intricate,[73] and his way of understanding the relationship between nature and human institutions is especially difficult for us today, who have expelled "nature" from respectable theoretical discourse. Yet he assailed the French revolutionaries for nothing more than their "unnatural" conduct, and if we need to learn what Burke thought, we cannot remain ignorant of the meaning of his attack on the French Revolution. Inheritance by the "method of nature" does not mean that we inherit our politics and constitutions from nature. Although we have a "natural sense of wrong and right,"[74] Burke does not say in the manner of Thomism that we have natural inclinations in our souls that are fulfilled in politics; the soul is not a theme of his.[75] Nor does he say with Aristotle that man is a political animal by nature, so that our political artifices would be the fulfillment of a natural potentiality. He says, instead, that "man is by his [natural] constitution a religious animal,"[76] since atheism is against our instincts as well as our reason. We are propelled, it seems, to the recognition of a superior will in order to avoid dependence on our own arbitrary will, a recognition which is a human instinct for human good. It is not that we seek to know God, as Thomas Aquinas said. When Burke attacked the French Revolution for doing

[72] *Works*, II, 307.
[73] *Works*, II, 307, 334.
[74] *Works*, II, 354; see II, 155; III, 92.
[75] See *Works*, II, 484; III, 86.
[76] *Works*, II, 363.

violence to our nature, he meant that it ignores or opposes the instincts we have for our own good, the natural affections for our families and neighborhoods, for "the little platoon," together with the check on such affections in our sense of justice and in our religion.[77]

We do not inherit *from* nature, but we inherit the products of human making according to laws of nature. Natural rights, which Burke deprecatingly calls "metaphysic rights," do not come to us directly, but "like rays of light which pierce into a dense medium, are, by the laws of nature, refracted from their straight line."[78] Taking a cue from this famous remark, we might say that for Burke laws of nature are laws of refraction. They are laws describing the ways in which men, making their own conventions, constitutions, or property, imitate or follow nature as nature conducts itself without reference to humans. For example, as we have seen, men making constitutions imitate nature in finding harmony through the struggle of its discordant powers and permanence through the rise and fall of its transitory parts. "Art is man's nature,"[79] Burke says, in reproach of the modern philosophers who place the "state of nature" outside civil society. Art (not choice) is nature's special gift to humans, but the gift is not used in a manner to preserve human specialness. All society is artificial, yet all artifice is according to natural law; the gift of art must be given back to nature. One wonders whether prudence is after all sovereign for Burke, if it must operate "under that discipline of nature."[80]

The sovereign rule of prudence is also a rule *for* prudence. It is prescription, "this great fundamental part of natural law,"[81] which describes the manner of growth of property and constitutions and lays down the method of inheritance. Strange to say, prescription before Burke was never considered to be unequivocally part of natural law, for it was not thought to be applicable in public law.[82] Burke borrowed the concept from Roman law, in which prescription gives title to

---

[77] *Works*, II, 320, 347, 410; V, 255.

[78] *Works*, II, 334.

[79] *Works*, III, 86.

[80] *Works*, III, 87; see I, 345; II, 369; VI, 21.

[81] *Works*, II, 422.

[82] Burke's appeal to the authority of Jean Domat (*Works*, II, 422) ignores Domat's refusal to apply prescription to public property; Jean Domat, *Les Lois Civiles dans l'ordre naturel*, III, vii, 5. A closer anticipation of Burke may be found in David Hume, *A Treatise of Human Nature*, III, ii, 3, 10; see also William Paley, *Principles of Moral and Political Philosophy* (1785), VI, 2. On prescription, see the excellent article of Paul Lucas, "On Edmund Burke's Doctrine of Prescription," *The Historical Journal*, XI (1968), 35–63; Harvey C. Mansfield, Jr., "Burke and Machiavelli on Principles in Politics," in *Edmund Burke: The Enlightenment and the Modern World*, ed. P. J. Stanlis (Detroit: University of Detroit Press, 1967), pp. 69–76, and *Statesmanship and Party Government* (Chicago: University of Chicago Press, 1965), pp. 221–23, 240.

property without a deed by long-continued use or takes it away despite a deed after long-continued disuse. This rule of private law was transformed by Burke into a rule of public law applicable to constitutions (not merely to the law of nations). Thus, a rule of private property becomes *the* rule for government, "the most solid of all titles, not only to property, but, which is to secure that property, to government"; "a title which is not the creature, but the master, of positive law," "the sacred rules of prescription."[83] If the problem of theory's intrusion into practice is the theme of Burke's political philosophy, prescription is his special discovery—one must say, since he could not abide the word "innovation," his grand reform.[84] It was merely a description of the working of the British constitution, he claimed; but as theory it was certainly new. Indeed, Burke had, he said, "a very full share" in the passage of the Nullum Tempus Act of 1769, by which he attempted to establish prescription as public law in Britain. Burke made this claim proudly in his splended self-defense against the Duke of Bedford, *A Letter to a Noble Lord,* but he did not similarly advertise the theoretical reform which justified the legal novelty (which went against the authority of Blackstone).[85] Nor did he remark that prescription became public law in 1769 not through prescription but by statute. That not merely *a* title, but the *most solid* title to property comes from long use rather than a deed implies that government, which issues deeds, is bound by long-continued practices rather than by principles. Property by prescription implies government without a founding or a theory: the best claim to rule comes not from establishing one's own claim as best but by securing the abandonment of rival claims. Yet it required a theory to show this, and even if Burke had tread softly to introduce it, even if his theory had fit neatly the shape of fact, it cannot be denied that his theory intrudes upon the prudence of statesmen.

Prescription follows nature but improves on it. Change, Burke says, is "the most powerful law of nature. . . . All we can do, and that human wisdom can do, is to provide that the change shall proceed by insensible degrees." Nature on its own might produce great and swift change, but such change imitated in human proceedings would breed a "black and sullen discontent" in those suddenly dispossessed of influence and, on the other side, intoxicate those who had been long

[83] *Works,* V, 137; VI, 80, 146; see II, 493 for Burke's statement of the revolutionaries' argument against prescription.
[84] *Works,* V, 120.
[85] *Works,* V, 137; Blackstone, *Commentaries on the Laws of England,* II, 263–64. See Burke's attempt to apply prescription to the Church, *Writings and Speeches,* II, 366.

depressed "with a large draught of new power."[86] Change there must be, but men must take care that it proceed by insensible degrees. Insensible change can be legal change, because it does not call the established laws or constitution into question. Or it can legalize change; it "mellows into legality governments that were violent in their commencement."[87] Agreeing, as was said above, with Machiavelli that all human things are in motion, Burke denies that the motion need be violent or revolutionary. For this reason prescriptive right is not the same as historical or traditional right. Prescription takes its bearing from current use, unless property or government has been recently usurped. It is opposed to historical claims that would overthrow established power, and it is sceptical of historical research that would confirm it.[88]

For Burke, then, prescription is a "great fundamental part of natural law." He does not quite say it is *the* fundamental part, and he does not specify the full content of natural law in the manner of more theoretical theorists such as Aquinas or Hobbes. He is satisfied that natural law be understood as a law beyond and above human legislation; he does not require that human law be seen as application of natural law. In the debate between Cicero and Hobbes as to whether "men have a right to make what laws they please," Burke is on the side of Cicero in denying this. He then says that "all human laws are, properly speaking, only declaratory; they may alter the mode and application, but have no power over the substance of original justice."[89] But since Burke has imported prescription into natural law itself, and has said little to establish the substance of original justice, it seems in effect that the mode and application, more than the substance, of natural law is to guide practice. Natural law is more means than ends because prescription, in order to exclude violent, comprehensive change, prevents the ends of politics from appearing in politics unrefracted by materials and circumstances. Prescription is prudence crystallized in theory. As such it is censor to the rest of natural law, so that natural law can speak in its own voice only "the principle of a superior law."[90] Human liberty is so far from opposed to the principle of a superior will that it cannot survive without one. Although society is the product of a contract among men, men cannot live freely if they

[86] *Works*, III, 340.
[87] *Works*, II, 435.
[88] *Works*, VI, 414.
[89] *Works*, VI, 21–22.
[90] *Works*, VI, 21; VII, 99–100, 504.

are free to make a new contract in every generation. Each generation must regard its liberties as an "entailed inheritance,"[91] as its property precisely because those liberties were not created by it. One may venture to conclude that at the center of Burke's political philosophy is the British constitution, not natural law. Natural law is the ground, but only because a constitution, made by accidents, needs a ground. However admirable it may be, the British constitution is not, for Burke, the rational state. But the ground of the constitution must be unseen and unfelt lest it upset the constitution that rests on it.

Here one might object that we are forgetting the "laws of commerce," which Burke, in a passage in his *Thoughts and Details on Scarcity* (1795), once equated, to the disgust of Karl Marx, with the "laws of nature, and consequently the laws of God."[92] The laws of commerce, it would seem, promote too much novel enterprise to be held accountable to the principle of prescription.[93] That is so, except insofar as prescription welcomes and justifies private enterprise without deeds or charters from the government. But the mobile property of merchants, together with the active abilities that create it, could be held in check and kept in balance, Burke believed, by the establishment of landed property and by the rule of gentlemen. With some basis in English experience, and some degree of hope, he joined together the supremacy of the landed interest, which he rightly said was recommended by "the practical politics of antiquity" (particularly Aristotle and Cicero), with a statement that could not be found, except as satire or disapproval, in ancient writers: "The love of lucre, though sometimes carried to a ridiculous, sometimes to a vicious, excess, is the grand cause of prosperity to all states."[94] While the landed interest should be supreme, it should not form a separate body in the nation, as in countries other than Britain; and though Burke endorsed the prejudices that gentlemen live by, he did not accept or share the gentleman's contempt for those who make money. He himself represented a merchants' constituency, Bristol, in Parliament from 1774 to 1780 (though not to its satisfaction), and, at his own estate in

[91] *Works*, II, 306.
[92] *Works*, V, 100; Marx, *Capital*, chap. 24, sec. 6. Marx apparently overlooked the following passage in Burke, which is more congenial to him: "Even commerce, and trade, and manufacture, the gods of our economical politicians, are themselves perhaps but creatures; and themselves but effects, which as first causes, we choose to worship" (*Works*, II, 351).
[93] *Works*, V, 207, 217, 256.
[94] *Works*, V, 313, 342.

Beaconsfield, he was active, as his letters attest, in the search for new methods (and greater returns) in agriculture.[95]

However one may connect Burke's doctrine of natural law to the natural law tradition, whether he was closer to Cicero or to Locke, it must be admitted that he makes most visible not that connection or his own allegiance within the tradition, but the peculiar features of natural law according to him. His natural law leaves sovereignty to prudence and gives prominence to circumstance; it does not demand transcendence of self-interested affections (including the love of lucre), which Burke emphatically labels "natural"; and it is more than tolerant of prejudice, it is positively hospitable to it. With a view to protecting the prejudices of gentlemen, Burke did not wish to show the British constitution in debt to philosophical tradition, though he did not hesitate to exclaim that Montesquieu, who held out that constitution to the admiration of mankind, was a man "tinctured with no national prejudice."[96]

"We are generally men of untaught feelings," Burke asserts of the British in a passage of the *Reflections on the Revolution in France,* congratulating his people on their imperviousness to the philosophy of enlightenment. We cherish our prejudices, he continues, "and to take more shame to ourselves, we cherish them because they are prejudices." "Our men of speculation" (one of his few approving references to this breed), instead of exploding general prejudices, use their sagacity to discover the latent wisdom in them.[97] Prejudice is not opposed to reason, but allied with it. Prejudice supplies the untaught, natural feelings that give permanence to reason, for "naked reason" is flighty; and at the same time "prejudice is of ready application in the emergency," whereas reason by itself is hesitant. Burke's frank recognition that politics is inseparable from prejudice, that society can never be rational and enlightened, reminds one of Aristotle; but his confidence that prejudice contains sufficient latent wisdom does not. For Aristotle, latent wisdom indeed exists in political opinion, but not in the uncontradicted seclusion that Burke seems to suppose. On the contrary, according to Aristotle political opinion typically asserts itself against an opponent, present or imagined; it has the character of debate. Any observation, not to mention speculative study, of political

[95] *Corr.,* II, 165–67, for example.
[96] *Works,* III, 113.
[97] *Works,* II, 359.

opinion reveals differences taking the form of contradictions, especially *the* typical difference in politics between the many and the few.
Burke leaves the obvious partisanship of prejudice out of account.
Although he often speaks of the few and the many, he does not stress
their difference of opinion, the gentleman's prejudice against the vulgar *versus* the people's resentment of privilege. As may be recalled,
Burke does not think that every man has a natural right nor the people
a natural desire to rule.[98] The people are content to let their wisdom
be latent rather than to assert it, and so the aristocracy can be bred
to rule without asserting its own distinctiveness.

Aristotle thought that political opinion becomes wisdom only if
partisan assertions are brought out for examination, corrected for their
partiality, and combined with truth from their opponents. He wrote
his *Politics* as if he were conducting a debate, and he implied that the
statesman could improve politics despite the ineradicability of prejudice by drawing out the latent implications of a prejudice which
might make it more wholesome. Burke, however, implies that the
wisdom in prejudice remains wisdom only so long as it is latent;
prejudice must not be disturbed, or natural feelings will be inflamed.
He seems to presuppose a fundamental cooperation between gentlemen and people, liable to disruption from outside but essentially un-
contentious. A "natural aristocracy" rules without asserting itself,
hence without imposing itself. But even if this were possible, Burke
took a risk in recommending that prejudice be left unenlightened, as
if he could be sure that prejudice would never bite. He knew that
"the will of the many, and their interest, must very often differ."[99]
But he supposed that it is "out of the power of man . . . to create a
prejudice . . . a king may make a nobleman but he cannot make a
Gentleman."[100] The slow, natural growth of prejudice in manners and
sentiments would render it harmless by habituating gentlemen and
people alike to the satisfaction of their wants within the bounds of
their natural affections. Philosophers and statesmen should leave prejudice to exercise its good effects uninstructed.

Yet Burke himself did not leave gentlemanly prejudice as he found
it. He once said that his chief employment was the "woeful one of
flapper," to awaken the gentleman in his party.[101] The very conception
of party that Burke elaborated in *Thoughts on the Cause of the Present*

[98] *Works*, II, 177, 332; III, 497.
[99] *Works*, II, 325.
[100] *Corr.*, VIII, 130.
[101] *Corr.*, III, 388–89.

Discontents was an implication of gentlemanly prejudice used to correct gentlemanly prejudice. "So to be patriots, as not to forget we are gentlemen" was Burke's summary of his advice.[102] Previously, in Britain and in other free countries, it had been taken for granted that a politician could not be both partisan and patriot, that open, committed partisanship could not, as a regular practice, be principled. Burke was the first to argue the contrary, that principled behavior in politicians must inevitably be partisan, and that partisanship is not only occasionally necessary in emergencies but useful and respectable in the ordinary working of the constitution. These beliefs are now held as universally and as thoughtlessly as were their contraries before Burke wrote, and insofar as Burke was responsible for the change, his theorizing had a mighty effect. But to make this change, Burke appealed to gentlemanly prejudice: ". . . not to forget we are gentlemen." Those politicians (Burke had his eye on Lord Chatham) forget they are gentlemen who pretend to put patriotic devotion to the public ahead of all private friendship and parade their "supernatural virtue" as a demanding qualification for high office. "When I see in any of these detached gentlemen of our times the angelic purity, power, and beneficence, I shall admit them to be angels. In the mean time we are born only to be men."[103] One is reminded of the passage in *The Federalist* No. 51, which says: "If men were angels, no government would be necessary." While in *The Federalist* the nonangelic nature of man justifies tolerance of ambition, for Burke it confirms the need for gentlemanly virtue to oppose hypocritical ambition. Party is informal, yet when made respectable it is no longer concealed or conspiratorial. With its source in private friendship and honorable attachments, party loyalty provides a visible measure of consistency in principle; not deserting one's friends becomes the mark of a patriot. In gentlemanly party politics Machiavellian flexibility is not required and not rewarded.

Gentlemanly virtue, for Burke, is manliness. It would not go too far to say that manliness is *the* virtue, according to Burke. It was the virtue he claimed for himself: in his progress of life, he asserted in *A Letter to a Noble Lord*, "I had no arts but manly arts."[104] And it was the virtue he set against the liberty propagated by the French revolutionaries: "I love a manly, moral, regulated liberty."[105] Manliness to

---

[102] *Works*, I, 379.

[103] *Works*, I, 378. On Burke's responsibility for the founding of party government, see Mansfield, *Statesmanship and Party Government*, esp. chap. 1; and John Brewer, "Rockingham, Burke and Whig Political Argument," *The Historical Journal*, XVIII (1975), 194–95.

[104] *Works*, V, 125; see II, 128.

[105] *Works*, II, 282; see I, 323, 370, 376, 451, 490; II, 287, 308, 339, 352; III, 438; V, 212.

Burke appears to be courage and prudence so combined that manly actions are open to public inspection without being subservient to public opinion. Having some admixture of Christian humility, manliness is not quite up to the pride of magnanimity;[106] but it is perhaps more effective in opposition to vanity for that reason, and also because it has the strength of a virtue that brings men together rather than elevating a few. Vanity and affected pity were the vices that Burke saw in the French doctrine of the rights of man; he tried to replace that doctrine with the "*real* rights of men*," the rights of manly men who can sustain the severe virtues as well as the liberal.[107] In our day manliness is losing its identification as male, but after the telling denunciation of democratic softness from authorities as diverse as Tocqueville and Nietzsche, we cannot afford not to reconsider Burke's principal value.

Burke, the champion of gentlemanly prudence, spent his political life beyond the limits of gentlemanly prudence, looking ahead to what his party could not see, urging it on to unaccustomed activity on uncongenial ground. One should say also that he devoted himself to securing and improving the boundaries of gentlemanly prudence, to keeping out subversive speculators and refashioning constitutional practices, such as party and impeachment, that would facilitate the rule of gentlemen. Having helped to found his party—by giving it a doctrine and a soul rather than by directing it—he abandoned it after the French Revolution and then attacked it. His colleagues could not see the difference between the American Revolution and the French; they did not appreciate the uniqueness of the latter event, the most complete revolution ever known. Burke's political philosophy centers on the defense of an actual constitution rather than the construction of an imaginary one. His theme is the sufficiency—rather, the perfection—of gentlemanly prudence. But his defense of his beloved gentlemen reveals their limitations, perhaps better than any revolutionary attack. For the revolutionaries found no suitable replacement for gentlemen; nor indeed have we, though we have sought among bureaucrats, technocrats, and democrats. One could almost define "gentlemen" by adding up everything that is lacking in bureaucrats, technocrats, and democrats. Burke's admiring view of them is clearer than that of their critics; the defects of gentlemen are to be seen in the need for his own contribution to their defense. That contribution went well beyond warning them of perils they were too dull to sense

[106] *Works*, I, 509; II, 536; III, 438.
[107] *Works*, II, 331, 418, 536, 537; V, 322.

and arousing them with fine phrases. Using what he once called "the seasonable energy of a single man,"[108] Burke tried to fortify the rule of gentlemen so as to make them less liable to subversion and attack. The result in the nineteenth century was both to fix them in place, immobile in their newly philosophical prejudice (the conservatives), and to loosen their attachments, trusting in the promise that reform would be the means of their conservation (the liberals).[109] Somewhat unwillingly, Burke bears testimony to the necessary imperfection of politics in the very midst of his inspiring speeches and noble deeds.

[108] *Works*, v, 78.

[109] Cf. Michel Ganzin, *La Pensée Politique d'Edmund Burke* (Paris: Pichon et Durand-Auzias, 1972), pp. 312–33.

A SKETCH OF BURKE'S LIFE

EDMUND BURKE was born in Dublin, Ireland, on January 12, 1729, the son of a prominent attorney. Although his mother was Roman Catholic, he was raised as an Anglican. He was sent to Ballitore School in County Kildare; there he met Richard Shackleton, the son of the headmaster, with whom he began a lifelong friendship. He then studied at Trinity College, Dublin, receiving an A.B. degree in January 1748. In 1750 he went to London to study law at the Middle Temple. But he apparently found study of the law too narrow (information on his life in the years from 1752 to 1757 is very scarce) and abandoned it, to the dismay of his father. He remained in London, turning to literary occupations. In March 1757 he married Jane Nugent and, for a time, the two lived with her father Christopher Nugent. They were joined by Edmund's younger brother Richard, and by Edmund's closest friend, William Burke, probably not a relation (though known as "Cousin Will"), whom he had met at the Temple.

In 1756 Edmund Burke published *A Vindication of Natural Society*, an ironic praise of "natural society" and an attack on civilization that parodied Bolingbroke's praise of natural religion and attack on revealed religion. In this first work Burke began the defense of the social and political artifices of civilization which was to claim his attention repeatedly for the rest of his life. Civilization, he thought, is built gradually over many ages with the aid of many minds; it must be

protected against "presumptuous and superficial" writers like Bolingbroke (as Burke later called him), who would attempt to remake all
laws and customs by a single act of legislation.

Burke's next publication was the only strictly theoretical work that
he ever wrote, *A Philosophical Inquiry into the Origin of Our Ideas of
the Sublime and Beautiful* (1757). Inspired by Locke and Montesquieu,
and reminiscent of Hume, this work drew praise from Kant. It is a
book of modern philosophy in the tradition of British sensualism,
opposed to "the Platonic theory of fitness and aptitude" which connects visible beauty to intelligible fitness or proportion. These books
won a reputation for Burke, but neither fame nor career. They were
printed by Dodsley, the most respectable of publishers in that time,
who also underwrote the *Annual Register,* founded in 1759 by Burke
and still regarded today as an accurate and impartial source for the
politics of its time. Burke also received a commission from Dodsley
for a *History of England* which he began but never finished. His attempt
was published posthumously as *An Essay towards an Abridgment of the
English History.*

After these modest successes and small failures in literary theory
and political commentary, Burke turned to politics. His genius was
political, and the literary fame he has gained is for the brilliant prose
of his political rhetoric. In 1759 he became private secretary to William
Gerard Hamilton, Member of Parliament and minor politician, and
accompanied him to Dublin, where Hamilton served as Chief Secretary
to the Lord Lieutenant of Ireland. There Burke had opportunity to
reflect on British misrule in Ireland and to develop his lifelong concern
for his native people. He began but did not complete his *Tract on the
Popery Laws in Ireland.* Back in London, he and Hamilton quarreled
violently over the nature of their relationship. Burke cut himself free,
abandoning a pension of £300 which was most of his regular income.
In July 1765 he was taken up very opportunely by the Marquess of
Rockingham, who made him his private secretary in the administration
he was forming. Burke was elected to Parliament in December 1765
through the influence of Lord Verney. The seat from the borough of
Wendover had been promised to William Burke, but "Cousin Will"
stepped aside for him.

Once in Parliament, Burke hurled himself into debate and achieved
an immediate and astonishing success. He soon distinguished himself
as one of the greatest orators in an age of great oratory. He was also
the greatest political pamphleteer in an age where the art of the pamphlet was practiced more widely and skillfully than in our day. All his

most famous writings are pamphlets—written speeches—on current political problems. Yet his rhetoric and his absorption in timely issues were directed by philosophical reflection and supported by vast learning. Burke wrote for the moment, but with all men and all time under his eye. A casual reader can sense the consistency of his career, but to find and explain that consistency is not easy, and scholars are divided over the character of his political philosophy, indeed, over the question of whether he has one. Burke himself took great pride in his consistency. In one of his later writings, *An Appeal from the New to the Old Whigs* (1791), he defended his consistency against the charges that he had abandoned his early principles and that he should have looked with favor on the French Revolution as he had on the American. The true statesman, he said, must rush to the defense of whatever is dear to him that is in danger—the British monarchy when monarchy is attacked by the French revolutionaries, Parliament when it is the victim of a court cabal, and the American colonies when they are the object of parliamentary interference. This appearance of imbalance is so far from inconsistency, he thought, that it is necessary to the true consistency of a statesman. Burke's own life may be examined as a series of episodes in each of which he tried to defend and confirm, in practice as well as in theory, an endangered institution of free government.

The first such institution was party. Burke had a subordinate and unofficial position in the first Rockingham administration of 1765–66. He did not hold office until the next Rockingham administration of 1782–83, in which he was made Paymaster-General of the forces, also a lesser role. He could have risen faster and gained office sooner but for his desire to maintain his political friendships. Such a display of party consistency was unusual in his day, when party association was thought to be evidence of lack of principle in politics.

Burke undertook to change this low estimation of party. In his *Thoughts on the Cause of the Present Discontents* (1770) he asserted that the constitution was being subverted by the "King's friends," a group in Parliament that always supported the government and boasted of its nonpartisanship. He then produced the first argument in the history of political philosophy for the respectability, not merely the necessity, of parties in politics. Reversing the prevailing opinion that parties were essentially evil and only occasionally good, he said they were "essentially necessary for the full performance of our public duty, accidentally liable to degenerate into faction." Burke served his party faithfully and busily from 1765 until the French Revolution. At that time he found it necessary to make it clear that partisanship has limits. When the leader of his party, Charles James Fox, showed that he was determined to support the cause of the revolutionaries, Burke broke with him in a celebrated scene in Parliament on May 6, 1791. With great reluctance, but with considerable energy, Burke turned his fire on the sympathizers with revolution in his old party.

No small part of Burke's conception of party was the dominance of landed gentry, which he thought natural and just. He was always content, while active in politics, to serve leaders from the great Whig families, men far less competent than he. He never took full advantage of the abundant opportunities in his day for obscure men of great talent to rise to high office. In his view, the safety of the constitution depended on the dull but reassuring leadership of propertied men from prominent families. Loyalty to them derived from the lesser loyalties that hold society together, and at the same time confirmed those loyalties.

Notwithstanding the "conservatism" of his beliefs ("conservatism" is a term not used until the early nineteenth century), Burke generally supported the American colonists before the Revolution. He spoke for repeal of the Stamp Act in 1766, yet also voted for the Declaratory Act as confirmation of Britain's constitutional right to tax the colonists. He served as agent for the New York Assembly to the British government from 1770 to 1775 and did his best, unsuccessfully, to calm both sides and keep them informed about each other.

On April 19, 1774, Burke delivered his *Speech on American Taxation*, his greatest speech yet, in which he tried to shift the debate over America from conflicting claims of constitutional rights to the prudence or imprudence of exercising those rights. Then, on March 22, 1775, Burke gave his *Speech on Conciliation with America*, a masterpiece of oratory that used to be studied by every American schoolchild. In it he asked Parliament to avoid the "great Serbonian bog" of theoretical rights and to practice tolerance and magnanimity. "A great empire and little minds go ill together," he said. When war came, the Rockingham party "seceded" from Parliament, refusing to attend. Burke defended this policy and again deplored the direct application of theory to politics, especially in lawyerly arguments, in his *Letter to the Sheriffs of Bristol* (1777).

Throughout his life, Burke kept a watchful eye on Irish affairs. Although he defended British sovereignty over Ireland, he was convinced that British rule there was oppressive. In his *Tracts on Popery Laws* he attacked the penal laws applied to Catholics and the many disabilities by which honors and offices were denied them. Later, he argued the wisdom of inviting the Irish to share in the advantages of the British constitution, in *A Letter to Sir Hercules Langrishe* (1792). To do this he could not, of course, suppose that the British constitution was already applicable to Ireland, and so in his writings on Ireland, as on India, he made frequent appeals to natural law. The natural law he relied on was that of Cicero, which establishes the "principle of a superior law," as opposed to that of Hobbes, which merely endorses the arbitrary will of human sovereigns.

In 1774 Burke accepted an invitation to stand for election at Bristol, a more popular district than Wendover, and one where he would face a contest. Burke won, but his successful colleague in the two-member district, Henry Cruger, a local merchant and political Radical, pledged himself to submit to the instructions of his constituents. Burke spoke in reply, and as he later said, he "was the first man who, on the hustings, at a popular election, rejected the authority of instructions from constituents; or who, in any place, has argued so fully against it." While admitting that a representative should reflect the feelings of the people, he asserted that he owes them his jugment on the common good, which may often diverge from their opinions. Burke did in fact displease the Bristol Radicals and merchants, the former by supporting relief for Catholics and the latter by concessions to Irish trade. He was forced to withdraw at Bristol in 1780, and thereafter to accept election in Lord Rockingham's borough of Malton until he retired in 1794.

Burke was also a leader in administrative reform of the constitution he so much admired. In his *Speech on the Economical Reform* (1780) he extended the argument he had made on behalf of parties ten years earlier. His aim now was to abolish many sinecures in the royal household and to centralize administration, partly in order to save money but still more to reduce the corrupting influence of the Crown. Burke's reform was intended to make it more difficult for the King's ministers to reward their compliant supporters in Parliament; and though it was modest (as Burke believed all reforms should be), its tendency was to compel the King to govern through public parties of well-born, proper-tied gentlemen. Burke did not accuse the sinecure-holders of lacking abilities; rather, it was their very abilities that made them subservient in order to get ahead. The defense of property against talent was a theme of Burke's politics which culminated in his writings against the French Revolution. When Burke joined Rockingham's second administration in 1782, he secured the enactment of a part of his reform.

This was the beginning of a long process of reform continuing through the nineteenth century which did not, however, sustain Burke's original intent of supporting gentlemanly rule.

For all his appreciation of tradition, Burke had a very advanced position in modern political economy. He wrote his *Thoughts and Details on Scarcity* (1795) to protest "indiscreet tampering" with trade, and asserted, by way of warning off governmental interference, that "the laws of commerce . . . are the laws of God." This statement drew an angry attack from Karl Marx, who accused Burke of sycophancy to the English bourgeoisie. However unfair this charge is, one may agree that, in economics, Burke was much closer to his friend Adam Smith than to Cicero.

India was a grand topic of Burke's life. Toward the end of his life (in 1796) he exclamed to a friend, concerning his consuming, unrelenting struggles on behalf of India: "Let everything I have done, said or written be forgotten but this." His interest in India was evidenced as early as 1766, when Lord Chatham sought more revenue for the British government from the East India Company. That company, Burke said later, had begun "in commerce and ended in empire," as it gradually took on functions of government in order to protect its trade. Burke (and the Rockingham party) at first went to the defense of the charter rights of companies against such exactions by government. In 1773 he continued to oppose, unsuccessfully, governmental regulation of the company.

As Burke became better acquainted with Indian affairs, however, he changed his mind. By 1782 he had become implacably hostile to Warren Hastings, Governor-General of India, and determined to bring him down together with the system, as Burke saw it, of British tyranny and corruption in India. With the aid of Philip Francis, an old enemy of Hastings in India, Burke pursued Hastings from 1782 to 1795, censuring him in eleven reports of a select committee in the House of Commons (1782–83) and presenting the case for Hastings' impeachment in Commons (1786–87).

In the impeachment Burke, at the height of his powers, confronted a formidable opponent in Hastings, whose administrative skill and political and military daring had saved the British Empire in India. Burke now demanded that the British government intervene to prevent the plunder of India and to restrict the East India Company to the business of trade. Indians, he asserted, deserve to be treated with the justice due them under natural law, even if this should harm British trade and endanger British rule, and despite the disinterest or hostility of the British public. Burke succeeded in having Hastings impeached in Commons, but suffered agonizing disappointment as Hastings was found not guilty after trial by the House of Lords. Burke's effort to secure a more regular place for impeachment in the British constitution (as complement to party) also failed.

The last, and climactic, episode of Burke's life was his defense of the British constitution against the French Revolution. Sooner than any other statesman in England, Burke concluded that the revolution was a profound and contagious evil which would subvert the manners and morals of Western civilization, thrust Europe (including Britain) under tyranny, and even change the constitution of the human mind. Burke first spoke up against the revolution in debate on February 2, 1790; then he composed his greatest work, *Reflections on the Revolution in France* (published November 1, 1790). Sequels to this work, scarcely less brilliant, followed at short intervals until Burke's death. Notable among them was *A Letter to a Noble Lord* (1796), in which Burke read a lesson to the young Duke of Bedford, the beneficiary of prodigious grants of property from Henry VIII, who had criticized Burke for accepting a small pension from the government.

Burke's *Reflections* immediately became a best-seller and roused furious controversy, notably between Burke and Tom Paine, whose *Rights of Man* was written in rebuttal. The French Revolution, Burke thought, had been brought about by the principles of the revolutionaries, which were conceived as abstractions but put into practice with terrible effect. As opposed to abstract rights of man justifying the destruction of Church, nobles, monarchy, and property, Burke set forth the "*real* rights of man," which are rights to particular reforms out of actual grievances. These real rights would have required considerable reform in France, but not the destruction of the "establishments" in society which make liberty a living inheritance rather than a slogan.

Burke died on July 9, 1797, at his country home in Beaconsfield, after three years of retirement from Parliament, saddened by the death of his son Richard in 1794 and by the triumph of the revolution he had nobly opposed.

Burke's

SELECTED CORRESPONDENCE

Private and Public Life

T HE LETTERS grouped together in this section mark milestones in Burke's life: his first job, his first quarrel, his appointment as secretary to Lord Rockingham, the death of Rockingham, the death of his son Richard, the receipt of a pension from the King, and Burke's own death. But, what is more interesting, they also contain Burke's reflections on the relationship between private and public life. Burke was not one to record an event without reflection, comment, or instruction, and in his own self-defense he could be a lavish and exuberant teacher. His very long draft of a letter to Dr. William Markham, an extraordinary document of self-exculpation, gets its length from Burke's desire to go beyond denial and excuse to the elaboration of standards by which his conduct ought to be judged. He defends his party (therefore, too, the very idea of partisanship), himself, and his "friends and relations."

The latter were William Burke, a friend and apparently no relation; and Richard Burke, Sr., Burke's younger brother. Burke lived *en famille* with these two, together with his wife and his son Richard, and apparently shared income and expenses in common. Little is known of this unusual arrangement, but if its purpose was to free Burke from financial worries, it cannot have succeeded. William and Richard, Sr., failed disastrously as speculators in the East and West Indies, bringing criticism and embarrassment to Edmund rather than security. Nonetheless, he lived with them in comity and friendship throughout his life, and also managed to purchase, with loans from other friends, an estate in Beaconsfield.

Besides needing the support of his kinsmen, Burke faced the problem of defining the conditions under which he would work for his
patron (see the exchange and violent break with William Gerard Hamilton). He would also lament that those in public life, especially in a
free country, come under attack for the conduct of their private lives,
in particular for "corruption" (see the exchange with Richard Shackleton, April 1770, and the letter to the Stewards of the Bell Club,
November 1, 1777). Burke spent his political life working under men
with more rank and less talent than he, whom he regarded as fitter
for public service than himself by virtue of their private station. Yet
it often fell to him to encourage such men to overcome the languor
induced by their very fitness and to claim the posts which others sought
eagerly to grasp (see the letter to the Duke of Richmond, September
1774).

To WILLIAM GERARD HAMILTON—[*March* 1763]

Corr. (1958), I, 163–66

William Gerard Hamilton (1729–96) was often called 'Single-speech Hamilton' from
having made a great reputation in the House of Commons with a brilliant maiden
speech, after which he was remarkably silent. Burke was introduced to him in 1759
and served him as a secretary for six years. At the end of two years' service as Chief
Secretary to the Lord Lieutenant of Ireland, Hamilton secured an important sinecure
post for himself, and secured for Burke as his protégé a pension of £300 a year on
the Irish Establishment. Burke, full of gratitude, wrote a formal letter of thanks, in
which, however, he marked out one important reservation he wished to make in his
further devotion of himself to his patron's affairs.

Dear Sir,

I am now on the point of acquiring through your friendship an
establishment which I am sensible is as much above my merits, as in
any other channel it may be above my reasonable expectations.—I
should think myself inexcusable in receiving this pension, and loading
your interest with so heavy a charge, without apprizing you of those
conditions on which alone I am able to take it; because, when I have
taken it, I ought no longer to consider myself as possessed of my
former freedom and independence.

I have often wished to explain myself fully to you on this point. It is against my general notions to trust to writing, where it is in one's power to confer otherwise. But neither do you hear, nor do I speak, on this subject, with the same ease with which we converse on others. This is but natural; and I have therefore chosen this method as less liable to misunderstanding and dispute; and hope you will be so indulgent to hear me with coolness and attention.

You may recollect when you did me the honour to take me as a companion in your studies, you found me with the little work we spoke of last Tuesday, as a sort of rent charge on my thoughts.[1] I informed you of this, and you acquiesced in it. You are now so generous, and it is but strict justice to allow that upon all occasions you have been so, to offer to free me from this burthen. But in fact though I am extremely desirous of deferring the accomplishment, I have no notion of entirely suppressing that work; and this upon two principles, not solely confined to that Work, but which extends much further, and indeed to the plan of my whole life.

Whatever advantages I have acquired, and even that advantage which I must reckon as the greatest and most pleasing of them, have been owing to some small degree of literary reputation. It will be hard to persuade me that any further services which your kindness may propose for me, or any in which my friends may wish to co-operate with you, will not be greatly facilitated by doing something to cultivate and keep alive the same reputation. I am fully sensible that this reputation may be at least as much hazarded as forwarded by new publications. But because a certain oblivion is the consequence, to writers of my inferior class, of an entire neglect of publication; I consider it as such a risk as some times must be run. For this purpose some short time at convenient intervals and especially at the dead time of the year, will be requisite, to study and consult proper books. These times, as you know very well, cannot be easily difined nor indeed, is it necessary they should. The matter may be very easily settled by a good understanding between ourselves, and by a discreet liberty, which I think you would not wish to restrain nor I to abuse. I am not so unreasonable

---

[1] The editors of *Corr.* (1844) were doubtless right in assuming this to be the *Essay towards an Abridgment of English History* (*Works* [Bohn], VI, 184–422, [Little, Brown], VII, 157–488), which Burke never finished. There have been wide differences of opinion as to the value of the *Abridgment*. G. M. Young thinks it nearly valueless, and asserts without offering any evidence that it is 'demonstrably a translation from the French' ('Burke', in *Proceedings of the British Academy*, XXIX, London, 1943, p. 6). Lord Acton, commenting on the story that Burke discontinued his History of England because Hume published his, said 'it is ever to be regretted that the reverse did not occur' (quoted in Herbert Butterfield, *Man on his Past*, Cambridge, 1955, p. 69).

and absurd enough to think I have any title to so considerable a share in your interest, as I have had, and hope still to have, without any or but an insignificant return on my side; especially as I am conscious that my best and most continued endeavours are of no very great value. I know that your business ought on all occasions to have the preference, to be the first and the last, and indeed in all respects the main concern. All I contend for is, that I may not be considered as absolutely excluded from all other thoughts in their proper time, and due subordination:—the fixing the times for them to be left entirely to yourself.

I do not remember that hitherto any pursuit has been stopped, or any plan left defective through my inattention, or through my attention to other matters; and I protest to God I have applied to whatever you have thought proper to set me, with a vigour and alacrity and even an eagerness that I never felt in any affair of my own whatsoever. If you have not observed this, you have not I think observd with your usual sagacity. But if you have observed it and attributed it to an interested design, which will cease when its end is in any degree answered, my mind bears me witness that you do not do me justice. I act almost always from my present impulse, and with little scheme or design, and perhaps generally with too little.—If you think what I have proposed unreasonable, my request is, that you will, which you may very easily do, get my Lord Halifax to postpone the Pension, and afterwards to drop it, we shall go on as before until some other more satisfactory matter occurs. For I should ill brook an accusation either direct or implied, that I had through your friendship acquired a considerable establishment and afterwards neglected to make any fair return in my power. The thought of this has given me great pain, and I could not be easy without coming to some explanation upon it. In the light I consider things, it can create no great difficulty: but it may possibly to you appear otherwise. Let this be how it will I can never forget the obligations, the very many and great obligations which I have already had to you, and which in any situation will always give you a right to call on me for any thing within my compass. If I do not often acknowledge my sense of them, it is because I know you are not very fond of professions, nor am I very clever at making them, you will take in good part this liberty which sincerely is not made for the purpose of exercizing my pen impertinently. Two words from you would settle the point one way or other.

I am with the utmost truth
Ever yours,
E BURKE

To WILLIAM GERARD HAMILTON—
[*ante* 12 *February* 1765]

Corr. (1958), I, 179–81

Burke is answering a stiff letter from his patron, Hamilton, who had been dismissed from his post of Chief Secretary to the Lord Lieutenant of Ireland in May 1764. Hamilton still held a seat in the British House of Commons, and wanted Burke to continue as his secretary—under terms to which Burke objected violently. The person who succeeded Burke as Hamilton's assistant—though his duties were of a rather different character—was apparently Samuel Johnson (*Life of Johnson*, I, 489–90, 519–20).

Dear Sir

Your Letter which I received about 4 o Clock yesterday seemed not to have been written with an intention of being answered. However on considering the matter this morning, I thought it respectful to you, and in a manner necessary to myself, to say something to those heavy charges which you have made against me in our last conversations, and which, with a polite acrimony in the expression you have thought proper to repeat in your Letter.

I should indeed be extremely unhappy if I felt any consciousness at all of that unkindness of which you say you have so lively a sense. In the six years during which I have had the honour of being connected with you I do not know that I have given you one just occasion of complaint: and if all things have not succeded every way to your wishes, I may appeal to your own equity and candour, whether the failure was owing to any thing wrong in my advice or inattention in my conduct. I can honestly affirm, and your heart will not contradict me, that in all cases I preferred your interest to my own. I made you and not myself the first object in every deliberation, I studied your advancement your fortune, and your reputation in every thing with zeal and earnestness, and sometimes with an anxiety which has made many of my hours miserable. No body could be more ready than I was, to acknowledge the obligations I had to you; and if I thought, as in some instances I did and do still think, I had cause of dissatisfaction I never exposed to others, or made yourself uneasy about them. I acted in every respect with a fidelity which, I trust, cannot be impeached. If there be any part of my conduct in life upon which I can look with entire satisfaction it is my behaviour with regard to you.

So far as to the past. With regard to the present, what is that unkindness and misbehaviour, of which you complain? My heart is full of friendship to you: and is there a single point which the best and most intelligent men have fixed as a proof of friendship and gratitude in which I have been dificient or in which I threaten a failure? What you blame is only this: That I will not consent to bind myself to you for no less a term than my whole life: in a sort of domestick situation, for a consideration to be taken out of your private fortune, that is, to circumscribe my hopes, to give up even the possibility of liberty, and absolutely to annihilate myself for ever. I beseech you, is the demand, or the refusal the act of unkindness. If ever such a test of friendship was proposed in any instance to any man living, I admit that my conduct has been unkind and if you please ungrateful.

If I had accepted your kind offers, and afterwards refused to abide by the condition you annex to them, you then would have had a good right to tax me with unkindness. But what have I done, but at the end of very long, however I confess unprofitable service, but to prefer my own liberty to the offers of advantage you are pleased to make me? and at the same time to tender you the continuance of those services (upon which partiality only induces you to set any value) in the most disinterested manner, as far as I can do it consistent with that freedom, to which for a long time I have determined to sacrifice every consideration; and which I never gave you the slightest assurance that I [had] any intention to surrender, whatever my private resolves may have been, in case an event had happened which, (so far as concerns myself) I rejoice never to have taken place. You are kind enough to say, that you look'd upon my friendship as valuable, but hint that it has not been lasting. I really do not know, when and by what act I broke it off. I should be wicked and mad to do it; unless you call that a lasting friendship which all mankind would call a settled servitude and which no ingenuity can distinguish from it. Once more put yourself in my situation and judge for me. If I have spoken too strongly, you will be so good to pardon a man on his defence, in one of the nicest questions to a mind that has any feeling. I meant to speak fully not to offend. I am not used to defend my conduct, nor do I intend for the future to fall into so bad a habit. I have been warmed to it by the imputation you threw on me, as if I deserted you on account solely of your want of success. On this however I shall say nothing, because perhaps I should grow still warmer, and I would not drop one loose word which might mark the least disrespect, and hurt a friendship which has been and I flatter myself will be a satisfaction and an honour to me. I beseech you, that you will judge of me with a little impartiality and temper. I hope I have said nothing in our last interview, which could urge you to the passion you speak of. If any thing fell which was strong in the expression, I beleive it was from you, and not from me; and it is right that I should bear more than I then heard.

I said nothing but what I took the liberty of mentioning to you a year ago in Dublin. I gave you no reason to think I had made any change in my resolution. We, notwithstanding, have ever since until within these few days proceeded as usual.

Permit me to do so again. No man living can have an higher veneration than I have for your abilities, or can set an higher value on your friendship, as a great private satisfaction, and a very honourable distinction.

I am much obliged to you for the favour you intend me in sending to me in three or four days, (if you do not send sooner) when you have had time to consider this matter coolly. I will again call at your door, and hope to be admitted. I beg it and intreat it. At the same time do justice to the single motive which I have for desiring this favour, and desiring it in this manner.

I have not wrote all this tiresome matter, in hopes of bringing on an altercation in writing, which you are so good to me as to decline personally, and which in either way I am most sollicitous to shun. What I say is, on reviewing it, little more than I have laid before you in another manner, it certainly requires no answer. I ask pardon for my prolixity, which my anxiety to stand well in your opinion has caused. I am with great truth,

> Your most affectionate
> > and most obliged humble Servant
> > > E BURKE

To the Right Honourable
  William Gerard Hamilton.

To JOHN MONCK MASON—[*post* 29 *May* 1765]

Corr. (1958), I, 195–98

John Monck Mason (1726–1809) had been three years ahead of Burke at Trinity College, had studied law at the Middle Temple, been called to the Irish Bar in 1752, and entered the Irish House of Commons in 1761. Burke writes to explain the grounds of his violent break with Hamilton.

My dear Mason, I am hardly able to tell you how much satisfaction I had in your Letter. Your approbation of my Conduct makes me believe much the better both of you and of myself; and I assure you that that approbation came to me very seasonably. Such proofs of a warm, sincere, and disinterested friendship were not wholly unnecessary to my support, at a time when I experienced such bitter Effects of the perfidy, and ingratitude, of other, much longer, and much closer, connections. The way in which you take up my affairs binds me to you in a manner I cannot express: For to tell you the Truth, I never can, (knowing, as I do, the principles upon which I always endeavour to act) submit to any sort of compromise on my Character; and I shall never therefore look upon those, who after hearing the whole story, do not think me *perfectly* in the right, and do not consider Hamilton as an infamous Scoundrel, to be in the smallest degree my friends, or even to be persons for whom I am bound to have the slightest Esteem, as fair or just estimaters of the Characters and Conduct of men. Situated as I am and feeling as I do, I should be just as well pleased that they totally condemned me, as that they should say that there were faults on both sides, or that it was a disputable Case, as I hear is I cannot forbear saying, the affected Language of some Persons. Having let you into this perhaps weak part of my Character, I must let you into another which is I confess full as weak and rather more blameable, that is some degree of mortification which I cannot avoid feeling on the Letters I receive almost daily and from several hands from Dublin, giving me an account of a violent outcry of ingratitude which is there raised against me. If the absurdity of an accusation were a sufficient antidote against the poison of it this would I suppose be the most innocent charge in the world: But if its absurdity weakens the force of it to the conviction of others it adds to my feeling of it, when I reflect that there is one person who has ever seen my face that can listen to such a Calumny. H's Emissaries do more for him than he has ever attempted to do for himself. He charges me with receiving that Pension during the Kings pleasure (in getting me which he had the least share of four who were engaged in it) not at all a favour, but as the consideration of a Bargain and sale of my Liberty and existence. It cannot be, at once a voluntary Benefit claiming gratitude, and a mercenary consideration exacting service. They may (if they are contented to Speak a consistent falshood) accuse me of breach of faith but they can never, without nonsense as well as injustice say I am ungrateful, until they can prove that some favour was intended to me. In regard to their own understanding they will be so gracious as to drop one or the other of the Charges. In modesty they ought to drop both of them unless serving their friend with six of the best years of my Life whilst he acquired at their expence a ministerial fortune and then after giving him my Labour, giving him also a Pension of 300 a year be not unless these be thought as great faults towards him, as perhaps they were towards the publick, and unless those delicate friends do not think their late grateful, sincere disinterested Secretary has not yet enough on their Establishment. You cannot avoid remarking my dear Mason, and I hope not without some indignation at the unparallel'd Singularity of my Situation. Was ever a man before me expected to enter into formal, direct, undisguised Slavery? Did ever a man before him confess an attempt to decoy a man into such an illegal Contract, not to say any thing of the impudence of regularly pleading it? If such an attempt, be wicked and unlawful (and I am sure no one ever doubted it), I have only to confess his Charge, and to admit myself his Dupe to make him pass on his own Shewing for the most consummate Villian that ever lived. The only difference between us is not whether he is not a rogue; for he not only admits but pleads the facts that demonstrate him to be so, but only whether I was such a fool as to sell myself absolutely for a consideration which so far from being adequate, (if any such could be adequate) [is] not even so much as certain. Not to value myself (as a gentleman a freeman a man of Education; and one pretending to Literature) is there any situation in Life so low or even so criminal, that can subject a man to the possibility of such an engagement? Would you dare attempt to bind your footman to such Terms? Will the Law suffer a felon sent to the Plantation to bind himself for his Life and to renounce all possibility either of elevation or quiet? And I am to defend myself for not doing, what no man is Sufferd to do and what it would be criminal in any man to Submit to. You will excuse me for this heat, which will in spite of me attend and injure a just cause whilst Common judgments look upon coolness, as a proof of innocence though it never fails to go along with guilt and ability. But this is the real State of the Affair.

H. indeed I hear has the impudence sometimes [to] pretend that my
going to Mr T.[1] is the Cause of our Rupture. This is I assure you an
abominable falshood. I never had more than a very slight acquaintance
with Mr T. till long after our rupture. O'Hara through whom a part
of the Negotiation passed will let you see that our rupture had no sort
of relation to him ⟨ . . . ⟩ But Ridge[2] will explain the point to you at
large. You will Shew this much as you like to any you think fit of our
common friends, meaning that H. should know in what a manner I
speak of him on all occasions.

You are my dear Mason by your Bedford connection involved in
the support of Ld W's government and I could heartily wish, that
your Task were less difficult, with an unsupported and beggard Lord
Lt attended with officers to do business at a doubtful time, the best
of them with middling ability and no experience. My Ld Lt himself
is a genteel man and of excellent Natural Sense is as univerally said.[3]
I wish it may turn out for your advantage, and that the barrack board[4]
may be not the seat of Bench but a Step of the Stairs. You know I
suppose that H. endeavourd by his connection with the Thynne to
intrude into that Family and wanted to stipulate for a month or six
Weeks service to get for a Cousin of his a Deenery, but I imagine they
hear on all hands.

If Mason was more willing than Flood to take Burke's side against Hamilton, he was
a good deal less disposed to congratulate him on his new patron Charles Townshend.
'I have no great reliance', he wrote 28 June, 'on the faith, or affection of men so
entirely devoted to Ambition as your late Master, or your new friend; but I hope I
wrong the latter; the other I have no doubts about, he has proved himself a thorough
rascal'.

To CHARLES O'HARA—11 *July* 1765

Corr. (1958), I, 211

Burke announces his new post as Secretary to Lord Rockingham to his Irish friend
Charles O'Hara, with whom he maintained a long and frequent correspondence. The
post of private secretary to the First Lord of the Treasury (as Rockingham was,
briefly, in 1765) was unofficial and unsalaried. Its status depended on the characters

[1] Charles Townshend (1725–67).

[2] John Ridge (*c.* 1728–96), Burke's lawyer and a trusted friend in Ireland.

[3] Burke is charitable. Horace Walpole (*Memoirs*, II, 126–7) desribed Weymouth as 'an inconsiderable, debauched young man, attached to the Bedfords, but so ruined by gaming, that
the moment before his exaltation he was setting out for France, to avoid his creditors'. Having
been appointed Lord Lieutenant at the end of May, Weymouth was removed in July, without
ever having crossed to Ireland.

[4] Mason became Commissioner and Overseer of the Barracks 23 April 1765.

of the men concerned and their relationship to each other: the private secretary might be a mere amanuensis, or, as Burke became, a confidential man of business to his principal. Rockingham did not secure a sinecure for Burke, as was customary, but some 'secret service' payments were made to him.

My dear Sir, My Letter by last post was a long one. This will be very short. The Papers shew you the ministerial Changes, in which you will be pleased to see your friend Conway in possession of the Seals. I have got an employment of a kind humble enough; but which may be worked into some sort of consideration, or at least advantage; Private Secretary to Lord Rockingham, who has the reputation of a man of honour and integrity; and with whom, they say, it is not difficult to live. Will is strongly talked of for a better thing. All my Speculations are in my last Letter. Adieu my dear Sir, Affectionately yours

E BURKE

July 11th 1765

To RICHARD SHACKLETON—19 *April* 1770

Corr. (1958), II, 129–31

Burke's Quaker schoolmate Richard Shackleton (1726–92) had been for many years his closest friend. In 1766 when Burke was enjoying his first considerable fame, an English person, never positively identified, applied to Shackleton through a third party for particulars of Burke's family, religion, and character. Not suspecting any evil, Shackleton wrote and sent his correspondent a sketch of his boyhood friend. The account was ultimately printed in the *London Evening Post* for 14–17 April 1770. Burke was irritated by the publication, perhaps chiefly because of what was said of the religion of his mother and his wife. Of Burke's mother Shackleton had written: 'She was of a *Popish family;* I cannot say whether she legally conformed to the Church of England, but she practised the duties of the *Romish religion* with a decent privacy'. Burke's wife Shackleton described, surely with the best intentions, as 'a genteel well-bred woman, of the Roman faith, whom he married neither for her *religion,* or her *money,* but from the natural impulse of youthful affection'.

My dear Shackleton,

You will be so good to excuse me for having so long delayed an answer to your Letter. If I could have served your friend I would have done it. But nothing could have been more improper than any applications, on the footing of friendship, to Lord Rockingham, in what relates to the disposal of his private fortune; or to ask that, as any kind of favour, which ought to be left to the principles of common dealing. Believe me, my friend, that this, and no want of an earnest desire of doing what might be acceptable to you, prevented the application you desired.

I confess a little weakness to you. I feel somewhat mortified at a paper written by you, which some officious person has thought proper to insert in the London Evening post of last Night. I am used to the most gross and virulent abuse daily repeated in the papers—I ought indeed rather have said, twice a day. But this abuse is loose and general invective. It affects very little either my own feelings, or the opinions of others, because it is thrown out by those that are known to be hired to the Office of my Enemies. But this appears in the Garb of professed apology and penegyrick. It is evidently written by an intimate friend. It is full of anecdotes and particulars of my Life. It therefore cuts deep. I am sure I have nothing in my family, my Circumstances, or my Conduct that an honest man ought to be ashamd of. But the more circumstances of all these which are brought out, the more materials are furnished for malice to work upon: and I assure you that it will manufacture them to the utmost. Hitherto, much as I have been abused, my Table and my bed were left sacred, but since it has so unfortunately happend, that my Wife, a quiet woman, confined to her family Cares and affections, has been dragged into a Newspaper, I own I feel a little hurt. A Rough publick man may be proof against all sorts of Buffets, and he has no business to be a publick man if he be not so. But there is as natural and proper a delicacy in the other Sex, which will not make it very pleasant to my Wife to be the daily subject of Grubstreet, and newspaper invectives; and at present, in Truth her health is little able to endure it. It is true, that you have said of me, ten thousand handsome things, which are infinitely beyond any thing I have deserved, or can deserve. But this is only the Language of friendship; which is always interpreted down to its proper Level, possibly below it, by the severe scrutiny of the publick. Indeed what you have said of my Modesty and moderation in Debate, will, I fear, take off not a little from the Authority of the rest. It is but too well known, that I debate with great Vehemence and asperity and with little management either of the opinions or persons of many of my adversaries. They deserve not much Quarter, and I give and receive but very little. Do not think my dear Shackleton that this is written with the least View of upbraiding you with what you have done, from the best and purest motives and in which you have erred only from a want of knowledge of the ill dispositions of the world, and the modes in which they execute their malice—I only write, that if your friend

Pike,[1] in whose hands I found there had been a Copy of this Paper, and who I suspect transmitted it to the Newspaper intends any thing more of that kind, that you would quietly restrain him. I mention this because the News writer desires a further correspondence with him. I can hardly think Abraham Rawlinson could have been the publisher.[2] As to the former Gentleman after what passed, when I was last in Dublin, I hardly thought he would have let any Copies out of his hands. I just forgot to mention that you are mistaken in some Circumstances; where you speak of my being made easy by Patronage &c. I assure you, that if you allude to a small pension which I had for a time, and resigned upon an overstrained point of honour[3]—I am to inform you I got that from the Patronage of no man living. It was indeed a defective performance of a bargain for full consideration. Nor have I had any advantage, except my Seat in Parliament, from the Patronage of any man; Whatever advantages I have had, have been from friends on my own Level; As to those that are called great, I never paid them any Court; perhaps since I must say it, they have had as much benefit from my Connection, as I have had. This for your private Satisfaction. Remember us all most cordially to Mrs Shackleton and to your father. Poor Richard is orderd to the Grenades, no pleasant place, nor pleasantly inhabited for him. I have not interest to prevent it. Adieu my Dear friend and believe me most faithfully and affectionately yours

EDM BURKE

Gregories
    April 19. 1770
    I am here for a day; just to see how things go on. Mrs Burke is too weak to come along with me. Adieu.

RICHARD SHACKLETON *to* EDMUND BURKE—
28 *April* 1770

Corr. (1958), II, 133–35

My dear Friend, If I may take the liberty still to call thee so, I have received thy Letter written in the vexation of thy spirit, cutting and

---

[1] Richard Pike (1748–1814) of Dublin, to whom Shackleton had given a copy of the sketch of Burke.

[2] Abraham Rawlinson (1709–80), a Lancaster merchant; probably the person who first requested the account.

[3] The pension Burke received in 1763 and resigned in 1765.

wounding in the tenderest parts, and ripping open a Sore which I thought was long ago healed, I know nothing in the world about the publication of that unfortunate paper, but what thou tells me; nor who could be the Publisher of it. I have used thee and thy family grossly ill. I acknowledged it as fully as I could. I am covered with Grief, Shame, and Confusion for it. It was done in the Simplicity of my heart: I mean the writing of it. The giving a Copy of it I will not call Indiscretion, but Madness and Folly. With the same Simplicity I before let thee Know how I came to write it, and why I gave a Copy of it. When I had given it to my Friend, and he had given a Copy to his Friend, it very probably circulated out of the power of either of us to recal. It passed like money through the hands of People, good and bad, friends and enemies: and because the matter was Gold though bunglingly coined, and possibly still more defaced in the circulation, it was too precious to be lost. I am sure I had no more thoughts of it's spreading as it has done, nor of it's ever being published, than I have of the Publication of this Letter. If what has been published varies at all from the Copy which I sent thee, or if I can do any thing by way of atonement or amendment, grant me this last favour of putting it in my power to do it. In a few days I expect to see Dick Pike, and purpose to make all the enquiry, and give all the charges necessary. I said thy letter cut and wounded me: it did indeed effectually. It was dictated by a perturbed mind: it was calculated to punish and fret me; and it has obtained its end. Thy family, thy circumstances, thy conduct, thy bed, thy board; I am indirectly or directly charged with defaming and vilifying them all; not indeed as a false friend, but as a very foolish one. I could bear even all this, whether deserved or not, from thee. Thou art so used to lay about thee, and give and take no Quarter with thy Enemies, that it is unsafe for thy friends to be near thee. If there be any of the language of Friendship in thy Letter, it is only like oil, to make the edge more keen: if the voice be any where like Jacob's the hands are Esau's. Thou art grown a rough publick man, sure enough—I say I could bear even this from thee; (for I know both my own heart and thine,) and if the affair lay only between ourselves, there might some time be an end of it. But thy mention of my interfering in thy domestick connexions and dragging the Partner of thy bed and the softener of thy busy Scenes of life into a News-Paper is wounding to the last degree. Whatever thou art pleased to think of me, I have, Perhaps, and (for aught I know) ever had as great delicacy in these matters as any man. Look into that ill-advised, impertinent Paper which I stupidly wrote, and see is there any thing that offends against the nicest delicacy. The truth is, this Paper and conduct of mine will (like most other things) bear a double construction. Taking a full view of it altogether, I cannot be reckoned exceedingly criminal: view it in a partial light (luce malignâ) and it will be deemed thy great misfortune that in the early part of thy Life, thou happened to have had any connexion with such low companions, such indiscreet Friends. I do in the sincerest and most earnest manner beg forgiveness of thy amiable companion, the bosom-Friend of my Friend, for having written any thing that could give her the most distant cause of uneasiness. As to any of her house being offended with me for taking the liberty of delineating thy character; be it known to them that not one of them all, nor I believe, any man living more zealously, more affectionately, more assiduously seeks and desires the welfare of Ned Burke than I do: and though in a way which neither he, or they may know much about, I am sure it is in sincerity; and I trust not altogether in vain. What is Flattery to Fools, is plain-dealing and Truth to a man of Sense, and a man of sense will not be hurt by it: The talents which God has given thee, the Powers which thou hast display'd, the high ground on which thou stands have rendered thee an object of Publick admiration: they that hate thee, yet admire thee. Hence naturally follows Envy. Why should thou expect to escape it? Thou knows far better than I how the greatest men among the gentiles felt and lamented it. The first Apostle among the Christians says that he approved himself in his office by honour and dishonour: by evil report and good report: as a Deceiver and yet true.[1] Wert thou my Inferior or my Equal, I might indulge in expatiating on this and such topicks: but when I look up to thee, thou seem so thoroughly to have anticipated in thy observation and experience all that I could say upon the subject, that any thing that I could drop would appear to myself more like the trite common-place declamation of a conceited Country-Pedant who loved to hear himself prate, than the pertinent and seasonable remarks of a rational Friend. I will therefore have done. I am sorry that we must lend Richard to the Barbarians on the other side of the Globe. Every one of us has his own perplexity. His remote destination, my home-confinement, thy complicated, arduous engagements embitter our several Cups of life, and fully prove to each of us that it is a Cup of Mixture. To live in the awful Fear of our Creator, and keep a Conscience void of offence, helps much to sweeten the Draught. Tell him my love and good wishes attend him there and

[1] II Corinthians, VI. 8.

back again. Remember me most affectionately to thy household: or rather desire them to forget me. My Father and my Wife are well, and preserve a sincere affection for you all. I am entirely convinced (and thought before) that thy application to Lord Rockingham upon the subject of my last would have been quite Improper. I mentioned in that Letter why I could not (nevertheless) well avoid moving it to thee. I am quite satisfied about the propriety of thy conduct respecting it, but not of my own; for I was a blockhead to meddle in it. I wrote thee a long letter before that, but thou dost not give me the satisfaction of knowing whether thou received it or not and it's like that if thou hast not been heartily vexed, I would have known as little for a long time to come about the fate of my last. However, this be assured of, that whether ever I see or hear from thee again, or whether this Letter closes our correspondence for life, I am with unabated, undiminished affection, thy sincere and faithful friend,

RICHD SHACKLETON.

Ballitore: 28th of 4th month 1770.

To RICHARD SHACKLETON—6 *May* 1770

Corr. (1958), II, 135–36

My dear friend, I am now in the place, from whence I was weak and blameable enough to write you a very angry, a very Cruel, and in all respects a very improper Letter. I will not be more dilatory in making all the amends in my power for the offence, than I was in offending. So I write immediately on the receipt of your Letter. But let my apology be, if it be one, that a Spirit, not naturally over patient had about that time ten thousand things to mortifye it; and this coming on the back of them did for a while put me beside myself. I assure you I am so concerned for what you have felt that I could not bear to read through your description of it. A little triffling mere imprudence, at worst, did by no means deserve anything like a reproof; much less so harsh an one. As to my Wife you needed to make no apology at all to her. She felt nothing but goodwishes and friendship to you, and is by no means liable to those Spurts of Passion to which I am unfortunately but too subject. In truth, the publication was soon forgot;—produced no sort of effect—but was born down the Torrent of such matter, where one succeeds and carries away the other *velut unda impellitur unda.*[1] Pray forget it, as the world has, and as I do; burn the Letter I wrote which deserves no better fate; and may I beg since it is one of the drawbacks on those who get a little consideration in the world, that every little matter relative to them, how unfit soever for the publick Eye, is dragged before it by one means or other, that you would commit to the same flames any other letters or papers of mine which you may find and which you think liable, through some accident to be so abused. It is hardly credible how many people live by such publications and how hard it is altogether to escape their interested diligence.

This winter has been laborious and busy enough. The Court scheme still predominates; though every name in the Kingdom respectable for publick Virtue, publick Service, or publick Talents is against it. The Pamphlet which I sent to you,[2] and which has been well received, will explain to you the Grounds of our proceeding, better than I can do in this place. It is the political Creed of our Party. Many parts will be unintelligible to you I confess for want of knowlege of particular persons and facts; but on the whole I think you must enter into the design. Read it with some attention.

My Brother is to leave us Shortly; but I trust in God his stay in that disagreeable part of the world will be short. Mrs Burke is recovering; she is now in the Country; and desires to be most sincerely and most cordially rememberd to you to Mrs Shackleton and to your father.

My little Boy joins us in the same good wishes in proportion to his knowlege and remembrance of you. He is a boy of good dispositions and no bad parts; he is now forward in Homer and Lucian and makes Latin verses that are not altogether detestable for his time. Adieu my dear Shackleton forgive one who if he is quick to offend is ready to attone, who loves, values, and esteems your abilities and your Virtues; and never can think of your early and continued friendship, but as one of the chief blessings of his Life. I am my dear friend, once more, truly and affectionately yours

EDM BURKE

Gregories May 6. 1770

Have we no hope of seeing you here this Summer?

---

[1] As wave is pushed on by wave; see Ovid, *Metamorphoses*, xv, 181.
[2] *Thoughts on the Cause of the Present Discontents.* It was published on 23 April.

To DR WILLIAM MARKHAM—[*post* 9 *November* 1771]

Corr. (1958), II, 252–86

This extremely long draft of a letter had its origin in a quarrel (acute but temporary) between Burke and his old friend William Markham (1719–1807, Bishop of Chester and Archbishop of York, 1777). The quarrel arose from Burke's distress at the widespread belief that he was the author of the letters of Junius, which were scurrilous, anonymous attacks on the government. Burke tried to get Markham in intervene with his friend Lord Mansfield, who had helped to spread this rumor. In response, Markham apparently (his letters have been destroyed) criticized both the public and private life of Edmund, William, and Richard. By doing so he called forth this remarkable justification.

My Lord

When your Lordship is pleased, so severely to censure almost every part of my Conduct and Character, I should be without all comfort, if my Conscience did not as clearly accquit, as you have decisively condemned me. . . . I will consider your Lordships heavy accusation under the three heads into which it sems to be divided.

1st my conduct in conjunction with my political connections; 2dly Certain matters which your Lordship charges to my particular account and lastly the various crimes which your Lordship has collected from the private conversations of my nearest freinds and relations. To all these I shall answer fully, distinctly and I trust satisfactorily.

Your Lordship, by ashuming the persons of others whose opinions you do not condemn, considers the measures of my party—"in which I have been so forward to take a lead, as running the extreme line of wickedness".

This is what your Lordship states as the description of our measures and, as to our morals, you describe them, (still stating the opinion of others of which you express no disaprobation) "as who first used their sovereign basely, and then sought their Justification in slandering his character". Heavy charges both on persons and actions! My Lord, if, by accident, you believe, that such charges on such men, as compose our party, are groundless, pray why could you not imagine with equal Justice, aided by a little of not unbecoming partiality, that my particular part in those Actions, reported from the same bad authority, was not more blameable than that of the rest of our Party? But if your Lordship (as you seem to do) rather inclines to give credit to these imputations, Then, my Lord, I do freely and chearfully take my share in the measures: I take it with such numbers and such Persons, both of our own and other bodies, that I am as well defended as respectable authority and awful example can make me. Your Lordship ought to pity me under the influence of so plausible and irresistable a seduction. But my Lord I do not secure a presumption in my favour merely in the number and weight of the present *opposition;* If we have "run the extreme Line of wickedness"; there are but few now in his Majestys service, who has not pushed us very hard in the race; some have gone over one part, some another, some almost over all the course along with us. I can recollect but a very few who can escape much better than I can, unless Errour in Conduct is to be rectified by inconsistency of Character.

Whenever your Lordship, or any body else, shall distinctly specify any one of those measures, be it what it may, I will engage to call out some person now high in his Majesties Service and favour, to whom I will commit the Cause; who must either disgrace himself, or fully vindicate our proceedings. If you do not harshly censure this ministerial Advocate, permit me to say, that your Lordships Justice must necessarily suffer us to escape. It is not, I am sure, the fortune and situation, but the Actions of men, which become the subjects of your indignation. I am really afraid to join in your Lordship censure of our conduct, least I should lean too heavy on some respectable persons in Authority; and thus again become taxed with "ill treating some of the highest people in the Kingdom".

You do not think I am going into the business of six years, This is infinite: No I shall go on general but very satisfactory grounds. If The measures we have carried into Legislative acts be so extremely wicked, why does not the court with the power of the Nation in their hands redress the Mischief by repealing our Acts and regulations? But they all stand; and whilst they do I must respect them as making a part of the established laws of our Country. If the Measures we have proposed and lost, or those which we have opposed without success, were so wicked; they were wicked only in the intention, we have failed in the act. If the Nation likes the proceedings they enjoy the Benefit of them, Posterity must judge of their intrinsic value, and of the Prudence, the Reach of thought, the decorum, consistency moderation and Justice with which they were conceived and conducted from the beginning to the End.

Upon the merit of the Ministerial Conduct that of the Opposition must finally stand or fall. The matter of some part of it is not left to the representations of those that your Lordship lives with. I must suppose you have not read the grounds, upon which the opposition to some of the capital measures of Administration have been justified,—works which ought to be perused by everyone before he peremtorily attributes to the extreme Line of Wickedness the conduct of Large Bodies of Men.

As to "my forwardness in taking the Lead in the measures of the party", I am not sure that I perfectly understand the nature of the Charge. I am no Leader my Lord, nor do I ever answer for the Conduct of any one but myself. If your meaning be that I commonly make the Motions; or am forward in laying the grounds for opposition, your Lordship is certainly misinformed. I generally speak in justification of the vote I am to give very late in the debate.[1] But if by *forwardness* and *lead*, you mean nothing more than that I do with all my heart, all my soul and all my strength support the measures I believe to be right, the fact is undoubtedly true, But before either the fact itself or the earnestness with which it is pursued be clearly censurable, the measures must be proved to be wrong or to be unimportant: My Lord it is not my interest in my own case nor my disposition in any case, to receive the assertions of Enemies as competent proof of either, and as yet I have heard nothing else.

After stating by an Aposiopesis, the force of which mode of speech no one better understands than your Lordship that our Party has run the extreme line of wickedness, in the same mode you speak of them as having used the K. "basely and then seeking their justification in slandering his character".

My Lord, in one thing you do me great Justice; you say that my opinion differs very widely from yours upon this subject, it does indeed, it differs as widely as the remotest extremes can differ. To speak fully to the point is difficult. To be wholly silent, impossible. The Charge is heavy; and it is as general as it is henious; like the former on the measures of the party it points to no one circumstance of action, time, or place which can particularize it. No defence can therefore be made, but by opposing to it the denial of both the propositions of which the charge is compounded; and by shewing, as far as general presumptions can goe, the utter improbability of the existence of any Truth in either of them. Indeed, my Lord you have been cruelly abused and imposed upon. I am sure I shall think myself happy if the unlucky subject of my defence however it may fail for myself, may be obliquely and accidentally the means of undeceiving you in a mistaken opinion of the best characters in the Kingdom.

[1] This is confirmed by Cavendish's *Debates, passim.*

Before I say a word further, I must observe that your Lordship is the very first from whom I ever knew, that such a charge was made. I never heard it in any conversation; I never read it in any of the numerous publications on the part of the Court. I have always heard Lord R. and his freinds censured for a Behaviour rather too reserved and managed for the purposes of Opposition. But I make no doubt that such discourses as you mention are held. They are held very improperly; They are held with more mischief of the persons, in whose favour they seem to be utter'd, than even of those whom they intend to injure.

Will you permit me to speak on this business with a frankness suitable to its importance. Indeed my Lord his Majesties servants have in my humble opinion been much too free with the sacred name of their Master, both in their Apologies for themselves and in their accusations of others. I wish the Gentlemen of the Court to consider seriously, how well they consult an honour in which we have, all of us, so great an Interest and in which they have so peculiar and religious a trust, when they can affirm, that Lord R. and his freinds, have treated the K. basely. By the tenour of the sentence I must conclude that this charge of base treatment is fixed at the time when Lord R. and his freinds had the honour to serve the Crown. Your Lordship will recollect that Lord R. was called into the Closet, a full year after his removal from office,[a] with large offers for himself and for his freinds and even with powers still more extensive. Do these persons so affectedly zealous reflect in what manner they consult the personal glory of their sovereign when they represent him as shewing such favour to, and putting such confidence in those who were capable of treating him with *baseness?* do they in such a Charge consult the future connexion that ought ever to exist between that *Glory,* and the possible *interest* of their Master, in case the convenience of his Service, should once more induce him to call any of these eminent persons who are charged with having treated him basely into employment! But if they choose, on a supposition of the validity of the charge, to suppose that such an arangement is impossible, is it then altogether for the Kings Advantage to persuade such, and so large bodies of men, they they are proscribed, and as it were disinherited by the common Protector and Father of all his Subjects?

Besides, let me say, that though on every account the Character of the Sovereign ought to be preserved inviolate and that too with the

[a] July. 1767. [Burke's note in the margin.]

utmost care and tenderness; yet there are other Characters to be preserved also. Characters in which though the subject has not an equal
he has yet a very considerable interest. Your Lordship will hardly
think it altogether prudent (I will go no further, for I dare not return
a word of the hard language I received) wantonly to toss great names
in peoples faces in order to put them out of Countenance and to oblige
them either from shame to abandon their defence; or from warmth
to say things which may be misinterpreted into a criminal disrespect.
The former is hardly fair in argument, nor the latter in morals (Though
it often may be meant innocently as in this case I am ready to believe
it.) It has the air of insidiously drawing men upon dangerous ground
in order to entrap them on it; and this, if I were in your Lordship
place and armed with your Authority from station and knowledge, I
would certainly say to those who have the Levity to hold such discourses.

I would also submit to your Lordships consideration whether it be
right to set the people upon too many enquiries into these matters
that trench so nearly upon Anecdote; Certainly my Lord the last thing
the people of England will suspect in Lord R. and his great freinds
is anything whatsoever of baseness either done or suffered. They will
enquire whence and how this surprizing charge has arisen and possibly
in the course of such an Enquiry their censure may fall not lightly
upon those who are capable of abusing either their Ears or the Ears
of their Sovereign with such a gross charge upon the best Subjects
that he has.

Any Prince might glory in having such Subjects. He might well
rejoice in finding, that the persons who have always been the truest
to the succession of his family, are at the same time distinguish'd
among his people, for their unspotted honour and integrity, for their
disinterested Love of their Country, and for every virtue publick and
private. No wise King of G.B. would think it for his credit to let it
go abroad that he considered himself or was considerd by others as
personally at variance with Lord R. a D. of R. a D. of P. an E. of D[2]
the families of the Cavendishes, with a Savill a Dowdswell and a very
long train of names who are the ornaments of his country in peace,
and to some of whom he owes some of the greatest Glories of his own
and his predecessors Reign in all the various services of the late war.

---

[2] Lord Rockingham, a Duke of Richmond, a Duke of Portland and an Earl of Dartmouth.

The Publick will not lightly believe, that the close Connections of the late D of N.[3] and the late D of Cumberland[4] have been capable of using basely a King of the Brunswick line.

As little will anyone credit the other part of the Charge, that they sought their justification in traducing his Majesties character. Till this day they have never heard of this charge and therefore most certainly never could be put to this Justification. But if you mean that they use it in defence of their measures in opposition; surely you cannot imagine that they are so miserably put to it for Argument as to have no other way of defending themselves but by traducing any Character whatsoever. If they are alleged to have used such Justification in Parliamentary debate; the time and occasion ought to be marked. If in writing, the piece ought to be shewn, and ought with some probability to be carried home to them. If in Conversation the informer ought to appear and make good the matter he delates. In no other way than one of these three can the Persons have committed the offence your Lordship mentions to be charged upon them.

Avoiding all offensive Terms or any kind of recrimination on their accusers, I simply say they deny the Truth of the Charge and I trust nobody can bring a shadow of proof for it. I am sorry that in your Lordships numerous freinds, you could find no one man under personal obligations to the Leader of that respectable party, who might long since have removed those impressions from your Lordships mind, and rendered my poor defence unnecessary.

I have said all I mean to say in vindication of my having gloried in my political connexions, and in the part I have taken along with them. My principles, indeed the principles of common sense lead me to act in Corps. Accident first threw me into this party. When I was again at Liberty Knowledge and reflection induced me to reenter it, principle and experience have confirmed me in it. Your Lordship will find it difficult to shew, where a man who wished to act systematically in publick business, could have aranged himself more reputably. By arranging myself with them I trust I have given some sort of security to the publick for my good Behaviour. That versatility those sudden evolutions which have something derogated from the credit of all publick professions are things not so easy in large Bodies, as when men act alone; or in light Squadrons. A man's virtue is best secured

[3] Thomas Pelham Holles, 1st Duke of Newcastle (1693–1768).
[4] William Augustus, Duke of Cumberland (1721–65), uncle of George III.

by shame, and best improved by Emulation in the Society of virtuous
men. Most of my publick procedings have been in the strictest concurrence with that party and with your Lordships Candour and mature
consideration I hope I may safely leave both the party and its
proceedings.

I now pass to the seperate account you have opened with myself for
matters of my own private conduct. Here my Lord you accuse me of
maltreating the greatest men in the Kingdom you particularise &c
&c——and you seem to think that I have not sufficiently "distinguished myself from useless declaimers who are valued only for Bear
Garden Talents", and that I have given the world an "impression of
me, as a man capable of things dangerous and desperate". This is the
peculium of blame which your Lordship has portioned out to me and
seperated from the common stock. Pardon me if I think you have your
accounts of me from men of little moderation; Indeed from a Kind
and Class of Enemies far below the common generosity of that adverse
character. Has your Lordship then found me in the innumerable conversations that we have had together for many years, (which I now
remember with a melancholly pleasure) an useless declaimer and distinguished by Bear Garden Talents? If your Lordship has not found
this in my conversation (you will not affirm that you have), why will
you so easily give credit to those who assert, that I am of another
Character wherever you do not happen to see me? My Lord I have
written some trifles, They are indeed full of imperfections, but they
are not altogether useless declamations, nor have they I think a great
deal of the scurrilities of the Bear Garden; some of them are written
too on a subject of publick controversy. But there I am safe enough,
what a man writes defends or accuses itself; what he speaks is but too
much at the mercy of narrators, and I have fallen amongst the very
worst of that odious band.

Hypocrisy is not cheap vice; nor can our natural Temper be masked
for many years together. I have not lived my Lord at any period of
my life nor do I live at present in societies where the talents your
Lordship alludes to are in any sort of request. I Live and have Lived
in Liberal and humanized company, who as they could never endure
such a character, would be infinitely surprized at this imputation upon
a person whom at least they tollerate.

As to some little occasional sallies out of serious business which you
have been ready to commend in other men and which when not ill
executed have been commended by all Ancient and modern cricks.
I am sure they are not without their use in popular debates. For my

own part in them I can only say that if I could receive any comfort under your Lordships displeasure I have the consolation not to be equally ill thought of by every body. You Know I am sure a person of Rank long removed from Publick Business in which he had much distinguished himself and who was equally distinguished for the Elegance of his manners and the well bred felicity of his Wit,[a] has a great deal more than once repeated without any very harsh Censure some of the Trifles which less grave occasions have drawn from me in the house. He has even condescended to say most obliging things to myself upon the Subject. That person I assure your Lordship is not so poor in the resources of real politeness as to be driven to supply his deficiencies out of the fund of ill placed Flattery. He is no way connected with me in party or otherwise. He is too considerable to be one of my admirers, and all I shall say is, He did not find in any of my little pleasanteries the relish of that celebrated academy from which your Lordship is pleased to derive them.

The attacks I have made are specified to be on Mr Grenville, Mr Rigby; Sir Wm Bagot and Lord Barrington. You could lengthen, you say, the catalogue; certainly you could; for I have had rather more altercations than are mentioned in this List, and your Lordship as certainly supposes me the aggressor in all of them. As to the first I only desire in common justice to me and even to Mr Grenville[5] that his court freinds will not be too superfluously Kind to his memory, that they will not resent any injuries to him for which he had no resentment himself. Perhaps your Lordship does not know, that I had the honour of being on the best terms with Mr Grenville which continued uninterrupted to his death, that he gave to my Kinsman Wm Burke and to me a pressing invitation to his house in the Country. That in his house in Town upon a Business too which most people would think delicate, we had a long Conversation wherein without any direliction of principle on either side, we settled the matter to mutual satisfaction, and that he afterwards was so obliging to enter upon a very curious and interesting conversation relative to many of the most essential particulars of his Ministry and Life. His Brother Lord Temple is Known to cherish the most affectionate reverence to his memory. I have the pleasure to assure your Lordship that I am at this instant in intimacy and on terms of freindship with Lord Temple,

[a] Lord Chesterfield. [Burke's note.]

[5] Burke had vigorously attacked George Grenville's American policy both in the House and in his *Observations on a Late Publication intituled the 'Present State of the Nation'*, 1769.

who most assuredly would not do me that honour, if he thought my difference in opinion with him or his Brother had ever carried me to lengths unjustifiable among Gentlemen. . . .

Now my Lord, at the black tail of this black catalogue of Accusations, let me stirr up the principle of Candour, which all this Slander has for a moment smothered in you, and ask you seriously, whether you beleive that in coming into the House of Commons, "I entered like a wolf" into a fold of Lambs, and with ferocious and savage fury "snapd now at one, now at another" of those meek and passive Creatures, without mercy fear or shame? Does not your Lordship think it possible that in such a place, where such matters are agitated as will call out all of the wild Beast that lurks in human nature, that there are other animals with Fangs and Claws besides me? Does your Lordship think it absolutely incredible, that attempts might be made to *pull me down;* and that I may have been necessitated to make some strong Efforts to *keep myself up?* Do you seriously think, that the Understandings of your Narrators are better disciplined in the Duties and Decorums of publick Life than mine? Do you imagine, that they are not equally liable to passions similar to mine, which may mislead them in the representation possibly in their conceptions of my Conduct? Have they not Interests far more considerable than mine, which may as naturally bias them, from the Strait Line of their Duty? You were "overborn", you say "when you" did me the very great Honor of becoming my advocate, "by the number of charges against me". I am sorry that you threw up your Brief so early and that I lost on such an insufficient Ground all the advantage of your Lordships goodness and Ability, Because it is evidently not the *number* but the truth of the Charges, that ought to prevail in any equal Tribunal. If it should be otherwise, nothing will save me, either now or in future; for you may be very sure, that as many as my actions are, just so many will be the Charges of my Enemies. Did your Lordship ever hear of a man acting in publick who was free from them? If I were with all Expressions of tenderness friendship and Compassion to write down but one half of the Language of thier Enemies, concerning any given publick person, whom *you* know and esteem, I am very much afraid, if I sent it to you, your Lordship would think it little else than a Libel. If I sent it to any of *themselves* you would think it a Gross insult. Suppose that one of the best friends they have, were to make such a collection for the Instruction and Entertainment of Lord Chatham, or Lord Mansfield, or the Duke of Grafton, or of Lord North. They are greater Men than I; they have the advantage of their Dignity; Worse things have been said of them. Your Lordship does not think that the Eminence of their Station ought to make the bearing of truth less necessary to them, or make it less proper for them to bear it with Temper; In what Light would you consider such a communication to these persons? even though it were made lest they should happen not to be apprised of the Tone of their Enemies, or be unacquainted with the Language of an uniform Series of 5 years daily newspapers?[a]

I know well enough what my Enemies say. I know too what my Conscience answers to their malice. My publick Conduct coextensive with my largest *relation* must be my Glory or my Shame. Has your Lordship found one single part of it to be praiseworthy?

If I act in party, you more than insinuate that the party runs the extreme line of wickedness; if I act alone, then I have some wickedness of Supererogation beyond that Line, some Eccentric Crimes to answer for. In every altercation I am the Aggressor; my debate is declamation; my Raillery the Bear Garden; In my Motions, I shew myself capable of "things dangerous and desperate." The daily conversations of my friends and Relations, are guilty of "all the Malignity of treason." My House—"by the deductions of no exceptionable Logic easily taken for an Hole of Adders." My lord all this, and more are your Sentiments of me, I trust expressed in Anger, and in the vehemence of a mistaken Zeal, from which no Talents nor Situation will always exempt even Men of Piety and Virtue. If indeed you censure many material parts of my little publick System, I do not wonder that you condemn the whole.

My Principles are all settled and arranged, and indeed at my time of Life, and after so much reading and reflection, I should be ashamed to be caught at hesitation and doubt, when I ought to be in the midst of Action, not, as I have seen some, to be, as Milton says *"unpractised and unprepared, and still to seek."*[6] However this necessary use of the principles I have, will not make me shut my Ears to others which as yet I have not; I only wish to act upon some that are rational.

"I illtreat the first Men in the Kingdom". If you shew me that in no Case this may be my Duty I will confess I am in the wrong. I am a respecter of Authority. But my Lord I execute my share of an important magistracy, and I conceive that it may happen to be part of my Office to accuse and even very ill treat the first Men in the

[a] The Bishop in his Letter states his fear that being always surrounded by admirers I do not know the Language of my Enemies. [Burke's note.]

[6] *Paradise Lost*, VIII, 197.

Kingdom; Would your Lordship have me so treat Clerks in office, who transcribe Letters, or Serjeants of the Guards who execute orders? "I attacked Lord Barrington." I did so, and let me add I attacked Lord Weymouth as much as Him; and I attackd Lord Hillsborough as much as either, though on another Ground. But I did this in a regular, sober, constitutional manner. However I bear your Censure the better as I am absolutely satisfied that to this minute you neither know a single Ground on which, I made the attacks, nor the temper with, which I conducted myself in any of the Proceedings upon which you charge me. I never made more than two motions.[7] As to that on St Georges fields, I did in effect repeat it,[8] and I never slept so happily as after I had discharged myself of that accusation. I now give over the pursuit, not as blameable but hopeless. It was indeed very nearly what your Lordship calls it a proceeding *"dangerous and desperate"*; *desperate* as to hope of success; dangerous as it has been a means of forfeiting your good opinions; To its Object it proved very innoxious. It has not diminished a Shilling of Lord Barringtons salary. But if it had succeeded, I have no doubt that very salutary Effects to the public, would have followed from it.

I acted to the best of my judgment. It would be hard to find a bad motive for my Conduct in this particular. I am a Man of none but civil talents, such as they are; and I can have no views from a state of disorder and confusion; no, not more than even your Lordship.

"Your Lordship tells me it is not what pretensions I may have but what the world will chuse to allow me". What Pretensions My Lord am I making to any thing that the world has to allow or to refuse? I make no Pretensions my Lord but those which, with Gods Blessing, no Power can take from me, those of doing my duty agreably to my own Ideas, within the Laws of the land, and the Rules and orders of the Body to which I belong; and I will do that Duty with such vigour, or such remission, as I may think, will best answer the purpose of my trust. If by Pretensions you mean Places, I sollicit none, and I really think I never shall; though I would very gladly serve the Crown and be of use to my own family, if I could do it with Honor. . . .

My Lord, this part of your letter is indeed very serious. The crimes are high; the Accuser of great Authority; and the persons accusd my nearest and dearest friends. You would think me I am sure the basest

---

[7] That of 8 March 1769 for an inquiry into the conduct of the Government during the riots in St George's Fields and that of 9 May 1770 for an inquiry into the causes of the late disorders in the colonies in North America.

[8] In the debate of 13 November 1770 on the Address.

of friends, the worst of Brothers, and the most unworthy and unnatural of all men if I took in very good part and as an act of kindness your Lordships charges against them.

My Lord, Mr Wm Burke the first you set to the bar, has had the closest and longest friendship for me, and has pursued it with such nobleness in all respects as has no example in these times and would have dignifyd the best periods of History. Whenever I was in question, he has been not only ready but earnest even to annihilate himself. And he has not been only earnest but fortunate in his endeavours in my favour. Looking back to the course of my life, I remember no one considerable benefit in the whole of it which I did not mediately or immediately derive from him. To him I owe my connexion with Lord Rockingham. To him I am indebted for my seat in Parliament. To him it is I must referr all the happiness and all the advantages I received from a long acquaintance with your Lordship. For me he gave up a respectable employment of a thousand pounds a year with other very fair pretensions; he gave up an employment which he filld with pleasure to himself, with great honour to his Abilities and with great satisfaction to his principal in Office.[9] Indeed he both held and quitted it with such a well arranged discharge of all his Dutys that a strict friendship subsists between him and the Principal he left from that moment even to this, amidst all the rage and confusion of parties. This employment too he held upon terms of Parliamentary freedom that were very agreeable and altogether singular. But he resignd it, to give an example and encouragement to me, not to grow fearfull or languid in the course to which he had always advisd me. To encourage me he gave his own Interest the first Stab—*Pæte non dolet*.[10] This my Lord was true friendship, and if I act an honourable part in life, the first of all benefits, it is in great measure due to him. He loved your Lordship too and would have died for you, I am thoroughly persuaded he would. He had the most ardent affection for you and the most unbounded confidence in you. If there was any difference between his regard for you and me, it is that there were certain disparities which made him look up to you with greater reverence. Such a friendship can grow in none but a soil favourable to and producing every kind of Virtue; and accordingly he has nothing like a fault about him that does not arise from the luxuriance of some generous quality. Do not "disinherit your Son" for anything Will Burke is capable of doing;

[9] General Conway.

[10] 'Paetus, it doesn't hurt': said by Arria to her husband, Caecina Paetus, to encourage him to commit suicide, while she stuck the knife into herself (Pliny, *Espistles*, III, 16, Sec. 13).

I look with pleasure and with the most auspicious hopes, and with I am sure very unaffected good wishes on your growing family. But if I was their father, my prayer in their favour would be for half his virtues. I would ask for no more, because I would wish a good man to be happy and prosperous in the World. My Lord I owe this honest testimony, all I can return for a friendship of which I can never make myself deserving. As to him, my Lord, I am not capable of telling you in what manner he felt your charges. He answers nothing to them. He only bids me tell you, that never being able to suppose himself in a situation of serious controversy with your Lordship, much less, as the Culprit in a *criminal accusation* for a matter of *state* brought by *you* upon his *private* conversation, he knows not what to say. He is at your Mercy. He really cannot put his pen to paper on this Subject tho he has two or three times attempted it. Permit me my Lord on this very serious head to lay before your Lordship a very few matters for your consideration; I feel myself as averse to the stating this matter to your Lordship in a Style of controversy as my friend is incapable of it. Will your Lordship then have the goodness to consider, that the conversations of your friend to which your Lordship gives in your passion such very hard names, have passd intirely *between you and him*, that they have passd in the freedom of friendship, in the openness of the most unreserved confidence. Is it true that no one was witness to any thing capable of such a construction out of the inmost recesses of your own family? Does your Lordship recollect, that there was any Stranger present, in any mixd company, either at your house or elsewhere, who heard any such conversation? Now my Lord if there be no such witness out of your own family (*te concute*)[11] might it not be rather, the intire confidence that Mr Burke reposed in your honour, than any indiscretion which had induced him to enter with you into topics in themselves delicate and extremely capable of misconstructions. I never will believe the loosest flow of the heart in all its temporary feelings to be indiscreet in conversation with you.

My Lord there is another consideration which I would beg leave to submit to you upon these supposed culpable conversations. I believe if you call to mind times and circumstances you will find that there could scarce have passd any private political conversation between W. Burke and your Lordship for near three years. A very hard Statute

[11] Examine yourself; see Horace, *Satires*, I, III, 34–5.

was made concerning words in the reign of K. Ch.2.[12] but hard as it was, it limited the prosecution to be within   [13] otherwise the Statute would not have been hard but intolerable, and the reason is extremely clear. Words are fugitive and the lapse of a little time may cancel such a variety of explanatory circumstances in the mind of the party accused as extremely to enfeeble, perhaps entirely to destroy a very full defence. Besides, the memory of the informer may be full as fallacious as that of the party chargd. If he has not set down the words, their true Spirit may well have escapd him. If he has, it furnishes a very just presumption, that he has stored up this invidious matter for so long a time not for the purposes of Justice but of malice. Your Lordship will tell me that you are not now making a Charge in a Court of Justice. Very true; but permit me to say, that the Equity and reason of these Rules ought to be carried into all personal Reproaches and revilings for supposed similar Offences so long passd. When any person has not *at the time expressd any disapprobation of these discourses*, every principle of justice precludes him and ought to stop his mouth for ever. Your Lordship does in effect admit that you heard without any marks of disapprobation discourses to which your Lordship now gives appellations that for your own sake I cannot bear to repeat. You say that a "dislike of Altercation, and a respect to your profession" hinderd you from expressing your Sentiments at the time. May I presume to differ in this point and to think that it was so far from being contrary to the Duties and decencies of your sacred profession, that nothing was more strictly within both, than to give grave and sober Counsel upon such occasions to those with whom you condescended to live. If the immediate moment was too sudden or the parties appeard too warm, Advice upon the next day would have been prudent from a wise man, proper from a friend; charitable from a divine; full as much so, pardon the weakness of my Judgment, as to keep charges of the kind in your own bosom, for upwards of two years, and then to produce those charges for the first time in the Spirit and language of the bitterest reproach not against the Speaker of the words, but against a third person (myself) in order to aggravate ac-

---

[12] 13 Car. II, St. I, c. i. (1661). The act to preserve the Person and Government of the King. It imposed among other things the penalties of praemunire on all who maintained in writing or speech various statements damaging to the restored monarchy. Prosecution had to be undertaken within six months of the offence.

[13] There is a space of two or three words at this point.

cusations against *me*, which you have carried on with much earnestness, though without any provocation real or pretended. My Lord there was no reason, drawn from profession or temper, (I beg leave to say) for your Silence and your forbearance at that time, that does not as strongly at least subsist against your reproaches and your warmth at this. If you thought these conversations unadvised, it was a reason for advice; if you thought they argued depravity it was a reason for rupture. You neither gave your Advice; shewd your disapprobation, or came to any Rupture. Far from it; after, long after any period you can assign, for such supposed conversation, much intercourse has passd between W Burke and your Lordship, and I do not remember that you have treated our common friend at any time of our long acquaintance with warmer demonstrations of affection; some of which when you please I will point out to your Lordships recollection. I therefore am obliged to conclude, that your Lordships memory has not done its Office quite perfectly on this occasion; and that the discourses which passd so long ago were of a different nature from what you consider them in the moment of your present zeal and warmth.

As to my Brother, I am bound to do him justice at the very least. He is too near to me to make it decent for me to speak what I think of him, and which others would say, with more propriety and with equal pleasure. I assure you my Lord, his Majesty has not those who serve him in the highest as he does in the lowest capacity, who are better affected to his Government, or more capable of doing it honour or Service. My Lord he heard with great astonishment, and some feeling your Lordships criminal accusations, so heavy in the matter and so unmanagd in the Epithets. He would immediately have answered for himself, but I interposed and took it into hands very equal to it, for it stands in need of no skill or ability. First my Lord I must observe, as in the Case of my Kinsman, so in that of my Brother, not one of the persons who make the charges upon me to alledge his conversation as the cause. This is your Lordships own, peculiar, and appropriate. My Lord, please to recollect in the next place that no *late* discourses of *his* could possibly give Offence or furnish ground for the late presumptions against *me*, for the justification of which presumption your Lordship has referrd to those supposed discourses of his. He is but just returned to the Kingdom after an absence of near two years. He was actually not returned to England at the time when this hue and cry of the Court was raised against me. So far as to the late *presumed* public conversations, in which my Lord it is simply, not improbable, but absolutely impossible he should have been the cause and ground of recent accusations against me.

But if your Lordship supposes that the impropriety and publicity of conversations in former days has made such an impression as to produce this effect at such a distance of time; be so good as to recollect the extreme improbability of the charge. A great part of the time he spent in England was, from, to us, a melancholy accident,[14] passd in his Bed or chair, some part in Ireland. My Lord his acquaintance beyond my closest connections is very limited. Who of those makes this charge upon him. Who is it that charges him except your Lordship? you indeed proceed against him in a manner, in which I do not so readily recognize your Lordships natural and usual generosity. You bring a charge upon him, which in your way of making it, it is impossible in case of the most perfect Innocence that he should be able to refute. The charge (dropping the handsome epithet) is not for indecorum or indiscretion, but for *falsehood*. The only defence therefore (if the fact of the words were once admitted) would be to plead that the words were *true*. My Lord, will you seriously say, that you would suffer him to alledge any sort of proofs of the truth of such an assertion as you suppose? Would you not consider the very attempt to be a new Offence, would you not consider it as an Offence ten times heavier than the first? Recollect that the informations for libels has lately been purged of the word *false*.[15] This (if legally) was very properly done, as the Lawyers have been in a practice of not giving Evidence to the falsehood, or admitting disculpatory Testimony to the truth. I confess I should carefully imitate this proceeding of the Lawyers in my intercourse with mankind, and would think it very unjust and improper in me to accuse any man with a departure from veracity, where his attempt to prove the truth would be more dangerous to him than his admitting the falsehood with which He stood charged. But my Lord my Brother puts himself on his defence and does totally deny the fact. Who out of your own family was present at any such discourse at any time? My Brother never had the honour of being often in your Lordships company; when he was he stood in some awe, tho in no sort of fear of you. He has had very few political discourses with you, and never any thing resembling a political dispute, but one. This was on your Lordships ending a conversation, of which I was

[14] His broken leg.
[15] In Rex *v.* Almon (*State Trials*, xx, 837) Lord Mansfield said that in the indictments for libel formerly 'they put in the word "false" but . . . it was left out many years ago; and the meaning of leaving this out is, that it is totally immaterial in point of proof, true or false'.

(as I am now) the unhappy Subject, with declaring that "Party operated to eradicate every virtue out of the heart of man". On that occasion, he grew into some warmth and retorted on other factions some of the charges your Lordship had made upon me. This my Lord, he never mentiond to me, untill his necessary justification drew it from him. He proceeded to justify the propriety of oppositions by the principles of the Revolution, in which he said they were founded. So far from blaming that glorious Event, or its sound principles, that he assumed them as the very ground of his argument. He asserts that he never had any other discourse with your Lordship about the Revolution. Consider my Lord, how easy it is for a passionate recollection of a passionate debate to confound matters strangely, suppose my Lord I was to say that the Revolution could not be supported unless some lesser modes of opposition could be also justified. My Lord I do say it; but I say it upon paper. This in conversations of years standing, the hearer might forget to have been an hypothetical proposition. The little piddling monosyllable—if—might slip out of the memory and the thing stand in all the glare of a criminal Offence, so dangerous it is to mention such things without their necessary Adjuncts; the time the occasion, the posture of the debate, the purpose of the Speaker. So dangerous after a long time past to mention them at all in a Style of accusation or reproach.

Supposing some impropriety in my Brothers language with regard to persons in power; I must beg leave to observe, that being utterd only to yourself, very vulgar generosity would as easily pardon the natural warmth of a Brother, as I do from my Soul and most unaffectedly forgive the reflection on me which gave occasion to that warmth in him. At any rate this imprudence never went beyond the very inside of your own family. Both my friends however do insist upon it, that such discourses as your Lordship supposes, may not be confounded with strong censures upon what are sometimes, though with great impropriety, called the Kings measures. However it is the only comfort they have if your Lordship persists in this charge, that you charge them with nothing in which by your Lordships own account they are not involved with the very best men, and best affected Subjects his Majesty can boast of.

With regard to these discourses of my Brother and my friend you say you "have done all you could, you did not publish them". I am always fond of doing justice to your Lordships actions. You did very rightly and wisely. If your Lordship takes the word—publishing, in the vulgar Sense, for making generally known, be pleased to reflect, if your Lordships Idea be founded, that they themselves held these discourses and very publickly in other places (as you infer by an Argument a fortiori from their private conversation in your house) then my Lord your publication of what they said to you, would be the most idle and superfluous piece of zeal in the world. They have saved you the invidious and unpleasant task of revealing private conversation. If your Lordship means by publication (as the Lawyers sometimes do) any communication, and would apply it as a discovery to persons in power, it would be a proceeding, I am sure, wholly shocking to the nobleness of your nature, to make any charge where by the circumstances, it is impossible to oppose to it any kind of defence. But if you meant by publication, a denunciation as a matter criminal, Your Lordship must have, while our Laws stand in Vigour quite other sort of matter, and other sort of proof, I assure you, than I think you could possibly bring upon the occasion.

Therefore whilst I do justice to the rectitude of your conduct I cannot acknowledge it as any thing of favour, kindness or friendship, and therefore I only wish you had not said "you had done all you could" for you could do nothing else in common sense and common Justice.

Almost every word in the last page but one of your letter carries a Sting with it. You charge my friends with   .[16]
This is all full of various, odd and complicated charges and insinuations, but all conveying matter of invidious and to us most dangerous reflexion, easily understood in the gross, though hard enough to be develloped into the particulars. However my Lord, my desire of giving complete satisfaction to your Lordship and to justice induces me to bring it into distinctness as well as I am able.[17]

By the discourses which your Lordship holds to be so obnoxious, and imprudent, I must suppose your Lordship must mean that my friends have at some time or other thrown out some very severe strictures on the memory of those princes who have so long since demised. I am compelled whether I will or no, to think this the Gist of the accusation, because some Gentlemen who have been considered I know not how justly, as professed and very publick advocates and admirers of that illustrious family, have had no sort of reason to think their persons to be obnoxious or their discourses to be imprudent. Nay some who were so attached to that family, as to hold close connections with such as pretended however falsely, to belong to it, have had no

---

[16] There is a space of several lines at this point.
[17] A space of uncertain length follows and the draft continues on a new sheet.

reason to repent of this their close connection and enthusiastick attachment. I will not say my Lord that my friends may not in argument where they thought things swayed too much to that side, have rather spoken disrespectfully, but they thought safely of a king an 100 years dead, I and others have heard them do it. People will say many things in Argument and when they are provoked by what they think extravagant Notions of their adversarys. Nay it is not uncommon, when Men are got into debates to take now one side, now another of a question, as the momentary humour of the Man, and the occasion called for, with all the Latitude, that the antiquated freedom and ease of English conversation among friends, did in former days encourage and excuse, and indeed in speaking to your Lordship they thought themselves, I dare say equally safe whether they commended or blamed any part or all of that individual family. As to Me My Lord on whom the Light thrown on my friends is brought to reflect with undiminished Lustre, I assure you that I have always spoken and thought on that subject with all that perfect calmness which belongs to it. My passions are not to be roused either on the side of partiality or on that of hatred, by those who lye in their cold lead quiet and innoxious in the Chapel of Henry 7[18] in the Churches of Windsor Castle or La Trappe.[19] Quorum cinis tegit appia atq. Latina.[20] My opinion of the truth and falsehood of facts related in History, is formed on the common rules of Criticism. My opinion of Characters on those rules, and on the common principles of morality. I have no side in these matters, as your Lordship has a little invidiously put it. But I will always speak what I think without caring one farthing what is the bon ton upon the subject either at Court in Coffee houses, untill all honest freedom of disquisition and all manly Liberty of speech shall by legal or other power be conclusively put an End to. Good reasons may exist for such a restraint; and perhaps we are at the Eve of it. But until the time does actually arrive, I shall cherish and cultivate in myself and those I live, a *decent* freedom of Speech in publick; *all* freedom of speech among confidential friends; where other principles than those of decorum are the Lawgivers. To this freedom your Lordships friends the antients (in a Language you understand much better than I do) gave

---

[18] Henry VII's Chapel, Westminster Abbey. Burke refers to the tombs of the Kings of England there and in Windsor Chapel.

[19] Burke seems to suggest that the tomb of James II was at the monastery of La Trappe in France. Though James visited and admired La Trappe no part of his remains were buried there.

[20] Burke misquotes the last line of Juvenal's first *Satire:* 'Whose ashes lie under the Flaminian and Latin roads'.

an Honourable name and classed it among the Virtues.[21] But whether a *Virtue*, or only an *Enjoyment* I assure your Lordship that neither Courts nor town Halls with all they could give of gold Boxes or Pensions could indemnify me for the want of an Hours use of it. You tell me that these historical discussions "are usually held the tests of Principles". Possibly they may. I However dont apprehend that I am responsible for the opinions of the Vulgar till I adopt them. My Lord I have not learned my publick principles, in any such wild, unsystematick, and preposterous a Mode. I have taken them from quite other Scources than those of Mr Carte[22] or Monr Rapin de Thoiras.[23] My principles enable me to form my judgement upon Men and Actions in History, just as they do in current life; and are not formed out of events and Characters, either present or past. History is a preceptor of Prudence not of principles. The principles of true politicks are those of morality enlarged, and I neither now do or ever will admit of any other. But when your Lordship speaks of tests of publick principles, there is one which you have not mentioned but which let me say is far above them all. The actions and Conduct of Men. Let mine and those of my friends speak for our publick principles. If the last 6 years are not enough, let us be on our trial for 6 more. That indeed is in the hands of providence not in ours. But I trust, that He who has made honest fame a lawful Object of prayer and pursuit, and the possession of   [24] to stand second in the order of his Blessings will give us means and Will to live down all charges and Aspersions. The principles that guide us in publick and in private, which as they are not of our devising but moulded into the nature and essence of things, will endure with the Sun and Moon, long very long after Whig and Tory, Stuart and Brunswick, and all such miserable Bubbles and playthings of the Hour are vanished from existence, and from memory. My friends and myself may sink into Errors and even into considerable faults; but I trust that these principles will buoy us up again, so that we shall have something to set against our imperfections, and stand with the world at least not as the worst Men or the worst Citizens of our day.

---

[21] See Aristotle, *Nicomachean Ethics*, IV, 7.

[22] Thomas Carte (1686–1754). His *History of England* in four volumes was published between 1747 and 1755.

[23] Paul de Rapin, usually called Rapin-Thoyras (1661–1725), Huguenot refugee. His *History of England*, first published in French in 1723–5 and later translated into English, and continued by Nicholas Tindal, won wide popularity.

[24] A word omitted.

My Lord in charging us with indiscretion, together with the word stuarts, you have coupled the revolution; If I were to guess at a charge of indiscretion, from the Credit and fortunes of Men, I should on this occasion suppose we had spoken too favourably of that Event. But do you mean the contrary? and under this and the foregoing words seriously intend to insinuate a charge of Jacobitism? Then be it so—I am afraid that our Enemies who do not allow us *common* Virtues, will hardly agree with you in giving us the Credit of so amazing, and *supernatural* a fidelity; that at the Expence of fame and fortune, and every thing dear to Man, we should choose to be attached to a person when He is deserted by the whole world and by himself. When He has, as I am told, not so much as a single Scotch, English, or Irish footman about him. Truly we never were so wonderfully dazzled with the splendours of actual royalty, as to be captivated with what is not even the shadow of it; nor ever was so in my time. If you mean that, not our *attachments* but our *principles* are of that sort; favourable to arbitrary powers, truely in our present connections, we have brought those principles to the very worst imaginable market, when the very best (in common opinion) was directly open before us. We have built our Chalcedon, with the chosen Port of the Universe full in our prospect.[25] But my Lord I must again attribute these reflections to an over warmth in your temper, or an Error in your Memory, or to both. My Brother and my friend or myself never have for a moment, thought other of the revolution than as of an Act just, necessary, and most Honourable to this nation whose Liberty and prosperity it has ensured to this time; and will for Ages, if its true principles be well adhered to. Your Lordship is more indulgent than we wish. I cannot admit that men have a Liberty of taking seriously and dogmatically what side they please in this question. I dont mean in this or in any thing to abridge any mans private Liberty. but I am sure that Man is not safely placed in any weighty publick trust in this Kingdom, who thinks of the revolution in any other manner than that which I have mentioned.

This is no matter of historical Criticism. It is a moral conclusion, on an undisputed fact. A Man who condemns the revolution has no longer any obnoxious persons to hand his principles on, and therefore, He and they may be made but too convenient to the executive powers of the time. But for this reason, He is much more dangerous than formerly to the Constitution and Liberties of his Country. Let me add

---

[25] The men who built Chalcedon were said to be blind, since they chose a poor site for their city, though the grander one that was later Byzantium was in full view across the Sea of Marmara. The story appears in Herodotus, IV, 144.

further, that a Man who praises the *fact* of the revolution, and abandons its *principles;* substituting the *instrumental* persons and establishments consequential to that Event, in the place of its true *Ends*, is as bad as the former. To me indeed He seems to be infinitely worse, as He can have no sound moral principles of any kind; nor [be] a fit servant for honest Government in any Mode whatever. The one has *lost* his Attachment; the last has *deserted* his principle; and the last is by far the most culpable and the most dangerous. These are, always were my sentiments and expression on the revolution, drawn from principles of publick Law and natural Justice, well Spun, and firmly wove together, not patched out of party coloured Rags, picked from the filthy Dunghills of old womens superstitions, and childrens Credulity; not from Fuller's warming pan,[26] or Oats plot,[27] Fergusons manifesto,[28] or manwarings Massacre,[29] no nor from the paltry memoirs of that Age, which I would as soon take for its History, as I would take the Authority of *the Whisperer*[30] for the Events of this Reign; or that of the pensioners of the present Court for the Character of King George the Second.[31]

I say nothing of W Bs early habits you know them. If I were to mention those of my Brother, his Education not so learned as yours had been however at least as much in the utmost Severity of Whig Principles.

But I say nothing of that inferrd Education, which is as Nothing— We came both of us pretty early into our own hands; and our principles

[26] William Fuller (1670–c. 1717) published in 1696 a false revelation about the 'warming pan plot', the story that James, the heir of James II, was a child smuggled into the palace in a warming pan.

[27] The notorious Popish Plot which Titus Oates falsely claimed to expose in 1678.

[28] The Declaration given out by the Duke of Monmouth at the outset of his abortive invasion of 1685 was written by Robert Ferguson, a discreditable Scottish adventurer. Macaulay called it 'a libel of the lowest class, both in sentiment and language' (*History of England*, ed. C. H. Firth, London, 1913–15, II, 564).

[29] Burke would seem to be referring to the allegations that the Irish Rebellion of 1641 began with a massacre of the Protestants of Ulster, a subject of much controversy at the time. It is not clear why he called it 'manwarings Massacre'; possibly Manwaring is a slip by him or the scribe for Mervyn, and the allusion is to Colonel Audley Mervyn's *An Exact Relation of all such occurrences as have happened in the severall Counties of Donegall, London-Derry, Tyrone, and Fermanagh in the North of Ireland, since the beginning of this horrid, bloody, and unparaleld rebellion there, begun in October last* [1641] . . . presented to the English House of Commons on 4 June 1642. For the whole question see W. Lecky, *History of Ireland* . . . (London, 1892), I, 46 ff.

[30] A scurrilous periodical written by William Moore which ran from 1770 to 1772. Sir William Meredith had complained of it in the House of Commons on 14 March 1770 (Cavendish, *Debates*, I, 514 ff.).

[31] Burke inserted 'Character of King George the second'; Court pamphleteers from John Douglas in his *Seasonable Hints from an honest man on the present important crisis of a new reign and a new Parliament* (1761) onwards had put forward the view that George II had been a king in toils to his oligarchic ministers.

are of our own putting together. Those who do not like them will have nothing to do with any of us. I thought however that we had in the main, the same principles with those of your Lordship and that this similarity in the great lines, was one of the grounds of your former kindness.

I have spoken fully to the first part of the Series of Charges on the principles of my friends, which are mine also. You mention at the End of the Roll of obnoxious tenets which my friends were so indiscreet as to utter in your Company in former times, the Irish Rebellion, by which I suppose you mean the great Rebellion of 1641. I all along suspected that your Lordship had mistaken *my* discourses with you for those of *my friends*. This convinces me of it. W.B. and my Brother most certainly never have spoken to you on the Subject. They know little or nothing of the Irish History. They have never thought on it at all; *I* have studied it with more Care than is common, and I have spoken to you on the Subject, I dare say 20 times. This mustard Bowl is *my* thunder.[32] "Me—Me—adsum qui feci, ille nec ausus nec potuit."[33] Indeed I *have* my opinion on that part of history, which I have often delivered to you; to every one I conversed with on the Subject, and which I mean still, to deliver whenever the occasion calls for it. Which is "That the Irish Rebellion of 1641 was not only (as our silly things called Historys call it), not utterly *unprovoked* but that no History, that I have ever read furnishes an Instance of any that was so *provoked*". And that "in almost all parts of it, it has been extremely and most absurdly misrepresented".

I assure you I am not singular in that opinion. Several now living think so. The late Mr York thought so and expressed himself so in debate in The House of Commons on the nullum tempus Bill,[34] as well as to myself in Conversation. I realy thought our History of Ireland so terribly defective that I did, and with success, urge a very learned and Ingenious friend of yours and mine in the University of Dublin[35] to undertake it. I dare say He will do it ably and faithfully, but if He

---

[32] The Oxford Dictionary defines mustard-bowl: 'a wooden bowl in which mustard-seed was pounded, proverbially referred to as the instrument for producing stage thunder'.

[33] 'Me, me, adsum, qui feci, in me convertite ferrum O Rutuli! mea fraus omnis; nihil iste nec ausus nec potuit'; see Virgil, *Aeneid*, IX, 427–9; Strike me! I am he who did the deed, turn your sword against me, Rutulians. All the offence is mine, *he* neither dared nor had the power to do you any injury.

[34] This is not directly borne out by Cavendish's report of Charles Yorke's speeches in the debate on the Nullum Tempus Bill on 24 February 1769 (Cavendish, *Debates*, I, 240 ff.) but there is a reference to Ireland in connexion with which he might well have made some such statement.

[35] Thomas Leland (1722–85), Fellow of Trinity College Dublin. His *History of Ireland from the Invasion of Henry II* . . . appeared in 1773.

thinks, that any thing unfavourable to his principles will be deduced, from telling the truth or cares for Vulgar Malignity on that occasion He is much more below the task than I can yet prevail on myself to think him.[36] As to my *principles* on this subject I must leave them to your mercy. I have told you what I know *to* be true in *fact*. If I were to reason on that Event, and to affirm it justifiable, you might say I shewd myself a friend to Rebellion. If I blamed it you might say I was attached to the doctrines of passive Obedience. This is an ugly Dilemma. I dont remember, to have said, either the one or the other: But if people must make a conclusion concerning my Character from what I did, do, and shall say on this subject, all that in Charity and Decency they *ought* to conclude is, that I am no lover of oppression nor believer in malignant fables, what they *will* conclude is their affair not mine. This was necessary to bring this charge and indeed all the others from my friends to the true object myself.

To the DUKE OF RICHMOND—[*post* 26 September 1774]

Corr. (1958), III, 38–40

An exhortation to Charles Lennox, 3rd Duke of Richmond (1735–1806), a somewhat independent member of the Rockingham party.

My dear Lord,

. . . It would give me very unfeigned concern for the sake of the publick that your Grace could ⟨seriously⟩ think or talk of being sick of Politics. Let me say that you have tolerable corroborants[1] for the Stomach. It is not for want of bitters that it is so weak. But in serious earnest you have less reason for this despondency, than most Men. Your constitution of Mind is such that you must have a pursuit, and in that which you have chosen you have obtain a very Splendid reputation which is no slight Object to every generous Spirit. You have exerted very great abilities, in a very excellent Cause, and with very noble associates. You have not disappointed your friends; nor have they disappointed you; and if on casting up the account you find your power in the State not equal to your services to the Publick you

---

[36] Burke was far from satisfied with Leland's performance. He told his son Richard twenty years later that he had gone over some of the materials for it with Leland: 'We agreed about them; but when he began to write history, he thought only of himself and his bookseller;—for his history was written at my earnest desire, but the mode of doing it varied from his first conceptions' (letter to Richard 20 March 1792, printed *Corr.* (1958), VII, 104).

[1] A strengthening agent, a tonic.

have notwithstanding an high Rank in your Country which Kings cannot take from you, and a fortune fully equal to your Station though not—it would be hard to find one—to the personal dignity of your mind. My dear Lord the whole mass of this taken together is not to be called unhappiness nor ought it to drive you from the publick Service. Private Life has sorrows of its own for which publick employment is not the worst of medicines. And you may have in other things as much vexation without the same Splendour. Your Birth will not suffer you to be private. It requires as much Struggle and violence to put yourself into private Life as to put me into publick. Pardon a slight comparison but it is as hard to sink a Cork as to buoy up a Lump of Lead.

To the STEWARDS OF THE BELL CLUB—1 *November* 1777

Corr. (1958), III, 394–98

The *Bristol Gazette* prefaced this letter with the statement that 'On Tuesday a very numerous and respectable meeting of the independent Citizens of Bristol was held at the Coopers Hall in King street, to commemorate the success at the late election of Henry Cruger and Edmund Burke, Esqrs. to be their Representatives in Parliament . . . and the following Letter from Mr Burke to the Stewards was read'. The portion printed here is from a draft version.

Beaconsfield, Nov. 1, 1977

Gentlemen,

. . . If it be true in any degree, that the Governors form the people, I am certain, it is as true, that the people in their Turn impart their Character to their Rulers. Such as you are, sooner or later must Parliament be. I therefore wish, that you at least, would not suffer yourselves to be amused by the Style, now grown so common, of railing at the corruption of Members of Parliament. This kind of general invective has no kind of Effect, that I know of, but to make you think ill of that very institution, which do what you will you must religiously preserve, or you must give over all thoughts of being a free people. An opinion of the indiscriminate corruption of the house of Commons will at length induce a disgust of Parliaments. They are the corruptors themselves who circulate this general charge of corruption. It is they, that have an Interest in confounding all distinctions, and involving the whole in one general Charge. They hope to corrupt private Life by the example of the publick; and having produced a despair, from a supposed general failure of principle, they hope, that they may persuade you, that since it is impossible to do any good, you may as well have your share in the profits of doing ill.

Where there are towards six hundred persons, with much temptation, and common frailty, Many will undoubtedly be moved from the line of Duty. But I have told you before, and I am not afraid to repeat it, that there are many more, amongst us who are free from all sorts of corruption, and of a very excellent publick spirit, than could well be expected. Since there is this difference, it is the Business of the constituents to distinguish, what it is the policy of some to confound. When you find men that you ought to trust, you must give them support; else it is not them that you desert, but yourselves that you betray. Nor is it at all difficult to make this distinction. The way to do it is quite plain and simple—It is to be attentive to the Conduct of men, and to judge of them by their actions; and by nothing else.

It is true, that many of our Brethren, from their habits of Life, and their not being on the actual Scene of Business, are not capable of forming an opinion upon every several Question of Law or politicks or, of course, of determining on a mans conduct with relation to such questions. But every man in the Club, and every man in the same situation in the Kingdom, is perfectly capable, as capable as if he were a Minister of State or a chief Justice, of determining whether publick men look most to their own Interest or to yours; or whether they act an uniform, clear, manly part in their station—whether the main drift of their Counsels, for any series of years, be wise or foolish, and whether things go well or ill in their hands.

You will therefore not listen to those who tell you, that these matters are above you and ought to be left entirely to those into whose hands the King has put them. The publick interest is more your Business than theirs; and it is from want of spirit, and not from want of ability, that you can become wholly unfit to argue or judge upon it. For in this very thing lies the difference between free men, and those that are not free. In a free Country, every man thinks he has a concern in all publick matters; that he has a right to form, and a right to deliver an opinion upon them. They sift, examine, and discuss them. They are curious, eager, attentive, and jealous; and by making such matters the daily subjects of their thoughts and discourses, vast numbers contract a very tolerable knowlege of them; and some a very considerable one. And this it is, that fills free Countries with men of ability in all Stations. Whereas in other Countries, none, but men whose Office calls them to it having much care or thought about publick affairs, and not daring to try the force of their opinions with one another,

ability of this sort is extremely rare in any station of Life. In free
Countries there is often found more real publick wisdom and sagacity
in Shops and manufactories than in the Cabinets of Princes, in Countries, where none dares to have an opinion until he comes into them.
Your whole importance therefore depends upon a constant discreet
use of your own reason. Otherwise you and your Country sink to
nothing. If upon any particular occasion you should be roused you
will not know what to do. Your fire will be a fire in Straw, fitter to
waste and consume yourselves than to warm or enliven any thing else.
You will be only a giddy Mob upon whom no sort of reliance is to be
had. You may disturb your Country but you never can reform your
Government. In other Nations they have for some time indulged themselves in a larger use of this manly Liberty than formerly they dared.

To the MARCHIONESS OF ROCKINGHAM—
27, 28 *September* 1780

Corr. (1958), IV, 299–302

Wednesday Septr 1780.

Madam,   The day of Surry Election.
. . . My brother and I will very gladly and very thankfully accept your
Ladyships most obliging invitation if it should be in our power. But
I am very fearful that it will not. This gives me great concern, on
account of the loss of an immediate satisfaction, one of the greatest I
could have: But as to my poor affairs I doubt things are not yet ripe
for a consideration of them, by my Lord Rockingham, or by any body
else, who may be still kind enough not to be tired of them and of me.
The late Business at Bristol has renewed in my Mind some cool and
serious reflexions. They had gone a good way during the Course of
last Winter: They proceeded further on account of many things which
I had observed towards the close of the Session; and they occupy my
Mind very much at present. I am indeed in that awkard State of
indecision, which does not become any person, and to which I am as
little disposed as any man living. I know, that it is not reason but
weakness which keeps me in publick Business. I am at length thoroughly convinced, that I can no longer do good to others or to myself
by a vain contention. I am told, that I am the single instance of a man
who had been any way eminently active in Parliament, and who had
been wholly left out on a General Election. I believe it is the Case;
and I am far from sure, that these very marked events are not hints

of a designation of providence, which a man is obliged to obey. The people of England have, even as a people, many Virtues—and have frequently stepped forward, as I am persuaded they would still, to screen an innocent man from oppression: But they are certainly not in the smallest degree to be depended upon by a person who engages in any difficult design to serve them. If there were any two Objects, upon which the people of England had *seemd* to set their hearts for some time past, they were, the reduction of the influence of the Crown, and the shortening the duration of Parliaments. Mr Sawbridge[1] moved the Latter, and I the former. We are both cast out of Parliament, in the two principal Cities, and most popular Elections in the Kingdom. There is no standing against the inference to be drawn from this extraordinary fact. If I were to come into Parliament by any of the little posterns or sallyports of the constitution, my moving such Bills as I formerly did, and as I have been desired to two Counties to do again, would be a piece of Buffoonery, to which I am little inclined to submit: To decline that Business would lay me open to misconstruction—I do not know how I can justifye myself to your Ladyship for having triffled away so much of your time on such a subject. I shall stop here; though I have much upon my Mind—I take the Liberty of enclosing to your Ladyship a Copy of a long Letter I have written to Bristol on the same subject, which, if your Ladyship finds any time exceedingly tedious on your hands, you may cast your Eye over with no more attention than such a thing merits.

Mrs Burke desires her humble respects to your Ladyship and Lord Rockingham. I must beg leave, again to renew my acknowlegements to your Ladyship for your goodness in thinking of me so favourably or indeed for thinking of me at all—and to wish, that in return for all your kindness, (and a better cannot be made to you, I am sure) that you may soon hear that admiral Keppel is returned triumphant Member for Surry. It will make Wimbledon more beautiful than ever. I have the honour to be with the most perfect and most grateful attachment

Madam
your Ladyships
most obedient
and faithful humble Servant

Beconsfield Septr 27. 1780. EDM BURKE

---

[1] Alderman John Sawbridge (1732–95), M.P. for London, who customarily made a motion for leave to bring in a Bill to shorten the duration of Parliament.

To LORD LOUGHBOROUGH—17 *July* 1782

Corr. (1958), V, 19–21

Alexander Wedderburn, 1st Baron Loughborough (1733–1805), was at this time Chief Justice of the Common Pleas.

My dear Lord

I received your very kind and obliging Letter from Beechwood,[1] and I thank you for it very sincerely. It was much the more acceptable on account of the place it came from, combined with the remembrance of the worthy Master. I met him since, in not so pleasant a place, under St James's Gate, and had a hearty shake of the hand. It was very good of you both in such a situation, formed for every kind of calm satisfaction, to throw a thought upon a scene so full of confusion as this, and on my poor part in it, which contrary to all order, is as troublesome as it is inconsiderable. I remember several years ago a few most pleasant days that I passed with you and Sir John under his noble Beech Trees, in a manner and with thoughts perfectly remote from my course of Life and the train of my Ideas ever since. Since then many Winters have snowed upon my head without making it in proportion wiser, and God knows whether I have done good to others in any proportion to the innumerable, unspeakable vexations which I have suffered, during that whole time. I cannot say that those troubles were not mixed with many consolations. But it requires, at least my whole stock of Philosophy, to bear up against the Events which have lately happened, and which have indeed gone very near to my heart. I have lost, and the public have lost, a friend.[2] But this was the hand of God manifestly, and according to the course and order of his Providence. I had no hand in it. But to think that all the Labours of his Life, and that all the Labours of my Life, should *in the very moment of their Success,* produce nothing better than the delivery of the power of this Kingdom into the hands of the E. of Shelburne, the very thing, (I am free to say to you and to every body,) the toils of a life ten times longer and ten times more important than mine would have been well employed to prevent—this I confess, is a sore, a very sore tryal. It really looks as if it were a call on me at least wholly to withdraw from all struggles in the political Line. This was the first impression on my Mind—I do not know how long it will continue.[3] We are naturally

---

[1] Loughborough's letter of 7 July was written from Sir John Sebright's seat.

[2] Lord Rockingham.

[3] Burke was still seriously considering retirement from politics, and discussing the idea with his friends, as late as May 1783. Dr Johnson was strongly opposed to retirement, which he said

changeable. There is a great deal of difficulty, at my time of Life, and in my circumstances in changing, even to a course, that would seem more suitable to decline and dissapointment. On the other hand, if we go on, there must be some sort of system. If so, all is to begin again, a great part of our construction is (what I call) sound. But there is a great and I fear an irreperable, Breach—with what to build it up that will bind and coalesce, I do not see.

Indeed I do not see any thing in a pleasant point of View. I bear up however better than my present style would seem to indicate. I do so rather by force of natural spirits, than by the aid of reason; though now and then reason whispers some sort of comfort even by suggesting ones own blindness; and that there is good ground to think, whatever appearances may be, that in some way or other, at some time or other, or in some place or other, the effect of right endeavours must be right. Nota est illis operis sui series, omniumque rerum per manus suas venturarum scintia in aperto est semper—Nobis ex abdito subit.[4]

Your Lordship sees, that like Hudibras discomfited and laid in the Stocks, that I

> comfort myself with ends of verse
> and sayings of Philosophers.[5]

I wish you most heartily a pleasant Circuit, moderate litigation and as little hanging as possible. Alas it is not worth while, to swing out of the world, those, you have to send away! When shall we have a Grand Jail delivery!

> I am with great Esteem and regard
> My dear Lord
> Your most obedient and humble Servant
> ED. B.

Whitehall July 17th 1782
Here still but out in Law.[6]

I forgot to tell you that I had a most friendly Note from Adam Smith at his departure for Scotland.

---

would be 'civil suicide' (Boswell, *Life of Johnson*, IV, 223 and n.).

[4] See Seneca, *De Beneficiis*, IV, XXXII, I; the exact wording of the original is 'nota enim illis est operis sui series, omniumque illis rerum per manus suas iturarum scientia in aperto semper est; nobis ex abdito subit, et, quae repentina putamus, illis provisa veniunt ac familiaria'. This has been translated: 'for the gods know well the complete evolution of their work, and the knowledge of all that will hereafter pass through their hands is always to them clearly revealed. The events that appear suddenly to us out of the unknown, and all that we count unexpected are to them familiar happenings, long foreseen'.

[5] *Hudibras*, Part I, Canto iii. Burke is not quoting exactly.

[6] Burke's office was officially vacated on 17 July 1782.

To EARL FITZWILLIAM—[*post* 4 *August* 1794]

Corr. (1958), VII, 567–69

William Fitzwilliam, 4th Earl Fitzwilliam (1748–1833), was Rockingham's nephew and Burke's close friend.

I know your Lordship does not expect an answer from me in my present condition: But I am able to do it, and I ought to do it. It has been my fate all my Life to receive obligations, and never to return them. I ought however to acknowlege them. Oh your Letter affected me to the very bottom of my Soul. It is, just like every thing that comes from you, full of Wisdom and goodness. You have touched the true point of comfort—that, for the little time I live, I ought to wish to resemble him that I have lost, and that I flatterd myself might live a long time, and live, under your patronage, an ornament and a Benefit to the world. His fortitude was indeed a true and glorious part of his Character—I trust in God he is now in a place where that virtue is useless. If I considerd his Loss as a mere act of the common Providence of God—I think I should instantly profit of your advice, and not suffer my heart to be torn to pieces as it is at present, not by grief but by remorse. I have not husbanded the Treasure that was in my hands. I squanderd it away in a manner, that when I look back, I can scarcely conceive. I threw him away by every species of Neglect and misman-agement—and what did I throw away in this frantick manner? It was not a pious Son, though he carried Piety to me and his Mother to a fault—to her—only to what was right—to me—to a Species of Idol-atry—But it was only in submission and piety he shewed himself a Son—It was a noble, generous, and Heroic friendship, he shewd to me;—This was among the causes of his being so little known to the world. But it is known to God; and will by him be rewarded, whilst I am left to the just punishment of a fruitless repentance.

My Dear Lord—you put him with all the Nobleness and generosity that belongs to you—into the way of turning his wonderful Qualities and dispositions, to the great advantage of this Nation,—perhaps of many Nations. He was pleased with his Election. You gave him a glimmering of publick hope before his death. Thank thank you— thank you—for that one short happy day to us both.[1] To reward you in full, may your Son grow up like him—but may he have a longer

---

[1] When Richard was elected on 18 July Edmund received an Address of Thanks for his services to the borough voted by the Bailiff and Burgesses of Malton. In replying to the Address Burke said that 'nothing had ever given him so great a Pleasure as the proceedings of that Day which he then declared to be *The Happiest of his Life*'.

life—may the order of Nature be kept, and may not you receive, as I have done from my Son, His Last breath!—but may he, in a Life of full prosperity, utility, and honour close the Eyes of his Mother and his father! You are more kind to me than I deserve—But I trust you will be paid in the way I wish. As for me, for whom you express such generous sollicitude, I am told by my Wife, that my living is necessary to her existence. I rather think so—and I owe much to a woman, whose equal is rarely found, and to the Mother of a Son that never had an equal. I use therefore every art and contrivance I can think of, to bear up against this Calamity, and against the sore reproaching feelings of my own Mind. I am told by some wise and good friends— that I ought to endeavour the prolongation of my being here, to suffer firmly whatever providence may have yet to impose for my ultimate good: Otherwise I had and have a serious Doubt, whether it is of good example to the world that I should conquer the just feelings that God and nature have implanted in me, and which indulged, would soon place me in the Grave of my dearest Son—and my unparralled friend. I feel this Doubt—But I give way to the better thoughts of others— who think there may be something in the world, ordaind by God, that I should do or suffer—and this I will submit to; and will, I hope, by his Grace, adore his justice for such a space as he pleases to give me, in a life of privacy humiliation, and penitence. Again and again my best thanks for the best and kindest Letter that was ever written. It is of great consolation to me.—My Son has left me a wonderful Legacy, in such a friend, and resemblance of him, as Dr Walker King. Just as he was going to be married, with every prospect of happiness, to a young woman that he dearly loves, and loves him, he came into this house of mourning—and has never left our side from the Moment of our Sons danger to this Hour. If any thing could console us, we have great consolations. Adieu! and may you be happy—and may I learn to be patiently and submissively miserable! Your unhappy but most faithful, affectionate and grateful friend

EDM BURKE

To WILLIAM PITT—31 *August* 1794

Corr. (1958), VII, 577

William Pitt (1759–1806) was Prime Minister at this time.

Dear Sir,

This morning I received your very Obliging Letter of the thirtieth of this Month, acquainting me with his Majesties most gracious dispositions towards the remains of this afflicted family.

You will be so kind as to lay me, with all possible humility, duty, and Gratitude, at his Majesties feet, and to express my deep and heartfelt sense of his Majesties Bounty and Beneficence; and the gracious condescension with which his Majesty has been pleased to distinguish me; at a time too, when neither I, nor any person to represent me; can aspire to the honour and happiness of rendering him any service whatsoever.

I have never presumed to apply for any thing. I never could so far flatter myself, as to think, that any thing done by me, in or out of Parliament, could attract the Royal Observation. In some instances of my publick conduct I might have erred. Few have been so long, (and in times and matters so arduous and critical) engaged in affairs, who can be certain that they have never made a mistake: But I am certain that my intentions have been always pure, with regard to the Crown and to the Country. It is upon these intentions, that his Majesty has been pleased to judge of my Conduct; and to reward them with his Royal acceptance, and Royal munificence. I could wish for ability to demonstrate the sincerity of my humble gratitude, by future active service. But I am denied this satisfaction. My time of Life, my bodily infirmity, and my broken state of Mind, leave me no other Capacity, than that of praying, which I do most fervently, for the prosperity and glory of his Majesties Reign; and that he may be made the grand instrument in the hand of Providence, for delivering the world from the grand Evil of our time, the greatest with which the Race of man was ever menaced.

I have the honour to be with the most perfect respect and affection

> Dear Sir
> Your most faithful
> and obliged humble Servant
> EDM BURKE

Beconsfield August 31. 1794.

The King commented on Burke's letter: 'Misfortunes are the greatest softeners of the human mind: and have in the instance of this distressed man made him own what his warmth of temper would not have allowed under other circumstances, viz, that he may have erred. One quality I take him to be very Susceptible of, that is gratitude, which I think covers many failings, and makes me therefore happy at being able to relieve him'.

FRENCH LAURENCE *to* EARL FITZWILLIAM— 9 *July* 1797

Corr. (1958), IX, 373–74

French Laurence (1757–1809) was a devoted disciple of Burke and one of the editors of his *Works*.

Beaconsfield July 9, 1797

My dear Lord,

Mr Nagle will have given your Lordship a short account of our poor friend's loss.[1] In the overwhelming affliction that surrounds me here, I have but one consolation, that I arrived in time for a last interview. I saw him, I talked with him; I saw him after He had ceased to talk at all; I joined in prayer with his other friends and family around his bed; I was present when the last breath passed so gently that no one can exactly say when he expired. When I first entered his room he seemed much better and stronger than he had been. From some confidential directions which he gave me I know that he considered his dissolution as fast approaching, but not so instant as it proved to be. He talked of public affairs and private with his accustomed interest and vivacity. He asked me if I had read Mr Grattan's address.[2] On being told that I had, he entered into a comment upon it, praising the brilliancy of some of the declarations, but censuring the false taste of the whole, particularly blaming, yet rather lamenting than blaming, more in sorrow than in anger the bad politics of beginning, continuing and ending with what is called parliamentary Reform. I observed to him the new and cruel difficulties which such intemperate declarations throw in your way, when turning to me he said, inform 'Lord Fitzwilliam from me, that it is my dying advice and request to him, steadily to pursue that course in which he now is. He can take no other, that will not be unworthy of him'. Mrs Burke, I believe, was then in the room. She can bear witness to the solemn injunction, of which I have

[1] Burke died shortly after midnight on the morning of 9 July.
[2] Grattan's address to the citizens of Dublin was published in the *Dublin Evening Post* of 1 July, which arrived in England on 5 July.

now acquitted myself. As I remember, this was almost if not quite the last thing which he said on public affairs.

His funeral (he told me,) he had by his will directed to be private; but he explained to me that he did not mean to preclude his friends from those last offices, which might be attended with gratification to them, though with no advantage to him. When the day of the interment will be, I am not certain. I do not mean to fix it till I hear whether Dr W. King can come here to consult upon the subject. In any event, it will not be earlier than *Saturday* next, perhaps not till Monday.[3] Will you my dear Lord, allow me to name your Lordship for one of the Pall-bearers, to shew the last respect to the memory of a man, who while living ever loved you most affectionately and ardently? It may however be right to advertize your Lordship that from some late most kind messages, and from his having borne the pall over poor young Richard, it will be impossible to pass over the Duke of Portland on this melancholy occasion.[4]

Mrs Burke, of whom you and Lady Fitzwilliam will I am sure be most anxious to hear, shews a fortitude truly worthy of the character which we have ever known her to possess. She feels that she has duties to discharge, for the sake of which she thinks herself bound to take every care of life, though in itself it has no longer any pleasure for her. Her behaviour is most unaffectedly heroic.

I shall protract my stay here till Wednesday and then must go to London for a day or two.

Oh! my dear Lord, what an incalculable loss have his family, his friends, and his countrymen suffered in that wonderful man, preeminent no less in virtues than in genius and in Learning! So kind to all connected with him, so partial to those whom he esteemed, ever preferring them in all things to himself; yet so zealous and resolute a champion in the cause of Justice, social order, morals and Religion. The private vanishes before the public calamity. When he fell, these kingdoms, Europe, the whole civilized world, lost the principal prop that remained, and were shaken to their very centers.

> Believe me to be
> My dear Lord
> Ever most gratefully and affectionately Yours
> FRENCH LAURENCE.

[3] The funeral was on Saturday 15 July at Beaconsfield.

[4] The pall bearers were : Windham, the Earl of Inchiquin, Earl Fitzwilliam, the Duke of Devonshire, Sir Gilbert Elliot, Henry Addington, the Duke of Portland, Lord Loughborough.

CHAPTER TWO

LITERARY FRIENDS
AND PHILOSOPHICAL CONCERNS

B URKE'S LITERARY and philosophical letters cover the span of his correspondence, from 1759 soon after he had published his *Essay on the Sublime and Beautiful* to 1797, just before his death. Burke was one of the original members of the Club, founded in 1764, which also included Dr. Samuel Johnson, James Boswell, Edmond Malone, Joshua Reynolds, and Burke's father-in-law, Dr. Christopher Nugent. Yet his letters to this illustrious group are disappointingly few. Two letters to Malone on Shakespeare and Joshua Reynolds are printed here, and one amusing reply from Burke to Boswell in reaction to Dr. Johnson's low opinion of Burke's wit.

We also see Burke advising the young painter James Barry, who was much troubled by an artistic temperament, as well as the poet William Richardson. Burke praises the historian William Robertson, the novelist Fanny Burney, and the translator of Tacitus, Arthur Murphy. He tells Arthur Young, the agriculturist, of his not-so-successful experiment of Young's theory about feeding carrots to pigs. And there are two exchanges with critics of Burke's *Reflections on the Revolution in France*, who soon become admirers: Friedrich Gentz, and James Mackintosh.

In sum, we would surely wish for more letters from Burke to "those who know how to make the Silence of their Closets more beneficial to the world than all the noise and Bustle of Courts, Senates and Camps." But for all his charm and good humor when away from politics, Burke was at home only when immersed in politics.

To ADAM SMITH—10 *September* 1759

Corr. (1958), I, 129–30

Adam Smith was Professor of Moral Philosophy at Glasgow when Burke's *Sublime and Beautiful* appeared. A remark of his that the author of that essay would be worthy of a university chair may be the origin of a particularly hardy legend that Burke once applied for the chair of Logic at Glasgow. When Smith's *Theory of Moral Sentiments* was published in 1759, David Hume made certain that a copy was sent to Burke. Burke wrote an appreciative letter to the author.

Sir

I am quite ashamed that the first Letter I have the honour of writing to you should be an apology for my conduct. It ought to be entirely taken up with my thanks to you for the satisfaction I received from your very agreeable and instructive work, but I cannot do that pleasing act of Justice without apologising at the same time for not having done it much earlier. When I received the Theory of Moral Sentiments from Mr Hume, I ran through it with great eagerness; I was immediately after hurried out of Town, and involved ever since in a Variety of troublesome affairs. My resolution was to defer my acknowlegements until I had read your book with proper care and attention; to do otherwise with so well studied a piece would be to treat it with great injustice. It was indeed an attention extremely well bestowed and abundantly repaid. I am not only pleased with the ingenuity of your Theory; I am convinced of its solidity and Truth; and I do not know that it ever cost me less trouble to admit so many things to which I had been a stranger before.[1] I have ever thought that the old Systems of morality were too contracted and that this Science could never stand well upon any narrower Basis than the whole of Human Nature. All the writers who have treated this Subject before you were like those Gothic Architects who were fond of turning great Vaults upon a single slender Pillar; There is art in this, and there is a degree of ingenuity without doubt; but it is not sensible, and it cannot long be pleasing. A theory like yours founded on the Nature of man, which is always the same, will last, when those that are founded on his opinions, which

---

[1] Burke's review of the book in the *Annual Register* for 1759 praises Smith's originality: 'this author has struck out a new, and at the same time a perfectly natural road of speculation on this subject. . . . We conceive, that here the theory is in all its essential parts just, and founded on truth and nature. The author seeks for the foundation of the just, the fit, the proper, the decent, in our most common and most allowed passions; and making approbation and disapprobation the tests of virtue and vice, and shewing that those are founded on sympathy, he raises from this simple truth, one of the most beautiful fabrics of moral theory, that has perhaps ever appeared'.

are always changing, will and must be forgotten. I own I am particularly pleased with those easy and happy illustrations from common Life and manners in which your work abounds more than any other that I know by far. They are indeed the fittest to explain those natural movements of the mind with which every Science relating to our Nature ought to begin. But one sees, that nothing is less used, than what lies directly in our way. Philosophers therefore very frequently miss a thousand things that might be of infinite advantage, *though the rude Swain treads daily on them with his clouted Shoon.*[2] It seems to require that infantine simplicity which despises nothing, to make a good Philosopher, as well as to make a good Christian. Besides so much powerful reasoning as your Book contains, there is so much elegant Painting of the manners and passions, that it is highly valuable even on that account. The stile is every where lively and elegant, and what is, I think equally important in a work of that kind, it is well varied; it is often sublime too, particularly in that fine Picture of the Stoic Philosophy towards the end of your first part which is dressed out in all the grandeur and Pomp that becomes that magnificent delusion. I have mentioned something of what affected me as Beauties in your work. I will take the Liberty to mention too what appeared to me as a sort of Fault. You are in some few Places, what Mr Locke is in most of his writings, rather a little too diffuse. This is however a fault of the generous kind, and infinitely preferable to the dry sterile manner, which those of dull imaginations are apt to fall into. To another I should apologise for a freedom of this Nature.

My delay on this occasion may I am afraid make it improper for me to ask any favour from you. But there is one, I have too much at heart not to sacrifice any propriety to attain it. It is, that whenever you come to Town, I may have the honour of being made personally known to you. I shall take the Liberty of putting this office on our friend Mr Hume who has already so much obliged me by giving me your Book. I am Sir with the truest esteem for your Work and your Character

your most obliged and
obedient Servant
EDM BURKE.

Wimple Street Cavendish Square
Westminster September 10th 1759

[2] *Comus*, ll. 634–5. Burke uses the quotation in a similar way in his Speech on Conciliation with the Colonies (*Works* [Bohn], I, 489; [Little, Brown], II, 154).

EDMUND *and* WILLIAM BURKE
to JAMES BARRY—[ante 19 *February* 1767]

Corr. (1958), I, 292–94

In the latter part of 1763 Burke's friend Dr. Joseph Fenn Sleigh had introduced to
him a young painter, James Barry (1741–1806), who was attempting to make his way
in Dublin. Sleigh hoped that Burke would help a countryman of talent, and Burke
welcomed the opportunity. He encouraged Barry to cross to England, and there found
him work with James Stuart (1713–88), the classical artist. He also introduced him
to the leading painters of the capital, and then, with the assistance of Will Burke,
sent him to Italy to study.

My dear Barry,

I am greatly in arrear to you on account of correspondence; but
not, I assure you, on account of regard, Esteem, and most sincere
good Wishes. My mind followed you to Paris, through your Alpine
Journey, and to Rome; You are an admirable Painter with your Pen,
as well as with your Pencil; and Every one to whom I shewd your
Letters, felt an interest in your little adventures, as well as a satisfaction
in your descriptions; because there is not only a Taste, but a feeling
in what you observe; something that shews you have an heart; and I
would have you by all means keep it. I thank you for Alexander;[1]
Reynolds[2] sets an high esteem on it, and thinks it admirably drawn,
and with great Spirit. He had it at his house for some time, and
returned it in a very fine frame; and it at present makes a capital
ornament of our little Dining Room between the two Doors. At Rome,
you are, I suppose, even still so much agitated by the Profusion of
fine things on every side of you, that you have hardly had time to sit
down to methodical and regular study; When you do, you will certainly
select the best parts of the best things, and attach yourself to them
wholly. You whose Letter would be the best direction in the world to
any young Painter, want none yourself from me, who know little of
the matter. But as you were always indulgent enough to bear my
humour under the Name of advice, you will permit me now, my dear
Barry, once more to wish you, in the beginning at least, to contract
the circle of your Studies; The extent and rapidity of your mind carries
you to too great a diversity of things; and to the completion of a whole,
before you are quite master of the parts in a degree equal to the Dignity
of your Ideas. This disposition arises from a generous impatience,
which is a fault almost Characteristic of great Genius. But it is a fault

[1] The copy Barry had made for the Burkes of a painting by Le Sueur.
[2] Joshua Reynolds (1723–92), the painter and lifelong friend of Burke.

nevertheless; and one which I am sure you will correct, when you consider, that there is a great deal of *mechanic* in your Profession, in which however the distinctive part of the Art consists, and without which the finest Ideas can only make a good Critic, not a painter. I confess I am not much desirous of your composing many pieces, for some time at least. Composition (though by some people placed formost in the list of the ingredients of an Artist,) I do not value near so highly. I know none, who attempts, that does not succeed tolerably in that part. But that exquisite masterly drawing, which is the glory of the great school where you are, has fallen to the lot of very few; Perhaps to none of the present age in its highest perfection. If I were to indulge a conjecture, I should attribute all that is called greatness of stile and manner in drawing, to this exact knowlege of the parts of the human body, of Anatomy, and perspective. For by knowing exactly and habitually, without the Labour of particular and occasional thinking, what was to be done in every figure they designed, they naturally attained a freedom and spirit of outline; because they could be daring without being absurd. Whereas ignorance, if it be cautious, is poor and timid. If bold, it is only blindly presumptuous. This minute and thorough knowlege of Anatomy and Practical as well as theoretical perspective, by which I mean to include foreshortening, is all the Effect of Labour and *use* in *particular* Studies, and not in general compositions. Notwithstanding your natural repugnance to handling of Carcasses, you ought to make the knife go with the pencil, and study Anatomy in real, and, if you can, in frequent dissections. You know that a man, who despises as you do, the minutiæ of the Art, is bound to be quite perfect in the noblest part of all; or he is nothing. Mediocrity is tolerable in middling things; not at all in the great. In the Course of the studies I speak of, it would be not amiss to paint pourtraits often and diligently; This I do not say, as wishing you to turn your Studies to Pourtrait Painting. Quite otherwise; but because many things in the human face will certainly escape you without some intermixture of that kind of Study. Well! I think I have said enough, to try your humility on this Subject. But I am thus troublesome, from a sincere anxiety for your success. I think you a man of honour, and of Genius; and I would not have your Talents lost to yourself, your friends, or your Country, by any means. You will then attribute my freedom to my sollicitude about you; and my sollicitude to my friendship. Be so good to continue your Letters and observations as usual. They are exceedingly grateful to us all, and we keep them by us. Since I saw you, I spent three months in Ireland. I had the pleasure of seeing

Sleigh but for a day or two. We talked a deal about you, and he loves
and esteems you extremely. I saw nothing, in the way of your Art,
there, which promised much. Those who seemed most forward in
Dublin, when we were there, are not at all advanced, and seem to
have little ambition. Here they are as you left them; Reynolds, every
now and then striking out some wonder. Barrett is fallen into the
painting of Views; It is the most called for and the most lucrative part
of his Business. He is a wonderful observer of the accidents of Nature,
and produces every day something new from that Scource—and indeed
is on the whole a delightful painter, and possessed of great rescources.
But I do not think he gets forward as much as his Genius would entitle
him to; as he is so far from studying, that he does not even look at
the Pictures of any of the great masters, either Italians or Dutch. A
man never can have any point of pride that is not pernicious to him.
He loves you and always enquires for you. He is now on a Night Piece,
is indeed noble in the conception and in the execution of the very first
merit. When I say he does not improve, I do not mean to say that he
is not the first we have in that way; but that his Capacity ought to
have carried him to equal any that ever painted Landscape. . . .

To JAMES BARRY—16 *September* 1769

Corr. (1958), II, 81–83

In reply to a letter from Barry written from Rome 8 July. Barry had complained of
a combination against him in which, he asserted, picture-dealers, ciceroni and artists
had entered 'so that I shall be surprised if you have not been frightened with the
terrible accounts given of me'. He lamented that he had not heard from the Burkes
for a long time and hoped that their silence was in no part due to malicious accounts
they had heard of him. Barry's subsequent career shows both how wise was the
warning Burke gave him and how far he was from being able to profit by it.

My dear Barry,

I am most exceedingly obliged to your friendship and partiality,
which attributed a Silence very blameable on our parts to a favourable
Cause; Let me add in some measure to its true Cause; a great deal of
occupation of various sorts, and some of them disagreeable enough.
As to any reports concerning your Conduct and Behaviour, you may
be very sure, they could have no kind of influence here; For none of
us are of such a make, as to trust to any ones report, of the Character
of a person whom we ourselves know. Until very lately, I had never
heard any thing of your proceedings from others; and when I did, it

was much less than I had known from yourself—that you had been upon ill Terms with the Artists and Virtuosi in Rome, without much mention of Cause or consequence. If you have improved these unfortunate Quarrels to your advancement in your Art you have turned a very disagreeable Circumstance to a very Capital advantage. However you may have succeeded in this uncommon attempt, permit me to suggest to you, with that friendly Liberty which you have always had the goodness to bear from me, that you cannot possibly have always the same success, either with regard to your fortune or your Reputation. Depend upon it, that you will find the same competitions, the same jealousies, the same Arts and Cabals, the same emulations of interest and of Fame, and the same Agitations and passions here that you have experienced in Italy; and if they have the same effect on your Temper, they will have just the same Effects on your Interest; and be your merit what it will, you will never be employd to paint a picture. It will be the same at London as at Rome; and the same in Paris as in London; for the world is pretty nearly alike in all its parts. Nay though it would perhaps be a little inconvenient to me, I had a thousand times rather you should fix your Residence in Rome than here, as I should not then have the mortification of seeing with my own Eyes a Genius of the first Rank, lost to the world, himself, and his friends—as I certainly must; if you do not assume a manner of acting and thinking here totally different from what your Letters from Rome have described to me. That you have had just subjects of indignation always, and of anger often, I do no ways doubt; who can live in the world without some trials of his Patience? But believe me, my dear Barry, that the arms with which the ill dispositions of the world are to be combated and the qualitys by which it is to be reconciled to us, and we reconciled to it, are moderation, gentleness, a little indulgence to others, and a great deal of distrust of ourselves; which are not qualities of a mean Spirit, as some may possibly think them; but virtues of a great and noble kind, and such as dignifye our Nature, as much as they contribute to our repose and fortune; for nothing can be so unworthy of a well composed Soul, as to pass away Life in bickerings and Litigations: in snarling, and scuffling with every one about us. Again, and again, Dear Barry, we must be at peace with our Species; if not for their sakes, yet very much for [our] own. Think what my feelings must be, from my unfeigned regard to you, and from my wishes that your Talents might be of use, when I see what the inevitable consequences must be, of your persevering in what has hitherto been your Course ever since I knew you, and which you will

permit me to trace out to you beforehand. You will come here; you
will observe what the Artists are doing, and you will sometimes speak
a disapprobation in plain words, and sometimes in a no less expressive
Silence. By degrees you will produce some of your own works. They
will be variously criticised; you will defend them; you will abuse those,
who have attacked you; Expostulations, discussions, Letters, possibly
challenges will go forward, you will shun your Brethren, they will
shun you—In the mean time Gentlemen will avoid your friendship
for fear of being engaged in your Quarrels, you will fall into distresses,
which will only aggravate your disposition to further quarrels; you
will be obliged for maintenance to do any thing for any body, your
very Talents will depart for want of hope and encouragement and you
will go out of the world fretted, disappointed, and ruined. Nothing
but my real regard for you could induce me to set these considerations
in this Light before you. Remember we are born to serve, or to adorn
our Country and not to contend with our fellow Citizens: and that in
particular, your Business is to paint and not to dispute.

What you mention about heads, hands, feet &c, I think is very
right; you cannot to be sure do without them; and you had better
purchase them at Rome than here; as usual you will draw for the
Charge.[1] If you think this a proper time to leave Rome, (a matter
which I leave entirely to yourself) I am quite of opinion you ought to
go to Venice. Farther I think it right to see Florence, and Bologna,
and that you cannot do better than take that Route to Venice. In short
do every thing that may contribute to your improvement, and I shall
rejoice to see you what Providence intended you a very great man.
This you were in your Ideas before you quitted this. You best know
how far you have studied, that is practised the Mechanic; despised
nothing till you had tried it; practised dissections with your own hands;
painted from Nature as well as from the statues, and pourtrait as well
as History, and this frequently. If you have done all this as I trust you
have you want nothing but a little prudence to fulfil all our Wishes.
This let me tell you is no small matter; for it is impossible for you to
find any persons any where more truly interested for you; to these
dispositions attribute every thing which may be a little harsh in this
Letter. We are thank God, all well and all most truly and sincerely

---

[1] Barry had written in his letter of 8 April (*Works*, I, 159): 'Now, for about eight pounds, I
can get fresh good casts of several heads, torsos, feet etc, that would be of the last importance
to me when I get home.'

yours. I seldom write so long a Letter take this as a sort of proof how much I am Dear Barry

Gregories Septr 15. 1769.
Direct as usual.

Your faithful friend
and humble Servant
EDM BURKE

To ARTHUR YOUNG—21 *October* 1770

Corr. (1958), II, 165–67

This letter would seem to be the first from Burke to the famous agriculturalist. Arthur Young (1741–1820) had begun his long series of works intended to popularize improved husbandry in England, with the *Farmer's Letters to the People of England* in 1767. The same year he wrote the first of his famous Tours, *Six Weeks Tour through the Southern Counties of England and Wales,* and in 1770 there appeared among other works his *Six Months Tour through the North of England.* After this letter was written Young visited Gregories. Though Burke considered himself a pupil of Young, it is noteworthy that his comments often showed more grasp of agricultural principles than those of his mentor, and while Young totally failed to make his farm pay, Burke was generally admitted to have been a successful practical farmer.

Sir,

I am sure you will have the goodness to excuse the trouble I am going to give you; and to which your knowlege and your communicative Character must necessary make you subject.

When I had the pleasure of seeing you last year, I told you that I had sown about an acre of Carrots[1] for a Trial. My Soil is a gravelly loam, tolerably deep, but in some places a little Stiff. As the seed was sown Late, the ground not very well prepared, and the year in general, I am told, not favourable to that Vegetable, my Crop was but indifferent. So far with regard to the Husbandry of that article. With regard to the oeconomy, the success was worse. I attempted to fatten two middle sized Bacon Hogs with Carrots; after having been two months, or near the matter, in the Stye, I found that, as they were young, they had grown pretty considerably; but continued as lean as when I put them up. I was obliged to have recourse to Barley meal, and in a short

[1] An account of these experiments is incorporated in Young's *Eastern Tour,* IV, 76–84 (Letter XXXI).

time they became as fat as I could wish though to all appearance no way helped by the previous use of Carrots.

He is but a poor Husbandman who is discouraged by one years ill success where he acts upon good authority,[2] or pursues a rational principle. Last Spring I sowed two acres with the same seed. The ground had received a years fallow one good Trench ploughing and two or three turnings in the common way; it was dunged early in the winter; so that the Earth was pretty well pulverised, and the dung thoroughly rotted and mixed, by the Spring. In the Summer they were twice handhoed; I fear not sufficiently; but the Crop is very large, and the Carrots, though not so sightly as the sand Carrots, full as rich in Colour, or indeed rather higher and finer; a most aromatic Smell, Firm, and admirably Tasted. I have sent two Waggon loads to London,[3] for which I had six pounds, fifteen. The back carriage of Coal ashes has paid my Charges.[4] I take it, that the Crop is, nowithstanding the many and heavy expences attending it, better than a Crop of Wheat, according to the usual produce of this part of the Country.

So far I am satisfied. Now comes the domestic use. Somewhat more than a fortnight ago I put up two Porkers of the Kensington Breed;[5] They have not made the smallest progress on the boiled Carrots, with which they have been fed very plentifully. Last year the Bailif attributed the failure to the Carrots having been overboiled; this year they have been boiled less; hitherto the Event has been the same. The price of Barley and Peas is this year so high, that I should wish to persevere, if there was the least chance for succeeding, as I have a very great quantity of Carrots, and the London Market will take off only those which have an handsome appearance. Now Sir Let me beg that you will be so obliging as to point out what degree of boiling the Carrots ought to have, or where you may suspect that my Errour lies. The year is so far advanced that I scarce dare to beg the favour of seeing you here. I have had a very uneasy Summer from a long illness of Mrs Burkes or I should have endeavourd at that honour before. Once

---

[2] Young had published in 1769 his *Essay on the Management of Hogs* in which he advocated the use of carrots for fattening. Later he himself changed his views on their use for pigs, and recommended them as good for men and horses only.

[3] Gregories, 24 miles from London, was near enough for the single journey to be made in the day by a two-horse wagon.

[4] Coal ash, now regarded as almost useless as a fertilizer, was much prized for this purpose in the eighteenth century, possibly because it was often mixed with wood ash.

[5] Research has failed to find any reference to this as a recognized breed of pig.

more I request your pardon for this Trouble and am with great Truth and Esteem

Sir

your most obliged

and obedient humble Servant

EDM BURKE

Beconsfield Octr 21. 1770.

I am to tell you that whilst I failed in fattening by Carrots I have this year Killed one fine porker of 20 Lb the Quarter,—and two of sixteen each. From Barley meal each fattend perfectly in little more than three weeks.

To DR WILLIAM ROBERTSON—9 *June* 1777

Corr. (1958), III, 350–52

William Robertson (1721–93), the Scottish historian, whose writings were well known to Burke, does not appear in the correspondence until this month. On 5 June 1777 he wrote to Burke from Edinburgh saying that he had desired William Strahan (1715–85), the printer, to send a copy of the *History of America* (2 vols., London, 1777) in testimony of respect to 'one of the best judges in the Kingdom of the subject on which it is written'.

Sir,

I am perfectly sensible of the very flattering distinction I have receivd in your thinking me worthy of so noble a present as that of your History of America. I have however sufferd my Gratitude to lie under Some suspicion by delaying my acknowlegment of so great a favour. But my delay was only to render my obligation to you more compleat, and my thanks to you, if possible, more merited. The close of the Session[1] brought a great deal of very troublesome though not important business upon me at once. I could not go through your work at one breath at that time; though I have done it since. I am now enabled to thank you, not only for the honour you have done me, but for the great satisfaction, and the infinite Variety and compass of instruction, I have receivd from your incomparable Work. Every thing has been done which was so naturally to be expected from the authour of the

[1] On 6 June.

History of Scotland and the Age of Charles the fifth.[2] I believe few
Books have done more than this, towards clearing up dark points,
correcting Errours, and removing prejudices. You have too the rare
secret of rekindling an Interest, in subjects that had been so often
treated, and in which every thing which could feed a vital flame,
appeard to have been consumed. I am sure I read many parts of your
history with that fresh concern, and anxiety, which attends those who
are not previously apprised of the Event. You have besides thrown
quite a new light on the present State of the Spanish provinces, and
furnished both materials and hints for a rational Theory of what may
be expected from them in future.

The part which I read with the greatest pleasure is the discussion
on the Manners and character of the Inhabitants of that new World.
I have always thought with you, that we possess at this time very great
advantages towards the knowlege of human Nature. We need no longer
go to History to trace it in all its stages and periods. History from its
comparative youth, is but a poor instructour. When the Ægyptians
called the Greeks children in Antiquities,[3] we may well call them
Children; and so we may call all these nations, which were able to
trace the progress of Society only within their own Limits. But now
the Great Map of Mankind is unrolld at once; and there is no state
or Gradation of barbarism, and no mode of refinement which we have
not at the same instant under our View. The very different Civility of
Europe and of China; The barbarism of Persia and Abyssinia. The
erratick manners of Tartary, and of arabia. The Savage State of North
America, and of New Zealand. Indeed you have made a noble use of
the advantages you have had. You have employd Philosophy to judge
on Manners; and from manners you have drawn new rescources for
Philosophy. I only think that in one or two points you have hardly
done justice to the savage Character.[4]

There remains before you a great field—Periculosae plenum opus
aleæ tractas, et incedis per ignes suppositos cineri doloso.[5] When even

---

[2] Burke was almost certainly the reviewer who praised the *History of Scotland* in the *Annual
Register* for 1759. It is probable, though far from certain, that he wrote its review of Robertson's
History of Charles V in 1769.

[3] Plato, *Timaeus*, 22.

[4] The long and favourable review of this book in the *Annual Register* for 1777 (pp. 214–34)
makes the same criticism: 'Dr Robertson has taken no notice of the eloquence or poetry of the
Americans, which are among the most distinguished properties of mankind in a state of savage
nature' (p. 218).

[5] You undertake a task full of risk, and tread upon fires hidden under deceptive ashes; see
Horace, *Odes*, II, i, 8.

these ashes will be spread out over the present fire God knows. I am
heartily sorry that we are now supplying you with that kind of dignity
and concern, which is purchased to History at the expence of Mankind.
I had rather by far that Dr Robertsons pen were only employd in
delineating the humble Scenes of political œconomy, and not the great
Events of a civil war. However if our Statesmen had read the book of
human nature instead of the Journals of the house of commons, and
history instead of Acts of Parliament, we should not by ⟨the latter⟩
have furnished out so ample a page in the former. For my part I have
not been, nor am I very forward in my speculations on this Subject.
All that I have ventured to make, have hitherto proved fallacious. I
confess I thought the Colonies left to themselves could not have made
any thing like the present resistance, to the whole power of this Country and its Allies; I did not think it could have been done without the
declared interference of the house of Bourbon. But I looked upon it
as very probable, that France and Spain would have before this taken
a decided part. In both these conjectures I have judged amiss. You
will smile when I send you a triffling temporary production,[6] made
for the occasion of a day, and to perish with it, in return for your
immortal Work. But our Exchange resembles the politicks of the times;
you send out solid wealth, the accumulation of Ages, and in return
you are to get a few flying leaves of poor American papers. However
you have the mercantile comfort of finding the Balance of Trade infinitely in your favour; and I console myself with the smugg consideration of uninformed natural acuteness, that I have my Warehouse
full of Goods at anothers Expence.

Adieu Sir! continue to instruct the world; and whilst we carry on
a poor unequal conflict with the passions and prejudices of our day,
perhaps with no better weapons, than other passions and prejudices
of our own, convey Wisdom at our Expence to future Generations! I
have the honour to be with the highest respect and Regard

Sir

your most obedient
and obliged humble Servant
EDM BURKE

Westmr June 9. 1777.

[6] The *Letter to the Sheriffs.*

To WILLIAM RICHARDSON—18 *June* 1777

Corr. (1958), III, 353–56

William Richardson (1743–1814) was Professor of Humanity at Glasgow from 1772. In 1774 he published *A Philosophical Analysis and Illustration of Some of Shakespeare's Dramatic Characters* (Macbeth, Hamlet, Jacques and Imogen), and also *Poems Chiefly Rural*. It is probably to these two volumes that Burke refers.

Sir,—I should be extremely concerned if you were to judge of the value which I set on the honour you have done me, by the lateness of my acknowledgment. I may be suspected of procrastination and negligence by those who know me, but never I trust of ingratitude. But neither the failing which I acknowledge, nor the vice which I abhor, was among the causes of my delay in answering your most obliging letter, and thanking you for your most acceptable present. My little occupations, which redoubled on me towards the close of the session, and my little private concerns, which I neglect during the time of parliamentary business, have not permitted me, until within these few days, to go through your two volumes, although their bulk and value are so very different. I have now read both with much pleasure and instruction. The poetry is graceful and affecting, and of a very happy turn. I could indeed wish that you had chosen to write in rhyme, as I doubt whether any poetry, except the dramatical, appears in its best form in blank verse; particularly in the lesser and lighter kinds. But in this however I shall not be very positive, as I know that I differ from the practice of great poets, and the decision of great judges.

You are certainly in the right, that the study of poetry is the study of human nature; and as this is the first object of philosophy, poetry will always rank first among human compositions. In that study you cannot have chosen a fitter object than Shakespeare. Your tracing that progress of corruption, by which the virtues of the mind are made to contribute to the completion of its depravity, is refined and deep; and tho' there are several ingenious moral criticisms on Macbeth, this seems to me quite new. In your examination of Hamlet, you have very well unravelled the mazes and perplexities of passion and character which appear in that play. You have really removed a great many difficulties which I found in it. Still, however, some remain; which, I suspect, have arisen from the poet's having a little forgotten himself, or perhaps (what I conceive is sometimes the case with Shakespeare) from his not having persevered through the play in the plan on which he had originally set out, and not having corrected the foregone part, to the new ideas he had adopted in the course of his work. Shakespeare having entered the most deeply perhaps of all the poets into human nature, is clearly the best subject for criticism. But it would be worthy of you, if in the course of your enquiries you would turn your attention to his faults, which are many of them, of a kind as peculiar as his excellencies; for I am far from sure that an indiscriminate admiration of this poet has not done something towards hurting our taste in England. But I ought to ask pardon for suggesting any thing on this subject to you, who are so perfect a master of it.[1]

I am much flattered by the good opinion which you are so indulgent as to express of the trifles I have written; and of my intentions in my very feeble endeavours in active life. However, in expressing your approbation, you seem to ascribe to me some writings, the honor of which belongs to somebody else, as I have not done any thing in that way. Indeed very many years are elapsed since I had leisure or inclination for any compositions, except a few which have an immediate relation to the unhappy concerns in which I take a part. Except two or three of such, I have written nothing, though many pieces to which I had no title, have been attributed to me. One of the inconsiderable papers which I have written, I now take the liberty of sending to you.[2] The principles on which it goes will make you the more indulgent to the execution. How could you think I could be indifferent to the opinions of a gentleman in your honourable and happy situation, secluded though you conceive it to be from the importance of political occupation? So far from it, that I look with a degree of admiration not wholly unmixed with envy, on the course of life you have chosen. As long as the original light is brighter than the reflected, as long as the instructor is wiser than the instructed, so long will your occupation be superior to ours. The contemplative virtue is in the order of things above the active; at least I have always thought it so.[3] It has as great a degree of perfection and independence as any thing given to man can have: the other, at best, is but a very gross and concrete body; constantly dependent; frequently defeated; always obstructed; and carries with it, even when most successful, such manifest debility and imperfection, as gives daily and hourly cause of disgust to any one

---

[1] Richardson apparently followed this suggestion. When he included the *Philosophical Analysis* in a volume of essays (1783 and later) he added an *Essay on the Faults of Shakespeare* (Donald Bryant, *Edmund Burke and his Literary Friends*, St Louis, 1939, pp. 243–6).

[2] Probably the *Letter to the Sheriffs.*

[3] Burke has often been reproached for undervaluing Theory.

who has but the faintest ideas of what excellence is. You will remember the beautiful lines that express that condition of life, so superior not only to the vices, but to the inferior and incomplete virtues:

Credibile est illos pariter vitiisque locisque
Altius humanis exeruisse caput.
Non Venus et vinum sublimia pectora fregit;
Officiumve fori, militiæve labor;
Nec levis ambitio, perfusaque gloria fuco,
Magnarumve fames solicitavit opum.[4]

and the rest that precede and follow them. You see, that by the art of quoting I have contrived to give some value to my letter. You will have the goodness to excuse its exorbitant length.

I have the honour to remain,
With the greatest esteem, Sir,
Your's, &c.
(Signed) EDMUND BURKE
Westminster, June 18, 1777.

To MISS FRANCES BURNEY—29 July 1782

Corr. (1958), V, 25–27

When Fanny Burney (1752–1840) had published her anonymous first novel *Evelina* in 1778, Burke had been one of its earliest and most enthusiastic admirers: '. . . he began it one morning at seven o'clock', the young authoress was told, 'and could not leave it a moment; he sat up all night reading it'. Fanny first met Burke at one of Sir Joshua Reynolds's dinners in the spring of 1782. She decided that she was in love with him: 'quite desperately and outrageously in love'. He was the '2d Man in this Kingdom . . . Dr Johnson I think the First of *every* Kingdom;—but I need not, I think, *name* Mr Burke for his next Neighbour,—such spirit, such intelligence,—so much energy when serious, so much pleasantry when sportive,—so manly in his address, so animated in his Conversation,—so eloquent in Argument, so exhilarating in trifling. . . .' Burke was as much impressed by Fanny's second novel, *Cecilia*, published in five volumes on 12 July 1782, as he had been by her first. He read it in three days, '. . . and you know I never parted with it from the time I first opened it'.

---

[4] 'Well may we believe they lifted up their heads alike above the frailties and the homes of men. Their lofty natures neither love nor wine did break, nor civil business nor the toils of war; no low ambition tempted them, nor glory's tinsel sheen, nor lust of hoarded pelf' (Ovid, *Fasti*, I, 299–304; in praise of the first astronomers).

Madam,

I should feel exceedingly to blame, if I could refuse to myself, the natural satisfaction, and to you, the just but poor return, of my best thanks for the very great instruction and entertainment I have received from the new present you have bestowd on the publick. There are few, I believe I may say fairly, there are none at all, that will not find themselves better informed concerning human Nature, and their stock of observation enrichd by reading your Cecilia. They certainly will, let their experience in Life and manner be what it may. The arrogance of age must submit to be taught by youth. You have crouded into a few small volumes an incredible variety of Characters; most of them well planned, well supported, and well contrasted with each other. If there be any fault in this respect, it is one, in which you are in no great danger of being imitated. Justly as your Characters are drawn, perhaps they are too numerous,—but I beg pardon; I fear it is quite in vain to preach oeconomy to those who are come young to excessive and sudden opulence. I might tresspass on your delicacy if I should fill my Letter to you with what I fill my conversation to others. I should be troublesome to you alone, if I should tell you all I feel and think, on the natural vein of humour, the tender pathetick, the comprehensive and noble moral, and the sagacious observation, that appear quite throughout that extraordinary performance. In an age distinguishd by producing extraordinary Women, I hardly dare to tell you where my opinion would place you amongst them—I respect your modesty, that will not endure the commendations which your merit forces from every body.

I have the honour to be with great gratitude, respect, and Esteem

Madam
your most obedient
and most humble Servant
EDM BURKE

Whitehall
July 29. 1782.

My best compliments and congratulations to Doctor Burney on the great honour acquired to his family.

Fanny was ecstatic over this letter of appreciation: 'For elegance of praise no such a one was ever written before'. It was used as a preface for later editions of *Cecilia*. No one but her father, Fanny wrote, 'could, at a Time of Business, disappointment, care and occupation such as His are now, have found time to read with such attention, and to commend with such good nature, a work so totally foreign to every thing that just now can come Home to his Business and bosom' (Joyce Hemlow, *The History of Fanny Burney*, p. 153).

To JAMES BOSWELL—4 *January* 1786

Corr. (1958), V, 248–50

Boswell had published his *Journal of a Tour to the Hebrides with Samuel Johnson* on 1 October 1785, and with the assistance of Edmond Malone (1741–1812) had corrected it for a second edition, published on 22 December. One passage in the work disturbed both men, who feared it would be offensive to Burke. In the record of a conversation with Dr Robertson, Johnson was reported as saying that Burke never succeeded as a wit: "'Tis low; 'tis conceit. I used to say, Burke never once made a good joke' (Boswell, *Life of Johnson*, V, 32). Boswell had demonstrated his own good intentions by affixing a long footnote to this passage in the first edition, trying to prove by numerous specimens of Burke's conversation that he was wittier than the Doctor allowed. Malone, in the second edition, considerably expanded the note—it ended by being an essay of nearly a thousand words—with still more specimens, many of them puns, to illustrate Burke's wit.

My dear Sir,

I give you many thanks for your present of the second Edition of your very entertaining Book.[1] By the Date of your Letter I find that I ought to have profited of your kindness much earlier than I had the good fortune to do: And therefore I may appear more slow in my acknowlegements than I ought to be for so valuable a mark of your attention.

I am extremely obliged to you and to Mr Malone (to whom I beg my best compliments) for your friendly sollicitude with regard to a point relating to me, about which I am myself not very anxious. The reputation for Wit (the *fama dicacis*)[2] is what I certainly am not entitled to; and, I think, I never aimed at. If I had been even so ambitious, I must shew myself as deficient in Judgment as I am in wit, if I thought that a Title to pleasantry could be made out by argument. The feelings of every one you live with must decide without appeal. I am therefore in no sort disposed to bring a writ of Errour on the Judgment pronounced upon me. I admit the Court to be competent; the proceedings regular; and the reporter learned and exact. This is not only what Justice, but what common policy requires: For if I were to weaken the authority which refuses me what I am not intitled to in a smaller

[1] Boswell had sent Burke a copy of the *Tour* on 20 December 1785, with a letter explaining the long footnote and confessing that it was only partly his own.

[2] See Horace, *Satires*, I, iv, 83.

Matter, I might undermine it, when it decides in my favour, in points where my claim is full as doubtful, and the Object of much greater moment.[3] I have other reasons besides, though of similar Nature, for my perfect acquiescence in this decision. I shall be well content to pass down to a long posterity in Doctor Johnsons authentick Judgment, and in your permanent record, as a dull fellow and a tiresome companion, when it shall be known through the same long period, that I have had such men as Mr Boswell and Mr Malone as my friendly counsel in the Cause which I have lost. This circumstance will furnish a strong presumptive proof of my being possessd of some qualities much more estimable than the Talent, which all their Eloquence was not able to protect. It will be thought that the body of the place was of some value, when Engineers of their Skill, were so earnest to defend a small, and, I fear untenable, outwork of my reputation. I have turned to Mr Malones Note. It is sound and judicious in every respect, in its general principles; though, by his partiality and condescension only applicable to me.

You see, My dear Sir, that Vanity always finds its consolation. But Wisdom might draw a Lesson even from this little Circumstance of which we have been too long in the discussion. I ought not to take this publick reprimand amiss. My companions have a right to expect, that, when my conversation is so little Seasond, as it is, with Wit, it should not, out of respect both to them and to myself, to be so light and careless, as it undoubtedly always has been, and is. It is not only in the other World, that 'we are to give an account of every Light word'.[4] I ought therefore to thank you for informing the World of this censure of our deceasd friend, that I may regulate myself accordingly. Those I have the honour to live with are too well instructed, not to know and feel, that, though pleasantry is not, prudence, and circumspection certainly are in a mans own power; and that if he has not the Talent to please, he ought to have the delicacy not to disgust his Company.[5] I am sure there are very few, (let them be qualified as they will) shall be indiscreet enough to interrupt, by the intrusion of their Ideas, the strong flow of your real Wit, and true humour, who will not be great Enemies to their own entertainment, as well as to the

---

[3] Johnson usually praised Burke's ability as a talker: 'When Burke does not descend to be merry, his conversation is very superiour indeed. There is no proportion between the powers which he shews in serious talk and in jocularity. When he lets himself down to that, he is in the kennel' (*Life of Johnson*, IV, 276).

[4] Matthew xii. 36.

[5] Burke's warmest admirers sometimes reproached him for his puns.

satisfactions of the rest of the Company. I am with sincere respect and regard

My dear Sir
Your most faithful
and obedient humble Servant
EDM BURKE

Beconsfield   Jany 4. 1786.

To EDMOND MALONE—[circa 29 November 1790]

Corr. (1958), VI, 181–82

Edmond Malone had been engaged for several years upon his edition of the *Plays and Poems of William Shakspeare*, published on 29 November 1790. In the preface he went out of his way to pay a compliment to Burke as 'a great orator, philosopher, and statesman, now living, whose talents and virtues are an honour to human nature' and who alone could compete with Dr Johnson to be called 'the brightest ornament of the eighteenth century'. Burke wrote to acknowedge his presentation copy of the monumental ten-volume work.

My dear Sir,

Upon my coming to my new Habitation in Town I found your valuable work upon my Table. I take it as a very good earnest of the instruction and pleasure that may be yet reserved for my declining years.

Though I have had many little arrangements to make both of a publick and a private nature, my occupations were not able to overrule my Curiosity, nor to prevent me from going thro' almost the whole of your able, exact, and interesting History of the Stage.[1] An History of the Stage is no trivial thing to those who wish to study Human nature in all Shapes and positions. It is of all things the most instructive, to see, not only the reflection of manners and Characters at several periods, but the modes of making this reflection, and the manner of adapting it, at those periods, to the Taste and disposition of mankind.

---

[1] The second part of the first volume of Malone's edition was devoted to an historical account of the English stage in more than three hundred pages. Boswell reported to Malone that at the meeting of the Literary Club on 30 November Burke spoke of '. . . the clearness and accuracy of your dramatick history'. At a dinner party on 4 December (Boswell reported) Burke also declared, '. . . he had read your *Henry VI.*, with all its accompanyment, and it was exceedingly well done'. In his best reportorial style Boswell quoted Burke's exact words: 'I have read his history of the stage, which is a very capital piece of criticism and antiquarianism. I shall now read all Shakespeare through, in a very different manner from what I have yet done, when I have got such a commentator'.

The Stage indeed may be considerd as the Republick of active Literature; and its History as the History of that State. The great events of political History when not combined with the same helps towards the Study of the manners and Characters of men, must be a study of an inferiour nature.

You have taken infinite pains, and pursued your Enquiries with great Sagacity, not only in this respect, but in such of your Notes as hitherto I have been able to peruse. You have earned your repose by publick Spirited Labour: But I cannot help hoping, that when you have given yourself the relaxation which you will find necessary to your health, if you are not called to exert your great Talents, and employ your great acquisitions, in the transitory service to your Country which is done in active Life, you will continue to do it that permanent Service which it receives from the Labours of those who know how to make the Silence of their Closets more beneficial to the world than all the noise and Bustle of Courts Senates and Camps.

I beg leave to send you a pamphlet which I have lately publishd. It is of an Edition, I think more correct than any of the first[2] and renderd more clear in points, where I thought on looking over again what I had written, there was some obscurity. Pray do not think my not having done this more early was owing to neglect or oblivion, or from any ⟨want⟩ of the highest and most sincere respect to you. But the Truth is (and I have no doubt you will beleive me,) that it was a point of delicacy which prevented me from doing myself that honour. I well knew that the publication of your Shakespeare was hourly expected, and I thought if I had sent that small *donum*, the fruit of a few Weeks, I might subject myself to the suspicion of a little Diomedean policy, in drawing from you a return of the value of an hundred Cows, for my nine. But you have led the way, and have sent me Gold, which I can only repay you in my Brass. But pray admit it on your Shelves and you will shew yourself generous in your acceptance as well as in your Gift.

Pray present my best respects to Lord and Lady Sunderlin, and to Miss Malone. I am with the most sincere affection and gratitude

My dear Sir
Your most faithful
and obliged humble Servant
EDM BURKE

[2] Presumably this was the 3rd or 4th edition of Burke's *Reflections on the Revolution in France.*

To JAMES BOSWELL—20 *July* 1791

Corr. (1958), VI, 299–300

Burke wrote in answer to Boswell's letter of 16 July in which Boswell asked for a precise account of Burke's praise of Boswell's *Life of Johnson* (newly published on May 16) to the King. Burke shows himself somewhat unappreciative of Boswell's extraordinary memory for conversations.

Dear Sir,

I am perfectly sensible of the favour you have done me by your obliging Letter, and by all the Kind things you are so good to report from others, and much more for those you are pleased to say of me yourself.

I wish you all happiness, whenever you retire to Auchinleck, from the entertainment of your friends and the applauses of the publick. We shall I trust find ourselves hereafter as much obliged to your invention as hitherto we have been to your recollection. I am sure that something original from you will be well received; Whether, in the present possession of the favourable opinion of the world as you are, it will be prudent for you to risque the further publication of anecdotes, you are infinitely more competent to judge than I am.

As to the conversation I had the honour of having with the King at his Levee with regard to your Work and to Johnson, I gave you the account of it with as much exactness at the time, as I am able ever to relate any thing; not being much in the habit of precision with regard to particular expressions. Since then other things, not of much moment I admit, have made my recollection of the conversation far worse than then it was. I am quite certain, that I am now far less able to furnish you with any detail of that matter; and that you have reason on occasions of this Nature, and indeed of any nature, rather to trust to your own Memory than mine. Be assured that this is the fact, and that I do not decline an Obedience to your Commands, either from Laziness or inattention to you. In the Substance of the conversation you are certainly right. The King by his manner of questioning me, seemd to be affected properly with the merit of your performance; and I said, what I thought, that I had not read any thing more entertaining; though I did not say to his Majesty, what nothing but the freedom of friendship could justify my saying to yourself, that many particulars there related might as well have been omitted; However in the multitude of readers perhaps some would have found a loss in their omission.

Mrs Burke finds some Benefit from the use of the seabathing and presents her compliments.

I have the honour to be with very great respect and regard

Dear Sir

Your most faithful

and obedient humble Servant

Margate July 20. 1791.   EDM BURKE

FRIEDRICH GENTZ *to* EDMUND BURKE—
8 *February* 1793

Corr. (1958), VII, 346–47

Friedrich Gentz (1764–1832), at this time a comparatively junior official in the service of the Prussian Government, had welcomed the outbreak of the French Revolution, and in December 1790 had described it as 'der erste praktische Triumph der Philosophie, das erste Beispiel einer Regierungsform, die auf Prinzipien und auf ein zusammenhängendes, konsequentes System gegründet wird' (*Briefe von und an Friedrich von Gentz*, ed. F. C. Wittichen, Munich and Berlin, 1909–13, I, 178–9). But his opinions gradually changed. He began reading the *Reflections* early in 1791 and in 1793 brought out his German translation of it under the title *Betrachtungen über die französische Revolution. Nach dem Englischen des Herrn Burke neu-bearbeitet, mit einer Einleitung, Anmerkungen . . . , von Friedrich Genz,* Berlin, 1793. In his later career as a political writer and close associate of Metternich he was an uncompromising opponent of liberal and revolutionary movements.

Sir!

Having finished a toil which afforded to me, nearly for two years, that precious enjoyment to converse with the most sublime genius of the age,[1] it is but very natural, I should wish to carry this labour of mine before the most competent judge, I can look for among the wise. I am certainly aware, the language I wrote in, is but little known to the nation, which is happy and glorious in Your possession, and also perhaps unknown to You: still I hope, there may be among Your acquaintance one willing to become my interpreter: and if not, I'll think myself sufficiently rewarded, whenever this undertaking does not entirely die away, unreguarded by You.

What power I had, I assumed, to deliver a faithful lively copy of my great Original. What I thought proper, in order to put German

---

[1] Gentz described his reactions of first reading the *Reflections* in April 1791: 'Ich lese dieses Buch, so sehr ich auch gegen die Grundsätze und gegen die Resultate desselben bin (ich habe es aber noch nicht ganz zu Ende), mit ungleich grösserem Vergnügen, als hundert seichte Lobreden der Revolution . . . ' (*Briefe von und an Gentz*, ed.Wittichen, I, 204).

readers into the just sense of Your book, and to make them fair judges about those refined ideas, which were too often misunderstood, I brought into annotations and annexed essays.[2] Nay, I was bold enough to entertain a doubt against a very few of Your opinions:[3] much oftener I ought to reinforce what Your experience, what Your consummated wisdom foretold us two years ago, by what the sad history of these last two years is compelled to remember.

So I went on warmly, zealously, I dare say enthusiastically. I served a fair cause. This is a time, where every man, conscious of his forces is obliged to pay a public tribute to reason—A time as well for Germany, as for the rest of Europe.

Inclination prompted me not less than duty and love of my country to enter the honourable carreer. I'll think myself arrived at its glorious aim, if my name should be found worthy, to be traced at the pedestal of Your statue.

I must not abuse any longer the advantage to be the contemporary of Burke—I only dare to wish, Sir, Your high and important occupations might leave You a moment's time to let me Know this letter did reach Your notice. In such a case my address is:

Genz, Conseiller de guerre et Secretaire privé au
Grand-Directoire des Finances, à Berlin

In every case I am respectfully, and with deeper sentiments of admiration, than any pen may utter

Sir!

Your most obedient
humble Servant
GENZ.

Berlin 8th february
1793:

To FRIEDRICH GENTZ—[*post* 8 *Feburary* 1793]

Corr. (1958), VII, 347–48

This is clearly the draft of a reply to the preceding letter. There is no proof that it was ever finished or sent.

[2] Gentz's translation was accompanied by five essays: on political liberty and its relation to government; on morality in revolutions; on the Declaration of Rights; a refutation of the *Vindiciae Gallicae* of James Mackintosh (1765–1822); and on national education in France.

[3] Gentz's notes and his essays were in places critical of Burke: in particular he disagreed with his concept of reason, and protested against his opinion of Rousseau.

Sir,

I am infinitely sensible of the honour you have done me in thinking my Sentiments worthy of being naturalised in Germany. Their good reception[1] must have been owing as much at least to the Translator as the author. I ought to be somewhat ashamed of my total ignorance of the German Language in which so many valuable works of all sorts have appeard; I am sure I am much mortified at it, as it prevents me from seeing how much my thoughts are improved in your hands. My Loss however is much greater in not being able to read the original pieces of yours which accompany that Translation.

To SIR LAWRENCE PARSONS—7 *March* 1793

Corr. (1958), VII, 358–60

Sir Lawrence Parsons, 5th Baronet (1758–1841), later (1807) 2nd Earl of Rosse, a respected independent member of the Irish House of Commons who sat for King's County, had sent Burke a copy of his pamphlet *Thoughts on Liberty and Equality. By a Member of Parliament*, Dublin, 1793.

Sir,

I am extremely flatterd to find that in the moment when you are doing such very essential Service to your Country[1] you have been so obliging as to turn any part of your thoughts towards me. It is unfortunate that after having enjoyd for so many ages the Benefits of civil Society, of which as you have well shewn property is the first origin, the continued Bond, and the ultimate End, one should be obliged at every turn to recur to the analysis of that society to convince men by abstract reasoning of the value of the benefits which they ought to know by feeling, and to enjoy with gratitude. The Evil of our time is in presumption and malice, the latter partly the Cause, partly the consequence of the former. There is no ignorance so mischeivous as that which arises from imperfect knowlege joind to a greater opinion of what is already obtaind than of what is yet to be acquired. A vast multitude of people have formed a mechanical Habit and facility of Style. Their readiness in expressing their conceptions

---

[1] There had been two German editions of the *Reflections* before Gentz's, both of which had been well received; but Gentz's translation sold twice as well as those of his predecessors (Frieda Braune, *Edmund Burke in Deutschland*, Heidelberg, 1917, pp. 19–20, 22).

[1] Parsons had made a much admired speech on the Catholic Relief Bill on 18 February (*Parliamentary Register of Ireland*, XIII, 203–19).

passes with them for a power of thinking. They are prompt to come out with their crude undigested and vulgar conceptions, which readers of the Same or a lower pitch, as well as the authours, consider as great discoveries. They look on those things as discoveries because no one had hitherto been so absurd as to spit out such nonsense. As these wonderful discoveries are made upon the most easy of all Subjects the finding fault, they have great advantages; Because faults cannot be denied to exist in all men and all establishments. It is awkard to admit faults and to reject a correction. Nobody has extricated himself better out of the difficulty than you have; particularly in the latter part of Your Pamphlet in which you reason concerning the collection and concentration of ability. It is wise and profound. Though so many have reasond on this Subject, your Book is in several parts quite new, and in all parts, the Argument is stated in a new and forcible manner. I see no marks of Haste in the Execution. I am sure that in the conception it is the product of a mind formed to the Habits of what Newton calls 'Patient thinking'.[2] We are almost perishing by the Press. It is fit, that if possible, we should be saved [by] it. I trust Ireland will take advantage of what is so well intended and executed with such superiour ability. I am sure she is a great and Essential part of our total Strength. If an intestine war of French Theory should rage within her own Bowels we shall labour terribly in the foreign War we are to carry on against the same Theory supported by all the rescources of that extensive Robbery to which this Theory has led the way.

Permit me to flatter myself that the honour you have done me on this occasion, may intitle me to the further satisfaction of which I am ambitious that of seeing you when you come to England.

> I have the honour to be with most perfect respect and Esteem
> Sir
>> Your most obedient
>> and humble Servant

Duke Street   EDM BURKE
March 7. 1793.

[2] Newton once described his own achievements as 'due to nothing but Industry and patient Thought' (*Four Letters from Sir Isaac Newton to Dr Bentley. Containing some Arguments in Proof of a Deity*, London, 1756, p. 2).

To ARTHUR MURPHY—8 *December* 1793

Corr. (1958), VII, 500–503

Burke is writing to thank Arthur Murphy for a present of his translation in four volumes of the *Works of Cornelius Tacitus* which he had dedicated to Burke.

My dear Sir,

I have not been as early as, to all appearance, I ought to have been, in my acknowledgments for your present. I received it in due time, but my delay was not from the want of a due sense of the value of what you have sent, or of the honour you have done me in sending it. But I have had some visitors to whom I was obliged to attend; and I have had some business to do, which, though it is not worth your while to be troubled with it, occupied almost every hour of the time I could spare from my guests: until yesterday, it was not in my power so much as to open your Tacitus.

I have read the first book through; besides dipping here and there into other parts. I am extremely delighted with it. You have done what hitherto, I think, has not been done in England: you have given us a translation of a Latin prose-writer which may be read with pleasure. It would be no compliment at all to prefer your translation to the last, which appeared with such a pomp of patronage. Gordon was an author fashionable in his time;[1] but he never wrote any thing worthy of much notice but that work,[2] by which he has obtained a kind of eminence in bad writing: so that one cannot pass it by with mere neglect. It is clear to me that he did not understand the language from which he ventured to translate; and that he had formed a very whimsical idea of excellence with regard to ours. His work is wholly remote from the genius of the tongue, in its purity, or in any of its jargons. It is not English, nor Irish, nor even his native Scotch. It is not fish, nor flesh, nor good red herring. Yours is written with facility and spirit, and you do not often depart from the genuine native idiom of the language. Without attempting, therefore, to modernize terms of art, or to disguise ancient customs under new habits, you have contrived things in such a manner that your readers will find themselves at home. The other translators do not familiarize you with ancient Rome: they carry

---

[1] Thomas Gordon (d. *c.* 1750) published his *Works of Tacitus* in two volumes: volume one *Containing the Annals. To which are prefixed Political Discourses Upon that Author* in 1728, dedicated to Sir Robert Walpole; volume two *Containing his Five Books of History, his Treatises on Germany, and Life of Agricola: with Political Discourses Upon that Author* in 1731, dedicated to Frederick, Prince of Wales.

[2] Gordon was also a writer of political and religious tracts.

you into a new world. By their uncouth modes of expression, they prevent you from taking an interest in any of its concerns. In spite of you, they turn your mind from the subject, to attend with disgust to their unskilful manner of treating it: from such authors we can learn nothing. I have always thought the world much obliged to good translators, like you. Such are some of the French. They who understand the original are not those who are under the smallest obligations to you; it is a great satisfaction to see the sense of one good author in the language of another. He is thus *alias et idem*.[3] Seeing your author in a new point of view, you become better acquainted with him: his thoughts make a new and deeper impression on the mind. I have always recommended it to young men in their studies, when they had made themselves thorough masters of a work in the original, then (but not till then) to read it in a translation, if in any modern language a readable translation was to be found. What I say of your translation is really no more than very cold justice to my sentiments of your great undertaking. I never expected to see so good a translation. I do not pretend that it is wholly free from faults; but at the same time I think it more easy to discover them than to correct them. There is a style, which daily gains ground amongst us, which I should be sorry to see farther advanced by the authority of a writer of your just reputation. The tendency of the mode to which I allude is, to establish two very different idioms amongst us, and to introduce a marked distinction between the English that is written and the English that is spoken. This practice, if grown a little more general, would confirm this distemper (such I must think it) in our language, and perhaps render it incurable.

From this feigned manner of *falsetto*, as I think the musicians call something of the same sort in singing, no one modern historian, Robertson only excepted, is perfectly free.[4] It is assumed, I know, to give dignity and variety to the style; but, whatever success the attempt may sometimes have, it is always obtained at the expence of purity, and of the graces that are natural and appropriate to our language. It is true, that when the exigence calls for auxiliaries of all sorts, and

---

[3] Different and the same.

[4] Burke probably wrote the enthusiastic reviews in the *Annual Register* of *The History of Scotland, during the reigns of Queen Mary and King James VI* . . . , London, 1759, and *The History of the reign of the Emperor Charles V* . . . , London, 1769, by William Robertson (1721–93). For his equally enthusiastic reception of Robertson's *History of America*, London, 1777, see above, p. 101. Gibbon was among those modern historians of whose style Burke disapproved; he is reported to have told Reynolds that 'it was very affected, mere frippery and tinsel' (J. Northcote, *The Life of Sir Joshua Reynolds* . . . , 2nd ed., London, 1818, II, 31).

common language becomes unequal to the demands of extraordinary thoughts, something ought to be conceded to the necessities which make 'Ambition Virtue:'[5] but the allowances to necessities ought not to grow into a practice. Those portents and prodigies ought not to grow too common. It you have here and there (much more rarely, however, than others of great and not unmerited fame) fallen into an error, which is not that of the dull or careless, you have an author who is himself guilty, in his own tongue, of the same fault in a very high degree. No author thinks more deeply or paints more strongly, but he seldom or ever expresses himself naturally. It is plain, that comparing him with Plautus and Terence, or the beautiful fragments of Publilius Syrus,[6] he did not write the language of good conversation. Cicero is much nearer to it. Tacitus and the writers of his time have fallen into that vice, by aiming at a poetical style. It is true, that eloquence in both modes of rhetorick is fundamentally the same; but the manner of handling is totally different, even where words and phrases may be transferred from the one of these departments of writing to the other.

I have accepted the licence you have allowed me, and blotted your book in such a manner that I must call for another for my shelves. I wish you would come hither for a day or two. Twenty coaches come almost to our very door. In an hour's conversation, we can do more than in twenty sheets of writing. Do come, and make us all happy. My affectionate compliments to our worthy Doctor. Pray believe me, with most sincere respect and regard, my dear Sir,

Your most faithful
and obedient humble servant,

Beaconsfield, Dec. 8, 1793.   EDMUND BURKE.

JAMES MACKINTOSH *to* EDMUND BURKE—
22 *December* 1796

Corr. (1958), IX, 192–94

James Mackintosh (1765–1832), later (1803) Sir James Mackintosh, published in 1791 his *Vindiciae Gallicae*, an able reply to Burke's *Reflections* from the standpoint of a moderate liberal. In November and December 1796 he published in the *Monthly Review* two unsigned articles on the *Two Letters on a Regicide Peace* in which he

---

[5] *Othello*, III, 3, 351.
[6] Publilius Syrus, a writer of Latin mimes in the first century B.C.

argued that the war with France was unjust and unnecessary, though he expressed his admiration for Burke's intellectual powers and literary style.

Sir

The liberty which I take in addressing you is so great and the nature of the address so peculiar that I certainly should not have hazarded such an address to a mind of a different Cast from yours.—From you however I venture to hope that a Simple and ingenuous Statement of my feelings will at least procure me pardon if I should fail in obtaining the success to which I presume to aspire.

From the earliest moments of reflexion your writings were my chief study and delight. The instruction which they contain is endeared to me by being entwined and interwoven in my mind with the recollection of those fresh and lively feelings of youth which are too pure and exquisite a pleasure to be twice tasted by the human heart.

The enthusiasm with which I then embraced them is now ripened into solid Conviction by the experience and meditation of more mature age. For a time indeed seduced by the love of what I thought liberty I ventured to oppose your Opinions without ever ceasing to venerate your character. I speak to state facts—not to flatter—You are above flattery. I am too proud to flatter even you.—Since that time a melancholy experience has undeceived me on many subjects on which I was the dupe of my enthusiasm.—I cannot say (and you would despise me if I dissembled) that I can even now assent to all your opinions on the present politics of Europe. But I can with truth affirm that I subscribe to your general Principles; that I consider them as the only solid foundation both of political Science and of political prudence; that I differ solely as to some applications of them which appear to my poor understanding not entirely accordant to the scheme and Spirit of your System; and that above all if the fatal necessity should arise (which God forbid) there is no Man in England more resolutely determined to Spill the last drop of his blood in defense of the Laws and Constitution of our Forefathers.

Even this much Sir I should not have said to you if you had been possessed of power.—I should for ever have imposed silence on my feelings if the act by which I now gratify them could be ascribed even by calumny herself to any base or unworthy motive.

But I hope that the pure desire of expressing my gratitude and veneration is at least a venial impropriety though it should overstep a little the bounds of Strict decorum. Suffer me then to express my Solicitude to be admitted to the honour of a few minutes conversation with you on some of your visits to town.—There are few boons in any man's Power to grant which will be a greater gratification to the Suitor.

Whatever may be the fate of this request I can only safely entrust the Construction of so Singular a Step as that which I now hazard to such a mind as yours; and I am perfectly confident that you will not so far punish my presumption as to expose me to the sneers of those who are less generous by disclosing any Circumstance of this address.

> I have the honour to be
> Sir
> with the most unfeigned and (suffer me
> to add) the most affectionate veneration
> Your faithful humble Servant,
> JAMES MACKINTOSH

No 14 Serle Street Lincolns Inn
22nd December 1796

To JAMES MACKINTOSH—23 December 1796

Corr. (1958), IX, 194–96

Sir

The very obliging Letter with which you have honoured me, is well calculated to stir up those remains of vanity, that I hoped had been nearly extinguished in a frame approaching to the dissolution of every thing that can feed that passion. But, in truth, it afforded me a more solid and more sensible consolation. The view of a vigorous mind subduing by its own constitutional force the maladies which that very force of constitution had produced, is, in itself, a Spectacle very pleasing and very instructive. It is not proper to say any more about myself, who have been, but rather to turn to you who *are*, and who probably *will* be, and from whom the world is yet to expect a great deal of instruction and a great deal of service. You have begun your Opposition by obtaining a great victory over yourself, and it shews how much your own Sagacity operating on your own experience is capable of adding to your very extraordinary natural Talents, and to your early errudition. It was the shew of virtue and the semblance of publick happiness that could alone mislead a mind like yours; and it is a better knowledge of their substance which alone has put you again in the way that leads the most securely and most certainly to your End. As it is on all hands allowed that you were the most able advocate for the cause which you supported, your sacrifice to truth and mature reflexion, adds much to your glory.

For my own part (if that were any thing) I am infinitely more pleased to find that you agree with me in several capital points than surprized that I have the misfortune to differ with you in some. When I myself differ with persons I so much respect of all Names and parties, it is but just (and, indeed, it costs me nothing to do it) that I should bear in others that disagreement in Sentiment and Opinions, which at any rate is so natural, and which perhaps arizes from a better view of things.

Tho' I see but very few persons, and have, since my misfortune[1] studiously declined all new acquaintances and never dine out of my own family, nor live at all in any of my usual societies, not even in those with which I was most closely connected, I shall certainly be as happy as I shall feel myself honoured by a visit from a distinguished person like you, whom I shall consider as an exception to my rule. I have no habitation in London, nor never go to that place but with great reluctance, and without suffering a great deal. Nothing but necessity calls me thither; but tho' I hardly dare to ask you to come so far, whenever it may suit you to visit this abode of sickness and infirmity, I shall be glad to see you. I dont know whether my friend Doctor Laurence and you have the happiness of being acquainted with each other; if not, I could wish it to be brought about. You might come together, and this might secure to you some entertainment which, my infirmity, that leaves me but a few easy hours in my best Days, will not afford me the means of giving you by those attentions that are your due.

You will have the goodness to excuse my making use of another hand to answer your Letter, but of late I have found it very irksome and inconvenient to me to stoop to my Desk. I therefore dictate from my Couch whatever I wish to say to my friends at a distance. I have the honour to be Sir, with great respect and regard

Your most obedient and very
much obliged humble servant,
EDM BURKE.

Beaconsfield
23d Decr 1796

[1] The loss of his son in 1794.

Mackintosh accepted Burke's invitation and spent a few days at Beaconsfield. A friend with whom he later discussed his impressions of Burke preserved them in a rough summary. Mackintosh, the friend reported, '. . . described, in glowing terms, the astonishing effusions of his mind in conversation: perfectly free from all taint of affectation; would enter, with cordial glee, into the sports of children, rolling about with them on the carpet, and pouring out, in his gambols, the sublimest images, mingled with the most wretched puns.—Anticipated his approaching dissolution with due solemnity but perfect composure;—minutely and accurately informed, to a wonderful exactness, with respect to every fact relative to the French Revolution. Burke said of Fox, with a deep sigh, "He is made to be loved" ' (Mackintosh, *Memoirs*, I, 91–2).

To EDMOND MALONE—4 *May* 1797

Corr. (1958), IX, 326–29

Burke writes to thank Malone, the famous Shakespearean scholar, for the gift of his edition of *The Works of Sir Joshua Reynolds* (2 vols., London, 1797).

My dear Sir,

I have received your valuable Present; very valuable indeed from what it contains of your own, as well as of the works of our inestimable Friend. Your Life of him is worthy of the subject, which is to say a great deal.[1] I have read over not only that Life but some part of the Discourses with an unusual sort of pleasure, partly because being faded a little on my memory they have a sort of appearance of novelty, partly by reviving recollections mixed with melancholly and satisfaction. The Flemish Journal I had never seen before—Your trace in that every where the Spirit of the Discourses supported by new examples: He is always the same Man, the same philosophical, the same artist-like critick, the same sagacious Observer, with the same minuteness without the smallest degree of trifling. I find but one thing material, which you have omitted in his Life—you state very properly how much he owed to the writings and conversation of Johnson;[2] and nothing shews more the greatness of Sir Joshua's Parts than his taking advantage of both; and making some application of them to his profession, when Johnson neither understood, nor desired to understand any thing of painting, and had no distinct Idea of its nomenclature even in those parts which had got most into use in common Life: But Though

---

[1] Malone's biographical introduction occupies the first sixty-eight pages of volume one.

[2] Reynolds himself acknowledged this indebtedness. He said of his own *Discourses:* 'Whatever merit they may have must be imputed, in a great measure, to the education which I may be said to have had under Dr Johnson . . . he qualified my mind to think justly' (*Boswell's Life of Johnson*, ed. G. B. Hill, rev. L. F. Powell, Oxford, 1934–51, III, 369 n.).

Johnson had done very much to enlarge and strengthen his habit of thinking, Sir J. did not owe his first rudiments of Speculation to him. He has always told me, that he owed his first dispositions to generalize—and to view things in the abstract to old Mr Mudge,[3] Prebendary of Exeter and brother to the celebrated mechanick of that name.[4]— I have seen myself Mr Mudge the clergyman at Sir Joshua's house. He was a learned and venerable old man, and as I thought very much conversant in the Platonick Philosophy and very fond of that method of philosophizing. He had been originally a dissenting minister, a description which at that time bred very considerable men both among those who adhered to it and those who left it. He had entirely cured himself of the unpleasant narrowness, which in the early part of his Life had distinguished these Gentlemen and was perfectly free from that ten times more dangerous enlargment, which has been since then their general characteristick. Sir J. Reynolds had always a great love for the whole of that Family; and took a great Interest in whatever related to them. His acquaintance with the Mudges ought to be reckoned among the earliest of his literary connexions. If the work should come to a second Edition, I hope you will not omit this very material circumstance in the Institution of a mind like that of our Friend. It was from him that I first got a view of the few, that have been published, of Mr Mudge's sermons[5] and on conversing afterwards with Mr Mudge I found great traces of Sir Joshua Reynold's in him, and, if I may say so, much of the manner of the master.[6] I cannot finish this part of my Letter without thanking you, for the very kind manner in which you are pleased to speak of me;[7] far indeed beyond any thing which I can have a claim to, except from your extraordinary good nature.

There is a matter, which I am now going to mention to you which is so full of delicacy, that I should not dare to touch it except through the confidential hand of our friend Dr King, who has been charitable enough to visit me here and so condescending as to employ himself for me in the manner that you see. You mention the Copy money for

[3] The Rev. Zachariah Mudge (1694–1769).

[4] Thomas Mudge (1717–94), appointed King's Watchmaker in 1776, was the son of Zachariah Mudge.

[5] Mudge published: *Liberty; a Sermon* . . . , London, 1731; *The Nature and Extent of Church-Authority. A Sermon* . . . , London, 1748; *Sermons on Different Subjects*, London, 1739.

[6] In his second edition Malone printed the present letter to this point (I, pp. xxxii–xxxv).

[7] Malone mentions that Reynolds was 'lavish in his encomiums' on Burke's *Reflections* (I, p. lvii), and when referring to Burke's anonymous obituary of Reynolds, Malone himself says: 'the hand of the great master, and the affectionate friend, is so visible, that it is scarcely necessary to inform the reader that it was written by Mr Burke' (I, p. lxviii).

which you have agreed with the Bookseller. If I were to consider, that the Life which you have written is entirely your own Work and that the compilation has been made and superintended by your own care in common justice the money is your property: but if you should consider yourself, perhaps too generously, as holding the money in trust for Lady Inchiquin as an executor, permit me to remind you of one circumstance and to entreat you to touch it as delicately as possible to Lady Inchiquin.—When one wishes to pay homage to the memory of departed Eminence in a friend with whose cast of complexion and turn of mind we are acquainted, we ought to do it in the way, in which, if living, we know that he would have desired. I can say with certainty that nothing would have given him more pleasure, than to be assured, that a monument should be erected to his memory in St Paul's Church.[8] He had too proper a sense of Reputation to give any such thing in charge to his Representatives. You remember that after his Death it was talked of in his Club[9] and in a manner resolved upon, that a monument should be erected for him, the basis of which should be laid in the subscriptions of the Club. As I was a large legatee[10] I was willing to subscribe £100. Now I do not know how the money arising from his Works can be so well employed, as in further contributing to his fame, in a way connected with the Arts and appropriate to his particular Relish. And if you do not chuse to make your own use of your own money I do not know in what way it can be better applied. I am sensible of the enormous price which the fashionable artists demand for works of this kind. But I know that there are others of less name but of merit, which Sir J. R. would not think contemptible who would execute a very handsome monument for £1500; towards making up which, besides the £350 and my £100, Lord and Lady Inchiquin would naturally wish to be very liberal contributors—The Club, his friends and his fame would do the rest—at least I fancy so.[11] All this however I submit to your judgment, without any reservation

[8] Reynolds, who thought that St Paul's looked 'forlorn and desolate', or at least 'destitute of ornaments suited to the magnificence of the fabrick', while Westminster Abbey was 'encumbered and overloaded with ornaments', successfully insisted that Dr Johnson's monument should be placed in St Paul's. Malone, in his second edition of the *Works of Reynolds* (II, 343) expressed the hope that monuments to both Reynolds and Burke would be erected in St Paul's.

[9] The Literary Club, of which Reynolds 'had the merit of being the first proposer'; see *Boswell's Life of Johnson*, I, 477.

[10] Reynolds had left Burke £2000, in addition to cancelling a bond for £2000.

[11] Reynold's monument, by John Flaxman (1755–1826), was erected in St Paul's Cathedral in 1813. Members of the Literary Club agreed to contribute '5 *guineas each* only as being likely to induce members to subscribe' (*Farington Diary*, ed. James Greig *et al*, London, 1922–8, III, 188).

of a further opinion of my own. You will speak to Mr Metcalfe about it of course.

As to myself in whom you are pleased to take an Interest, my health is so variable that I do not know well what to say upon the subject. When I wish to turn my thoughts abroad I see nothing but what tends to make my retreat even into the feelings of my own illness a sort of consolation. Great means of Power destroyed by mean, pusillanimous and most mistaken measures in the use of them. Every thing menacing from abroad, every thing convulsed within,—the violent convulsions of feeble nerves—As to what has happened in Ireland I expected nothing else from what has been done in that country—There I doubt we do not so much agree about the cause as we must concur in sorrow concerning the melancholly fact of the situation of that country. I shall therefore say no more upon this subject; but most cordially wish for success in all your most virtuous and liberal pursuits, as long as the state of the World will permit you to continue them.

> I have the honour to be, my dear Sir,
> Your most faithful and affectionate
> and obliged humble Servant

Bath 4th May. 1797.   ED. BURKE

At some time Burke set down the following 'few hints' on Reynolds's character for Malone's use:

Sir Jos Reynolds.

He was a great generaliser, and was fond of reducing every thing to one System more perhaps than the variety of principles which operate as in the human mind and in every human Work will properly endure. But this disposition to abstractions generalizing and classifica[tions] is the great glory of the human mind, that indeed which most disting[uishe]s man from other animals and is the Scource of every thing that can be called Science. I beleive his early acquaintance with Mr Mudge of Exeter, a very Learnd and thinking man, and much inclined to Philosophise in the Spirit of the Platonists, disposed him to this habit. He certainly by that means Liberalized in an high degree the Theory of his own Art; if he had been more Methodically instituted in the early part of his Life, and if he had possessed more leisure for Study and reflexion he would in my opinion have pursued this method with great success. [He] had a strong turn for humour and well saw the weak sides of things. Was *timid*—enjoyd every Circumstance of his good fortune and had no affectation on that Subject. I do not know a fault or weakness of his that he did not convert into something that bordered on a virtue instead of pushing it to the confines of a Vice.

TOLERATION AND RELIGION

THESE LETTERS bear on the difficult and disputed question of
Burke's religion. Burke was not a devout believer, and none of
his letters could be called devotional. In recognizing "the principle of
a superior will" he was in some sense religious, but in what sense
precisely? From the first he seems to have been preoccupied with the
problem of the "Diversities of Sects and opinions amongst us," as he
says in a letter written at age fifteen to his Quaker friend Richard
Shackleton. How could a free society secure the benefit—or, better to
say, supply the necessity—of a *superior* will in view of the exclusiveness
of sects and religions, which derive from the exclusiveness of *one*
superior will?

Burke was not tempted by the eighteenth-century solution of deism,
which attempted to define a God that would be superior without being
exclusive. Nor, convinced as he was of the necessity and benefits of
religion, did he adopt our twentieth-century liberal indifference, in
which the state leaves religion itself as a matter for private choice. He
held to both establishment and toleration: establishment of the Church
of England (even in Ireland) so as to enforce the principle of a superior
will, and yet toleration of dissenters and Catholics (not to mention
"Jews, Mahometans and even Pagans") to respect the diversity of
sects, ultimately the freedom of human opinion. This freedom deserves
respect when it is exercised by *prescription*, that is, when it is exercised
not by a willful individual but by a long-standing community. "I can
never think any man an Heretick . . . by *education*" (Letter to William
Burgh). This thought is elaborated in Burke's letter to Viscount Ken-

mare protesting an alleged reform of the penal laws affecting Catholics in Ireland. Yet while defending toleration, Burke found it necessary to reproach the Protestant dissenters who were the main beneficiaries of toleration. The dissenters, in their exclusiveness, remained anti-Catholic (letters to James Boswell and Dr. John Erskine), and yet in their universalism were carried away by zeal for toleration so as to attack all establishment of religion and to demand toleration as an abstract right (letter to John Noble).

To RICHARD SHACKLETON—15 October 1744

Corr. (1958), I, 32–4

When Burke left Ballitore School for Trinity College at age 15 he returned to live in his father's house at Arran Quay, Dublin. Richard Shackleton (1726–92) remained at Ballitore, about 30 miles distant. This is one item of an active correspondence.

Arran Quay October 15th 1744

The hurry of Examinations is at length over, and I sit down to write to Dear Dick with much greater pleasure since No business interrupts, or hinders me speaking my thoughts with the freedom of an undisturbed mind.

I am entirely of your opinion concerning being diligent. I know that it's the gate by which we must pass to knowledge and fortune, that without it we are both unserviceable to ourselves and our fellow-Creatures and a burthen to the Earth; Knowledge is Doubtless the greatest acquisition we can make because it is what Denominates us men and as you remark'd is the most essential difference between us and the brute-Beasts. I shall say no more about it, for fear I should be ask'd the question why I dont follow what I so much approve and be more Studious? Perhaps bona videoque proboque deteriora sequor,[1] is applicable to me. I know what is Good like the Athenians, but Dont practice like the Lacædemonians.[2] What would not I give to have my Spirits a little more settled? I am too giddy, this is the bane of my Life, it hurries me from my Studies to triffles and I am afraid it will hinder me from knowing any thing thoroughly. I have a Superficial knowlege of many things but Scarce the bottom of any, so that I have

[1] I see and approve the good; I follow the worse. See Ovid, *Metamorphoses*, VII, 20–21.
[2] Cicero, *De Senectute*, XVIII.

no manner of right you the preference to give me in the first.—As to the second I told you my opinion when I had last the pleasure of ⟨see⟩ing you, I have no relish at all for that sort of Life so that I may say with Cowley If eer Ambition did my &c³

What made you stop short in the middle of your discourse? I am sure I should not be displeased at hearing all the praises you could possibly bestow on a belief which you profess and which you believe to be the true and pure Doctrine of Christ, we take different Roads tis true⁴ and since our intention is to please him who suffered the punishment of our sins to justifie us, He will I believe consider us accordingly, and receive us into that glory which was not merited by our own good Deeds but by his sufferings which attone for our Crimes. Far be it from me to exclude from Salvation such as beleive not as I do, but indeed it is a melancholy thing to consider the Diversities of Sects and opinions amongst us, Men should not for ⟨sm⟩all matters commit so great a Crime as breaking the unity of the Church, and I am Sure if the Spirit of humility the greatest of Christian virtues was our guide, our Sects and Religions would be much fewer. Give me leave to add also that since it is our misfortune to have so many different opinions we should not hide our Talent in the earth but exert it with all diligence in the great Affair for the Acomplishment of which we were sent into the world to wit Salvation. God all merciful, all good, has given us a guide, a Talent to direct us in the slippery paths of the world, let us then my Dear friend earnestly and heartily set to work praying the Divine being of his infinite mercy to help us in our Undertaking by the saving and enlightening assistance of his holy Spirit, while we seek what manner of Serving him will most please our great Creator, for it is impossible that all can be equally pleasing to him, who has declar'd that as there is but one God so there is but one faith, and one Baptism. O my friend what so⟨rt of⟩ an account will those have to give who as if they were asleep pass their lives without the least consideration of this, will it be a sufficient excuse for them to say in that way no, no, it is the business of every one to search whether their way be good, and if any man who knows this to be his Duty as there is no Christian but does, if (I say) he willingly neglects this and

---

³   If e'er Ambition did my fancy cheat
                           With any wish so mean as to be great,
                           Continue Heaven still from me to remove
                           The humble blessings of the life I love.
                                    Cowley, *Several Discourses by Way of Essays in Verse
                                         and Prose*, VI, 'Of Greatness'.

⁴ Shackleton was a devout Quaker.

be found in a wrong way he will not be held guiltless before God. Then, my Dear Dick let us take this into Consideration for indeed it is a Serious affair and worth the attention even of our whole lives and implore the assistance of the holy Spirit which leads into all Truth and endeavour to walk piously and Godlily in the path our great Redeemer has shew'd us confiding very little in our Strength but Casting ourselves upon him who died for us, and with great humility asking his assistance in knowing what manner of serving him will best please him that we may not be in the Number of those whose ignorance is justly imputed to themselves. If we do this I do not in the least doubt but that 'God of his great mercy will guide us in the right road.' I very m⟨uch⟩ approve of the method you laid down for our Correspondence I will as much as I can observe it. I must own that I cant with any freedom write better so you must excuse me in that part. And in point of Stile but I hope to improve in that by Degrees: I do not know to whom I can write with greater freedom and less regularity than to you for as the thoughts come Crouding into my head I cann⟨ot⟩ forbear putting 'em down be they in what order o⟨r disorder⟩ they will. You will excuse me for this and for what ⟨mistakes⟩ and incongruities you may find in my future ⟨letters⟩ because you will beleive that whether what I say ⟨be well or⟩ ill express'd it comes from a sincere heart and f⟨rom one⟩ who is sincerely your friend. God gives me good r⟨esolves⟩ sometimes and I lead a better life, they last for a ⟨time or⟩ so, sometimes more sometimes less and then thr⟨ough⟩ the fickleness of my temper and too great confiden⟨ce in my⟩self I fall into my old Courses, ay often far wo⟨rse. You⟩ see my weakness Dear Dick and my failings p⟨lead⟩ and pray for me, we will pray for one another rec⟨ipro⟩cally: Praise be to his holy name for all things, for every impulse of his Grace he gives me I praise him and trust that he will continue em to me, and make me persevere in 'em. Let us lead the best life we can and ma⟨ke⟩ it our Study to please him the best we can both in faith and works. I could write a great deal more with pleasure. I dare not say you would be tired with reading but that I find my Paper almost gone.—. . .

To WILLIAM BURGH—*9 February* 1775

Corr. (1958), III, 110–13

William Burgh (1741–1808), who lived at York, was a layman with theological interests. William Mason (1724–97) described him as 'a young man of the quickest parts and most general knowledge I ever met with' (Walpole, *Corr.*, ed. W. S. Lewis, XXVIII, 200). He owned estates in Ireland and was a member of the Irish House of Commons from 1769–76. In June 1774 he published anonymously a *Scriptural Confutation of the Arguments against the One Godhead . . . by the Reverend Mr Lindsey*. Burke evidently read the book and expressed a desire to meet the unknown author; for on 23 July Burgh wrote to him from Scarborough, disclosing his identity, reminding Burke that he had shown some kindness to the author when a boy, and regretting that distance prevented his taking advantage of Burke's invitation. In 1775 Burgh brought out a second edition, this time under his own name and with a dedication to Burke. On 30 January Mason sent Burke a proof of this dedication, and a few days later, on the eve of leaving town, wrote again asking him to express any objections and to return the proof to Mr Burgh in York.

Dear Sir,

I beg you will not think that my delay in returning you the proof sheet of your most ingenious and most obliging dedication could proceed from a want of the liveliest Sensibility to the great honour you have done me. I now return the proof, with my sincerest and most grateful Acknowledgments.

Some topicks are touched in that dedication, on which I could wish to explain myself to you. I should have been glad to do it through Mr Mason; but to my great Loss, on this, and many other accounts, he left town suddenly. Indeed, at that time and ever since, the pressure of American business on one hand and a petition against my election on the other, left me not a single minute at my disposal[1]—and I have now little leisure enough to explain myself clearly on some points in that dedication, which I either misunderstand, or they go upon a misapprehension of some part of my public conduct. For which reason I wish, if I might presume to interfere, that they may be a little altered.

It is certain that I have, to the best of my power, supported the establishment of the Church, upon grounds and principles, which I am happy to find countenanced by your approbation.[2] This you have been told; but you have not heard that I supported also the petition of the dissenters, for a larger toleration than they enjoy at present,

[1] From the meeting of Parliament of 19 January there had been important debates on American policy centering around the petitions of the merchants, Lord Chatham's proposed settlement, and the parliamentary Address supporting the ministry. The select committee on the Bristol election petition began its sittings on 10 February; so that Burke was occupied in preparing his case before that day.

[2] Particularly in February 1772 when he opposed the relaxation of the Thirty-nine Articles as a test of faith for clergymen of the Church of England (*Parliamentary History*, XVII, 275–89). The Rev. Theophilus Lindsey (1723–1808) is said to have been present at this debate and to have been offended by Burke's opposition (Sir Philip Magnus, *Edmund Burke*, pp. 69, 313–14).

under the letter of the act of K. William.[3] In fact my opinion in favour of toleration goes far beyond the limits of that act; which was no more than a provision for certain sets of men, under certain circumstances; and by no means, what is commonly called, an act of toleration. I am greatly deceived if my opinions on this subject are not consistent with the strictest, and the best supported Church-establishment. I cannot consider our dissenters, of almost any kind, as schismaticks; whatever some of their Leaders might originally have been in the eye of him, who alone knows, whether they acted under the direction of such conscience as they had, or at the instigation of pride and passion. There are many things among most of them, which I rather *dislike*, than dare to *condemn*. My ideas of toleration go far beyond even theirs. I would give a full civil protection, in which I include an immunity, from all disturbance of their publick religious worship, and a power of teaching in schools, as well as Temples, to Jews Mahometans and even Pagans; especially if they are already possessed of any of those advantages by long and prescriptive usage; which is as sacred in this exercise of Rights, as in any other. Much more am I inclined to tolerate those, whom I look upon as our brethren; I mean all those who profess our common hope; extending to all the reformed and unreformed Churches, both at home and abroad; in one of whom I find any thing capitally amiss, but their mutual hatred of each other. I can never think any man an Heretick, or schismatick by *education*. It must be, as I conceive, by an act, in which his *own choice*, (influenced by blamable passions,) is more concerned, than it can be, by his early prejudices, and his being aggregated to bodies, for whom men natu-rally form a great degree of reverence and affection. This is my opinion; and my conduct has been conformable to it. Another age will see it more general; and I think that this general affection to religion will never introduce indifference; but will rather encrease real Zeal, Chris-tian fervour, and pious emulation; that it will make a common cause against Epicurism, and every thing that corrupts the mind, and renders it unworthy of its family. But toleration does not exclude rational preference, either as to modes, or opinions; and all the lawful and honest means which may be used for the support of that preference.

I should be happy to converse with you, and such as you, on these subjects, and to unlearn my mistaken opinions; if such they should be; for how ever erroneous, I believe there is no evil ingredient in

[3] Although supporting subscription to the Thirty-nine Articles by clergy of the Church of England, Burke was in favour of relaxing this requirement for Protestant dissenting ministers and schoolmasters (*Parliamentary History*, XVII, 770–83).

them. In looking over that dedication, if you should agree with me, that there are some expressions that carry with them an idea of my pushing my ideas of Church establishment further than I do, you will naturally soften or change them accordingly. I do not very well know how to excuse the great Liberty I take in troubling you with observations, where I ought to speak only my obligations. Be assured that I feel myself extreamly honoured by your good opinion, and shall be made very happy by your friendship. I am, with the greatest esteem

Westminster Feb. 9. 1775

To JAMES BOSWELL—1 *March* 1779

Corr. (1958), IV, 44–7

When the English Acts relaxing the penal laws against Roman Catholics were passed in the Spring of 1778 it was understood that similar legislation for Scotland was to follow. The prospect called forth an organized opposition, and in February there were anti-Catholic riots in Edinburgh and Glasgow. The Government gave way before this demonstration of popular feeling and abandoned its intention of changing the Scottish penal laws. James Boswell had written to ask Burke whether his party, now in opposition, would acquiesce in this shift of policy.

My dear Sir

Your goodness is indeed inexhaustible; But great as my faults are they do not make such a demand upon it as you imagine. I have had the misfortune of missing the third Letter you speak of; and before your last, only *one* came to my hands. But as I was not so early as I ought to have been in acknowleging the honour of that one, my fault is greater than I fear I am able to attone for; and I tell you of the failure of the other, because I do not wish that my crime should have any aggravation.

I had heard some account of the Subject of your Letter before I receivd it from you. It would have been against the Spirit of the act of Union if Scotland did not, at some time or other partake of the disorders that prevail in the constitution of the British Family. I do confess indeed, that I did not expect, that our dear Sister, who in the rigour of her Prudery, had shewn such outrageous Zeal, and decreed such severe penances against other frail and offending parts of the houshold, should make such a slip herself as to give her a fair Title to the Stool and white Sheet.[1] But these things will happen as long as the very best of us are only made up of mere rebellious flesh and blood.

As to the Riot which has been ⟨Performed⟩, and the rebellion which is threatned, they have at least the advantage of diversifying the Scene of our modern contentions. A religious war was not exactly the thing I expected in my time. I thought it possible, that even at the other side of the Tweed, a man might be allowd to say his prayers in Latin without any gross violation of the native, inherent, essential privileges and immunities of the broad Scotch. I admit, that the Ears of heaven may be more delighted with these accents; yet as the other Tongue may be as intelligible there (though not so pleasing) I think a little of it might be borne at Edinburgh without making a very serious quarrel of the matter. The Romans of our day are not quite so dangerous an Enemy to Galgacus[2] and his Warriours, as they were 1700 years ago; or as some of their descendents were a century or two since; I cannot conceive, that Bishop Hay[3] is so dreadful a person as Julius Agricola; or that Mr Macdonald with all his Grocery,[4] and Mr Bagnal with all his crockery Ware,[5] are altogether so formidable as Sextus the fifth with his Bulls.[6]

You certainly have a right to a rebellion in your Town; and of course we must leave the matter and fashion of that gratification to your own Choice. But without presuming to arraign any ones fancy, I confess, that the American rebellion is more to my Taste than that which you are cooking in the North. I think it ⟨behoves⟩ as well to resist an act

---

[1] An allusion to the stool of repentance in Scottish churches, where sinners did penance in a white sheet.

[2] Calgacus, the Caledonian chief defeated by Julius Agricola; he is known only from Tacitus.

[3] George Hay (1729–1811), Roman Catholic Bishop of Daulis and Vicar Apostolic of the Lowland District of Scotland. The Edinburgh mob had plundered this chapel, house and library. Burke had probably met him when he had come to London with Lord Linton. This visit was in connexion with the loyal address of the Roman Catholics of 3 April 1778, which Burke had drafted. Hay and Linton were in London again in January 1779 to press for the amendment of the Scottish penal laws.

[4] In the Edinburgh riots a mob had attacked the shop of Daniel Macdonald, a Roman Catholic grocer.

[5] The pottery works of Robert Bagnal had been destroyed in the Glasgow riot of 9 February. Bagnal was a Roman Catholic and had allowed one of his workshops to be used as a chapel.

[6] Sixtus V was Pope from 1585 to 1590. Burke probably means Pius V, who issued the Bull excommunicating and deposing Queen Elizabeth.

of Taxation as an act of Toleration; and it would hurt me rather more to have the Excise in my own house,[7] than the Mass in my Neighbours. I take it for granted, that there are good reasons for every thing you do. But I am apt to be as much puzzled with moral Mysteries as others are with religious. I do not yet clearly comprehend, why it should be right, to burn mens houses and to despoil them of their Goods, because somebody is supposed to intend them an Act of Kindness; and I should not think the difficulty perfectly removed, though it were proved beyond contradiction, that the sufferers were consenting to, or even actually desirous of such a Benefit. Full as little do I understand why the University should share the Fate of the Masshouses; and why the use of the Citadel of Edinburgh should be to afford a place of refuge to your most learned professors and most eminent Writers.[8] But time I suppose will clear up all those deep Mysteries.

You ask me, whether, after His Majesties Ministers have given up the Scotch toleration Bill, any other Members intend to bring it in? Indeed I am so struck with the admiration of this heroic act of Magnanimity in our Ministers, that I do not aspire to the most distant imitation of it. Besides being at 400 good Miles distance from the coercive Arm of the Edinburgh powers, I *will not* ⟨tell⟩ what I intend to do, or to give my reasons for it, (as Falstaff says) on compulsion, though they were as plenty as Blackberries;[9] and as to what others intend to do, I really do not know. Oh poor Government, how art thou fallen! That Government which so many wise Tories and good nursing loyalists have been cramming and nourishing into Strength, has been so overfed, and so diseased by high living, that instead of standing firm on its legs by all the good things that have been put into its belly, it is got so gouty, that it can hardly be supported by crutches! However, we continue the old Course without being discouraged by Events; and are dying according to art and by the best rules that are possible. . . .

I dined with your friend Dr Johnson on Saturday at Sir Joshua's.[10] We had a very good day, as we had not a sentence, word, syllable,

---

[7] The excise was notoriously unpopular in Scotland; it was hated everywhere because it was collected by means of a system of inspectorship which on occasion brought the excise officer literally into the taxpayer's house.

[8] In the Edinburgh riots Burke's friend William Robertson (1721–93), the historian, Principal of Edinburgh University, had ordered the college gates closed and placed a guard of 200 men within; Catholics of the city were offered refuge in Edinburgh Castle.

[9] *Henry IV, Pt I*, II, 4.

[10] Sir Joshua Reynolds (1723–92).

Letter, comma, or tittle, of any of the Elements that make politicks. Adieu and believe me with Great Esteem and regard

Dear Sir

your most faithful

and obedient humble Servant

EDM BURKE

Westminister

Monday March 1. 1779

To DR JOHN ERSKINE—12 *June* 1779

Corr. (1958), IV, 83–8

Burke's somewhat delayed reply to John Erskine's letter of 24 April. Erskine (1721–1803), Doctor of Divinity of Glasgow University, was Minister of Old Greyfriars, Edinburgh. He was one of the ablest leaders of the Scottish Church.

Sir

I am honoured with your very obliging Letter by Lord Balgony, together with the four pieces which you have been so good as to send along with it. Nothing but the uncommon urgency of publick business could have prevented me from immediately waiting on Lord Balgony to pay my respects to his Lordship, and to make my acknowledgments for his great politeness on the occasion. I am besides to thank you Sir, for giving me an opportunity of being known to a person whose Character must naturally make me ambitious of his acquaintance.

The Sentiments expressed in your pamphlet, so far as they regard America are very honourable to you; They discover a great deal of that enlarged Benevolence of heart, which is very rarely separated from Sound political judgment, and is certainly the best substitute, that can be conceived, where that Judgment is wanting. In other particulars, that relate to the internal regulation of this Kingdom, you will have the goodness to excuse me, if I have the misfortune of differing with you, in no small degree. I do not presume to ensure you, who have so much better reason undoubtedly for the opinions you entertain, than I am able to give for mine. To speak only for myself, and my own private feelings, I assure you, that I should think myself, irrational and inconsistent (to say no worse) if I refused to apply my Ideas of Civil to religious Liberty. When I could so far subdue the ambition, natural to mankind, in giving up, as I did with great Chearfulness, very flattering powers and very colourable Rights, of the Nation of which I am a Citizen, and the Legislature of which I am a Member, in favour of the happiness of a very distant part of Mankind, I should find it difficult to trace the order and connexion of my principles, if I were capable of denying indulgencies infinitely smaller, to my immediate Countrymen; when too, these indulgencies were to be allowed, without abandoning any one object of honour, profit, or pleasure. I wish, along with you, that we may not be so far Englishmen or Scotchmen as to forget that we are Men. I wish that we may not be so far Presbeterians, or Episcopals as to forget that we are Christians, the one being our common bond of humanity, as the other is our common bond of religion. I am by choice and by Taste, as well as by Education, a very attached Member of the Establish[ed] Church of England. But it is far from my wish, as I thank God it is from my power, to persecute you, who probably differ from me in a great many points: I wish it were equally out of my power to persecute any Roman Catholick. He has as much a right to my benevolence, as even you Sir, and no man can have a better claim to universal Esteem and regard. I hope too, that you will not think it any sort of derogation from the deference which I ought to pay to your Judgment that I think myself obliged in conscience, to take my opinions of Mens principles rather from themselves, than from you. I keep at the same time, I assure you, very just weights and Measures; and as I do not take my Ideas of the Churches of France and of Italy from the Pulpits of Edinburgh, so I shall most certainly not apply to the Consistory at Rome or to the College of Sorbonne at Paris, for the Doctrines and Genius of the Church of Scotland.

I have lived long enough, and largely enough in the World, to know for certain, that the Religion, which (I believe most firmly) the divine wisdom has introduced into it, for its improvement, and not for its depravation, contains, in all its parts, so much of good, as not wholly to disapoint the wise purposes for which Religion was intended, and abundantly to merit all the Esteem and veneration I can bestow upon it. Perhaps I sometimes think I see many strong Marks of human Error and infirmity in all its Divisions; tho' I can much more easily support the Modesty which induces me to treat them all with respect, than the presumption which leads me to find fault with any of them. It is in this manner I think of the whole Christian Church; I mean the Great Bodies of the East and West, including all their particular descriptions; which I am willing to consider, rather as divisions, made for convenience and order, than Seperations, from a diversity of Nature, or from irreconcileable contradiction in principles. I think so of the whole and of all the considerable parts of those who profess our common Hope; having at the same time, that degree of respect for all other religions, even for those who have nothing better than mere human Reason, or the unregulated instincts of human Nature, for their Basis, that I could not prevail on myself to bestow on the Synagogue, the Mosque or the Pogoda, the language which your Pulpits lavish upon a great part of the Christian world.

If on Account of such Sentiments, people call me a Roman Catholick, it will give me not the smallest degree of disturbance. They do me too much honour, who aggregate me as as Member to any one of those respectable Societies which compose the body of Christianity. Wherever they choose to place me, I am sure to be found in extraordinary good Company. I do not aspire to the Glory of being a distinguishd Zealot for any National Church, untill I can be much more certain than I am, that I can do it honour by my doctrine or my Life, or serve it in some more reputable and effectual manner than by a passionate proceeding against those who are of another description.

I have read the pamphlet and Sermons which you were so obliging as to send me. They are in many respects written with the Ability and Skill that may be expected from Men of learned Education, and who are in the exercise of an Authority over the Minds of others. But I confess I am somewhat surprised, that you should think they serve as proofs of the *Moderation* of the Writers and preachers of them. If I had the Ability, which I have not, or the wish, which I hope I never shall have, for exciting popular tumults for the destruction of any set of people, I could not desire anything more elaborately composed, or more powerfully drawn from all the Sources of Eloquence for that purpose, than *some* of the pieces you have sent me. It is not a cold caution for moderating our Anger, or a refinement on the difference between a detestation of a Mans principles and an hatred of his person, that can save the objects of those sanguinary invectives from the blind fury of the Multitude. To represent a Man as immoral by his religion, perfidious by his principles, a Murderer on point of conscience, an Enemy from Piety to the foundations of all social intercourse, and then to tell us, that we are to offer no Violence to such a person, under favour, appears to me rather an additional insult and mockery, than any sort of corrective of the injury we do our Neighbour by the Character we give him.

He must indeed be unacquainted with human Nature, who will from thence infer that the Authors of those pieces intend all the Mischief they produce. I know the contrary. They have but *one* Object in their View. It is dear to them. They raise imaginary fears about it; they have the common apprehensions of jealous Men. They imagine a combination of all the world to rob them of their beloved possession. They of course suppose all sorts, even of preventive Hostility to be self defence; and this just and laudable principle of self preservation, if not guided with great judgment, is liable to be the most mischievous thing in the world; for the rights of self preservation, being the same thing as necessity, are circumscribed by no Law; and therefore it is proper that the existence of the Case should be very clearly and solidly proved, before Men can have any permission to act upon it. We soon forget what another may suffer, when the question is about our own safety; we therefore ought not to be hasty in taking Men to be Enemies, because against Enemies it is easy to believe any ill, and the rules of Hostility admit of almost every sort of Violence. I really believe those Gentlemen are in earnest when they talk of self preservation—but fear, which is always cruel, is not always founded.

It would, I likewise admit, be altogether unfair to attribute to these particular Sermons, the robberies and burnings, and other outrages committed at Edinburgh and Glascow, because all these Enormities were perpetrated before the Sermons were preached, and there were afterwards, few or no houses of any mark, or any quantity of valuable Effects left, upon which the populace could exert their Zeal.[1] But I cannot be equally sure, that some *similar* writings or discourses have not been the very natural causes of these disorders: nor can I by any means agree with Dr Macfarlane,[2] that Men, when they wish to free themselves from the Terrour of penal Laws, and the odium of being supposed the just object of them, when they earnestly sollicit to have that Stigma taken off, and to recommend themselves to their Government by dutifull applications, can be said to bring their Misfortunes on themselves, if on that account, a furious and bigotted set of Miscreants choose to rob them of their Goods, and to burn their houses. I really should be shocked at that Gentlemans assertion, if I considered it as a deliberate proposition, or any more than an Effect of that sudden

---

[1] Burke was mistaken in thinking the sermons had been preached after the riots.

[2] Dr John Macfarlan (1740–88), Minister of the Canongate, Edinburgh, had published *A Defence of the Clergy of Scotland, who had Appeared in Opposition to the Intention of an Unlimited Repeal of the Penal Laws against Roman Catholics* (Edinburgh, 1778).

warmth which sometimes surprises the reason of the most prudent and equitable Men.

I greatly fear, that I have trespassed on your time and patience very unwarrantably especially as all discourse on the present subject is just now Superfluous. The matter of the contest is over for this year, perhaps for ever. You have in Scotland obtained a great Victory over those who differed from you in opinion. In England however we have been still better off; for we have obtained *two* Victories, though indeed of a nature very different from yours—Victories not over our Enemies, but over our own passions and prejudices; having passed, in the last Session, a Bill for the relief of Roman Catholicks; and in the present for the relief of protestant dissenting Ministers, many of whom are of your particular discipline and persuasion.[3] On this latter, Sir, you will permit me to give you my hearty congratulations.

It is unlucky that matters of difference should make the discourse much longer than the pleasant Topics on which we are agreed. I mean pleasant as to the principle, for nothing is so perfectly disagreeable as the present aspect of things with regard to the publick, in which (however odious it may sound) I include our brethren in America, whether they find it their Interest to embody under our Monarchy, or to regulate themselves in Republics of their own. In either Case, I do not like to part with my Interest in, and my communion with them. They are still Englishmen by blood, and freemen by principle. I cannot help thinking, that we should have far more Glory, and far more advantage too, (but even publick Glory is publick advantage) in letting them govern themselves under the protection of England as friends, than to attempt a conquest over them as Enemies, whilst they have France for their Protector. I say this even in Case of possible success, which in my opinion, knowing as I do the consequences, would be worse than any defeat which could befal us. I think we might have kept them very easily; but when the natural Bonds of dominion are so broken, it is better, I am sure, to look for a friendship that will hold, than an Authority that will not; But at present America is in a state of dreadful confusion of which we cannot in the least profit. I am sorry to tell you that by the complexion of the House of Commons last Night, I see no sort of prospect that all the humiliations which have impaired our strength will increase our Wisdom. Permit me to

[3] An Act for the further Relief of Protestant Dissenting Ministers and Schoolmasters (19 Geo. III, c. 44). Burke supported the oath to be taken by those benefitting from the Act. On this issue he found himself on the same side as Lord North and opposed by Fox and Lord John Cavendish.

apoligise once more for this first and last trouble I give you, and be assured, that I have the honour to be with the greatest Esteem and respect

                              Sir your most Obedient and humble Servant
                                                                    E B

12th June 1779
Charles St St James's Square
To. The Revd Dr Erskine Edinburgh

To VISCOUNT KENMARE—21 *February* 1782

Corr. (1958), IV, 405–18

Thomas Browne, 4th Viscount Kenmare (1726–95), a Catholic peer whose estates were in County Kerry, Ireland. He had written to Burke about a Bill for the further relaxation of penal laws brought before the Irish Commons by Luke Gardiner (1745–98).

                                                        Charles Street
My Lord,   Feb. 21. 1782.
    I am much obliged to your Lordship for your communication of the heads of Mr Gardiners Bill. I had receivd it in an earlier stage of its progress from Mr Braughall; and I am still in that Gentlemans Debt, as I have not made him the proper return for the favour he has done me. Business to which I was more immediately called, and in which my Sentiments had the weight of *one* Vote, occupied me every moment since I receivd his Letter. This first morning which I can call my own, I give with great cheerfulness to the Subject on which Your Lordship has done me the honour of desiring my opinion.
    I have read the heads of the Bill with the amendments. Your Lordship is too well acquainted with men and with affairs, to imagine, that any true Judgement can can formed on the value of a great measure of policy from the perusal of a piece of paper. At present I am much in the dark with regard to the State of the Country, which the intended Law is to be applied to. It is not easy for me to determine, whether or no it was wise, for the sake of expunging the black Letter of Laws, which menacing as they were in the Language, were every day fading into disuse, solemnly to reaffirm the principles, and to reenact the provisions, of a Code of Statutes, by which you are totally excluded from the *priveleges* of the *commonwealth* from the highest to the Lowest; from the most *material* of the civil professions; from the *army;* and

even from Education, where alone Education is to be had.[1] Whether this scheme of indulgence, grounded at once on contempt and Jealousy, has a tendency gradually to produce *something better* and more liberal, I cannot tell, for want of knowing the actual Map of the Country. If *this should be the Case*, it was right in you to accept it such as it is. But if this should be one of the experiments, which have sometimes been made before the Temper of the Nation was ripe for a real reformation, I think it may possibly have ill Effects, by disposing the penal matter in a more Systematick order, and thereby fixing a permanent Bar against any thing that is *truly substantial*.

The whole merit or demerit of the measure depends upon the plans and dispositions of those by whom the act was made, concurring with the general Temper of the protestants of Ireland, and their aptitude to admit in time of some part of that *equality*, without which you never can be *fellow citizens*. Of all this I am wholly ignorant. All my correspondence with men of publick importance in Ireland has for some time totally ceased. On the first Bill for the relief of the Roman Catholicks of Ireland, I was, without any call of mine, consulted both on your side of the Water and on this. On the present occasion, I have not heard a word from one man in Office; and I know as little of the Intentions of British Government, as I know of the Temper of the Irish parliament. Your Lordship mentions, that opposition is expected from the Archbishop of Cashell. If I am rightly informed, he has obtaind that high and Lucrative Office under the Crown, by the Credit of his Uncle Mr Ellis,[2] who has himself an high and tolerably profitable Office under the King, who has been for many years constantly in such Offices; and, I am told looks to the peerage. Opposition too is hinted from other persons, who hold great places, and multiplied great emolluments under the Government. I do not find, that any opposition was made by the principal persons of the minority in the House of Commons, or that any is apprehended from them in the house of Lords. The whole of the difficulty seems to Lie with the principal men in Government, under whose protection this Bill is supposed to be brought in. This violent opposition and cordial support coming from one and the same quarter, appears to me something Mysterious, and hinders me from being able to make any clear Judgment of the merit of the present measure as compared with the actual State of the Country, and the general Views of Government; without which, one can say nothing that may not be very erroneous.

[1] i.e. abroad.
[2] Welbore Ellis (1713–1802), M.P. for Weymouth, later (1794) 1st Baron Mendip.

To look at the Bill in the abstract, it is neither more nor less than a renewd act of universal, unmitigated, indispensible, exceptionless, disqualification. One would imagine, that a Bill inflicting such a multitude of incapacities, had followd on the heels of a conquest made by a very fierce Enemy under the impression of recent animosity and resentment. No man, in reading that Bill, could imagine he was reading an act of amnesty and indulgence, following a recital of the good behavior of those who are the Objects of it, which recital stood at the head of this Bill as it was first introduced, but, I suppose, for its incongruity with the body of the piece, was afterwards omitted. This I say on memory. It however still recites the oath; and, that Catholics 'ought to be considerd as being good and loyal Subjects to his Majesty, his Crown and Government'. Then follows an universal exclusion 'of those good and loyal subjects' from every, even the lowest Office of Trust or profit, from any Vote at an election, from any privelege in a Town Corporate from being even a Freeman of such corporation, from serving on Grand Juries, from a Vote at a *Vestry*, from having a Gun in his house, from being Barrister Attorney or Solicitor &c &c &c. This has surely much more the air of a Table of proscription than of an act of Grace. What must we suppose the laws concerning those good subjects to have been of which this is a relaxation!

I know well enough, that there is a Cant current about the difference between an exclusion from employments, even to the most rigorous extent, and an exclusion from the natural Benefits arising from a mans own industry. I allow, that under some Circumstances, the difference is very material in point of justice; and that there are considerations, which may render it advisable for a wise Government to keep the leading parts of every Branch of civil and military administration in hands of the best Trust. But a *total* exclusion from the commonwealth is a very different thing. When a Government subsists, as Governments formerly did, on an *Estate of its own*, with but few and inconsiderable revenues drawn from the Subject, then, the few offices which subsisted were naturally at the disposal of those who paid the salaries out of their *own* pocket, and there, an exclusive preference could hardly merit the name of a proscription. Almost the whole produce of a mans industry remaind in his own purse to maintain his family. When a very great portion of the Labour of individuals goes to the State, and is by the State again refunded to individuals, through the medium of Offices, and in this circuitous progress from the publick to the private fund, indemnifies the families from whom it is taken, an equitable Ballance between the Government and the Subject is established. But if a great body of the people who contribute to this State Lottery are excluded from all the prizes, the stopping the Circulation with regard to them may be a most cruel hardship, amounting, in effect, to being double and trebled Taxed; and will be felt as such, to the very quick, by all the families high and low of those hundreds of thousands, who are denied their chance, in the returned fruits of their own Industry. This is the thing meant, by those who look upon the publick Revenue only as a spoil; and will naturally wish to have as few as possible concerned in the division of the Booty. If a State should be so unhappy as to think it cannot subsist without such a barbarous proscription, the persons so proscribed ought to be indemnified by the remission of a large part of their Taxes, by an immunity from Offices of publick burthen, by an exemption from being pressed into any military or naval service. Common sense and common justice dictate, this at least, as some sort of compensation for their slavery. How many families are incapable of existing, if the little Offices of the revenue, and little military commissions are denied them? To deny them at home, and to make the happiness of acquiring some of them somewhere else, felony or high Treason, is a piece of cruelty in which, till very lately, I did not suppose this age capable of persisting. Formerly a similarity of religion made a sort of Country for a man in some quarter or other. A refugee for religion was a protected Character. Now their reception is cold indeed; and therefore as the asylum abroad is destroyd, the hardship at home is doubled.

This hardship is the more intollerable, because the professions are shut up. The Church is so of Course. Much is to be said on that subject with regard to them and to the protestant dissenters. But that is a chapter by itself. I am sure I wish well to that Church and think its Ministers among the very best Citizens of your Country. However such as it is, a great walk of Life is forbidden Ground to seventeen hundred thousand of the Inhabitants of Ireland. Why are they excluded from the Law? do not they expend money in their suits? why may not they indemnifye themselves by profiting, in the persons of some, for the losses incurred by others? Why may not they have persons of confidence, whom they may if they please, employ in the Agency of their affairs. The exclusion from the Law, from Grand Juries, from Sheriffships, and under sheriffships, as well as from freedom in any corporation, may subject them to dreadful hardships; as it may exclude them wholly from all that is beneficial, and expose them to all that is mischievous, in a Trial by Jury. This was manifestly within my own observation; for I was three times in Ireland from the year 1760 to the year 1767; where I had sufficient means of information concerning the inhuman proceedings, (among which were many cruel murders, besides an infinity of other outrages and oppressions, unknown before in a civilized age) which prevailed during that period, in consequence of a pretended conspiracy among Roman Catholicks against the Kings Government. I could dilate on the mischiefs that *may* happen, from those which *have* happend, upon this head of disqualification, if it were at all necessary.

The head of the exclusion from *Votes* for Members of Parliament is closely connected with the former. When you cast your Eye on the Statute book, you will see, that no Catholick, even in the ferocious act of Queen Anne, was disabled from Voting on account of his *religion*.[3] The only ⟨conditions⟩ required for that privelege, were the oaths of allegiance and abjuration; both oaths relative to a *civil* concern. Parliament has since added another oath of the same kind;[4] and yet an House of Commons adding to the securities of Government, in proportion as its danger is confessedly lessend, and professing both confidence and indulgence, in effect takes away the privelege, left by an act, full of Jealousy, and professing persecution. The taking away of a Vote is the taking away the Shield which the subject has, not only against the oppressions of power, but of that worst of all oppressions, the persecutions of private Society, and private manners. No candidate for parliamentary influence is obliged to the least attention towards them, either in Cities or Counties; on the contrary, if they should become obnoxious to any bigotted, or any malignant people among whom they live, it will become the Interest of those who court popular favour, to use the numberless means, which always reside in Magistracy and influence, to oppress them. The proceedings in a certain County in Munster, during that unfortunate period I have mentiond, reads a Strong Lecture on the cruelty of depriving men of that Shield, on account of their speculative opinions. The protestants of Ireland feel well and naturally on the hardship of their being bound by Laws for which they do not directly or indirectly Vote. The bounds of those matters are Nice and hard to settle in Theory; and perhaps they have been pushed too far. But how they can avoid the necessary application in the Case of others toward them I know not. It is true, the words of this act do not create a disability, but they clearly and evidently suppose it. There are few Catholick Freeholders to take the Benefit

---

[3] Roman Catholics had not been deprived of the franchise until 1728, though after 1704 (by 2 Anne c. 6—'the ferocious act') they could only vote if they took the oath of abjuration.

[4] By an Act of 1774.

of the privelege, if they were admitted to partake it: but the manner in which this very right in Freeholders at large is defended, is not on the Idea, that they do really and truly represent the people, but that all people being capable of obtaining freeholds, all those, who by their industry and sobriety merit this privelege, have the means of arriving at Votes. It is the same with the Corporations.

The Laws against foreign Education, I find are reenacted. They are clearly, the very worst part of the old Code. Besides your Laity, you have the Succession to about four thousand Clergymen to provide for. These, having no lucrative livings in Prospect, are taken very much out of the Lower orders of the people. At home, they have no means whatsoever provided for their obtaining a *clerical* Education, or indeed any Education at all. When I was in Paris, about seven years ago, I looked at every thing, and lived with every kind of people, as well as my time admitted. I saw there the Irish College of the Lombard, which seemd to me a very good place of Education, under excellent orders and regulations, and under the Government of a prudent and learned man.[5] This College was possessed of an annual fixed revenue of more than a thousand pound a year—the greatest part of which had arisen from the Legacies and benefactions of persons educated in that College, and who had obtaind promotions in France, from whence they made this grateful return. One in particular, I remember to the amount of ten thousand Livres annually, as it is recorded on the Donors monument in their Chappel. It has been the Custom for poor persons in Ireland to pick up such knowlege of the Latin Tongue, as, under the general discouragements and occasional pursuits of Magistracy, they were able to acquire, and receiving orders at home were sent abroad to obtain a clerical Education. By officiating in petty Chaplainships, and performing now and then, certain offices of religion for small gratuities, they receivd the means of maintaining themselves, until they were able to compleat their Education. Through such difficulties and discouragements, many of them have arrived at a very considerable proficiency, so as to be marked and distinguished abroad; who afterwards by being sunk in the most abject poverty, despised and ill treated by the higher orders among Protestants, and not much better esteemed or treated even by the few persons of fortune of their own persuasion, and contracting the habits and ways of thinking of the poor and uneducated, among whom they were obliged to live, in a few years retained little or no traces of the Talents and acquirements

[5] The Rev. Lawrence Kelly (*c.* 1720–77), Rector of the College from 1769 until his death.

which distinguished them in the early period of their Lives. Can we with justice, cut them off from the use of places of Education founded, for the greater part from the œconomy of poverty and Exile, without providing something that is equivalent at home? Whilst this restraint of foreign and domestick Education, was a part of an horrible and impious System of Servitude, the Member was well fitted to the body. To render men patient under a deprivation of all the rights of human nature, every thing which could give them the knowlege or feeling of these rights, was rationally forbidden. To render humanity fit to be insulted, it was fit that it should be degraded. But when we profess to restore men to the capacity for property, it is equally irrational and unjust, to deny them the power of improving their minds, as well as their fortunes. Indeed, I have ever thought that the prohibition of the means of improving our rational Nature to be the worst species of Tyranny, that the insolence and perverseness of mankind ever dared to exercise. This goes to all men in all situations, to whom Education can be denied. Your Lordship mentions a proposal which came from my friend the Provost, whose benevolence and enlarged spirit, I am perfectly convinced of, which is the proposal of erecting a few sizar-ships in the College for the education, I suppose, of Roman Catholick Clergymen. He certainly meant it well. But coming from such a man as he is, it is a strong instance of the danger of suffering any description of men to fall into entire contempt. The charities intended for them, are not perceivd to be fresh insults; and the true Nature of their wants and necessities being unknown, remedies wholly unsuitable to the nature of their complaint are provided for them. It is to feed a sick Gentû with Beef Broth, and to foment his Wounds with Brandy. If the other parts of the university were open to them, as well on the foundation as otherwise, the offering of sizarships would be a pro-portiond part of a *general* kindness. But when every thing liberal is withheld, and only that which is servile is permitted, it is easy to conceive upon what footing they must be in such a place. Mr Hutchinson[6] must well know, the regard and honour I have for him, and he does not think my dissenting from him in this particular, arises from a disregard of his opinions; It only shews, that, I think, he has lived in Ireland. To have any respect for the Character and person of a popish priest there—Oh! it is an uphill work indeed! But until we come to respect what stands in a respectable light with *others*, we are very deficient in the Temper which qualifies us to make any Laws or

[6] John Hely Hutchinson (1724–94), Provost of Trinity College, Dublin; M.P. for Cork in the Irish Parliament; and an old friend of Burke.

regulations about them. It even disqualifies us from being charitable towards them with any Effect or Judgment.

When we are to provide for the Education of any body of men, we ought seriously to consider the particular functions they are to perform in Life. A Roman Catholick Clergyman is the Minister of a very ritual Religion; and by his profession subject to many restraints. His Life, is a life full of strict observances; and his Duties of a laborious nature towards himself, and of the highest possible trust towards others. The duty of *confession* alone is sufficient to set in the strongest light, the necessity of his having an appropriated mode of Education. The Theological opinions and the peculiar Rites of one religion never can be properly taught in Universities founded for the purposes, and on the principles of another, which in many points is directly opposite. If a Roman Catholick Priest, intended for Celibacy, and the Function of confession, is not strictly bred, in a seminary where these things are respected, inculcated, and enforced, as sacred, and not made the subject of derision and obloquy, he will be ill fitted for the former, and the Latter will be indeed, in his hands, a terrible Instrument. There is a great resemblance between the whole frame and constitution of the Greek and Latin Churches—The secular Clergy in the former, *by being married,* living under little restraint, and having no particular Education suited to their function, are universally fallen into such contempt, that they are never permitted to aspire to the dignities of their own Church; and it is not held respectful to them to call them *Papas,* by their true and antient appellation; but those who wish to address them with civility, always call them Hieromonachi. In consequence of this disrespect, which I venture to say, in *such a Church,* must be the consequence of a secular Life, a very great degeneracy from reputable Christian manners, has taken place throughout that great Member of the Christian Church. It *was so* with the Latin Church, before the *restraint on Marriage.* Even that restraint gave rise to the greatest disorders before the Council of Trent, which, together with the emulation raised, and the good example given by the reformed Churches, wherever they were in View of each other, has brought on that happy amendment, which we see in the Latin communion both at home and abroad. The Council of Trent has wisely introduced the discipline of *Seminaries,* by which Priests are not trusted for a Clerical institution even to the severe discipline of their own Colleges; but after they pass through them, are frequently, if not for the greater part, obliged to pass through peculiar methods, having their particular ritual Function in View. It is in a great measure to this, and to similar methods used in *foreign education*, that the Popish Clergy of Ireland, miserably provided for, living among *low* and ill regulated people, without any discipline of sufficient force to secure good manners, have been hinderd from becoming an intollerable nuisance to the country, instead of being, as, I conceive, they generally are, of very great Service to it. The Ministers of Protestant Churches require a different mode of education, more Liberal, and more fit for the ordinary intercourse of Life, and having little hold on the minds of the people by external Ceremonies, extraordinary observances, or seperate habits of Living, they make up the deficiency, by cultivating their minds by all kinds of ornamental Learning, to which the Liberal provision made in England and Ireland for the parochial Clergy, and the comparative lightness of parochial Duties, enables the greater part of them, in some considerable degree, to accomplish; to say nothing of the ample Church preferments with little or no Duties annexed. This learning, which I believe to be pretty general, together with an higher situation, and more chastened by the opinions of mankind, forms a sufficient security for their morals, and their sustaining their Clerical Character with dignity. It is not necessary to observe, that all these things are however collateral to their function; and that except in preaching, which may be, and is supplied, and often best supplied, out of printed Books, little else is necessary to a protestant Minister than to be able to read the English Language; I mean for the exercise of his Function, not to the scrutiny at his admittance. But a popish parson in Ireland, may do very well without any considerable Classical erudition, or any proficiency in pure or mixed Mathematics, or any knowledge of civil History. Even if they should possess these acquisitions (as at first many of them do) they soon lose them in the painful Course of professional and parochial Duties; but they must have all the *knowlege*, and what is to them more important than the Knowlege, the *discipline* necessary to those Duties. All modes of Education conducted by those, whose minds are cast in another mold, as I may say, and whose original ways of thinking are formed upon the reverse pattern, must be, to *them*, not only useless, but mischeivous—just as I should suppose the Education in a popish ecclesiastical Seminary would be ill fitted for a protestant Clergyman. Here it would be much more so, as in the Case of the Protestant it only requires to *reject*, in the other little for his purpose is acquired.

All this, my Lord, I know very well, will pass for nothing with those who *wish*, that the popish Clergy should be illiterate, dissolute, and in a Situation to produce contempt and detestation. Their minds are wholly taken up with party squabbles, and I have neither leisure nor inclination to apply any part of what I have to say, to those, who never think of religion, or of the commonwealth, in any other light, than as they tend to the prevalence of some Faction in either. I speak, on a supposition, that there is a disposition,—*to take the State in the Condition in which it is found,*—and to improve it *in that State*, to the best advantage. Hitherto the plan for the Government of Ireland has been to sacrifice the civil prosperity of the Nation to its religious improvement. But if people in power there, are, at length, come to entertain other Ideas, they will consider the good order, decorum, Virtue, and morality, of every *description* of men among them, as of infinitely greater importance, than the struggle (for it is nothing better) to change those *descriptions*, by means, which put to hazard Objects, which, in my poor opinion, are of more importance to religion and the State, than all the polemical matter which has ever been agitated among men from the beginning of the world to this hour. On this Idea, an Education, fitted to each order and division of men, such as they are found, will be thought an affair rather to be encouraged than discountenanced; and until Institutions at home, suitable to the occasions and necessities of the people, and which are armed, as abroad they are, with authority to coerce the young men to be formed in them by a strict and severe discipline, the means they have at present of a cheap and effectual Education in other Countries will not continue to be prohibited by penalties, and modes of inquisition, not fit to be mentiond to Ears, that are organized to the chaste sounds of equity and Justice.

Before I had written thus far, I learned more at large, than I had it from your Lordship, of the Scheme for giving to the Castle the patronage of the presiding Members of the Catholick Clergy. At first I could scarcely credit it; for I believe it is the first time, that the presentation to other peoples Alms has been desired in any Country. If the State provides a suitable maintenance and Temporality to those governing members, and to the Clergy under them, I should think the project, however improper in other respects, to be by no means unjust; But to deprive a *poor* people, who maintain a *second set of Clergy* out of the miserable remains of what is left after Taxing and Tything, to deprive them of the disposition of their own Charities among their own Communion, would in my opinion be an intollerable hardship. Never were the Members of one religious Sect fit to appoint the Pastors to another. Those who have no regard to their welfare, reputation, or internal quiet, will not appoint such as are proper. The

Seraglio of Constantinople, is as equitable as we are, whether Catholicks or Protestants; and where their own Sect is concerned full as religious; But the sport which they make of the miserable Dignities of the Greek Church, the little factions of the *Haram* to which they make them subservient, the continual Sale to which they expose and reexpose the same dignity, and by which they squeeze all the inferior orders of the clergy, is, (for I have had particular means of being acquainted with it) nearly equal to all the other oppressions together, exercised by the Mussulmen over the unhappy Members of the Oriental Church. It is a great deal, to suppose, that even the present Castle would nominate Bishops for the Roman Church of Ireland with a religious regard for its welfare. Perhaps they cannot, perhaps they dare not do it. But suppose them as well inclined, as I know, that *I* am, to do them all kind of Justice, I declare *I* would not, if it were in my power, take it upon myself. I know I ought not to do it. *I belong to another community;* and it would be an intollerable usurpation in me to affect such an authority where I conferred no Benefit, or even if I did confer, (as in some degree the Seraglio does,) temporal advantages. But allowing, that the present Castle finds itself fit, to administer the Government of a Church, which they solemnly forswear, and forswear with very hard words, and many evil Epithets, and that as often as they qualifye themselves for the power, which is to give this very patronage, or to give any thing else that they desire; yet they cannot ensure themselves, that a man like the late Lord Chesterfield will not succeed to them.[7] This man, whilst he was duping the Credulity of Papists with fine words in private, and commending their good behaviour during a rebellion in Great Britain, as it well deserved to be commended and rewarded was capable, of urging penal Laws against them in a Speech from the Throne, and stimulating with provocatives, the wearied and half exhausted bigottry of the then parliament of Ireland.[8] They set to work, but they were at a loss what to do; for they had already almost gone through every contrivance which could waste the vigour of their Country; but after much struggling they produced a child of their old Age the shocking and unnatural act about Marriages, which tended to finish the Scheme for making the people, not only two distinct parties for ever, but keeping them as two distinct

[7] Philip Dormer Stanhope, 4th Earl of Chesterfield (1694–1773) had been Lord Lieutenant of Ireland 1745–6.

[8] Chesterfield had suggested in October 1745 that the Irish Parliament might consider strengthening the penal laws.

species, in the same Land.[9] Mr Gardiners humanity was shocked with it,[10] as one of the worst parts of that truly barbarous System, if one could well settle the preference where almost all the parts were outrages on the rights of humanity and the Laws of Nature.

Suppose an atheist, playing the Part of a Bigot, should be in power again in that Country, do you believe, that he would faithfully and religiously administer the trust of appointing Pastors to a Church, which wanting every other support, stands in tenfold need of Ministers, who will be dear to the people committed to their charge, and who will exercise a really paternal authority amongst them? But if the superior power were always in a disposition to dispense conscientiously, and like an upright Trustee and Guardian these rights which he holds for those, with whom he is at variance, has he the capacity and means of doing it? How can the Lord Lieutenant form the least judgment on their merits, so as to discern, which of the Popish priests is fit to be made a Bishop? It cannot be; the Idea is ridiculous. He will hand them over to Lords Lieutenants of Counties, Justices of peace and other persons, who for the purpose of vexing and turning to derision this miserable people, will pick out the worst and most obnoxious they can find among the Clergy, to set over the rest. Whoever is a complainant against his Brethren will always be considerd as persecuted; whoever is censured by his superiors will be looked upon as oppressed; whoever is careless in his opinions, and loose in his morals—will be called a Liberal man, and will be supposed to have incurred hatred because he was not a Bigot. Informers, Talebearers, perverse and obstinate men, flatterers, who turn their back upon their flock, and court the protestant Gentlemen of the Country—will be the Object of preferment. And then I run no risque in foretelling that whatever order quiet and Morality you have in the Country, will be lost. *A popish Clergy, who are not restraind by the most austere subordination, will become a Nuisance, a real publick Grievance of the heaviest kind in any Country that entertains them;* and instead of the great Benefit which Ireland does, and has long derived from them, if they are educated without any Idea of discipline and obedience, and then put under Bishops, who do not owe their station to their Good opinion, and whom they cannot respect, that Nation will see disorders, of which, bad as things are, it has yet no Idea. I do not say this, as

---

[9] The statute (19 Geo. II, c. 13) enacted that every marriage between a Roman Catholic and a Protestant, or between two Protestants if celebrated by a Catholic priest, should be null and void.

[10] Intermarriage was permitted under Gardiner's Bill as printed at the end of 1781.

thinking the leading men in Ireland would exercise this Trust worse than others. Not at all. No man, no set of men living, are fit to administer the affairs, or regulate the interior œconomy of a Church to which they are Enemies.

As to Government, if I might recommend a prudent caution to them, it would be to innovate, as little as possible, upon speculation, in establishments, from which as they stand, they experience no material inconvenience to the repose of the Country. *Quieta non movere*.[11] I could say a great deal more. But I am tired; and I am afraid your Lordship is tired too. I have not sat to this letter a single quarter of an hour without interruption. It has grown long, and probably contains many repetitions, from my total want of leisure to digest and consolidate my thoughts; and as to my expressions, I could wish to be able perhaps to measure them more exactly—but my intentions are fair— and I certainly mean to offend nobody. However, in the disorder in which this matter lies, I ⟨must⟩ request the favour of your Lordship by no means to put what I have written into any indiscreet hands whatsoever. If your Lordship thinks it worth your while, you will get it legibly copied, and shew it to Mr Eden, to Mr Gardiner, and to any other Gentlemen in Office, or in Parliament, (and particularly to the Speaker)[12] that you think proper. Beyond this I would not have it go— because I have already experienced the mischief of letting abroad a Letter carelessly penned; for, having with more familiarity than I confess I was intitled to, a good while ago happend to mention my name with that of a Gentleman of great consideration in Ireland, I am afraid I do not to this minute stand very well with him; and I am extremely sorry for it, for I am sure I wish for his friendship and good opinion.[13]

Thinking over this matter more maturely, I see no reason for altering my opinion in any part. The act, as far as it goes, is good undoubtedly. It amounts I think very nearly to a toleration with respect to religious Ceremonies. But it puts a new bolt on Civil Rights; and rivetts it I am afraid to the Old one in such a manner, that neither, I fear, will be easily loosend. What I could have wished would be to see the *civil advantages* take the lead. The other I conceive would follow, in a manner, of Course. For by what I have observed, it is pride, arrogance, and a spirit of domination, and not a bigotted spirit of religion, that has caused and kept up these oppressive Statutes. I am sure I have

---

[11] Let sleeping dogs lie.

[12] Edmund Sexton Pery (1719–1806), Speaker of the Irish House.

[13] A facetious reference to John Scott in the *Letter to Thomas Burgh* had offended him.

known those, who have oppressed papists in their civil rights, exceedingly indulgent to their religious ceremonies; who even wished them to continue, in order to furnish pretences for oppression; and who never saw a man, by converting, escape out of their power, but with grudging and regret. I have known men to whom, I am not uncharitable in saying, (though they are dead,) that they would become papists, in order to oppress protestants; if by being protestants, it was not in their power ⟨to oppress⟩ papists. It is ⟨injustice, and not a⟩ mistaken conscience, that has been the principle of persecution, at least so far as it has fallen under my observation. However as I begun; so I end. I do not know the map of the Country. Mr Gardiner who conducts this very great and difficult work, and those who support him are better judges of the Business than I can pretend to be, who have not set my foot in Ireland these sixteen years. I have been given to understand, that I am not considerd as a friend to that Country, and I know that pains have been taken to diminish and even wholly to destroy any little Credit I might have had there by the partiality, (which went at least as far as it ought to go) that I was once thought to have to the place of my Birth. I am so convinced of the weakness of interfering in any Business without the opinion of the people in whose affairs I interfere, that I do not know how to acquit myself in what I have now done.

I have the honour to be with high regard and Esteem

My Lord your Lordships most obedient and humble Servant

EDM BURKE

To JOHN NOBLE—14 *March* 1790

Corr. (1958), VI, 100–104

In his speech in the debate on the repeal of the Test and Corporation Acts on 2 March, Burke protested against the Dissenters basing their claims on abstract rights, and joined in the cry of 'Church in danger' by offering evidence of the avowed intentions of leading non-conformist spokesmen to subvert the Establishment. However, he made an attempt to distinguish the body of the Dissenters (whom he praised) from their leaders, and declared that if the former 'would come fairly forward, and let their actual desire and meaning be ascertained he would meet them. He, for one', he said, 'should be glad to sift their object, and if it were such as a rational legislature could safely grant, he, at least, should have no objection' (*Parliamentary History*, XXVIII, 441). Burke's old Bristol friend John Noble (1743–1828) apparently interpreted this as a hint that Burke was willing to act on behalf of the 'respectable' rank and file, and in a letter (missing) he seems to have suggested that Burke himself move a smaller, but significant, alteration in the law.

Beconsfield March 14. 1790.

My dear Sir,

. . . As to the Corporation clause you wish me to bring in,[1] you may be perfectly sure, that the house at this time will not hear of it. I think I know the disposition and temper of Parliament—and if ever there was a time, peculiarly unfavourable, to any alteration, in any thing which touches Church or State, it is this Moment. The Majority in *both* Houses, is strongly of opinion, that the Minority which appeard in *one* of them ought, for some Space, to lay asleep all discussions of the kind: There are very few things I should not most gladly do to fall in with your wishes: But I beg you to consider, that such an attempt, in *me*, would look like a mean unworthy Stroke of policy to make amends for the opinion I lately gave; and to insinuate myself into the favour of a powerful party, which I was afraid I had offended. To make myself contemptible or ridiculous, would not be the way to serve any person. My conduct would appear in that view to the dissenters themselves, in common with the rest of the world.

I certainly never had any ill wishes to these Gentlemen as a *body;* and there are not persons on earth I love and respect more than I do some individuals amongst them. A day may come for removing this Barrier. But I am sure it is not likely to come soon, if some of the most active and leading among the Dissenters do not alter their Conduct. As long as they continue to claim what they desire as a *Right;* so long will they find it difficult to obtain it.[2] Parliament will not hear of an *abstract principle*, which must render it impossible to annexe any qualification Whatsoever to the capacity of exercising a publick Trust; and I am myself much of the same Mind; though I would have these

[1] Fox's motion of 2 March was lost by a vote of 294 to 105. Burke did not vote in the divisions, and had opposed the motion in debate, on the grounds that repeal was inexpedient at this time (*Parliamentary History*, XXVIII, 432–43). Apparently Noble had suggested that Burke bring in a fresh motion for repealing section nine of the Corporation Act (13 Car. II, st ii. c. I), which stipulated that no one could hold a municipal office who did not take the sacrament in the Church of England. This section had, in fact, been rendered void in practice by successive indemnity acts since 16 Geo. II, c. 30, although it was not finally repealed until 1828 (9 Geo. VI, c. 17).

[2] The tone of the Dissenters' campaign of 1789–90 had been much more strident than that of previous campaigns. For example, the Bristol Dissenters referred to the Test and Corporation Acts as depriving 'persons of their religious persuasions, of their just and natural rights' (*St James's Chronicle*, 8–10 October 1789).

qualifications as few and as moderate as possible. This high claim of *Right*, leaves with Parliament no *discretionary* power whatsoever concerning almost any part of *Legislation;* which is almost all of it, conversant in qualifying, and limiting some *Right or other of mans original Nature*. As long as principal Leading men among the dissenters make *associations* on this Subject;[3] so long will they keep up the general Alarm. As long as they shew, not a cool, temperate, conscientious dissent, but a warm, animated and acrimonious Hostility against the Church establishment, and by all their words and actions manifest a settled design of subverting it, so long will they, in my poor opinion, be met, in any attempt whatsoever of the least consequence, with a decided opposition like that of Tuesday Sennight.[4] Let me assure you, that the corporation part of the proposed Repeal was what gave the greatest alarm, on account of the late Conduct of the dissenters, which, publickly and declaredly, went to make a subservience to *their* Views and purposes the *sole* condition, by which (to their power) any Member could sit in Parliament.[5] This had great weight, with many; and amongst others with me; as I saw plainly, that between different ecclesiastical parties, not a shadow of Liberty would be left to the House; and that every claim in individuals to publick confidence from *General* Service, would be wholly swallowed up in this *particular* merit or demerit. In such a dilemma We might choose our *Church* Interest—but we must forget that we had a *Country*. I must add, that the eager manner in which several dissenting Teachers shewed themselves disposed to connect themselves in Sentiment and by imitation, (and perhaps by something more) with what was done and is doing in France, did very much indispose me to any concurrence with them. That peoples (The French peoples) great Object seemd to me to be, to *destroy their Church*— that is, to plunder it but to effect *this*, they did not scruple to destroy all the other *powers*, and all the other *Interests*, in their Country. I

---

[3] For these associations, organized on a national scale in the autumn of 1789, see Henriques, *Religious Toleration in England*, pp. 63–4. The Revolution Society, organized in 1788, also had repeal as one of its principal aims (Eugene C. Black, *The Association*, Cambridge, Mass., 1963, pp. 214–15).

[4] i.e. in the debate of 2 March.

[5] The 'Committee to conduct the Application to Parliament for Repeal of the Corporation and Test Acts', set up by the Presbyterians, Baptists and Congregationalists in 1786, had in December 1788 decided to urge the dissenting interest to support candidates who approved of these aims in the next General Election. Pitt in particular had complained of their activities in this regard in the debate (*Parliamentary History*, XXVIII, 408–9), but it seems clear there had also been pressure on the other side, since several members reported that they were compelled to vote *against* repeal because of instructions from their constituents.

should be sorry to find, in such a scuffle, the City of Bristol, in one year, fourteen hundred and fifteen Ships short of her usual Entries, as the City of Bordeaux declares herself to have been.[6] People begin these things without seeing, or therefore providing against, their consequences; and those who countenance great commotions in their beginnings, are those, who in the End, smart most for them in their fortunes. It has happend so in France and elsewhere. I will not trouble you further. I opend myself to Harford[7] very much at large when he was in Town; and he is thoroughly master of all my thoughts on this Subject. Shew these few and short hints to whomsoever of my freinds you think proper.

I do not know whether the dissenters will hereafter think me their wellwisher: But whether they think it or not, I am so. I am naturally inclined to those who do not command. My opinion is, that they will always be found very *weak* when they put their Cause upon a *Trial of Strength;* and that, to carry their point, they must change their whole plan. That they must cease to *alarm* the Church establishment; which many people believe (and I among the rest) to be connected, in its safety or danger, with many *other* establishments which form parts of our constitution. They will consider the Church, as a *jealous friend* to be *reconciled*, and not as an *adversary* that must be *vanquished*. With this principle, for some years pursued, and with some correspondent moderation on the part of the Church; (which is much their Interest also) I should hope, that this last Battle (the Victory and the defeat) may be forgotten; and means of settlement, better than a sacramental Test,[8] may be found for the security of the civil establishment of the Church, and for a share in publick emolluments and

---

[6] The Chamber of Commerce of Bordeaux wrote to Necker, on 30 September 1789, complaining of 'les sacrifices énormes sur le prix des marchandises; les ventes forcées et ruineuses; la cessation des spéculations ordinaires; l'avilissement du papier sur la capitale; l'impossibilité de ne placer qu'à grandes pertes; et l'interruption totale du mouvement qui seul donne la vie' (M. Lhéritier, *Liberté (1789–1790): Les Girondins: Bordeaux et la Révolution française*, Paris, 1947, p. 115). At that date, and perhaps even in the spring of 1790, these conditions are rather to be attributed to the economic crisis than to the Revolution.

[7] Joseph Harford (1741–1802), one of the two proposers of Burke's candidacy at Bristol in 1774 and subsequently one of his closest Bristol friends; the connexion, like that with Noble, had been maintained after Burke ceased to sit for Bristol. Harford had been a Dissenter but was now an Anglican.

[8] Burke himself in the debate on 2 March suggested replacing the sacramental test with an elaborate oath not to attack the Church of England (*Parliamentary History*, XXVIII, 441–2). This solution was adopted, in a much modified form, at the repeal in 1828.

Trusts to be given to the Dissenters to the full extent of their rational desires. Adieu, my dear Sir; all here salute you and Mrs Noble, and beleive me ever most faithfully and affectionately yours

EDM BURKE

CHAPTER FOUR

PARTY

THE POLITICS OF FRIENDSHIP AND PRINCIPLE

W HEN BURKE became a Member of Parliament in January 1766, he had already been the Marquis of Rockingham's man of business since June of the preceding year. After Rockingham's brief ministry had fallen in July 1766, Burke continued to serve and support him until Rockingham died in 1782, even though Rockingham was able to form only one other brief ministry just before his death. This long tour of opposition and subordination were justified by Burke in the notion of party explained in the following letters as well as in his *Thoughts on the Cause of the Present Discontents* (1770).

"Formed opposition" was considered disreputable, even unconstitutional, in Burke's day because it seemed to imply disloyalty to the King or, more likely, a wicked, ambitious attempt to dictate his choice of ministers. It was acceptable, if not agreeable, for a politician to oppose the government on his own or with a few supporters temporarily, because this did not subtract from the King's freedom of maneuver. Such freedom, however, was understood by Burke to support a system of favoritism, and he undertook to change the prevailing view of party and opposition. With Rockingham's leadership and Burke's arguments, their party set out to distinguish itself from other aristocratic factions in Parliament by standing together for principle and refusing to succumb to blandishments and temptations that would give office to some but divide the party. Precisely because their party was "formed," because they acted on a "plan of connection," Burke argued, they could not justly be accused of ambition. Those like Lord

Chatham who always acted an independent role, while claiming to put "measures over men," were themselves ambitious and were encouraging ambition in others, because their independence, in practice, made a virtue of inconsistency.

Parties would not serve mere ambition if they were led by men whose wealth and standing placed them above the goals of ordinary ambition, men such as the Whig grandees whom Burke served. Such men did not need office and did not crave it. As Charles James Fox told Burke, they were "as unfit to storm a citadel as they would be proper for the defence of it." Burke was faced, then, with the continuing need to goad his chosen superiors to action; he had, he said, for many years as his chief employment, "that woful one, of a *flapper*." A truer independence than Lord Chatham's could only be found in duller talents than his. The mutual friendship of these men, aided by their willing "flappers," however more brilliant than they, would keep ambition in thrall to principle as much as it can be in politics.

Burke's several references to the "Bute faction" or "Bute party" need to be explained. The Earl of Bute, First Lord of the Treasury in 1762–63, was known to be the King's favorite and assumed, by the Rockingham party and others in opposition, to be at the head of a "scheme of private influence" by which every succeeding ministry in the 1760s was governed. This assumption has been shown to be wrong, but for Burke it was the scheme or the system of influence that mattered, not Bute. He was more opposed to those who claimed independence, like Chatham and the Grenvilles, than to those who labored in subservience. He himself chose subordination rather than subservience, and he chose carefully. His long letter to the Duke of Portland from his constituency at Bristol in 1780 seems at first to tell how he would lose at Bristol, but then proceeds to show why Bristol would lose him.

To CHARLES O'HARA—*23 December* [1766]

Corr. (1958), 1, 284–85

A letter to Burke's Irish friend on the current political situation. The Rockingham party had been in opposition since July 1766, and return to power now seemed more and more remote. Burke offers a brief appreciation of opposition.

My dear Sir,   We receivd last Night your Letters of the 6th and 12th. We are not surprised to find you take an interest in our affairs. I know not how, but our own little concerns grow important in our Eyes, when we find others anxious about them and our conduct grows more firm and assured, when judicious friends go along with us in our Notions. I think we are very, very far from port; but we keep the open Sea; far likewise from rocks and sands and shelves, and all the mischiefs of an unfaithful Coast. I see, that an union of the Corps in opposition (I mean the Grenvilles, the Bedfords, and ourselves) is an affair of infinite difficulty; and without such an union, our opposition may be respectable, but never can be effective. In the mean time, I should conceive, that Lord Chatham gathers strength; not only from our total disunion, but from the immense services he has done the Bute party. Lord Bute, to be sure, is uncertain and unquiet in his Nature; but who *will* do more, who *can* do more to satisfie him, than the present Minister? I therefore take it for granted, that he will continue his year at least. But if he should fall then, or even before that time, I cannot conceive that *we* shall rise by his fall. The Bedfords and Grenvilles, as a set of people at once more bold and more tractable than our party will be preferred to us, and will run their Course as others have done theirs. It may possibly, in the revolution of this Political Platonick year, come again to our turn. But I see this Event, (if I see it at all) at the End of a very long Visto. The View is dim and remote; and we do nothing in the world to bring it nearer, or to make it more certain. This disposition, which is become the principle of our party, I confess, from constitution and opinion, I like:[1] Not that I am enamourd of adversity, or that I love opposition. On the contrary it would be convenient enough to get into office; and opposition never was to me a desirable thing; because I like to see some effect of what I am doing, and this method however pleasant is barren and unproductive, and at best, but preventive of mischief; but then the walk is certain; there are no contradictions to reconcile; no cross points of honour or interest to adjust; all is clear and open; and the wear and tear of mind, which is saved by keeping aloof from crooked politicks, is a consideration absolutely inestimable. Believe me, I who lived with *your friend*[2] so many years feel it so; and bless Providence

---

[1] Burke told his friends at the Literary Club in 1778: 'I believe in any body of men in England I should have been in the Minority; I have always been in the Minority' (*Life of Johnson*, III, 235).

[2] William Gerard Hamilton.

every day and every hour to find myself deliverd from thoughts and from Characters of that kind. Will feels so exactly as I do, that if———³ does not go out in a very short time indeed, he will get away from a situation of Nicety, and fix himself upon more decided Ground. He has staid so long in Babylon, merely in compliance with the desires of his friends.⁴ . . .

To CHARLES O'HARA—11 *December* [1767]

Corr. (1958), I, 339–40

More on acting in opposition.

My dear Sir,

. . . I forgot to mention to you, that the Bedfords and Grenvilles are on this occasion all to pieces. Ld Temple is gone to the Country despairing of the Commonwealth. Grenville has not been in the house for some days; but I hear his *ton* is to take the matter quietly, and to wait Events; and in this, I apprehend, he is right. As to our Corps, which are the *Enfans perdus* of Politicks; we stay just where we were; keeping a distance from all others, shunning, and shunned by them. If we must be dupes, thank God, it is to our rectitude, and not to our politicks, or if you like it better, to our roguery; and I assure you both Will and I feel inexpressible comfort in finding ourselves among a set of men willing to go on all together on a plan of clear consistent conduct. For myself I really have no hopes. Every body congratulated me on coming into the House of Commons, as being in the certain Road of a great and speedy fortune; and when I began to be heard with some little attention, every one of my friends was sanguine. But in truth I never was so myself. I came into Parliament not at all as a place of preferment, but of refuge; I was pushed into it; and I must have been a Member, and that too with some Eclat, or be a little worse than nothing; Such were the attempts, made to ruin me when I first began to meddle in Business. But I considerd my situation on the side of fortune as very precarious. I lookd on myself, with this New Duty on me, as on a man devoted; and Thinking in this manner, nothing has happend that I did not expect, and was not well prepared for.

³ General Henry Seymour Conway (1719–95).
⁴ Will Burke had been feeling the discomfort of his situation ever since the Rockingham group had lost power in July. Conway, his superior, remained in office; Edmund, a much closer friend, was deeply committed to Rockingham and opposition.

Therefore my dear Sir, cheer up; nothing very much amiss can happen us, whilst it pleases God that we keep our health, our good humour, and our inward peace; None of which is, as yet gone from us. I write, and blot in some sort of confusion—being just risen from an heavy dinner—and in some hurry—Adieu and believe me most sincerely and affectionately yours.

E BURKE

Charles Street S. J. Square
11. Decr

To RICHARD SHACKLETON—1 *May* 1768

Corr. (1958), I, 350–51

My dear Shackleton,

. . . I know your kindness makes you wish now and then to hear of my Situation. It is, politically, just what is was; There is nothing to alter the position of our party; which is, (or rather keeps itself,) at some distance from the Court. I think we act on a right principle; as far as any thing can approach to what is exactly right, in so strange a time as this; It is a pleasure to act with men who mean fairly, and who carry on publick business with, at least, a considerable mixture of publick principle, and with attention to honest fame. I shewed to some of them and among others to Ld Rockingham part of a Letter which you wrote to me some time ago;[1] and they were much pleased, both with the manner and the Substance of it; Ld Rockm desired me to give him a Copy. We have attempted things last Session which have got us Credit with the weighty and sober part of the Nation; I imagine we shall pursue them further, and even against ministerial power, may possibly succeed, from the weight of the measures, and the diligence of the pursuit. You have not enough of the detail to render this perfectly intelligible; I only mention it to you just to point out, that our political Body is not unprofitably or unreputably employd. As to myself, I am by the Kindness of some very singular friends in a way very agreeable

[1] Burke is probably referring to a letter Shackleton wrote to Richard Burke 22 November 1767, containing a passage very complimentary to both Burke and his party: 'Ned is tied (I trust) by the noblest bonds to the Good of his Country and the Cause of Religion and Virtue. . . . From my heart I believe that great are the purposes for which he was sent into life, and endowed with such talents as he is possessed of. . . .' After describing the truly Moral Man, conducted by a higher power 'thro' the intricate, treacherous Road of life', Shackleton concluded: 'Happy is he. May this be the happiness of my Friend and all of his Friends'.

to me. I am again elected on the same interest. I have made a push with all I could collect of my own, and the aid of my friends to cast a little root in the Country. I have purchased an house, with an Estate of about 600 acres of Land in Buckinghamshire 24 Miles from London; where I now am;[2] It is a place exceedingly pleasant; and I propose, God willing, to become a farmer in good earnest. You who are classical will not be displeased to hear, that it was formerly the Seat of Waller the Poet, whose house, or part of it, makes at present the Farmhouse within an hundred yards of me. When you take a Journey to England you are obliged by Tenure, to come and pay due homage to the Capital Seat of your once favourite Poet.

To the MARQUESS OF ROCKINGHAM—9 July 1769

Corr. (1958), II, 43–6

William Burke had written to Rockingham on July 7 to tell him of Lord Chatham's reappearance after his illness and his audience with the King on July 6. Lord Chatham (William Pitt, 1708–78) was no longer in the ministry at this time, and although known to be disagreeable to the King, he was assumed by Burke to be cooperating in the 'Scheme of private influence' conducted on behalf of the King. Burke also refers to a movement in Buckinghamshire to petition the Crown against the action of the House of Commons on the Middlesex election, in declaring John Wilkes disqualified.

My dear Lord,

I was on the point of sitting down to trouble your Lordship with a word or two more on the subject of your last Letter; when I heard from Will Burke, that he had seen Lord Chatham pass by on his return from St James's, and that he had certainly been in the closet. He did not continue there above twenty minutes. It is not yet known whether he was sent for, or went of his own meer motion. If he was sent for, the shortness of the conference seems to indicate that nothing at all has been settled. If he was not sent for, it was only, humbly to

---

[2] The financing of this purchase has been much discussed. Dixon Wecter (*Edmund Burke and His Kinsmen*, Boulder, Colorado, 1939, pp. 27–8) summarizes such evidence as he can find bearing on the problem, and speaks of this account Burke gives to Shackleton as 'a little disingenuous'. One of the friends who assisted Burke was certainly Will Burke, who must have put at least as much money into the estate as Edmund did. He had inherited something at his father's death in 1764, and was speculating, still successfully, in East India stock, with Lord Verney's backing. The assertion has been made that Lord Rockingham assisted the purchase. There is no authority for supposing it, and Burke told Shackleton (letter of 19 April 1770) that he had had no advantage 'except my Seat in Parliament from the Patronage of any man; Whatever advantges I have had, have been from friends on my own Level'.

Lay a reprimand at the feet of his most gracious Master, and to talk
some significant, pompous, creeping, explanatory, ambiguous matter,
in the true Chathamic Style; and thats all. If indeed a change is thought
on, I make no Doubt but they will aim at the Choice of him as the
puller down of the old, and the Architect of the New Fabrick. If so,
the Building will not, I suspect, be executed in a very workmanlike
manner; and can hardly be such as your Lordship will choose to be
lodged in, though you should be invited to the State Apartment in it;
which however will not be the Event, whether the arrangement is
made agreeably to the inclinations of Lord Chatham or those who
employ him. The plan of the Court (coinciding sufficiently with his
Dispositions, but totally adverse to your principles and wishes) would
be to keep the gross of the present ministry as the Body of the place;
and to Buttress it up with the Grenvilles and the Shelburne people.
This arrangement would, partly resist, and partly dissipate the present
storm. It would give them a degree of present strength, much wanting
in this ugly Crisis of their affairs, and which, it must be admitted, is
considerable, without subjecting them to the Effects of that plan of
connection which is the greatest of all possible Terrours to the Bute
faction. Whatever they may do or threaten at Court, I should fancy
your Lordships Conduct will not be affected by it one way or the
other. If I have any guess from publick appearance or private information, It is steadily adverse (as far as there is steadiness in any of its
dispositions) to your Lordship, to your friends, and to your principles.
Your strength is of another kind; and I trust, a better. The sole method
of operating upon them, because they have no other standard of respect, is by fear. They will never give your Lordship Credit for your
moderation. Your doing but little will be attributed to your not being
in a Situation to do more; With regard to your own friends a certain
delicacy of management, (which is one of the things in which you
excell) is certainly very proper, and much in the Tenour of your whole
Conduct; but so far as the Court is concerned, the most Effectual
method seems to be far the best; and I could wish your Lordship to
choose such time, place, and manner, for carrying through the Business concerning the right of Election, as will have most of a sober and
well conducted Energy in it, without the smallest regard to their
opinions or their representations. Far from shunning the appearance
of a lead in this business, it would be every way better that they
thought the whole manœuvre, as much owing to your Lordships weight
in your County, and to your Activity in exerting it, as to the general
Sense and Inclination of the people, merely left to themselves. It is

the true Terrour of those who take the Lead in the Scheme of private Influence, to find that the people have their Leaders too, in whom they repose a perfect confidence.

I had lately a short Letter from the D. of Richmond. As the disposition to do something relative to the right of Election seems to spread and grow warmer every day, he desired to know from me what your inclinations were with regard to this point. I informed his Grace of the Substance of your Lordships Letter in the shortest manner I was able; That you were far from adverse to some proceeding; but that you wished it on a plan more limited than that of the Middlesex and London, and confined nearly, if not entirely to that single interesting point; that you seemd to prefer the method of instruction to that of Petition, (at least in your own County) but that you had said nothing of a definitive resolution upon that Subject in your Letter to me. As to the rest, I wrote pretty nearly in Substance the same to his Grace, that I had done to your Lordship: Might I presume to suggest that just at this time he may possibly expect to hear from your Lordship by the first safe conveyance. If the Letter be given to his Porter it will be sent by the Coach to Goodwood.

I saw a person who may be supposed to talk pretty much the Language of the Butes, when I was in Town last Wednesday. The Ministers are extremely alarmed at the late proceedings in London and Surry,[1] and not less so at the late advices from America.[2] In this staggering situation I imagine They would derive great comfort and some support, by finding a slurr cast upon the mode of Petitioning. They have great terrour from the Circumstance of bringing the discontents of the people directly home to the King; From instructions they have but little apprehension; they are a good deal worn out, and as such are hardly fit to be employd on a Business, new, unprecedented, and nationally alarming; and they know besides, I suppose from experience, that nothing much affects at   [3] but what is directly seen and heard; and in truth this is the Case of most weak and inexperienced people. It is from the fears of the adversary that sometimes one must take a direction for the operations against him. I beg pardon for opening this affair again to your Lordship, especially as you have friends near you among Whom it will be discussed to your Satisfaction

---

[1] The meetings called to agree to petitions to the Crown.

[2] Though the Ministry had decided to repeal the Townshend duties (apart from that on tea) when Parliament reassembled, and a circular letter to this effect had been sent to the Governors of the American Colonies dated 13 May, the dissatisfaction of the Colonies showed no sign of abating and disturbing evidence of their ill-will continued to come in during July and August.

[3] At Court.

in every particular. Your Lordship has seen the Buckinghamshire advertisement.[4] Lord Verney opened the Matter to the grand Jury[5] by telling them that several respectable Gentlemen and freeholders had applied to him to propose a meeting on the Judgment in favour of Colonel Luttrel, That he had declined taking it upon him as Member for the County, but that in that Capacity he was very willing to *attend* the meeting, and to act in conformity to their determination. There was some, though but a feeble opposition to the meeting; when it came to the Question 11 were for it; only three against. One was neuter. The Sheriff refused to advertise on which they agreed to do it without him. The meeting is put off until, I think, the twelfth of September, or thereabouts. This measure of delay I attribute to the Politicks of Stow.[6] The reason assigned is, that the Freeholders may be able to get their harvest in, and come in greater Numbers and with less inconvenience to the meeting. But the former I imagine to be the true reason; unless perhaps they may be willing to see what Course is taken in Yorkshire before they begin to move.

I got a letter since I began this from Charles Townshend (Tommy's Brother)[7] he says, that Pitt seemed to be in remarkable good humour on coming out of the Closet. I hear too[8] that Lord Hertford,[9] whose eldest hope[10] has been for a long time talking opposition Language in all companies, has been at Stow. If this be true, it is probably settled for a Family System,[11] which in my opinion precludes all possibility of a good Event. Had the first Offer gone elsewhere, they might have fallen into a plan of yours with Credit to themselves, and possibly with advantage to the publick. This could not be the event either in point of reputation or safety, if under the direction of Lord Chatham, and the Lead of the Grenvilles your Lordship and your friends were to make a part of an arrangement. The Court alone can profit of any movements of Lord Chatham: and he is always their rescourse when

[4] It first appeared in the *Public Advertiser* on 10 July, but it was dated 4 July.

[5] As foreman.

[6] Stowe, the Buckinghamshire seat of Earl Temple (Richard Grenville Temple, 2nd Earl Temple, 1711–79), who, with the rest of the Grenville family, had a strong political influence in the county.

[7] Charles Townshend (1736–99), 2nd son of the Hon. Thomas Townshend (1701–80).

[8] Also from Townshend's letter.

[9] Francis Seymour Conway (1718–94), 1st Earl and later (1793) 1st Marquess of Hertford; at this time Lord Chamberlain of the Household.

[10] Francis Seymour Conway, Lord Beauchamp (1743–1822), later (1794) 2nd Marquess of Hertford; M.P. for Orford.

[11] i.e. a Ministry based on the alliance of George Grenville, his brother Lord Temple and their brother-in-law Lord Chatham. In fact these three were temporarily drawing together in opposition.

they are run hard. I never attempt to write any thing like News to your Lordship, that when it is done, I do not begin to think myself very foolish, considering my own distant Situation, and the limping method of conveyance. You have all this undoubtedly more fully and authentically from others, as well as much earlier. However I take my Chance and am with the greatest Respect and affection

My dear Lord
your ever obedient
and obligd humble Servant

Gregories July 9. 1769   EDM BURKE
Sunday.

To CHARLES O'HARA—28 *August* 1769

Corr. (1958), II, 57–8

In reply to a letter from O'Hara written from Manchester on 20 August, on his way back to Ireland after a visit to the Burkes. O'Hara had obviously been uneasy about Burke's efforts to persuade Rockingham to change his mind on the question of a petition from Yorkshire, for he wrote, in a manner Burke calls 'reserved'.

My dear Charles, We have had stormy weather; and it has been so very violent, that we were not without some uneasy sensations concerning your safety; concluding that about the time of these Tempests you must have been at sea. We shall not be altogether free from apprehensions until we hear from you. Most heartily we thank you for your Letter from Manchester. There is a great Spirit all over the Northern part of the Kingdom, which if improved, supported, and rightly directed, could not fail of being infinitely useful. But God has given different Spirits to different men. The profligate and inconsiderate are bold, adventurous, and pushing. Honest men slow, backward and irresolute. In order to do Evil in the End, the dashers take noble steps; pretend good; and sometimes do it. The others are so fearful of doing ill, that they very frequently fall short of doing the good that is in their power. The world is thus constituted; and it is jest to murmur at the Course of human Nature and affairs. Considerations of this kind, you may be assured, will hinder me from pushing the Business you hint at with any improper importunity; indeed with any importunity at all. This resolution has been in a great measure formed upon your former opinion. In what you wrote last you were reserved; But the matter is of so interesting a Nature that when you are at leisure, and can do it safely, I shall be obliged to you for being more explicit. I wish to know it indeed from curiosity principaly, not much for the direction of my Conduct; for the Line I have chalked out for myself is so very simple, that a Child cannot go astray in it. . . .

To CHARLES O'HARA—27 September 1769

Corr. (1958), II, 85–6

Burke contrasts the Rockingham party to the Grenvilles.

My dear Sir,

. . . I am now at Lord Rockinghams. I left Buckinghamshire about a week ago; after having done my part in the Petition which was going forward there. Our meeting was not a bad one; though there is no inconsiderable Court and a very considerable Tory interest in that County. Lord Temple was very active amongst us. He brought G. G's eldest son[1] with him, and answerd for his Brothers approbation of our proceedings. This was indeed in the Inn after dinner; not in the Town Hall, to which, I suppose upon some point of delicacy about Peerage, he did not come. This Delicacy, if there had been any Ground for it, ought to have ran through the whole proceeding; and it would have had more decorum, and more weight too, for G.G. to have answerd for the Earls his Brothers, than one of them for him. However, though I saw well enough the politick motives which influenced this Style of proceeding, I took no Notice of it. It was our Business to shew no distrust or uneasiness, whilst we were carrying on a measure so necessary to the publick, with our Joint forces. But I could not help being inwardly affected with the extreme difference between the Spirit of that political School, and the party with which we act. We are diffident, scrupulous, timid, and slow in coming to a resolution; But when once we have engaged, we are not only much in earnest and very direct in our proceeding, but sufficiently bold and active in our Conduct. As for our Allies their manner is quite different; they resolve early and with boldness; but in the prosecution of business, they are never fair and direct; they have a thousand underplots and oblique views; one of them always reserves himself while another acts; and they frequently dissipate and lose their publick object; tho' they have the art sooner or later of securing their private and real Ends. I have lately seen

[1] George Grenville's eldest son, George Grenville (1753–1813).

enough both of the one and the other. You know how much I felt
from the slowness and irresolution of some of our best friends. Even
to this moment, there are some of them who cannot be prevailed upon
to take that lead, which is natural to their situation, and necessary to
their Consequence. But in the main, things are flowing into the right
channel; and will go, I hope, down an Easy declivity for the future.
On my coming here I found the Petition determined on and prepared;
a Very manly and proper piece;[2] and I think much the best of any
which has yet appeard; and there is a Spirit in the County fully adequate to the support of it. The meeting, which is held this day, must
be very great in point of Number, and still more considerable from
the opulence both landed and commercial of those who compose it.
Lord Rockingham does not think it right to be at the meeting; and
on the whole I am satisfied he has reason. The day before I departed
from the South, I saw my old friend William O'Hara.[3] He is come
over for his health. He is as thin as a whipping post; but otherwise
seemd tolerably well and in Spirits. I do not know whether he has
been yet at Gregories. Adieu my very dear friend—and believe me
ever yours.

Wentworth Septr 27. 1769.

To the MARQUESS OF ROCKINGHAM—29 October 1769

Corr. (1958), II, 100–101

Burke again describes the character of the party led by Rockingham.

My dear Lord,
   I am infinitely obliged to your Lordship for your long and satisfactory Letter; which I concealed or communicated in the manner I
thought most agreeable to your wishes. I found Lord Albemarle had
not received the Copy your Lordship intended for him; I therefore
shewed him mine, and let Mason make a copy of it, for Keppel and
Saunders, when they should come to Town. I shewed it besides to
Lord J. Cav. and Lord Frederick.[1] They all concurred very nearly in
Sentiment with your Lordship upon every particular; There was some

---

[2] The Yorkshire petition concentrated on one point, that of the Middlesex Election, but was
strong in expression and, like that of Westminster, demanded the dissolution of Parliament
(*Annual Register*, 1769, pp. 205–6).

[3] William Henry King O'Hara (1750–80), O'Hara's younger son.

[1] Lord Frederick Cavendish (1729–1803), M.P. for Derby, third son of the 3rd Duke of
Devonshire.

doubt whether our two friends ought not to pay the Visit which it seems is desired,[2] in order to hear at least what Style he uses, and what sentiments he would be believed to entertain; but they will do nothing without your desire. For my own part, the more I think of it, the more perfectly I am convinced, that we ought to take no sort of Notice of him, but to proceed exactly as if no such man existed in the world. For though, according to Lord Cambdens Phrase, Lord Chatham has had a wonderful resurrection to health, his resurrection to Credit, and consequence, and to the power of doing mischief, (without which last his resurrection will be incomplete) must be owing to your Lordship and your friends. It ought never to be forgotten, how much the Late Duke of Newcastle hurt himself, in his Interest very often, in his reputation almost always, by his Itch of Negotiation. If Lord C. has any thing to communicate to these Gentlemen he may send for them. This union of the three Brothers[3] will distract the Country as much in future, as there dissentions did formerly. I quite agree with your Lordship that Grenville is the most temperate and manageable of the Three; but he is no longer George Grenville, a disengaged individual; but one of the Triumvirate; to whom, by the way, he brings all the following that they possess. Nothing can be said of him, but what may be said with equal Truth of the other two; from whom I really believe he will never disconnect himself. All these considerations make me wish, as ardently as your Lordships partiality can do, that my little Scheme was in a way of being speedily completed,[4] I see, I feel, the necessity of justifying to our friends and to the world, the refusal, which is inevitable, of what will be thought very advantageous Offers. This can only be done by shewing the ground upon which the Party stands; and how different its constitution, as well as the persons who compose it are from the Bedfords, and Grenvilles, and other knots, who are combined for no publick purpose; but only as a means of furthering with joint strength, their private and individual advantage. I am afraid I shall never compass this design to my Mind. Hitherto I have been so variously distracted that I have made but little progress, indeed none. But to day I began to set to work a little seriously. But in order to produce something, which, by being timely, may be useful I must beg to be excused from going to Yorkshire in the next month. This would break me to pieces;

---

[2] Whether Admiral Keppel and Sir Charles Saunders should call upon Chatham.
[3] Lord Chatham, Lord Temple, and George Grenville, the latter two brothers and Chatham their brother-in-law.
[4] His pamphlet, *Thoughts on the Cause of the Present Discontents*.

and I think I may do more service here. Perhaps I may be able to send something for your consideration at that meeting. . . .

To the MARQUESS OF ROCKINGHAM— [post 6 *November* 1769]

Corr. (1958), II, 108–9

With this undated letter went "a good part" of Burke's pamphlet, *Thoughts on the Cause of the Present Discontents.*

My dear Lord

I send you a good part of what I had been meditating about the System of the Court, and which you were so earnest to see carried into Execution. I thought it better to let you see what was finished, rather than to postpone it until the Whole was completed. The design appears distinctly enough from what has been done. If you and your friends approve of it, you will be so good to send it back with your observations as soon as possible, that it may go to the press; when I have go thro' the concluding part, you shall have that also; and on its return, it shall follow the rest.

It will be a matter very proper for the consideration of your Lordship and your friends, whether a thing of this Nature should appear at all. It is in the first place a formal attack upon that Object which has been nearest and dearest to the Court since the beginning of the reign— and of Course, if this thing should be supposed to express your Sentiments, must put you on Terms irreconcileably bad, with the Court and every one of its adherents. I foresee at the same time, that the other—bodies who compose the opposition will desire "not to be comprehended in those declarations" as G.G. said upon such an occasion two years ago.[1] So that you irritate past forgiveness the Court party, and you do not conciliate all the opposition. Besides I am very far from confident, that the doctrines avowed in this piece (though as clear to me as first principles) will be considerd as well founded; or that they will be at all popular. If so, we lose upon every Side.

As to myself, I am indifferent about the Event. Only for my Credit, (as I fear, from some particular opinions, and from this extensive previous Communication, I shall be considerd as the authour) I wish that if our friends approve the design, I may have some tolerable

---

[1] Probably in George Grenville's speech of 24 November 1767, when he attacked Dowdeswell's views on American policy, though the exact phrase does not occur in any of the reports.

support in Parliament, from the innumerable attacks it will bring upon me. If this be successful with the publick, I shall have enough of Odium; I could wish it a little divided, if the Sentiments should belong to others as well as to myself. For it is upon this presumption and with this View only that I mean to publish. In order that it should be truly the Common Cause—make it at your meeting what you please— let me know what ought to be left out, what softend, and what strengthend. On reading it to Will and Dick they thought some things a little too Ludicrous; I thought it much otherwise: for I could rather wish that more had occurred to me (as more would had my Spirits been high) for I know how ill a long detail of Politicks not animated by a direct controversy, wants every kind of help, to make it tolerable.

The whole is in a manner new Cast, something to the prejudice of the order which if I can, I will rectifye; though I fear this will be difficult. The former Scheme would no ways answer, and I wish I had entirely thrown it aside, as it has embarrassed me a good deal. The whole attack on Pitts Conduct must be omitted, or we shall draw the Cry of the world upon us—as if we meant directly to quarrel with all mankind . . .

To the MARQUESS OF ROCKINGHAM—29 December 1770

Corr. (1958), II, 174–76

Beconsfield Decr 29. 1770.

My dear Lord

I thought it unnecessary to trouble your Lordship with a Letter by Montagu.[1] He was quite fresh from the Scene of action, and quite as competent a Judge of the interesting Events which had just passed upon it, as I could possibly be. I had written too, and pretty fully, the night before he left us.[2] Sunday morning I left Town myself; and have since heard nothing except by the Newspaper. My chief anxiety at present is on account of Lady Rockinghams health, and your ease of mind; and if I can be well satisfied on these points, I shall be much less sollicitous about the rest.

[1] Frederick Montagu (1733–1800), M.P. for Higham Ferrers, a supporter of the Rockingham party.

[2] The 'interesting events' which Montagu could report were presumably the recent changes in the Administration.

The day before I came out of Town I walked with Mr Dowdeswell[3] to Dunnings[4] Chambers. He admitted, that the Bill,[5] a Draft of which we left with him, was very unexceptionable in point of Form; if the bringing in such a Bill at all were an advisable measure. He seemed to think, that the juridical Duel between Lord Mansfield and Lord Cambden which is to be waged at the meeting after Christmas, might supply the place of such a Bill. At least he wished to have it postponed, until the Event of that Combat should be known. Mr Dowdeswel observd that this legal contest, let the event be what it may, could have no other influence on the Bill, than, from the extreme contrariety in opinion, so strenuously maintaind upon both sides by two great men, and so powerfully supported by authorities living and dead, at least on one side, to evince the absolute necessity of bringing the Law to something fixed and certain. He seemd on the whole rather to assent to this; and the Style of his conversation was moderate and fair. Dowdeswell agreed with him so far as to think it right to let this grand exhibition of the Law Masters have the *pas;* provided they did not keep the Spectators too long in Expectation. He was certainly right; it might look as if we were running races; and making the discussion, rather a contention for popular applause, than a ground of serious relief to the Subject. But this can postpone the Business for a very little time only; both of us most heartily agree with your Lordship, that we ought by no means to suffer ourselves to be bullied or chicaned out of our Bill. I remember when it was thought to be a sort of Trespass and usurpation on the right of another, if your Lordship or your friends, attempted to do anything which might be beneficial or pleasing to the publick. Some are still of the same disposition.

Things are just now, I think, at a critical a point as they have been for a long time; especially with regard to your Lordship. The manner in which the body of the Grenvilles are at present disposed, one may say upon the Wing, if not actually flown;[6] The Corporation of London (whatever it may be) possessd much more entirely than ever by the Shelburne faction;[7] Lord Chatham endeavouring to discredit you with

---

[3] William Dowdeswell (1721–75), Burke's friend and a Rockingham supporter.

[4] John Dunning (1731–83), later (1782) 1st Baron Ashburton, M.P. for Calne, had been Solicitor General 1768–70. He was a close personal friend of Shelburne and one of the chief legal advisers of the popular party at this time.

[5] The Jury Bill to determine the rights of juries in trials for libel.

[6] Lord North had written to the King on 16 November after the death of George Grenville: 'Lord North thinks there is an opening to acquire not only Mr Wedderburn, but all Mr Grenville's friends'. Wedderburn accepted the position of Solicitor General in January 1771.

[7] Alderman James Townsend and his friends in the City, who were closely linked with Shelburne, were in process of breaking with Wilkes and his personal supporters.

the people, and what is worse, to weaken you within yourselves; The Court irreconcileable to you, and professing itself so; and the sober, large-acred part of the Nation, whom you have most studied to please, and whom it is the most reputable to please, either entirely indifferent about us, or of no considerable weight in the publick Scale; In such a situation it will require not only great address but great activity to bring about any thing considerable either for the party or the publick. To lye by occasionally may be prudent for an individual; it never can do for a party; which will immediately putrifye and dissipate, if not kept healthy and compact by continual agitation and enterprise. I do not exclude a total Secession on proper Ground from my Idea of activity. Something of constant and systematical writing seems to me of absolute necessity. We lost much of the advantage of the Last pamphlet,[8] because the Idea was not kept up by a continued succession of papers, seconding and enforcing the same principle. For want of something of this Kind, every thing you have done or sufferd in the common Cause, had perishd as Soon as it is known; and however it may have served the Nation, certainly operates nothing at all in favour of the party. The more you are confined in your operations, by the delicate principles you profess, the more necessary it becomes to push with the utmost Vigour the few means that you have permitted to yourselves. I do not say this from the least glimmering of hope, that any thing which may be done by the best judged and most active endeavours, can be attended with Success; but solely, that in the Triumph of this mischievous System which you oppose, nobody may be able justly to reproach your Lordship or your friends with having omitted any one justifiable or rational attempt to destroy it. In all sorts of Circumstances reputation is a great deal; in bad circumstances it is every thing.

I saw an account of a new law-arrangement in the papers of this day. Though there are some things in it which must be mistaken, on the whole it seems to be likely enough. If this should be the fact, it is plaine that they intend to fight the weapons through with Lord Chatham and his people as well as with your Lordship. From the whole aspect of their conduct compared with what it was sometime ago, it is clear to me, that Lord Bute is no longer the adviser, but that his System is got into firmer and abler hands. While I write this, I learn, that there is no truth in the Law arrangement which has appeard

[8] *Thoughts on the Cause of the Present Discontents.*

in the late papers.[9] If so, I should hope, that our friends in that profession, when they have sufficiently reconnoitred the Ground, and pleased themselves with the free and fashionable air of disconnection, while it serves them for variety and pleasure, will at length come into proper winter quarters; such I mean as are good for the Society; though not for the *provisiade*. I was mentioning to Dowdeswell my astonishment at that sort of part, which by leaving a mans inclinations doubtful, after a Choice once made, takes off the grace of conduct, both before and after the hesitation, even though a man should return to the right way. I have always thought a Lady of a determined Character of Freedom; more excusable than, a perpetual Coquette, who can never come to a final determination what she shall be. I do not well know to what End I am running on upon the Conduct of these people, which after all one must bear, or direct if they can. To providence, and your Lordships temper and management I commit them. May I flatter myself with the hope of hearing from your Lordship and that you will have occasion to possess yourself in good humour enough to attend to all these serious Levities? I am My dear Lord

> your ever attachd
> and obedient humble Servant
> EDM BURKE

To WILLIAM BAKER—1 *October* 1771

Corr. (1958), II, 242–43

William Baker (1743–1824) and Joseph Martin (1726–76), Members of Parliament and supporters of the Rockingham party, had been persuaded by Rockingham to stand for the office of Sheriff in the City of London. After being elected, they had met with considerable hostility from the popular party supporting John Wilkes.

My dear Sir,

Excuse, I pray you my seeming, indeed only seeming inattention, for a day or two, to your Letter and your Business. It was not in my power to disengage myself until now; and now that I am disengaged, and have fully considerd the matter, I do entirely agree with you and our worthy friend Martin, that no Notice can be specifically taken of

[9] The Great Seal had been in Commission since the death of Charles Yorke on 20 January 1770. Lord Mansfield, who had been acting as Speaker of the House of Lords, had for some time been restive, and rumours of the appointment of a Chancellor became frequent in the Press. No appointment was, however, made until 23 January 1771, when Henry Bathurst (1714–94), created the following day 1st Baron Apsley and later (1775) 2nd Earl Bathurst, was appointed.

Charges or insinuations of an anonymous writer in any answer published in your own Names. Indeed these charges or insinuations, or be they what they will, do not go to any one point in your publick conduct. They tend to let down and depreciate the merit of actions which they confess to be in themselves meritorious. They indeed attack your *Motives* for taking Office; and they abuse your connections. When you come to your return for the Civilities which you may receive from the Livery,[1] I think it will not be very difficult to vindicate *motives*, when neither particular actions, nor general Character can possibly be questiond. You may safely appeal to both of these for an explanation of your Motives. As for your connexions; I take it for granted, you are not ashamed, to have acted in the best of Causes with the best of men; Men of untainted honour both publick and private; men (as Sir G. Savile expressed it) of hereditary principles of Liberty; of disinterested, clear, steady, uniform conduct, known friends and protectors of the constitutional and commercial interests of this Kingdom and its colonies; and one may fairly add, that no man could think of depreciating that body, or could endeavour to alienate the minds of the Livery from them, who had any sincere intentions towards the publick good; as none can wish better to it than these Gentlemen; and none have half the power of doing real service to the Country. These are my sincere Sentiments; I am persuaded they are yours; and if such a declaration is consistent with Truth, it is not inconsistent with propriety and prudence. Let those who are ashamed of the persons or the designs of their party, shuffle away their connections with it, and while they cabal in private, disavow one another in publick. The connexion and friendship of good men is their glory. It is a thing which bad men cannot long mimick; No wonder they should look upon it with malignity and envy. I am heartily concerned, that you and Martin do not think of going further in that Corporation. If I lament, I do not blame it; you might do great service; but I do not know whether it would not be too dearly bought by the sacrifice of the health and satisfaction of two such men. However you will not suffer yourselves to be run down; you feel but too sensibly that you do not live in *republica Platonis;* and it is necessary, that you should not suffer yourself to be besmeared by the *Fæx Romuli.*[2] I am sure you are convinced of the propriety of standing steadily and firmly on your own ground, and keeping, as the military men call it, a good countenance to the Enemy, I need not suggest to either of you any thing relative to the

---

[1] On the termination of their year of office as Sheriffs.
[2] Dregs of the populace. See Cicero *Ad Atticum*, 2. i. 8.

timing or any other part of the management. You have yourselves the "Spirit of the occasion" as much as any men I ever knew. Remember me to Martin and believe me with great regard

Dear Baker
Your most obedient Servant
and sincere friend
EDM BURKE

Beconsfield Tuesday Evening
October 1. 1771.

To the DUKE OF RICHMOND—[post 15 November 1772]

Corr. (1958), II, 372–78

An undated draft for a letter in response to the Duke of Richmond, who in a discouraged tone had resisted Burke's urgings to return from the country and had lamented the party's refusal to follow his advice in 1767. Richmond said: 'You say the Party is an object of too much importance to be let go to pieces. Indeed Burke you have more merit than any man in keeping us together, but I believe our greatest Bond is the Pride of the individuals, which Unfortunately tho' it keeps us from breaking, hinders us from acting like men of Sense'.

My dear Lord,

I am much obliged to your Grace for your very kind Letter of the 15th which I received by the Machine. Whatever others might have imagined I never thought your Grace too tenacious of your opinion. If you had rather leand to that extreme I should not have esteemd you the less for it. I have seen so many woful examples of the Effect of Levity, both that which arises from Temper, and that which is owing to Interest, that a small degree of obstinacy is a Quality not very odious in my Eyes, whether it be complexional or from principle. When a man makes great sacrifices to his honest opinion, it is no wonder that he should grow fond of it. I am sure that nothing can hinder the possession of publick Spirit from being very suspicious except great consistency; Those who do not much admire the security itself nor perhaps the Virtue it secures will represent it as a mark, as an obstinate and intractable disposition. Those who think in that manner of your Grace form that opinion on your steady attachment to your principles. They know nothing of your compliance and practicability in carrying on Business among your friends. I can bear witness that it has always been full as much as was necessary towards keeping a great System well compacted together in all its parts. I have known some good Effects of that practicability, I agree too, that there has been instances where we may now have reason to wish you had less facility. After all, Every political question that I have ever known, has had so much of the pro and con in it, that nothing but the success could decide which proposition ought to have been adopted. People in a constant minority can have no success; and therefore have not even that uncertain way of solving any problem of political Conduct. I believe we have had more divisions among ourselves than we ought to have had; and have made many mistakes in our Conduct, both as a body and as individuals. Comparing our proceedings with any abstract standard, we have been very faulty and imperfect; but if you try yourselves by comparison with any other existing body of men; I believe you will find a more decent regular consistent, and prudent series of proceeding among yourselves than among any of them or all of those put together. Have you in any place where you have had an Interest undone yourselves so compleatly, as a certain party which was lately in possession of the Corporation of London?[1] a Set of Gentlemen who cannot plead innocence and simplicity as an excuse for their innumerable Blunders. In the house of Lords, have the chiefs of you ever passed such injudicious motions, paid so little attention to your mutual honour, or contrived to reconcile your proceedings at one time to your declarations at another with so little finesse and dexterity as some persons of very high Name in this Country?[2] You have not, like them, while they were miserably distracted among themselves, formed a thousand childish and mischievous plots to break to pieces the only people who could possibly serve them, and in whom if they had common sense they would for their own Sakes have placed great confidence as well as have endeavourd to acquire the like from them by every method of fair and conciliatory conduct. If you look turning from them to the factions that make what is called administration, surely you are guiltless of that Tissue of absurdities by which Government that by mear abuses can hardly be more than odious, has been renderd the most contemptible thing in the world. Look at home one has much to complain of. Look abroad one has ten times more. So that on the whole I am inclined to think that the faults in your body are no more than the ordinary frailties of human Nature, some of them too inseperably attached to the Cause of all your strength and reputation. You are in general somewhat Languid, scrupulous and

[1] The Chatham-Shelburne group and their supporters in the City.
[2] Again the Chatham-Shelburne group.

unsystematick. But men of high Birth and great property are rarely as enterprising as others and for reasons that are very natural; Men of integrity are curious, sometimes too curious, in the Choice of means; and great Bodies can seldom be brought to System and discipline, except by Instruments that while you are out of Government, you have not in your power. However with all these faults it is better you should be rich and honest and numerous than needy, and profligate and composed of a few desperate politicians though they have advantages in their own way which you must always want. It is with such reflexions I compose and comfort myself in the occasional dejections and vexations that I am subject to, like other men and which your Grace has seen but too much of and they will in my cool moments always put me at ease and reconcile me to everything you do, as long as I can act in publick whether I agree in opinion with the rest of you or not.

As to your Graces situation in the party and in the world, it would be the greatest injustice, for Lord Rm not to say that he Sees and feels his obligations to you in their full extent; and has spoke a thousand [times] as he ought of the unparralled part you have acted. His nearest and oldest friends are, much in the same degree, your own. There can be but one opinion on your Conduct and abilities. With regard to others Your Grace is very sensible that you have not made your Court to the world by forming yourself to a flattering exterior but you put me in mind of Mr Wilkes's observation when he makes love, that he will engage in such a pursuit against the handsomest fellow in England, and only desires a month start of his Rival on account of his face; your month is past; and if your Grace does not, every one else does remark, how much you grow on the publick by the exertion of real Talents and substantial Virtue. You know you have already some fruits of them, and you will gather in such fruits every day until your Barns are full as they can hold. One thing and but one I see against it which is, that your Grace dissipates your mind with too great a variety of minute pursuits, all of which from the natural Vehemence of your Temper you follow almost with equal passion. It is wise indeed considering the many many positive vexations, and the unnumerable bitter disappointments of pleasure in the world to have as many rescources of satisfaction as possible within ones power. When we concenter the mind on one sole object that object and Life itself must go together. But though it is right to have reserves of employment still some one object must be kept principal; greatly and eminently so; and the other masses and figures must preserve their due subordination to make out the grand composition of an important Life, upon those sound principles which your Grace would require in some of those arts that you protect. Your publick business with all its discouragements and mortifications ought to be so much principal figures with you that the rest in comparison of it should be next to nothing; and even in that principal figure of publick Life it will be necessary to avoid the exquisiteness of an over attention to smaller parts and to over precision and to a spirit of detail, which acute understandings and precise reasonings, which without great Care all are apt to get into, and which, gives in some degree a Sort of hardness and what you connoisseurs call the dry manner to all our Actions; Your Grace has abundant reason not to be ⟨discouraged⟩ from the great exhibition that I wish to see you chiefly intent. In the Course of publick business, by degrees your Grace developes your true Character. You would be in a bad condition, if with the doors shut after the manner of the French, but on the principles of the English constitution, you were to be tried only by your peers. But this is not so. Business, by degrees, brings various kinds and descriptions of men into contact with you; and they all go off with the best impressions and communicate them to the world. Why have I rambled thus far—why truly, because it became an amusement to my mind, and that I see your Grace wants some amusement too? but is the indulgence of a Loquacious vein any amusement? I will try by going on further. I agree with your Grace, that our Condition is very bad. It is certainly so. It can be conceald neither from friends nor Enemies. The time for Secession is past, and no other such opportunity is in prospect. It would have done I am persuaded, but none of our friends are to blame for the rejection of that Idea; on the first proposal Lord Temple, Lord Lyttelton, and Lord Camden shewed such invincible repugnance to it that in your then situation, it could not be thought of; and it was impossible at that time to take a seperate walk from them.[3] With regard to the Transaction of 1767.[4] I do recollect, that I as well as others did in some particulars differ from your Graces opinion. I think you will do me the justice to believe that it was not out of any particular regard to Bedford House. Indeed independently of my former observations

3 Richmond had argued that they should have 'seceded,' that is, refused to attend sessions of Parliament, immediately after the Middlesex Election.
[4] The abortive negotiations of July 1767 for bringing the Rockingham group and others into Administration, in which Richmond had been critical of the handling of the matter by Rockingham.

I saw clearly during the supper at Lord Rockinghams[5] not only the most unamiable dispositions, but a behaviour in some of them that was scarcely polite, and a reserve, which Wine circulated briskly until the sunbeams drove us from it, was not able to dispel though these people are, not indeed candid but naturally very loose and careless talkers. But I thought I saw too, that the whole Treaty on the part of the Duke of Grafton and Lord Camden and much more of another was merely an imposition both on you and on Conway, principally meant to bring the Latter to act the part he did afterwards; I can scarcely forbear being still of opinion they never meant to bring you in except on Terms that when they became explicit you could neither have accepted nor rejected without great detriment and disgrace to you. I conclude this not only from the Closet disavowal in the middle of your proceedings but from a conversation with General Conway a few days after all was broke off in which he very frankly told me, that the intention never was to bring in the whole even of your body, but about half a dozen (I think) of the principal people, and to let you make way for the rest as opportunities should offer. Constituted as the remaining part of the ministry was this was no real plan of power which would enable you to serve your ⟨Cause⟩. Your Grace I dare say recollects, that we did all in effect and substance, at last accede to your Grace's opinion, when after a long consultation protracted to near two o Clock in the morning,[6] and after frequent Messages backward and forward, your Grace at length carried the ultimatum to General Conway, and never received an answer from that day to this. On the whole I saw so little real intention towards you at that time either in the D. of G. or Lord Camden or General Conway or in the first movers that I cannot without great difficulty, attribute our present condition to our rejection of the proposals of the Court; for in Effect if they had been such as your Grace thought them the Treaty never could have broken off on account of Bedford house which had broken with you and that in a manner equally violent and scandalous before that Business concluded.

Your Grace remember well the Character of the D. of N. who always treated with his Enemies in beginning by putting himself into their

[5] This supper took place on 3 July 1767, when Rockingham informed the members of the Bedford Group that Grafton had invited him to join the Administration. Of the Bedfords, only Gower and Weymouth are known to have been present.

[6] On 20 July 1767.

power and offering more than they would think of asking; and whose
jealousy little short of Phrensy of Lord Rm about Objects which he
neither would nor could have held, drove him headlong into any snare
his adversaries laid for him. Lord Albemarle too had his attentions to
the D of Bedford; but I must say with as great as just suspicions of
him and his, as with attachment to you in the total. Yet it was very
necessary to look to both these persons; and they, at least one of them
and the most material, required nothing more than an empty compliment; and this the Court knew or might have known as well as we
did.

But whether I am mistaken or not the thing being past, it only gives
me pain [to] attribute our misfortunes to our faults, where circumstances will not suffer our repentance to amend them. Bad they are
indeed; But where things are desperate with regard to power, they are
not always in a Situation the most unfavourable to Character. Decorum, firmness, consistency, Courage, patient manly perseverance those
are the Virtues of despair; They are worth something surely; and none
has profited of that situation so much as your Grace nor could you
have shewn of what materials you are made in any other. Persons in
your Station of Life ought [to] have long Views. You people of great
families and hereditary Trusts and fortunes are not like such as I am,
who whatever we may be by the Rapidity of our growth and of the
fruit we bear, flatter ourselves that while we creep on the Ground we
belly into melons that are exquisite for size and flavour, yet still we
are but annual plants that perish with our Season and leave no sort
of Traces behind us. You if you are what you ought to be are the great
Oaks that shade a Country and perpetuate your benefits from Generation to Generation. In my Eye—The immediate power of a D. of
Richmond or a Marquis of Rm is not so much of moment but if their
conduct and example hands down their principles to their successors;
then their houses become the publick repositories and offices of Record
for the constitution, Not like the Tower or Rolls Chappel where it is
searched for and sometimes in Vain, in rotten parchments under drip-
ping and perishing Walls; but in full vigour and acting with vital
Energy and power in the Characters of the leading men and natural
interests of the Country. It has been remarked that there were two
eminent families at Rome that for several Ages were distinguished
uniformly, by opposite Characters and principles. The Claudian and
Valerian. The former were high and haughty but publick spirited,

firm, and active and attached to the aristocracy. The latter were popular in their Tempers manners and principles. So far this remark; but I add that any one who looks attentively to their History will see that the ballance of that famous constitution was kept up for some ages by the personal Characters, dispositions, and traditionary politicks of certain families as by any thing in the Laws and order of the State. So that I do not look upon your time or lives lost, if in this sliding away from the genuine Spirit of the Country, certain parties if possible, if not the heads of certain families should make it their Business by the whole Course of their Lives principally by their Example to mould into their very vital Stamina of their descendants those principles which ought to be transmitted pure and ⟨uncorrupted⟩ to posterity. Neither Lord R. or your Grace have children; however you do not want successors of your Blood; nor I trust heirs of your Qualities, and your Virtues, and of the power which sooner or later will be derived from them. This I say to comfort myself and possibly your Grace in the present Melancholy View of our Affairs; Although the field is lost all is not lost[7]—to give you a Line of your Milton who has somewhat reconciled you to Poetry—and he is an able Advocate. For the rest— I can only tell your Grace, that

To the MARQUESS OF ROCKINGHAM—[24 January 1775]

Corr. (1958), III, 106–8

An undated letter referring to petitions from London and Bristol merchants protesting the results of British Policy in America. Burke urges Rockingham to lead.

My dear Lord,

I received your Lordships Letter, and, as the Merchants say, Note the Contents. Mr Wooldridge,[1] one of the Committee of the London Petitioners, wished to speak with me this day at one of Clock. I shall suggest your Lordships Idea to him; it is undoubtedly a right one. But I think the Petition should be a little varied in the Prayer, on account of our manner of proceeding. When I see Mr Wooldridge I shall endeavour to persuade him, either to decline being heard at all

---

[7] *Paradise Lost*, I, 105–6.

[1] Thomas Wooldridge (d. *c.* 1794), London merchant and Alderman (1776), with property in Staffordshire.

upon the Petition before us, or to present a petition praying the house not to enter upon any proceeding with regard to America, until they are heard on their first Petition.[2]

I passed rather a sleepless Night; and I could not help rolling over in my Mind, our conversation at Richmond house. I cannot help continuing, however with the defference, I owe, and most cheerfully pay, to your Lordships judgment, very strongly in opinion, that a plan of inaction, under our present Circumstances, is not at all in our power, and indeed not at all to be adopted if it were. There are others in the world, who will not be inactive because we are so; and who will be the more active, when they see us disposed to lye by. The question then is, whether your Lordship chooses to lead, or to be led; to lay down proper Ground yourself, or stand in an awkard and distressing situation on the Ground which will be prepared for you, and which, you can neither remain upon or quit, without great inconvenience and discredit. If then things are in such a situation, as without all question they are—The only way to keep your Lordship in the publick Eye, and to keep you advantageously in it, must be to resolve to take the lead yourself.

The strong part taken the first day of the Session, and the unusual mode of protesting on the address, indicated a Vigorous Campain.[3] Indeed nothing but a resolution to make it such could have justified so early and so determined a Step; to fall off immediately, and to do just nothing at all, seems very inconsistent with such a beginning.

To wait until there is more ripeness in the publick discontents is to let the Ministry compleat their measure without putting in on our part any thing like a Caveat against it, or making any sort of resolution against the Conduct which has led us into all these difficulties. The Business will be done. It will be done on Monday at farthest. Then the Cry will be 'all is over, we must reconcile our Minds to it, as well as we can'. I confess I do not entirely enter into the Idea of waiting until the publick discontents grow riper. They never did, do, or will, ripen to any purpose unless they are matured by proper means. To be useful they must have their direction given to them; and hope must

---

[2] The petitioners from London and Bristol had failed in their attempt to gain the promise of a hearing during the debate on American policy which was due to take place on 26 January. The two courses of action which Burke now proposed as alternatives were in fact both taken.

[3] The nine peers who had voted against the Lords' Address of Thanks on 30 November 1774 exercised their right to record a protest against the implied 'approbation of the system adopted with regard to the colonies' (*Parliamentary History*, XVIII, 37–8). The protest was described in the *Annual Register*, 1775, p. 43, as 'the first we remember to have heard of upon an address, and that too very strong and pointed'.

be held out somewhere—else the miseries of the Manufacturers will be considerd as the inevitable consequences of a natural decay of Trade, and *will* be borne, as *such* a decay *must* be borne.

Forgive this detail. I am much afraid, that your Lordships only two friends, that speak in the house of Lords,[4] will be much discouraged— and in the house of Commons we shall moulder to nothing.

I am my dear Lord
ever your Lordship's
faithful and oblig'd humble Servant
EDM BURKE

Tuesday morn ten o'Clock.

Possibly as a result of Burke's plea, Rockingham proposed a meeting of his friends on 29 January to consider plans for the debate which was expected to follow Lord Dartmouth's presentation of American papers on 2 February. Richmond declined to come up for such a meeting, since Rockingham had 'determin'd after full consideration that we ought not to get the start of Lord Chatham or run races with him as to Motions'. He suggested, however, that Chatham might be invited to 'meet and consult on what may be proper to be done' on the 2nd. Rockingham called on Shelburne, and through him put before Chatham a motion that 'the Ministry and the late Laws are *in great measure* the cause of the criminal State attributed to America'. Chatham, however, acted independently once again.

To the DUKE OF RICHMOND—[26 *September* 1775]

Corr. (1958), III, 217–18

Burke, disappointed by Rockingham's inaction, saw a ray of hope in the possibility of opposition to the ministry in Ireland, if Richmond could bring pressure on his relatives there.

My dear Lord

I should hardly take the liberty of troubling your Grace at this time, if I were not most thoroughly perswaded, that there is a very particular call of honour and conscience, on all those of your Graces situation and of your sentiments, to do something towards preventing the ruin of your Country; which If I am not quite Visionary, is approaching with the greatest rapidity. There is a short interval between this and the meeting of Parliament. Much may depend upon the use which shall be made of it.

[4] Burke presumably refers to the Duke of Richmond and George Montagu, 4th Duke of Manchester (1737–88).

I am perfectly sensible of the greatness of the difficulties, and the weakness and fewness of the helps in every publick affair which you can undertake. I am sensible too of the shocking indifference and newtrality of a great part of the Nation. But a Speculative despair is unpardonable where it is our duty to Act. I cannot think the people at large wholly to blame; or if they were, it is to no purpose to blame them. For Gods sake my dear Lord endeavour to mend them. I must beg leave to put you in mind, without meaning, I am sure, to censure the body of our friends, much less the most active among them, but I must put you in mind, that no regular or sustained endeavours of any kind have been used to dispose the people to a better sense of their Condition. Any Election must be lost; any family Interest in a Country would melt away, if greater pains, infinitely greater were not employed to carry on and support them, than have ever been employed in this End and object of all Elections, and in this most important Interest of the Nation and of every individual in it. The people are not answerable for their present supine acquiescence. Indeed they are not. God and nature never made them to think or to Act without Guidance and direction. They have obeyed the only impulse they have received. When they resist such endeavours as ought to be used, by those who by their Rank and fortune in the Country, by the goodness of their Characters, and their experience in their affairs are their Natural Leaders, then it will be time enough to despair and to let their Blood lie upon their own heads. I must again beg your Grace not to think that in excusing the people I mean to blame our friends. Very far from it. Our inactivity has arisen solely from a natural and most pardonable Error, (an Error however) that it was enough to attend diligently, and to be active in Parliament. . . .

To the MARQUESS OF ROCKINGHAM—6 January 1777

Corr. (1958), III, 308–15

During the parliamentary recess, from 13 December 1776 to 21 January 1777, the strategy of opposition was considered at length by the Whig leaders. They had already begun a tentative 'secession' from Parliament. In the Lords on 31 October the Duke of Manchester had described the amendment to the Address as 'the last attempt', and had announced his determination in the future to 'lament . . . in silence' (*Parliamentary History*, XVIII, 1372). In the Commons Lord John Cavendish had vainly moved on 6 November for a reconsideration of American policy, after which 'a sort of partial secession' began (*Annual Register*, 1777, pp. 48–9). By the first week of the new year, when Rockingham was in Yorkshire, discussions were in full swing; and Burke was preparing a systematic plan of action in case the Whig leaders chose to launch a vigorous campaign. Shortly before 6 January he discussed the situation with Portland and Frederick Montagu; and Portland took away the 'heads' of the discussion, probably for the use of Burke and other friends. Burke also showed Portland an *Address* which they might present to the King; and, at Portland's suggestion, he sent it to Richmond. At this stage Burke wrote his long letter of 6 January to Rockingham enclosing the proposed *Address*.

My dear Lord

I am afraid that I ought rather beg your pardon for troubling you at all in this Season of repose, than to apologize for having been so long silent on the approaching Business. It comes upon us; not indeed in the most agreeable manner; but it does come upon us: and I believe your friends in general are in expectation of finding your Lordship resolved in what way you are to meet it. The deliberation is full of difficulties; but the decision is necessary.

The affairs of America seem to be drawing towards a Crisis. The Howes are by this time in possession of, or able to awe, the whole Middle Coast of America, from Delaware to the Western Boundary of Massachusets Bay; The Naval Barrier on the Side of Canada is broken; a great Tract of Country is open to the supply of the Troops; The River Hudson opens a way into the heart of the Provinces; and nothing, in all probability can prevent an early and offensive Campain. What the Americans have done, is, in their Circumstances truly astonishing. It is indeed infinitely more than I expected from them. But having done so much, for some short time I entertained an opinion, that they might do more. But it is now evident, that they cannot look standing Armies in the Face. They are inferior in everything, even in Numbers; I mean the numbers of those, whom they keep to constant duty and in regular pay. These seem by the best accounts, not to be above ten or twelve thousand men, at most, in their grand Army. The rest are Militia; and not wonderfully well composed, or disciplind. They decline a general engagement; prudently enough, if their Object had been to make the war attend upon a Treaty for good Terms of Subjection: But where they look further, this will not do. An army that is obliged, at all times and in all situations to decline an Engagement may delay their ruin, but never can defend their Country. Foreign assistance they have little or none; nor are they likely to have more. France, in Effect has no King; nor any Minister, accredited enough either with the Court or Nation, to undertake a design of great Magnitude. In this State of things I persuade myself, that Franklin is come to Paris, to draw from that Court a definite and satisfactory answer, concerning the support of the Colonies. If he cannot get such an answer, (and I am of opinion, that at present he cannot) then it is to be presumed, that he is authorised to negotiate with Lord Stormont[1] on the Basis of a dependance on this Crown. This I take to be his Errand; for I never can beleive, that he is come thither, as a fugitive from his Cause in the hour of its distress; or that he is going to conclude a Long life, which has brightend every hour it has continued, with so foul and so dishonourable a flight.[2] On this supposition, I thought it not wholly impossible that the Whigg party might be made a sort of Mediatours of the Peace. It is unnatural, that in making an accommodation the Americans should not choose, rather to give Credit and support to those who all along have supported them, than to throw themselves wholly on the Mercy of their bitter, uniform, and systematick Enemies. It is indeed the Victorious Enemy who has the Terms to offer; the vanquishd party and their friends being, both of them reduced in their power; And it is certain, that those who are utterly broken and subdued, have no option. But as this is hardly yet the Case of the Americans, in this middle state of their affairs, (much impaird but not perfectly ruind) one would think it must be their Interest, to provide, if possible, some further security for the Terms which they may obtain from their Enemies. If the Congress could be brought to declare in favour of those Terms for which 108 Members of the House of Commons voted last year,[3] with some Civility to the Party which held out those Terms, it would undoubtedly have an Effect to revive the Cause of our Liberties in England, and to give the Colonies some sort of mooring and anchorage in this Country. It seemd to me, that Franklin might be made to feel the propriety of such a Step; and as I have an acquaintance with him I had for a Moment a strong desire of taking a Turn to Paris. Every thing else failing, one might obtain a better knowlege of the general Aspect of things abroad than I beleive any of us possess at present. The Duke of Portland approved the Idea. But when I had conversed with the very few of your Lordships friends who were in Town, and considerd a little more maturely the constant Temper and standing Maxims of the Party, I laid aside the design; not being desirous of risquing the displeasure

[1] Viscount Stormont (1727–96), at this time British Ambassador in Paris.

[2] Benjamin Franklin's motives in going to Paris were misinterpreted. A letter from New York, printed in *Bonner and Middleton's Bristol Journal*, 21 December 1776, for example, suggested that he and other Americans had gone to France 'to secure their dollars'.

[3] Burke probably refers to his own conciliatory proposals of 16 November 1775 which were lost by 105–210 (*Journals of the House of Commons*, XXXV, 448).

of those, for whose sake alone I wished to take that fatiguing Journey at this Severe Season of the Year.

The D. of Portland has taken with him some heads of deliberation, which were the result of a discourse with his Grace and Mr Mountagu at Burlington House. It seemd essential to the Cause, that your Lordship should meet your friends with some settled Plan, either of action or inaction. Your friends will certainly require such a plan; and I am sure the state of affairs requires it, whether they call for it or not.

As to the Measure of a Secession with reasons, after rolling the matter in my head a good deal, and turning it an hundred ways, I confess I still think it the most advisable; notwithstanding the serious Objections which lie against it; and indeed the extreme uncertainty of the Effect of all political Maneuvres; especially at this time. It provides for your honour. I know of nothing else which can do this. It is something; and perhaps all that can be done under our present Circumstances. Some precaution in this respect is not without its motives. That very Estimation, for which you have sacrificed every thing else, is in some danger of suffering in the General Wreck; and perhaps it is likely to suffer the more, because you have hitherto confided more than was quite prudent, in the clearness of your own intentions, and the solidity of the popular Judgment upon them. The former indeed is out of the power of Events; but the latter is full of Levity, and the very creature of Fortune. However such as it is, (and for one I do not think I am inclined to overvalue it) both our Interest and our Duty make it necessary for us to attend to it very carefully as long as we act a part in publick. The Measure you take for this purpose may produce no *immediate* Effect; but with regard to the *party*, and the *principles*, for whose sake the party exists, all hope of their preservation, or recovery, depends upon your preserving your Reputation.

By the conversation of some friends, it seemd as if they were willing to fall in with this design, because it promised to emancipate them from the servitude of irksome Business, and to afford them an opportunity of retiring to ease and Tranquility. It that be their Object in the Secession and representation, there surely never were means worse chosen to obtain their End; and if this be any part of the project, it were a thousand times better it were never undertaken.

The Measure is not only unusual, and as such critical, but it is in its own Nature, strong and vehement in an high degree. The propriety therefore of adopting it depends entirely upon the Spirit with which it is supported and followed. To pursue violent measures with langour and irresolution is not very consistent in Speculation; and it is not more reputable or safe in practice. If your Lordships friends do not go to this Business with their whole hearts; if they do not feel themselves uneasy without it; if they do not undertake it with a certain degree of Zeal, and even warmth and indignation at the present state of things, it had better be removed wholly out of our thoughts. A measure of less strength, and more in the beaten Circle of affairs, if supported with spirit and industry, would be, on all accounts, infinitely more eligible.

We are to consider, that in this undertaking we have something against us. We have the weight of King, Lords, and Commons in the other Scale. We have against us, within a triffle, the whole Body of the Law. We oppose the more considerable part of the Landed and mercantile Interests. We contend in a manner against the whole Church. We set our face against great Armies flushed with Victory; and Navies who have tasted of civil Spoil, and have a strong appetite for more. Our strength, whatever it is, must depend for a good part of its effect upon Events not very probable. In such a situation such a Step requires, not only great Magnanimity, but unwearied activity and perseverance, with a good deal too of dexterity and management to improve every accident in our favour.

The delivery of this Paper[4] may have very important consequences. It is true that the Court may pass it over in Silence with a real or affected contempt. But this I do not think so likely. If they do take notice of it, the mildest Course will be such an address from Parliament, as the house of Commons made to the King on the London remonstrance in the year 1769.[5] This address will be followd by addresses of a similar tendency from all parts of the Kingdom in order to overpower you with what they will endeavour to pass as the united Voice and Sense of the Nation. But if they intend to proceed further and to take steps of a more decisive Nature, you are then, not to consider what they may legally and justly do, but what a Parliament, omnipotent in power, inflamed with party rage, and personal resentment, operating under the implicit military obedience of Court dis-

---

[4] The enclosed *Address to the King*. In its final form this was printed in *Works* (Bohn), V, 460–76; (Little, Brown), VI, 161–82.

[5] At the height of the discontents in 1769 the City of London had addressed an extremely strong petition to the King, accusing his ministers of corruption, illegality and military tyranny. When this was disregarded, the City, on 6 March 1770, addressed a Remonstrance, reiterating the charges. The King on 14 March replied, calling the Remonstrance disrespectful and unconstitutional. After several days of discussion in Parliament a loyal Address was drawn up expressing concern and indignation at the 'insidious suggestions of those ill designing men' (*Parliamentary History*, XVI, 892–902).

cipline, is capable of. Though they have made some successful Experiments on Juries, they will hardly trust enough to them, to order a prosecution for a supposed Libel.[6] They may proceed, in two ways; either by an *impeachment*, in which the Tories may retort on the Whiggs, (but with better success, though in a worse Cause) the proceedings in the Case of Sacheverell.[7] Or they may, without this Form, proceed, as against the Bishop of Rochester, by a Bill of Pains and Penalties more or less grievous.[8] The similarity of the Cases, or the justice, is (as I said) out of the Question; the *mode* of proceeding has several, very antient, and very recent, precedents. None of these Methods is impossible. The Court may select three or four of the most distinguished among you for the Victims; and therefore nothing is more remote from the Tendency of the proposed act, than any Idea of retirement or repose. On the contrary, you have all of you, as principals or auxiliaries, a much hotter and more dangerous conflict in all probability to undergo than any you have been yet engaged in. The only question is, whether the risque ought to be run for the chance (and it is no more) of recalling the people of England to their antient principles, and to that personal Interest which formerly they took in all publick affairs?

At any Rate I am sure it is right, if we take this Step, to take it with a full View of the Consequences; and with Minds and Measures in a State of preparation to meet them. It is not becoming, that your boldness should arise from a want of foresight. It is more reputable, and certainly it is more safe too, that it should be grounded on the evident necessity of encountering the dangers which you foresee. Your Lordship will have the goodness to excuse me if I state in strong Terms, the difficulties attending a Measure, which on the whole I heartily concurr in. But, as from my want of importance, I can be personally little subject to the most trying part of the consequences, it is as little my desire to urge others to dangers, in which I am myself to have so inconsiderable a share.

If this measure should be thought too great for our Strength, or the dispositions of the time, then the point will be to consider, what is to be done in Parliament. A weak, irregular, desultory, peevish opposition

---

[6] Burke probably refers to Lord Mansfield's famous judgment of 1771 denying the right of juries to decide whether an alleged libel was in fact libellous.

[7] Dr Henry Sacheverell (*c.* 1674–1724) was impeached in 1710 for the expression of opinions subversive of the Revolution Settlement.

[8] Francis Atterbury, Bishop of Rochester (1662–1732), was banished and deprived of his preferments by a Bill of Pains and Penalties in 1722, when the evidence seemed inadequate for the courts to convict him of treasonable Jacobite activities.

there, will be as much too little as the other may be too big. Our Scheme ought to be such, as to have in it a *Succession* of Measures; else it is impossible to secure any thing like a regular attendance through the Session; and without a tolerably uniform attendance, opposition will always carry a disreputable air; neither will it be possible without that attendance to persuade the people that we are in Earnest. Above all a Motion should be well digested for the first day. There is one thing in particular, I wish to recommend to your Lordships consideration; that is the opening of the doors of the House of Commons.[9] Without this I am clearly convinced, it will be in the power of Ministry to make our opposition appear without doors just in what light they please. To obtain a Gallery is the easiest thing in the world if we are satisfied to cultivate the Esteem of our adversaries by the resolution and energy with which we act against them; but if their satisfaction and good humour be any part of our Object the attempt, I admit, is idle. I had some conversation before I left Town with the Duke of Manchester. He is of opinion, that if you adhere to your resolution of seceding, you ought not to appear on the first day of the meeting. He thinks it can have no Effect except to break the continuity of your conduct, and thereby to weaken and fritter away the impression of it. It certainly will seem odd, to give solemn reasons for a discontinuance of your attendance in Parliament, after having two or three times returned to it, and immediately after a vigorous act of opposition. As to Trials of the Temper of the house, there have been of that sort so many already, that I see no reason for making another, that would not hold equally good for another after that; particularly as nothing has happend in the least calculated to alter the disposition of the house. If the Secession were to be *general;* such at attendance followd by such an Act would have force; but being in its own Nature incomplete and broken, to break it further by retreats and returns to the Charge, must entirely destroy its effect. I confess I am quite of the D. of Manchesters opinion in this point.

I send your Lordship a corrected Copy of the paper. Your Lordship will be so good to communicate it, if you should approve the alterations to Lord John Cavendish and Sir Geo. Savile. I shewd it to the D. of Portland before his Grace left Town—and at his (the D. of P's) desire I have sent it to the Duke of Richmond. The principal Alteration is in the page last but one. It is made to remove a difficulty which had

[9] The public gallery was generally closed in the 1770's, by use of the Standing Order prohibiting the entry of strangers while the House was sitting. It was, however, a matter for the vote of the House.

been suggested to Sir Geo Savile and which he thought had a good deal in it. I think it much the better for that alteration. Indeed it may want still more corrections, in order to adapt it to the present, or probable future State of things.

What shall I say in excuse for this long letter which frightens me when I look back upon it? Your Lordship will take it, and all in it, with your usual incomparable Temper, which carries you through so much both from Enemies and friends. My most humble Respects to my Lady Rockingham, and beleive me with the highest regard ever

My dear Lord
your Lordships
obedient and obliged humble Servant

Beconsfield Jany 6. 1777   EDM BURKE
Monday Night.

I hear that Dr Franklin has had a most extraordinary reception at Paris from all ranks of People.

To CHARLES JAMES FOX—8 October 1777

Corr. (1958), III, 380–85

On 8 September Fox (1749–1806) had written to Burke from Chatsworth that since Parliament would meet late, he was setting out on the 10th for a visit to friends in Ireland with John Townshend (1757–1833). He commented on the prevailing opinion that the Opposition 'must wait for events to form a plan of operations', and added that this had always been the excuse for indolence. He concluded: 'I have been living here some time with the very pleasant and very amiable people but altogether as unfit to storm a citadel as they would be proper for the defence of it'.

My dear Charles

I am, on many accounts, exceedingly pleased with your Journey to Ireland. I do not think it was possible to dispose better of the interval between this and the meeting of Parliament. I told you as much, in the same general terms, by the post. My opinion of the infidelity of that conveyance hinderd me from being particular. I now sit down with malice prepense, to kill you with a very long letter; and must take my chance for some safe method of conveying the dose. Before I say any thing to you of the place you are in, or the business of it, on which by the way a great deal may be said, I will turn myself to the concluding part of your letter from Chatsworth.

You are sensible, that I do not differ from you in many things; and most certainly I do not dissent from the main of your doctrine concerning the Heresy of depending upon contingencies. You must recollect how uniform my sentiments have been on that Subject. I have ever wishd a settled plan of our own, founded in the very essence of the American Business, wholly unconnected with the Events of the war, and framed in such a manner as to keep up our Credit and maintain our System at home, in spite of any thing which may happen abroad. I am now convinced by a long and somewhat vexatious experience that such a plan is absolutely impracticable. I think with you, that some faults in the constitution of those whom we most love and trust are among the causes of this impracticability. They are faults too, that one can hardly wish them perfectly cured of, as I am afraid they are intimately connected with honest disinterested intentions, plentiful fortunes, assured rank, and quiet homes. A great deal of activity and enterprize can scarcely ever be expected from such men, unless some horrible calamity is just over their heads; or unless they suffer some gross personal insults from power, the resentment of which may be as unquiet and stimulating a principle in their minds, as ambition is in those of a different complexion. To say the truth, I cannot greatly blame them. We live at a time, when men are not repaid in fame, for what they sacrifice in Interest or repose. On the whole, when I consider of what discordant, and particularly of what fleeting materials the opposition has been all along composed, and at the same time review what Lord Rockingham has done, with that and with his own shatterd constitution, for these last twelve years, I confess I am rather surprized that he has done so much and perseverd so long, than that he has felt now and then some cold fits, and that he grows somewhat languid and desponding at last. I know that he and those who are most prevalent with him, though they are not thought so much devoted to popularity as others, do very much look to the people; and more than I think is wise in them, who do so little to guide and direct the public opinion. Without this, they act indeed; but they act as it were from compulsion, and because it is impossible in their situation to avoid taking some part. All this it is impossible to change, and to no purpose to complain of.

As to that popular humour which is the medium we float in, if I can discern any thing at all of its present state, it is far worse than I have ever known, or could ever imagine it. The faults of the people are not *popular* vices; at least they are not such as grow out of what we used to take to be the English temper and Character. The greatest number have a sort of an heavy lumpish acquiescence in Government, without much respect or esteem for those that compose it. I really cannot avoid making some very unpleasant prognostics from this disposition of the people. I think that many of the Symptoms must have struck you. I will mention one or two that are to me very remarkable. You must know that at Bristol we grow, as an Election Interest, and even as a party Interest, rather stronger than we were when I was chosen. We have just now a Majority in the Corporation. In this state of matters what think you they have done? They have voted their freedom to Lord Sandwich and Lord Suffolk—to the first at the very moment when the American Privateers were domineering in the Irish Sea and taking the Bristol traders in the Bristol Channel—to the latter when his remonstrances on the subject of Captures were the jest of Paris and of Europe. This fine step was taken, it seems, in honour of the zeal of these two profound Statesmen in the prosecution of John the Painter—So totally negligent are they of every thing essential; and so long, and so deeply affected with Trash and most low and contemptible; Just as if they thought the merit of Sir John Fielding[1] was ⟨the⟩ most shining point in the Character of great Ministers, in the most critical of all times and of all others the most deeply interesting to the commercial world! My best friends in the Corporation had no other doubts on the occasion, than whether it did not belong to me, by right of my representative capacity, to be the bearer of this auspicious Compliment. In addition to this, if it could receive any addition, they now employ me to sollicit as a favour of no small magnitude, that after the example of Newcastle they may be sufferd to arm Vessels for their own defence in the Channel. Their Memorial under the Seal of Merchants-hall is now lying on the Table before me. Not a Soul has the least Sensibility on finding themselves, now for the first time, obliged to act as if the Community were dissolved, and after enormous payments towards the common protection, to defend each part as if it were a separate State.

I don't mention Bristol, as if that were the part furthest gone in this mortification. Far from it. I know that there is rather a little more life in us than in any other place. In Liverpoole they are literally almost ruined by this American War; but they love it as they suffer from it. In short from whatever I see and from whatever Quarter I ahear, I am convinced that every thing that is not absolute Stagnation, is evidently a party Spirit, very adverse to our politics and to the

[1] (d. 1780), the celebrated blind magistrate.

principles from whence they arise. There are most manifest marks of
the resurrection of the Tory party. They no longer criticize, as all
disengaged people in the world will, on the acts of Government; but
they are silent under every evil, and hide and cover up every ministerial
blunder and misfortune with the officious zeal of men, who think they
have a party of their own to support in power. The Tories do universally
think their power and consequence involved in the Success of this
American business. The Clergy are astonishingly warm in it—and
what the Tories are when embodied, united with their natural head
the Crown, and animated by their Clergy, no man knows better than
yourself. As to the Whigs I think them far from extinct. They are
what they always were (except by the able use of opportunities) by
far the weakest party in this Country. They have not yet learnd the
application of their principles to the present state of things; and as to
the dissenters, the main effective part of the Whig strength, they are,
to use a favourite expression of our American Campaign Style—not
at all *in force.* They will do very little; and as far as I can discern, are
rather intimidated than provoked at the denunciations of the Court
in the Archbishop of Yorks Sermon.[2] I thought that Sermon rather
imprudent when I first saw it—But it seems to have done its business.

In this temper of the people, I do not wholly wonder that our
Northern friends[3] look a little towards Events. In war particularly I
am afraid it must be so. There is something so weighty and decisive
in the Events of war, something that so completely overpowers the
imagination of the Vulgar, that all Counsels must in a great degree be
subordinate to and attendant on them. I am sure it was so in the last
war[4] very eminently. So that on the whole, what with the temper of
the people, the temper of our own friends, and the domineering necessities of war, we must quietly give up all Ideas of any settled,
preconcerted plan. We shall be lucky enough, if keeping ourselves
attentive and alert, we can contrive to profit of the occasions as they
arise; tho I am sensible, that those who are best provided with a general
Scheme, are fittest to take advantage of all contingencies. However,
to act with any people with the least degree of comfort, I believe we
must contrive a little to assimilate to their Character. We must gravitate

---

[2] William Markham, Burke's old friend, had become Archbishop of York at the beginning
of 1777. On 21 February he preached a sermon before the Society for the Propagation of the
Gospel warning his hearers of the dangers of faction and the limits of toleration, attacking the
Whig support of the American cause, and threatening the Dissenters for their share in it. The
sermon was published and caused much controversy.

[3] Particularly Rockingham and the Cavendishes.

[4] The Seven Years War.

towards them, if we would keep in the same System, or expect that they would approach towards us. They are indeed worthy of much concession and management. I am quite convinced that they are the honestest public men that ever appeard in this Country, and I am sure that they are the wisest by far of those who appear in it at present. Not one of those who are continually complaining of them, but are themselves just as chargeable with all their faults, and have a decent stock of their own into the bargain. They are, (our friends) I admit, as you very truly represent them, but indifferently qualifyd for storming a Citadel. After all, God knows whether this Citadel is to be stormed by them or by anybody else, by the means they use or by any means. I know that as they are, abstractedly speaking, to blame, so there are those who cry out against them for it, not with a friendly complaint as we do, but with the bitterness of Enemies.[5] But I know too that those who blame them for want of Enterprize have shewn no activity at all against the common Enemy; All their Skill and all their Spirit has been shewn only in weakning, dividing, and indeed destroying their Allies. What they are, and what we are, is now pretty evidently experienced, and it is certain, that partly by our common faults, but much more by the difficulties of our Situation, and some circumstances of unavoidable misfortune, we are in little better than a sort of Cul-de-Sac. For my part, I do all I can to give ease to my mind in this strange position. I remember some years ago, when I was pressing some points with much eagerness and anxiety, and complaining with great vexation to the Duke of Richmond of the little progress I made, he told me kindly and I believe very truly, that, tho he was far from thinking so himself, other people could not be persuaded, I had not some latent private Interest in pushing these matters, which I urged with an earnestness so extreme, and so much approaching to passion. He was certainly in the right. I am thoroughly resolved to give both to myself and my friends, less vexation on these subjects than hitherto I have done; much less indeed.

If *you* should grow too earnest, you will be still more inexcusable than I was. Your having enterd into Affairs so much younger ought to make them too familiar to you, to be a cause of much agitation, and you have much more day before you for your work. Do not be in haste. Lay your foundations deep in public opinion. Though (as you are sensible) I have never given you the least hint of advice about joining yourself in a declared connexion with our party, nor do I now—

[5] Burke probably refers both to Chatham and his friends and to their radical allies in the City.

yet as I love that party very well, and am clear that you are better able to serve them than any man I know, I wish that things should be so kept, as to leave you mutually very open to one another in all changes and contingencies. And I wish this the rather, because in order to be very great, as I am anxious that you should be, (always presuming that you are disposed to make a good use of power) you will certainly want some better support than merely that of the Crown. For I much doubt, whether, with all your parts, you are the man formed for acquiring real interior favour in this Court or in any. I therefore wish you a firm ground in the Country; and I do not know so firm and sound a bottom to build on as our party. Well, I have done with this matter; and you think I ought to have finished it long ago. . . .

To WILLIAM BAKER—[12 *October* 1777]

Corr. (1958), III, 388–89

On 9 October William Baker, since early in the year again a Member of Parliament, had written a short letter to Burke from his home at Bayfordbury, asking whether 'our friends . . . the real friends to their Country'—whom Baker defined as Savile, Rockingham, the Cavendishes and Burke—were making any plans for the parliamentary session now six weeks away. 'We seem hitherto to have been wasting our Powder in Holiday Fireworks, and shall find ourselves in want of it in the time of actual Service'.

My dear Baker

I received your Letter yesterday. But as the post does not go from hence on Saturday Nights, it was not in my power to give you an answer until this day. This day I am sure I can give you no answer that will be at all satisfactory. One Word upon Business, from any one of the party, great or small, I have not heard since the hour of our dispersion at Westminster at the close of the last Session. I do not consider the two Letters I received from Lord Rockingham and the D. of Richmond as an exception to this, as they said no more of publick affairs, than just what was sufficient to express something very like their entire despondency about them.

Such is my situation, and my knowlege of these matters, and with this degree of knowlege, and in this situation I shall remain until time brings us all together, and Events supply occasions for action or resolution. I am quite satisfied that it never can be otherwise. Alas my dear friend those whom you and I trust, and whom the publick ought to love and trust, have not that trust and confidence in themselves, which their merits authorise, and which the necessities of the Country absolutely demand. Ill success, ill health, minds too delicate for the rough and toilsome Business of our time, a want of the stimulus of ambition, a degeneracy of the Nation, which they are not lofty enough to despise, nor skillful enough to cure, have, all together, I am afraid contributed very much to weaken the Spring of Characters, whose fault it never was to be too elastick and too firmly braced. But still, as you say, they are our only hope; on my conscience, I think the best men, that ever were. We must therefore bear their infirmities for their Virtues, and wait their time patiently. I believe you known that my cheif employment for many years has been that woful one, of a *flapper*.[1] I begin to think it time to leave it off. It only defeats its own purpose when given too long and too liberally; and I am persuaded that the men who will not move, when you want to teize them out of their inactivity, will begin to reproach yours, when you let them alone. Perhaps this would not, after all, be so right; if one had in his own Mind a distinct plan, which he could propose to others, and make it a point with them to pursue. I do not remember to have found myself at a loss in my own Mind about our Conduct, until now. I confess it; I do not know how to push others to resolution, whilst I am unresolved myself. It would give me infinite satisfaction if you would turn your thoughts to something on which we might confer. For I am like a dried spunge, I have nothing in me, and am ready to drink up a great deal. In War, *Events* do every thing. Ones *principles* ought not to be led by them; but I fear ones *conduct* must, more or less—for the gross of the people are our instruments, and their love or hatred, their distrust or Confidence, are wholly governed by the last Flanders Mail or New York Pacquet. Whatever becomes of War, and peace, of the good or ill humour of the people continue my dear Baker your old partiality to me. I can only merit it, by faithful regards to you. Mrs Burke desires her best respects to Mrs Baker. Gregory and Jack Bourke

---

[1] A person who arouses the attention or jogs the memory; in Jonathan Swift, *Gulliver's Travels*, III, 2, a remembrancer of heedless philosophers.

came here yesterday, and they both desire to be rememberd to you.
I am ever with

the greatest truth and esteem
My dear Sir
your most faithful
and affectionate humble Servant
EDM BURKE

Beaconsfield
Oct 12 1777

To the MARQUESS OF ROCKINGHAM—5 *November* 1777

Corr. (1958), III, 398–400

On 26 October Rockingham had written to Burke from Wentworth and expressed
his belief that the Whigs should not 'over hurry' public opinion, which needed time
to appreciate the losses of war. Burke's reply, while yielding to Rockingham's inclination for the moment, attempts to instruct him on the general necessity of activity.

My dear Lord,
    This may possibly reach you before you sett out on your Journey
Southward, and I hope but a little time before you begin to move. I
have not seen or heard from very many of your Lordships friends;
but I know that some of the most zealously attached to you, and to
the common Cause, are earnest that something Systematick may be
determined on before we walk into the great Rooms at Westminster.
In particular, I have receivd Some very earnest and anxious Letters
from Baker on that Subject. I confess, that for my own part I do most
perfectly agree with your Lordship in every particular of your Letter.
No man I believe less chooses to determine any part of his *principles*
by Events; but our *Conduct* must be so governed; because the people,
by whom and for whom we do, and ought to work, are entirely governd
by nothing else. We have indeed nothing for our present comfort, and
no scource for our future hope, but by preserving our reputation;
which cannot be done by the innocence of our intentions, but by the
rational activity of our exertions. To make our activity rational, there
must be some disposition in the minds of the many to cooperate; and
something or other conspiring in the Circumstances. None of these
occur. The wild tumult of Joy that the News of Sunday[1] caused in

[1] The defeat of Washington by Howe, as reported from New York; according to the Duke
of Manchester, London went mad at the news.

the Minds of all sorts of people indicates nothing right in their Character and disposition. Yet as the few who are not to be moved, want comfort; it will be necessary not to carry the appearance of too much despondency; but to appear to be doing something, lest they should conclude, perhaps sooner than they ought, that nothing can be done. And your Lordship knows but too well what a propensity there is in every routed party to throw the blame of their misfortunes, upon something improperly done or omitted by those who lead them. There is indeed among your friends an unusual spirit, which would counteract that natural propensity, if they were left to themselves. But there are persons, who do nothing themselves, and complain a great deal, who to my knowlege labour day and night to infuse Jealousies and uneasinesses amongst them, on this sole principle, that there is too much languor inactivity and remissness in the whole Tenour of our Character. That they succeed to some degree I know to a certainty. Several of our friends, that are very high amongst us, and ought to be still higher than they are, and assume more lead than they do, are of opinion, that these malignant endeavours signifye nothing, and that after all, mens reputation will depend on their own Conduct, and not on the representations of others. I am quite of that Sentiment; provided you allow ten or a dozen years for the operation. But in the mean time opportunities are gone and the fate of Nations and Systems decided. In my thoughts a *practical* reputation, to do any good, must be in possession, not in expectancy; and must coexist with every moment of our action. I say all this; because though I heartily concur in the very sound and wise principles of your Lordships Letter; yet I would have the temporising, which I know to be necessary, rather evident to others, than proposed by you; and that it should seem the result of prudence, rather than of complexion. Let people stand still; but Let them stop themselves, rather by the great dyke before them, than by your bridle. Lord Chathams figure has been for some time exposed to several; The blood of St Januarius began to Liquefie.[2] He was perfectly alive; very full of conversation; nowise communicative; and fully resolved to go down to the house of Lords on the first day of the Session. But I am afraid, that the present American News will put as many folds of Flannel about him, as their are linnen Fillets round an Ægyptian Mummy; but like a true obeyer of the Laws *he*

---

[2] Januarius, the patron saint of Naples, suffered martyrdom in the third century. Miracles were attributed to him during his lifetime; and in later centuries relics of his blood were said to liquefy at certain times.

will be buried in Woollen.[3] Adieu my Lord! God bless you, remember my most humble Duty to My Lady Rockingham. Here I am ready for your Commands as usual and ever with the most sincere and affectionate attachment

My dear Lord
your Lordships most oblig'd
and obedient humble Servant,
EDM BURKE

Beconsfield Nov. 5. 1777

To RICHARD SHACKLETON—25 *May* 1779

Corr. (1958), IV, 78–80

This is Burke's answer to Shackleton's letter of 10 April informing Burke of his retirement from the Ballitore School and that his son Abraham was now its Master, the third Shackleton to hold that position. Burke delivers some important general thoughts on parties.

My dear friend,

I do most heartily congratulate you on your enjoyment of the greatest good fortune which can attend our time of Life, I mean a retreat from Care and toil, with the View of a Child entering into active life with a fair prospect in his turn of enjoying the same repose and in the same place. If I had less interest than I really have in this Situation of your affairs, merely as a situation it could not fail to give me pleasure. May you grow more and more pleased with the satisfaction which you so well deserve both you and your excellent Wife! Give in my Name all sorts of felicitation to the third Shackleton; who, I have no doubt will fill his place as well as the two first; and better he cannot. That young Gentleman has been always a very great favourite of mine, on account of his excellent good parts, and the oppenness and the Liberality of Nature that I observed in him. These dispositions will ensure much happiness to you and to himself; and will enable him to supply many Virtuous and useful Citizens to his Country. I hope he will help to fill up the succession of the World in its progress to better things publick and private than we have the fortune to see at this moment.

[3] Chatham's theatrical appearances in Parliament, with much flannel to protect his gout, suggest to Burke an observance of the statutes of 1666 and 1678 requiring bodies for burial to be shrouded in woollen cloth.

Your sollicitude about my Son is very kind and flattering to us both. It does not become me to say all I think of him. My partiality may naturally influence my judgment in such a Case: But to you I may perhaps be allowd to express myself as I think and as I feel on any Subject. I thank God he much more than answers my hopes of him. I do not know how I could wish him to be in any particular whatsoever other than what he is. He has been for some time in the Inns of Court, and intends himself for that profession which is so leading, in this Country, and which has this peculiar advantage, that even a failure in it stands almost as a sort of qualification for other things.[1] Whether he will ever desire, or ever have it in his Choice, to engage further in publick affairs is more than I am able to foresee. If he should, I am sure that your kind admonitions will have their full Effect upon a constitution of mind very well disposed to receive every lesson of Virtue. What you say about his engaging in parties may be right for any thing I know to the Contrary. The Nature, composition, Objects, and quality, of the parties which may exist in his time, or in the form of commonwealth he may live to see, are not easy to be guessed at. It must be wholly left to himself; and must depend upon the future State of things, and the Situation in which he is found relatively to them. Humana *qua parte* locatus es in re?[2]—is the best rule both in morals and in prudence; and the progressive Sagacity, that keeps company with times and occasions, and decides upon things in their existing position, is that alone which can give true propriety, Grace, and effect to a mans conduct. It is very hard to anticipate the occasion; and to live by a rule more general. As to parties, there is much discussion about them in political morality. But whatever their merits may be, they have always existed and always will; and as far as my own observation has gone, I have observed but three sorts of men that have kept out of them. Those who profess nothing but a pursuit of their own Interest, and who avow their resolution of attaching themselves to the present possession of power, in whose ever hands it is, or however it may be used. The other sort are ambitious men, of light or no principles, who in their turns make use of all parties, and therefore avoid entering into what may be construed an engagement with any. Such was, in a great measure, the late Earl of Chatham; who expected a very blind submission of men to him, without con-

---

[1] Richard Burke, Jr, had been admitted to the Middle Temple on 22 November 1775, and was called to the Bar on 24 November 1780.

[2] At what point of the human commonwealth have you been stationed? See Persius, *Satires*, III, 72.

sidering himself as having any reciprocal obligation to them. It is true, that he very often rewarded such submission in a very splendid manner; but with very little marks of respect or regard to the Objects of his favour, and as he put a real confidence in no man, he had very few feelings of resentment against those who the most bitterly opposed, or most basely betrayd him. The other sort is hardly worth mentioning, being composed only of four or five Country Gentlemen of little Efficiency in publick Business. It is but a few days ago, that a very wise and a very good man, the Duke of Portland, said to me in a conversation on this Subject, that he never knew any man disclaim party, who was not *of* a party, that he was ashamed of. But thus much I allow, that men ought to be circumspect, and cautious of entering into this Species of political relation, because it cannot easily be broke, without loss of reputation, nor, (many times) perseverd in, without giving up much of that practicability, which the variable nature of affairs may require; as well as of that regard to a mans own personal consideration, which, (in a due subordination to publick good), a man may very fairly aim at. All acting in Corps tends to reduce the consideration of an individual who is of any distinguishd Value. As to myself, and the part I have taken in my time, I apprehend, there was very little choice. Things soon fell into two very distinct Systems. The principle upon which this Empire was to be governd made a discrimination of the most marked nature. I cannot think that I have been in the wrong so far as the publick was concernd, and as to my own annihilation by it with regard to all the Objects of men in publick life, it is of too small importance to spend many words upon it. In the Course I have taken I have met, and do daily meet so many vexations, that I may with truth assure you, that my situation is any thing rather than enviable; though it is my happiness to act with those that are far the best that probably ever were engaged in the publick service of this Country, at any time. So little satisfaction have I that I should not hesitate a moment to retire from publick Business—if I was not in some doubt of the Duty a man has that goes a certain length in those things; and if it were not from an observation that there are often obscure vexations and contests in the most private life, which may as efectually destroy a mans peace as any thing which happens in publick contentions. Adieu my dear friend—enjoy your Natural and deserved happiness, renew mine and my Wifes best wishes to Mrs Shackleton and the young pair. Both Richards join most cordially in them. I am always My dear Shackleton

Yours affectionately
and faithfully
EDM BURKE

May 25. 1779.

To the DUKE OF PORTLAND—3 September 1780

Corr. (1958), IV, 266–75

Burke arrived in Bristol on 18 August; Parliament was dissolved on 1 September. He had, therefore, had little time to devote to canvassing his constituency before he had to determine whether it was wise to contest an election at all, or whether to surrender his proud title of being the representative of the second city of the kingdom, to which he had been elected in 1774. Burke recognized that his chance of retaining his seat was slight, although his attention to national issues and his devotion to the lesser interests of his constituents had been exemplary. It is true that he was attacked for helping to remove the restrictions on Irish trade, for his refusal to oppose Lord Beauchamp's Bill, and for his advocacy of toleration for Roman Catholics. But his political weakness at Bristol cannot be explained merely by adducing the hostility he had incurred on these questions, for his personal influence in the city was much stronger in 1780 than it had been in 1774; he had in fact created a valuable personal following, and captured control of the Corporation. His real difficulty lay in the virtual impossibility of two Whigs being chosen at Bristol; the election of 1774 in which the radical Henry Cruger had been elected with him, and ahead of him, had been exceptional.

My dear Lord,

I receivd the Notice which your Grace was so very obliging and considerate to send to Champion. I am sorry that the Parliament is dissolved so early.[1] Since I came hither I have made no small progress in removing the ill Effects of the long, but on my part unavoidable, Neglect of my Interest in this City.[2] A want of a diligent attention on my side, and a want of decision on the side of my friends has made a certain length of time absolutely necessary to the recovery of our Ground. I wish to give your Grace in a very few words, as nearly as

---

[1] The dissolution of Parliament over a year before its legal termination, was without recent precedent.

[2] Burke had not visited Bristol since August 1776. The other three candidates, Brickdale, Combe and Cruger, being Bristol men closely associated with the city's affairs, were much better placed for the purpose of courting the voters.

I am able to comprehend it, the State of things here. Our grand division is of Whiggs and Tories. The Latter have made a constant unremitting canvass from the End of the last Election, and have receivd all possible assistance from the Treasury. They have accordingly had a uniform growth of Strength; and their confidence in it has been so great, that they have started two Candidates on that Interest, Brickdale and Coombes. The latter has been furnished with a compleat suit of armour from the Tower; having been lately made, and I conceive for the purpose of this contest, Treasurer of the Ordnance;[3] a place, which is called twelve hundred pounds a year. Many of that party dislike extremely the Idea of their starting two Candidates; not that they think it impossible to carry both; but they must carry them through a severe Struggle which from the Ballance of parties, they are persuaded cannot end with this Election. They are therefore for a compromise—those who think so are the most considerable, but by no means the most active and efficient of the party. They told me their sentiments, and told me at the same time that on such a compromise between Whigg and Tory they would certainly give the preference to me and to my friends; as they made no scruple to declare, that they neither loved nor respected Mr Cruger, nor most of his friends, even though no party matter were in question. There is one great Obstacle to this compromise on their side, that the person whom it would in prudence be most advisable for them to give up, is much the most favourite object with their richest and proudest people—of all those indeed, who rather look to the Court than to the general Interest of the Tory party. Brickdale has far the greatest Natural Strength, and deserves the most to have it, having long served that party and fought their Battles at a very great expence. He has most of the middling and lower part of the Tories, and indeed I look on his Election as the only sure one among the four pretenders.

As to the Whiggs, or such as call themselves so, they are intirely, and as I conceive irretrievably, divided. The most opulent, the most sober, the most understanding part are for me, and with a Zeal, constancy, and friendship that I shall never know how sufficiently to acknowlege. If the Whigg Merchants could make a Member, I should be chosen without all doubt or controversy. There is however among the opulent part of this City, a very large body that can scarcely be called of any party. They never have taken, and never will take any side with the smallest degree of Vigour or firmness. I am informed,

---

[3] An office which Burke had hoped to abolish.

that they lean to our friends; but we shall never derive any real advantage from it. They are all for a compromise; but their compromising Spirit hinders them from doing any thing towards it. Such is the State of my Strength with regard to the grand parties; and if a compromise between them can take place, I shall be on firm Ground, at least I think so. I should have many more of the second Tory Votes than Cruger, all indeed that the principal Merchants of that description can influence. If no compromise can take place then a Battle must be fought at an immense Expence, and with a very uncertain Issue. I should think it uncertain, though the whole Whigg strength of this City was perfectly united. But if it should continue, as it is, divided, then Cruger carries off such a Body of the low Voters, that I concurr, on full deliberation, with all my friends, that it is far better for me to make no Trial at all than to be disgraced in the manner we probably should be. It may appear extraordinary, how a man of no sort of Parliamentary value, of very indifferent Character, on whose word no man has a reliance, whose understanding is superficial, and felt to be so in the extreme; and who is now not worth a Shilling, should have such an Interest. The fact is he originally, and whilst his Circumstances were still good was put up as the head of the revolt from the old united Interests: He was on the Ground before me. So that they have an attachment to him as a party leader, which he has cultivated by a diligent attendance on *them*, and a total Neglect of attendance in Parliament. He makes them speeches which your Grace and I would think gross affronts to them; but there is an instinctive Sympathy between them, and he falls into their ways not through policy, but through conformity of Character. They are totally indifferent about any principles political or moral, or about the neglect or performance of publick Duty of any kind with respect to the State, or with respect to Commerce; What has more weight than all, he tells them (and it is the only Truth he does tell them) that if *he* were out of the way there would not be for a long time any contested Election in Bristol. This dreadful prospect of stopping the Aletap has as much Effect in this City as in any other you are acquainted with. Our friends wishing the peace of the City, and Mr Crugers dreading it as the greatest of all possible Evils, makes these lower Voters to look upon me and on all my friends with a very unfavourable Eye.

There is another Circumstance of his Strength and my weakness; It is, that those middling Tradesmen, who are, and from many Circumstances, must be the managers and intermediate people in all the Parishes, though well enough affected to the old joint (or seemingly joint) Interest, yet if there must be a seperation, in their hearts prefer Mr Cruger; as they think that he contributes far more to their importance than I do—and importance in the person made and the makers is all they look to, never extending their consideration beyond Bristol in any matter of Election. Of this Number is the *Watts*, whom I wished your Graces friend in Nottingham to write to. In all, but Election politicks, he is a very fair man. But I find, that he is so compleat a Jockey, that he has suppressed the Letters he receivd from Nottingham, which could not fail to have weight; and has suppressd the Letter I wrote to him to remove impressions which he lamented as prevailing against me, and of which he was himself very considerably the Cause—though he thought proper totally to disclaim their influence upon himself. All Low politicians play tricks; and this is with very few exceptions the disposition of most of the managers. They wish a junction; but if the united body was to be hard pressd, it is quite clear to us, that they would look for the least chance of Crugers safety, at the Expence of my certain destruction. As to Cruger himself, and his Committee, they have several Months ago positively refused all sort of union with me and my friends; and one of the principal of them spoke to the same effect to me, since my arrival. I believe their managers would actually compel them to a junction, if such a junction, so obtaind, and with such persons, could be relied on so as to make the obtaining it an Object to us. But we should get nothing by it but the power of fighting a doubtful Battle with allies, whose fidelity is a great deal worse than doubtful.

When I told your Grace, that Mr Cruger is not worth a farthing, and that he has very few men of fortune in his Interest, it will naturally occur to you to ask why he is so eager to venture into a most expensive contest for the sake of the precarious advantage of a seat in Parliament? The answer is, he has a father in Law of very Ample fortune, they talk of so much as fourscore thousand pound. This man refusing upon the original application to advance any thing towards the last Election, was drawn on Step by Step to spend three thousand five hundred pound. He is now very nearly as tenacious of money, and as unwilling to engage for any thing positive, as he was then; but he permits the Business to go on; and those who govern this man still more governable than parsimonious, are confident that they shall gradually draw out of him as much as their exigencies may require; and as they fight with other mens money, and have no conscience of their own, they are very indifferent about any thing he may suffer in Mind or purse.

Besides these two Capital divisions of Whigg and Tory, we are subdivided variously into political and religious bodies. The latter are more guided by the spirit of those religious descriptions than, I beleive, they are in any other part of England; and their preachers have more weight with them. The Majority of the Corporation are with me; and this would be decisive, if the election depended upon Corporate acts; but as it depends in a great measure upon the seperate Interests of the Members of the Corporation, and my friends being only in a Majority, the Effect is considerably weakend, and is indeed hardly felt. The presbyterians are in general Sound, and in our Interest. So are the Quakers, to about two or three; but the Quakers are not very active; and where Interests are nearly balanced, they are much inclined to caution. The Baptists and anabaptists were originally disposed to Cruger and continue, through the means of one of their Ministers,[4] (who is an Abingdonian[5] &c &c &c.) much his friends, and ill enough affected to me. I had the most of them in the last Election rather upon the principle of Junction with Cruger than from any good liking to our politicks.

There is one Sect (if they may be so called,) behind; pretty numerous; and still more under the discipline of their Teachers than any of the rest—that is the sect of the Methodists. I am not yet quite certain what part they will take, except that negative certainty, that they will not take it for me. I had one Parson (Roquet)[6] among them much my friend and of no small weight with them but he has been dead It is near five years since. Wesley carried over that set of men to the Court, and to all the slavish doctrines of Charles the 2ds reign in their utmost extent.[7] Cruger boasts, that he has obtaind his support; I should not think this impossible, for one of the Votes at least, from the known Versatility of the man; though it is not long since he preached a sermon recommending the support of what he calls Government. Perhaps Cruger may have given him private satisfaction on this head.

On a view of the whole, there is no reconciling my friends with Crugers principal people. Ours think ill of them; and they think too well of us.

---

[4] Probably Caleb Evans (1737–91), a pro-American in politics.
[5] i.e. a follower of Willoughby Bertie, 4th Earl of Abingdon (1740–99). Abingdon had published a pamphlet against Burke in 1775.
[6] James Rouquet (c. 1729–76), curate of St Werburgh, Bristol, and Vicar of West Harptree.
[7] John Wesley (1703–91) had initially been favourably disposed to the American cause, but a reading of Dr Johnson's *Taxation No Tyranny* in 1775 had converted him to the support of Government. He based a pamphlet on Johnson's and five thousand copies of it were purchased by the ministerialists of Bristol in 1780 to distribute to the voters.

On this View we have but two things to think of; first to make a compromise between the parties, by each withdrawing a Candidate. On this Business they are employd this day. The other is to make an honourable retreat. For this purpose they have applied to the Sheriffs to call a meeting for the nomination of Candidates. It will be next Tuesday; and if no compromise takes place, I shall there take my leave.

I intended to say but a few words; but I grew unawares into length. Indeed I am not sorry that I have done so; as I owe to your Grace and to our principal friends an account of the loss of the post which I was to defend; and I trust I shall be acquitted on my Court martial.

In all affairs of this kind, I do not like to throw up in a Pett. If I go off it will be on rational motives, and not from passion. I hope that in all Election and in all other matters I consider *myself* in but a secondary light. Although by various accidents I think it very imprudent to fight this Battle at this time, I think this Interest, which may hereafter be very useful to the Cause, too valuable to be thrown away. It is strong; it is reputable; it is growing; and one of my principal reasons for not trying it now, is lest it should be blighted before it comes to that maturity, to which, with tolerable management, it *must* arrive. And though *I* never can bring myself, (if I were to look so far before me) to think again of a place, in which I have been once rejected, it may afford *you* another, and perhaps a better Member. If the Gentleman from whose house I write, should think it worth his while, you could not have a better man than Mr Harford; He has a great bottom for Confidence. He has a firm Integrity; very enlarged notions; and one of the most solid and well cultivated understandings I have met with. Unluckily he is now Sheriff; and this takes away the weight of his personal Canvass from one of the most considerable Parishes here, as well as his influence in all. This is a great blow to our Interest. The other Sheriff too is my friend, and thus both are disabled. A personal Canvass is of the last degree of importance here.

There is another reason why I must decline standing. The expence would in all probability be dreadful. Men attentive to their Credit, though they would subscribe Liberally, would not and ought not to engage to an indefinite Charge. I believe they would risque any thing, in Case the Success was clear or even very probable. Mr Harford offerd to lay down three hundred for his Share, in Case of a contest; and I beleive many others would behave in such a Case with sufficient spirit. It was hinted to me before I came hither, that no subscription could go on with the least Spirit in a second expensive contest, if I did not myself take a lead in it, in some sort of proportion to my Interest. I could not resist it, and accordingly engaged for a thousand pound, hoping that my friends, who were disburthend of me for the last Parliament as well as the two preceding, might very well levy on the Gentleman or Gentlemen who came in by that opening, the sum wanted in support of the general Interest and Cause. This expence has been so levied in almost all Cases, and has been considerd, as in effect comparatively it is, bringing in a Member without expence; and thus a little well divided charge arranges many. However when I came to reflect upon all circumstances, I was frightned at the Rashness of the undertaking; which however, would not have been an undertaking at all, without great prospect of success. In that Case the thousand pound, if the party thought it proper to look for a seat for me, might be equivalent to a saving of two, supposing a Seat to be a Gift worth three thousand pound. But I have never applied for one; having felt an infinite satisfaction, that now for three parliaments I have never been the means of streightning the Parliamentary Interest of my friends, however unprofitable I may have been to them in other respects. It grieves me so much to lie as a weight on that Interest, that I do declare to you, I would not desire, no nor even accept of a seat, so compleatly sick I am of this game of politicks (taking all my Circumstances together) if I had not a certainty, that the News of my being totally shut out of Parliament might kill Will Burke; who is firmly persuaded, that all his hope of success in India is founded on the opinion, of some sort of consequence he is thought to derive, from my being in some sort of publick situation.

My friends yesterday made a last effort, proposing on one hand to Cruger, to induce him to resign his pretensions, to pay all his charges incurred, and to give him two thousand pounds more to aid him in getting a seat in any other place. This proposal was rejected last Night by his Committee; most of his friends acknowleging at the same time, that without the aid of mine they are apprehensive they shall lose the Election. On the other hand they have made a proposal to the high party to withdraw one of their Candidates, on a Condition, that if they support me with their Interest, ours will be thrown into their scale and thereby we shall secure the peace of the City for several Elections. I think they can do nothing more—nor am I willing to press them. This sort of fights grow less and less agreeable to my Temper, or suitable to my years. After being so many years known to the publick, to be obliged [to] fight ones way at every new contest like a new man, is not pleasant; and one begins to want the Talents, as well as the inclination for these combats. Oldish men are not more fit to court the people than the Ladies—nor is it very becoming—Turpe senex Miles, turpe senilis Amor.[8] I have a notion that men who take an enlarged line on publick Business, and upon Grounds of some depth, and that require at every instant, the appearance of doing something, in *appearance* wrong, in order to do what is really and *substantially* right, ought not to sit for these great busy places. Besides their local agency is vexatious, and sometimes humiliating. I have lookd back at my Conduct and its relation to the publick for some years past; and if I had followd the humours of this town, which are called opinions, I should have been more frequently wrong, than even if I had been guided by the Court; for I should have fallen into not a few of their Mistakes, and have had an whole Class of Errors of another kind to answer for into the Bargain. Indeed as I grow older, my temper grows in some Sort the more different from that of old men. I hope I never shall reject the principles of general publick prudence; Those which go under the description of the moral Virtue of that name; but as to the prudence of giving up the principle to the means, I confess I grow ten times more restive than ever. I shall always follow the popular humour, and endeavour to lead it to right points, at any expence of private Interest, or party Interest, which I consider as nothing in comparison—But as to leaving to the Crowd, to choose for me, what principles I ought to hold, or what Course I ought to pursue for their benefit—I had much rather, innocently and obscurely, mix with them, with the utter ruin of all my hopes, (which hopes are my all) than to betray them by learning lessons from them. They are naturally proud, tyrannical, and ignorant; bad scholars and worse Masters. I wish these my opinions and resolutions to be well known to any friend of mine who may have thoughts of bringing me into Parliament; that hereafter the language of some people in a dressing Room may not give them uneasiness about my Conduct, as in former times, when I represented other people, it has done; and God forbid that any man, or set of men, who take me, should not know, what they may think, the worst of me: For I must fairly say, that what many of them have called my passions, are my principles; and I shall act just as I have done, though perhaps more systematically, if God gives me Life, and they furnish me with the situation to act in. If this be disagreeable, with ten thousand thanks, I give up all.

[8] Shameful an old man a soldier, shameful an old man's love; see Ovid, *Amores*, I, ix, 4.

I am just come from dinner with Alderman Smith;[9] the father of the City; much I believe my friend—as far as age and indolence will permit him to be so. He and others begin to be sensible of the effects of that indolence, and I beleive will exert themselves heartily to put things upon a better footing. It is odd to say it, but I do not think there has been a moment, no not the moment of triumph at the last Election, in which I stood better with every respectable person in this City, from which I am going to be driven. I am sure the Troops will rally again; I am sure they will be stronger than ever; and I am equally sure, that the party here will be made infinitely more systematick than it has been formerly, or than it is in other places. If it cannot be purified from the gross matter, by which it is debased and renderd useless in other places, I think I shall take care, that it shall not exist in this place at all. In a word, I mean to bring it to act in concert with the rational and sober Whiggs, in a word with all of you, and to be entirely connected and of a piece with you. This I am persuaded may be done, and if it can, my Loss will be yours and the publick Gain.

I beg your Graces pardon for the Blotts in this Letter; the bad writing, hardly indeed legible, and the obscurity with which I have huddled many things together—But I have been so broken in upon at every page and almost every line that I wonder how I have got through it so well.

I have not time to write to Lord Rockingham at any length—I therefore beg the favour of your Grace to give him too the Trouble of reading this Stuff. I am with the sincerest respect and affection

My dear lord
your Graces
most obedient and humble Servant

Bristol Septr 3. 1780   EDM BURKE

[9] Alderman Morgan Smith (d. 1781), the senior member of the Corporation.

CHAPTER FIVE

AMERICA

BURKE AS AGENT AND REPRESENTATIVE

IN HIS LETTERS on America, we see Burke both as agent of the colony of New York and as representative for Bristol. He was made agent for New York in 1771 (letter to John Cruger), and he was elected from Bristol in 1774. Burke's first speech in the House of Commons in 1766 (for which we have an actor's applause in the letter from David Garrick) was on America, and America remained his primary concern until the outbreak of war in 1775 imposed silence on the subject.

In his *Speech to the Electors of Bristol at the Conclusion of the Poll* (1774), Burke made a point of the difference between agent and representative which can be seen in his letters. As agent, he acknowledged himself to be in total dependence to the people of the colony as distinguished from its "executive government" (letter to James De Lancey). As representative in Parliament, he was willing to assert that "All direction of publick humour and opinion must originate in a few" (letter to Rockingham, 1775). In other letters we have accounts of the Stamp Act crisis in 1765, the reaction to the passage of the Boston Port Bill in 1774, and to the Battle of Lexington and Concord in 1775; and we have Burke's forecast of the Battle of Bunker Hill, also in 1775. The last letter, to William Windham, written in 1797, the year Burke died, touches on a fundamental question in his life which Burke never treated thematically—the question whether the American and French Revolutions were so similar that it was inconsistent for Burke to consent to the former and oppose the latter.

To CHARLES O'HARA—31 *December* [1765]

Corr. (1958), I, 228–30

A letter to Burke's old friend in Ireland. Burke had just been elected to the House of Commons, and the House had been considering the riots and disturbances in America consequent to the Stamp Act.

My dear Sir,   I do not know how to thank you sufficiently for having rememberd me so often and so kindly in the midst of that hurry of Business you must have been in. It is but a poor return I can make you. I am myself as much occupied as you have been; and, I am sure, I am far less able to fill up the vacant moments, by furnishing entertaining accounts of any publick *occurrences* (if I may venture to use a word which our great Statesman G. Grenville has proscribed).[1] At present there is a sort of Cessation from the exterior operations of Politicks; and it will continue during the recess. However, in this narrow but dreadful interval, preparations are making on all hands. There are wonderful materials of combustion at hand; and surely, since this monarchy, a more material point never came under the consideration of Parliament. I mean the Conduct which is to be held with regard to America. And there are difficulties in plenty interior and exterior. Administration has not yet conclusively (I imagine) fixed upon their plan in this respect, as every days information from abroad may necessitate some alteration. In the mean time the Grenvillians rejoice and Triumph as if they had obtained some capital advantage, by the confusions into which they have thrown every thing. With regard to myself and my private opinion, my resolution is taken; and if the Point is put in any way in which the affirmative or Negative become the Test of my Voting I shall certainly vote according to them; though some of my very best friends should determine to the Contrary. You will think me ridiculous; but I do not look upon this as a common question. One thing however is fortunate to you, though without any merits of your own, that the Liberties, (or what shadows of Liberty there are) of Ireland have been saved in America. . . .

[1] Will Burke wrote his friend Macartney 21 December 1765 that Grenville, protesting against the discreet language in which the Speech from the Throne treated events in North America, 'harrangued upon the impropriety of terming the disturbances in N.A. *occurences;* he called them a rebellion. . . '.

To CHARLES O'HARA—18 [*January* 1766]

Corr. (1958), I, 231–33

Burke's modest account of his first speech in Parliament.

My dear Sir,

Last Tuesday we drew up the Curtain,[1] and discoverd the Great Commoner, attended by his Train, *solus*. From better correspondents you have heard of that most extraordinary day; of Mr Pitts disclaimer of the Late ministry and all their Works; his good opinion and his doubts of the present; and his strong reiterated declaration of our having no right to impose an interior Tax on the Colonies. This proposition and some others similar to it, brought on an altercation of several hours between him and G. Grenville. They were both heated to a great degree; Pitt as much, as contempt, very strongly marked, would suffer him. The ministers Messrs Conway and Dowdeswell did just what was necessary and no more; leaving Pitt to do Grenvilles Business. Conway went perhaps too far in his compliments to Pitt; and his declared resolution to yield his place to him. The day ended a little awkwardly; for the address being carried without any Dissent, The friends of Government went off, and Rigby finding a thin house carried a motion for printing the Papers. This had been the same day refused by the Lords on a motion of the D. of Bedford. You see this was getting into a scrape, and the worse scrape, as the Lives of some in America would be endangerd by such a publication. Yesterday it was set to rights; in the intervening time between that and the first day it had been carried to refer the dangerous Papers to the Speaker, that he might cut out the parts which might expose those who communicated intelligence to Government, to the resentment of the populace in America; Yesterday the Speaker was of opinion that no precaution of that kind would be sufficient for the purpose. And Mr Dowdeswell moved, on the Speakers report, to discharge the order for printing. This brought on a Debate which lasted till near ten. Mr Conway never shone so much; He was attacked on every side and supported himself with so much spirit, energy, Modesty, and good humour, as drew more and sincerer applause from the house than ever I knew a man to receive. He made an apology on being attacked for

---

[1] Parliament met 14 January, and Conway presented to the House papers on the American disturbances.

adulation to Pitt. He made his apology with so much dignity as not only fully to bring back what he might have lost by his first declarations on the Subject, but to get him new Credit. Rigby said some Good things; that he had heard of a Doctor malgré lui, but never before of a Minister malgré lui, and that on such compulsion he never could expect a good Physician or a good statesman. That day I took my first trial. Sr Wm Meredith desired me to present the Manchester Petition;[2] I know not what struck me, but I took a sudden resolution to say something about it, though I had got it but that moment, and had scarcely time to read it, short as it was; I did say something; what it was, I know not upon my honour; I felt like a man drunk. Lord Frederick Campbell[3] made me some answer to which I replied; ill enough too; but I was by this time pretty well on my Legs; Mr Grenville answerd; and I was now heated, and could have been much better, but Sr G. Saville[4] caught the Speakers eye before me; and it was then thought better not to proceed further, as it would keep off the business of the day. However I had now grown a little stouter, though still giddy, and affected with a swimming in my head; So that I ventured up again on the motion, and spoke some minutes, poorly, but not quite so ill as before. All I hoped was to plunge in, and get off the first horrors; I had no hopes of making a figure. I find my Voice not strong enough to fill the house; but I shall endeavour to raise it as high as it will bear. This is prattling like a Child to a father. Whenever I enter into these minutiae about myself I beg you throw my Letter into the fire. All here are yours. The last bell rings. We are in an odd posture. Adieu.

18.

O'Hara did not agree to the suppression of all personal *minutiae*. They are a part of friendship, he told Burke in his letter of 25 January, and 'that severity of restraint which may guard against them, is no more to my taste, than platonic love was formerly'. He both encouraged and warned Burke about his speaking: 'your voice will form from practice, your manner will improve, the great point you are to attend to is temper. Was it not Jephson that usd to tell you that in some circumstances you had an air of anger. Get rid of this air'.

[2] A petition from the merchants of Manchester complaining of the decay in the trade to the North American colonies, owing to the restrictions laid on it by government. It was one of ten similar petitions presented the same day.

[3] (1729–1816).

[4] Sir George Savile, 8th Baronet (1726–84), M.P. for Yorkshire and a leading member of the Rockingham party.

DAVID GARRICK *to* EDMUND BURKE—18 *January* [1766]

Corr. (1958), I, 233

A note of congratulation from the famous actor.

Janu the 18
Saturday

My dear Sir

In the first place—I am very sorry that I can't dine with you—I had forgot an Engagement of a fortnight's standing that I had made, and was reminded of it by a Card at my return last Night from the house of Commons—where, I had the honour and Pleasure of Enjoying Your Virgin Eloquence! I most sincerely congratulate you upon it— I am very Nice and very hard to please and where my friends are concern'd most Hyper-critical—I pronounce that you will answer the warmest Wishes of your Warmest friend—I was much pleas'd—I have much to say, which you will politely listen to, and forget the next moment, however you shall have it— . . .

To JOHN CRUGER—9 *June* 1771

Corr. (1958), II, 213

Burke's first formal letter as Agent to the General Assembly of the Province of New York, to which he had been unanimously elected on 21 December 1770.

Sir

I am very happy in the unanimous Testimony of the Gentlemen of the Assembly of New York in favour of my Endeavours to serve the publick. Such a Testimony from so large and respectable a part of my fellow Subjects perswades me that I have not been mistaken in the Line of Conduct I have pursued; and it will be a strong motive with me for persevering in the same Course. How long it may be consistent with the Duties of my situation to continue my little Offices to the Province I know not. But the Obligation you have conferred upon me by this mark of your good opinion is such, that I think myself intitled to claim the honour of some relation to New York; and that you will therefore have a right to call upon me for all the Attention I can shew, in whatever situation I may be. I have the honour to be with great regard and Esteem

Sir

your most Obedient and most humble Servant

E. B.

Beaconsfield June 9th 1771—

To JAMES DE LANCEY—4 *December* 1771

Corr. (1958), II, 289–91

In the letter to which this is a reply De Lancey had evidently drawn Burke's attention to the pressure which the Secretary of State and the Board of Trade were exerting upon the Northern Colonies to bring their method of electing Agents into line with that employed by the West Indian and Southern Colonies. As early as 8 April 1769— before Burke became Agent—the New York Assembly had refused to consider such a change. The matter had been reopened in 1771 over the credentials of Benjamin Franklin as Agent for Massachusetts. Burke, Franklin and the Assemblies they represented had similar views on the issue.

To
James Delancy Esqr at New York—

Dear Sir

I have not delayed my Answer to your last Letter, from any want of a due Sense of its Importance. The appointment of their Agent's cannot be a matter of Indifference to the Colonies. But Lord Hillsborough continued untill very lately in Ireland. Mr Pownal for sometime sayed nothing to me upon the Subject. It was no business of mine to be forward in entering upon so delicate a topic. I was sure if the Ideas you mentioned to me were seriously entertained by Ministry I shoud hear of it in a reasonable time.

At length Mr Pownal called upon me, and opened the matter from himself. He speaks of it rather as a scheme under deliberation than as a point actually determined. He is of opinion, that the Governour and Council ought to have their part in the nomination of the Provincial Agents or at least a negative on the choice of the Representative Assembly. He thinks that as the Agent is called, not the Agent of that Assembly but of the Province, the consent of all the parts which compose the Legislature is proper, in order to invest him with the

Compleat Authority of the Body he is intended to represent. He thinks, such a joint concurrence in the nomination wou'd be very serviceable to the Colony, as the Agent appearing in the fullness of his Character, wou'd act with much greater weight in all his transactions with Office. Lastly, He rests upon the Equity of admitting the Consent of the Governour and Council to the appointment of the Agent, as their concurrence is necessary to charge the province with his Salary and expences. This is the Substance of which Mr Pownal urged in favour of the proposed Alteration.

As He seemed desirous of hearing my Sentiments, I gave them to him very freely. I told him, that I looked upon the Agent for a Colony under whatever name he might be described, as in Effect *Agent for the House of Representative only;* that is a person appointed by them to take care of the interests of *the people* of the province as *contradistinguishd from its executive Government.*

In this Light, his business was always seperate from that of the Governours, and might in many Cases be opposite to his Interests and his Wishes. The Agent might even be employed to make complaints against him for Maladministration in his Office. I thought it ridiculous to expect that such a charge shoud be pushed with vigour and Effect by a person who was, in substance the representative rather of the Governour complained of, than the Colony complaining. By the new plan, the Governour (by his own vote and that of the Council) would have two parts, to one of the people, in this nomination. If his Conduct became never so unacceptable to the province, it would be totally out of their power to remove the Agent. Perhaps the very circumstance of his being unpleasing to them might become a reason for refusing the Governours consent to an Act for displacing him.

I have always been and shall ever be earnest to preserve the Constitutional dependence of the Colonies on the Crown, and Legislature of this Kingdom, and a friend to every just and honourable measure that tends to secure it. But this I consider in Effect, as a destruction of one of the most necessary Mediums of Communication between the Colonies and the parent Country. The provinces ought in my opinion to have *a direct* intercourse with Ministry and Parliament here, by some person who might be truely confidential with them who appoint him. Who might be entrusted with the strength and weakness of their Cause in all controverted points; and who might represent their own Sentiments in their own way. The intervention of the Governours in the Nomination would totally frustrate their purposes. If the Colony differed from the Governour, one can conceive nothing more improper than an Agents confidential between two contending and perhaps very hostile parties.

I confess I could not see what the Governour had to do with this Appointment. No part of his Correspondence I apprehend passes through the provincial Agent. With regard to the Arguments drawn from the Concurrence of the Governour and Council in granting the Supply for the Salary and Charges of the Agent, I thought it one of those Arguments, which by proving too much proves nothing at all. For if concurrence in the Grant of Salary implies the propriety of a similar concurrence in the Appointment of the Officer, to whom Salary is paid, then the Assembly, who have a part and the most essential part, in the granting a Salary to the Governour, ought to have a part in the nomination. But as this is against all usage, and against all reason, in most of the Colonies, the Argument is full as little valid in the Case of Agent as of Governour. If your Agent does not depend totally on the Colony for his Election, and for his continuance, He must be something more than useless to you. He will be to all intents and purposes an Officer of the Crown. However this business rests upon your own Judgment. Only I must, if this New plan shoud take place consider it as so much a ministerial Affair, that in my present situation I coud not honourably think of continuing to take care of the Charge of your business. . . .

To the COMMITTEE OF CORRESPONDENCE OF THE GENERAL ASSEMBLY OF NEW YORK—6 April 1774

Corr. (1958), II, 526–29

In this letter Burke gives an account of the first of the three Acts passed in an attempt to reduce Boston to order. This was the so-called Boston Port Act, removing the Customs Officers from the Port and prohibiting the landing of merchandise there. Burke's account of events is lucid and balanced, as he claims 'without heightenings or without palliation', and he seeks to make clear his own beliefs and those of his political friends as to the basis on which these relations should rest. No letter to Burke from New York on the subject of the disorders caused by the attempts to export teas to the Colonies survives earlier than one of 4 May from John Cruger who informed him: 'The Ship with the East Companys tea on board arrived at Sandy hook about two weeks ago. She did not come up higher but there Refitted and sailed again for England. The ship London Capn Chambers (one of our ships in that trade) arrived here from London the Captain of which had Imprudently taken on board and brought in here Eighteen boxes of fine Tea, Notice of which was sent from Philadelphia. On his arrival the Captain was Charged therewith, the proof being Very Plain he did not Deny it. A number of people went on board the Ship and many more

attending it was taken upon deck the boxes opened the tea trown into the River, thus
are the minds of the people Agitated against the Importation of Tea Subject to a duty.'

To The Gentlemen of the Committee &c   New York

April 6th 1774

Gentlemen

Since I had the honour of writing to you last Nothing new has occurred
relative to the publick affairs of the Province. The Lords of Trade
have been almost wholly occupied on the Papers and Letters received
from the Colonies, and on the measures which have been proposed to
Parliament in consequence of the Materials laid before the two houses.[1]

The Subject was ample and serious. Lord Norths Speech,[2] on the
first opening of the matter, turned on the absolute necessity of doing
something immediate and effectual. For things were come to such a
pass, by the evil disposition, the turbulent Conduct, and the dark
designs of many in the Colonies, that the deliberation was no longer
upon the degrees of Freedom or restraint in which they were to be
held, but whether they should be totally seperated from their connexion with, and dependence on the parent Country of Great Britain—
And that according to the Part which Gentlemen should take for or
against the measure to be proposed, a Judgement would be formed
of their disposition to or against that connexion and dependence. This
Topic was strongly insisted upon, and stated in the same invidious
light by other persons in Office, and in general by most of those who
declared themselves in favour of the Ministerial proceedings. On the
first day appointed for the Consideration of the papers Lord North
spoke of the indispensible Necessity of vigorous measures; but in a
tone more languid and moderate than is usual in the expression of
such Ideas. The outline, of what has since appeared, though faintly
and imperfectly, was chalked out from the beginning.

The air of Languor however wore off in the progress of the Business.
The Ministry seem to be better arranged than they appeared to be at
first; Lord North has assumed a Style of more authority, and more
decision; and the Bill laying Boston under a commercial interdict
during the Kings Pleasure has been proposed, and supported quite
through, with expressions of the utmost firmness and resolution. The
House was not as much animated as I have seen it upon other occasions

---

[1] In order to deal with the crisis in relations with the North Americans caused by the Colonists'
resistance to the landing of the East India Company's tea a message from the Crown was sent
to both Houses on 7 March, with voluminous illustrative documents.

[2] 14 March.

of a similar Nature; It did however very readily concur in the proposition that was moved; not so much from any predilection, that I could observe, to the particular measure which was adopted; as from a general Notion, that *some Act* of Power was become necessary; and that the hands of Government ought to be strengthened, by affording an entire Credit to the opinions of Ministry in the *Choice of that Act;* as the best pledge of the future support the House was to give in the effectual Execution of any coercive proceeding.

The popular current, both within doors and without, at present sets strongly against America. There were not indeed wanting some few persons in the House of Commons, who disapproved of the Bill, and who expressed their disapprobation in the strongest and most explicit Terms. But their Arguments upon this point made so little impression that it was not thought advisable to divide the House. Those who spoke in opposition, did it, more for the acquittal of their own honour, and discharge of their own consciences, by delivering their free sentiments on so critical an occasion than from any sort of hope they entertained of bringing any considerable Number to their opinion; or even of keeping in that opinion several of those who had formerly concurred in the same general Line of Policy with regard to the Colonies.

The Gentlemen who spoke against the Bill rejected that State of the question by which it was invidiously presumed, that those who opposed the Bill were for giving up the constitutional superiority of this Country.[3] That imputation will always be cast off with disdain by every good Englishman. Every good Englishman, as such, must be a friend to the Colonies; and all the true friends to the Colonies, the only *true* friends they have had, or ever can have in England have laid and will lay down the proper subordination of America, as a fundamental, incontrovertible Maxim, in the Government of this Empire. This Idea, to which they tenaciously adhere in the full extent of the proposition, they are of opinion is nothing derogatory to the real essential Rights of mankind which tend to their peace and prosperity, and without the Enjoyment of which no honest Man can wish the dependance of one Country upon another. Very unfortunately, in my poor thoughts, the advice of that sort of Temperate Men has been little attended to, on this side of the Atlantick and rather less on the other. This has brought on misunderstandings and heats, where nothing should exist but that harmony and good correspondence which

---

[3] For example, William Dowdeswell (*Parliamentary History*, XVII, 1179–81). Burke himself spoke on the third reading (*ibid.* XVII, 1182–5).

ought naturally to arise from the entire agreement of their real interests. . . .

The MARQUESS OF ROCKINGHAM *to* EDMUND BURKE—[22 *March* 1775]

Corr. (1958), III, 139

On 22 March 1775 Burke delivered his famous Speech on Conciliation with America. Rockingham began a letter of congratulation:

Dear Burke

I left the House of Commons after the conclusion of your speech— I just staid long enough to see Jenkinson get up to answer you, and I went out with a croud, who seemed to shew by their conduct that they had no expectation of an adequate reply, at least not from that gentleman.

What may have passed since, I dont know, I shall have hopes of hearing something till near one o'clock, and if not, I must content myself with going quietly to bed, and shall be very very anxious to hear a full account tomorrow morning.

I never felt a more complete satisfaction on hearing any speech, than I did on hearing yours this day, the matter and the manner were equally perfect, and in spite of envy and malice and in spite of all politicks, I will venture to prognosticate that there will be but one opinion, in regard to the wonderful ability of the performance.

I confess I carry my sanguine

To CHARLES O'HARA—[*circa* 28 *May* 1775]

Corr. (1958), III, 160–62

Burke gives his friend an account of the Battle of Lexington and Concord.

My dear friend,

. . . All our prospects of American reconciliation are, I fear, over. Blood has been shed. The sluice is opend—Where, when, or how it will be stopped God only knows. A detachment was sent to destroy a Magazine which the Americans were forming at a Village called Concord. It proceeded with secrecy and dispatch. But the Americans were alert and conveyd their Stores, all to four pieces of Cannon and some flour, to a more distant Town called Worcester. The Country was not embodied; but they rose, without concert, order, or officers, and fell upon the Troops on their return. Lord Percy[1] was sent out to sustain the first Party, which without his Assistance, would, most certainly, never have returned. He too would have been defeated; if it had not been for two pieces of Artillery, which he had the precaution to take, and which were well served. The Troops behavd well; and retreated thirteen Miles in pretty good order, it was a fatiguing day for them. Their loss did not exceed 70 killed; and probably about the same Number wounded. The Provincials harrassed them the whole way. Their loss was thirty nine. During the time of this strange irregular engagement, which continued almost the whole day of the 19th of April, expresses were sent to every part of America with astonishing rapidity—and the whole Northern part of the Continent was immediately under arms. So that by the 26th of the same Month upwards of twenty thousand men were assembled in the Towns of Cambridge, Roxbury, Watertown, and other Villages in the Neighbourhood of Boston; who have blocked up all the Avenues to that place. There is one principal Camp of 2000 Men; there are three or four smaller; The rest are cantond in all the adjacent Country, wherever they can find any sort of roof to cover them. My informant,[2] who is a sober, intelligent man, was at the Headquarters of their army on the twenty seventh. He says, that they are at least as numerous, as I have told you they were; They were then in a good deal of disorder; but that their Officers were very active in making proper dispositions. A Mr Pribble[3] is the Commander in chief. They have much confidence in him, as he has served a good deal, and with reputation. But he was very ill when my man came away; and a Mr Ward[4] commanded in his Place. Ward has great popularity, and is a steady, sensible, and temperate man; but without much military experience; However they have under him several Officers of competent Skill; and Col. Putnam[5] from Connecticut, who has a considerable Military Character, joined them before the 27th. He marched from Connecticut at the head of about 6000 men, with great diligence, on the first news of hostilities; but he told my informant that he had left them at about 35 Miles distance, fearing that he could not obtain subsistence for them, if he

---

[1] 1742–1817, eldest son of the Duke of Northumberland.
[2] Not identified.
[3] Jedediah Preble (1707–84).
[4] Artemas Ward (1727–1800).
[5] Israel Putnam (1718–90).

marched them further. But he proceeded himself to the head quarters of the Massachusets Army, in order to assist with his advice. He was much disposed to an immediate attack on Genl Gage,[6] but Ward and the rest were unwilling to expose the people of Boston to the Carnage which might ensue; and Gage, looking on that People as hostages in his hands, will not suffer one of them to go out. In this strange situation things were on the 29th of last Month. The news of this Breach raised the people wherever it arrived. At New York (as I am told in Letters from Bristol) the populace broke open the provincial Stores and began to arm; They likewise unloaded two Vessels going with Provisions to the Kings Troops. Every thing was every where in a confusion not to be described. The Ministers have had as yet no account.[7] It is odd, that they should have their advices sent by a Merchant-man, and a bad sailor; for by Bristol Correspondents Captain passed by their advice Schooner. Adieu my dear friend we do most passionately long to see you. Remember us to Ridge and Charles.

All the Inhabitants of the seaport Towns in the Massachusets are leaving their habitations and retiring into the Country. The populous Town of Marblehead was almost a desert.

To RICHARD CHAMPION—28 *June* [1775]

Corr. (1958), III, 175–76

Richard Champion (1743–91), a Quaker, was a Bristol merchant in the American trade and also a china manufacturer. In 1774 he had invited Burke to stand for election at Bristol. Thereafter he became a fast friend and a frequent correspondent.

My dear Sir,

I am sincerely thankful to you for your Care in supplying us with the earliest intelligence at this important Crisis. I have by me your Letter of the twenty seventh which came to me by the same conveyance which brought two others—which I take it for granted were all that you sent.[1] I believe it is a very certain and very expeditious method of sending news.[2] Things seem to be proceeding in America as might be expected. Causes will produce their Effects. Ministry have thrown

[6] General Thomas Gage (1721–87).
[7] Gage's official despatch reached Lord Dartmouth on 10 June.

[1] Champion had written on 20 June to Burke and to Rockingham, reporting the latest news from America, especially the warlike spirit in Philadelphia and New York.
[2] Burke may be referring to the new 'Bristol Diligence, or Flying Post Chaise' advertised in April 1775 as making the journey to London in sixteen hours.

out of their hands, one by one, every advantage which they have had in this Contest. They seem to have still one Left, in the apparent want of System shewn by the Congress, in suffering the Kings Forces to possess themselves of New York, infinitely the most important Post in America. I read this resolution with some Surprise[3]—They seem to have forgot that they are in Rebellion, and have done so much as to necessitate the doing a great deal more. Their Idea of a defensive war is quite ridiculous. Indeed, if this Step of theirs manifests a design of pacific Measures, it is very happy, and greatly to be applauded. But if it be the Effect only of a scrupulous timidity in the pursuit of Violence, it is triffling and contradictory, and can hardly fail of bringing with it its own Punishment. Whatever be done, God send us Peace. I wish that this Country had been wise enough to have laid the Ground for it by accepting my Resolutions. Apropos of them—Have my friends got my Speech[4] in Bristol and has it been circulated there. If it has what do the moderate people say to it?

Since you are gratified by hearing of us, I have the pleasure of assuring you that we are in perfect health, I bless God, all and some. I rejoice sincerely that your family is so. . . .

My dear Sir
most faithfully yours

June 28. Tuesday.   EDM BURKE

To RICHARD CHAMPION—19 *July* 1775

Corr. (1958), III, 179–80

Champion was by now sending regular information, as it arrived at Bristol, to several leaders of the Opposition. On 15 July he had written to Rockingham (probably also to Burke, although this letter is missing) enclosing copies of 'the Proclamation, which came this morning by a Vessel arrived a few hours ago from Boston'. This proclamation issued on 12 June by General Gage with the authorization of Lord Dartmouth, offered pardon to all those who should lay down their arms and return to peaceable duties, excepting only John Hancock (1737–93) and Samuel Adams (1722–1803). Champion commented on the exclusion of Hancock from this pardon, and reported that the troops being shipped to New York were now ordered to join those at Boston and to march out with them. If this happened, Champion believed that a bloody action must be expected.

[3] On 15 May the New Yorkers asked Congress how they should conduct themselves towards British troops in the city; and a resolution was passed that only defensive action should be taken—that is, troops could remain peaceably in barracks, but should be resisted if they attempted to erect fortifications and communications or engage in hostile acts.

[4] Burke's *Speech on Conciliation with America* had been published May 22, 1775.

My dear Champion,

I thank you for your kind and frequent remembrances. Things are
come to a Crisis in America. I confess to you that I cannot avoid a
very great degree of uneasiness in this most anxious interval. An
Engagement must instantly follow this Proclamation of Gages.[1] If he
should succeed, and beat the raw American Troops, which from his
superiority in discipline and artillery, as well as his present considerable Numbers, I think he probably will; then we shall be so elevated
here as to throw all moderation behind us, and plunge ourselves into
a War which cannot be ended by many such Battles, though they
should all terminate in so many Victories. If we are beat, America is
gone irrecoverably. I am astonishd at the exception of Handcock and
Adams when joind with a declaration of a similar guilt in all who shall
correspond with them or give them even sustenance. The Congress
in included in this description. It is in this as well in many other
particulars very unaccountable. Things look gloomy. However they
have a more cheerful aspect to those who know them better—for I
am told by one who has lately seen Lord North, that he has never
seen him or any body else in higher Spirits.

I thank you heartily for your Turtle. If you can make any good use
of it at Bristol—pray do. If not you will send it to Maidenhead[2]—all
conveyances are uncertain—but Turtles and Men must run their risque.
My Brother is washing himself at Brighthelmstone.[3] All here salute
you and yours affectionately. Pray remember me to all friends as I
ought to be rememberd to them. When I see them at my Levee, with
Dr Tucker, I shall know how to compliment them better. There
is Wit at the End of the Pamphlet, and it made me laugh heartily.[4]
The rest did not alter any of my opinions. I am dear Champion

faithfully yours
EDM BURKE

Butlers Court   July 19. 1775.

---

[1] Burke's prediction of an immediate engagement was strikingly confirmed; and in fact the
first rumours of Bunker Hill had reached London from Ireland on 18 July.

[2] Maidenhead would be the nearest stopping point for Beaconsfield on the Bristol-London
route.

[3] Brighton was a favourite resort of Richard—for gambling as well as for bathing.

[4] At the end of his *Letter to Edmund Burke,* just published, Dean Josiah Tucker (1712–99)
had described an imaginary levee to be held by Burke when the North ministry had been turned
out. Most of the pamphlet was a criticism of Burke's Speech on Conciliation; and it also referred
to his 'Abuse and Scurrility' directed at Tucker in the earlier speech of 19 April 1774.

To CHARLES O'HARA—26 *July* 1775

Corr. (1958), III, 181–82

My dear friend,

I am caught in my Roothouse[1] by a shower of Rain; and here very luckily I find the instruments of writing; and they tell me, or something else tells me, that I cannot employ them better, than in acknowleging the receipt of your Letter and in pressing you to make good the most acceptable part of it. We really long inexpressibly to see you. We have amusements enough; real comforts and satisfactions very few. The sight of such a friend as you, though for no more than the short interval between this and the meeting of your Parliament[2] (possibly of ours too) would make our leisure a real repose; and would enable us to look Business in the face with a little more spirit, when the disagreeable and hopeless hour of Business arrives. You see we are actually engaged in a civil War; and with little, very little hopes of any peace; and in my poor opinion with full Cause to despair of any that shall restore the antient confidence and harmony of the parts of this Empire. For one I am sure I have labourd as much as any body to procure it; and upon the only Terms of honour and safety I know of, that is to give them our own constitution or what is most substantial in it. How could you imagine that I had in my thoughts any thing of the Theoretical seperation of a power of Taxing from Legislation.[3] I have no opinion about it. These things depend on conventions real or understood, upon practice, accident, the humour or Genius of those who Govern or are governd, and may be, as they are, modified to infinity. No bounds ever were set to the Parliamentary power over the Colonies; for how could that have been but by *special Convention.* No such convention ever has been; but the reason and nature of things, and the growth of the Colonies ought to have taught Parliament to have set bounds to the exercise of its own power. I never ask what Government may do in *Theory,* except *Theory* be the *Object;* When one talks of *Practice* they must act according to circumstances. If you think it worth your while to read that Speech over again you will find that principle to be the Key of it.

[1] According to Mrs Champion, writing two years later, Burke's roothouse was about a mile from the house, at the far end of a wood on the garden side.

[2] The Irish Parliament was to reassemble on 10 October.

[3] In his letter of 5, 18 June O'Hara, who had been reading Burke's Speech on Conciliation, wrote: 'You have sugested one idea to me . . . that taxation is not comprizd within the term Legislative supremacy'.

You will see by the Gazette, that there has been another, but a more regular, and far more bloody engagement. Two such Victories, as Mrs B. observes after Pyrrhus, would ruin Genl Gage. He has lost in killed and wounded, a thousand men; and got nothing in the world, but a security from some Batteries which those he calls rebells were erecting against him. It was only a successful sally of a beseigd Garrison. Pray Pray come to us. All here are yours and not less Charles's the younger.

E B.

July 26. 1775

To CHARLES O'HARA—[17] *August* 1775

Corr. (1958), III, 185–88

My dear friend,
. . . The Spirit of America is incredible. Who do you think the Mr Mifflin,[1] Aid de Camp to Washington, is?—A very grave and staunch Quaker, of large fortune and much consequence. What think you of that political Enthusiasm, which is able to overpower so much religious Fanaticism? Washington himself is a man of good Military experience, prudent and Cautious, and who yet stakes a fortune of about 5000 a year. God knows they are very inferiour in all human rescources. But a remote and difficult Country, and such a Spirit as now animates them, may do strange things. Our Victories can only complete our Ruin. I have much to say to you, on the part which Ireland has acted in this Business—but I have tired you, and it is late. Adieu my dear friend—God give you health and peace of mind, and the fortune long to survive these Calamities. All here most cordially salute the Charles's.

Thursday Augst. 20. 1775.

To the MARQUESS OF ROCKINGHAM—[22,] 23 *August* 1775

Corr. (1958), III, 189–94

My dear Lord,
    When I was last in Town I wrote a short Letter by Mr Thesiger. But I opend all I had in my thoughts so fully to Lord John Cavendish

---

[1] Thomas Mifflin (1744–1800).

who was then setting out for the North, that I do not know whether it be necessary to trouble your Lordship any further upon the unhappy subject of that Letter and conversation. However if I did not write something on that Subject, I should be incapable of writing at all. It has, I confess taken entire possession of my Mind.

We are at length actually involved in that War, which your Lordship to your infinite honour, has made so many efforts to keep at a distance. It has come upon us in a manner more disagreeable and unpromising than the most gloomy prognostick had ever foretold it. Your Lordships observation on the general Temper of the Nation at this Crisis is certainly just. If any indication is to be taken from external appearances, the King is entirely satisfied with the present State of his Government. His Spirits, at his Levees, at the play, everywhere, seem to be remarkably good. His Ministers too are perfectly at their Ease. Most of them are amusing themselves in the Country, while England is disfurnished of its forces in the face of armed Europe; and Gibraltar and Minorca are deliverd over to the Custody of Foreigners.[1] They are at their Ease relative to the only point which could give them anxiety. They are assured of their places. I made no particular reflexions on Jenkinsons getting into Port.[2] I had reason to know the exact Value of the places which were exchanged. They differ but a triffle in emollument; and when a secure Tenure may be had without a material diminution of income, a man of less practice in that way than Jenkinson, would hardly refuse to accommodate the arrangements of a particular friend, by such an option as he has made. Besides he is now ready for another place during pleasure; which in due time may furnish the matter of another exchange; and so on ad infinitum.

As to the good people of England, they seem to partake every day more and more of the Character of that administration which they have been induced to tolerate. I am satisfied, that within a few years there has been a great Change in the National Character. We seem no longer that eager, inquisitive, jealous, fiery people, which we have been formerly, and which we have been, a very short time ago. The people look back without pleasure or indignation, and forward without hope or fear. No man commends the measures which have been pursued, or expects any good from those which are in preparation; But it is a cold Languid opinion; like what men discover in affairs that do not concern them. It excites to no passion; It prompts to no Action.

[1] The Hanoverian troops.
[2] A shift of offices by Charles Jenkinson (1729–1808), one of the "King's friends."

In all this State of things, I find my observation and intelligence perfectly agrees with your Lordships; In one point indeed I have the misfortune to differ. I do not think that Weeks, or even Months, or years, will bring the Monarch, the Ministers, or the people, to feeling. To bring the people to a feeling, such a feeling I mean, as tends to amendment or alteration of System, there must be plan and management. All direction of publick humour and opinion must originate in a few. Perhaps a great deal of that humour and opinion themselves must be owing to such direction. Events supply materials. Times furnish dispositions; but Conduct alone can bring them to bear to any useful purpose. I never yet knew an instance of any general Temper in the Nation, that might not have been tolerably well traced to some particular persons. If things are left to themselves, It is my clear opinion, that a nation may slide down fair and softly from the highest point of Grandeur and prosperity to the lowest state of imbecillity and meanness, without any ones marking a particular period in this declension; without asking a question about it; or in the least speculating on any of the innumerable acts which have stolen in this silent and insensible revolution. Every event so prepares the Subsequent, that when it arrives, it produces no surprise, nor any extraordinary alarm. I am certain, that if pains, great and immediate pains, are not taken to prevent it such must be the fate of this Country. We look to the Merchants in vain. They are gone from us, and from themselves. They consider America as lost, and they look to administration for an indemnity. Hopes are accordingly held out to them, that some equivalent for their Debts will be provided. In the mean time the leading men among them are kept full fed with Contracts, remittances, and Jobbs of all descriptions; and they are indefatigable in their endeavours to keep the others quiet with the prospect of their share in those emolluments, of which they see their advisers already so amply in possession. They all, or the greater Number of them, begin to snuff the cadaverous Haut Gout of a Lucrative War. War indeed is become a sort of substitute for Commerce. The freighting Business never was so lively on account of the prodigious taking up for Transport service. Great orders for Provisions and Stores of all Kinds. New cloathing for the Troops, and the intended six thousand Canadians,[3] puts life into the Woollen Manufacture; and the Number of men of War orderd to be equipped, has given a pretence for such a quantity of Nails and other Iron work as to keep the midland parts tolerably quiet. All this

[3] In July, Dartmouth had asked Carleton to raise six thousand troops in Canada. He could not secure three hundred.

with the incredible encrease of the Northern Market since the peace
between Russia and the Port,[4] keeps up the Spirits of the Mercantile
World and induces them to consider the American War not so much
as their Calamity as their rescource in an inevitable distress. This is
the State of most—not of *all* the Merchants.

All this however would not be of so much consequence. The great
Evil and danger will be the full and decided engagement of Parliament
in this War. Then we shall be thoroughly dipped; and there will be
no way of getting out, but by disgracing England or enslaving America.
In that State Ministry has a lease of power as long as the War continues.
The hinge between War and peace is indeed a dangerous Juncture to
Ministers. But a determined State of one or the Other is a pretty safe
position. When their Cause however absurdly, is made the Cause of
the Nation, the popular Cry will be with them. The Style will be that
their hands must be strengthend by an unreserved Confidence. When
that Cry is once raised, and raised it infallibly will be, if not prevented,
the puny Voice of reason will not be heard. As sure as we have now
an Existence, if the meeting of Parliament should catch your Lordship
and your friends in an unprepared State, nothing but disgrace and
ruin can attend the Cause you are at the head of. Parliament will
plunge over head and Ears. They will Vote the war with every supply
of domestick and foreign force. They will pass an act of attainder.
They will lay their hand upon the press. The Ministers will even
procure addresses from those very Merchants who last Session harrassed them with Petitions. And then what is left for us, but to spin
out of our own Bowels, under the frowns of the Court and the hisses
of the people, the little, slender, thread of a peevish and captious
opposition, unworthy of our Cause and ourselves, and without Credit,
concurrence, or popularity in the Nation? I hope I am as little awed
out of my senses by the fear of Vulgar opinion as most of my acquaintance. I think, on a fair occasion, I could look it in the face. But
speaking of the prudential consideration, we know that all opposition
is absolutely crippled, if it can obtain no kind of support without
Doors. If this should be found impracticable I must revert to my old
opinion, that much the most effectual, and much the most honourable
Course is, without the obligation of a formal Secession, to absent
ourselves from Parliament. My experience is worth Nothing, if it has
not made it as clear to me as the Sun, that in affairs, like these, a

---

[4] Richard Champion, writing to Messrs Willing Morris and Co. on 26 August 1775, referred
to the 'amazing Trade carried on with Poland and Russia' as helping greatly to offset the stoppage
in the American trade.

feeble opposition is the greatest Service which can be done to Ministry; and surely if there be a state of decided disgrace, it is to add to the power of your Enemies, by every step you take to distress them.

I am confident, that your Lordship considers my importunity with your usual goodness. You will not attribute my earnestness to any improper Cause. I shall therefore make no apology for urging again and again how necessary it is for your Lordship and your great friends, most seriously to take under immediate deliberation, what you are to do in this Crisis. Nothing like it has happend in your political Life. I protest to God, I think that your reputation, your Duty, and the Duty and honour of all who profess your sentiments, from the highest to the Lowest of us, demand at this time one honest, hearty effort, in order to avert the heavy calamities that are impending, to keep our hands from blood, and if possible to keep the poor, giddy, thoughtless people of our Country from plunging headlong into this impious War. If the attempt is necessary it is honourable. You will at least have the comfort that nothing has been left undone on your part to prevent the worst mischief that can befal the publick. Then and not before you may shake the dust from your feet and leave the people and their leaders to their own conduct and fortune.

I see indeed many, many difficulties in the way. But we have known as great or greater give way to a regular series of judicious and active exertions. This is no time for taking publick Business in its Course and order, and only as a part in the Scheme of Life, which comes and goes at its proper periods and is mixed in with the other occupations and amusements. It calls for the whole of the best of us; and every thing Else however just or even laudable at another time ought to give way to this great, urgent, instant concern. Indeed, my Dear Lord, you are called upon in a very peculiar manner. America is yours. You have saved it once; and you may very possibly save it again. The people of that Country are worth preserving, and preserving if possible to England.

I believe your Lordship remembers, that last year, or the year before, I am not certain which, you fixed your Quarters for a while in London, and sent circular Letters to your friends, who were concerned in the Business on which you came to Town. It was on occasion of the Irish Absentee Tax.[5] Your friends met, and the attempt was defeated. It may be worth your Lordships consideration, whether you ought not as soon as possible to draw your principal friends together.

[5] In November 1773.

It may be there examined whether a larger meeting might not be expedient, to see whether some plan could not be thought of for doing something in the Counties and Towns. The October meeting at Newmarket will be too late in the year, and then the Business of the meeting would take up too much time from the other.

It might be objected to doing any thing is this immature condition of the publick temper, that the Interest of your Lordships friends might suffer in making an attempt which might be vigorously and rather generally opposed and counterworked. On ordinary occasions this might be a matter of very serious consideration. The risque ought to be proportiond to the Object. But this is no ordinary occasion. In the first place, I lay it down that the present State of opposition is so bad, that the worst judged and most untimely exertions, would only vary the mode of its utter dissolution. Such a state of things justifies any hazard. But supposing our Condition better what is an interest cultivated for, but its aptness for publick purposes? and for what publick purpose do Gentlemen wait, that will be more worthy of the use of all the Interest they have? I should certainly consider the affair as desperate, if your success in such an Effort depended on any thing like an unanimous concurrence in the Nation. But in Times of Trouble this is impossible. In such times it is not necessary. A Minority cannot make or carry on a War. But a Minority well composed and acting steadily may clog a War in such a manner, as to make it not very easy to proceed. When you once begin to shew yourselves, many will be animated to join you, who are now faint and uncertain. Your adversaries will rouse the spirit of your friends; and the very contest will excite that concern and Curiosity in the Nation, the want of which is now the worst part of the publick distemper. . . .

GENERAL JAMES OGLETHORPE *to* EDMUND BURKE— 30 *May* 1777

Corr. (1958), III, 343–44

General Oglethorpe (1696–1785), the founder of Georgia, was now over eighty. He was well known in the circle around Dr Johnson; but no letters to or from Burke other than the exchange printed here are known to exist.

Sir

It's as improper to commend a Man to his Face: as to abuse him behind his Back.

I did not dare tell you the Transports I felt in reading Your Letter to Bristol.[1] That particular Paragraph, which Exhorts the Uniting honest Men in defence of Virtue, regardless of Parties, and Prejudices,[2] is most Excellent, and I hope it will be followed. The Number of honest Men in England is Great, and their Influence much Greater, and I dare say they Rejoice to hear, that the Names you mention Join with you in saving the Kingdom, and us All from Destruction. Excuse me for troubling you and believe me to be,

Sir,

Your very Humble Servant
J OGLETHORPE

Lower Grovenor—
Street, 30th May
1777.

To GENERAL JAMES OGLETHORPE—2 *June* 1777

Corr. (1958), III, 344

Sir

I must consider the triffling hurt in my right hand, which has disabled it for some days, as a great misfortune. It prevented me from a more early acknowledgment of the most flattering mark of honour which I ever received. Such a Testimony to the *uprightness* of a mans Conduct, is second only to the approbation of his own Conscience; but such partiality to his *endeavours* is a satisfaction which he is not to draw from his own self Love. However from *you* I have some pretensions to favour. The weakest defender of the rights of the Colonies naturally claims some merit with one of the most distinguished of their founders. May you see the Colony, planned by your Sagacity, and planted by your care, become once more a free and flourishing Member of a free and flourishing Empire! But if this be too much to hope from a Country, which seems to have forgot the true source of its dignity and greatness, may you never have the misfortune of having led Englishmen into servitude and misery in a strange land! But better things, I trust, await your honourable Age, and their generous Youth.

---

[1] Burke's *A Letter to the Sheriffs of Bristol, on the Affairs of America*, published May 8, 1777.
[2] The third or fourth paragraph from the end. Both have this theme.

I am happy in having known and admired the last of the English Legislators in America; and am with great sincerity and Esteem always Sir your most obedient and much obliged humble Servant

Westminster June 2. 1777

From the planting of Georgia 45
Genl Oglethorpe.

To WILLIAM WINDHAM—12 *February* [1797]

Corr. (1958), IX, 240–41

Windham (1750–1810) was an M.P. and Burke's friend and disciple in his later years. Burke makes a brief reference to the problem of his consistency in consenting to the American Revolution and opposing the French.

My dear Friend

How can I find thanks any way proportioned to your unwearied kindness. I must be silent and restrain my busts of Gratitude as you desire me to restrain the busts of my Stomach: In the latter I will do what I can. I received your Letter when I was half the channel over in Mr Erskines Pamphlet, which would have landed me safely in a good harbour of the Republick one and indivisible and that too, as Mr Erskine says, upon my own principles.[1] The Pamphlet is better written and less full of Vanity than I expected to find it; but it is the old matter new hashed up—France would have been very good if she had not been provoked by the wickedness of Great Britain and other powers who are confederates not against her ambition but against her Liberty—That she was right in every point and at all times and with all Nations.—That the cure for all disorders consists in your making your Representation at home as like hers as possible—In making Peace with her by giving her all that you offer and all that she demands—That by excluding her from all the Continental powers she will become well disposed to you; and that you and she will become Guardians of liberty throughout the world. And as to our safety, it will be perfect provided we do nothing to provoke that irresistible power—and lastly, in which alone I think with him, that for making such a peace it is proper that Mr Fox and his Friends should come into power. I think

[1] Thomas Erskine (1750–1823). His pamphlet, *A View of the Causes and Consequences of the Present War with France*, referred to 'the immense magazine of military and political wisdom' to be found in Burke's writings, and argued that what he had said of the need for conciliating America in the 1770s might be applied to France in the 1790s.

this is a just Analysis of Mr Erskine's pamphlet which he says he has formed on my Opinions, not with relation to France, but with relation to America.

I am to observe once for all, that these Gentlemen put the case of France and America exactly upon a Par, and always have done so. I leave them to rejoice in that discovery and in my inconsistency, and the antidote they have found in one part of my writings against the poison that exists in another. You will observe, that *their* Alliance with France, and a change in this Constitution are things that always go hand in hand, and I think, consistently enough. The only point upon which he is strong, but on which I dont think he makes the most is Mr Pitts having refused to make proffers of Peace whilst our affairs were in a prosperous condition.[2] When He allows that any Peace at all can be made with the Regicide powers that is likely to be safe and lasting. But Mr Pitt unfortunately is in the condition of 'Paulo pur-gante'.[3] He cannot make peace and he will not make war 'Deus dabit his quoque finem'[4] which I beleive I will not live to see. I wish [I] may live to make my final protest against the proceedings of both factions. God bless you and reserve you to better times, for which bettering of the times your preservation may be very essential. I con-tinue just as I was, with the difference of a bad Night—Doctor Parry had just given me a purgative Medicine, and I assure you I implicitly obey his directions. I cannot yet walk or stand firm, but I can read upon my back and dictate as I do now, whilst all the great hunters are driving their Spears into a dead Boar. Once more God bless you and for the few moments I have to live, beleive me devotedly

Yours
EDM BURKE

Bath
   12th Feby.

[2] In 1793.
[3] In Matthew Prior's poem 'Paulo Purganti and his Wife'.
[4] To this, too, God will grant an end; see Virgil, *Aeneid*, I, 199.

CHAPTER SIX

REFORM AND REVOLUTION

BURKE DID NOT NEED the French Revolution to teach him the difference between due reform and destructive revolution. Already we have seen him deplore the extension of theory into practice in regard to America: "I never ask what government may do in *Theory*, except *Theory* be the object . . ." (letter to Charles O'Hara, July 26, 1775, Chapter 5 above). We see him now (Letter to Joseph Harford, 1780) declaiming against "*Visionary* Politicians" who indulge themselves with speculations and startle others with the idea of innovation.

Yet the French Revolution to which Burke was hostile in his first reaction (letter to the Earl of Charlemont, August 9, 1789), impelled him to develop this distinction with the amazing penetration, illustration, and pointed application of which he was capable. "You may have made a Revolution, but not a Reformation" (letter to Depont, 1789). Burke admits the possible justice of the violent overthrow of a positively vicious and abusive government, but he denies that the French monarchy was in that condition. The way to reform is not to change everything in a vain attempt at "Theoretick Perfection," but to keep the form while improving the substance (letter to Joseph Harford, 1780). The virtues necessary to reform are prudence, to recognize what is good and and what is possible in the circumstances, and moderation, to qualify oneself for the use of power. In the face of a people's craving for "splendid and perilous extremes," the statesman must "dare to be fearful." Burke states the principle of these virtues clearly, concisely, and, as is his custom, in the middle of a practical lesson: "Nothing is good, but in proportion, and with Reference" (letter to Depont).

We learn Burke's low opinion of Voltaire and Rousseau, by contrast with his high opinion of Montesquieu (letter to Unknown, 1790), not to mention his contempt for Tom Paine (letter to William Smith, 1791). Burke's exchanges with his coadjutor Philip Francis and with Captain Thomas Mercer reveal the difficulty of convincing reformers and partisans of liberty that the French Revolution was wrong and vicious at its center. That vicious center, according to Burke, was its assault on property, especially property in long possessions to which owners have a prescriptive right if not a clear title (Burke does not object to "old violence"). Respect for property is both the security of liberty and the assurance of a moderate use of it. Such respect is infinitely superior to "that sublime, abstract, metaphysic reversionary contingent humanity" which the revolutionaries profess and act upon. This virtue flatters the passions; it explodes or discredits the virtues by which men restrain their passions and become human. The revolutionaries learned it from the Parisian Philosophers (letter to Rivarol, 1791). Burke's humanity is shown in his early, determined opposition to the slave trade, as well as in the moderation of his plan of reform (letter to Dundas, 1792).

To the CHAIRMAN OF THE BUCKINGHAMSHIRE MEETING—12 April 1780

Corr. (1958), IV, 226–29

The first county meeting in Buckinghamshire was held on 26 February in the midst of debate over two proposals of reform, "economical" or administrative reform, for which Burke had been working, and a more radical parliamentary reform put forth by Charles Stanhope (1753–1816), styled Viscount Mahon, and William Petty (1737–1805), 2nd Earl of Shelburne. A petition was adopted and a committee appointed of which both Edmund and Richard Burke, Sr, were members. Lord Temple, to whom Burke gave this letter, threw his great influence against any radical program. Lord Mahon, however, when he could not persuade the committee to adopt his proposal, determined to raise the matter at the second meeting on 13 April. Burke wrote this to oppose him.

Sir,

Having heard yesterday by mere accident that there is an intention of laying before the county meeting *new matter which is not contained in our petition,* and the consideration of which had been deferred to a fitter time by a majority of our committee in London; permit me to take this method of submitting to you my reasons for thinking, with our committee, that nothing ought to be hastily determined upon the subject.

Our petition arose naturally from distresses which we *felt;* and the requests which we made were in effect nothing more, than that such things should be done in parliament, as it was evidently the duty of parliament to do. But the affair, which will be proposed to you by a person of rank and ability,[1] is an alteration in the constitution of parliament itself. It is impossible for you to have a subject before you of more importance, and that requires a more cool and more mature consideration, both on its own account, and for the credit of our sobriety of mind who are to resolve upon it.

The county will, in some way or other, be called upon to declare it your opinion, that the House of Commons is not sufficiently numerous, and that the elections are not sufficiently frequent: that a hundred new knights of the shire ought to be added; and that we are to have a new election once in three years for certain, and as much oftener as the king pleases. Such will be the state of things, if the proposition made shall take effect.

All this may be proper. But, as an honest man, I cannot possibly give my vote for it until I have considered it more fully. I will not deny that our constitution may have faults; and that those faults, when found, ought to be corrected; but, on the whole, that constitution has been our own pride, and an object of admiration to all other nations. It is not everything which appears at first view to be faulty in such a complicated plan that is to be determined to be so in reality. To enable us to correct the constitution, the whole constitution must be viewed together; and it must be compared with the actual state of the people, and the circumstances of the time. For that which, taken singly and by itself, may appear to be wrong, when considered with relation to other things may be perfectly right; or at least such as ought to be patiently endured, as the means of preventing something that is worse. So far with regard to what at first view may appear a *distemper* in the constitution. As to the *remedy* of that distemper, an equal caution

---

[1] Lord Mahon.

ought to be used; because this latter consideration is not single and separate, no more than the former. There are many things in reformation which would be proper to be done, if other things can be done along with them; but which, if they cannot be so accompanied, ought not to be done at all. I therefore wish, when any new matter of this deep nature is proposed to me, to have the whole scheme distinctly in my view, and full time to consider of it. Please God, I will walk with caution whenever I am not able clearly to see my way before me.

I am now growing old. I have from my very early youth been conversant in reading and thinking upon the subject of our laws and constitution, as well as upon those of other times, and other countries. I have been for fifteen years a very laborious member of parliament; and in that time have had great opportunities of seeing with my own eyes the working of the machine of our government, and remarking where it went smoothly and did its business, and where it checked in its movements, or where it damaged its work. I have also had and used the opportunities of conversing with men of the greatest wisdom and fullest experience in those matters; and I do declare to you most solemnly and most truly, that on the result of all this reading, thinking, experience, and communication, I am not able to come to an immediate resolution in favour of a change of the ground-work of our constitution; and, in particular, that in the present state of the country, in the present state of our representation, in the present state of our rights and modes of electing, in the present state of the several prevalent interests, in the present state of the affairs and manners of this country, the addition of a hundred knights of the shire, and hurrying election on election, will be things advantageous to liberty or good government.

This is the present condition of my mind; and this is my apology for not going as fast as others may choose to go in this business. I do not by any means reject the propositions—much less to I condemn the gentlemen who, with equal good intentions, with much better abilities, and with infinitely greater personal weight and consideration than mine, are of opinion, that this matter ought to be decided upon instantly.

I most heartily wish that the deliberate sense of the kingdom on the great subject should be known. When it is known it *must* be prevalent. It would be dreadful indeed, if there was any power in the nation capable of resisting its unanimous desire, or even the desire of any very great and decided majority of the people. The people may be deceived in their choice of an object. But I can scarcely conceive any choice they can make to be so very mischievous as the existence of any human force capable of resisting it. It will certainly be the duty of every man, in the situation to which God has called him, to give his best opinion and advice upon the matter; it will *not* be his duty, let him think what he will, to use any violent or any fraudulent means of counteracting the general wish, or even of employing the legal and constructive organ of expressing the people's sense against the sense which they do actually entertain.

In order that the real sense of the people should be known upon so great an affair as this, it is of absolute necessity that timely notice should be given; that the matter should be prepared in open committees, from a choice into which no class or description of men is to be excluded—and the subsequent county meetings should be as full, and as well attended, as possible. Without these precautions the true sense of the people will ever be uncertain. Sure I am, that no precipitate resolution on a great change in the fundamental constitution of any country can ever be called the real sense of the people.

I trust it will not be taken amiss, if, as an inhabitant and freeholder of this county, (one indeed among the most inconsiderable,) I assert my right of dissenting (as I do dissent fully and directly) from any resolution whatsoever on the subject of an alteration in the representation and election of the kingdom *at this time.* By preserving this right, and exercising it with temper and moderation, I trust I cannot offend the noble proposer,[2] for whom no man professes, or feels, more respect and regard than I do. A want of concurrence in *everything* which *can* be proposed will in no sort weaken the energy, or distract the efforts, of men of upright intentions upon those points in which they are agreed. Assemblies that are met, and with a resolution to be all of a mind, are assemblies that can have no opinion at all of their own. The first proposer of any measure must be their master. I do not know that an amicable variety of sentiment, conducted with mutual goodwill, has any sort of resemblance to discord; or that it can give any advantage whatsoever to the enemies of our common cause. On the contrary, a forced and fictitious agreement (which every universal agreement must be) is not becoming the cause of freedom. If, however, any evil should arise from it, (which I confess I do not foresee,) I am happy that those who have brought forward new and arduous matter, when very great doubts, and some diversity of opinion, must be foreknown, are of authority and weight enough to stand against the consequences.

[2] Lord Mahon.

I humbly lay these my sentiments before the county. They are not taken up to serve any interests of my own, or to be subservient to the interests of any man or set of men under heaven. I could wish to be able to attend our meeting, or that I had time to reason this matter more fully by letter; but I am detained here upon our business. What you have already put upon us is as much as we can do. If we are prevented from going through it with any effect, I fear it will be in part owing, not more to the resistance of the enemies of our cause, than to our imposing on ourselves such tasks as no human faculties, employed as we are, can be equal to. Our worthy members[3] have shown distinguished ability and zeal in support of our petition. I am just going down to a bill brought in to frustrate a capital part of your desires. The minister is preparing to transfer the cognizance of the public accounts from those whom you and the constitution have chosen to control them to unknown persons, creatures of his own.[4] For so much he annihilates parliament.

> I have the honour, &c.
>
> Charles Street,   EDMUND BURKE.
> 12th April, 1780.

To JOSEPH HARFORD—27 September 1780

Corr. (1958), IV, 294–98

Burke comments to his Bristol friend on his loss of the election there and on the divisions in his own party over reform which might make him content to stay out of Parliament.

To Mr Harford Sheriff of Bristol.

My dear Sir

The fatigues of the Election are over; and I congratulate you on your return to quiet. I congratulate you too on the order, vigour, and spirit of decision, that shortened your work, and rendered the Election itself less tedious to the City and less vexatious and expensive to the Parties than it would have been but for your exertions. Give my best compliments on this occasion to your Colleague.

As to the Event of The Election, it has been just what it *ought to be*. It was the natural result of the conduct of *all* parties; and it may have a tendency to reform the conduct of *some of* them. The Tories

---

[3] Lord Verney and Thomas Grenville.
[4] The Commissioners of Accounts established by Lord North's ministry.

have not acquired a great deal of Glory by the Victory they have obtained, and by the use they have made of their strength. On the other hand, I am perfectly convinced that the defeat both of Mr Cruger and myself was a thing proper and necessary. If *I* had not been defeated, the Whigs never could be taught the necessity of Vigour, activity, Vigilance, and foresight. If *Mr Cruger* had not been defeated, his friends could not have had the *Chance* they now have, of being cured of presumption, and weak crooked politicks. *Both parties* could never have been taught the necessity of cordial Union, the Mischief of Gentlemens neglecting to cultivate an Interest among the common people, and the madness of the common peoples dream, that they could be any thing without the Aid of better fortunes and better heads than their own—None of us could be *practically* taught these essential Truths, but by the *Aid* of a defeat.

One great advantage towards our converting our loss into profit is, that we have lost neither temper nor Credit by it. At present all our prospects depend upon the use we make of these Circumstances. Our Numbers, though respectable, are not large. But then all the flesh we have is sound, and firm, and fit for action; and it is my earnest Wish, that no accession, however flattering, may be admitted, if it tends more to swell our Bulk than to augment our force. If it be, you will find it a weight to carry, not strength to carry away any thing else.

One thing, my dear friend, your manly sense will guard you against— the admitting any *Visionary* Politicians amongst us. We are sufficiently secured, (by our exclusion from the Court), from the *mercenary* of that Tribe. But the Bane of the Whiggs has been the admission among them of the Corps of Schemers; who in reality, and at bottom, mean little more than to indulge themselves with Speculations; but who do us infinite Mischief, by persuading many sober and well meaning people, that we have designs inconsistent with the Constitution left us by our forefathers. You know how many are startled with the Idea of innovation. Would to God it were in our power to keep things *where they are*, in point of *form;* provided we were able to improve them in point of *Substance.* The *Machine itself* is well enough to answer any good purpose, provided the *materials* were sound. But what signifies the Arrangement of rottenness?

It is our business to take care, that we who are Electors, or corporate Magistrates, or Freeholders, or Members of Parliament, or Peers, (or whatever we may be,) that we hold good principles, and that we steadily oppose all bad principles and bad men. If the Nation at large has *disposition* enough for this End, its *form* of Government is, in my opinion, fully sufficient for it. But if the *general* disposition be *against* a virtuous and manly line of publick conduct, there is no *form* into which it can be thrown that will improve its Nature or add to its Energy. I know that many Gentlemen in other parts of the Kingdom think it practicable to make the remedy of our publick disorders *attend* on an alteration in our actual constitution, and to bring about the former as a consequence of the Latter. But I believe that no people, who could think of deferring the redress of such Grievances as ours, and the Animadversion on such palpable misconduct as there has been lately in our Affairs, untill the material Alterations in the Constitution which they propose can be brought about; will ever do any mighty matter when they have carried these alterations; even if they should find themselves *able* to carry them.

As to myself, I am come to no resolution relative to my making one in the consultation of these matters. I believe, that without much intrigue, I might contrive to come into Parliament through some door or other. But when I consider on one hand, the power and prostitution of the faction which has long domineerd, and does still domineer in this Country, and on the other, the strange distraction not only in Interests, but in views and plans of conduct, that prevails among those who oppose that faction, I do, something more than, hesitate about the wisdom and propriety of *my* making one in this general Scene of confusion. I will say nothing about that Tail, which draggles in the dirt, and which every party in every state *must* carry about it; *That* can only flirt a little of the Mud in our faces now and then. It is no great matter. But some of our *capital* Men entertain thoughts so very different from mine, that if I come into Parliament, I must either fly in the face of the clearest lights of my own understanding, and the firmest conviction of my own conscience, or I must oppose those for whom I have the highest value. The D. of Richmond has *voluntarily proposed* to open the Election of England to all those, without exception, who have [the] qualification of being 18 years old; and has swept away at one stroke all the privileges of Freeholders, Cities, and Burroughs throughout the Kingdom, and sends every Member of Parliament, every year, to the Judgment and discretion of such Electors. Sir Geo: Saville has *consented* to *adopt*, the Scheme of *more frequent Elections* as a remedy for disorders, which in my opinion, have a great part of their Root in *Elections themselves;* and while the Duke of Richmond proposes to annihilate the Freeholders, Sir Geo: Saville consents to a plan for a vast encrease of their *power* by choice of an hundred new Knights of the Shire. Which of these am I to adhere to? or shall

I put myself into the graceful situation of opposing both? If I am asked who the D. of Richmond and Sir G: Saville are, and what is my own inward opinion of them, I must fairly say, that I look upon them to be the first Men of their Age and their Country; that I do not know Men of more parts or more honour; of the latter you remember, what I said in the Guildhall, and I cannot retract a word of it.

In this situation with regard to those whom I esteem the most, how shall I act with those for whom I have no Esteem at all? Such there are, not only in the Ministry, but in the opposition. There is indeed the M. of Rockingham and there are some more, with whom I do not think I differ materially; but I am quite certain, that though they make our greatest Number, yet it is a Number by no means sufficient with any Effect to oppose the Court, with little or no aid we have from the people. These are my thoughts; or rather a very small part of the inducements, which make me content, I had almost said desirous, of continuing where the larger part of our City was of opinion I ought to continue.

On recollection, I have perhaps gone further than I intended on the subject of my difference with my friends; and since I have troubled you with so long a letter I ought to take the Benefit of your present patience and explain myself a little.

As to the shortening the duration of Parliaments, I confess I see no cause to change or to modifye my opinion on that subject. The reason remains the same; the Desires of the people go along with the reason of the thing. I do not know any thing more *practically* unpopular. It is true, that many people are fond of *talking* on short parliaments, as a subject of ingenuity; and they will come to resolutions on the point, if any one wishes that they should; but when they come to the Touchstone, to *the Election itself* they vomit up all these Notions. You have, I dare say, remarked that, (except in one place only) not *one* Candidate has ventured, in an Advertisement, or in a declaration from the Hustings, to say one Syllable on the subject of short Parliaments, nor has any one Elector thought proper to propose a Test, or to give an Instruction, or even the Slightest recommendation of such a Measure. You know how every one in Bristol feels upon that matter; and I have reason to be persuaded, that they do not all differ from the Majority of the Kingdom.

As to *some* remedy to the present State of the representation, I do by no means object to it. But it is an Affair of great difficulty; and to be touched with great delicacy; and by an hand of great power. Power and delicacy do not often unite. But without great power, I do not

hesitate to say, it *cannot* be done. By power I mean the *executive* power
of the Kingdom. It is, (according to my Ideas of such a reformation)
a thing in which the executive Government is more concerned (in all
matters of detail it is much concerned) that it is in short Parliaments;
and I know that in business of this sort, if Administration does not
concurr, they are able to defeat the Scheme, even though it should be
carried by a Majority in Parliament; and not only to defeat it, but to
render it in a short time odious and contemptible. The people shew
no disposition to exert themselves for putting power into the hands
of those from whom they expect the performance of Tasks that require
a great deal of strength; and that too a strength regular, systematick,
and progressive. If they can find none to Trust there is an End of this
and of all Questions of reformation. . . .

To the EARL OF CHARLEMONT—9 *August* 1789

Corr. (1958), VI, 9–10

Burke's first recorded comment on the French Revolution is not a welcoming one.
He gives to it James Caulfeild, 1st Earl of Charlemont (1728–99), an Irish Opposition
peer.

My dearest Lord,

I think your Lordship has acted with your usual Zeal and judgment
in establishing a Whigg Club in Dublin.[1] These meetings prevent the
evaporation of Principle in Individuals and give them joint force, and
enliven their exertions by emulation. You see the matter in its true
light and with your usual discernment. Party is absolutely necessary
at this time.[2] I thought it always so in this Country ever since I have
had any thing to do in publick Business; and I rather fear, that there
is not virtue enough in this Period to support party, than that party
should become necessary on account of the want of Virtue to support
itself by individual exertions. As to us here our thoughts of every thing
at home are suspended, by our astonishment at the wonderful Spec-

---

[1] Charlemont wrote to Burke on 4 July: 'In order to bring and to keep our Forces together,
I have lately forwarded the Institution of a *Whig Club*, which will, I think, be of considerable
Utility'. His club was modelled on the English Whig Club founded by the Opposition leaders
after the electoral disaster of 1784.

[2] Charlemont had been reluctant to grant this for Ireland: 'Indeed I once flattered myself,
as I am but too apt to do, that there was in this Country a Fund of public Virtue sufficient to
render unnecessary it's far unequal Succedaneum Party Principle—Sad Experience has however
convinced me of my Error—We are as corrupt as our Neighbours, and as we participate of the
same Dissease, We must have Recourse to the same Remedies—Self Interest must be made a
Motive to Patriotism, and Party Honour must supply the vacant Place of Public Virtue'.

tacle which is exhibited in a Neighbouring and rival Country[3]—what Spectators, and what actors! England gazing with astonishment at a French struggle for Liberty and not knowing whether to blame or to applaud! The thing indeed, though I thought I saw something like it in progress for several years,[4] has still something in it paradoxical and Mysterious. The spirit it is impossible not to admire; but the old Parisian ferocity has broken out in a shocking manner. It is true, that this may be no more than a sudden explosion: If so no indication can be taken from it. But if it should be character rather than accident, then that people are not fit for Liberty, and must have a Strong hand like that of their former masters to coerce them. Men must have a certain fund of natural moderation to qualifye them for Freedom, else it become noxious to themselves and a perfect Nuisance to every body else. What will be the Event it is hard I think still to say. To form a solid constitution requires Wisdom as well as spirit, and whether the French have wise heads among them, or if they possess such whether they have authority equal to their wisdom, is to be seen; In the mean time the progress of this whole affair is one of the most curious matters of Speculation that ever was exhibited. . . .

To WILLIAM WINDHAM—27 September 1789

Corr. (1958), VI, 24–6

Burke answers Windham's letter of 15 September, with its brief and optimistic comments upon France.

My dear Sir

It is very true, that I promised myself the satisfaction of seeing you very soon after your return from the Land of Liberty. I am sure I was very glad of your *safe* return from it; for though I had no doubt of

[3] The storming of the Bastille had been described in London newspapers as early as 18 July, and since then much attention had been given to events in France, in particular to the revival of popular violence in Paris with the murder of Foullon and Bertier and to the numerous outbreaks of rioting and arson in the provinces.

[4] As early as 1769 Burke, after describing the financial difficulties of France, wrote, '. . . no man, I believe, who has considered their affairs with any degree of attention or information, but must hourly look for some extraordinary convulsion in that whole system; the effect of which on France, and even on all Europe, it is difficult to conjecture' (*Observations on a Late Publication Intituled The Present State of the Nation* in *Works*, Bohn, I, 230; Little, Brown, I, 331). This crisis was overcome and Tom Paine alleged that in 1788 and 1789 Burke did not reveal in his conversation any anticipation of French domestic troubles. Indeed, Paine complained in the opening pages of the *Rights of Man*, 'There was a time when it was impossible to make Mr Burke believe there would be any revolution in France. His opinion then was, that the French had neither the spirit to undertake it, nor fortitude to support it . . .'.

your prudence, where no Duty called you to the utterance of dangerous Truths, yet I could not feel perfectly at my Ease for the situation of any friend, in a Country where the people, along with their political servitude, have thrown off the Yoke of Laws and morals. I could certainly wish to talk over the details and circumstances with you— But the main matter consists in the results, and in the general impression made upon you by what you have seen and heard; and this you have been so kind to communicate. That they should settle their constitution, without much struggle, on paper, I can easily believe; because at present the Interests of the Crown have no party, certainly no armed party, to support them; But I have great doubts whether any form of Government which they can establish will procure obedience; especially obedience in the article of Taxations. In the destruction of the old Revenue constitution they find no difficulties—but with what to supply them is the Opus.[1] You are undoubtedly better able to judge; but it does not appear to me, that the National assembly have one Jot more power than the King; whilst they lead or follow the popular voice, in the subversion of all orders, distinctions, priveleges impositions, Tythes, and rents,[2] they appear omnipotent; but I very much question, whether they are in a condition to exercise any function of decided authority—or even whether they are possessed of any real deliberative capacity, or the exercise of free Judgment in any point whatsoever; as there is a Mob of their constituents ready to Hang them if They should deviate into moderation, or in the least depart from the Spirit of those they represent. What has happend puts all speculation to the blush; but still I should doubt, whether in the End France is susceptible of the Democracy that is the Spirit, and in a good measure too, the form, of the constitution they have in hand: It is except the Idea of the Crowns being hereditary much more truly democratical than that of North America. My Son has got a Letter from France which paints the miserable and precarious situation of all people of property in dreadful colours. Indeed the particular details leave no doubt of it. Pray let me hear from you again for I fear it will not be in my power to go to you or to our friend Dudley North—and I wish much to know whether the measures of the Enemies of honour and common sense have made any way at Norwich; for I had much rather you were the Spectator, than the Victim of popular madness.

[1] On 9 June the National Assembly voted that the existing taxes, not having been consented to by the nation, were illegal; nevertheless they were to be raised as formerly so long as the Assembly remained in session.

[2] By the decisions of the night of 4 August and the subsequent decrees of 5–11 August.

Adieu my dear freind and beleive me, ever with the most sincere attachment truly Yours

EDM BURKE

Beconsfield Septr 27. 1789.

To EARL FITZWILLIAM—12 *November* 1789

Corr. (1958), VI, 34–7

Another early comment of Burke's on the French Revolution.

My dear Lord,

. . . As to France, if I were to give way to the speculations which arise in my Mind from the present State of things, and from the Causes which have given rise to it and which now begin to be unfolded, I should think it a country undone; and irretrievable for a very long Course of time. I confess I am very sorry for it. I should certainly wish to see France circumscribed within moderate bounds. The interest of this Country requires, perhaps the Interests of mankind require, that she should not be in a condition despotically to give the Law to Europe: But I think I see many inconveniencies, not only to Europe at large, but to this Country in particular from the total political extinction of a great civilized Nation situated in the heart of this our Western System. There seems no Energy in the French Monarchy able to revive the Royal Authority. Its chief supports, the Nobility and the Clergy, are extinguished; and extinguished by the ill-judged acts of the Crown itself.[1] The King is heavy, inert, inexperienced, timid, without rescources, even if he were not a prisoner—and his Ministers, who have no real support either in his power or his attachment to them, and are men of no extraordinary capacity in themselves suited to an exigency, that calls for the greatest Courage and the highest Strains of Policy, can do very little to aid the King, the Country or themselves. The National assembly is nothing more than an organ of the Will of the Burghers of Paris; and they are so, because the feelings of the Burghers of Paris do not differ much from those of the generality of the French Nation. They are indeed in such a situation in France that a publick Bankruptcy seems the only remedy for the distempers of their Finance, and a civil war the only chance

---

[1] Burke is referring specifically to the decisions of the Royal Council first to double the representation of the Third Estate and then to permit the Three Estates to fuse into a single body, thus destroying any chance of a veto by the two privileged Orders.

for producing order in their Government. But they want Courage of understanding to decide upon the former, and there is not union enough between individuals or descriptions of men to produce the latter; For there are some sorts of general convulsions that require particular combinations and coherencies. As to the pillage of the Church,[2] this will prove the reverse of a rescource, either to their Finances or their Government. This is the only thing that is quite certain. The turning such multitudes out of their condition, such a convulsion in property, and of course in all the Revenues which arise out of the expenditure of property, the leaving such an extent of Landed Interest without any owner concerned in its preservation or melioration,[3] must infinitely encrease those publick disorders and that national imbecillity which are so strongly stated in the answer of the Ministers to the application made to them on the Comte de Mirabeaus motion. I wish your Lordship to look at that answer. All these things have happend out of the ordinary Course of Speculation. They may alter their aspect contrary to all the speculations which naturally arise from their present State. There is much in Fortune, or in more proper Language, in the overruling and mysterious disposition of Providence. One man may change all. But when and where and how is this man to appear. My Brother who is, thank God now quite well, and Mrs Burke present their best compliments to your Lordship and Lady Fitzwilliam. My Son who respects and loves your Lordship as he ought to do is in Town. I am ever

My dear Lord
your Lordship's
Most faithfully and affectionately

Beconsfield Nov. 12 1789   EDM BURKE

To CHARLES-JEAN-FRANÇOIS DEPONT— [*November* 1789]

Corr. (1958), IV, 39–50

Depont (1767–96) was a young man who had visited the Burkes in 1785. On November 4, 1789, he wrote to Burke to ask his assurance that the revolution in France would

---

[2] A decree of 2 November put the possessions of the Church at the disposition of the nation.
[3] So far no decision had been made about disposing of the property of the Church; the first sales were authorized by the decree of 19 December under the description of *biens nationaux*, and the whole was put up for sale on 9 June 1790. Once sales had begun, the property passed rapidly into private hands.

succeed. Burke's reply is his first considered judgment on the French Revolution. It was to be followed, in November 1790, by a still more considered judgment, his *Reflections on the Revolution in France*, which took the form of a letter to Depont.

Dear Sir,

We are extremely happy in your giving us leave to promise ourselves a renewal of the pleasure we formerly had in your Company at Beconsfield and in London. It was too lively to be speedily forgotten on our part; and we are highly flatter'd to find that You keep so exactly in your Memory all the particulars of the few attentions which You were so good to accept from us during your stay in England. We indulge ourselves in the hope, that you will be able to execute what you intend in our favour; and that we shall be more fortunate in the coming Spring, than we were in the last.

You have reason to imagine that I have not been as early as I ought in acquainting you with my thankful acceptance of the Correspondence you have been pleased to Offer. Do not think me insensible to the honour you have done me. I confess I did hesitate for a time, on a doubt, whether it would be prudent to yield to my earnest desire of such a Correspondence.

Your frank and ingenuous manner of writing, would be ill answer'd by a cold, dry, and guarded reserve on my part. It would indeed be adverse to my habits and my Nature to make use of that sort of Caution in my intercourse with any friend. Besides as you are pleased to think that your splendid flame of Liberty was first lighted up at My faint and glimmering taper, I thought you had a right to call upon me for my undisguised sentiments on whatever related to that Subject. On the other hand, I was not without apprehension, that in this free mode of intercourse, I might say something not only disagreeable to Your formed opinions, upon points, on which of all others we are most impatient of Contradiction, but not pleasing to the Power which should happen to be prevalent at the time of your receiving my letter. I was well aware, that, in Seasons of Jealousy, suspicion is vigilant and active; that it is not extremely scrupulous in its means of Enquiry;[1] not perfectly equitable in its Judgments; and not altogether deliberate in its Resolutions. In the ill connected and inconclusive logick of the Passions, whatever may appear blameable, is easily transferr'd from

---

[1] Burke's suspicions that correspondence was regularly opened in France, as had been the practice of the *ancien régime*, may have been sharpened by the debate on the subject in the National Assembly, 25–27 July, in which the practice was generally defended by deputies of all shades of opinion, on the grounds that such action was permissible in a state of war and France was in fact in that condition (*Journal des débats*, I, 255, 263–4).

the guilty Writer to the innocent Receiver. It is an aukward, as well as unpleasant Accident; but it is one that has sometimes happen'd. A Man may be made a Martyr to tenets the most opposite to his own. At length a friend of mine, lately come from Paris, informed me that heats are beginning to abate, and that intercourse is thought to be more safe. This has given me some Courage; and the Reflexion, that the sentiments of a Person of no more consideration than I am either Abroad or at home, could be of little consequence to the success of any Cause or any Party, has at length decided me to accept of the honour you are willing to confer upon me.

You may easily believe, that I have had my Eyes turned with great Curiosity to the astonishing scene now displayed in France. It has certainly given rise in my Mind to many Reflexions, and to some Emotions. These are natural and unavoidable; but it would ill become Me to be too ready in forming a positive opinion upon matters transacted in a Country, with the correct, political Map of which I must be very imperfectly acquainted. Things indeed have already happen'd so much beyond the scope of all speculation, that persons of infinitely more sagacity than I am ought to be ashamed of any thing like confidence in their reasoning upon the operation of any principle or the effect of any measure. It would become me least of all to be so confident, who ought at my time of life, to have well learn'd the important lesson of self distrust; A lesson of no small Value in company with the best information; but which alone can make any sort of amends for our not having learn'd other lessons so well as it was our business to learn them. I beg you, once for all, to apply this corrective of the diffidence I have on my own Judgment to whatever I may happen to say with more positiveness than suits my knowledge and situation. If I should seem any where to express myself in the language of disapprobation, be so good to consider it as no more than the expression of doubt.

You hope, Sir, that I think the French deserving of Liberty? I certainly do. I certainly think that all Men who desire it, deserve it. It is not the Reward of our Merit or the acquisition of our Industry. It is our Inheritance. It is the birthright of our Species. We cannot forfeit our right to it, but by what forfeits our title to the privileges of our kind; I mean the abuse or oblivion of our rational faculties, and a ferocious indocility, which makes us prompt to wrong and Violence, destroys our social Nature, and transforms us into something little better than the description of Wild beasts. To Men so degraded, a state of strong constraint is a sort of necessary substitute for freedom;

since, bad as it is, it may deliver them in some Measure from the worst of all Slavery, that is the despotism of their own blind and brutal passions.

You have kindly said, that You began to love freedom from Your intercourse with Me. This is the more necessary because of all the loose Terms in the world Liberty is the most indefinite. Permit me then to continue our conversation, and to tell You what the freedom is that I love and that to which I think all men intitled. It is not solitary, unconnected, individual, selfish Liberty. As if every Man was to regulate the whole of his Conduct by his own will. The Liberty I mean is *social* freedom. It is that state of things in which Liberty is secured by the equality of Restraint; A Constitution of things in which the liberty of no one Man, and no body of Men and no Number of men can find Means to trespass on the liberty of any Person or any description of Persons in the Society. This kind of liberty is indeed but another name for Justice, ascertained by wise Laws, and secured by well constructed institutions. I am sure, that Liberty, so incorporated, and in a manner, identified, with justice, must be infinitely dear to every one, who is capable of conceiving what it is. But whenever a separation is made between Liberty and Justice, neither is, in my opinion, safe. I do not believe that Men ever did submit, certain I am that they never ought to have submitted, to the arbitrary pleasure of one Man, but under circumstances in which the arbitrary pleasure of many Persons in the Community, pressed with an intolerable hardship upon the just and equal Rights of their fellows. Such a choice might be made as among Evils. The moment *Will* is set above Reason and Justice in any Community, a great Question may arise in sober Minds, in what part or portion of the Community that dangerous dominion of *Will* may be the least Mischievously placed.

If I think all men who cultivate Justice entitled to Liberty, and when joined in States, entitled to a Constitution framed to perpetuate and secure it; You may be assured, Sir, that I think Your Countrymen eminently worthy of a blessing, which is peculiarly adapted to noble, generous and humane Natures. Such I found the French, when more than fifteen Years ago, I had the happiness, tho' but for too short a time, of visiting your Country;[2] and I trust their Character is not alter'd since that period.

I have nothing to check my wishes towards the establishment of a solid and rational scheme of Liberty in France. On the subject of the

[2] In 1773.

Relative power of Nations I may have my prejudices; but I envy internal freedom, security, and good order to none. When therefore I shall learn, that in France, the Citizen, by whatever description he is qualified, is in a perfect state of legal security, with regard to his life, to his property, to the uncontrolled disposal of his Person, to the free use of his Industry and his faculties;—When I hear that he is protected in the beneficial Enjoyment of the Estates, to which, by the course of settled Law, he was born, or is provided with a fair compensation for them;—that he is maintain'd in the full fruition of the advantages belonging to the state and condition of life, in which he had lawfully engaged himself, or is supplied with a substantial, equitable Equivalent;—When I am assured, that a simple Citizen may decently express his sentiments upon Publick Affairs, without hazard to his life or safety, even tho' against a predominant and fashionable opinion; When I know all this of France, I shall be as well pleased as every one must be, who has not forgot the general communion of Mankind, nor lost his natural sympathy in local and accidental connexions.

If a Constitution is settled in France upon those principles and calculated for those ends, I believe there is no Man in this Country whose heart and Voice would not go along with You. I am sure it will give me, for one, an heartfelt pleasure when I hear, that, in France, the great publick Assemblies, the natural securities for individual freedom, are perfectly free themselves; when there can be no suspicion, that they are under the coercion of a Military Power of any description;[3] When it may be truly said, that no armed force can be seen which is not called into existence by their creative Voice, and which must not instantly disappear at their dissolving word,—When such Assemblies after being freely chosen shall proceed with the weight of Magistracy and not with the arts of Candidates; When they do not find themselves under the necessity of feeding one part of the Community[4] at the grievous Charge of other parts as necessitous as those who are so fed;—When they are not obliged, (in order to flatter those who have their lives in their disposal) to tolerate acts of doubtful

[3] Burke seems to suppose that the Assembly was under the threat of 'Military Power', by which he can only mean the National Guard. In fact this was its chief defence against the threat of mob violence.

[4] The Government, in the hope of preventing further disorder, took special measures to ensure the supply of grain to Paris.

influence on Commerce and on Agriculture, and for the sake of a precarious Relief under temporary scarcity, to sow (if I may be allowed the expression) the seeds of lasting want;—When they are not compell'd daily to stimulate an irregular and juvenile imagination for supplies, which they are not in a condition, firmly to demand;—When they are not obliged to diet the State from hand to Mouth, upon the casual alms of Choice, fancy, Vanity, or Caprice,[5] on which plan the value of the object to the Publick which Receives, often bears no sort of porportion to the loss of the Individual who gives;—When they are not necessitated to call for contributions to be estimated on the conscience of the Contributor,[6] by which the most pernicious sorts of exemptions and immunities may be establish'd; by which Virtue is taxed, and Vice privileged; and honour and Publick spirit are obliged to bear the burthens of Craft, selfishness and avarice; When they shall not be driven to be the instruments of the Violence of others, from a sense of their own weakness; and from a want of Authority to Assess equal and proportion'd Charges upon all, they are not compelled to lay a strong hand upon the entire possessions of a part;—When under the exigencies of the State (aggravated if not caused by the imbecillity of their own Government, and of all Government) they are not obliged to Resort to *confiscation* to supply the defect of *taxation,* and thereby to hold out a pernicious example to teach the different descriptions of the Community, to prey upon one another;—When they abstain religiously from all general and extrajudicial declarations concerning the property of the Subject;[7]—When they look with horrour upon all Arbitrary decisions in their Legislative Capacity, striking at prescriptive Right, long undisturbed Possession, opposing an uninterrupted stream of Regular judicial determinations, by which sort of decisions they are conscious no Man's possession could be safe, and Individual Property, to the very idea would be extinguish'd;—When I see your great Sovereign Bodies, Your now Supreme Power; in this condition of deliberative freedom, and guided by these or similar principles in

[5] The *dons patriotiques,* free gifts of money or articles of value from individuals and groups for the immediate necessities of the state, which the National Assembly had encouraged since September.

[6] A *contribution patriotique* of a quarter of the income was decreed on 6 October. Since it was to be paid over the period up to 1 April 1792 this reduced the annual rate to 8.33 percent. In fact only a small porportion of what was hoped for was ever paid.

[7] Burke must be referring to the night of the Fourth of August and the subsequent legislation abolishing seigneurial dues and privileges.

acting and forbearing, I shall be happy to behold in Assemblies, whose name is venerable to my understanding, and dear to My heart, an Authority, a dignity, and a Moderation, which in all Countries, and Governments ought ever to accompany the collected Reason and Representative Majesty of the Commonwealth.

I shall rejoice no less in seeing a Judicial Power establish'd in France, correspondent to such a Legislature as I have presumed to hint at, and worthy to second it in its endeavours to secure the freedom and property of the Subject. When your Courts of Justice shall obtain an ascertain'd Condition[8] before they are made to decide on the condition of other Men;—When they shall not be called upon to take cognizance of publick Offences, whilst they themselves are consider'd only to exist as a tolerated abuse;—When under doubts on the legality of their Rules of decision, their forms and modes of proceeding, and even of the validity of that system of Authority to which they owe their existence; When amidst circumstances of Suspense, fear, and humiliation, they shall not be put to judge on the Lives, Liberties, Properties or estimation of their fellow Citizens;—When they are not called upon to put any Man to his trial upon undefined Crimes of State, not ascertain'd by any previous Rule, Statute or course of precedent;[9]— When Victims shall not be snatched from the fury of the People, to be brought before a Tribunal itself subject to the effects of the same fury, and where the acquittal of the Parties accused might only place the Judge in the situation of the Criminal;—When I see Tribunals placed in this state of Independence of every thing but Law, and with a clear Law for their direction,—as a true lover of equal Justice, (under the Shadow of which alone, true liberty can live) I shall Rejoice in seeing such a happy order establish'd in France as much as I do in my consciousness, that an order of the same kind, or one not very Remote from it, has been long settled, and I hope on a firm foundation in England. I am not so narrow minded as to be unable to conceive, that the same Object may be attain'd in many ways, and perhaps in ways very different from those which we have follow'd in this Country. If this real *practical* Liberty, with a Government powerful to Protect, impotent to invade it, be establish'd, or is in a fair train of being establish'd in the Democracy, or rather collection of Democracies,

---

[8] This and the following passage refer to the situation of the *parlements*. Their vacations were prolonged by a decree of 3 November and their judicial functions were left to the *chambres de vacation*. This situation was only a provisional one, to last until a new system of courts had been set up.

[9] There were repeated discussions in the Assembly as to what court should try those accused of the new crime of *lèse-nation* (invented on analogy with *lèse-majesté*).

which seem to be chosen for the future frame of Society in France,[10]
it is not my having long enjoyed a sober share of freedom under a
qualified Monarchy that shall render Me incapable of admiring and
praising your System of Republicks. I shall rejoice, even tho' England
should hereafter be reckon'd only as one among the happy Nations;
and should no longer retain her proud distinction, her Monopoly of
fame for a practical Constitution, in which the grand secret had been
found of reconciling a Government of real energy for all foreign and
all domestick Purposes, with the most perfect security to the liberty
and safety of Individuals. The Government whatever its name or form
may be, that shall be found, substantially and practically, to unite
these advantages, will most Merit the applause of all discerning Men.

But if (for in my present want of information I must only speak
hypothetically) neither your great Assemblies, nor your Judicatures
nor your Municipalities Act and forbear to Act in the particulars, upon
the principles, and in the spirit that I have stated, I must delay my
congratulations on your acquisition of Liberty. You may have made a
Revolution, but not a Reformation. You may have subverted Monarchy, but not recover'd freedom.

You see, Sir, that I have nearly confined myself in my few observations, on what has been done, and is doing in France, to the topics
of the liberty, property, and safety of the Subject. I have not said much
on the influence of the present measures upon your Country as a State.
It is not my business, as a Citizen of the World; and it is unnecesary
to take up much time about it, as it is sufficiently visible.

You are now to live in a new order of things; under a plan of
Government of which no Man can speak from experience. Your talents,
Your publick spirit, and your fortune give you fair pretensions to a
considerable share in it. Your settlement may be at hand; But that it
is still at some distance is more likely. The French may be yet to go
through more transmigrations. They may pass, as one of our Poets
says, 'thro' many varieties of untried being'[11] before their State obtains
its final form. In that progress thro' Chaos and darkness, you will find
it necessary (at all times it is more or less so) to fix Rules and to keep
your life and Conduct in some steady course. You have theories enough
concerning the Rights of Men. It may not be amiss to add a small

[10] Burke has in mind the proposals for the establishment of municipalities and the electoral
and administrative assemblies which were presented to the Assembly on 29 September. The
relevant legislation was passed on 14 and 22 December.

[11] See Addison, *Cato*, V, I, II. Burke quotes this line in a similar context at the end of the
Reflections.

degree of attention to their Nature and disposition. It is with Man in the concrete, it is with common human life and human Actions you are to be concerned. I have taken so many liberties with You, that I am almost got the length of venturing to suggest something which may appear in the assuming tone of advice. You will however be so good as to receive my very few hints with your usual indulgence, tho' some of them I confess are not in the taste of this enlighten'd age, and indeed are no better than the late ripe fruit of mere experience.— Never wholly seperate in your Mind the merits of any Political Question from the Men who are concerned in it. You will be told, that if a measure is good, what have you [to] do with the Character and views of those who bring it forward. But designing Men never seperate their Plans from their Interests; and if You assist them in their Schemes, You will find the pretended good in the end thrown aside or perverted, and the interested object alone compassed, and that perhaps thro' Your means. The power of bad Men is no indifferent thing.

At this Moment, you may not perceive the full sense of this Rule, but you will recollect it, when the Cases are before you; You will then see and find its use. It will often keep your Virtue from becoming a tool of the Ambition and ill designs of others. Let me add, what, I think has some connexion with the Rule I mention: That you ought not to be so fond of any Political Object, as not to think the means of compassing it a serious consideration. No Man is less disposed than I am to put You under the Tuition of a petty Pedantick scruple in the management of arduous affairs: All I recommend is, that whenever the sacrifice of any subordinate point of Morality, or of honour, or even of common liberal sentiment and feeling is called for, one ought to be tolerably sure, that the object is worth it. Nothing is good, but in proportion, and with Reference. There are several who give an air of consequence to very petty designs and Actions, by the Crimes thro' which they make their way to their objects. Whatever is obtain'd smoothly and by easy means appears of no value in their Eyes. But when violent Methods are in agitation, one ought to be pretty clear, that there are no others to which we can Resort, and that a predilection from Character to such Methods is not the true cause of their being proposed. The State was Reformed by Sylla and by Caesar; But the Cornelian Law and the Julian Law were not worth the proscription. The Pride of the Roman Nobility deserved a check; But I cannot, for that Reason admire the Conduct of Cinna, and Marius, and Saturninus.[12]

I admit that Evils may be so very great and urgent that other Evils are to be submitted to for the mere hope of their Removal. A War, for instance, may be necessary, and we know what are the Rights of War, But before we use those Rights, We ought to be clearly in the state which alone can justify them; and not, in the very fold of Peace and security, by a bloody sophistry, to act towards any persons, at once as Citizens and as Enemies; and without the necessary formalities and evident distinctive lines of War, to exercise upon our Countrymen the most dreadful of all hostilities. Strong Party contentions, and a very violent opposition to our desires and opinions, are not War, nor can justify any one of its operations.

One form of Government may be better than another; and this difference may be worth a struggle. I think so. I do not mean to treat any of those forms, which are often the contrivances of deep human Wisdom (not the Rights of Men, as some people, in my opinion, not very wisely, talk of them) with slight or disrespect; Nor do I mean to level them.

A positively Vicious and abusive Government ought to be chang'd, and if necessary, by Violence, if it cannot be, (as sometimes it is the case) Reformed: But when the Question is concerning the more or the less *perfection* in the organization of a Government, the allowance to *means* is not of so much latitude. There is, by the essential fundamental Constitution of things a radical infirmity in all human contrivances, and the weakness is often so attached to the very perfection of our political Mechanism, that some defect in it, something that stops short of its principle, something that controls, that mitigates, that moderates it, becomes a necessary corrective to the Evils that the Theoretick Perfection would produce. I am pretty sure it often is so, and this truth may be exemplified abundantly.

It is true, that every defect is not of course, such a corrective as I state; but supposing it is not, an imperfect good is still a good; The defect may be tolerable, and may be Removed at some future time. In that Case, Prudence (in all things a Virtue, in Politicks the first of Virtues) will lead us rather to acquiesce in some qualified plan that

[12] The allusion is to events in Roman history between about 120 and 44 B.C. Lucius Cornelius Cinna, Caius Marius and Lucius Appuleius Saturninus, were all leaders of the popular party in the conflicts preceding the civil wars and enacted punitive legislation against the senatorial class.

does not come up to the full perfection of the abstract Idea, than to push for the more perfect, which cannot be attain'd without tearing to pieces the whole contexture of the Commonwealth, and creating an heart-ache in a thousand worthy bosoms. In that case combining the means and end, the less perfect is the more desirable. The *means* to any end, being first in order, are *immediate* in their good or their Evil, they are always, in a manner, *certainties;* The *End* is doubly problematical; first whether it is to be attain'd; then, whether supposing it obtaind, we obtain the true object we sought for.

But allow it in any degree probable, that theoretick and practical Perfection may differ, that an object pure and absolute may not be so good as one lower'd, mixed, and qualified, then, what we abate in our demand in favour of moderation and Justice and tenderness to Individuals, would be neither more nor less than a real improvement which a wise Legislator would make if he had no collateral Motive whatsoever, and only look'd in the formation of his Scheme, to its own independent Ends and purposes. Would it then be right to make way, thro' Temerity and Crime, to a form of things, which when obtained, evident Reason, perhaps imperious Necessity would compel us to alter, with the disgrace of inconsistency in our Conduct, and want of foresight in our designs.

Believe me, Sir, in all changes in the State, Moderation is a Virtue not only Amiable but powerful. It is a disposing, arranging, conciliating, cementing Virtue. In the formation of New Constitutions it is in its Province: Great Powers reside in those who can make great Changes. Their own Moderation is their only check; and if this Virtue is not paramount in their minds, their Acts will taste more of their Power than of their Wisdom or their benevolence. Whatever they do will be in extremes; it will be crude, harsh, precipitate. It will be submitted to with grudging and Reluctance; Revenge will be smother'd and hoarded; and the duration of schemes made in that temper will be as precarious as their Establishment was odious. This Virtue of Moderation (which times and Situations will clearly distinguish from the counterfeits of pusillanimity and indecision) is the Virtue only of superior Minds. It requires deep Courage, and full of ⟨Ref⟩lexion, to be temperate, when the voice of Multitudes (the speci⟨ous⟩ ⟨m⟩imick of fame and Reputation) passes Judgment against you; ⟨the⟩impetuous desires of an unthinking Publick will ensure no course but what conducts to splendid and perilous extremes. Then to dare to be fearful, when all about you are full of presumption and confidence, and when those who are bold at the hazard of others, would punish your caution as disaffection, is to shew a Mind prepared for its trial; it discovers in the midst of general levity, a self possessing and collected Character which sooner or later bids fair to attract every thing to it, as to a Center. If however the Tempest should prove to be so very violent that it would make Publick Prudence itself unseasonable, and therefore little less than madness for the Individual and the Publick too, perhaps a Young Man could not do better than to retreat for a while into Study—to leave the field to those whose duty or inclination, or the Necessities of their Condition, have put them in possession of it;—and wait for the settlement of such a Commonwealth as an honest Man may act in with satisfaction and Credit. This he can never do when those who counsel the Publick or the Prince are under terror, let the authority under which they are made to speak other than the dictates of their conscience, be never so imposing in its name and attributes.

This Moderation is no Enemy to Zeal and Enthusiasm. There is room enough for them; for the restraint is no more than the restraint of principle, and the restraint of Reason.

I have been led further than I intended. But every days account shews more and more, in my opinion, the ill consequence of keeping good principles and good general views within no bounds. Pardon the liberty I have taken; though it seems somewhat singular, that I, whose opinions have so little weight in my own Country, where I have some share in a Publick Trust, should write as if it were possible they should affect one Man, with regard to Affairs in which I have no concern. But for the present, my time is my own, and to tire your patience is the only injury I can do You.

To UNKNOWN—[*January* 1790]

Corr. (1958), VI, 78–82

It is not known to whom or precisely when this letter was written, but it was probably composed at the time when Burke became alarmed at the extent of English sympathy for the French Revolution.

With regard to the state of things in France, I am afraid that, as matters appear to me at present, I cannot at all agree with you, until at least my information is as good as yours. I hope you do not think me weak enough to form my opinion of what is doing there upon the representations in newspapers, much less upon those of the newspapers of a country in which the true spirit of the several transactions cannot be generally known. English newspapers, however, do not, I believe, lead the opinions of people here; but, as I conceive, rather follow the current of the notions most prevalent. As for me, I have read, and with some attention, the authorised, or rather the equally authentic documents on this subject, from the first instructions to the representatives of the several orders[1] down to this time. What else I have read has been for the greater part on the side of those who have a considerable share in the formation and conduct of public measures.[2] A great many of the most decisive events, I conceive, are not disputed as facts, though, as usual, there is some dispute about their causes, and their tendency. On comparing the whole of fact, of public document, and of what can be discerned of the general temper of the French people, I perfectly agree with you that there is very little likelihood of the old government's regaining its former authority. Were the king to escape from his palace where he is now in reality a prisoner with his wife and almost his whole family, to what place could he fly? Every town in France is a Paris. I see no way, by which a second revolution can be accomplished. The only chance seems to consist in the extreme instability of every species of power, and the uncertainty of every kind of speculation. In this I agree with you; in most other particulars I can by no means go so far. That a police is established at Paris, I can readily believe. They have an army, as I hear, of six thousand men, apparently under their command. They have some militia too in pretty constant service; and this militia may be augmented to almost any given number for any exigency. They have the means of preserving quiet; and since they have completely obtained their ends, they must have the disposition. A total anarchy is a self-destructive thing. But if the same ends should hereafter require the same courses, which have been already pursued, there is no doubt but the same ferocious delight in murder and the same savage cruelty will be again renewed. If any of those horrid deeds, which surely have not been misrepresented to us, were the acts of the rulers, what are we to think of an armed people under such rulers? Or if, (which possibly may be the case) there is in reality and substance no ruler, and that the chiefs are driven before the people rather than lead them; and if

[1] Probably a summary of the *cahiers de doléances* drawn up by the separate Orders at the time of the election of the Estates General.

[2] Burke later mentions having read, before he first spoke against the Revolution on 9 February, 'some pieces supposed to have been written by the Comte de Mirabeau' (probably in the *Courier de Provence*, edited by Mirabeau) and the proceedings of the National Assembly (probably parts, at least, of the *Procès-verbal*).

the armed corps are composed of men who have no fixed principle of obedience, and are embodied only by the prevalence of some general inclination; who can repute himself safe among a people so furious and senseless? As to the destruction of the *Bastile*, of which you speak, we both know it was a thing in itself of no consequence whatever. The *Bastile* was at first intended as a citadel undoubtedly; and when it was built, it might serve the purposes of a citadel. Of late, in that view, it was ridiculous. It could not contain any garrison sufficient to awe such a city as Paris. As a prison, it was of as little importance.[3] Give despotism, and the prisons of despotism will not be wanting, any more than lamp-irons will be wanting to democratic fury. . . .[4]

In all appearance, the new system is a most bungling, and un-workmanlike performance. I confess I see no principle of coherence, cooperation, or just subordination of parts in this whole project, nor any the least aptitude to the condition and wants of the state to which it is applied, nor any thing well imagined for the formation, provision, or direction of a common force. The direct contrary appears to me. I think it carries evident marks of the incurable ignorance of this most unenlightened age, the least qualified for legislation that perhaps has been since the first formation of civil society. . . .

Man is a gregarious animal. He will by degrees provide some convenience suitable to this his natural disposition; and this strange thing may, some time or other, assume a more habitable form. The fish will at length make a shell which will fit him. I beg pardon for dwelling so long and employing so much thought upon a subject, on which its contrivers have evidently employed so little. I cannot think with you, that the assembly have done much. They have, indeed, *undone* a great deal, and so completely broken up their country as a state, that I assure you, there are few here such *antigallicans* as not to feel some pity of the deplorable view of the wreck of France. I confess to you that, till I saw it, I could not conceive that any men in public could have shewn so little mercy to their country. You say, my dear sir, that they read Montesquieu—I believe not. If they do, they do not understand him. He is often obscure; sometimes misled by system; but, on the whole, a learned, and ingenious writer, and sometimes a most profound thinker. Sure it is, that they have not followed him in any one thing they have done. Had he lived at this time, he would certainly

---

[3] At the time of its fall the Bastille contained only seven prisoners: four forgers, two lunatics and one dissipated young noble incarcerated at the request of his family. It had already been decided, before the Revolution, to pull it down, as useless and in the way of urban development.

[4] The projecting iron brackets holding the street lamps of Paris proved handy gibbets.

be among the fugitives from France. With regard to the other writers you speak of, I do believe the directors of the present system to be influenced by them. Such masters, such scholars. Who ever dreamt of Voltaire and Rousseau as legislators? The first has the merit of writing agreeably; and nobody has every united blasphemy and obscenity so happily together. The other was not a little deranged in his intellects, to my almost certain knowledge.[5] But he saw things in bold and uncommon lights, and he was very eloquent—But as to the rest! —I have read long since the *Contrat Social*. It has left very few traces upon my mind.[6] I thought it a performance of little or no merit; and little did I conceive, that it could ever make revolutions, and give law to nations. But so it is. I see some people here are willing that we should become their scholars too, and reform our state on the French model. They have begun; and it is high time for those who wish to preserve *morem majorum*, to look about them.

It seems clear that by the end of 1789 Burke had already made up his mind about the French Revolution. It required one more provocation to determine him to make a public stand. This was provided when he returned to London in mid-January for the meeting of Parliament on the 21st. On the night of his arrival he read for the first time Dr Price's sermon and the Revolution Society's correspondence with the National Assembly. He immediately began making notes for a public answer, presumably in some such form as was finally embodied in the *Reflections*. His first impulse was to avoid parliamentary discussion of the subject. The Government supporter who moved the Address of Thanks at the opening of Parliament vigorously condemned the Revolution, but Burke told friends two days later that he thought this speech imprudent— he himself would have said 'ten times as much' had he thought it proper, but for the moment he saw no need of interfering. Two weeks later, however, in the Committee on the Army Estimates on 5 February, Fox reintroduced the subject, going out of his way three times to praise the Revolution. Burke was not present on this occasion, and Fox later insisted that he had heard only a garbled and distorted ministerial version of what was said. In the continuation of the debate on 9 February, Fox praised the Revolution with rather less restraint, saying he 'exulted' in it 'from feelings and from principle'; he applauded the French guards for their refusal to obey the Court in the previous July. Pitt also spoke at some length, saying that he looked forward to the day when a reconstructed and free France 'would stand forward as one of the most brilliant powers in Europe'. Only after this flood of praise and speculation about the future of the Revolution did Burke himself take up the subject, delivering a solemn warning against revolutionary principles. The substance of his speech in this debate was published on 20 February.

---

[5] Burke was a friend of Hume at the time when Hume brought Rousseau to England in 1766, but he does not claim a personal acquaintance with Rousseau.

[6] Burke reviewed Rousseau's *Letter to d'Alembert* in the *Annual Register* for 1759 and *Emile* in that for 1762. Both reviews were sharply critical, though not in the denunciatory style of the famous passage in the *Letter to a Member of the National Assembly*.

PHILIP FRANCIS *to* EDMUND BURKE—19 *February* 1790

Corr. (1958), VI, 85–7

Philip Francis (1740–1818), M.P., had been a friend of Burke's since 1773, and since 1785 had been his indispensable assistant in the prosecution of Warren Hastings. Burke evidently sent Francis first the manuscript draft and then the proofs of his *Reflections on the Revolution in France*, and asked for comment.

19th Feburary. 1790

My dear Mr. Burke,

I am sorry you should have had the trouble of sending for the printed paper you lent me yesterday, though, I own, I cannot much regret even a fault of my own, that helps to delay the publication of that paper. I know with certainty that I am the only friend, and many there are, who ever ventures to contradict or oppose you, face to face, on Subjects of this nature. They either care too little for *you*, or too much for *themselves*, to run the risk of giving you immediate offence, for the sake of any subsequent or remote advantage you might derive from it. But what they withhold from *you* they communicate very liberally to *me*, because they think or pretend that I have some influence over you, which I have not, but which, on the present occasion, I most devoutly wish I had. I am not afraid of exasperating you against me at any given moment, because I know you will cool again, and place it all to the right account. It is the proper province and ought to be the priviledge of an inferior to criticise and advise. The best possible Critic of the Iliad, would be ipso facto, and by virtue of that very character, incapable of being the author of it. Standing as I do in this relation to you, you would renounce your superiority if you refused to be advised by me. Waving all discussion concerning the Substance and general tendency of this printed Letter, I must declare my opinion that what I have seen of it, is very loosely put together. In point of writing at least the manuscript you shewed me first, was much less exceptionable. Remember that this is one of the most singular, that it may be the most distinguished and ought to be one of the most deliberate acts of your life. Your writings have hitherto been the delight and instruction of your own Country. You now undertake to correct and instruct another Nation, and your appeal in effect is to all Europe. Allowing you the liberty to do so in an extreme case, you cannot deny that it ought to be done with special deliberation in the choice of the topics, and with no less care and circumspection in the use you make of them. Have you thoroughly considered whether it be worthy of Mr Burke, of a Privy Councillor, of a man so high and considerable in the House of Commons as you are, and holding the station you have obtained in the opinion of the world to enter into a war of Pamphlets with Doctor Price? If he answers you as assuredly he will (and so will many others) can you refuse to reply to a person whom you have attacked? If you do you are defeated in a battle of your own provoking, and driven to fly from ground of your own choosing. If you do not, where is such a contest to lead you, but into a vile and disgraceful, tho' it were ever so victorious, an altercation? '*Dii Meliora*' that if you will do it, away with all jest and sneer and sarcasm. Let every thing you say be grave, direct and serious. In a case so interesting as the errors of a great nation, and the calamities of great individuals, and feeling them so deeply as you profess to do, all manner of insinuation is improper, all jibe and nickname prohibited. In my opinion all that you say of the Queen[1] is pure foppery. If she be a perfect female character you ought to take your ground upon her virtues. If she be the reverse it is ridiculous in any but a Lover, to place her personal charms in opposition to her crimes. Either way I know the argument must proceed upon a supposition; for neither have you said anything to establish her moral merits, nor have her accusers formally tried and convicted her of guilt. On this subject, however, you cannot but know that the opinion of the world is not lately but has been many years decided. But in effect when you assert her claim to protection and respect on no other topics but those of gallantry and beauty and personal accomplishments, you virtually abandon the proof and assertion of her innocence, which you know is the point substantially in question. Pray, Sir, how long have you felt yourself so desperately disposed to admire the Ladies of Germany?[2] I despise and abhor, as much as you can do, all personal insult and outrage even to guilt itself, if I see it, where it ought to be, dejected and helpless; but it is in vain to expect that I or any reasonable man shall regret the sufferings of a Messalina,[3] as I should those of a Mrs Crewe[4] or a Mrs Burke, I mean of all that is beautiful or virtuous amongst women. Is it nothing but outside? Have they no moral minds? Or are you such a determined Champion of Beauty as to draw your Sword in defense of any jade upon Earth provided she be handsome? Look back, I beseech you and deliberate a little, before you determine

[1] The famous passage describing Marie Antoinette.
[2] An allusion to the Opposition's criticism of Queen Charlotte's activity during the Regency crisis, and to Burke's suspicions that she was protecting Hastings.
[3] The third wife of the Emperor Claudius, notorious for profligacy, avarice and ambition.
[4] Frances Anne, *née* Greville (d. 1818), one of the most prominent Whig hostesses.

that this is an office that perfectly becomes you. If I stop here it is not for want of a multitude of objections. The mischief you are going to do yourself is, to my apprehension, palpable. It is visible. It will be audible. I snuff it in the wind. I taste it already. I feel it in every sense and so will you hereafter when I *vow to God* (a most elegant phrase) it will be no sort of consolation to me to reflect that I did every thing in my power to prevent it. I wish you were at the De-l. for giving me all this trouble. And so farewell

P. FRANCIS.

To PHILIP FRANCIS—20 *February* [1790]

Corr. (1958), VI, 88–92

Gerard Street Feb. 20. 1/2 after 8.

My dear Sir,

I sat up rather late at Carlton House, and on my return hither. I found your Letter on my Table. I have not slept since. You will therefore excuse me if you find any thing confused, or otherwise expressed than I could wish in speaking to you upon a matter which interests you from your regard to me. There are some things in your Letter for which I must thank you; there are others which I must answer; Some things bear the marks of friendly admonition; others bear some resemblance to the Tone of accusation.

You are the only friend I have who will dare to give me advice. I must then have something terrible in me, which intimidates all others who know me from giving me the only unequivocal mark of their regard. Whatever this Rough and menacing manner may be, I must search myself upon it; and when I discover it, old as I am, I must endeavour to correct it. I flatterd myself however, that you at least would not have thought my other friends altogether justified in with-holding from me their services of this Kind. You certainly do not always convey to me your opinions with the greatest possible Tenderness, and management; and yet I do not recollect since I first had the pleasure of your acquaintance that there has been an heat or a coolness of a single days duration on my side during that whole time. I believe your memory cannot present to you an instance of it. I ill deserve friends, if I throw them away on account of the Candour and simplicity of their good nature. In particular you know, that you have in some instances favourd me with your Instructions relative to things I was preparing for the publick. If I did not in every instance agree with you, I think you had on the whole sufficient proofs of my docility to make you believe that I received your corrections not only without offence, but with no small degree of Gratitude.

Your remarks upon the two first Sheets of my Paris Letter relate to the Composition and the matter. The composition you say is loose; and I am quite sure it is. I never intended it should be otherwise; for purporting to be, what in Truth it originally was, a Letter to a friend, I had no Idea of digesting it in a Systematick order. The Style is open to correction, and wants it. My natural Style of Writing is somewhat careless; and I should be happy in receiving your advice towards making it as little viscious as such a Style is capable of being made. The general Character and colour of a Style which grows out of the Writers peculiar Turn of mind and habit of expressing his thoughts must be attended to in all corrections. It is not the insertion of a piece of Stuff though of a better kind which is at all times an improvement.

Your main Objections are however of a much deeper Nature, and go to the Political opinions and moral Sentiments of the piece; in which I find, (though with no sort of surprise, having often talked with you on the Subject) that we differ only in every thing. You say 'The mischief you are going to do yourself is to my apprehension palpable. I snuff it in the wind; and my Taste sickens at it.' This anticipated Stench that turns your Stomach at such a distance must be nauseous indeed. You seem to think I shall incur great (and not wholly undeserved) infamy by this publication. This makes it a matter of some delicacy to me to suppress what I have written; for I must admit in my own feeling, and in that of those who have seen this piece, that my Sentiments and opinions deserve the infamy with which they are threatned. If they do not, I know nothing more than that I oppose the prejudices and inclinations of many people. This I was well aware of from the beginning, and it was in order to oppose those inclinations and prejudices, that I proposed to publish my Letter. I really am perfectly astonish'd how you could dream with my paper in your hand—that I found no other Cause than the Beauty of the Queen of France (now I suppose pretty much faded) for disapproving the Conduct which has been held towards her, and for expressing my own particular feelings. I am not to order the Natural Sympathies of my own Breast, and of every honest breast to wait until the Tales and all the anecdotes of the Coffeehouses of Paris and of the dissenting meeting houses of London are scoured of all the slander of those who calumniate persons, that afterwards they may murder them with impunity? I know nothing of your Story of Messalina.[1] Am I obliged to prove juridically the Virtues of all those I shall see suffering every kind of wrong, and contumely, and risk of Life, before I endeavour to interest others in their sufferings, and before I endeavour to excite an horrour against midnight assassins at back stairs,[2] and their more wicked abettors in Pulpits? What, are not high Rank, great Splendour of descent, great personal Elegance and outward accomplishments ingredients of moment in forming the interest we take in the Misfortunes of Men?[3] The minds of those who do not feel thus are not even Dramatically right. 'Whats Hecuba to him or he to Hecuba that he should weep for her?'[4] Why because she was Hecuba, the Queen of Troy, the Wife of Priam, and sufferd in the close of Life a thousand Calamities. I felt too for Hecuba when I read the fine Tragedy of Euripides upon her Story: and I never enquired into the Anecdotes of the Court or City of Troy before I gave way to the Sentiments which the author wished to inspire; nor do I remember that he ever said one word of her Virtues. It is for those who applaud or palliate assassination, regicide, and base insults to Women of illustrious place, to prove the Crimes in the sufferers which they allege to justifye their own. But if they had proved fornication on any such Woman, taking the manners of the world and the manners of France, I shall never put it in a parralel with Assassination. No! I have no such inverted Scale of Faults in my heart or my head. You find it perfectly ridiculous, and unfit for me in particular, to take these things as my ingredients of Commiseration. Pray why so? Is it absurd in me, to think that the Chivalrous Spirit which dictated a veneration for Women of condition

---

[1] Burke cannot mean that he has never heard any story about Messalina; but that he gives no credit to similar stories about Marie Antoinette. It is highly improbable that he had heard none of those spread in the libellous pamphlets circulated by her enemies at Court. Indeed, in the *Reflections* he refers to the 'slanders of those who bring us their anecdotes with the attestation of the flower-du-luce on their shoulder' (*Works*, Bohn, II, 356; Little, Brown, III, 342), which is certainly a reference to the *Mémoires* of Jeanne de Saint-Rémy de Valois, Comtesse de La Motte (1756–91) who had been branded for her part in the Diamond Necklace affair.

[2] Burke is referring to the incident of 6 October 1789 described in the *Reflections* (*Works*, Bohn, II, 343–4; Little, Brown, III, 325), when members of the mob broke into the Queen's chamber and the guard at the door was supposedly killed. The accuracy of his account was subsequently challenged, and Richard, writing from Coblenz, said he had met the guard whom Burke had thus done away with.

[3] Burke makes a similar comment in the *Reflections*, shortly before his description of Marie Antoinete: 'I confess to you, Sir, that the exalted rank of the persons suffering, and particularly the sex, the beauty, and the amiable qualities of the descendant of so many kings and emperors . . . instead of being a subject of exultation, adds not a little to my sensibility on that most melancholy occasion' (*Works*, Bohn, II, 347; Little, Brown, III, 330).

[4] *Hamlet*, II, ii, 564–5.

and of Beauty, without any consideration whatsoever of enjoying them, was the great Scource of those manners which have been the Pride and ornament of Europe for so many ages? And am I not to lament that I have lived to see those manners extinguishd in so shocking a manner by mean speculations of Finance and the false Science of a sordid and degenerate Philosophy? I tell you again that the recollection of the manner in which I saw the Queen of France in the year 1774[5] and the contrast between that brilliancy, Splendour, and beauty, with the prostrate Homage of a Nation to her, compared with the abominable Scene of 1789 which I was describing did draw Tears from me and wetted my Paper. These Tears came again into my Eyes almost as often as I lookd at the description. They may again. You do not believe this fact, or that these are my real feelings, but that the whole is affected, or as you express it, 'downright Foppery'. My friend, I tell you it is truth—and that it is true, and will be true, when you and I are no more, and will exist as long as men—with their Natural feelings exist. I shall say no more on this Foppery of mine.—Oh by the way—you ask me how long I have been an admirer of German Ladies? Always the same. Present me the Idea of such massacres about any German Lady here, and such attempts to assassinate her, and such a Triumphal procession from Windsor to the old Jewry—and I assure you I shall be quite as full of natural concern and just indignation. As to the other points they deserve serious consideration and they shall have it. I certainly cannot profit quite as much by your assistance as if we agreed. In that case every correction would be forwarding the design. We should work with one common View. But it is impossible that any man can correct a Work according to its true Spirit who is opposed to its object; or can help the expression of what he thinks ought not to be expressed at all.

I should agree with You about the vileness of the Controversy with such Miscreants as the Revolution society and the National assembly, and I know very well that they, as well as their Allies the Indian delinquents, will darken the air with their arrows. But I do not yet think, they have the advowson of reputation. I shall try that point. My dear sir you think of nothing but controversies. 'I challenge into the field of Battle and retire defeated' &ca &ca. If their having the last word be a defeat they most assuredly will defeat me. But I intend no controversy with Dr Price or Lord Shelburne or any other of their

[5] A slip for 1773.

set.[6] I mean to set in a full View the danger from their wicked principles and their black hearts; I intend to state the true principles of our constitution in Church and state—upon Grounds opposite to theirs. If any one be the better for the example made of them, and for this exposition, well and good. I mean to do my best to expose them to the hatred, ridicule, and contempt of the whole world; as I shall always expose such, calumniators, hypocrites sowers of sedition, and approvers of murder and all its Triumphs. When I have done that, they may have the field to themselves and I care very little how they Triumph over me, since I hope they will not be able to draw me at their heels and carry my head in Triumph on their Poles. I have been interrupted and have said enough. Adieu. Believe me always sensible of your friendship although it is impossible that a greater difference can exist on Earth between any Sentiments on those Subjects than unfortunately for me there is between yours and mine.

To CAPTAIN THOMAS MERCER—26 *February* 1790

Corr. (1958), VI, 92–8

Burke's attack on the principles of the French Revolution in the debate on the Army Estimates advertised to the world that there were serious divisions within the Opposition. It surprised many contemporaries, who had been accustomed to regarding Burke as a liberal and a reformer. Thomas Mercer (*c.* 1733–1801) of Arno's Vale, near Newry, County Down, was apparently a rather recent acquaintance of Burke's. Shocked by Burke's comments upon the French Revolution, which he had read in English newspapers, Mercer wrote from Newry on 19 February expressing his wonder at '. . . the imputation to you of sentiments exceedingly inimical to what is thought by many a most glorious revolution in France'. He protested against Burke's charges that the French had subverted their ancient government and church, observing that both deserved it; then proceeded to justify revolution as the only way to shake the hold of despotism, and concluded that the new French Government promised to be truly representative, the only type 'fit for rational beings to live under and submit to'.

Dear Sir,

The speedy answer I return to your letter, I hope, will convince you of the high value I set upon the regard you are so good to express for me, and the obliging trouble which you take to inform my judgment upon matters in which we are all very deeply concerned. I think

[6] William Petty, formerly Fitzmaurice, 2nd Earl of Shelburne (1737–1805), who had been created Marquess of Lansdowne in 1784, was a promoter of parliamentary reform and a protector of Price, Priestley and other radical dissenters.

perfectly well of your heart and your principles, and of the strength of your natural understanding, which, according to your opportunities, you have not been wanting in pains to improve. If you are mistaken, it is perhaps owing to the impression almost inevitably made by the various careless conversations which we are engaged in through life; conversations in which those who propagate their doctrines have not been called upon for much reflection concerning their end and tendency; and in which those, who imperceptibly imbibe the doctrines taught, are not required, by a particular duty, very closely to examine them, or to act from the impressions they receive. I am obliged to *act*, and am therefore bound to call my principles and sentiments to a strict account. As far as my share of a public trust goes, I am in *trust* religiously to maintain the rights and properties of all descriptions of people in the *possession* which legally they hold; and in the *rule* by which alone they can be secure in any possession. I do not find myself at liberty, either as a man, or as a trustee for men, to take a *vested* property from one man, and to give it to another, because *I* think that the portion of one is too great, and that of another too small. From my first juvenile rudiments of speculative study to the grey hairs of my present experience, I have never learned any thing else. I can never be taught any thing else by *reason;* and when *force* comes, I shall consider whether I am to submit to it, or how I am to resist it. This I am very sure of, that an early guard against the manifest tendency of a contrary doctrine is the only way by which those who love order can be prepared to resist such force.

The calling men by the names of 'pampered and luxurious prelates',[1] &c. is in you no more than a mark of your dislike to intemperance and idle expence; but in others it is used for other purposes. It is often used to extinguish the sense of justice in our minds, and the natural feelings of humanity in our bosoms. Such language does not mitigate the cruel effects of reducing men of opulent condition, and their innumerable dependents, to the last distress. If I were to adopt the plan of a spoliatory reformation, I should probably employ such language; but it would aggravate instead of extenuating my guilt in overturning the sacred principles of property.

[1] Mercer had written: 'For the rest—if to take from pampered and luxurious prelates a part of those sumptuous livings which were accumulated in the times of ignorance and superstition, and to provide for the more comfortable subsistence of parish priests, be the subversion of a church, millions of good men and good Christians will heartily wish (for the honour of true religion, distinct from pageantry and hypocrisy) that all such may in this manner be speedily subverted'.

Sir, I say that church and state, and human society too, for which church and state are made, are subverted by such doctrines, joined to such practices, as leave no foundation for property in *long possessions*. My dear Captain Mercer, it is not my calling the use you make of your plate in your house, either of dwelling or of prayer, 'pageantry and hypocrisy', that can justify me in taking from you your own property, and your own liberty to use your own property according to your own ideas of ornament. When you find me attempting to break into your house to take your plate, under any pretence whatsoever, but most of all under pretence of purity of religion and Christian charity, shoot me for a robber and an hypocrite, as in that case I shall certainly be. The 'true Christian Religion' never taught me any such practices, nor did the religion of my nature, nor any religion, nor any law.

Let those who never abstained from a full meal, and as much wine as they could swallow, for a single day of their whole lives, satirize 'luxurious and pampered prelates', if they will. Let them abuse such prelates, and such lords, and such squires, provided it be only to correct their vices. I care not much about the language of this moral satire, if they go no further than satire. But there are occasions when the language of Falstaff, reproaching the Londoners, whom he robbed in their way to Canterbury, with the gorbellies and their city luxury, is not so becoming.

It is not calling the landed estates, possessed by old *prescriptive rights*, the 'accumulations of ignorance and superstition', that can support me in shaking that grand title, which supersedes all other title, and which all my studies of general jurisprudence have taught me to consider as one principal cause of the formation of states; I mean the ascertaining and securing *prescription*. But these are donations made in 'ages of ignorance and superstition'. Be it so. It proves that these donations were made long ago; and this is *prescription;* and this gives right and title. It is possible that many estates about you were originally obtained by arms, that is, by violence, a thing almost as bad as supersitition,[2] and not much short of ignorance: but it is *old violence;* and that which might be wrong in the beginning, is consecrated by time, and becomes lawful. This may be supersitition in me, and ignorance; but I had rather remain in ignorance and superstition than

[2] Many of the estates in Ulster had passed into protestant and English hands after the overwhelming defeat of the Irish revolt of 1598 and the 'plantation' of the province under James I; others had changed hands by force as a result of the Cromwellian and Williamite reconquests of Ireland.

be enlightened and purified out of the first principles of law and natural justice. I never will suffer you, if I can help it, to be deprived of the well-earned fruits of your industry, because others may want your fortune more than you do, and may have laboured, and so now labour, in vain, to acquire even a subsistence. Nor on the contrary, if success had less smiled on your endeavours, and you had come home insolvent, would I take from any 'pampered and luxurious lord' in your neighbourhood one acre of his land, or one spoon from his sideboard, to compensate your losses, though incurred (as they would have been incurred) in the course of a well-spent, virtuous, and industrious life. God is the distributor of his own blessings. I will not impiously attempt to usurp his throne, but will keep according to the subordinate place and trust in which he has stationed me, to secure the order of property which I find established in my country. No guiltless man has ever been, nor ever will, I trust, be able to say with truth, that he has been obliged to retrench a dish at his table for any reformations of mine.[3]

You pay me the compliment to suppose me a foe to tyranny and oppression,[4] and you are therefore surprized at the sentiments I have lately delivered in Parliament. I am that determined foe to tyranny, or I greatly deceive myself in my character: and I am sure I am an ideot in my conduct. It is because I am, and mean to continue so, that I abominate the example of France for this country. I know that tyranny seldom attacks the poor, never in the first instance. They are not its proper prey. It falls on the wealthy and the great, whom by rendering objects of envy, and otherwise obnoxious to the multitude, they may more easily destroy; and, when they are destroyed, that multitude which was led to that ill work by the arts of bad men, is itself undone for ever.

I hate tyranny, at least I think so; but I hate it most of all where most are concerned in it. The tyranny of a multitude is a multiplied tyranny. If, as society is constituted in these large countries of France and England, full of unequal property, I must make my choice (which God avert!) between the despotism of a single person, or of the many, my election is made. As much injustice and tyranny has been practised in a few months by a French democracy, as in all the arbitrary monarchies in Europe in the forty years of my observation. I speak of

---

[3] Burke is referring to his Establishment Acts of 1782 and 1783, and to his reform of the Pay Office.

[4] Mercer had written: 'I had long considered you the determined enemy of tyranny and oppression of every kind—the friend of man—and of every thing which might promote his felicity'.

publick glaring acts of tyranny; I say nothing of the common effects of old abusive governments, because I do not know that as bad may not be found in the new. This democracy begins very ill; and I feel no security, that what has been rapacious and bloody in its commencement, will be mild and protecting in its final settlement. They cannot, indeed, in future, rob so much, because they have left little that can be taken. I go to the full length of my principle. I should think the government of the deposed King of France,[5] or of the late King of Prussia,[6] or the present Emperor,[7] or the present Czarina,[8] none of them, perhaps, perfectly good people, to be far better than the government of twenty-four millions of men, *all as good as you;* and I do not know any body better; supposing that those twenty-four millions would be subject, as infallibly they would, to the same unrestrained, though virtuous, impulses; because it is plain, that their majority would think every thing justified by their warm good intentions—they would heat one another by their common zeal—counsel and advice would be lost on them—they would not listen to temperate individuals, and they would be less capable, infinitely, of moderation, than the most heady of those princes.

What have I to do with France, but as the common interest of humanity, and its example to this country, engages me? I know France, by observation and enquiry, pretty tolerably for a stranger: and I am not a man to fall in love with the faults or follies of the old or new government. You reason as if I were running a parallel between its former abusive government and the present tyranny. What had all this to do with the opinions I delivered in Parliament, which ran a parallel between the liberty they might have had, and this frantic delusion. This is the way by which you blind and deceive yourself, and beat the air in your argument with me. Why do you instruct me on a state of the case which has no existence? You know how to reason very well. What most of the newspapers make me say, I know not, nor do I much care. I don't think, however, they have thus stated me. There is a very fair *abstract* of my speech printed in a little pamphlet,[9] which I would send you if it were worth putting you to the expence.

[5] Louis XVI. Burke takes the assumption of power by the National Assembly to be equivalent to Louis XVI's deposition.
[6] Frederick II.
[7] Burke must mean Joseph II, who had in fact died on 20 February, although the news had not yet appeared in the English press.
[8] Catherine II.
[9] Burke himself had been responsible for the publication of the *Substance of the Speech of the Right Honourable Edmund Burke, in the Debate on the Army Estimates,* published on 20 February.

To discuss the affairs of France and its Revolution would require a volume, perhaps many volumes. Your general reflections about revolutions may be right or wrong:[10] they conclude nothing. I don't find myself disposed to controvert them, for I do not think they apply to the present affairs, nay, I am sure they do not. I conceive you have got very imperfect accounts of these transactions. I believe I am much more exactly informed of them.

I am sorry, indeed, to find that our opinions do differ essentially, fundamentally, and are at the utmost possible distance from each other,[11] if I understand you or myself clearly on this subject. Your freedom is far from displeasing to me; I love it; for I always wish to know the full of what is in the mind of the friend I converse with. I give you mine as freely; and I hope I shall offend you as little as you do me. I shall have no objection to your shewing my letter to as many as you please. I have no secrets with regard to the public. I have never shrunk from obloquy; and I have never courted popular applause. If I have met with any share of it, '*non recepi sed rapui*'.[12] No difference of opinion, however, shall hinder me from cultivating your friendship, while you permit me to do so. I have not written this to discuss these matters in a prolonged controversy (I wish we may never say more about them), but to comply with your commands, which ever shall have due weight with me. I am most respectfully, and

most affectionately your's,
EDMD BURKE

London,
February 26, 1790.

Mercer was neither crushed nor converted by Burke's letter. He composed a ten-page answer to it in August 1790, but did not forward it to Burke until 8 November, after seeing advertisements for the publication of the *Reflections*.

[10] A revolution, Mercer told Burke, 'cannot be effected without some convulsion; nor is it possible so to order the matter, but in some cases many individuals may suffer injury and outrage; and this, as far as it goes, is to be lamented. But, if it ends in freedom, in the deliverance of a nation from the despotism of one man, no price can be thought too dear to pay for it'.

[11] Mercer concluded his letter: 'Perhaps you will cheer me with an assurance that we do not differ widely; than which nothing would be a more exhilirating [sic] cordial to one, who has the honour to be, with every possible respect, Your most faithful and Humble servant'.

[12] The verbs are reversed; the source has not been found.

To ADREIN-JEAN-FRANÇOIS DUPORT—
[*post* 29 *March* 1790]

Corr. (1958), VI, 104–9

Adrien-Jean-Françoise Duport (1759–98) was *conseiller au parlement* at Paris before the Revolution. Elected to the Estates General by the *noblesse* of Paris, he joined the Third Estate and became prominent among the moderate reformers, taking a leading part in the discussion of judicial reforms. His speech on *Principes et plan sur l'éta-blissement de l'ordre judiciaire* was printed by order of the Assembly. A long note on page 105 has almost the character of a public letter of remonstrance to Burke for his lack of sympathy with the Revolution; in this letter Burke replies to him.

Sir,

I have received your speech upon your proposed organisation of Courts of Judicature under the new Constitution of France. I am extremely obliged to you for the honour you have done me by this mark of your attention. I am not less sensible to the polite manner in which you are pleased to express yourself to me personally in stating your disapprobation of the sentiments I entertain upon the affairs of France.

A difference in opinion from a Gentleman of your merit and abilities, in one point of view, I must always think a misfortune. But whatever the errours of my speech might have been, I faithfully assure you, they are entirely my own, and have not been infused into my mind, as you supposed by any representation of the Refugees from France, in London.

I do not recollect, that previous to my declaring my thoughts in my place upon occasion of the Army debate, I had spoken to one French person except to one French Gentleman, with some of whose family I had an acquaintance. This Gentleman was not a Refugee, but had come hither upon business, wholly unrelated to Politicks. On the subject of that business alone, as well as I can remember, I had conversed with him at that time.

I had then scarcely read any thing upon the subject, except the general Instructions given to the Representatives; and the proceedings of the National Assembly, extremely at variance with those instructions; and some pieces supposed to be written by the Comte de Mirabeau; together with the facts which appear'd uncontradicted in some foreign and domestick papers. From them I had formed my opinions.

Since that time I have read more largely; I have also sometimes had the honour (but not so often as I wished) of meeting Persons of your Nation, of great merit and distinction, Exiles of Virtue and Patriotism, whom it can never be to the glory or the advantage of any Country to have driven from its bosom. All worthy people here, and of all descriptions and ranks, and without any distinction of Party, wish to testify their great respect for those illustrious Refugees and to afford them all the consolations in their power. I have found these Gentlemen ardent Lovers of the Country which is the origin of their being, and their sufferings. They lament (I take it for granted else I should think otherwise of them than I do) the destruction of the unity of the Kingdom; the total subversion of the monarchy, the imprisonment of their Sovereign and their Queen, and the daily insults and humiliations to which these revered personages are exposed in their unmerited Captivity. They are deeply affected, to be sure, with the not much less captivated condition of the National Assembly; with the publick bankruptcy, and all the evils which in consequence have fallen upon Individuals, upon publick Bodies, and on the State. They are generally reserved on these subjects; but I hope you do not think that it is necessary for the Refugees to tell us, how they ought to feel in all these particulars.

In some of these sentiments, as an Englishman, I cannot sympathize with them so much as I sincerely do in others. The reduction of the late formidable power of France by dismemberment and its partition into a multitude of Republicks,[1] each of which seems to have seized and appropriated to themselves, portions of the Revenue or to have abolish'd them, sets this Country pretty much at ease. As the best Roman Patriots did not however, with old Cato, wish the total destruction of Carthage, there are many here who are not perfectly sure, that the proceedings of its National Assembly may not reduce our late Rival, France, to a still lower condition than is good for the total balance of Europe, and consequently for our welfare. On this political question however, which is not without its difficulties, I form no Judgment.

In your plan of Judicature, I acknowlege with pleasure the work of a powerful and comprehensive understanding. But I can say nothing further of it. One can form no judgment of these things in the abstract. How this project falls on all the other members of the system (if system it be) of your new Constitution, is impossible for me, who know that

---

[1] As Burke thought had been done by the decree of 22 December 1789, establishing electoral and administrative assemblies and by the formal division of France into departments in the decree of 26 February. In the *Reflections* he repeats this complaint that France had been broken into separate and independent republics (*Works*, Bohn, II, 452–3, 457; Little, Brown, III, 479, 480).

Constitution only on paper, to form even a tolerable guess. Perhaps Sir, it may not be quite easy for yourself to estimate its probable effects in that relation; I can draw no lights from my experience in the Judicature of this Country to determine. Our Juries, for instance, are placed in very different relations and are combined with an order of things so totally unlike your whole project, that no argument from their known effect in England can be safely drawn as to their probable effect in the experimental establishments in France.

On the whole Sir, give me leave to express my surprize that a Man of your capacity can condescend to amuse yourself so seriously, not to say laboriously about the Constitution of Tribunals to try property in a Country where the foundations of property are destroyed, about the administration of Justice, in a Country where the people appear to be ignorant of its first elemental principles. How can you think it worth your valuable time and pains to regulate the modes and forms in which a savage people are to be called methodically to assassinate and to rob, instead of doing the same thing by the present short, summary, and I really think, more tolerable process. What does it signify to the cause of humanity when a Man is to die like Monsr Foulon[2] or like Monsr Favras?[3] Whether a Man is to be turned out of his house by an arbitrary Vote of an Assembly, by the iniquitous Judgment of a Court, or the plain violence of a Mob. Ought not some Teacher appear, by some religious influence, to pave the way for the entry of a rational Judicature such a one as it was said formerly—

[4] Is it not necessary that there should first be some dawnings of Civilization in the Country? That your People should be made Men before they are constituted Magistrates; that they should have some faint, obscure notions of Justice before they are made Judges?

Forms are not without their value; but they hold a low place indeed in the scale of moral agency. They are but instruments at best. Where the idea of Justice is generally recognized and prevalent you can hardly constitute a Judicature in such a manner that the ends of publick order should not in a good degree be answer'd by it. But when Men are destitute not only of all wise and sound discipline on this subject but

[2] Joseph-François Foullon (1717–89) was appointed Controller General on 12 July 1789 after the dismissal of Necker. He was captured by a mob on 22 July 1789, hanged from a *lanterne*, and his decapitated head, the mouth stuffed with straw, carried in triumph through Paris on the end of a pike.

[3] Thomas de Mahy, Marquis de Favras (1744–90), Colonel in the Swiss Guard of the Comte de Provence, was arrested in December 1789 and charged with plotting counter-revolution. He was sentenced to death and hanged before the Hôtel de Ville on 19 February.

[4] There is a gap—of about one line—in the MS at this point.

have the natural rude unplanted sense of Justice extirpated out of their minds and a sort of artificial ignorance and systematick barbarism substituted in their place, the most plausible formalities can be of no use but to give something of a colour to wrong and violence. The more popular such a form of Judicature is made, the worse it is, because the more loose, headlong and unrestrained their outrages are likely to become towards the objects of their malignity, rapacity, revenge or envy.

A People who thirst for blood and confiscation in the bosom of Peace, who could endure even to hear of a maxim that the goods of any one Citizen possessed by a long acknowledged legal title belong to the State, and that those who assume the exercise of sovereign Authority are free to take it from him and to make such a distribution of it as they please, such a People are not fit to sit in a seat of Judgment, or for any other function, because they despise the very foundation of social Union. Those who have the temper of Tyrants are only made for the condition of Slaves. It is good for themselves and for every one else that they should be so.

I confess to you Sir, that from what passes in a manner before my eyes (for the industry of your publications brings every thing into view) I think of all the Countries I have ever seen, heard, or read of, France as it is likely to be constituted, is the very last in which a considerate Man would wish to have his lot cast, or to have his life, liberty or property depending upon any of their formalities which may be established.

Thinking well, as you are pleased to do, of my general intentions you are surprized that I should be adverse to proceedings so favourable to the cause of *humanity*. You will pardon me, if on my side, I am a little surprized to find however they may be supported on other grounds; they are to be justified by any sentiments of humanity or a love for our species. It is a thing of course that all publick Men, in all their actions hold out some prospect of publick good, but men who pursue their plans by violent stretches of arbitrary power to the utter ruin of multitudes of people, and make no great scruple of shedding blood out of battle, are generally rather thought deep and daring politicians than Men who ought to value themselves upon the tenderness and humanity of their dispositions. I confess to you that I have no great opinion of that sublime abstract, metaphysic reversionary, contingent humanity, which in *cold blood* can subject the *present time*, and those whom we *daily see and converse with*, to *immediate* calamities in favour of the future and uncertain benefit of persons who *only exist in idea*.

This may be something above, and better; but it is by no means the same thing with humanity. These notions of mine may be the effect of weakness, ignorance, and old prejudice (that Enemy of the National Assembly to which it gives no quarter) but I cannot help my Nature. I cannot think well of that speculative good which is to be produced by a great deal of practical evil. I think it possible that plans which beggar the present generation for the sake of enriching the future may produce what they seek, but they may also fail, and the evil is certain. I cannot prevail on myself to stand by and applaud those who are engaged at such a Table, where men so freely game away the substance and the blood of others. Our first trust is the happiness of our own time.

Excuse the liberty I take. It certainly means no personal offence to you. But we are in a crisis, where there is no trifling. It is plain that you have among You those who are strongly tinctured with a most dangerous spirit

To UNKNOWN—26 January 1791

Corr. (1958), VI, 214–16

The anonymous author of a pamphlet entitled *A Comparison of the Opinions of Mr Burke and Mnsr Rousseau* (London, 1791) sent Burke a copy with a letter dated 18 January. He identified himself only as one who had 'pass'd many pleasant hours in your society and looks forward to the continuance of your friendship'. According to his Preface, the object of his work was to show that 'Rousseau and Burke are too much of the same opinion on Government Reform, to be so differently esteemed by the French Assembly'. For Rousseau's principles he relied almost wholly upon the *Considérations sur le gouvernement de Pologne*, from which he selected many passages which anticipated Burke's arguments in the *Reflections*. The parallel he drew between Rousseau's advice on the reform of the Polish constitution and the opinions of Burke might seem justified, and has been noticed by others since then. But since Burke was about to denounce Rousseau in his *Letter to a Member of the National Assembly*, he might have found the pamphlet embarrassing. In this letter he does not refer to the general subject of the pamphlet, but picks up for comment a merely incidental reference to his own religious views.

Dear Sir

I am extremely happy and much flatterd, to find that the Gentleman, who, without putting his name to his very ingenious and well written pamphlet and letter, is pleased to think so favourably of me, is among my acquaintance. I hope on my coming to Town I may be permitted to thank him for the Sentiments, which, upon acquaintance with myself, my conduct, and my writings he is so kind to entertain of them all.

You have made me acquainted with the Criticisms which have appeard upon my Letter. I really had not read any of them, though they have all been sent to my house. I had said nearly all that I had to say upon the subject of France; and I resolved, when I knew I was not likely to alter my own opinions, or to change those of my adversaries, not to be tempted into any further controversy.

By your Book, I perceive, that one of the Topics of those who write against me is my religion. They can do nothing in a publick discussion without something personal about their adversary. I do not think I have said any thing concerning theological tenets, or the parties they have given rise to, beyond expressions of general goodwill to them all, whatever little goodwill they may bear to one another. I have been baptised and educated in the Church of England; and have seen no cause to abandon that communion. When I do, I shall act upon my conviction or my mistake. I think that Church harmonises with our civil constitution, with the frame and fashion of our Society, and with the general Temper of the people. I think it is better calculated, all circumstances considerd, for keeping peace amongst the different sects, and of affording to them a reasonable protection, than any other System. Being something in a middle, it is better disposed to moderate. As to the rest, I see some things in all the subdivisions of our common principle which I might wish were otherwise than they are; I do not know any of them that does not peculiarly possess something that is good and laudable, and which those who differ from it might adopt to their advantage: but these are notions, in which, whether the matter of them be civil or religious, men may and commonly do, indulge themselves, without causing them to separate from those with whom they are associated by the arrangements of providence. My particular religious sentiments are not of much importance to anyone but myself. I am attached to Christianity at large; much from conviction; more from affection. I would risque a great deal to prevent its being extinguishd any where or in any of its shapes. As to the Sects and parties, that (happily, or unhappily, or with a mixed effect) divide that religious commonwealth, I do not perceive any thing in any of them so very evil, as to induce a man, reasonably and conscientiously, to give his hand to the destruction of the publick happiness, and to the breaking up the foundations of social order, for the sake of destroying this or that description. For this opinion I may be censured. I endeavour every day to live more and more to myself and less to popularity. But if I must have a reference to the judgment of others, I would say to my Censors, that they may think what they please of my religion, so long as they do not imagine it authorises me to betray, to rob, to murder, and to rebel without cause. To the contrary of all these my principles lead me. I am afraid, that some individuals in parties (no whole parties I am sure) find such crimes very reconcileable with their tenets, or rather with their dispositions to which they have the secret of bending their opinions.

I beg pardon for the trouble I have given you, but you have brought it upon yourself. I have the honour to be with great acknowlegement for your kindness and politeness, and with sincere respect for your Talents

Dear Sir
Your most obedient
and obliged humble Servant
EDM BURKE

Beconsfield Jan. 26. 1791.

To the CHEVALIER DE LA BINTINAYE—[March 1791]

Corr. (1958), VI, 241–43

Agathon-Marie-René de la Bintinaye (b. 1758) was a former naval commander and an émigré from France.

Dear sir,

I had the honour to receive your most friendly and obliging Letter from Brussels. You greatly overrate the value of the very few attentions which I had the means of showing you whilst you remaind in London. I do most sincerely lament the sad occasion that produced our acquaintance. In so great a publick disaster however I feel this consolation, that I had an opportunity of seeing undeserved afliction borne with a manly constancy; and that the same courage which produced your honourable wounds, and sustaind you under them, has enabled you to support your reverse of fortune with the dignity which becomes those who suffer in the Cause of honour and Virtue. I should be happy to send you a Copy of the Letter which I wrote to a person of distinction in Paris[1] in answer to one from him. But as I had my doubts, whether what I wrote, in the present Temper of the times and the present

---

[1] The *Letter to a Member of the National Assembly.*

posture of affairs, might be useful in the publication I left the matter
to the Gentlemans own discretion, promising not to disperse any copies
without his leave. This, I hope, my dear Sir, will plead my excuse to
you. I did hear that a Translation of that Letter was preparing at
Paris. If this be the Case, you will see it very soon. It will, I am afraid,
afford you no very great satisfaction. Some part of the letter was to
exculpate myself, (or rather perhaps to apologize) from some faults,
which the Gentleman found in my Pamphlet. The rest was to shew,
from the actual State of France, (as well as I was able to enter into
its condition) the utter impossibility of a counter revolution from any
internal Cause. You know Sir, that no party can act without a resolute,
vigorous, zealous, and enterprising chief. The chief of every monarchical party must be the monarch himself: at least he must lend himself
readily to the spirit and energy of others. You have a well intentiond
and virtuous prince—But minds like his, bred with no other view
than to a safe and languid domination, are not made for breaking their
prisons, terrifying their Enemies and animating their friends: Besides,
in a Wife and children he has given Hostages to his Enemies. If the
King can do nothing in his situation the wonder is not great. It is
much greater, in all appearance, that not one man is it to be found in
the numerous Nobility of France, who to great military Talents adds
any sort of lead, consideration, or following, in the Country, or
in the Army. To strengthen itself the Monarchy had weakend every
other force: To unite the Nation to itself, it had dissolved all other
ties. When the chain, which held the people to the Prince was once
broken, the whole frame of the commonwealth was found in a State
of disconnection. There was neither force nor union any where to
sustain, the Monarchy, or the Nobility, or the Church. As to great
and commanding Talents they are the Gift of Providence in some way
unknown to us. They rise where they are least expected. They fail
when every thing seems disposed to produce them, or at least to call
them forth. Your sole hope seems to me to rest in the disposition of
the Neighbouring powers and in their ability to yield you assistance.
I can conjecture nothing with certainty of this in either of the points.
But at present I see nothing, that in the smallest degree, looks that
way. In the mean time the usurpation gathers strength by continuance;
and credit by success. People will look to power; and join, or at least
accommodate themselves, to it. I confess, I am astonishd at the blindness of the States of Europe, who are contending with each other
about points of trivial importance, and on old, worn out principles

and Topics of Policy, when the very existence of all of them is menaced, by a new Evil, which none of the antient Maxims are of the least importance in dissipating. But in all these things we must acknowlege, and revere in silence, a superiour hand. In the Spirit of this submission, I however, am so far from blaming every sort of endeavour, that I much lament the remissness of the Gentlemen of France. Their adversaries have seized upon all the Newspapers which circulate within this Kingdom, and that from Hence are dispersed all over Europe. That they are masters of the Presses of Paris is a thing of Course: But surely the oppressed party might, amongst them, maintain a person here to whom they might transmit a true State of affairs. The Emissaries of the Usurpation here are exceedingly active in propagating Stories which tend to alienate the minds of people of this Country from the suffering Cause. Not one french Refugee has intelligence or spirit enough to contradict them. I have done all, which the common Duties of Humanity can claim from one who has not the honour of being a Subject of France. I have Duties and occupations at home, publick and private, which will not suffer me to continue longer with my thoughts abroad. But if any Gentleman from France would undertake such a Task with proper materials from it, he should have my best advice. The Expence of such a person stationd here would not be great; and surely, reduced as the Noblesse of France, not expatriated, is, yet enough remains to them to do this and more. If their avarice or their dissipation will afford nothing to their honour or their safety—their Case is additionally deplorable.

My Wife and my Son always preserve the most respectful and affectionate remembrance of you, of the Bishop, and of Mademoiselle de Cicé. I have ⟨had⟩ a Letter from the Vicomte with a very satisfactory memor⟨ial⟩. I have given him an answer and have taken the Liberty of putting further Questions to him. I have the honour ⟨to⟩ be with the most cordial and respectful attachment

Dear Sir
Your most faithful
and obedient humble Servant
EDM BURKE

Duke Street March 1791.

Bintinaye's association with Burke was largely responsible for his appointment as a representative of the French Princes later in the year.

To CLAUDE-FRANÇOIS DE RIVAROL—1 *June* 1791

Corr. (1958), VI, 265–70

Claude-François de Rivarol (1762-1848), known variously as the Chevalier, the Vi-comte and the Comte de Rivarol, was the brother of the better-known royalist writer Antoine de Rivarol (1753–1801), also called both the Chevalier and the Comte de Rivarol. He was a captain in the infantry in 1788, and on the outbreak of the Revolution co-operated with his brother in various royalist publications, but emigrated in 1790. In early 1791 he was an agent for the *émigré* Princes at Brussels.

I am much obliged to you for your very polite and flattering attention to me, and to the piece which you are pleased to regard with so much indulgence. It is an endeavour very well intended, but I am conscious very inadequate to the great interests of this Kingdom, and of mankind, which it proposes to assert.

I have seen tho' too late to profit of them, your brother's admirable annals,[1] which may rank with those of Tacitus. If there is indeed a strong coincidence in our way of thinking I ought to be very proud of that circumstance. If I had seen his performance before I had written on the same subject, I should rather have chosen to enrich my pamphlet with quotations from thence, than have ventured to express the thoughts in which we agreed, in worse words of my own. I thank you too for the elegant Poem which you have done me the honour to transmit to me with your letter.[2] So far as I am capable of forming any judgment upon French poetry, the verses are spirited and well turned; and the author possesses the art of interesting the passions which is the triumph of that Kind of eloquence. I wish without disguising my real Sentiments, I could go as far in my approbation of the general tendency of one of these pieces, and of the policy of such publications at such a time as this; Forgive me, sir, if I take the liberty of suggesting to your superior judgement as well as to that of the emperors advisers,[3] that it is not very easy to suppress (by the methods lately used) what you call 'the *monkish fury*'[4] without exciting fury of another Kind; a sort of fury which will perhaps be found more untractable than the other, and which may be carried to much greater

---

[1] *Le journal politique national.*

[2] Evidently Rivarol had sent Burke a copy of his book of poems *Les Chartreux, poëme et autres pièces fugitives*, a 4th edition of which had appeared in Paris in 1789.

[3] Burke is writing on the assumption that the new Emperor, Leopold II, might decide to imitate the anti-clerical policy of his brother Joseph II, who had died on 20 February 1790.

[4] Rivarol's poem tells the story of a young man compelled by his father to take vows in a Carthusian house and to foresake his beloved. She seeks him out and passes a year with him in a secret dungeon and an ecstasy of love. The birth of a child brings about their betrayal and the Carthusian Fathers descend on them and beat all three to death.

lengths. In such a dilemma, it would not misbecome a great statesman seriously to consider which he has it in charge to support and to the country, which it is his duty to preserve in peace and prosperity. That fury which arises in the minds of men on being stripped of their goods, and turned out of their houses by acts of power, and our sympathy with them under Such wrongs, are feelings implanted in us by our creator to be (under the direction of his laws) the means of our preservation. Such fury and such sympathy are things very different from men's imaginary political systems concerning governments. They arise out of instinctive principles of self deffence and are executive powers under the legislation of nature, enforcing its first law. This principle Prince and Commonwealth (whatever they may think their Rights) cannot always attack with perfect impunity.

If Princes will in cold blood and from mistaken ideas of policy excite the passion of [the] multitude against particular descriptions of men whether they be priests or nobility, in order to avail themselves of the assistance of that multitude in their enterprises against those classes. Let them recollect that they call in the aid of an ally more dangerous to themselves than those whom they are desirous of oppressing.

The Netherlands have been but newly recovered to the Emperor.[5] He owes that recovery to a concurrence of very extraordinary circumstances, and he had made great sacrifices to his object. Is it really his interest to have it understood that he means to repeat the very proceedings which have excited all the late troubles in his territories? Can it be true that he means to draw up the very same floodgates which have let loose the deluge that has overwhelmed the great Monarchy in his neighbourhood? Does he think, if he means to encourage the spirit which prevails in France, that it will be exerted in his favour or to answer his purposes? Whilst he is destroying prejudices which (under good management) may become the surest support of his government, Is he not afraid that the discussion may go farther than he wishes? If he excites men to inquire too scrupulously into the foundation of all old opinion, may he not have reason to apprehend that several will see as little use in Monarchs as in Monks? The question is not whether they will argue logically or not; but whether the turn of mind which leads to such discussion may not become as fatal to the former as to the latter. He may trust in the fine army he has assembled. But fine armies have been seduced from their allegiance; and the seducers are not far from him. He may fortify his frontier.

[5] In 1790.

But fortresses have been betrayed by their garrisons and garrisons overpowered by burghers. Those of the democratick faction in the netherlands have always an armed ally more conveniently situated to assist them than the Emperor is conveniently situated to assist himself. Would not prudence rather dictate to that great Sovereign, the surest mode of fortification? Would not prudence direct him, I say, to fortify himself in the heart of his people, by repairing rather than by destroying those dykes and barriers, which prejudice might rise in his favour and which cost nothing to his treasury, either in the construction or reparation. It were better to forget once for all, the *Encyclopedie* and the whole body of Economists and to revert to those old rules and principles which have hitherto made princes great and nations happy. Let not a Prince circumstanced like him weakly fall in love either with Monks or nobles; Still less let him violently hate them. In his Netherlands he possesses the most populous the best cultivated, and the most flourishing country in Europe; a country from which at this day, and even in England we are to learn the perfect practice of the best of arts that of agriculture. If he has a people like the Flemings, industrious frugal, easy, obedient, what is [it] to him whether they are fond of Monks, or love ringing of bells and lighting of candles, or not? A wise Prince, as I hope, the Emperor is, will study the genius of his people; he will indulge them in their humours, he will preserve them in their privileges; he will act upon the *circumstances of his states as he finds them;* and whilst thus acting upon the practical principles of a practical policy, he is the happy Prince of an happy people. He will not care what the Condorcets and the Raynals, and the whole flight of the magpies and Jays of philosophy may fancy and chatter concerning his conduct and character.

Well it is for the Emperor that the late rebellion of the Netherlands was a *rebellion against innovation.* When therefore he returned to the possession of his estates (an event which no man wished more sincerely than I did) he found none of the ancient land-marks removed. He found every thing, except the natural effect of a transient storm, exactly as it was on the day of the revolt. Would the King of France, supposing his restoration probable, find his Kingdom in the same condition? Oh no, Sir! Many long, long labours would be required to restore that country to any sort of good order. Why? Because their rebellion is the direct contrary to that of Flanders. It is a *revolt of innovation,* and thereby the very elements of Society have been confounded and dissipated. Small politicians will certainly recommend to him to nourish a democratick party in order to curb the Aristocratick and the Clerical. In general, all policy founded on discord is perilous to the Prince and fatal to the country. The support of the permanent orders in their places and the reconciling them all to his government, will be his best security, either for governing quietly in his own person, or for leaving any sure succession to his posterity. Corporations which have a perpetual succession, and hereditary nobles who themselves exist by Succession are the true guardians of Monarchical succession. On such orders and institutions alone an hereditary monarch can stand. What they call the *Démocratie Royale* in France is laughed at by the very authors, as an absurd Chimera. Where all things else are elective, you may call a King hereditary: but he is for the present only a cypher, and all the Succession is not supported by any analogy in the State nor combined with any Sentiment whatsoever existing in the minds of the people, It is a solitary, unsupported, anomalous thing.

The story you tell of the *Chartreux* in the time of Charles the fifth may be true for any thing I know to the contrary. But what inference can be drawn from it? Why should it be necessary to influence the people at such a time as this[6] to rob the Chartreux who had no hand in that murder? Were the Chartreux that I have seen at Paris employed in committing or meditating murders? Are they so at *la Trappe* or at the *Grande Chartreuse*, or any where else? Inferences will be made from such a story, I don't mean logical but practical; inferences which will harden the hearts of men in this age of spoil, not only against them, but against a considerable portion of the human race. Some of these Monks in a sudden transport of fury murdered somebody in the time of Charles the fifth—what then? I am certain that not only in the time of Charles the fifth but now and at all times, and in all countries and in the bosom of the dearest relations of life, the most dreadfull tragedies have been and are daily acted. Is it right to bring forth these examples to make us abhor those relations?

You observe that a Sequestration from the connexions of society makes the heart cold and unfeeling. I beleive it may have that tendency—though this is more than I find to be fact from the result of my observations and enquiries. But in the theory it seems probable. However as the greatest crimes do not arise so much from a want of feeling for others as from an over sensibility for ourselves and an over indulgence to our own desires, Very sequester'd people (such as the Chartreux) as they are less touched with the Sympathies which Soften

---

[6] Burke apparently did not notice, as Rivarol pointed out in a note to the French translation of this letter, that Rivarol's poems were first published in 1782, before the Revolution. Nonetheless, Burke's criticism remains pertinent.

the manners, are less engaged in the passions which agitate the mind. The best virtues can hardly be found among them; But crimes must be more rare in that form of Society than in the active world. If I were to trust to my own observation, and give a verdict on it, I must depose that in my experience, I have found that those who were most indulgent to themselves, were (in the mass) less kind to others than those who have lived a life nearer to self denial. I go further, in my experience, I have observed that a luxurious softness of manners hardens the heart at least as much as an overdone abstinence. I question much whether moral policy will justify us in an endeavour to interest the heart in favour of immoral, irregular and illegal actions, on account of particular touching circumstances that may happen to attend the commission or the punishment of them. I know, Poets are apt enough to chuse Such Subjects in order to excite the high relish arising from the mixed sensations which will arise in that anxious embarassment of the mind, whenever it finds itself in a locality where vices and virtues meet near their confines—where

> mire Sagaces falleret hospites
> discrimen obscurum. . .[7]

I think of late that the Parisian Philosophers have done upon meditated System, what the Poets are naturally led to by a desire of flattering the passions. To you, as a Poet, this is to be allowed. To Philosophers one cannot be so indulgent. For perhaps ladies ought not 'to love too well' like the Phædras and Myrrhas of old, or the ancient or Modern Eloyses.[8] They had better not pursue their lovers into convents of Carthusians nor follow them in disguise to camps and slaughter houses. But I have observed that the Philosophers in order to insinuate their polluted Atheism into young minds, systematically flatter all their passions natural and unnatural. They explode or render odious or contemptible that class of virtues which restrain the appetite. These are at least nine out of ten of the virtues. In the place of all these they substitute a virtue which they call humanity or benevolence. By these means, their morality has no idea in it of restraint, or indeed of a distinct settled principle of any kind. When their disciples are thus left free and guided only by present feeling, they are no longer to be depended on for good or evil. The men who to day snatch the

---

[7] The difference, not recognized, would deceive knowing strangers; see Horace, *Odes*, II, v, 22–3.

[8] Phaedra, the wife of Theseus, loved her stepson Hippolytus. Myrrha had an unnatural passion for her father Cinyrs. The two Eloises are presumably Abelard's beloved and the heroine of Rousseau's *Nouvelle Héloise*.

worst criminals from justice, will murder the most innocent persons to morrow.

I assure you, Sir that this letter has been written six weeks ago given to be copied and I really thought sent to you. Looking on my papers, I found my memory had betrayed me and that you have an apparent reason to complain of my neglect. You have in the late events done yourself great honour as I hear. Do not be discouraged. The value of such services will one day or other be known and acknowledged. I have the honour to be with most sincere respect

your most obedient
humble servant
signed EDM. BURKE.

Dated. June 1st 1791.

Rivarol in his reply maintained his original position firmly, though politely. He denounced the *philosophe* as violently as Burke had done: 'C'est un vrai sauvage au milieu de la société'. But he was also critical of aristocrats, whom he condemned as the true enemies of royalism. He defended his original views about the social ill-effects of solitude and celibacy, and described his poem as a mere literary effusion.

To WILLIAM SMITH—22 *July* 1791

Corr. (1958), VI, 302–4

William Smith (1766–1836), later (1808) 2nd Baronet, was a young Irish barrister who in 1791 published an anonymous tract entitled *The Rights of Citizens. Being an Examination of Mr Paine's Principles Touching Government. By a Barrister.* He sent a copy to Burke along with a letter (MS missing) on 30 June, requesting his approval and indirectly asking for permission to dedicate the pamphlet to him. A second edition, which appeared later in the year, contained Smith's letter of 30 June, Burke's reply and a dedication to Burke dated 4 November.

Sir,

. . . You talk of Paine with more respect than he deserves: He is utterly incapable of comprehending his subject. He has not even a moderate portion of learning of any kind. He has learnd the instrumental part of literature, a style, and a method of disposing his ideas, without having ever made a previous preparation of Study or thinking—for the use of it. Junius, and other sharply penn'd libels of our time have furnishd a stock to the adventurers in composition; which gives what they write an air, (and it is but an air) of art and skill;—but as to the rest, Payne possesses nothing more than what a man whose audacity makes him careless of logical consequences, and his total want of honour and morality makes indifferent as to political consequences, may very easily write. They indeed who seriously write upon a principle of levelling ought to be answerd by the Magistrate—and not by the Speculatist.[1] The People whom he would corrupt, and who are very corruptible, can very readily comprehend what flatters their vices and falls in with their ignorance; but that process of reasoning, which would shew to the poorest, how much his poverty is comparative riches in his state of subordination, to what it would be in such an equality as is recommended to him, is quite out of his reach, even if it were pleasing to his pride; because it involves in it a long and labourd analysis of Society. If he will not receive it on authority he is incapable of receiving it at all; and where a man is incapable of receiving a Benefit through his reason, he must be made to receive it thro' his fears. Here the Magistrate must stand in the place of the Professor. They who cannot or will not be taught, must be coerced.

With more of your approbation than I can presume to lay any claim to, I meet something of your censure which I perhaps better deserve. You think that my way of treating these subjects is too much in the *concrete* in which I *ramble* in too large a share of circumstances, feelings &c &c; however I console myself in this, because I think before you have done—you condemn the abstract mode perhaps as much as I do; and I am the less ashamed of being in the wrong, when I am so in such very good company. But surely you forget, that I was throwing out reflexions upon a political event, and not reading a lecture upon theorism and principles of Government. How I should treat such a subject is not for me to say, for I never had that intention. The event itself was of a very mixed nature; and the observations upon it were, of course, of a mixed nature too. On all this however I hope I shall have the pleasure of conversing with you more fully at Beconsfield, on your return, if you should go to the continent as early as you intend. But I hope somethng may keep you in London 'till I can get to town. I shall be ambitious of improving the acquaintance with which you flatter me.[2]

[1] In the *Appeal from the New to the Old Whigs* (1791), after quoting a series of passages from Paine (but not naming him as their author), Burke says: 'I will not attempt in the smallest degree to refute them. This will probably be done (if such writings shall be thought to deserve any other than the refutation of criminal justice) by others . . .' (*Works*, Bohn, III, 75–6; Little, Brown, IV, 161). Paine made a vigorous response to this remark in the preface to the second part of the *Rights of Man*.

[2] Smith did pay a visit to the Burkes. Richard, Jr, recalled it in a letter dated 'Dublin, Tuesday', written some time in 1792: '. . . on the day when I sat next you at Beaconsfield, it seemed to me that we made as much progress in intimacy as could well be made in an afternoon; especially by two lemonade drinkers, which I remember we were at the time'.

To HENRY DUNDAS—9 April 1792

Corr. (1958), VII, 122–25

The slave trade had been under attack in the House of Commons since 1788. Burke had from the first been among those who favored its abolition. On 2 April 1792 the opponents of the trade had their first success. Although they failed to carry a motion for its immediate abolition, the House accepted the principle of gradual abolition. Henry Dundas (1742–1811), Secretary of State for Home Affairs, had been a powerful influence behind this compromise. On 4 April he had been pressed to produce a plan for gradual abolition, and the House had agreed to consider the matter again on 18 April.

Dear Sir,

I should have been punctual in sending you the sketch I promised of my old African Code,[1] if some friends from London had not come in upon me last Saturday, and engaged me till noon this day; I send this pacquet by one of them, who is still here. If what I send be, as under present circumstances it must be, imperfect, you will excuse it, as being done near twelve years ago. About four years since I made an abstract of it, upon which I cannot at present lay my hands; but I hope the marginal heads will in some measure supply it.

If the African trade could be considered with regard to itself only, and as a single object, I should think the utter abolition to be, on the whole, more advisable than any scheme of regulation and reform. Rather than suffer it to continue as it is, I heartily wish it at an end. What has been lately done has been done by a popular spirit,[2] which seldom calls for, and indeed very rarely relishes, a system made up of a great variety of parts, and which is to operate its effect in a great length of time. The people like short methods; the consequences of which they sometimes have reason to repent of. Abolition is but a single act. To prove the nature of the trade, and to expose it properly, required, indeed, a vast collection of materials, which have been laboriously collected, and compiled with great judgment.[3] It required also much perseverance and address to excite the spirit which has been excited without-doors, and which has carried it through. The greatest eloquence ever displayed in the House has been employed to second the efforts which have been made abroad. All this, however, leads but

---

[1] The Code is printed in *Works* (Bohn), V, 524–44; (Little, Brown), VI, 262–89.

[2] In 1788 one hundred and three petitions had been presented against the slave trade; in 1792 five hundred and nineteen.

[3] The Society for the Abolition of the Slave Trade had collected evidence. Its activities had been followed by prolonged inquiries into the trade by a committee of the Privy Council and by the House of Commons.

to one single resolve. When this was done, all was done. I speak of absolute and immediate abolition, the point which the first motions went to, and which is in effect still pressed; though in this session, according to order, it cannot take effect. A *remote* and a *gradual* abolition, though they may be connected, are not the same thing. The idea of the House seems to me, if I rightly comprehend it, that the two things are to be combined; that is to say, that the trade is gradually to decline, and to cease entirely at a determinate period. To make the abolition gradual, the regulations must operate as a strong discouragement. But it is much to be feared, that a trade continued and discouraged, and with a sentence of death passed upon it, will perpetuate much ill blood between those who struggle for the abolition, and those who contend for an effectual continuance.

At the time when I formed the plan which I have the honour to transmit to you, an abolition of the slave trade would have appeared a very chimerical project. My plan, therefore, supposes the continued existence of that commerce. Taking for my basis, that I had an incurable evil to deal with, I cast about how I should make it as small an evil as possible, and draw out of it some collateral good.

In turning the matter over in my mind at that time, and since, I never was able to consider the African trade upon a ground disconnected with the employment of negroes in the West Indies, and distinct from their condition in the plantations whereon they serve. I conceived that the true origin of the trade was not in the place it was begun at, but at the place of its final destination. I therefore was, and still am, of opinion, that the whole work ought to be taken up together; and that a gradual abolition of slavery in the West Indies ought to go hand in hand with anything which should be done with regard to its supply from the coast of Africa. I could not trust a cessation of the demand for this supply to the mere operation of any abstract principle, (such as, that if their supply was cut off, the planters would encourage and produce an effectual population,) knowing that nothing can be more uncertain than the operation of general principles, if they are not embodied in specific regulations. I am very apprehensive that so long as the slavery continues some means for its supply will be found. If so, I am persuaded that it is better to allow the evil, in order to correct it, than by endeavouring to forbid, what we cannot be able wholly to prevent, to leave it under an illegal, and therefore an unreformed, existence. It is not, that my plan does not lead to the extinction of the slave trade; but it is through a very slow progress, the chief effect of which is to be operated in our own plantations by rendering, in a length of time, all foreign supply unnecessary. It was my wish, whilst the slavery continued, and the consequent commerce, to take such measures as to civilize the coast of Africa by the trade, which now renders it more barbarous; and to lead by degrees to a more reputable, and, possibly, a more profitable, connexion with it, than we maintain at present.

I am sure that you will consider, as a mark of my confidence in yours and Mr Pitt's honour and generosity, that I venture to put into your hands a scheme composed of many and intricate combinations, without a full explanatory preface, or any attendant notes, to point out the principles upon which I proceeded in every regulation, which I have proposed towards the civilization and gradual manumission of negroes in the two hemispheres. I confess, I trust infinitely more (according to the sound principles of those who ever have at any time meliorated the state of mankind) to the effect and influence of religion, than to all the rest of the regulations put together.

Whenever, in my proposed reformation, we take our *point of departure* from a state of slavery, we must precede the donation of freedom by disposing the minds of the objects to a disposition to receive it without danger to themselves or to us. The process of bringing *free* savages to order and civilization is very different. When a state of slavery is that upon which we are to work, the very means which lead to liberty must partake of compulsion. The minds of men being crippled with that restraint can do nothing for themselves; everything must be done for them. The regulations can owe little to consent. Everything must be the creature of power. Hence it is, that regulations must be multiplied; particularly as you have two parties to deal with. The planter you must at once restrain and support; and you must control, at the same time that you ease, the servant. This necessarily makes the work a matter of care, labour, and expense. It becomes in its nature complex. But I think neither the object impracticable nor the expense intolerable; and I am fully convinced that the cause of humanity would be far more benefited by the continuance of the trade and servitude, regulated and reformed, than by the total destruction of both or either. What I propose, however, is but a beginning of a course of measures, which an experience of the effects of the evil and the reform will enable the legislature hereafter to supply and correct.

I need not observe to you, that the forms are often neglected, penalties not provided, &c. &c. &c. But all this is merely mechanical, and what a couple of days' application would set to rights.

I have seen what has been done by the West Indian assemblies. It is arrant trifling. They have done little; and what they have done is good for nothing; for it is totally destitute of an *executory* principle. This is the point to which I have applied my whole diligence. It is easy enough to say what shall be done:—to cause it to be done,—*Hic labor, hoc opus.*[4]

I ought not to apologize for letting this scheme lie beyond the period of the *Horatian* keeping[5]—I ought much more to entreat an excuse for producing it now. Its whole value (if it has any) is the coherence and mutual dependency of parts in the scheme; separately they can be of little or no use.

I have the honour to be, with very great respect and regard,
>   Dear Sir,
>   Your most faithful and obedient humble servant,
Beaconsfield,   EDMUND BURKE.
Easter-Monday night, 1792.

On 23 April Dundas produced resolutions to abolish the slave trade in 1800 and to regulate it in the intervening period. On 27 April the House voted to terminate it in 1796. The House of Lords, however, insisted on holding its own inquiry so that no immediate action was taken. Burke's African Code exercised some influence on later anti-slavery thought; as late as 1822 William Wilberforce considered using it as a plan of emancipation.

[4] Hic opus, hic labor est; this is the task, this the toil. See Virgil, *Aeneid*, VI, 129.
[5] Nine years; see Horace, *Ars poetica*, 388.

CHAPTER SEVEN

COUNTERREVOLUTION

C OUNTERREVOLUTION," now used politically only by Marxists, was a new term discovered in the French Revolution to describe the intent of opponents of the Revolution. It was used both by friends of the Revolution such as Tom Paine (in a letter to Burke, *Corr.*, 1958, VI, 72), and by its enemies such as Burke himself (*Corr.*, 1958, VI, 241, 475). The term presupposes that the French Revolution is not merely *a* revolution but *the* Revolution, so that opposition to it is not merely defense of the prior regime or revolutionary in another direction but resistance to *the* Revolution which is more revolutionary than any prior revolution. Since the French Revolution, partisans of that revolution or one like it or one improving on it have been known as "revolutionaries," as if all revolution fundamentally tended in one direction—toward democracy. Revolutionaries of the right have to be specified as such, and they are understood, they understand themselves, as counterrevolutionaries opposed to the fundamental revolution.

In *A Letter to a Noble Lord* (1796), Burke wrote, "Before this of France, the annals of all time have not furnished an instance of a *complete* revolution." He then added that the Revolution "seems to have extended even to the mind of man." This was a possibility that Kant had already seen and claimed for himself, also one that Hegel and German idealism were to develop. Burke turned to counterrevolutionary politics, some might wish to think, with an inkling that to forestall this grand movement of thought and all its vast consequences would be a clear benefit to the human race. As Burke became alienated from Charles James Fox and other partisans of the French Revolution in his own party (the break with Fox came in May 1791), he made his influence felt not so much in private deliberations and parliamentary speeches as in the scorching pamphlets on the Revolution, beginning with *Reflections on the Revolution in France* (1790), which have made his fame secure. His letters begin to reflect his writings more than before, and although some modulations can be found (for example, the criticism of Louis XVI in his letter to the Chevalier de la Bintinaye, March 1791; see above, chapter 6), we begin to see in his letters the outlines of famous arguments and the first formulations of his best passages.

Because the French Revolution is a complete revolution, it is very powerful. Despite the fact that it was imposed from Paris and "bears no one character of a National Act," one cannot expect it to be overthrown from within France (letters to Lord Grenville and to the Chevalier de Grave, 1792). A policy of intervention from outside is necessary; England and its allies must fight an offensive war against it (letter to Sir Lawrence Parsons, 1797). Also, because the French Revolution is complete, it is contagious. "No lines of demarcation can bound the Jacobin Empire" (letter to the Comte de Mercy-Argentau, 1793). "No man's fireside is safe from the effects of a political revolution" (letter to Lord Loughborough, 1794). That revolution cannot be opposed successfully with a policy of neutrality, as Pitt first attempted, or with peace negotiations after a period of war, the "Regicide Peace" that Burke denounced in 1796.

Burke was dismayed and disheartened by his inability, despite the full exercise of his gifts and virtues, to persuade his country and his government that the danger and the evil from the French Revolution were as deep as he saw them. As he was dying, he wrote to his friend: "But all is over with the world in which I, and your Lordship at a later period, were born, and in which we wished to die" (letter to Lord Fitzwilliam, 1797).

To Richard Burke, Jr—*26 September* 1791

Corr. (1958), VI, 409–14

Burke comments to his son, now in Coblenz at the headquarters of the French *émigrés*, on the hesitations of the Austrian Emperor Leopold II. He stresses that the Bourbon princes, the Comte de Provence and the Comte d'Artois, brothers of King Louis XVI who were preparing an army to invade France and overthrow the Revolution, must pledge to establish a free constitution.

. . . The Truth is, I am afraid, that the Emperor and some of his Ministers though he does not approve; (as he cannot approve) of the destruction of the monarchy, is infinitely pleased with the Robbery of the Church property and the humiliation of the Gentry; and that in that lust of philosophick spoliation, and equalization, he forgets that he cuts down the supports of Monarchy, and indeed destroys those principles of property, order and regularity for which alone any rational man can wish Monarchy to exist. But the difference among the race who have got the present Education, is only, whether the same Robbery is to be committed, by the despotism of an individual or that of a multitude; and therefore, that the Emperor has made the Parade of a threatning, and of a threatning only, that this vile assembly may be induced to treat, to secure some affluence and Liberty to the King and Queen, leaving the Church robbed, and the Nobility beggard and degraded. This is what we fear. It is what we ought to do our best to prevent; and to engage the Emperor in a System of politicks more conformable to the true Interests, Rights, and duties of Sovereigns. I have read the declaration of the Bourbon Princes.[1] You have, if you are still at Coblentz by this a very Rude sketch of a Bill of Rights,[2] which ought to be agreed to in a General meeting of Princes, nobles, and Magistrates. I think it well penned,[3] and in many points very right, and proper. But the Ton is not just what one would wish in all points. In some things it is dangerously defective. They ought to promise, distinctly, and without ambiguity, that they mean, 1 when the Monarchy as the essential Basis shall be restored, to secure with it, a free constitution, 2 and that for this purpose they will cause at a meeting of the States freely chosen according to the antient Legal order, to vote by order—3 all Lettres de Cachet and other means of

[1] The Declaration of Pillnitz of 27 August, between Austria and Prussia, was circulated in a *Lettre de Monsieur, et de M. le Comte d'Artois au Roi leur Frère* dated from Coblenz 10 September. The Princes announced that all the powers of Europe were engaged to employ their forces to assist the King of France, and called on him not to accept the Constitution.

[2] Presumably this was in a letter from Edmund to Richard which is now missing.

[3] i.e. the Declaration of the Princes, not Burke's own sketch of a Bill of Rights.

arbitrary imprisonment to be abolishd. 4 That all Taxation shall be by the said States conjointly with the King. 5. That responsibility shall be establishd, and the publick Revenue put out of the power of abuse and malversation; 6. a canonical 'synod of the Gallican Church to reform all abuses' and (as unfortunately the K has lost all reputation) they should pledge themselves, with their Lives and fortunes, to support, along with their King those conditions and the wise order, which can alone support a free and vigorous Government. Without such a declaration or to that Effect they can hope no converts.[4] For my part for one, though I make no doubt of preferring the antient Course, or almost any other to this vile chimera, and sick mans dream of Government yet I could not actively, or with a good heart, and clear conscience, go to the establishment of a monarchical despotism in the place of this system of Anarchy. I should think myself obligd to withdraw myself wholly from such a competition and give repose to my age. . . .

To HENRY DUNDAS—30 *September* 1791

Corr. (1958), VI, 418–22

Dundas was Secretary for Home affairs and Pitt's leading adviser.

Dear Sir,

After some deliberation concerning the propriety of complying with your request, I send you the Letter I received from one of the dearest friends I have in the world,[1] and one of the best men that exists in it, or I believe ever did. All the competition I know is between him and the Duke of Portland. This is not party Language; for with them party connection is much to my sorrow suspended, and probably never can be revived. The cause which seperated me from their party would I believe seperate me almost from mankind. As yet I have heard nothing from the Duke of Portland; though he told a friend of ours,[2] that he meant to write to me, and very fully, on the subject of my late and former publication.[3] The two excellent persons I speak of are not

---

[4] The *Lettre* of Provence and Artois promised that restoration of the full powers of the French Monarchy would not mean the establishment of tyranny. It did not, however, contain any of the specific assurances listed by Burke.

[1] Earl Fitzwilliam's letter of 18 September.

[2] Presumably French Laurence.

[3] *The Reflections on the Revolution in France* (1790) and *The Appeal from the New to the Old Whigs* (1791).

infected, nor ever were, in the slightest degree with the new doctrines. I think they hate them as much as I do; but the point which causes our difference is, that they cannot be brought to think that there is any danger of the prevalence of such doctrines in England, or of their being ever reduced to practice. They will not do any thing which may seem to condemn a friend[4] whom they love and admire, and who, in Truth, in many points, well merits affection and admiration, when they think, that the worst he has done is to throw out some expressions not so well considerd. In that View of things, they will never disavow a person so circumstanced, from any dread of the ill Spirit which has lately appeared with so much force; but which, they are of opinion (an opinion very different from mine) is likely to evaporate and to expire of itself. I find, that this Idea is not only prevalent amongst many of my friends, but among many, if not all, of yours. When I find this to be the Case, I ought to be diffident of my own Judgment. If, indeed, I could prevail on myself to think our fate likely to be decided merely by what happens in England, I should not perhaps differ from this general Sentiment. But I never can leave France, (where these pernicious Theories have been nursed to maturity, and for the *first* time reduced to *practice*) out of the question. I cannot leave out of my calculation, the Effect in this Country of the Success and even temporary stability of the same System in that very neighbouring Nation which the other day I could see so clearly from the Pier of Ramsgate. With me this Effect is no matter of Doubt at all. The British constitution will be fought for, and conquerd, not here but in France. There the cause of all Monarcheis, and of all Republicks too constituted upon antient models, are upon their Trial. Nothing internal in France can of itself produce any change. This I lay down as a certainty. I consider it as a matter of equal certainty, that if it stands there, it *must* prevail here. I have, from the very first, attended with more care than is common the effects of this French malady on the minds of men in England and Ireland. The only thing which kept some people hesitating, and unwilling to adopt their System, was a doubt whether so new, and apparently so desperate attempt, as that of altering the whole Frame of Society in the greatest Country in Europe, could be at all realized. It has been realized beyond the imagination of any one. I find the operation of that *fact* only, that is the two years existence of that state of things, makes a very great, (and to me a very alarming,) impression on the minds of some people,

[4] Fox.

in every other respect rational and sober; persons who, indeed, from many Circumstances, are the very last from whom I should expect this determination. They say, it is an *experiment* towards obtaining a greater degree of happiness for men, than had ever yet been attempted; and that it would be a great Pity, that it should not have what it promises to have, such a duration as is necessary to give fair play to an experiment which naturally demands time for its full operation. These people are, from its success, become a kind of converts to it in spite of every contradiction from their heads and their hearts. Success is dazzling in all things. In political and military affairs it is in a manner irresistible. It becomes a decisive Test of the wisdom of the plan and the ability of the managers.

The Gentlemen I allude to are individuals, but individuals of no slight importance. But what I look to with seriousness is the Phalanx of Party which exists in the body of the dissenters, who are, at the very least, nine tenths of them entirely devoted, some with greater some with less zeal, to the principles of the French Revolution.[5] I think, they compose a more active, a more spirited, and a more united body, than the Jacobites ever were; and as to the Republicans, (except in the time of the great troubles, near an hundred and fifty years ago) they never formed themselves into any thing like a party, until within these two years they were embodied under the French standard. Until then they were individuals who hung upon the whigg party, and by that party were lookd upon as absurd and visionary men of no sort of consequence. But things are since much changed with them. Even consider them under the impression of a late check from the populace. Look at the declaration of the Yorkshire Dissenters,[6] publishd by their order, and signed, with the same authority, by Mr Satchheard.[7] This declaration has been enclosd to me, and I fancy to every Member of Parliament. It is intended to quiet the publick mind concerning their

[5] This is an exaggeration; very few of the Dissenters seem to have wholly accepted revolutionary ideas. See also Burke's *Thoughts on French Affairs* (*Works*, Bohn, III, 354; Little, Brown, IV, 324).

[6] This 'Address to the People of England' was adopted unanimously 'At the Regular Quarterly Meeting of the Committee of Protestant Dissenting Laymen and Ministers of the three Denominations for the West Riding of the County of York' at Wakefield on 1 September, and (from what Burke says of it below), probably published as a broadside or a pamphlet. It appeared as an advertisement in the *Morning Chronicle* of 19 September and in other papers about the same time; it is reprinted in the *Gentleman's Magazine*, 1791, LXI, pt II, 924–6.

[7] Watson Scatcherd (d. 1817) of Morley, Yorkshire, barrister and J.P., signed the Address as Chairman of the Meeting (*ibid.* 1817, LXXXVII, pt I, 374).

Conduct and designs. They endeavor, of Course, to make it as plausible as they can. Yet the Style and manner at every turn, discover them;[8] and their professions with regard to our present constitution, are replete with so many insinuations of a desire of various changes, as makes me think their paper, considering the guarded Nature of an expurgatory declaration, one of the worst indications they have ever yet furnishd of their disposition. With all their simulation and dissimulation, the strength of their Zeal gets the better of their fraudulent prudence. In their postscript, where, as Lord Bacon observes, cunning men state their true object,[9] they publickly adopt Priestley and his Cause; They give him compliments of condolence and encouragement, and declare him a *Martyr*—a Martyr to what?

The Evil does not exist the less, because the fire of their intemperate Zeal has been turned upon themselves by the intemperate Zeal of others, and for the present they are obliged to cover it with ashes. For my part, I shall never think that a party, of at least seven hundred thousand Souls, with such recruits as they can pick up, in this Kingdom, and with a body united with them in Sentiments and principles, and more susceptible of violent passions, can be in the present state of things, a ground, upon which one can rest in perfect Security. A foreign factious connexion is in the very essence of their politicks. Their Object is avowedly to abolish all national distinctions and local interests and prejudices, and to merge them all in one Interest and one Cause, which they call the rights of man. They wish to break down all Barriers which tend to seperate them from the Counsels, designs, and assistance, of the republican, atheistical, faction of Fanaticks in France. France, in the very plenitude of any power which she possessd in this Century, would be no Object of serious alarm to England, if she had no connexion with parties in this Kingdom: With a connexion here which considers the predominant power in France as their natural friend and ally, I should think Three or four departments in Normandy more formidable than the whole of that once great Monarchy. At this moment I think, There is no danger from them.

[8] The Address congratulates 'the inhabitants of a neighbouring country on their late deliverance from the power of a despotic government, and their present flattering prospect of being blessed with the possession of legal liberty. . . . In this auspicious change we anticipate a glorious addition to the general happiness of mankind. We exult in the reflexion that we live in an age which has produced a body of legislators, who, by directly disclaiming all offensive wars, have presented a new example to an admiring world' (*ibid.* 1791, LXI, pt II, 925–6).

[9] The remark is in Bacon's essay 'Of Cunning'.

But our danger must be from our not looking beyond the moment. How variable and unstable popular humour is, and how capable those who today cry up Church and King, are the next of crying them down with equal rage, are things not at all necessary to be stated to one of your Sense and experience. What then is to be done? Very little can be done *at home* in my opinion. Our Laws, which are so vigorous and effective in the punishment of Treason, when it is got under, and even during the conflict, are feeble indeed in preventing Treasonable machinations. I think, on the whole View of affairs, that this Temper in our Laws is for the better, though, in critical times, inconveniencies may happen from it. Even if any measure of domestick policy were proper to be pursued, perhaps both Ministry and opposition would be shy in provoking the dissenters. But the root of the Evil is *abroad;* and the way to secure us at *home* is to deprive mischeivous factions of their *foreign* alliances. The present opportunity seems to me astonishingly favourable to this policy. If missed, it cannot easily be recoverd. Europe is in profound peace. All its powers are, with an unanimity without example, indisposed to this French System. A few months may change a situation and dispositions so rarely found and combined. They look to England—Without being satisfied of her goodwishes they will not move. Will you permit me to remind you of what I had the honour of laying before you in a short conversation, and of stating more at large to Mr Pitt and Lord Grenville. It is in substance, that the Emperors Ministers, for purposes and from Characters, which I mentiond in detail, counteract all his designs; and that, perhaps more from inconstancy than ill design, he has delayed a Business of the speedy execution of which he had given the fullest hopes. The K. of Prussia engaged, as I understand, at his (the Emperors) desire; and he has a full right to demand of him, that he may not appear a Dupe in the Eyes of all Europe. The best manner of suggesting to him, what I beleive, he is very desirous of doing, must be left to you. This seems to me to be the most effectual way of acting; so as to effect an Object agreeable, I am sure, to sound policy, and at the same time tending to preserve the neutrality you wish to keep. May I beg Your goodnature to excuse this trouble to your patience and to believe me with great Respect and regard

> Dear Sir
> Your most faithful
> and obliged humble Servant
> EDM BURKE.

Beconsfield Sept. 30. 1791.

My Son is this instant returned and in good health.

Rt Honble Henry Dundas

To the KING of POLAND—28 February 1792

Corr. (1958), VII, 76–7

On 3 May 1791 Poland had adopted a new constitution of moderate character. Burke had praised it in the *Appeal from the New to the Old Whigs*. Stanislaus Augustus (1732–98), King of Poland, wishing to express his appreciation of Burke's views, sent Burke a letter in English with a gold medal.

Sir,
. . . Hitherto the Body of the Nation has seconded your Endeavours. The exertion of one Virtue is always a pledge for the Exertion of another. I shall not therefore, for a moment, suffer myself to apprehend, that the Polish Nation will not add constancy to their Zeal, and, that recruited as it is, in the powers of its activity, it will not continue to second your Majesty in giving perfection and stability to the great work which has been carried so far. I will go further and indulge myself in the hope, that no one Individual will remain in such a state of delusion as to imagine, that, under whatever description he may be known, he is, in reality, a Nobleman, a Gentleman, or even a Citizen in any commonwealth, who is continually subjected to the Will of foreign powers. No individual will continue to form so erroneous an Estimate of things, as to feel himself miserable and degraded, because his countrymen are elevated and happy. It is a poor exaltation which consists only in the depression of other men. I love Nobility. I should be ashamed to say so, if I did not know what it is that I love. He alone is noble, that is so reputed by those, who, by being free, are capable of forming an opinion. Such a people are alone competent to bestow a due Estimation upon Rank and Titles. He is noble, who has a priority amongst Freemen; not he who has a sort of wild Liberty among Slaves. One so circumstanced, is not so much like a person noble from his Rank, as one, who has escaped from his lot in the general bondage, by injustice, Violence, and wrong. There is no Nobility where there is no possible Standard for a comparison among Ranks. To think otherwise, is to think very differently from Your

Majesty. You delight, and therefore the world delights in you, to be considerd as the father not the proprietor of your people. . . .

To LORD GRENVILLE—18 *August* 1792

Corr. (1958), VII, 173–78

William Wyndham Grenville, 1st Baron Grenville (1759–1834), was Foreign Secretary in Pitt's ministry.

My Lord,

I do not know whether I can perfectly justify myself in venturing to trouble your Lordship, in my imperfect state of knowlege, with any suggestion of mine: But I trust that however weak you may find my Notions, you will believe that [they] are formed with general good intentions, and that they are laid before you with all possible respect to yourself and to your Colleagues, and with real good wishes for whatever may contribute to your reputation in the Conduct of the King's Business.

The late shocking, though long expected Event at Paris, has rendered, in my opinion, every step that shall be taken with regard to France at this conjuncture extremely delicate.

The part of a neutral Power is in itself delicate; but particularly so in a Case in which it is impossible to suppose that in this Neutrality there should not be some lurking wish in favor of one of the Parties in the Contest. The Conduct of such a Power will be looked up to with hope and fear during the Contention. Every thing which such a power says or does will be construed by an application to the Circumstances.

The present Circumstances are an Attack upon the King of France's Palace; the murder of all who were found in it—the imprisonment of the King—His Suspension, stated by the Faction itself as a Deposition—Acts of violence which have obliged the majority of the National Assembly to absent themselves from their functions[1]—add to these the intention, not in the least ambiguous, the bringing the King and Queen to a Trial, the resolution expressed by many, of putting them to death with or without that formality. The effect of these things, from their very nature, and from the nature of Men, as well as from the principle on which they are done, at a time when theories are rashly formed and readily pass from speculation into practice, and

---

[1] Only about a third of the members of the Legislative Assembly were attending its sittings.

when ill Examples, at all times apt to infect, are so unusually contagious, it is unnecessary for me to state to one of your Lordship's
sagacity and penetration.

This last Revolution, whatever name it may assume, at present bears
no one Character of a National Act. It is the Act only of some desperate
Persons, Inhabitants of one City only, instigating and hiring at an
enormous Expence, the lowest of the people, to destroy the Monarch
and Monarchy, with whatever else is respectable in Society. Not one
Officer of the National Guards of Paris, which Officers are composed
of nothing higher than good Tradesmen, has appeared in this Business.[2] It is not yet adopted throughout France by any one Class of
People. No regular Government of any Country has yet an Object
with which they can decently treat in France, or to which they can
rationally make any official Declaration whatsoever.

In such a state of things to address the present heads of the Insurrection put by them into the nominal administrative Departments of
State Office, is to give a direct sanction to their Authority on the part
of the Court of Great Britain. To this time the King of France's name
has appeared to every public Act and Instrument; and all Office transactions to our Court, and to every other foreign Court, have appeared
in their usual form. If we pleased it was in our power to shut our eyes
to every thing else: But this is now no longer possible. I should therefore beg leave to submit it to consideration, whether, to recognize the
Leaders in the late murderous Insurrection, as the actual Governors
of France, is not at best, a little premature. Perhaps it may be a doubt,
as a matter of sound policy, whether more would not be lost by this
hasty recognition on the side of the great, settled, and acknowleged
powers, than we can hope to gain by pressing to pay our court to this,
at best, unformed and embryo Potentate.

I take it for granted, that it will not be easy for Lord Gower[3] to
continue in his present Situation. If it were even thought for the dignity
of this Crown, no man of honor and spirit would submit to it. It is a
sacrifice too great to be made of all generous and noble feeling. I
should humbly propose it for consideration, whether on his retreat,
great reserve ought not to be used with regard to *any Declaration*. If
any person standing in the place of a Minister should apply to him

[2] The commander of the National Guard, Jean-Antoine Galyot, Marquis de Mandat (1731–
92), who had arranged for the National Guard to take part in the defence of the Tuileries, had
been summoned early on 10 August to the Hôtel de Ville, removed from his command and
murdered. As a result the National Guard played no official part in the events which followed.
[3] George Granville Leveson Gower, styled Earl Gower (1758–1833), the British Ambassador
in France.

for an Explanation, he ought, in my poor opinion, to be *absolutely silent*. But if that should not be thought the best course, he might say that he had leave to return on his private Affairs. The King of Spain has no Minister at Paris, yet his neutrality has hitherto been complete.[4] The neutrality of this Court has already been more than once declared.[5] At *this moment*, any overprompt and affected new Declaration on that subject, made to the persons who have lately vaulted into the seat of Government after committing so many atrocious Acts and threatening more, would have all *the force and effect of a Declaration in their favour*. Although it should be covered with mollifying Expressions with regard to the King's personal safety (which will be considered as nothing but a sacrifice to Decorum and Ceremony and as mere words of course) it will appear to the Jacobine Faction as *a direct recommendation to their meditated Act of Regicide*, knowing, as the World does, their dispositions, their menaces, their preparations, and the whole train of the existing circumstances. In that Case to say, 'I hope you mean no ill, and I recommend it to you to do no ill,—but do what you please, you have nothing to fear from me', would be plainly to call upon them to proceed to any lengths their wickedness might carry them.

It is a great doubt with me whether a Declaration to this new Power, a Creature almost literally of yesterday, and a Creature of treasonable and murderous Riot of the lowest people in one City, is not a substantial breach of the neutrality promised to the power to whom originally the neutrality was assured, on the interposition of *foreign* powers, namely, to the most Christian King. To take the first opportunity with the most extraordinary haste, to remove all fears from the minds of his Assassins, is tantamount to taking a part against him. Much I fear, that, tho' nothing could be more remote from the intention of this Court, yet if such a Declaration were made, and if the Act of atrocity apprehended, should actually take place, we shall be considered as ready Accomplices in it; and *a sort of Accessories before the fact;* particularly when no Declaration on the part of our Court has been called for by the new power, and that as yet they have no Minister at this Court. If the step of the recal of our Minister (supposing such a step in contemplation) should produce any fears in them—I see no use in removing these fears. On our part, the Navy of France is not so formidable, that I think we have any just ground of apprehension that she will make war upon us. It is not the enmity, but the friendship

---

[4] Spain had recalled her Ambassador in August 1791 and was represented at Paris by a chargé d'affaires.

[5] e.g. after the Declaration of Pillnitz.

of France that is truly terrible. Her intercourse, her example, the spread of her doctrines, are the most dreadful of her Arms.

I do not see what a Nation loses in reputation or in safety, by keeping its conduct in its own power. I think such a state of freedom in the use of a moral and politic reserve in such unheard of circumstances, can be well justified to any Sovereign abroad, or to any party or person at home. I perceive, that much pains are taken by the Jacobins of England, to propagate a notion that one State has not a right to interfere according to its discretion, in the interior Affairs of another. This strange notion can only be supported by a confusion of ideas, and by not distinguishing the Case of promoting Rebellion and sedition in a neighbouring country, and taking a part in the divisions of a Country, when they do prevail and are actually formed. In the first Case there is undoubtedly more difficulty than in the second, in which there is clearly no difficulty at all. To interfere in such dissentions requires great prudence and circumspection, and a serious attention to justice and to the policy of one's own Country, as well as to that of Europe. But an abstract principle of public law, forbidding such interference, is not supported by the reason of that law, nor by the Authorities on the Subject, nor by the practice of this Kingdom, nor by that of any civilized Nation in the World. This Nation owes its Laws and Liberties, his Majesty owes the Throne on which he sits, to the contrary principle. The several Treaties of Guarantee to the protestant Succession, more than once reclaimed, affirm the principle of interference which in a manner forms the basis of the public Law of Europe. A more mischievous idea cannot exist than that any degree of wickedness, violence and oppression may prevail in a Country, that the most abominable, murderous and exterminatory Rebellions may rage in it, or the most atrocious and bloody tyranny may domineer, and that no neighbouring power can take cognizance of either, or afford succour to the miserable Sufferers.

I trust your Lordship will have the goodness to excuse the freedom taken by an old Member of Parliament. The habits of the House of Commons teach a liberty, perhaps improper, with regard to Office. But be assured, there is nothing in mine, that has the smallest mixture of hostility—and it will I trust appear that my motives are candid and friendly, if ever this Affair should come into discussion in the House of Commons, and I should feel myself called on to deliver my opinion. If I were, as formerly I have been, in systematic Opposition (most assuredly I am not so now) I had much rather, according to my practice in more instances than one, respectfully to state a doubt to Ministers

CHAPTER SEVEN

whilst a measure is depending, than to reproach them afterwards with its consequences, in my place. What I write will, I hope, at worst, be thought the intrusion of an importunate friend. I am thoroughly convinced that the faction of the English Jacobins, though a little under a Cloud for the present, is neither destroyed nor disheartened: The fire is still alive under the Ashes: Every encouragement direct or indirect, given to their Brethren in France, stirs and animates the Embers. *So sure as we have an existence, if these things should go on in France, as go on they may, so sure it is that in the ripeness of their time, the same Tragedies will be acted in England.* Carra and Condorcet, and Santerre and Manuel, and Petion[6] and their Brethren the Priestleys, the Coopers and the Watts', the Deputies of the Body of the Dissenters and others at Manchester, who embraced Carra in the midst of the Jacobin Club,[7] the Revolution Society that receivd Petion in London[8] the whole race of the *affiliated*, who are numerous and powerful, whose principles, dispositions and wishes, are the very same, are closely connected as ever, and they do not fail to mark and to use every thing that shews a remissness, or any equivocal appearance in Government, to their advantage. I conceive that the Duke of Brunswick is as much fighting the Battle of the Crown of England as the Duke of Cumberland did at Culloden.[9] I conceive that any unnecessary Declarations on our part, will be to him, and to those who are disposed to put a bound to this Empire of Anarchy and Assassination, a signal discouragement. The Cause of my dread, and perhaps over officious anxiety at this time, has arisen from what (you will have the goodness to pardon me) I thought *rather too much readiness to declare on other occasions.* Perhaps I talk of a thing not at all in contemplation. I have never heard that it was. If no thoughts of the kind have been entertained,

[6] All radical revolutionaries: Jean-Louis Carra (1742–93); the Marquis de Condorcet; Antoine-Joseph Santerre (1752–1809); Pierre-Louis Manuel (1751–93); Jérôme Pétion (1756–94), Mayor of Paris 1791–2.
[7] Thomas Cooper (1759–1839) and James Watt (1769–1848), son of the engineer, had presented the Address of the Manchester Constitutional Society to the Jacobin Club (*Societé des amis de la constitution, séante aux Jacobins, a Paris. Discours de M.M. Cooper et Watt . . . le 13 avril 1792*, Paris, 1792). Burke had attacked Cooper and Watt in his speech of 30 April, to which Cooper was to reply in a pamphlet, *A Reply to Mr Burke's Invective against Mr Cooper, and Mr Watt*, London, 1792.
[8] At the celebration of the anniversary of the Revolution of 1688 on 4 November 1791.
[9] Charles William Ferdinand, Duke of Brunswick (1735–1806), commander of the Prussian invasion of France. The Duke of Cumberland commanded the British King's forces at the Battle of Culloden in 1746, where the Jacobite pretender was defeated.

your Lordship will be pleased to consider this as waste paper. It is at any rate but as a hint to yourself and requires no Answer.

I have the honor to be &c
Beconsfield Aug. 18. 1792.

Grenville replied on 6 September that a decision on the points raised by Burke had already been reached. In fact a dispatch had been sent to Lord Gower on 17 August, instructing him to return to England, reiterating the King's neutrality in the internal affairs of France and his 'solicitude for the personal situation of Their Most Christian Majesties, and their royal family'.

To the CHEVALIER DE GRAVE—*24 August* 1792

Corr. (1958), VII, 182–83

Pierre-Marie, Chevalier de Grave (1755–1823), had been appointed French Minister of War on 9 March and had resigned on 8 May. He retired to England, whence he addressed a letter to the Legislative Assembly, dated 6 August.

Sir

I am obliged to you for the honor you have done me in sending me your Letter to the President of the National assembly. The Picture you have drawn of the Calamitous State of your Country must deeply affect every mind out of which the Spirit of System has not effaced all the genuine Sentiments of Natural Humanity. It is impossible, Sir, not to take a particular Interest in men who have made Sacrifices to their honour, even where we may differ in opinion about the exact propriety of their Conduct. I really do justice to the purity of your motives in your acceptance and in your resignation of the place you held in one of the late transitory administrations. In great Revolutions and in Critical situations like those which France has for some time experienced great Errours are, in a manner, unavoidable. He knows little of Mankind, and feels less for them, who is not Sensible of this, and who will not make a liberal allowance for our common and inevitable infirmity. It is enough, if Errours are not Shewn in Crimes, and if by obstinacy, mistake is not heightned into madness. I believe that your acceptance of Ministry, under Circumstances in which it was evidently impossible to perform its Duties, and in which no degree of reputation could be obtained, was imputable to the dreadful Necessities of the time, and to a laudable desire of preventing as much Evil

as may be, where to do good was hopeless. Such a necessity will often
involve the best of men in the worst of Systems. In that Light I consider
the new Constitution of France in all its parts. Nothing has happen'd
but what was the Natural and inevitable Effect of that fatal Constitution, and its absurd and wicked principles. Nothing has been the
Effect of accident; Every Successive Event was the direct result of
that which preceeded it; and the whole, the Effect of the false Basis
on which that constitution was originally laid. A more deplorable
monument of the weakness and malignity of which the Human mind
is capable, never has been raised in any time or in any Country. I am
sure it gives me Sincere Sorrow, that you, together with so many
thousands of worthy Patriots, have been sacrificed to that Idol. You
Speak of returning to France when such a party as you describe is
formed *in* France. Such a party can never be formed there. The predominant faction have taken good care, that their body politick Should
not contain within itself any remedy for its own distempers. As their
contrivance imitates Nature in nothing else, so neither does it in this
great Circumstance, of Self healing powers and properties.

I shall go to Bath towards the End of next week; but my Stay there
will not be very long. On my return, if it Suits your convenience to
do me the honor, I shall be happy to receive you and pay you my
respects in this place.

> I have the honor to [be] with very great respect
> Sir your most Obedient
> and Humble Servant
> > E: BURKE

Beaconsfield
August 24 92

To EARL FITZWILLIAM—29 *November* 1792

Corr. (1958), VII, 306–18

Burke describes his efforts to stir the British government to action after the failure
of the Prussian invasion to France. He is trying to secure the support of his friend
Lord Fitzwilliam for a broader ministry that would include the antirevolutionary
'Portland Whigs'.

My dear Lord,
   There is a part of the Subject of your Letter on which I ought to
postpone doing any thing until you get to Town, or until Richard

arrives from Ireland. I was in some hopes of seeing your Lordship in London when I was there. A part of your Letter to the Duke of Portland which his Grace shewed me was the only thing I found in London to give me satisfaction. The Ideas are just, sound, comprehensive, manly, and what, a while ago, I should have called the Sentiments of an Englishman, and of an Englishman of the first rank; But I am afraid, that in a very short time we shall look in vain for that Character in any Rank: for if it appears but in a few, and in those few, is to be suppressed almost as soon as it appears, in a short time the very traces of it will not remain. The whole nation will change its Character, if it has not changed it, as I strongly suspect it has, already. The Liberty which appears amongst us is not English Liberty; the policy which is in fashion is not English Policy—The Spirit (if such it may be called) which influences most of those you converse with, is not English Spirit. When I last went to Town I found the Duke of Portland, Lord Loughborough, Windham, and Lord Malmsbury exactly in the Sentiments of your Letter. There was not an Iota of difference between any of them and myself upon the aspect of foreign affairs, and its influence upon the very being of this Country. But far otherwise with many others. They have the same fears and apprehensions that we have; but they are fears that do not lead to any provision for safety—They are such, as aggravate the danger, as make indeed an essential part of it,—and if they continue to prevail, will I apprehend, make it inevitable. The moment an Englishman thinks that the French possession of the Netherlands, and their exerting an absolute Empire at Sea, is to be borne without even an attempt at resistance, and that we may secure ourselves from the effect of their arms and intrigues by the prosecution of a few of their Libellers, it is all over with us. I think Europe recoverable yet. But it must be by a great and speedy Effort of *this Country.* This can never be done but by the extinction, or at least by the suspension, of Parties amongst us. Whatever our Sentiments or likings may be in this point we ought to act as if we were but one man. If the French arms and principles (which are things inseperable) are not, in their prevalence, the greatest of all Evils, I really think, that such an Effort on the part of this Country ought not to be attempted; for I am well aware, that by the cruel neutrality which has been so much in fashion, we have been brought into very great difficulties: But these very difficulties are amongst the motives to exertion. I know, that what cripples the Duke of Portland is his Doubt of getting any considerable number of his friends to fall in with him, if he should suspend active opposition upon the principle of supporting Ministry, in defending this Kingdom, and its former allies on the Continent, against the prevalence of France. In my opinion, there is no place for triffling in the present Crisis. Those who are called your friends ought to have a faithful opinion given to them, and a decided example set before their Eyes.—And if they choose to adopt other opinions, and to follow other leaders, you lose nothing by discovering who do and who do not belong to you. There are times in which, of all things, this is the most necessary to be known. People who do not agree in principle are not of the same party. Oh! take care, that you do not lose the importance which you have as individuals, by looking towards a party, which, for your principles and your Objects, has no existence. I shall not easily believe, that, if the name of a party had never been heard of in the Country, the part which Lord Fitzwilliam and the Duke of Portland, and some others whom I could name, would take, must not have great weight in the support of any measure, and a large share of influence on the publick mind. Many, if not most, of those who really love you, trust you, and think with you, would tread in your footsteps. At any Rate you would deprive of the Credit of your names, and the assistance of your fortunes, those who are pursuing measures of your Ruin. I say eminently, for *your* Ruin; for though it is beyond all doubt, that their projects extend much farther, you are the persons more particularly struck at, and who will fall the first Victims to their success. The way, and the only way you have to be united amongst yourselves is to seperate yourselves from those who are adverse to you—for otherwise this false appearance of union is itself a Scource of the greatest distraction, and of a distraction the more fatal, because the persons who work against you are in your own bosom. I believe, that no greater differences in political System ever did exist among the most adverse nominal descriptions of men, than prevail at this hour between the two divisions of those who affect to be considerd of as the same party. How is it possible that you can have a consultation on any plan of action when the Objects you have in view are in direct contradiction to one another? My dear Lord, forgive me, if I repeat it—This is no moment for triffling. You are to provide, and that *speedily* too, for the salvation of yourselves, your wives, your posterity. At any rate, those whose opinion cannot prevail, on some occasions, are obliged publickly to make their protestation. Acquit yourselves from any share in the ruin of your Country. I remember a saying of Keppels.[1] Somebody told him that he

---

[1] Augustus Keppel, 1st Viscount Keppel (1725–86).

wonderd we should divide when we shewed such weak Numbers. He answerd, that we did not divide to shew our Numbers but to shew ourselves. I forget what the Case was. I suppose it was important. If it was, I think his answer and our Conduct was very proper. Since I returned from London The Duke of Portland I find has seen Mr Fox. Before I make any remark on what passed at that interview, I wish to give you an account of the Motives which called me to London immediately on my return from Bath—what made me go there a second time; and what was done during my continuance there. I think it my Duty to account with you for my Conduct; but if it be not a strict Duty, it is enforced by a motive commonly much stronger: It is a great satisfaction to me.

On that unparalleled Event of the King of Prussias negotiation with an army which he came to fight, and which was every thing but surrenderd to him, I felt the Evil which I had long dreaded come much more close to us. I felt the Country to be in no State of Offence or defence, political, military, or naval. The Ministers by their neutrality, (which they had persevered in with the most pedantick exactness, and in which they were at least encouraged, if not led into, by the most energetick part of the opposition, and the acquiescence of the whole) had broken the continuity and chain of their connexions with the continent; and of course there was no sort of reciprocal confidence or communication between this Court and any other in Europe. An universal weakness appeared to me to be the result of that neutrality, which by taking away the connexion with Great Britain, took away the cement which held together all other States. In great emergencies mere complaint and mutual accusation rather aggravates than removes the Evil. I therefore, instead of blaming Ministry or opposition, set myself to think in what manner they might in future cooperate to the correction of former Errours and to the recovery of our former place in Europe. For this purpose I considerd of two plans; one for our external affairs; one for putting our domestick affairs into such a situation, as might best forward and concur with the former. I send you what occurred to me on the foreign affairs.[2] I shewd it to Lord Camden,[3] then at Bath; and I talked to him a great deal about the internal State of things. He spoke with a great deal of apparent openness. But at the same time declared, that he took no part in Cabinet or very little, and only remaind in his place until he could accommodate Mr Pitt with the disposal of that Office. He shewd no

---

[2] Burke's *Heads for Consideration on the Present State of Affairs.*
[3] Charles Pratt, 1st Earl Camden (1714–94), Lord President of the Council.

desire of having it communicated to his Colleagues in Office; and so the affair dropped until my return to this place.

To say that I was somewhat uneasy would but ill paint the State of my Mind. It was for some time a question with me, whether I should not leave things to take their Course, and lie still upon the Strand, until the Tide, which already appeared to me to ride as a Bore,[4] should cover me and every body else. However this thought was not of many hours duration. The very morning after my return, I went to London. I was resolved to try whether there was a pulse of Life beating in any one person of any description; or whether Life could be infused into any of them.

First I went to the Minister.[5] I took occasion from my being of the Committee for the French refugees, to try whether he would relish for them an Establishment in Canada, since it was evident that private Benevolence, which might be adequate to a temporary relief, was utterly incompetent to a permanent settlement. My plan, which was founded on something nearly approaching to despair of the foreign Courts resolution to shake the present state of things in France, was well received by him both as a plan and on the principle. He seemd to have very little hopes. I did not enter further into a Business, for which I plainly saw he was not ripe, on which I did not think he wished to pursue the conversation, and on which I wished to take, as far as I could, the Sense of some others before I opend myself further to him. This reserve I chiefly used with regard to the interiour State of things. By word of mouth I explaind myself as little with regard to the foreign—but as my sentiments on foreign affairs required no sort of concurrence of others, I put a Copy of the Memorial I send to your Lordship into his hands.[6] He received it very civilly and said he would read it with attention and Interest.

I left my name at Lord Loughboroughs. The next morning I saw him and Windham. They were both strongly impressed with the danger impending over Europe and this Country by the prevalence of French arms and principles. I do not think I have ever seen them both so animated. I well knew the general Ideas of your Lordship and the Duke of Portland. We were all of opinion, that every thing depended on the resolution of Ministers to act with Vigour and with a prompt decision. My opinion was, grounded both on the nature of

---

[4] 'A tide-wave of extraordinary height, caused either by the meeting of two tides, or by the rushing of the tide up a narrowing estuary' (*Oxford English Dictionary*).

[5] Pitt. Burke probably saw him on 9 November.

[6] Again, *Heads for Consideration on the Present State of Affairs.*

things, and on the direct declarations of some of them, that their inertness and want of all mental as well as active rescource, was owing to a consciousness of the Fundamental weakness of their System, and its want of Basis in the strong permanent aristocratick Interests of the Country.—The Conduct which they ought to hold was in my opinion so clear and self evident, that if they were assured of a support in a Line of measures against the doctrinal arms of France, (which went as those of Mahomed, the Rights of man in one hand, and the Sword in the other)—they might be brought to act in a very different sort of Spirit from any they had hitherto Shewn. Lord Loughborough thought so too; and he was of opinion, in which we concurred with him, that nothing relative to support could be done in the way of *Official coalition*—in any shape whatsoever. Much less could it be ïor the publick Interest that an active opposition, for the purpose of changing the Ministry, or even for disabling it in its operations, should be continued. He thought that these two latter points should be distinctly known to them, to the Party, and to the world; because he was sure, that in so very critical a time as this, nothing ought to be done which could make the motives to the support of Ministers in the smallest degree equivocal. We readily, as Your Lordship may well believe, fell in with sentiments so rational and so honourable. The thing which pressed upon us was, the urgency of the present Crisis, which made the conduct to be held by Ministers, with relation to foreign affairs, to depend upon the use of a day, perhaps of an hour. It was therefore thought expedient, that Windham and I should go to the Ministers; that we should sound them, and try to discover, whether they thought, that so strong and decided a line of conduct with respect to foreign affairs and domestick or both, might probably be called for, as to make some support, more extensive than the ordinary force of Government, necessary to them? To state, that we were there without authority, but not destitute of observation of dispositions or knowlege of Sentiments; That we could speak from that observation and knowlege, that any opposition, the Tendency of which would be to weaken Government as such, or which should have for its Object a change of Ministry, was not thought, at this Crisis, advisable; That therefore to give the greater Credit and efficacy to the support, it was to have no relation whatsoever to official arrangements; but that it would necessarily require a fair communication of the substance of the measures on which this support would be required, and as much and as fair information on the subject as certain necessary official and Cabinet reserves would admit. We went to Mr Pitt and Lord Grenville and saw them together.[7] The next morning we saw Lord Hawkesbury.[8] Our conversation was to the Purport I have stated it. The two first received the communication with civility—(Windham thinks it amounted to something more) They were not very explicit with regard to the Vigour of any measures which they might pursue as to interiour or exteriour Objects—But they did not deny, that such might be necessary—and desired, as they found that we tried the Ground rather than spoke from any direct authority, that they might have some more certain and definite assurances of support from the heads of the party before the meeting of Parliament (if such should be resolved on) than we were, at that time, empowerd to give them. Lord Hawkesbury, without, in effect, saying much more than the others did, was apparently Less guarded; and seemd extremely earnest, that such a good understanding, as we expressed our wish for, could be realized. During these conversations, I mentiond the grounds upon which I went—that is to say, the necessity, which this time imposed upon all men, of putting an End to differences of all sorts; That, as the main attack of the common Enemy was upon all Kings; it behoved honest men, whether Ministers or not, to endeavour in the first place, to put an End to the differences in the Royal family. That the payment of the Princes Debts, if the Prince should shew practicability as a Son, and the King as a father, instead of seperating them in affection or Interest, might tend to bring them together[9]—and I indicated some of the outlines of the plan, I had formed upon that subject, which, I conceived, would, without unpopularity or uneasiness in Parliament, accomplish an happy arrangement of this matter. I hope to talk to your Lordship more fully on this project. The next step was to put an End to the divisions in Parliament as much as possible. This was the direct Object of the conference. For this purpose I stated, that in my opinion, no measures ought to be omitted to gain over Mr Fox, of which, I said, I did not despair—but at which they shook their heads. The last, and not the least important was the settlement of the disputes which existed in Ireland. On this last I had something like a plan, which was very simple and could not fail in my opinion of success. After a good deal of talk on all these Subjects we parted. The next Step was to be made by us.

[7] On 13 November.

[8] Charles Jenkinson (1729–1808), 1st Baron Hawkesbury (1786), President of the Committee for Trade and Plantations in Pitt's cabinet.

[9] The Prince's debts were not paid until 1795.

We had in this first, taken a very bold Step indeed, and which, in the moment, we knew could not be justified by the common rules of prudence. But we thought the Case out of these Rules; because we thought it a very uncommon, and a very urgent Case; and that in endeavouring to bring parties together, we were to apply first to those who were nearest at hand. The French arms would not wait, nor their intrigues be suspended, on account of the mode of our deliberations. But the very next day, I lost no time in communicating the whole matter, just as it was, to the Duke of Portland, who expressed to me his fullest approbation of what we had done. He seemd to feel the importance of the Crisis full as strongly as Lord Loughborough, Mr Windham, and myself had done. He went without delay to Town, for the purpose, I imagine of conferring with his friends upon it—and expressed to Windham the same full approbation which he had been kind enough to express to me. I found, that Lord L.[10] expected me to return to Town, to a dinner at his House, at which our common friends were to be. The first thing I did, on going to Town a seconde time in consequence of this invitation, was to call at Burlington House. I there found Adam[11] and Tom Grenville[12] with the Duke. The discourse could turn but upon one Subject. Grenville seemd strongly under the impression of the General alarm. When I said, that measures ought to be taken to resist the Progress of the Enemy at home and abroad; or, to try some way of treating with their Leaders at home and abroad, for some safety to our Lives—He said there was a third way, that is, to wait Events; and to let things take their Course; that the Nation would not, at this time, second or support any Efforts, either on the Part of Ministry, or minority, or on both, which might tend to involve us in a War with France;—That perhaps when Holland was attacked they might be roused;—That to make any opposition to the Progress of French power, at this time, would be impracticable; and that to shake their System in France itself, was so evidently out of all hope, (the attempt having been made and failed) that it might be advisable to recognize that Republick, and to treat with it, concerning the Countries of which it seemd resolved to take possession.[13] This last part I am not quite so clear about; either that he did not express himself very distinctly, or that I do not carry away what he said very correctly. But this, I think, substantially was his opinion,

[10] Alexander Wedderburn (1733–1805), 1st Baron Loughborough.
[11] William Adam (1751–1839), M.P.
[12] Thomas Grenville (1755–1846), M.P.
[13] This was the view of Fox.

as to the measure of the recognition—As to the rest, I have no doubt.
I am sorry to say, he is not the only person who holds the same
Language. The Duke of Portland combated those opinions, (which
suppose, or must produce, the utter annihilation of this Kingdom as
a State) with as much energy, and as decisively, as I have ever heard
him argue against any thing in my Life. I had the Satisfaction to find,
that I agreed with him to a Tittle, in all the Sentiments expressed in
the Memorial I send you, as well as in that, which I wrote about a
year ago. Your Lordship recollects, that I put it into your hands; That
you had not time to read it; and that I took it away again to shew it
to Ministers and to the King, on whom it produced no effect. I will
send you a copy if you please.

The Duke of Portland was thus disposed, when we went to the
dinner, where we had Lord Stormont, Lord Carlisle, Lord Malmsbury,
Lord Portchester Mr Windham, and Mr Anstruther, with the Duke.
I felt, with a degree of satisfaction which I had not experienced for a
long time, myself, as in old times, with so many friends, consulting
about the Common good. We seemd all getting together again. I hope
it is not for my final exclusion; though I much fear it is the last time
we shall meet in that manner; or, at least, in the manner and on the
Terms I flatterd myself we had met. I rather think, the Majority was
quite right. But in such meetings the Minority usually decides; if any
thing at all can be supposed decided, where the Spirit of Doubt and
indecision seemd to predominate. I think the D. of P. felt embarrassed.
As to foreign affairs, (in which no man can persuade me, that all our
domestick interests are not included) by an almost general consent,
they were entirely postponed, as things, which they thought it hardly
safe even to discuss. With regard to the suspension of opposition,
Lord Stormont took the lead in Objecting to it; not as from his own
opinion, but from the difficulty of bringing others to it, Who, if Lord
Thurlow (he expressed him, not by name, but by description) should
hold out an hope of driving out the Ministers upon any particular
Question, could hardly relish any understood arrangement which was
to preclude them from taking it up in the Line of opposition. He
mentiond, as an example, the Forest Bill. He thought, and in this the
concurrence was pretty general, that you are bound to support the
Proclamation,[14] and all its fair consequences;—but as *he* did not think
you bound to more, that it would hardly be prudent to go beyond it;
but to leave every thing else as open to opposition as before. I do not

[14] A Proclamation against Seditious Writings.

say, that the company gave into the limitation. They all admitted, that to the Proclamation and its consequences they were bound in honour; but as to the going further, I rather imagine, nay I am sure, that Lord Loughborough, Lord Malmsbury, Mr Windham, Mr Anstruther and myself were for it. Lord Portchester was undecided. The D. of Portland did not strongly express his Sentiments; But on further conversation with him, I find, that his Sense of what he is bound to in the support of the Proclamation is very large, and that it includes every thing which can be done against the extending French influence abroad or at home, not excepting a war against that power. However, I do not find, that the rest of the company did at all consider it in that comprehensive View, but rather the contrary; and indeed I do not myself imagine, that it fairly bears so very lax a construction. If it did, I should find myself nearly satisfied. The result of the whole on my Mind is this, that Mr Windham and I are not authorised to give to the Ministers at present any very distinct Ideas of support, beyond what they may conclude from your conduct at the End of the last Session; and that nothing more of a confidential communication is opend between you.

So far as to what was done; or more correctly speaking, what was not done, at that days meeting. Before I came off, which was late in the day following, I heard that Mr Fox had arrived in Town. I knew that a communication with him, in order to discover his Sentiments was desired by the D. of P. and indeed was earnestly wished by all I conversed with. For my own part, I was not, when I first went to Town, without strong hopes that he would come right. I flatterd myself, that the Villainy and illiberality of the faction predominant in France, that the nastiness and Turpitude of the thing, that their compound of baseness and cruelty, (mud and blood) would have become disgustful to his Taste; and that the successful progress of this vile and odious scheme, so as to overturn the ballance of Europe, and even to touch this Country to the Quick, would have roused his sense of the national honour. I thought that he had, as many others had, an honourable retreat before him; and that he would avail himself of it to reunite himself with his oldest and best friends, who, he knew, abhorred the proceedings in France, and trembled at the progress of the arms of that people. The overturning of the first constitution, and the murder and proscription of the persons who had been concerned in framing it, would have given him a fair opportunity of choosing better ground, without any imputation of inconsistency. My first conversation with Windham damped me a little in these expectations. He had, not long since, seen Fox. He found him no way alterd. His opinion was, that the danger to this Country chiefly consisted in the growth of Tory principles, and that what happend in France was likely to be useful to us in keeping alive and invigorating the Spirit of Liberty. He was disposed to lower and palliate whatever seemd shocking in their procedure. I was informed too, (not by Windham, but by perfectly good authority) that he has lived, more than with any body, with the Ladies here belonging to Monsr L'Egalité—and was of frequent parties with them, with the Bishop of Autun,[15] and Chauvelin;[16] persons with whom scarcely any body else chooses to converse. I found too, that Erskine, who is outrageously French, tells every where, uncontradicted, that he has gone over his Brief with Mr Fox for Paines defence; and that he has receivd more important and useful instructions from him for that defence than he could have drawn from the whole Bar.[17]

What passed at the Duke of Portlands with Mr Fox I would not be supposed to attempt at Stating with precision:—I have it at second hand from Windham through Dr Laurence.[18] I understand that he says, he apprehends no danger to the internal State of this Kingdom; which however he checks, by saying that he has not lived much about for a good while past. That he is of opinion we ought to recognize the French Republick; and that having done this we ought to inform that Republick, that we shall not quietly see them add the Austrian Netherlands to their dominions—That however these Countries are not to be restored to the Emperour but left to choose a Government for themselves. He did not say who were to be the persons, to elect this

---

[15] Talleyrand.

[16] François-Bernard, Marquis de Chauvelin (1766–1832), the French Minister in London. Talleyrand was acting as his secretary.

[17] Paine (in France since 13 September) was tried for sedition *in absentia* on 18 December, and convicted and outlawed. Thomas Erskine was the Chief Counsel for the defence.

[18] Portland saw Fox on 24 and 25 November. The Duke reported to Fitzwilliam: 'The disposition and temper of his mind seemed to me so much more warped than it was in the beginning of the year when *we* conversed with Him upon the subjects of the French Revolution and Association of the Friends of the People—He appeared so little affected by the horrors which the former had produced in the course of the summer, He is so Hostile to, what he calls, the cause of Kings, and consequently so satisfied and pleased with the failure of the Prussian and Austrian Powers, that He is in a manner insensible to the Effects of the increasing power of France, and to that Lust of Dominion which is to me as evident in their present Republican Government as in the Zenith of their Monarchical Glory. His Eyes appeared to be not at all more open than they were in the Spring to the danger to which this Country is exposed by the inundation of Levelling Doctrines and the support they derive from the success of the French Arms; the interest he used to profess for the preservation of the Constitution seemed much less lively, and I am sorry to say, that I fear I observed Symptoms of no very strong indisposition to submit to the experiment of a new and possibly a Republican form of Government'.

Government. That as to the interiour affairs he thought satisfaction ought to be given to the Catholicks in Ireland; That in England the Test ought to be repealed. That in Scotland the Boroughs ought to be settled according to Sheridans Bill.[19] As to the rest a regular opposition was to be carried on as usual. What was said, or whether any thing was said, upon these several Heads, as yet I do not know. As to all the interiour regulations, I do not mean to trouble your Lordship with any sentiments of mine at present. The foreign state of things almost exclusively occupies my thoughts. Mr Foxes scheme of taking the Netherlands from the Emperor and erecting them into some fashion of a Republick, nominally independent, is not likely to cause any difference between him, and his friends in France. It is exactly the Scheme they propose themselves, and which they, and all the world think is their mode of extending an universal Empire.[20] No man can dream that in the present State of things or any which can be divined in future that such a Republick can be really and substantially independent. It must cling to that power to which it owes its origin; and thus France will be augmented by the finest addition which it has ever received—and Great Britain is to cede in one day to that nation the Object for which she carried on so many wars during an hundred years. That Holland must not follow, it is ridiculous to imagine. Gentlemen say, that when Holland is attacked this Nation may be roused—But if we wait till then, its rousing will be in vain. It may as well continue its slumbers. To attack Holland, in the actual State of Affairs and to take it, is one and the same thing. It cannot cost three weeks, especially if the frosts should set in sharply. I know the Statholder[21] has taken the alarm. It is plain he has, by the reclamation made to this Court.[22] But under that sense of danger on the Part of Holland, and the promise of executing the Guarantee on the part of this Court, not the least preparation is made either by Sea or Land

[19] A bill to reform the Scottish Burghs had first been introduced by Sheridan on 17 June 1788.

[20] On 16 November the French Executive Council to gain the support of Antwerp opened the Scheldt estuary to the shipping of all nations—an act which violated international treaties and was a direct challenge to Holland. On 19 November the French Convention adopted a decree offering assistance to all peoples who wished to regain their freedom. Shortly afterwards, finding that establishing the independence of conquered areas presented many difficulties, France began a policy of annexation. It was these acts which drove the Pitt Administration in the direction of war with France. On 29 November Lord Grenville informed Chauvelin that the edict of 16 November and the decree of 19 November must be revoked.

[21] William V (1748–1806).

[22] The Dutch Government had wished the British Government to take some action 'to deter the French from any attempt against Holland'. The result was the publication on 16 November of a Declaration of the British Government 'of inviolable friendship' with Holland and a determination to fulfil the Treaty of Alliance of 1788.

by the Dutch for their own Defence, or by England for their support. We are not to arm to save it; but, if we can, to reconquer it; very different things! and the last in a manner a thing desperate. What Mr Fox proposes on System, others concur in from Temper—that is from indolence, timidity, and want of all mental rescource. It seems we do not dare in this State, to fit out a fleet even of Observation to second our Negotiation in favour of our Allies,—or, if it should be necessary, (God knows how soon it may become so) for our own proper defence. France is drawing her Nets round us on every side; and she has a party to destroy us within the Toils. As to the growth of this contagion within our walls, as a meer domestick Evil, and unconnected with a dangerous foreign power, I have ever had little comparative apprehension; But combined with the foreign forces—there—there is the danger. If France goes on to break down every power in Europe, to disgrace and to disable us, and to render us afraid even of every provident means of personal safety,—it is impossible for the present order of things to subsist. If it does, it must subsist at her pleasure, and we well know what that pleasure is. All this I do not say, to cause an unmeaning alarm; but to submit to your better judgment, whether any time ought to be lost in putting yourselves in some proper array; knowing who are or are not with you—and making yourselves rather a small well orderd Phalanx, that an apparently great, but confused, and radically discordant Corps. Party ought to be made for politicks: not politicks for Party purposes. I really think I stand very nearly acquitted to my own Conscience, as having left little undone, within my power, to save the Country to which I belong; the order of things to which I was born; and the friends I love. On quitting Town I told the D. of P. that he knew where I was, and that I was always ready for every good word and work which he should please to command. I am very old; but as yet healthy, and neither wholly unfit, according to my Measure, nor indisposed to action, and I have a Son to second me; I trust in God I have.

I will write again to Bintinaye. I think their Schemes perfectly foolish. York City is the only place for them in the North. But I know no place very good for strangers but Bath. As to the Lay Committee I know not how it is conducted. At first I know they were falling from Blunder to Blunder: but I hear they are at length taking some rational direction. I shall write to Walker King about it. I am ever my Dear Lord most faithfully and affectionately your ever obliged

and humble Servant

Beconsfield Novr 29. 1792   EDM BURKE

To FLORIMOND-CLAUDE, COMTE DE MERCY-ARGENTEAU—[*circa* 6 *August* 1793]

Corr. (1958), VII, 386–93

Mercy-Argenteau (1727–94) was representing the Austrian Emperor at Brussels, and Burke had written to him on behalf of his young kinsman James Nagle. Now he explains the nature of the war against Jacobinism.

Sir,

I am infinitely obliged to your Excellency for your generous Intentions with regard to my young relation Nagle. Whenever he comes to possess enough of the French or German Languages to be fit to be presented to your Excellency he will sollicit that honour, if his military destination should permit him to profit of your condescension and goodness. General Count Dalton has been so very kind as to give him his first commission in his own Regiment. I hope that in Course of time your Excellencies powerful protection and his own good behaviour in endeavouring to merit that enviable distinction will ensure his future advancement. It is a thing about which I am anxious, as I am much deceived if he is not a good Lad.

I shall always recollect with the highest satisfaction the morning which you did me the honour to spend at my house;[1] and if it has given any thing like a favourable impression of me and my Intentions to one of your Excellencies judgment, experience, and knowlege of men and affairs, I shall remember it with as much Pride as Gratitude. If any thing in my conversation has merited your regard I think it must be the openness and freedom with which I commonly express my sentiments. You are too wise a man not to know that such freedom is not without its use; and that by encouraging it, men of true ability are enabled to profit by hints thrown out by understandings much inferiour to their own, and which they who first produce them are by themselves unable to turn to the best account. I am sure there is one Circumstance which will induce your Excellency to forgive the freedom that I used formerly or that I may now use, it is the perfect deference that every thing I suggest is submitted to your Judgment.

I flatter myself too, that you are pleased with my Zeal in this Cause. I certainly, look upon it to be the Cause of Humanity itself. I perfectly concur with you in that opinion provided I understand, as I trust I do, the true object of the War. I do not exclude from amongst the just Objects of such a confederacy as the present, the ordinary securities

---

[1] On Mercy-Argenteau's visit to England in August 1791.

which nations must take against their mutual ambition Let their internal constitutions be of what nature they will. But the present Evil of our time, though in a great measure an Evil of ambition, is not one of common political ambition; but in many respects entirely different. It is not the Cause of Nation as against nation, but as you well observe, the cause of mankind against those who have projected the subversion of that order of things under which our part of the world has so long flourishd, and indeed been in a progressive State of improvement, the Limits of which, if it had not been thus rudely stopped, it would not have been easy for the imagination to fix. If I conceive rightly of the Spirit of the present combination it is not at War with France but with Jacobinism. They cannot think it right that a second Kingdom should be struck out of the System of Europe,[2] either by destroying its independence, or by suffering it to have such a form in its independence, as to keep it as a perpetual Fund of Revolutions, in the very center of Europe; in that Region, which alone touches almost every other, and must influence even where she does not come in contact. As long as Jacobinism subsists there, in any form, or under any modification, it is not, in my opinion, the gaining a fortified place or two, more or less, or the annexing to the Dominion of the allied powers this or that Territorial district, that can save Europe, or any of its Members.[3] We are at war with a principle, and an example, which there is no shutting out by Fortresses or excluding by Territorial Limits. No lines of demarcation can bound the Jacobin Empire. It must be extirpated in the place of its origin, or it will not be confined to that place. In the whole Circle of military arrangements, and of political Expedients, I fear that there cannot be found any sort of *merely defensive plan* of the least force against the Effect of the Example which has been given in France. That Example has shewn, for the first time in the History of the world, that it is very possible to subvert the whole Frame and order of the best constructed States by corrupting the common people with the Spoil of the superiour Classes. It is by that instrument, that the French Orators have accomplished their purpose, to the Ruin of France; and it is by that instrument, that, if they can establish themselves in France, however broken or curtailed by themselves or others, that, sooner or later, they will subvert every Government in Europe. The Effect of erroneous Doctrines may be

---

[2] Burke presumably regarded Poland as the first.

[3] It had been accepted in principle since the beginning of the campaign of 1793 that the allies, and in particular Austria, should receive indemnities of territory in northern France. The extent of these indemnities had not yet been decided.

soon done away: But the example of successful pillage is of a nature more permanent, more applicable to use, and a thing which speaks more forcibly to the interests and passions of the corrupt and unthinking part of Mankind than a thousand Theories. Nothing can weaken the lesson contained in that example but to make as strong an example on the other side. The Leaders in France must be made to feel, in order that all the rest there and in other Countries may be made to see, that such spoil is no sure possession. It will be proper to let the Leaders of such Factions know, that, when they shake the property of others, they can never convert their Spoil into property in their own Favour, either in the specifick Object of their Robbery, or in any representative which they may choose to give it. The people at large in all Countries ought to be made sensible that the Symbols of publick Robbery never can have the Sanction and the currency that belong exclusively to the Symbols of publick faith. If any Government should be settled in France upon any other Idea than that of the faithful restitution of all property of all descriptions and that of the rigorous and exemplary punishment of the principal authours and contrivers of its Ruin, I am convinc'd to a certainty, that property, and along with property, Government, must fall, (in the same manner in which they have both fallen in France) in every other State in Europe. I am convinced, that twenty years would be too long a period to fix for such an Event, under the operation of such Causes as are now at work. As to France itself, no Form of Government which human wit can contrive, or human force compel, can have a longer duration there, than those miserable tottering Constitutions, which have been erected on false foundations for these four years past have had; as the new, or the restoration of the old Government, will be deprived of that solid foundation which connects property with the safety of the State. If the old proprietors (of whatever name) be not restored, an immense mass of Possession will be thrown into hands who have been enriched by the subversion of the Monarchy, and who never can be trusted for its support. Nothing I am persuaded can be done with the smallest prospect of permanence, but by completely counteracting all those crude Systems with which mankind has been surfeited, and by putting every thing without exception as nearly as possible upon its former Basis. When this, (the short and simple method) for which we have no need to have recourse to abstruse Philosophy or intricate Politicks, we may then talk with safety, upon some practical principles, of reforming what may be amiss, with the comfortable assurance to honest, who are the only wise men, that if they should not be able to make any reformation whatsoever in the antient order of things, the worst abuses which ever attended it would be ten thousand times better for the people than all the boasted reforms in the Scheme of innovation. It is very fortunate for those who may have the happiness of contributing to the Settlement of France (in which your Excellency may have a share which I envy to you) that the fraudulent currency funded upon this Robbery has, of itself, sunk so very low, as to leave but one, that that a very short, step to its utter annihilation. The utter destruction of Assignats and the restoration of order in Europe are one and the same thing. A reasonable publick Credit, and some retribution to those who have sufferd by its destruction, may be hoped for, when this immense mass of fraud and violence, which has usurped its place, is totally destroyd, so as not to Leave the slightest trace of its ever having existed.

It is the contempt of Property, and the setting up against its principle, certain pretended advantages of the State, (which by the way exists only for its conservation) that has led to all the other Evils which have ruined France, and brought all Europe into the most imminent danger. The beginning of the whole mischief was a false Idea, that there is a difference in property according to the description of the persons who hold it under the Laws, and that the despoiling a Minister of Religion is not the same Robbery with the Pillage of other Men. They, who thro' weakness gave way to the ill designs of bad men in that confiscation, were not long before they practically found their Errour. The spoil of the Royal Domaine soon followd the seizure of the Estates of the Church. The appenages of the Kings Brothers immediately came on the heels of the usurpation of the Royal Domaine; The property of the Nobility survived but a short time the appenages of the Princes of the Blood Royal.[4] At length the monied and the moveable property tumbled on the ruin of the immoveable property— and at this day, no Magazine, from the Warehouses of the East India company[5] to the Grocers and the Bakers shop, possesses the smallest degree of safety. I am perfectly persuaded, that there does not exist the smallest chance, under the most favourable issue of military op-

---

[4] The lands of the Church in France became the property of the nation by a decree of 2 November 1789. On 9 May 1790 the Constituent Assembly declared that the Crownlands also belonged to the nation. The grants of lands as apanages made to the King's brothers the Comte de Provence and the Comte d'Artois in 1771 and 1773, together with the seventeenth-century apanage of the Duc d'Orléans, were abolished by a decree of 13 August 1790. No sequestration from the nobility as a whole had been attempted, although the goods of émigrés had been confiscated under the law of 8 April 1792.

[5] The monopoly of the French East India Company had been abolished in April 1790. The Company was finally wound up in August 1793.

erations, of restoring Monarchy, order, Law and religion in France, but by doing justice, under wise Regulations, to those Ecclesiasticks who have been robbed of their Estates by the most wicked and the most foolish of all men, by those who took the lead in the constituting assembly.

In this opinion give me Leave to assure your Excellency I am far from single. It is the decided Sense of all thinking men, who are well affected to the Cause of order, in this Country. The necessity of providing for such French Ecclesiasticks as are in the British Dominion, has often led the conversation to that subject. We have had opportunities of knowing and considering them, in all points of View; and, if their reestablishment were not a valid claim of Justice, yet their personal merits, and the rules of sound policy, would strongly recommend it. We did not believe, before we had an opportunity of seeing it realized before our Eyes, that, in such a multitude of men, so much real Virtue had existed in the world. We are convinced, that a number of persons so disposed and so qualified as they are, if restored to their Country their property, and the influence which property in good hands carries with it, would be a necessary supplement to the use of arms; and that, under a Wise administration, they might do great things indeed for restoring France to the civilized World. Without this help such a deplorable Havock is made in the minds of men (in both Sexes) in France, still more than in the external order of things, and the Evil is so great and spreading, that a remedy is impossible on any other Terms.

Perhaps to a mind formed like that of your Excellency to give a preference to that kind of policy which is most connected with generosity, honour, and justice, the opinions of people in England ought to have some weight, partly that we cannot be supposed influenced in this point by the Spirit of Sect, and partly, because we may be supposed to have made a sort of equitable purchase of a right to a voice in their affairs. The maintenance of these worthy and meritorious persons, Scanty as it is for each individual, has already cost us upwards of seventy thousand pound sterling.[6] Unfortunately this Kind of Rescourse cannot continue long. Surely it is as reasonable that they should be maintained from their own Property as from Yours, or from our English Charity.

It is with a real Satisfaction, and which highly enhances the pleasure we feel from the glory of your arms, that you have gone before me in

---

[6] £41,000 had been raised by a national collection carried out by the Church of England and other religious bodies and £34,000 had come from subscriptions.

the restitution of some kinds of property in Conde and Valenciennes.[7] If Providence should so far favour the allied Arms, that the whole of the French Netherlands should be reduced the restitution of all kinds of Ecclesiastick Estates, would form a very essential rescource for many that are now upon your and upon our hands.

Since I have taken the Liberty of troubling you so far, you will excuse me, if, once for all, I trespass a little longer on your generous indulgence. There is a matter essential enough to justifye a good deal of discourse. I shall however touch only on a very few heads, which I leave entirely to your Excellencies more mature consideration.

It is a thing singular in our age, and, I believe, without example in any, that in so large and important a part of Europe as France, no person, and no Body politick whatsoever, is recognized in the Character of its Lawful Government, or as representing that Government. It is not necessary to point out to one of your Sagacity the fatal consequences of this State of things, and its Effect upon the Reputation of the great powers engaged in this War. These powers appear with regard to France in no other way than in the light of an Enemy to the Nation universally, and not, as when they made the Declaration of last Summer, as the Enemy only of a pernicious faction Tyrannizing in that Country;[8] a light in which no belligerent power ever did appear if he could possibly avoid it. Indeed, not to recognize the Government in the legal successor to the Monarchy is virtually to acknowlege the usurpation;[9] and to justifye the murder, or what is worse than the Murder, the deposition and pretended Trial of the King. I am afraid too that it is a principal Cause of the dreadful Treatment of the now King[10] and particularly of that of the Queen, whose Situation Grief, Horrour, and indignation leave me no power of describing[11]—nor is it necessary to any one, much less to you. Several of the most sensible and dispassionate observers are astonishd at this procedure. They are astonished at the situation of the Brothers of the late King, two mild and benevolent Princes, and worthy of a better destiny. They feel the

[7] A proclamation had been issued at Condé on 20 July announcing that claims for the re-establishment of suppressed religious foundations would be considered and that property sequestered from *émigrés* would be restored.

[8] In a declaration issued on 4 August 1792 the Emperor and the King of Prussia stated that they were not 'at war with the French nation' but intended 'to come to its assistance'.

[9] Following the execution of Louis XVI, his brother the Comte de Provence declared himself Regent of France for the late King's eight-year-old son, and made the Comte d'Artois 'Lieutenant-General of the Kingdom'. Russia was the only major power to recognize the Regent.

[10] The young son of Louis XVI had been taken from his family on 3 July and was kept in the Temple, where he was brutally treated.

[11] On 1 August the Convention decreed that Marie Antoinette should be kept in confinement in the Conciergerie, and brought before the Revolutionary Tribunal.

same as to the Nobility of France, who have comported themselves so as to merit the esteem and respect of all honourable and feeling minds. It is wonderful that amongst such a vast multitude of Gentlemen as we have seen here, some of them too very young and who have not had time to have their principles confirmed, not one of them, notwithstanding the pressure of very urgent circumstances have been known to do a single Low and unworthy action. These as far we know are treated, some with more, some with less attention. The persons are more considerd than the Cause; none are taken up, as our natural Allies, and as sufferers in a cause which we have in common. They are treated just as fugitives or exiles in an ordinary Local and domestick dispute in which there is no general concern. This is my opinion, both with regard to the Princes and the Crown party in France is a dangerous mistake. The late King fell, because the Rebels thought that in him they should be able to extinguish the Monarchy, as they conceivd that the regards of other powers were personal only and not political. To say the Truth, appearances seem too much to favour that opinion. They are therefore encouraged to take every step which their malice, baseness, and wicked policy can suggest with the Queen and those precious parts of the Royal Family which are in their hands. As to those abroad, they conceive that no Interest is taken in them—and that the sole Objects of any sort of Care are those whom they may treat as they please. They would cease to heap indignities on those personages, and hourly to threaten them with Death, if they saw that the Monarchy was treated as existing in all, who, by the Laws and by proximity of blood, had an Interest in it. The Monarchy must exist somewhere in act and representation: But the Throne cannot be represented by a Prison. Its virtue and operation must be where it can act and appear, if not with suitable Dignity, at least with Freedom. Monsieur is, by the Reason and necessity of the Case, stronger than all Law, Regent of that Kingdom. If I were to speak my wishes, and what would perhaps be best if France were any way settled, the Queen would be Regent. What is there to prevent it, if that Event, which cannot be brought about but by the great powers, (I mean the Settlement of France) should take place? In the mean time the Monarchy as well as the Monarch ought not to be reputed to be imprisond in the Conciergerie, and all the States of the Kingdom suffer a total eclipse.

It is to the Emperour that the world looks for the protection of the Cause of all government, in the protection of the Monarchy of France. His personal Virtues, His Rank in Europe, his relation to the Queen

Dowager and the young King, make him the fittest to authorise this arrangement provisionally.[12] No person can now or hereafter hope to be Regent or any thing else against his Will. The French Monarchy, if it ever can be restored, languishing, feeble, and tottering, with an infant King, and a convalescent Royalty, will for a long time be rather an Object of Protection than of Jealousy, in any of its Magistracies, to him or to any foreign power.

Excuse, Sir, this long Letter. My Mind has for some time sufferd too much anxiety and agitation to enable me properly to compress and digest my thoughts. I cannot see the Dignity of a great Kingdom, and with its dignity, all its virtue, imprisond or exiled, without great pain. I cannot help making their Care my own, and that of my friends who adhere to the same Cause; and whilst I feel my share in the Common gratitude of Europe to his Imperial Majesty, to his Ministers and his Generals, for the security which for the time we enjoy, like the rest of mankind, I look for the most of future Service to the same Quarter from whence we have receivd most for the time past.

Be pleased Sir, to do me the honour to accept my assurances of the most respectful attachment and beleive me

Sir

Your Excellencies

most obedient

and faithful humble Servant

EDM BURKE

To HENRY DUNDAS—8 October 1793

Corr. (1958), VII, 445–46

The traditional British objective in eighteenth-century wars against France had been the acquisition of French colonies, especially those in the West Indies. By the autumn of 1793 it was becoming clear that the British Government still regarded the West Indies as an important theatre of war and were prepared to divert what Burke regarded as excessive military resources from Europe to the Caribbean.

---

[12] The Emperor Francis II was the nephew of Marie Antoinette and the cousin of the Dauphin, whom Royalists now called 'Louis XVII'. The Emperor had told the Comte de Provence on 13 July that he would not recognize him as Regent, that he would not permit the French Princes to join the Austrian army in France, and that he would continue to take possession of French towns in his own name and not in that of the French Monarchy.

My dear Sir,

Excuse the trouble I again take the Liberty of giving you. It arises from my extreme anxiety about the Object of our common sollicitude; and my clear and decided conviction, that there is one part of the War, which instead of being postponed and considerd in a secondary light, ought to have priority over every other, and requires our most early and our most careful attention; I mean La Vendée. Hitherto, the Business of Toulon only excepted, every thing has been done in in the Style of indiscriminate Hostility to the Nation without distinction of persons, parties, or Principles. It has fared accordingly. Millions have been spent by the Allies, Torrents of blood have been spilled, and little progress has been made, considering the immense weight of united Europe employd in this Effort. In Poitou a War has been maintaind for eight months, the means adverted to, with astonishing success. This is a War directly against Jacobinism and its principle. It strikes at the Enemy in his weakest and most vulnerable part. At La Vendée with infinitely less Charge, we make an impression likely to be decisive. This goes to the heart of the Business. I am [far] from being sure that the Expedition talked of to Martineque furnishes any advantage,[1] equally probable, and equally conclusive as to the general Issue of the War, though at some time or other it might be a very proper Measure. That Island is in a State very different from what it was when the defence was in the hands of the Proprietors.[2] All operations continued for a long time, as at the Havannah between the Tropics are devourers of men at a rate scarcely credible.[3] However these things may not be incompatible. But the Vendée is first amongst the first. Minutes there are precious—and permit me to hint that not a moments time ought to be lost in sending supplies thither, with such officers as can be found here, or called from the Netherlands[4] as well as some Clergy from Jersey. To own their Cause is surely necessary to get others engaged, as well as for our own honour and consistency that we may not seem to have one set of politicks and principles on the Meditterranean another on the Ocean.

[1] Active steps were being taken to assemble an expeditionary force for the West Indies.
[2] An attempt to take Martinique in June had already failed when it met stiff resistance from the Republican régime established there.
[3] During the siege of Havana in Cuba in 1762 over five thousand British soldiers had died of disease.
[4] Burke means French émigré officers.

Again excuse this Liberty. I have the honour to be with much respect and regard

My dear Sir
Your most faithful
and obedient humble Servant

Beconsfield Oct. 8. 1793.   EDM BURKE

Qu. Whether supposing, (what I hope will not be the case) that La Vendée does not preengage every force we can spare, Guadaloupe ought not to precede Martinique as an Island at least equally good and more easily reduced.[5]

To WILLIAM WINDHAM—[circa 10 November 1793]

Corr. (1958), VII, 480–82

My dear Sir

I received your second very kind and very satisfactory Letter, just as I was going to thank you for your first.

I do confess, that I feel myself gradually sinking into something like despondency. It is not from the Events of War; which, as one might expect, have been chequerd. A little security towards a defensive is promised to us in the Netherlands. The affair of Weissenburg[1] seems to me one of the finest things in military History. I can scarcely, as an operation of War, imagine any thing beyond it. But it is not from our defeats, that my hopes are damped, but from our Successes. If we had been only beaten, better conduct and greater force, with our share of the Chances, might set us right again. But I see nothing, which all the Successes we have had, and much greater than I dare to look for, can do towards bringing things to the conclusion we wish, as long as the plan we have pursued and still pursue, is perseverd in. When I have the pleasure of seeing you, we will talk over this matter in the Detail.

---

[5] The important sugar-producing island of Guadeloupe was thought to be much less easily defensible than Martinique, 'one of the strongest countries in the world' (Bryan Edwards, *The History, civil and commercial, of the British Colonies in the West Indies*, 4th ed., London, 1807, III, 437).

[1] On October 13 the Austrian army operating on the Rhine under the command of General Würmser drove the French out of their strongly fortified positions at Wissembourg.

I agree with you, that the proclamation[2] is well drawn: Perhaps too well drawn, as it shews too much art. I admit that it seems, more than any thing else that has yet appeard, to depart from the unfortunate plan of making war against France, and to direct it where it ought to be directed, to the relief of the oppressed, and to the destruction of Jacobinism. I wish however that nothing had been said about indemnity. It is a thing unheard of in this Stage of a War; and as in fact we have no pledge whatever in our hands but Toulon, it looks as if we meant to keep that place, and the ships in its harbour for that indemnity though surrenderd to our faith upon very different Terms.[3] This previous demand of indemnity, which has a sort of appearance, (even so much as perhaps to hazard the whole effect of the Declaration) of Fairness, is yet so very loose and general that I scarce know what it is that we and the allied Courts may not claim under it.[4] The worst of the matter is that the only Object which we have hitherto pursued, is the previous security of the indemnification.

The thing however that perfectly sickens me in this Declaration is its total disagreement with every thing we have done or (so far as I see) that we are going to do. We promise protection and assistance to those who shall endeavour the Restoration of Monarchy in that Country; Yet, though Poitou is in a manner at our door and they have for eight months carried on a War on the principles we have pointed out— not a man, not a Ship not an article of Stores has been yet sent to these brave unfortunate people; all the force we can spare was destined for our indemnity;[5] and when now released, I do not know with what prudence, from the Flemish Service—it is intended again to go the West Indies. No talk, nor no thought of giving the least of the succour we stand engaged for, and which common justice and common policy ought to have induced us to send though we were under no positive engagement at all. This, joined with our refusing to recognise that Monarchy in those who have a right to exercise its authority is a

---

[2] A Declaration published October 29 in which the British government disclaimed any intention of interfering in the internal affairs of France after the war, but offered its friendship to all Frenchmen who supported a 'Monarchical Government'.

[3] In his Proclamation on taking possession of Toulon Admiral Hood had promised that he held it 'in Trust only for Louis XVII until Peace shall be re-established in France . . .'

[4] The Declaration stated that Britain looked for 'a just Indemnification . . . not such as the Expences, the Risques, and the Sacrifices of the War might justify, but such as his Majesty thinks himself under the indispensable Necessity of requiring . . .'

[5] Burke is implying that any French islands captured in the West Indies would be kept as a British indemnity.

defeasance to our Declaration which nothing but a total Change of conduct can cancell. However though I am grieved beyond measure, and mortified at this proceeding, our only hopes are from these people. The conduct of our late party is so absurd, contradictory, and self destructive, that I cannot easily express it—But on all these matters we shall talk seriously when we meet which I trust will be soon. Oh! what you say of the Queen in your two Letters is like what I should expect from your feelings on that, the most dreadful Scene, that ever was exhibited to the world! Stupified as I was at the enormous wickedness of the actors, as well as at the *nature* of it, which was worse, in my opinion, than its *magnitude*, and astonishd at the sustaind fortitude and patience of the sufferer, yet my indignation, at the unfeeling manner in which it has been received by the Princes of her own House,[6] has perhaps been the strongest of my Emotions on this occasion. The wicked faction at Paris have obtained the only end they could have proposed to themselves by this savage proceeding, the rendering vile and contemptible the Royal Character. The execution of a King or Queen by the hands of the common hangman, as the Lowest and vilest of criminals, will produce no more effect than one of the periodical hangings at the old Baily. I am quite of your mind that there is something that mingles more of disgust, and of compassion, with our horrour in this Barbarity even more than in the murder of the King. In fact Women, and such Women are more out of the Field in such contentions as brought on these Events—and the Circumstances themselves were much worse. Sure some Justice ought to be done to a character which does so much more than Justice to the nature we belong to. . . .

To WILLIAM WINDHAM—25 *November* 1793

Corr. (1958), VII, 489–91

November 25, 1793.

Since I wrote last, the outside of affairs is a good deal mended,[1] but they will not bear inspection. Our politics want directness and sim-

---

[6] The Imperial Court at Vienna had done nothing to mark the Queen's death, beyond the customary observance of Court mourning.

[1] Reports had been appearing in the English press of successes won north of the Loire by the rebels from the Vendée and of the preparation of a British expedition to link up with them by a landing on the coast of Brittany or Normandy. Burke had made some suggestions about the expedition in a memorandum dated 19 November.

plicity. A spirit of chicane, or something very like it, predominates in all that is done, either by our allies or by ourselves. Westminster-hall has ruined Whitehall; and there are many things in which we proceed more like lawyers than statesmen. If this distemper is not cured, I undertake to say, with the more positive assurance, that nothing but shame and destruction can be the result of all our operations in the field and in the cabinet. All the misfortunes of the war have arisen from this very intricacy and ambiguity in our politics; and yet, though this is as visible as I think it is real, I do not find the smallest disposition to make any alteration in the system. I have the greatest possible desire of talking with you on this subject. I think something ought to be done, and I know that I cannot act alone. If I had not always felt this, all that has happened within these three months would have convinced me of it. The very existence of human affairs, in their ancient and happy order, depends upon the existence of this ministry, but it does not depend on their existence only in their ministerial situation and capacity, but on their doing their duty in it. They are certainly bewildered in the labyrinth of their own politics. What you observe is most true; they think they can defend themselves the better by taking part of the ground of their adversary. But that is a woful mistake. He is consistent and they are not. He is strengthened by their concessions. He avails hmself of what they yield, and contends with advantage for the rest. As to the affairs of France, into which they have entered at last, it is plain to me that they are wholly confounded by their magnitude. The crimes that accumulated on each other astonish them. These crimes produce the effects which their authors propose by them. They fill our ministers, and I believe the ministers of other courts, not with indignation and manly resentment, but with an abject terror. They are oppressed by these crimes—they cry quarter—and then they talk a feeling language of mercy; but it is not mercy to the innocent and virtuous sufferers, but to base, cruel, and relentless tyrants. I shall explain myself more fully when we meet.[2] People talk of the cruelty of punishing a revolutionary tribunal, and the authors of the denunciation of an infant king, concerning offences that the voice of humanity cannot utter, in order to criminate his own mother,[3] at the very moment (this very moment) when they turn out of the house,

---

[2] Burke's discussion of this point in his *Remarks on the Policy of the Allies* is apparently addressed to Windham (*Works*, Bohn, III, 450–7; Little, Brown, IV, 460–70).

[3] The last article of charge against the Queen was 'That finally, Marie Antoinette is such an adept in all sorts of crimes, that, forgetting her situation of mother, she committed indecencies with her own son, too shocking to mention'.

which they have given them in the king's name and taken credit for it, six hundred and eighty virtuous and religious men, in the beginning of a winter, which threatens no small rigour, without a place to hide their heads in.[4]

I am mortified at all this, and I believe I express myself with some confusion about it. But we must endeavour to make our complaints rather effectual than loud. The other faction is dreadful indeed. It consists of two parts; one of which is feebly and unsystematically right, the other regularly, uniformly, and actively wrong; and, what is natural, that which is the most steady and energetic, gives the law to that which is lax and wavering. The entire unfolding of the Jacobin system has made no change in them whatsoever. Not one of them has been converted; no, nor even shaken; and those who coincide with us in the absolute necessity of this war (to which, however, they give but a very trimming and ambiguous support), are become far more attached than ever to their Jacobin friends,[5] are animated with much greater rage than ever against the ministers, and are become not much less irritated against those of their old friends who act decidedly and honestly in favour of their principles. This state of things requires to be handled according to its true nature. If you and I take the steps we ought to take, there is yet a chance that all may be right. For God's sake come, and come speedily, for no time is to be lost!

Ever most faithfully yours,
EDMUND BURKE

To LORD LOUGHBOROUGH—19 *October* 1794

Corr. (1958), VIII, 43–45

Alexander Wedderburn, 1st Baron Loughborough (1733–1805), had been the first of the Portland Whigs to accept office in Pitt's Government. In January 1793, with Burke's enthusiastic support, he had accepted the office of Lord Chancellor, and since then had acted as an intermediary between the Portland Whigs and Pitt.

[4] Burke believed that the French refugee clergy were about to be turned out of the King's House at Winchester.
[5] An attempt to reconcile Fox and the Duke of Portland was being made at this time, but it ended in failure.

My dear Lord,

I am to inform you, that your goodnatured presentation has had its full Effect, and that Mr Etty is Parson of Whitchurch.[1] By that one arrangement your Lordship has the satisfaction of making several people happy, the person who resignd the living not the least so.[2] Your Protegee is much attachd to a very pleasing young Woman, the daughter of a worthy Clergyman in this Neighbourhood.[3] Without this preferment there was no hope of their Union. All the parties have a considerable degree of merit; and they feel much gratitude for the happiness they enjoy, and the good prospect, which in their Estimate, lies before them. I am sure I am myself extremely obliged to you on this occasion, and should think myself much to blame, if I neglected to make you my best acknowlegements.

We must enjoy those transient satisfactions as they arise, without enquiring too minutely into their probable duration. God knows how long the Church Establishment, on which these people exist, and to which such multitudes are now breeding up, is likely to last. But whenever that goes it will go with every thing else.

When that grand period will arrive, it is not easy to foresee with exactness: But there are plain and evident marks of its approaching. I dont mean, that they appear in the Event of this or that measure (tho' the prospect in that point of View is gloomy enough) but in the dispositions of men which prepare bad Events and improve accidental misfortune into Systematick ruin. I very much doubt, whether in any Country, they who have the charge of us the poor flock, are sufficiently aware of the Giant strides with which the great overbearing Mastercalamity of the time is advancing towards us. All you the Great act just as if you thought a thousand things were to be feard or pursued for their own seperate sakes, when in reality, none are worth notice, otherwise than as they tend to promote or to resist the Cause of Jacobinism. What amazes me, even to consternation and Horrour, is, that people, otherwise of the very best understandings, proceed exactly

---

[1] The Rev. James Etty (c. 1771–1805), Rector of Wooburn, Buckinghamshire, had just become Rector of Whitchurch, Oxfordshire, a valuable living in the gift of the Lord Chancellor.

[2] The Rev. Robert Stebbing (c. 1720–1800), Rector of Beaconsfield, had been Rector of Whitchurch since 1784, succeeding the Rev. Andrew Etty (d. 1784), James Etty's father. Stebbing and Etty were related, and Etty had acted as curate at Beaconsfield.

[3] Etty married Miss Middleton (d. 1804), daughter of the Rev. John Middleton, Vicar of Penn, on 30 June 1796.

as if every thing stood in the situation, in which you and I saw them
thirty year ago, at a time when very great Errours led but to very
slight consequences; and not as they are now, when very slight mistakes lead to incalculable Evils. Then the greatest changes which could
be apprehended, could very little affect the domestick happiness of
the greater part of mankind—now no mans Fireside is safe from the
Effects of a political revolution. . . .

To WILLIAM SMITH—29 *January* 1795

Corr. (1958), VIII, 127–33

William Smith (1766–1836) was an Irish M.P., a pamphleteer, and an admirer of
Burke.

My dear Sir,
    Your Letter is, to myself, infinitely obliging; With regard to you,
I can find no fault with it, except that of a Tone of Humility and
disqualification, which neither your rank, nor the place your are in,
nor the profession you belong to, nor your very extraordinary Learning
and Talents will, in propriety, demand, or perhaps admit. These dispositions will be still less proper, if you should feel them in the extent
your Modesty leads you to talk of them. You have certainly given by
far too strong a proof of self diffidence by asking the opinion of a man
circumstanced as I am, on the important subject of your Letter. You
are far more capable of forming just conceptions upon it than I can
be. However since you are pleased to command me to lay before you
my thoughts, as materials upon which your better Judgment may
operate, I shall obey you, and submit them, with great deference, to
your melioration or rejection.
    But first permit me to put myself in the right. I, owe you an answer
to your former Letter. It did not desire one but it deserved it. If not
for an answer, it called for an acknowledgement. It was a new favour;
and indeed I should be worse than insensible, if I did not consider
the honours you have heaped upon me, with no sparing hand, with
a becoming Gratitude. But your Letter arrived to me at a time, when
the closing of my long and last Business in Life, a Business extremely
complex, and full of difficulties and vexations of all sorts, occupied
me, in manner, which those who have not seen the interiour as well
as exteriour of it, cannot easily imagine. I confess that in the Crisis
of that rude conflict I neglected many things that well deserved my

best attention; none that deservd it better, or have caused me more regret in the Neglect than your Letter. The instant that Business was over, and the house had passed its judgment on the conduct of the managers,[1] I lost no time to execute what for years I had resolved on. It was to quit my publick Station, and to seek that Tranquility in my very advanced Age, which after a very tempestuous Life I thought myself intitled. But God has thought fit, (and I unfeignedly acknowlege his Justice) to dispose of things otherwise. So heavy a Calamity has fallen upon me as to disable me for Business, and to disqualifye me for repose.[2] The existence I have I do not know that I can call Life. Accordingly I do not meddle with any one Measure of Government, though, for what reasons I know not, you seem to suppose me deeply in the secret of affairs. I only know, so far as your side of the Water is concernd, that your present excellent Lord Lieutenant,[3] (the best man, in every relation, that I have ever been acquainted with) has perfectly pure intentions with regard to Ireland; and of Course, that he wishes cordially well to those, who form the great Mass of its Inhabitants, and who, as they are well or ill managed, must form an important part of its strength or weakness. If with regard to that great Object he has carried over any ready made System, I assure you, it is perfectly unknown to me. I am very much retired from the world and live in much ignorance. This I hope will form my humble apology if I should err in the Notions I entertain of the Question which is so soon to become the subject of your deliberations: at the same [time] accept it as an apology for my Neglects.

You need make no apology for your attachment to the religious description you belong to. It proves (as in you it is sincere) your attachment to the great points in which the leading divisions are agreed, when the lesser, in which they differ, are so dear to you. I shall never call any religious opinions which appear important to serious and pious minds things of no consideration. Nothing is so fatal to Religion as indifference which is, at least, half Infidelity. As long as men hold Charity and justice to be essential integrant parts of religion; there can be little danger from a strong attachment to particular Tenets in faith. This I am perfectly sure in your Case: But I am not equally sure, that either Zeal for the Tenets of Faith, or the smallest degree of Charity or justice, have much influenced the Gentlemen, who, under

[1] On June 20, 1794, Burke received the thanks of the House of Commons as one of the Managers of Warren Hastings' trial for impeachment.
[2] The death of his son Richard on August 2, 1794.
[3] Fitzwilliam arrived in Dublin on 4 January.

pretexts of Zeal, have resisted the enfranchisment of their Country. My dear Son, who was a person of discernment, as well as clear and acute in his expression, said in a Letter of his which I have seen 'that in order to grace their Cause and to draw some respect to their persons, they pretend to be Bigots'.[4] But here I take it we have not much to do with the Theological Tenets, on the one side of the Question or the other. The point itself is practically decided. That Religion is owned by the State. Except in a settled maintenence, it is protected. A great deal of the Rubbish, which, as a nuisance long obstructed the way, is removed. One impediment remaind longer, as a matter to justifye the proscription of the body of our Country, after the rest had been abandond as untenable Ground. But the Business of the Pope, (that mixed person of politicks and religion) has long ceased to be a Bugbear; for some time past he has ceased to be even a colourable pretext. This was well known when the Catholicks of these Kingdoms, for our amusement, were obliged, on oath to disclaim him in his political Capacity, which implied an allowance for them to recognize him in some sort of ecclesiastical superiority.[5] It was a compromise of the old Dispute.

For my part, I confess, I wish that we had been less eager in this point. I dont think indeed that much mischief will happen from it, if things are otherwise properly managed. Too nice an Inquisition ought not to be made into opinions that are dying away of themselves. Had we lived an hundred and fifty years ago, I should have been as earnest and anxious as any one for this sort of Abjuration: But living at the time in which I live, and obliged to speculate forward instead of backward, I must fairly say, I could well endure the existence of every sort of collateral aid, which opinion might, in the now State of things, afford to authority. I must see much more danger, than in my Life I have seen, or than others will venture seriously to affirm that they see, in the Pope aforesaid, (though a foreign power and with his long tail of etceteras) before I should be active in weakening any hold which Government might think it prudent to resort to in the management of that large part of the Kings subjects. I do not choose to direct all my precautions to the part where the danger does not press—and to

---

[4] This letter of Richard's has not been found.

[5] By an 'act to enable His Majesty's subjects of whatever persuasion to testify their allegiance to him' (13 and 14 Geo. III, C. 35), Catholics were permitted to take the oath of allegiance and make a declaration. A person making the declaration promised to maintain 'the succession of the crown in His Majesty's family', denied that the Pope had any civil authority within the realm and repudiated the doctrines that the Pope could depose excommunicated sovereigns, that faith need not be kept with heretics and that 'it was lawful to murder and destroy' them.

leave myself open and unguarded, where I am not only really, but visibly attackd.

My whole politicks, at present, center in one point; and to this the merit or demerit of every measure, (with me) is referable: that is, what will most promote or depress the Cause of Jacobinism?—What is Jacobinism? It is an attempt (hitherto but too successful) to eradicate prejudice out of the minds of men, for the purpose of putting all power and authority into the hands of the persons capable of occasionally enlightening the minds of the people. For this purpose the Jacobins have resolved to destroy the whole frame and fabrick of the old Societies of the world, and to regenerate them after their fashion: To obtain an army for this purpose, they every where engage the poor by holding out to them as a bribe, the spoils of the Rich. This I take to be a fair description of the principles and leading maxims of the enlightend of our day, who are commonly called Jacobins.

As the grand prejudice, and that which holds all the other prejudices together, the first, last, and middle Object of their Hostility, is Religion. With that they are at inexpiable war. They make no distinction of Sects. A Christian, as such, is to them an Enemy. What then is left to a real Christian, (Christian as a believer and as a Statesman) but to make a league between all the grand divisions of that name, to protect and to cherish them all; and by no means to proscribe in any manner, more or less any member of our common party. The divisions which formerly prevailed in the Church, with all their overdone Zeal, only purified and ventilated, our common faith; because there was no common Enemy arrayed and embattled to take advantage of their dissensions: But now nothing but inevitable ruin will be the consequence of our Quarrels. I think we may dispute, rail, persecute, and provoke the Catholicks out of their prejeudices; But it is not in ours that they will take refuge. If any thing is, one more than another, out of the power of man, it is to *create* a prejudice. Somebody has said that a King may make a nobleman but he cannot make a Gentleman.

All the principal religions in Europe stand upon one common bottom. The support, that the whole, or the favourd parts, may have in the secret dispensations of Providence, it is impossible to tell: But humanly speaking, they are all *prescriptive* religions. They have all stood long enough, to make prescription, and its train of legitimate prejudices, their main Stay. The people, who compose the four Grand divisions of Christianity,[6] have now their religion as an habit, and upon

---

[6] Calvinist, Catholic, Lutheran and Orthodox.

authority, and not on disputation—as all men, who have their religion derived from their parents, and the fruits of the Education, *must* have it; however the one, more than the other, may be able to reconcile his faith to his own Reason, or to that of other men: Depend upon it, they must all be supported; or they must all fall in the crash of a common Ruin. The Catholicks are the far more numerous part of the Christians in your Country; and how can Christianity (that is now the point in Issue) be supported, under the persecution, or even under the discountenance of the greater number of Christians? It is a great Truth, and which, in one of the Debates I stated as strongly as I could to the House of Commons in the last Session, that if the Catholick religion is destroyd by the Infidels it is a most contemptible and absurd Idea, that, this, or any Protestant church, can survive that Event.[7] Therefore, my humble, but decided opinion is, that all the three religions, prevalent more or less in various parts of these Islands, ought all, in subordination to the legal establishments, as they stand in the several Countries, by all countenanced, protected, and cherished, and that in Ireland particularly, the R.C. Religion should be upheld in high respect and veneration; and should be, in its place, provided with all the means of making it a blessing to the people who profess it. That it ought to be cherished as a good, (though not as the most preferable good, if a Choice was now to be made) and not tolerated as an inevitable Evil. If this be my opinions to the Catholick religion, as a Sect—you must see, that I must be to the last degree adverse to put a man upon that account, upon a bad footing with relation to the priveleges which the fundamental Laws of this Country give him as a subject. I am the more serious on the positive encouragement to be given to this religion, (always however as secondary) because the serious and earnest belief and practice of it by its professors forms, as things stand, the most effectual Barrier, if not the sole Barrier, against Jacobinism. The Catholicks form the great body of the lower Ranks of your community; and no small part of those Classes of the middling that come nearest to them. You know, that the seduction of that part of mankind from the principles of religion, morality, subordination, and social order, is the great Object of the Jacobins. Let them grow lax, sceptical, careless and indifferent with regard to religion, and, so sure as we have an existence, it is not a Zealous Anglican or Scottish Church principle, but direct Jacobinism which will enter that Breach. Two hundred years dreadfully spent in experiments to force that peo-

---

[7] Nothing exactly corresponding with this reference has been found in the printed versions of Burke's speeches during the 1794 session.

ple to change the form of their Religion have proved fruitless. You have now your choice for full four fifths of your people, the Catholick religion or Jacobinism. If things appear to you to stand on this alternative; I think you will not be long in making your option.

You have made, as you naturally do, a very able analysis of Powers; and have seperated, as the things are seperable, civil from political-powers. You start too a question whether the civil can be secured without some share in the political. For my part, as abstract Questions, I should find some difficulty in an attempt to resolve them; But, as applied to the state of Ireland, to the form of our commonwealth, to the parties that divide us, and to the dispositions of the leading men in these parties, I cannot hesitate to lay before you my opinion, that whilst any kind of discouragements and disqualifications remain on the Catholicks, an handle will be made by a factious power utterly to defeat the Benefits of any civil rights they may apparently possess. I need not go to very remote times for my Examples. It was within the Course of about a twelvemonth, that after Parliament had been led into a Step, quite unparralleld in its records,[8] after they had resisted all concession and even hearing, with an Obstinacy equal to any thing that could have actuated a party domination in the 2d or 8th of Q. Ann;[9] after the strange adventure of the Grand Juries;[10] and after Parliament had listend to the Sovereign pleading for the emancipation of his subjects, it was after all this, that such a grudging and discontent was expressed as must justly have alarmed, as it did extremely alarm, the whole of the Catholick body—and I remember but one period in my whole life, (I mean the savage period between 1761 and 1767)[11] in which they have been more harshly and more contumeliously treated than since the last partial enlargement—and thus I am convinced it will be, by paroxysms, as long as any Stigma remains on them, and whilst they are considerd as no better than half Citizens. If they are kept such for any length of time they will be made whole Jacobins. Against this Grand and dreadful Evil of our time (I do not love to

[8] On 20 February 1792 the Irish House of Commons rejected a petition presented on behalf of the Roman Catholics of Ireland requesting a further relaxation of the Penal Laws and a share in the elective franchise.

[9] One of the most comprehensive and severe acts against the Irish Roman Catholic was An Act to Prevent the Further Growth of Popery, passed in 1704 (2 Anne, c. 6). Five years later is was amended by 8 Anne, c. 3.

[10] In the summer of 1792 a number of Grand Juries protested against the plan to hold a Catholic Convention in Dublin as an attempt to overawe the legislature.

[11] When the Irish Parliament enacted severe legislation, which was vigorously enforced, to check the agrarian disturbances in Munster known as 'The Whiteboy Movement'. Burke himself was in Ireland in the early sixties as secretary to William Gerard Hamilton, the Chief Secretary.

cheat myself or others) I do not know any solid Security whatsoever: But I am quite certain, that what will come nearest to it, is to interest as many as you can in the present order of things, religiously, civilly, politically—by all the ties and principles by which mankind are held. This is like to be effectual policy. I am sure it is honourable policy— and it is better to fail, if fail we must, in the paths of direct and manly, than of low and crooked wisdom.

As to the capacity of sitting in Parliament after all the capacities for voting, for the Army, for the Navy for the professions, for civil Offices, it is a dispute *de Lana caprina*[12] in my poor opinion, at least on the part of those who oppose it. In the first place this admission to Office and this exclusion from Parliament, on the principle of an exclusion from political power, is the very reverse of the principle of the English Test act. If I were to form a judgment from Experience rather than Theory, I should doubt much whether the capacity for or even the possession of a seat in Parliament did really convey much of power to be properly called political. I have sat there with some Observation for nine and twenty years or thereabouts. The power of a Member of Parliament is uncertain and indirect—and, if power rather than splendour and fame were the Object, I should think that any of the principal Clerks in Office, to say nothing of their superiours, (several of whom are disqualified by Law for seats in Parliament) possess far more power than nine tenths of the Members of the House of Commons. I might say this of Men who seemd from their fortunes, their weight in their Country, and their Talents, to be persons of figure there; and persons too not in opposition to the prevailing party in Government.

But be they what they will, on a fair canvass of the several prevalent Parliamentary Interests in Ireland, I cannot, out of the three hundred Members, of whom the Irish Parliament is composed, discover that above three or at the utmost four Catholicks, would be returned to the House of Commons: But suppose they should amount to thirty that is to a tenth part (a thing I hold impossible for a long series of years, and never very likely to happen) what is [this] to those, who are to balance them in the one house and the clear and settled Majority in the other—for I think it absolutely impossible, that in the Course of many years above four or five Peers should be created of that Communion. In fact the exclusion of them seems to be only to mark jealousy and suspicion, and not to provide security in any way. But I return to the old Ground—the danger is not there.—These are things

---

[12] About a goat's wool: that is, about something worthless. See Horace, *Epistles*, I, xviii, 15.

long since done away. The grand controversy is no longer between you and them. Forgive this length. My Pen has insensibly run on— You are yourself to blame, if you are much fatigued.—I congratulate you on the auspicious opening of your Session. Surely Great Britain and Ireland ought to join in wreathing a never fading Garland for the head of Grattan. Adieu! my dear Sir—good Night to you—I never can have any—Yours always most

sincerely
EDM BURKE

Jany 29. 1795.
twelve at Night

To FRENCH LAURENCE—1 *March* 1797

Corr. (1958), IX, 263–67

My dear friend,

In the hurry in which your business engages you I ought to be thankful to you rather that you write at all, than that you do not write fully. The only thing that I have to blame is, that you have not sent me word whether you have received or not the Pacquets which contained Sir L: Parsons's Letter to me on the state of Ireland. A word would have done this. There is but one Opinion, and there can be but one Opinion, on the manner on which the safety of Ireland was provided for. It was certainly the grossest of all abuses, of Parliamentary confidence, for the Government to take the opportunity of the general wish to support them in order to produce, not a silence upon their neglects, or a pretention of them in a general Compliment, but a direct Panegeric upon the vigilance of those, who, to the knowledge of every member who voted, had been sleeping in profound security. You see by Sir L: Parsons's Letter the reasons which influence the votes of several of those who consented on political motives against their Opinion, to subscribe to this shameful Panegeric.[1] I do admit that the members were in a dilemma with regard to a general address of support and confidence; and here it was that the Castle was so

---

[1] Sir Laurence Parsons (1758–1841), an Irish M.P., had written to Burke about an address of thanks to the King from the Irish Parliament, implying approval of the peace negotiations of the British government with the French, and of its measures for the defense of Ireland against the French.

infinitely culpable in pushing the matter further, for which, in my Opinion, no good political motive could be assigned.

If the Parliament of Ireland has not done its duty in the melancholly state in which the two Kingdoms stand related to one another, in which no degree of subordination is provided for, I am sure the Parliament of England cannot do much Good by an impotent interference, even if it should interfere at all. We must consider our condition. It is not the invasion of Ireland only that is threatened, but of this Kingdom also; and I am by no means apprized, or of Ability to resist this double attack, but this I know that the Partizans of France are not one Jot more likely to defend us from it than those who have hitherto (with whatever incapacity) been the Enemies of that power. You know better than any one what I think of the conduct of Mr Pitt in the whole of the War which has passed, and what is likely to come in the War which he is going rather to suffer than to pursue. I have no partiality at all to him or to his measures against which latter nothing but the accelerated motion of my illness could have hindered me from publishing my Opinion before this time, but between my disapprobation of Mr Pitts measure and my horrour of those, of Mr Fox there is some difference. I have attended very carefully to all Mr Fox's declarations upon occasion of the Treaty Debate.[2] I have not forgot to compare them with the uniform tenour of his Speeches at the time of his Election, and between those two periods.[3] I find in all that tremendous consistency which makes me look on his power as one of the most dreadful evils which could fall upon the Country. I have compared those Speeches with those of the Peers and Commoners that adhered to him in Parliament; I find them all in exact unison with those of their Chief. I have looked at two of the Pamphlets which have been written under his inspection by his closest friends, and for the avowed purposes of his exaltation—I mean those of Mr O'Brien,[4] and Mr Erskine;[5] the one, in fewer and distincter words; the other with more Verbiage, avowing the principles of the French Revolution, con-

---

[2] Fox spoke at length in the debate of 30 December 1796 on the failure of the Peace Negotiations (*Parliamentary History*, XXXII, 1466–93).

[3] Between the General Election of 1796 and the close of the year.

[4] Dennis O'Bryen (1755–1832) had recently published *Utrum Horum? The Government or the Country*, London, 1796. His aims were to show that the continuation of the war would lead to the ruin of the country but that the best peace which could be expected from the existing ministry would be an ever greater calamity than the continuation of the war.

[5] Thomas Erskine (1750–1823), the famous advocate, published on February 11 his pamphlet, *A View of the Causes and Consequences of the Present War with France*. In it he argued that an honourable peace with France could be obtained and that peace should be followed by Parliamentary reform in England.

demning the councils of this Nation for our not taking an active part in favour of it, by overawing those Powers who might seem disposed to prevent its march and the consequences of that march. I see them disclaim all Alliance with the Powers of Europe, and, in effect, that placing ourselves in a state of Vassalage to France on pretence of a Communion with them and an alienation from all others, upon the supposed principles of Freedom. I find, as the result of all this Speculation that Mr Fox is to be forced upon the King, (and upon no small part I think the majority) of this Nation, as a person agreeable to the French Republick for his uniform friendship to her, and his disposition to abandon the publick faith given to our Allies and to seperate himself wholely from them. Accordingly, they propose, (as he had before proposed,) to deliver a Country belonging to our Allies, and indeed, a great deal more, which they who can speak no language but the new French, choose to call Belgium,[6] but which neither by that name, nor with any certain bounds or limits, is to be found in any Map. You, who are conversant in Science, know how near the adoption of a new Nomenclator, approaches to the adaption of a new System. These new Appellations have been adopted in order to support the new System of giving to modern France the limits of antient Gaul, the Northern part of which had been antiently called Gallia Belgica. I say nothing of their new Christening the United States of the Netherlands into the Batavian Republick,[7] in order to render it under the false name of a Confederate, and dependant on that Republick which they affect to form on the maxims of the Commonwealth of Rome. As to the rest of Europe they are profoundly silent. This is a Summary of their foreign Politicks—On this principle they propose to make their Peace: But, these Politics are not so foreign as to be supposed to have no influence on the domestic, for Mr Fox proposes and has reiteratedly pledged himself to make some undefined changes in the Constitution, the nature of which he has never discovered; but he has not been equally reserved as to the effects which he states to be to make the influence of what He calls the People *every thing*, and that of the Crown—*Nothing*, which I conceive to be the definition of a compleat Democracy, or I do not know what a Democracy is. It is for this grand end, he proposes that kind of Peace which he recommends and is one of the chief advantages which he expects and very rationally expects

---

[6] The Austrian Netherlands, described by the revolutionaries as Belgium, were annexed by France in 1795.

[7] After being conquered by France in 1795, the United Provinces were termed the Batavian Republic.

at some period or other from such an arrangement. A Peace with the Regicides may be made with more honour to himself personally by Mr Fox than by Mr Pitt. He would be consistent with himself first and last. He would dissociate himself from Europe and Join in whatever unequal league and with whatever consequences to the Glory, and safety and the fundamental policy of this Country with the new Powers of France; but the Country must appear in the character of a Renegade confessing its violence and injustice, and must abandon all its maxims. Of the two, I think it very probable that the Regicides of France would prefer Mr Fox as Minister. It is very natural, and indeed, if we once place ourselves in a state of inferiority they will now, and at all times, in effect, name a minister to this Country. There never has been a superiour power who would suffer a dependant Province substantially to name its own Minister. From my part, if I were to count myself amongst the living I should make it one of my chief objections to have Mr Fox Minister, that He is, and that his conduct and opinions have been acceptable to this cruel, imperious, and oppressive Master. However, in reality, neither this declaimer and sophister, nor the declaimer and Sophister his rival, can make any Peace which will not carry shame and ruin on the very front of it. I call them Sophisters and declaimers because they have melted down all the faculties that God has given them into those characters; and in proportion to their perfection in those they sink in every other respect. Neither of them have even the shadow of a statesman. I shall say no more on this melancholly Subject being convinced that the evil is incurable and that the very abilities of the persons concerned tend to render all change impossible from the presumption which they excite in themselves and the admiration which they cause in their blind followers. I see, that unless Mr Pitt takes a much more decided tone, the Minority will every day encrease, and the depreciation of publick Credit will go on more rapidly. He must make up his mind so as to declare whether he means in good earnest and at whatever charge to support the only Ally we have, or he will see his cause, if any cause he has totally ruined, and even that Majority in which he vainly trusts and which he vainly hopes to keep by prevaricating compliances, melt away under his Eyes.

Give my most sincere love to Lord Fitzwilliam and assure him that living or dying I am entirely his. That if I live for any little time longer, I shall live praying for him. If I die, the first among my dying vows, will be for his happiness and prosperity and that God will keep him in the same virtuous Course in which he has hitherto run, but, with better fortune. The state of my health is exactly this. I enjoy much longer intervals of ease, I thank God, than I did some time ago and my Nights are a good deal better, but the radical complaint remains, tho' with less noise in the Symptoms. My head is perfectly releived from that Giddiness which alarmed me more than any other Symptom—I am told by others that my Strength is increased—I am by no means equally sensible of it myself, tho the weakness does not seem to be any thing so considerable as when it was complicated in the Giddiness.

Such is my real state, or such it appears to myself without any exaggeration one way or the other. Mrs Burke's complaints still continue, tho' she holds up much better than could be expected.

Ever Affectionately yours

Bath 1st March   E B
   1797

To GEORGE CANNING—1 *March* 1797

Corr. (1958), IX, 267–70

George Canning (1770–1827), the future Prime Minister, as a school boy and undergraduate was a strong Whig. He was, however, alarmed by the French Revolution and radical agitation in England, and he entered Parliament at the beginning of 1794 as a strong supporter of Pitt. When he made his maiden speech on 27 January, Burke came across the House and said, 'I lament that the Debate upon this subject is at an end—I want to say *aloud* to tell the House what I think of you—I would get up on purpose to do so—but that I think that would look as if I thought you *wanted* help. It is more dignified to let you *go alone*'. On 11 March 1797 Canning wrote to the Rev. William Leigh, 'Tho it is not true, as you have heard—that I have been writing to Mr. Burke my sentiments on the present state of politicks—though he has written his to me.—My letter to him, (to which I owe his answer), was simply five lines, inclosing a packet which had come for him, under my cover, from the Continent.— His answer is in truth, a very valuable piece of writing and full of good sense, and spirit, and truth.—Though I am not sure that it is wholly unmixed with speculations of a more gloomy cast than are justified by the actual situation and prospects of the Country.—I will send you the letter some day or other, (for it is one that I shall most assuredly preserve as long as I live—one of the last letters perhaps of one of the greatest men of his time)—but I cannot part with it just at present'.

Dear Sir

I am infinitely obliged to you for the generous partiality which you have shewn in the vigour of your Life and abilities towards my declining person, and my worn out faculties which, at best, were very unequal to the favourable estimate you are pleased to make of them.

The Pamphlets, which you were so good to send to me, are on the Subject of the general Revolution which has been finished in France, and is in the course of its accompaniment every where else. It is a subject which I cannot contemplate, even, at the moment of my probable departure, without a deeper interest than I ought perhaps to take in any human affairs, my Notions may be weak and Heterodox; but the confidence you are pleased to repose in my intentions induces me to expose them to you with more freedom perhaps than prudence. I think I see nothing short of the total and inevitable ruin of the Kingdom, even in the means that seem to be provided for its safety. When I see an Army, amounting, as I hear, in both Kingdoms to 150,000 Men, who, by the very terms and conditions of their Service, cannot strike a blow at any Enemy,[1] I see already a fatal termination of the War. What has an Enemy to fear from a Nation who confines herself to an inert, passive, domestic, defence? By continually threatening, tho' without ever striking a blow, and by the demonstration of the smallest forces, they can ruin you in your resources of Revenue and of Credit. This is a matter of demonstration, if not, of intuitive certainty. To say that this is more agreeable to the People, is to say nothing, when the question is concerning, not their humour, but their existence. When Ministers have failed in other sorts of attempts, this may be an excuse for the failure; but it can be none for having disarmed the Nation under a false appearance of putting it in a military posture. But I will say no more, because, either the hint will suffice, or a long and laboured detail will be necessary, which, tho' I have the matter present to my mind, in my present state, and with a Strong Paroxism of my disorder, tis impossible for me to enter upon; but the whole scheme, of, what is called defence, must be altered before the end of this Session, or nothing but the extraordinary Providence of God, can save us.

I do not altogether like the complexion of Monday's debate.[2] Mr Pitt must much more distinctly avow his cause, his principles, and his Allies, than He did in that Debate, or his Enemies will every day gain some new advantage over him; and all the Shabby part of his

[1] More militia had been recruited in 1796 with terms of service limited to home defense.

[2] On 26 February the Privy Council had issued an order empowering the Bank of England to refuse cash payments. On Monday, 28 February, the House of Commons debated a message from the King informing it that this step had been taken. During the debate Sheridan argued that specie should not be exported for the use of the Emperor.

friends, which always form a very large part of those who belong to the Men in Power, will, by degrees, desert him. Some much more distinctive lines, than hitherto have been traced, must be drawn between him and his Adversaries, else he will find the publick favour towards him grow cooler every day untill there is a total indifference in whose hands the Ministry shall be placed: For at the very hour in which I write, I have reason to be quite sure, that He owes the adherence of many People in Parliament and of more out of it [more] to a dread of certain chiefs of the Opposition, than to any zeal in his favour. As to the present flurry about publick Credit, there is no cause, I think, for alarm, unless the means that are taken to support it, should not undermine its foundations. There is the same Quantity of Gold and Silver in the Country, (or nearly the same quantity) that there was a month ago. The National income is the same, and the Stock of individuals, whether in Land or Goods, is not impaired. Credit has long been overstrained, a cause and consequence of National prosperity, and National exertion. If the last is a fruitless exertion, as I think it is, any solid and permanent remedy will be utterly impracticable. But, for the present, if the general interest is appealed to in support of Credit, Credit will be supported, and Cash will, by degrees, reappear, from the necessity of its reappearance but if a low Paper Currency is once admitted, the Market will be overloaded, Gold and silver will be more and more withheld and if Guinea Notes, or any thing resembling them, are once put into Currency, you will never see a Guinea; whereas if you keep the Currency where it is and support it with vigour, necessity will draw out the Gold and silver. Excuse, I beg you, these crude ideas. No man wishes more than I do, that all my ideas should be found vain and frivolous upon experience. Your usual goodness will induce you to pardon my freedom. Be assured my dear Sir, That no Man has a higher value than I have for your virtues and talents, or is more desirous of keeping a place in your kind estimation. I have the honour to be with the highest respect and regard, Dear Sir,

> Your most faithful
> and obliged humble Servant

Bath   EDM BURKE
  1st March 97

P.S: You will excuse my using the hand of a confidential friend, as I have not been able for a long time to do any thing more than dictate.

Almost thirty years later, in the debate on the Bank Charter and Promissory Notes Acts in February 1826, Canning quoted Burke's opinions and referred to this letter: 'I came, Sir, into parliament, two years before that great man retired from public life. I had the good fortune to enjoy, during the short remainder of his natural life, a small portion of his private friendship. A letter—the only letter which I ever received from him—and which I have treasured up as a memorial of departed genius, was on this very subject. It was written at Bath, on that bed of sickness from which he never afterwards rose. After discussing the arguments for and against the measure of the Bank restriction, the letter concluded with this remarkable sentence—"Tell Mr Pitt, that if he consents to the issue of one-pound notes, he will never see a guinea again" (hear, hear!). Mr Burke, like most prophets, was not believed at the time of uttering his predictions. One-pound notes were issued in abundance; they expelled, as had been foretold, guineas from circulation. . . .'

To SIR LAWRENCE PARSONS—8 *March* 1797

Corr. (1958), IX, 277–80

On 31 January Sir Lawrence Parsons, 5th Baronet (1758–1841), later (1807) 2nd Earl of Rosse, an able and independent-minded Irish M.P. who was Colonel of the King's County Militia, wrote a long and powerful letter to Burke on 'Ireland's deficiency in military force' which had been revealed by the threat of a French landing in Munster. Though theoretically there were 40,000 troops in the country, when the sick and untrained and the forces stationed in Ulster were deducted, only 16,000 men could be mustered for the defence of the south. Moreover the forces in Ireland were badly equipped, their artillery and medical services being seriously inadequate. Parsons advocated the adoption of a 'grand scale of defence' which would have involved raising more men and building extensive fortifications. He also was in favour of Catholic emancipation, both as 'a fair reward for approved loyalty' and as facilitating 'the great levies which times require'. He urged Burke 'day after day to represent our danger until measures are taken to countervail it'. He also urged in the Irish House of Commons on 21 and 24 February that additional forces should be raised for the defence of Ireland.

Dear Sir

You cannot overrate my regard for Ireland, As it is the Country to which I am bound by my earliest instincts, and as it is a part, which I cannot seperate, even in thought, of this great Empire, to the head of which I am bound by my maturest habits, by duty and by gratitude: But you may easily overrate, (as you do,) my ability to serve it. I am sunk deep in age and still more sunk in Affliction and infirmity. I was brought to this place,[1] with very little hopes of recovery, as my last resource, and here I have lain a long time in a state of utter inability for any exertion of mind or body, having been reduced nearly to the

[1] Bath.

last extremity. It was in that condition, and in this place, that I received the honour of your Letter, full, as I might justly expect of public spirited anxiety for your Country and of many just views of what is proper in its present situation. I do not find any inconsistency, that is a moral or political inconsistency, between your publick Votes and your private sentiments. Without condemning a different proceeding in other Gentlemen, I know nothing more consistent with the character of a man of honour and virtue than to conceal the faults and errors of a Government, which circumstances oblige him to support from fear of worse evils and a full exposure of the same neglects and mismanagements in an amicable manner to those in whose power it is to correct them, and who having omitted the performance of their duty in prevention, are but the more bound to the duty of furnishing a remedy. However, you have totally mistaken in your application to me, tho' I am infinitely sensible of the honour you have done me by that Application. When I was in a much better state of health, than I have long since enjoyed, I never had any communication whatsoever, with the men in power, except one Gentleman in Office,[2] who sometimes from compassion visits me, as an old and infirm friend, but with whom I do not talk on public business. His Majesty's principal Minister I have not so much as seen, to the best of my recollection, for nearly 3 years. All I can do is to give you merely a private Opinion, and you have every title, that it should be a fair one. I do not enter into the circumstances of the measures which have been taken for the defence of either kingdom. I am afraid that the descent of the Enemy in Ireland was not credited, and therefore could not be provided for. A Naval defence must be in its nature in the highest degree uncertain; but if it were better, than it is, it must be perfectly ruinous, to keep the most formidable Navy that Great Britain ever possessed, meerly as a Coast guard. It is wholely to mistake the nature and purpose of a Naval force.—It is also my poor opinion, but formed upon an attentive consideration of the subject, begun several years ago upon something of a similar occasion,[3] that it is impossible to secure the Coast of these kingdoms particularly the South west Coast of Ireland by any fortifications. That the very attempt would be mischievous, and possibly ruinous, if extended beyond a few Naval Stations. I am in the same errour, if it be an errour, with regard to all the other modes of passive defence, such as old and new Militias, for home service. Yeomen Cavalry, and Infantry, Volunteers &ca except in such

[2] Windham.
[3] Probably when a Franco-Spanish invasion was threatened in 1779.

small numbers as may be subservient to a vigilant Police: For by keeping up in the two Kingdoms the expence of an Army of *200,000* Men, who, by the very terms of their service, cannot strike a blow at an enemy except at his pleasure—That Enemy may compleatly ruin our finances and destroy our public Credit, even by the menaces of his hostility, without putting to the risk, or expence of a single hostile step. I wish we may not already have experienced the ill effects of this policy, so contrary to all the rules and principles hitherto observed in War. I am sure it is directly contrary to the Policy and proceeding of this Country in any period of its former Wars, where our best defence has been ever found in the offensive measures we have pursued against our Enemies. But now it has happened, that our apprehensions are increased as might have been expected in the exact proportion to the magnitude of the mistaken provision that is made for our safety. I am very well aware that the seed of this mistaken policy has not been sown at this time, but at this time it has been watered and manured to the growth in which we see it. Can that Nation expect even the shadow of an honourable and advantageous peace who is resolved not to strike one preventive blow at an Enemy, and, which, with the burthen of an Army and a Navy, which well managed and jointly employed, might go a great way in giving Laws to the world, employs the Navy, meerly as an outwork, and the Army, meerly as a Garrison to cover the most extensive Coast, taking the two Islands together, which the same measurement of Land affords upon the habitable Globe. Nothing gives me greater grief than that I have not strength enough to protest at large and in the most publick manner against putting these Islands into a state of Siege, whilst almost all Europe is conquered before our Eyes, and every Port with which we can maintain a Commercal intercourse with the world, has fallen or is falling into the hands of those Enemies, whose own territory we consider as sacred.

I beg pardon for the freedom which your liberality of sentiment has encouraged me to take with you. I am an old Man, and have old Notions; and if you reject my Opinions, will be so good at least, as to pardon my weakness. I have the honour to be, with the highest respect and regard

Dear Sir
Your most faithful humble
Servant
EDM BURKE

Bath 8th March
1797

To WILLIAM WINDHAM—30 *March* 1797

Corr. (1958), IX, 299–302

Bath, March 30, 1797.

My dear Friend,

Though my mind is full indeed of all that is going on, in a strange kind of harmony of discord, between both sides of the House, I thought it unnecessary to trouble you with any of my melancholy reflections upon that sad subject. The opposition have never manifested, at least not in so great a degree, or so avowedly, their ill-intentions to their country, as to its credit, its finances, or its policy,—I may almost say, to its being. They have gone so far as to attempt to force the bank paper, which they had done every thing to depreciate, upon the soldiers and the sailors;[1] and thus, by discontenting these descriptions, to leave it without an army or a navy, or, perhaps, what would be worse, an army and navy full of mutiny and sedition. To the plausible part of their objections an answer is made; but nothing is said, within or without the House, to expose the designs which have given rise to this sort of discussion. In debate, as in war, we confine ourselves to a poor, disgraceful, and ruinous defensive. What is the reason that Mr Pitt does not avow the principle of a firm and effective alliance with the Emperor? Why does he continually postpone a full declaration of his sentiments on that head? Why does he suffer an ally of Great Britain, who, while he is such, is an integrant part of the strength of Great Britain, and in a manner part of Great Britain itself, to be called a foreign power, and the assistance afforded him to be considered as money thrown away, as if we had no relation whatsoever to him? Since we are resolved to make no active use of our own forces, he is the only energetic portion of the British power; and the question is, whether, in such a war as this, we ought to disarm that portion of our strength which alone discovers any life. The consequence of all this must be as fatal to Mr Pitt as to the king and the nation. He cannot make peace, because he will not make war. He will be beaten out of all his entrenchments. The enemy is turning his flanks. I find he is left alone to make his defence, and perhaps he chooses to be so; but it has a very ill aspect to those who speculate on the duration of a ministry.

[1] On 24 March when the Bank Indemnity Bill was in committee, the Opposition criticized a clause permitting the Bank to retain a sufficient quantity of specie to enable the Government to pay the Army and Navy in cash. In the course of the discussion Pitt explained that most of the payments to the forces would be made in paper.

These speculators multiply. They increase the confidence of the leaders of opposition, and they add to the number of their followers. All this arises, as I conceive, from Mr Pitt's considering the part he has taken in this war as the effect of a dire necessity, and not of a manly and deliberate choice. But when a man shows no zeal for his own cause, we are not to be surprised that no others will show any zeal for his person. He would not consider those who are attached to him *from principle*, to be his friends, and he will find that he has a very insecure hold of those whose attachment is wholly *without principle*. They who make a man an idol, when he is off his pedestal will treat him with all the contempt with which blind and angry worshippers treat an idol that is fallen.

You are the only person who has taken a manly part; and I can truly assure you, that your enemies are so far from beng exasperated, that they are rather softened by this conduct. It is the only conduct that can mitigate the animosity of enemies like yours.

Ireland is in a truly unpleasant situation. The government is losing the hearts of the people, if it has not quite lost them, by the falsehood of its maxims, and their total ignorance in the art of governing. The opposition in that country, as well as in this, is running the whole course of Jacobinism, and losing credit amongst the sober people, as the other loses credit with the people at large. It is a general bankruptcy of reputation on both parties. They must be singularly unfortunate who think to govern by dinners and bows, and who mistake the oil which facilitates the motion, for the machine itself. It is a terrible thing for government to put its confidence in a handful of people of fortune, separate from all holdings and dependencies. A full levée is not a complete army. I know very well that when they disarm a whole province, they think that all is well; but to take away arms, is not to destroy disaffection. It has cast deep roots in the principles and habits of the majority amongst the lower and middle classes of the whole Protestant part of Ireland. The Catholics, who are intermingled with them, are more or less tainted. In the other parts of Ireland, (some in Dublin only excepted,) the Catholics, who are in a manner the whole people, are as yet sound: but they may be provoked, as all men easily may be, out of their principles. I do not allude to the granting or withholding the matters of privilege, &c., which are in discussion between them and the Castle.[2] In themselves, I consider them of very little moment, the one way or the other. But the principle is what

---

[2] The Irish Administration.

sticks with me; which principle is the avowal of a direct, determined hostility to those who compose the infinitely larger part of the people; and that part, upon whose fidelity, let what will be the thought of it, the whole strength of government ultimately rests. But I have done with this topic, and perhaps for ever, though I receive letters from the fast friends of the Catholics to solicit government here to consider their true interests. Neglect, contumely, and insult, were never the ways of keeping friends; and they had nothing to force against an enemy.

I suspect, though Woodford has said nothing of it, and perhaps the more for his having said nothing of it, that the perfidious and cowardly design of destroying the French corps in our service still goes on.[3] A part of the aim, I suspect, is at yourself. It will undoubtedly require the utmost diligence and firmness, as well as so much temper as can consist with those qualities, to carry you through. God Almighty direct you, for this matter is almost above my hand.

It is evident that the opposition have directly, and without any management at all, embraced the French interests, and mean to shake our credit and resources at home, and destroy all possibility of connexion abroad. It is equally plain that, except by yourself, they are not met manfully upon either of these grounds. Their best fire is only to cover a retreat. What is the reason that Gifford's book[4] is not strongly recommended and circulated by them and theirs? There are but a very few pages in that book to which I do not heartily subscribe; but *they* ought to subscribe to the whole of it, unless they choose to be considered as criminals soliciting for a pardon, rather than as innocent men making a defence. However, I have great satisfaction in telling you, that your manly way of proceeding augments the number of your favourers every day; and not only your nature, but your policy, will induce you to proceed in the same course. I have attempted to resume my work, but the variable state of my health continually calls me from it; otherwise, our scheme of defence, founded solely upon fear and meanness, would not be persisted in. Adieu! and believe me ever with the truest, most affectionate, and most grateful attachment,

My dear friend,
Yours, most sincerely
EDM. BURKE.

[3] The French troops loyal to the monarchy who fought with the British and were maintained by them, until November 1796, when four units were disbanded.

[4] At the end of March John Gifford (1758–1818), an Anti-Jacobin writer, published *A Letter to the Hon. T. Erskine; containing some Strictures on his View of the Causes and Consequences of the Present War with France.* Towards the end of April it had reached a fifth edition.

Five o'clock.
My last night was pretty good, but I have not passed an equally good day. My strength, however, improves. Otherwise, I make no great progress. Mrs Burke, thank God, is, on the whole, rather better than when we came here.

To EARL FITZWILLIAM—26 *April* [1797]

Corr. (1958), IX, 317

My dear Lord,

I have no great heart to write in the present State of things. The quick succession of every sort of calamity and disgrace both foreign and domestick has quite overwhelmed my feeble constancy, which, one way or other, has, to this time, kept itself erect. The evil effect of our narrow System of inert and passive defence has already appeard in its operation even on our misapplied means, and the instruments of that false and pusillanimous System. Indeed it is impossible, that a stagnant military force, in times like the present at least, perhaps at any time, should not corrupt and putrifye. The temporary quiet in our marine has been bought at the expence of all future discipline.[1] The concessions are of such a nature, as, I am afraid, take away the possibility of reestablishing it, though *all* the art and management should be used, not part of which, I am persuaded, will be put in practice. A spirit of fear and compromise, if it deserves the name of a spirit, is become universal, or indeed is rather made so. What shall we be under an abject and ignominious peace, if cowardice is the principle of our War. But all is over with the world in which I, and your Lordship at a later period, were born, and in which we wished to die. This is most certain:—and yet I heartily agree with you, that you ought to act in your private Affairs, as if it were to continue for ever. You perform a present Duty—and as to the future it must be committed to the disposal of Providence.

As to the poor friend, so many years known to you only by obligations for which he could make no return—The shadow of him exists. Though the muscular flesh be wasted and indeed almost wholly gone, Some Strength is recoverd and on the whole, the radical malady, (not

---

[1] On April 16 the crews of the British fleet at Spithead refused to obey orders and petitioned for an increase of pay. On April 23 they were informed their grievances would be redressed, at which 'The men gave three cheers and declared they were ready to obey orders'.

to be conquerd at my time of Life) excepted, I feel better. Mrs Burke is better of her cold—and we both cordially salute Lady Fitzwilliam. May the God who has made you what you are, preserve to better times.

Ever truly, affectionately and gratefully Yours
EDM BURKE

April 26, 1796.

CHAPTER EIGHT

INDIA

BURKE'S MONUMENT

N EAR THE END of his life Burke wrote to his friend and literary
executor French Laurence with the gravest urgency, commanding him to publish after his death a record of his actions in the
impeachment of Warren Hastings, Governor-General of India. "Let
my endeavours to save the Nation from that Shame and Guilt, be my
monument," he wrote; "The only one I ever will have. Let every thing
I have done, said, or written be forgotten but this" (letter to Laurence,
July 1796). Empire, he added, was not delivered into British hands
to serve merely as an opportunity of gratifying "the lowest of their
passions." But when, in 1782, Burke decided seriously to pursue Hastings and his regime in India, he knew that he had not only to oppose
Hastings' criminal greed but to do so against "the most perfect indifference" of his countrymen, who did not care how their empire
was acquired and maintained (letters to William Eden and to William
Baker, 1784). As he told the niece of Sir Joshua Reynolds, "I have
no party in this Business . . . but among a set of people, who have
none of your Lilies and Roses in their faces; but who are the images
of the great Pattern as well as you and I" (letter to Miss Mary Palmer,
1786).

Besides leaving this great moral example of justice done to a subject
race against powerful perpetrators and despite public indifference,
Burke wished also to establish impeachment as a political precedent.
In *Thoughts on the Cause of the Present Discontents* (1770), he spoke of
impeachment as "that great guardian of the purity of the constitution."

While fixing the charges against Hastings in the House of Commons, and during his trial in the House of Lords, Burke repeatedly protested against the notion advanced by legalistic neutrals as well as Hastings' partisans that the proof required be the same as would convict in an ordinary case of law (letters to Philip Francis, 1785, and to Thomas Burgh, 1787). To require strictly legal proof would be to forget the political or constitutional character of impeachment, and to reduce it to redundancy. Taking British and American constitutional practice as a whole, Burke has not prevailed on this point. Yet he may be right. It is hard to see how the moral example of impeachment can be effectual without the political means to defeat legal chicanery aided by prominent status and excused by popular indifference.

To JOHN BOURKE—[*November* 1777]

Corr. (1958), III, 402–3

Bourke (*c.* 1722–1806) was a London merchant and a distant kinsman of Burke's. Burke speaks of a long letter by his friend Philip Francis (1740–1818) opposing the reorganization of the collection of revenue in India being undertaken by Warren Hastings [1732–1818], the Governor-General.

Becd Wednesday.

My dear John

I give you a thousand thanks for the papers you have been so good as to put into my hands. I wished to keep them a little longer; but I husbanded my time as well as I could; and when my Company went to bed spent the greatest part of the Night in reading them. This morning I went through the whole. I dont know that I ever read any State paper drawn with more ability; and indeed I have seldom read a paper of any kind with more pleasure.

In general I perfectly agree with Mr Francis, that a nice Scrutiny into the property and Tenures of an whole Nation is almost always more alarming to the people, than advantagious to Government. It is never undertaken without some suspicion at least of an attempt to impose some new Burthen upon them. Mr F. is a better judge than I can possibly be of the politicks which have given rise to such a measure. Upon that Subject therefore, I can form no opinion but what

I take from his authority. The Idea of forcing every thing to an artificial
equality has something, at first View, very captivating in it. It has all
the appearance imaginable of Justice and good order; and very many
persons, without any sort of partial purposes, have been led to adopt
such Schemes and to pursue them with great earnestness and warmth.
Though I have no doubt, that the minute, laborious, and very expensive *Cadastre*,[1] which was made by the later King of Sardinia,[2] has
done no sort of good, and that after all his pains, a few years will
restore all things to their first inequality, yet it has been the admiration
of half the reforming Financiers of Europe. I mean the Official Financiers, as well as the speculative. You know that it is this very rage for
equality, which has blown up the Flames of this present cursed War
in America. I am, for one, entirely satisfied, that the inequality, which
grows out of the *nature of things* by time, custom, succession, accumulation, permutation, and improvement of property, is much nearer
that true equality, which is the foundation of equity and just policy,
than any thing which can be contrived by the Tricks and devices of
human skill. What does it amount to, after some little jumbling, but
that some men have better Estates than others. I am certain that when
the financial System is but tolerably planned it will catch property in
spite of all its doublings; and sooner or later those who have most will
pay most; and this is the effective quality which circumstances will
bring about of themselves if they are left to their own operation. . . .

To WILLIAM EDEN—17 *May* 1784

Corr. (1958), V, 150–51

William Eden (1744–1814), later (1789) 1st Baron Auckland, M.P., had served Lord
North as an Under-Secretary of State and as Chief Secretary in Ireland, and had
returned to office as Vice-Treasurer of Ireland in the Fox-North coalition. Burke
writes just after Pitt's great victory in the general election of 1784.

My dear Sir,—I am obliged to you for thinking of me in the midst of
your cabbage garden: I never have been called away from mine with
so much reluctance in my whole life. It is not pleasant to play the
captive part in a triumphal procession, especially when the weather
is hot and the ways dusty. I agree with you that our first days will be
employed in the display and insolence of victory. If insolence and

---

[1] Survey of taxable land.
[2] Charles Emmanuel III (1701–73), who ruled from 1730 to 1773.

reason were terms that could agree, I should say that they have reason for their insolence. The humour (for I must not call it madness) of the people has much exceeded my apprehensions, and you know I have not been very sanguine.

My accounts from India do not at all differ from yours. I do not believe that those who act as Ministers will much dispute the Company's affairs. The delusion has done all that the authors and abettors proposed, and they will not endeavour to keep it up only to embarrass themselves: for no Government can find it either for its interest or credit to support a fictitious solvency in the Company, the effect of which must be to bring a real bankruptcy on the Exchequer, and that in no great length of time. You are certainly right: the havock and destruction of the species made in the East Indies does by no means touch the humanity of our countrymen, who, if the whole Gentoo[1] race had but one neck, would see it cut with the most perfect indifference.[2] To their own interest they have sensibility enough, but then it is only in the moment of suffering. Until the House shall adopt the true state of the East India affairs the nation will not see them; and the Ministers, who in general terms will be ready enough to admit the difficulties and embarrassments in that part of the world, will never suffer a clear and distinct statement of them to be made.[3] I shall, indeed, be much disappointed if they suffer a single East India paper to be laid before their Parliament. I find that you and others think rather better of this new chosen body than I am able to do. I am glad that your opinion is so favourable, for it will make your exertion more lively and effectual.

For my part, I despair totally of anything which can be done in future, if we do not commence our proceedings by a strong defence of our past conduct, and by as strong a crimination of those who have caballed you out of your power, and have libelled you out of your reputation. If this preliminary point were once well secured, the mode of our opposition would, in my opinion, be of less moment, and might even be left to the guidance of events. If something of the kind be

---

[1] Hindu.

[2] Burke is adapting the saying which Suetonius attributes to Caligula.

[3] Burke's 'Ninth Report' began with an assertion of the crying need for a discussion of the Indian problem in plain language: 'Your committee have endeavoured to perform this task in plain and popular language, knowing that nothing has alienated the House from inquiries, absolutely necessary for the performance of one of the most essential of all its duties, so much as the technical language of the Company's records; as the Indian names of persons, of offices, of the tenure and qualities of estates, and of all the varied branches of their intricate revenue. This language is, indeed, of necessary use in the executive department of the Company's affairs; but it is not necessary to parliament' (*Works*, Bohn, IV, 1–2; Little, Brown, VIII, 3–4).

not adopted, I have no confidence in any mode of opposition whatever. Whenever business is put into any sort of train, I think I may take the part which may be allotted to me; till then I have no great ambition.

> Ever most faithfully
> and affectionately yours,
> ED. BURKE.

17th May, 1784.

To WILLIAM BAKER—22 *June* 1784

Corr. (1958), V, 154–56

Burke carried out the intention he had mentioned to William Eden of preparing for his party a 'strong defense of our past conduct'. On June 14 he introduced a motion in Commons setting out a defense of the Fox-North Coalition (*Journals of the House of Commons*, XL, 198–204). William Baker (1743–1824), M.P., a loyal follower of Rockingham and friend of Burke, had written to Burke in appreciation of this action, and Burke now replies.

My dear Baker,

I am sincerely sorry for the cause of your confinement. I hope soon to hear better news; and that the Object of your family sollicitude, will leave you at leisure to think of other things, and to think of him with more Tranquillity.

As to the publick Object of your Care, it is certainly not in my power to give you any comfort about it. I consider the House of Commons as something worse than extinguishd. We have been labouring for near twenty years to make it independent; and as soon as we had accomplishd what we had in view, we found that its independence led to its destruction. The people did not like our work; and they joind the Court to pull it down. The demolition is very complete. Others may be more sanguine; but for me to look forward to the Event of another twenty years toil—it is quite ridiculous. I am sure the Task was more easy at first than it is now. The examples which have been made must operate. I can conceive that men of spirit might be persuaded to persevere in a great and worthy undertaking for many years, at the hazard, and even with the certainty of the utmost indignation of a Court; but to become Objects of that indignation only to expose themselves to popular indignation, and to be rejected by both Court and Country, is more perhaps than any one could expect; certainly a great deal more than one will meet, except perhaps in three or four men, who will be more marked for their singularity and obstinacy, than pitied for their feeble good intentions. It is rather difficult to form a judgment of an whole people. But at present the picture of the English Nation does not appear to me in a very favourable light. I do not conceive them to be under any delusion at all. If I am not mistaken, they are perfectly well aware of the Nature and Tendency of what they have done, and they by no means repent of it. To be sure they do not intend, formally to deliver over themselves and their posterity to servitude. This is not their primary intention. But they are so fond of aggrandizing the Crown, and of humbling every thing which does not derive its importance directly from that Scource, that they are totally indifferent to the consequences. A More frightful Symptom, in my Mind, than this, appears in the Nation at present; to which I do not think any thing was correspondent, even in the worst times of the Roman Republick. That is that all the Tyranny, robbery, and destruction of mankind practised by the Company and their servants in the East, is popular and pleasing in this Country; and that the Court and Ministry who evidently abet that iniquitous System, are somewhat the better liked on that account. The factions of the great gave countenance to the ruin of the provinces in the days of the Roman domination; But such men as Verres, and such practices as his, were always odious to the people at Large.[1]

You ask me why my Motion was not supported by the party? Truly I can give no good reason for it. Such was their pleasure. If I had followed the prevailing opinion I never would have made that Motion. But I was resolved to take my own way, and to leave them to take theirs. So I made the motion; and the Event is such as you have seen. I am happy to find you think me in the Right: I am sure I should not have slept as well as I have done since that time, if I had been persuaded to omit a protest against the doctrines in the Speech from the Throne, and a defence of the worthy persons with whom I had the honour of acting in the last Parliament, and who had no longer any parliamentary means of defending themselves. A certain Routine, of Conduct, some weak hopes of the present parliament, an expectation that the popular tide would turn; that we must not too strongly oppose ourselves to the prevailing humour, and many other Topics of the same Metal, not in my opinion at all worthy of our Cause, of ourselves, or of the occasion, prevented several from coinciding with me with regard to

[1] For a discussion of the influence of Cicero's orations against Verres upon Burke, see H. V. Canter, 'The Impeachments of Verres and Hastings, Cicero and Burke', *Classical Journal*, IX (February 1914), 199–211.

the seasonableness of our making our defence, or of our setting our faces against the first declaration of the New Doctrines. For my own part I was thoroughly convinced, not only of the rectitude, but of the prudence and propriety of the act; and I am so little ashamed of the reception which my Motion met with (which was indeed with apparent uneasiness on our side, and with all kind of Boyish petulance and insolence on the other) that I am resolved to reprint it in a seperate Pamphlet with Notes and references; to send it to every part of the Kingdom; and to get it translated into French, and to circulate it in every Country in Europe.[2] It may be perhaps the last free act we shall [be] permitted to do: and that last act ought not to be such as to disgrace all the Rest. Adieu my dear friend and beleive me ever

> most faithfully
> and affectionately Yours &c
> EDM BURKE

Beconsfield June 22d 1784.

To LORD THURLOW—[14 *December* 1784]

Corr. (1958), V, 203–05

An unfinished draft of a letter to Edward Thurlow, 1st Baron Thurlow (1731–1806), Lord Chancellor in Pitt's ministry. The Board of Control supervising the East India Company had just decided to pay the debts of the Nawab of Arcot out of revenues of the Carnatic in Southern India. Burke believed that the debts were in many cases fraudulent, that the Carnatic—already devastated by four years of war—was incapable of paying the Nawab's debts, and that the Government was rewarding the political and financial support it had received from some of the larger creditors of the Nawab during the 1784 election. See Burke's *Speech on the Nabob of Arcot's Debts* (*Works*, Bohn, III, 116–268).

My dear Lord,

I am very happy if I have been able to suggest any hints which may put a mind so vigorous and sagacious as yours in the way of Enquiry. It is the whole of what I can pretend to. The rest will be furnishd from your own rescources. I just wish to add in the same Character

[2] Burke prepared this pamphlet, which he entitled *A Representation to His Majesty moved in the House of Commons by the Right Hon. Edmund Burke, and seconded by William Windham, Esq. on Monday, June 14, 1784, and negatived. With a Preface and Notes* (*Works*, Bohn, II, 248–76; Little, Brown, II, 537–76).

of an Index to facts that in stating my Objections to the Scheme of double loading the possible revenues of a Country actually ruined with Charges not eventual and contingent but certain and the Charges not defined nor authenticated, I only touched upon what I considerd the radical Cause of all the other Evils; that is the great enormous and disproportiond momentum of private Interest weighing and operating against the publick. But I assure your Lordship, that there are other Circumstances in that arrangement, which for their extent and quality would be found full as exceptionable; and such indeed as no Temperate Government would adopt, without a great deal of consideration; in which consideration I include all adverse remark; as an essential part of every discussion of a matter so new and which is to have its effect on an Object so remote from our feelings and our information. It is a matter delicate indeed.

With regard to the Object of your present Enquiry, I shall be able to furnish your Lordship with heads may be as material with regard to the prosperity of our Northern as what shall be done with relation to the Subject of our last Night's conversation may be to that of the Southern part of our possessions in India; and though in the result we may differ, and in the difference the power of representing only is on my side, and that of acting is on yours, and notwithstanding your previous good opinion of the parties concernd, I am not afraid of putting a possible adversary both of power and Talents, in possession of my Case;[1] rather than that an actual able and powerful Minister should be misled by the only way in which he can be misled a misinformation concerning fact.

I have been myself in the very Circumstances in which Your Lordship stands with regard to Mr Hastings that is under the strongest prejudice in his favour, raised as yours may be by strong and often repeated confident general panegyrics. But at length without any other intervening Cause whatsoever, than an Inquiry which a particular duty in Parliament obliged me to undertake,[2] I found the extreme danger of following what is called Character, where given by the Creatures

---

[1] Thurlow was in fact in close contact with Major Scott, Hastings' chief proponent, whom he convinced that Hastings was about to be given an English peerage. After having dinner alone with the Chancellor on 6 December, Scott wrote to Hastings, on 7 December, 'He is a glorious Fellow—and fit to be a minister—He says we shall be held contemptible through Europe if you are not supported and honoured'. Apparently Scott was as ignorant as Burke that the Chancellor was giving audiences to them both.

[2] His duty as a member of the Select Committee.

and Agents of persons at a distance—whose whole being depends upon the service done by such representations.

I am no Enemy of that man—he never gave me Cause directly or indirectly he is nec odio nec beneficio mihi cognitus.[3] He never gave and never refused to give because probably I never asked any thing from him for any friend I have in the World;[4] I dont recollect that I have ever seen him, I am sure I never conversed with him. Nor have I more Enmity to him than I have to the Creditors of the Nabob of Arcot; if the dispute was between him and them and not between them and the native Inhabitants I should not think it worth my while to walk across the Street to give them a moments trouble.

But of some things I am certain. I know that the Country under his Care is sacked and pillaged and I know he is the Government and I know a great deal more. I have not in Town nor could I if in the Country, instantly put together the matters of which I made collection when I intended to move an impeachment against him.[5] But I conceive I can speak with tolerable accuracy to many things from my Memory.

I have said this in Justice to myself and to my Motives a justice which no man who had observed the process and Train of my Conduct I flatter can refuse me, I shall wait on your Lordship to talk over that affair this Evening or when you please. I shall cheerfully stay in Town. . . .

To PHILIP FRANCIS—10 December 1785

Corr. (1958), V, 241–44

Burke discusses with Francis the question whether charges of impeachment against Hastings should be narrowed to those which could gain the widest consent, that is, to charges strictly provable in law.

---

[3] Known to me neither for good nor ill. The source of this quotation has not been traced.

[4] Speculation on the influence of William Burke on Edmund's crusade against Hastings was freely indulged in by the Burkes' more hostile critics. There is evidence that William was convinced that Hastings was the enemy of his first employer, the Raja of Tanjore; but the allegation, made, for example, by Charles M'Cormick (*Memoirs of Edmund Burke*, London, 1797, pp. 214–15), that Edmund's resentment was engendered by Hastings's obstruction of William's interests as Paymaster, seems to be without foundation.

[5] This would seem to confirm the widespread rumours that Burke had been contemplating a Bill of Pains and Penalties against Hastings in the early months of 1783. In April 1783 Burke had 'pledged himself . . . that he would bring to justice, as far as in him lay, the greatest delinquent that India ever saw' (*Parliamentary History*, XXIII, 800).

Beaconsfield 10th Decr 1785

I shall be happy to see you and Mr Fox here any day this week; the sooner the better. I shall now say a few words on the business-part of our correspondence. I entertained not the least doubt that Mr Fox would take his part in the Bengal question, which *must* be brought on. He is certainly right. We ought to be very careful not to charge what we are unable to prove. I only think it odd, after all that has passed, how he, or any body, can make any doubt of our exactness in this particular. If we understand by proof the establishment of fact by evidence agreeable to the nature of the transaction and the principles of Jurisprudence, I think we can be under no difficulty. Most of the facts, upon which we proceed, are confessed; some of them are boasted of. The labour will be on the *criminality* of the facts, where proof, as I apprehend, will not be contested. Guilt *resides* in the *intention*. But as we are before a tribunal, which having conceived a favourable opinion of Hastings (or what is of more moment, very favourable wishes for him) they will not judge of his intentions by the acts, but they will qualify his Acts by his presumed intentions. It is on this preposterous mode of judging that he has built all the Apologies for his conduct, which I have seen. Excuses, which in any criminal court would be considered with pity as the Straws, at which poor wretches drowning will catch, and which are such as no prosecuter thinks it worth his while to reply to, will be admitted in such a House of Commons as ours as a solid defence. Mere impudence, which in all other cases would be thought infinitely to aggravate guilt, will with us be considered as the tone of innocence and conscious virtue. These are difficulties not arising from the Nature of our case, but the circumstances of the time; they are of a sort, that no care in the formation or execution of our plan can possibly remove. And in my opinion, after making these difficulties, to show that we are aware of them, they ought to make no part of our consideration. We know that we bring before a bribed tribunal a prejudged cause. In that situation all that we have to do is to make a case strong in proof and in importance, and to draw inferences from it justifiable in logick, policy and criminal justice. As to all the rest, it is vain and idle.

Perhaps my plan may not be the best for drawing in the greatest concurrence upon the vote, and making, what is called, a respectable Minority. I should admit, if there were a prospect of such a minority as is nearly tantamount to a majority, and, in a second trial, is in a manner sure to produce one, the plan ought to have numbers in view, as a principal consideration. With such a prospect before you, it is very often necessary to take away something from the force of your charge, in order to secure its effect. In the course of a long administration, such as that of Mr Hastings, which has been coexistent with several administrations at home,[1] it has happened that some are involved with him in one sort of business, who stand clear in others; in which again a different description may feel themselves (or friends, who are as themselves) directly or indirectly affected; to say nothing of the private favours, which such multitudes have received; (which makes at once Mr Hastings's crime and his indemnity;) and in which every party without distinction is engaged in one or other of its members. Parties themselves have been so perfectly jumbled and confounded, that it is morally impossible to find any combination of them, who can march with the whole body in orderly array upon the expedition before us. With other prospects than ours, I know that we ought to exert all our dexterity in our selection, and not to aim a shot at the hunted deer, except where you are sure not to hit any other. This necessity I have experienced and submitted to (as in common sense I ought) in many instances. But all the reasons for such a conduct failing here, I find myself not in the least inclined to abandon any one solid ground of Charge, which I have taken up in any report, speech or publick proceeding whatsoever, or which I find strongly marked in the Records, which I have by me. My reason is this. A parliamentary criminal proceeding is not in its nature within the ordinary resort of the law. Even in a temper less favourable to Indian delinquency than what is now generally prevalent, the people at large would not consider one or two acts, however striking, perhaps not three or four, as sufficient to call forth the reserved justice of the State. I confess, I partake myself so far of that coarse vulgar equity, that if I found the general tenour of a man's conduct unexceptionable, I should hardly think the extreme remedies fit to be resorted to on account of some wrong actions during many years continuance in an arduous command. Of this I am certain, that *a general evil intention*, manifested through a long series and a great variety of acts, ought to have much greater weight with a *publick political* tribunal, than such detached and unrelated Offences, into which common human infirmity has often betrayed the most splendid characters in History. Such a series of offences, manifesting

[1] Hastings had been Governor and Governor General of Bengal from 1772 until he left India on 7 February 1785: that is, during the Administrations of North, Rockingham, Shelburne, the Coalition and William Pitt.

a *corrupt, habitual,* evil intention, may be produced; and nothing but a series of such facts can furnish, in my opinon, a satisfactory proof of it.

In that case I am little disposed to weaken my cause in order to strengthen the importance of an adequate support. Shall we abandon the substance of our charge (which is in the multitude and the perseverance in offences) to fall in with Lord Titius, or Mr Caius, when Lord Titius or Mr Caius are unable to give us Substantial aid in the few mutilated particulars they leave us to proceed upon? Our friend,[2] you say, is to consult many. He, who is to please many in a business, which, in the first instance, he makes his own, may be in the Right to do so, though this perhaps is doubtful. But any man, whose only object is to acquit *himself* properly, ought to abstain from that general Consultation as from a poison. Speaking for myself, my business is not to consider what will convict Mr Hastings, (a thing we all know to be impracticable) but what will acquit and justify myself to those few persons and to those distant times, which may take a concern in these affairs and the Actors in them. Those, who may think otherwise, may have, (I ought to say they undoubtedly have) intentions as good as mine, and a judgment much superiour, for the regulation of their own particular conduct. It might not become a man, situated like Mr Fox, to move without a considerable retinue. He is in the right not to appear weak, if possible, because the opinion of strength leads to further strength; and without that strength the manly scheme of politicks, in which he is engaged can never become prevalent. In a party-light, and as a question to draw numbers, whatever modification we may bestow upon our motion, a worse cannot be chosen out of the whole bundle of political measures. It is therefore my opinion that the wisest course for Mr Fox to pursue is, not to consider it as such. But, as my intention is known and declared, and as I never stated it to be conceived in concert with any one, he will naturally support the question as concurrent with his own opinion and with his own principles, and not as a point he means to exert strength to carry; for this the known state of the country will be his justification. Mr Fox, with regard to himself, has nothing at all to embarrass him in this business; but, as he means to call in the aid of other opinions, it is impossible for us to blend ourselves with them. They will not digest several very important matters, which you and I may think essential. They, who could wish that nothing at all were done, will wish to have as little done as can be. Do not we know that one or two, otherwise cordially

[2] Fox.

with us, are of the very party with Mr Hastings, and have publickly
made his Panegyrick; and would not suffer even a remedial act, which
was supposed to be grounded in some of its provisions on his misconduct?[3] Do not we know that others, who were so far deluded by
those, who every way betrayed them, as in effect to renew the trust
given to Mr Hastings, after they had accumulated materials for his
prosecution, will cordially advise a revision of those matters, which
they have been at least induced to tolerate?[4] If therefore we do not
resolve (I mean, if you and I *dually* do not resolve) to consult only
the cause, and not the support, I pledge myself to you, that we shall
neither have cause, nor support. Whereas if the matter is planned and
settled without them, only taking care that they are well instructed,
there are many things, which they could never permit in consultation,
which in debate they must support, or disgrace themselves for ever.

To MISS MARY PALMER—19 *January* 1786

Corr. (1958), v, 252–57

Mary Palmer (1751–1820), Sir Joshua Reynolds's niece, had lived with her uncle
almost continuously since 1773 and was well acquainted with all the Burkes. Evidently
she was disturbed by the manner in which one of her correspondents in India spoke
of Edmund's activities. Edmund tried to reply to the correspondent through her.

My dear Miss Palmer,

How could you apologize, and apologize to me too, for an act of
good nature and kindness? I hear enough of my faults from my Enemies; shall I not bear to hear them from my friends? Shall I bear
wounds in the field of Battle, and quarrel with my Surgeons, who
open them only to heal them, in my Tent? Tell your worthy correspondent, who is so good as to take an Interest in me, that I am truly
thankful, to him or her (whoever it may be) for their obliging sollicitude. I am an old acquaintance of your House; I believe of not much
less than thirty years standing;[1] though a much later personal acquaintance of *yours;* and you, according to your ages, are best Judges,

---

[3] Before the summer recess of 1783, there had been strong rumours that the Coalition intended
to remove Hastings and the Supreme Council from India by act of Parliament. No bill for this
purpose was ever introduced, and the project may well have been defeated, as Burke here seems
to imply, by opposition within the Government.

[4] Burke would seem to be referring to the reappointment of Hastings in the Regulating Act
of 1781, after the Secret Committee had 'accumulated materials for his prosecution'. In fact at
the time the Act was passed, the Secret Committee had not yet turned its attention to Hastings.

---

[1] Edmond Malone reported that the friendship of Burke and Reynolds had begun in 1758.

whether I am that very intemperate man, that I am described to be in the cool and moderate Climate of Bengal. I am far from the least Title to *Great;* perhaps I am not much nearer to that of *good,* though I endeavour all I can at the latter—nothing at all, I assure you at the former. However I am not, at my years, a person of a childish credulity—nor apt to run away with every report. Having been employd for years in the Business of arranging and stating, as well as collecting, *Evidence,* it would not much become me, of all men, to be light and careless about matter of fact. It is indeed much the Interest of those on whom facts bear hard, so to represent me; and I do not blame them for doing the only thing which can be done in their Cause. It is not uncommon, nor blameable, to make use of a *report,* when a motion is made in the House of Commons, for papers that may, verify, contradict, or qualifye the matter of the report, according to its nature. Almost all motions for papers are made upon that Ground. However, I am, perhaps, the only active man in the House, that never did make a motion, without a very good previous knowlege of the paper I moved for. I will tell you this Business just as it is. I found, that they had received at the India House, a paper of Instructions from Mr Hastings to Mr Bristow,[2] one of which was to apprehend, and to put to Death a certain Gentleman 'called' Almas Âli Khân.[3] I had a copy of that curious secret instruction in my Pocket. I moved, that this Instruction should be laid before the House;[4] stating, as my Ground, the precarious

[2] John Bristow (1750–1802), Resident at Lucknow.

[3] (d. 1808), the most influential revenue farmer in Oudh. Burke is referring to the seventh item of the instructions from Hastings to Bristow, dated 23 October 1782. In this item, Hastings instructed Bristow to see that any engagement between the Nawab Wazir and Almas 'however exceptional' was faithfully observed, and continued: 'If he [Almas] has been guilty of any criminal offence to the Nabob his master, for which no immunity is provided in the engagement, or he shall break any one of the conditions of it, I do most strictly enjoin you, and it must be your special care to endeavour, either by force or surprize, to secure his person, and bring him to justice: by bringing him to justice, I mean that you urge the Nabob, on due conviction, to punish him with death, as a necessary example to deter others from the commission of the like crimes; nor must you desist till this is effected.—I cannot prescribe the means: but to guard myself against that obloquy to which I may be exposed by a forced misconstruction of this order, by those who may hereafter be employed in searching our records for cavils and informations against me, I think it proper to forbid, and protest against, the use of any fraudulent artifice or treachery to accomplish the end which I have prescribed; and as you alone are privy to the order, you will of course observe the greatest secrecy that it may not transpire: but I repeat my recommendation of it as one of the first and most essential duties of your office' (*An Authentic Copy of the Correspondence in India between the Country Powers and the honourable the East India Company's Servants,* 6 vols, London, 1787, II, 99–111). In his answer to the 16th Article of Impeachment, one of the 'Misdemeanours in Oude', in the autumn of 1787, Hastings admitted the instruction but stressed the conditional clauses at the beginning enjoining Bristow to act only if Almas had been guilty of a criminal offence (*Journals of the House of Lords,* XXXVIII, 47).

[4] Burke's motion on 30 July 1784 produced a stormy scene (*Parliamentary History,* XXIV, 1252–62). After calling Hastings 'the scourge of India' and accusing him of reducing the whole country to 'a waste, a howling desert', Burke was finally shouted down; the order of the day was read, and the debate stopped.

Tenure, on which people of distinction in that Country, held their honours, fortunes, and lives;—but never, either directly or indirectly, said one word of his Wife, children, parents, or relations; not having reason to know, that he had any Wife—nor having, receivd any report, made directly to me, or thro' the intervention of any other person, that should lead me to such a concluson. If I had mentiond any such thing it must have been a mere fiction of my own brain.[5] My motion, which stands on the Journals,[6] will verifye this; in which there is not a word of his Widow—nor of his Death—but solely of the *Order* to seize upon him, and to cause him to be put to death. The paper was given. It appeard just as I had represented. It was printed by order of the House. It excited a general indignation; and the Newspapers fell to work on that ground, to frame petitions from his Wife and Children &ca &c—The only favour I have to beg of my friends, is, that they will form their Judgments of me, by what the records of Parliament, and not the fictions of Newspapers, relate concerning me. In those records, they will find eleven pretty large Volumes;[7] *some* of which are *entirely* mine; and the materials of *all* of which I have diligently perused, and compared—and if on collation with the authorities at home or abroad, they find, that I have abused the Trust placed in me by Parliament, by recording rumours, instead of facts, taken from official Papers, or oral Evidence judicially given at a Committee Table, I shall be very ready to excuse them in supposing me to be, what, at my age, and with my very large experience, it is very unfit I should be, a man of a giddy credulous nature, apt to be run away with every idle rumour, and to commit myself rashly upon it. I certainly do not expect, (and I should be a fool if I did) that the reports of my conduct and Character, from the Bengal Gentlemen in London, to the Bengal Gentlemen at Calcutta, should be favourable to me. Mr Hastings has given their stations to several of them; and if they wish to imitate his Conduct—it is certain that they can never have me for

---

[5] Burke had been much incensed by the sensational treatment of the episode in the Opposition press; the *English Chronicle* for 31 July–3 August 1784, for example, printed a letter from the 'wife' of Almas begging for the life of the 'father of my children' and describing how Almas had been "immediately strangled'—phrases which must have amused those conversant with Indian affairs, since Almas was still alive and known to be a eunuch.

[6] 'Ordered, That there be laid before this House, Copies of all Letters, Instructions, or Minutes relative to the Seizure of the Person of a Native of India, resident in the Country of Oude, called Almass Ali Khan, and for putting the said Native to Death' (*Journals of the House of Commons*, XL, 386).

[7] *The Reports from the Select Committee, appointed to take into consideration the State of the Administration of Justice in the Provinces of Bengal, Bahar, and Orissa*. The First Report was delivered on 5 February 1782, the Eleventh on 18 and 20 November 1783. The Ninth and Eleventh Reports were printed in Burke's *Works* as his.

their friend. I have not fallen into any Traps laid by their Patron against my reputation; He was *very* near falling into a Trap, laid, not by me, but by himself; and from which he escaped, if he has escaped, by greater Trap mechanists than he has ever been, or can be.[8] I know him very well; though never having seen him, but in the dusk of one Evening, in a walk with you and your Uncle,[9] and in the midst of a squadron; I am sure I could not distinguish his face; but I know him in his actions and his writings. I likewise am an old acquaintance of Almas ali Khân of whom there is a great deal in the Papers before our Committee not yet reported—and on the whole, perhaps, there are not very many Gentlemen at Calcutta, so well informed of the State of the upper provinces, as I am; at least to a certain period—and that I am as little likely to fall into a gross Errour, as to persons or factors, as any of them. Your correspondent says, and does me only Justice in saying, that 'I do all the good in my power to the party I represent'. But I must beg leave to inform you, that in India affairs, I have not acted at all with any party from the beginning to the End. I know of no party which goes in a body upon this subject; they are all so distracted with personal considerations; and that perhaps may be among the causes of the Cry against myself in particular. I began this India Business in the administration of Lord North to which in all its periods [I was] in direct opposition, and acted in it with several of those who voted on his side of the House;[10] and against some of my own description, who have been among the Loudest against me on that account.[11] I have no party in this Business, my dear Miss Palmer, but among a set of people, who have none of your Lilies and Roses in their faces; but who are the images of the great Pattern as well as you and I. I know what I am doing; whether the white people like it or not. They hear, it seems, at Calcutta, that 'I am declined in popular favour'. That cannot be; for I never had any to lose. I never conformed myself to the humours of the people. I cannot say that opinion is indifferent to me: but I will take it, if I can, as my companion; never as my Guide. I see, that the same imputation of *intemperance* has been laid upon me by a Gentleman, at the meeting to remonstrate against

[8] Burke seems to imply that Hastings's misdeeds had forced the Coalition to plan measures for his punishment, from which he only escaped by alliance with the new Administration.

[9] Hastings had been in England between 1765 and 1769. Reynolds had painted his portrait in 1766 and it appears that the two men met socially on occasions during the Impeachment.

[10] Notably Charles Jenkinson and Lord Loughborough.

[11] Burke seems to be exaggerating. He was widely blamed for the consequences of Fox's India Bills, but it is difficult to think of any members of the Rockingham group who differed substantially with him over India 'in the administration of Lord North'.

Mr Pitts bill.[12] It is natural, for his connexions, that he should do so; and should take an occasion (from a measure I abhor, and certainly had no share in, except in expressing my detestation of it, and hoping, that no man who had a regard to his Character would suffer himself to be ballotted for the execution of it) to cast reflexions upon me, rather than upon those whose act he opposes. I have always wished, that no man should be prosecuted for offences, but before Tribunals known to the Law; and that when inquisitions were made, they should be into the actions, and not the fortunes, of persons under accusation.[13] I never found men guilty in the Mass; nor proceeded against their Estates, without knowing whether I had any fault to find with their proceedings. I found the general Tenour of the Companies internal and external System to be bad. The actors and advisers of that Evil System; I knew; I pointed out; and would have punishd if I could. But I never wished to make a previous Enquiry into what they were worth, in order to drive them to a composition for the delinquencies, I should presume from the degree of their power in ransoming themselves. There are those, who like neither the Methods of the present Ministry nor mine—but some lately returnd, I am sure, would greatly prefer that of the persons now in power to mine. They, therefore, support the Ministry and they persecute me, in the only way they can, by their calumnies. As to the Gentlemen who serve in India, as a *body*, I have nothing to say to them; because I have nothing to say to men in *bodies*. I attach myself to the guilty, where alone guilt can lie, *individually;* and if the Servants in general think, that my charges against Sir Elijah Impey,[14] Mr Hastings, and Mr Benfield,[15] are ill founded, or frivolous, it would give me a worse opinion of them than I have yet entertaind, who have a most sincere Esteem for several of them. Is not this, my dear Miss Palmer, a strange ⟨account⟩ to you, who care not three Straws for such things? But it is written *thro'* you, not *to* you; and I wish you to send it (blots and all, for I have written in a good deal of haste) to your Indian friend. It is, as a friend to you, I write it—from my real love to all of your Connexions; who, (if I had taken ways to power which I never could prevail on myself to

[12] On 25 July 1785 there was a meeting of protest at Calcutta against the 'inquisitional' clauses of Pitt's India Act. Burke joined in the general objections to the clause setting up a special tribunal for Indian offences.

[13] Clauses of Pitt's Act required Company Servants to deliver an inventory of their property on returning home. These clauses were never enforced, and were repealed in the Bengal Judicature Act of 1786.

[14] (1732–1809), Chief Justice of the Supreme Court at Calcutta.

[15] Paul Benfield (1741–1810), M.P., largest creditor of the Nawab of Arcot.

take) would have found some results from my goodwishes to some of them; as well as to other persons in India; I, whom you know, to be so *far from* a general Enemy, and persecutor of any description of men, that I would not hurt any Creature on earth, 'till I found him intollerable to every other Creature. My dearest Miss Palmer, God bless you; and send you friend home to you Rich and innocent; and may you long enjoy your own swe⟨et⟩ repose; and the love and esteem of all those who know how to value, elegance, Taste, abilities, and simplicity. I am ever

Your affectionate friend
EDM BURKE

Beconsfield Jany 19. 1786.

To HENRY DUNDAS—25 *March* 1787

Corr. (1958), V, 312–15

This is the first of a long series of letters between Burke and Henry Dundas, the most influential member of Pitt's cabinet on matters concerning India. By 25 March five Charges against Hastings had been passed, and there could be no real doubt that a trial would take place in the House of Lords. But, if the main crisis had been surmounted, Burke was keenly concerned about certain other problems, such as the timing of the final vote of impeachment and the extraction of evidence from reluctant Company Servants. To carry his points he required the support of Pitt, and to obtain this he corresponded with Dundas, the Minister primarily responsible for India affairs. Pitt and Dundas had voted for most of the Charges and were, in general, willing to give Burke the assistance he required. On certain issues, however, they disagreed with him. Pitt believed that the reputation of the House of Commons was at stake, and his interpretation of constitutional practice was sometimes stricter than Burke's.

Sir,

I have the honour of transmitting to you the Copies of Mr Andersons and Mr Middletons Letters to the Court of directors which I received from the Secretary to the India House.[1] Along with them I send a Copy of my own Letter to the Chairman written in consequence of this communication. You perceive the manner in which Anderson fights off. As to Hastings and the Rest, their answers probably are

[1] David Anderson (1751–1825), one of Hastings's most intimate and trusted friends, served as the Company's envoy to Mahadaji Sindhia of Gwalior and as President of the Bengal Committee of Revenue. In his letter to the Court of Directors of 23 March he said, 'as my Correspondence was very voluminous, and the Copies kept by me are interspersed in Books containing other extraneous Letters and Papers, it will necessarily require a very long Time before the Whole can be selected and copied'. On the same day Nathaniel Middleton replied that he had already handed over all correspondence carried on in his 'Official Capacity'.

not yet received; but I presume, when they come they will be of the same evasive Nature with that of Anderson.

The Business of the impeachment grows hourly to be more and more critical to the House of Commons, and to all the parties in it.[2] Two things things will be necessary; a strong case; and a full attendance. It will not be for the Interest of Justice, or of any of those engaged in our common Cause in this Instance, that upon any overnice distinctions, any point, strong in criminality, and in proof, should be given up. It is upon this principle, that the charges must be drawn; and if, on submitting them to Common Lawyers and Civilians the best we can procure, the impeachment on those points can be supported, I am sure, that not one Vote in the House of Commons will be gained by narrowing our Ground,[3] whilst we shall appear with a more feeble and unimpressive Case before the House of Lords than that which we are entitled to upon the original Merits. In order to bring about the great primary Object of a strong case, I wish that the Substance of the Charge should be either left to my own discretion, or, what I should like much better, that we should find some way of previously settling our plan of Conduct. It is but too obvious that a few words snatched behind the Speakers Chair can never put things on a clear and decisive footing. Publick consultations on our Legs in the House of Commons must be still more unoperative. This mode of proceeding can neither be right in itself, nor safe for the Business. I am obliged therefore to call on you for a full hours uninterrupted conversation, upon what is done already, and on what yet remains to do. The aspect of the House of Commons is enough to satisfye me, that very good reasons may exist in your Mind, why our conferences should not be very frequent or very publick. The time and place you will therefore settle according to your own conveniency. I have no Managements. If no arrangement can be made we shall be more distracted by occasional agreement, than by uniform difference. In a situation like ours, a temporary confidence, for Business and accommodation, is necessary to people otherwise adverse, but who happen to coincide in some one important point.

Without such communication, I shall certainly proceed with firmness and consistency, as far as my own Judgment can serve me for a

---

[2] On 22 March Burke announced that the House would be asked to approve the report from the Committee of the Whole House, who had been considering the Charges. He also let it be known that he hoped Hastings would be formally impeached at the same time.

[3] Burke was trying to refute Pitt's criticisms in the debate of 22 March, that the Charges were too vague (*Parliamentary History*, XXVI, 779).

guide. But I wish to clear myself of all part of the blame which may hereafter be imputed to me, for pursuing a Course, which any untoward Event may denominate imprudent and unadvised.

As to the material point of Numbers, means are using on our side to call in as many as the Lax discipline of oppositions can secure; and it is thought we shall muster pretty strong. On a view of various Lists, some who can judge on that Subject much better than I am able to do, are sanguine as to the Majority. With regard to your friends, you will excuse the Liberty I take in suggesting, that the Idea of wholly seperating the Man from the Minister, if carried substantially into effect, cannot fail of being infinitely mischeivous, however, the internal Circumstances of administration may make some appearance of that kind in some degree, or for some time, expedient; but even that appearance ought not to continue for too long a time, or to be at all overdone. For if Mr Pitt does not very speedily himself understand, and give others to understand likewise, that his personal Reputation is committed in this Business (as most manifestly it is) I am very far from venturing to answer for the ultimate Success, especially when I consider the constitution of the Late Minorities, combined with the political description of the absentees.[4] But I think it impossible, that all this should not be felt by you and Mr Pitt. I shall therefore only beg leave to add, that if ever there was a common National Cause totally seperated from Party it is this. A body of men, united in a close connexion of common guilt and common apprehension of danger in the moment, with a strong and just confidence of future power if they escape it, and possessd of a measure of wealth and influence which perhaps you yourself have not calculated at any thing like its just magnitude, is not forming, but actually formed in this Country. This faction is at present ranged under Hastings as an Indian leader; and it will have very soon, if it has not already, an English Leader of considerable enterprise and no contemptible influence.[5] If this faction should now obtain a Triumph it will be very quickly too strong for your Ministry. I will go further, and assert without the least shadow of hesitation, that they will turn out too strong for any one description of national Interest that exists, or, on any probable speculation that can exist in our time. Nothing can rescue the Country out of their

---

[4] James Duff, 2nd Earl Fife (1729–1809), M.P. for Elginshire, a close political associate of Dundas, wrote on 3 March, 'many of Mr Pitt's friends voted in the Minority, and none of what they call the Court People were present'.

[5] Probably a reference to Lord Shelburne (now Marquess of Lansdowne), whom Burke and his friends increasingly regarded as the leading figure among those favourable to Hastings.

hands, but our vigorous use of the present fortunate moment, which if once lost is never to be recoverd, of effectually breaking up this corrupt combination by effectually crushing the Leader and principal Members of the Corps. Their Triumph will not be over us, who are not the Keepers of the parliamentary force, but over you; and it is not you ⟨who⟩ will govern them, but they who will tyrannise over you and over the publick along with you. You have a vindictive set to deal with, and you have gone too far to be forgiven. I do not know, whether, setting aside the honour and justice of the Nation deeply involved in this Business, you will think the political Hints that I have given you to be of importance. Whatever they may be, you, who hold power, and are likely to hold it, are much more concerned in the question than I am. I have the honour to be with very great Respect

Sir your most obedient
and humble Servant
EDM BURKE

Gerard Street Soho
Sunday March 25. 178⟨7⟩.

To THOMAS BURGH—1 *July* 1787

Corr. (1958), V, 340–42

Burgh (1754–1832) was an Irish M.P. and a friend of Burke's.

My dear Sir,
  I am not a little flatterd by your very goodnatured and very agreeable Letter. I don't think that the Interest which general Humanity leads you to take in our proceedings loses any part of its merit by being seasond by private friendship. To me at least it ought not; and it does not. In my turn, I assure you, that the effect at Old-town[1] of what we do at Westminster is a valuable addition to our satisfaction in having so prosperously arrived at the first Stage of our long Indian Journey. Here our Caravan may take up its rest for a while, and our Camels may unload and drink. One great point we have secured. The House of Commons has cleared itself of the stain which its' Eastern Government has fixed upon this Nation. Perhaps we may consider it as some addition to the Success we have had, that this House of Commons, chosen for the express purpose of discrediting the last, has acquitted

---

[1] Burgh's country seat was at Old Town, County Kildare.

its predecessor with honour—and has justified by something much stronger than resolutions, the ground upon which the late Parliament stood and fell; and it has prosecuted the very delinquent which it was (very near expressly) chosen to protect and exalt. In other things this Parliament is faithful to the principles of its institution. In this respect it has certanly failed. What the House of Lords will do I am wholly unable to divine. If I did not trust, so much as I do, to the intrinsick radical Strength of the Cause, I might be alarmed at the known disposition of very many of the Judges. I am sorry to say that the most sacred part of that house is precisely that in which we can confide the least. The humility of the Bishops will leave the honour of vindicating the Christian religion to others. I speak of five or six of the leading men on that Bench[2]—of the rest we must hope the best, or persuade ourselves to do so. I hear much of an Intention to bind us down to certain unknown and unprecedented rules of pleading, and to an unparliamentary, and indeed impracticable strictness of Evidence. But I am not greatly affected with all these denunciations. We have had much boasting from that faction as a preliminary to every defeat which they sufferd in the House of Commons. But if they give us, what I think they cannot refuse, Westminster hall for the place of Trial, the Lords will not dare in the face of England and in the face of Europe, every peer rising individually in his place, to tell the Commons of Great Britain that they have brought to their Bar a false or frivolous accusation; nor, admitting the facts, in their judicial Capacity, will they venture to affirm, that those things which touch the natural feelings of mankind as the most enormous Crimes, are in their Lordships judgment meritorious actions—for merely innocent they certainly cannot be. I believe their Lordships to be bold and chivalrous personages—But I think, when it comes to the point, notwithstanding the kind of valour which many will wish to assume, they will feel some check at the moment, when they are called upon to act as men of principle and honour or to charge themselves with as heavy a loading of infamy as any with which a set of men ever sent down their names to posterity. With regard to their *present* dispositions, I have no doubt that the speculation in Ireland is right. I am far from holding your intelligence with regard to certain things lightly. You certainly are

---

[2] When Hastings's Impeachment ended in 1795, none of the bishops found him guilty on any of the Articles. William Markham, Archbishop of York, was a keen partisan of Hastings, perhaps influenced by his son William, who had been in India. John Warren (1730–1800), Bishop of Bangor, and Samuel Horsley (1733–1806), Bishop of Rochester, attended the Trial sufficiently assiduously to take part in the verdict.

often much better informed, than we are here in general, of the true
secret springs of action in the recesses of our politicks, and are far
better able to prognosticate the Issue of most of our Measures. But
in this point I rather hope your politicians will be found mistaken.
They are a little Shelburnized; and this may make them a little more
sanguine. You know, that Lord Lansdownes people supported Hastings with great Zeal, and with no small expectation of putting themselves at the head of the Indian Interests.[3] I have troubled you enough
on that Business. As to what you say of the politicks of Ireland, I have
no doubt that yourself and your connexions will always act the steady
and honourable part that becomes you. I could wish indeed that some
System existed to which such principles and conduct could be more
usefully referred. But in that respect we must rest contented; for I
believe after all, that Systems must arise out of Events, rather than
preexist and guide them as they happen; though the Latter would be
infinitely the most desirable. You will tell the Duke of Leinster how
true a Sense my Son and I have of his reception of us. You will of
Course put Mrs Burgh in mind of her Guests. She is the most respectable (I say this in defiance of her time of Life) and the most
amiable Woman I ever knew; fit for every situation of Life, the Sun-
shine or the Shade, for a princess or a Shepherdess. I wish something
might call you and her towards our Woods. I need not tell you how
happy Mrs Burke and all here would be to receive you both. Adieu
and believe me

My dear Sir
Your most affectionate
and obliged humble Servant
EDM BURKE

T. Burgh Esqr
Beconsfield   July 1. 1787.

To the EARL OF CHARLEMONT—10 *July* 1789

Corr. (1958), VI, 1–4

James Caulfeild, 1st Earl of Charlemont (1728–99), was one of Burke's oldest and
closest Irish friends. As the leading Opposition peer in Ireland he had played a

---

[3] There is little evidence for these suspicions of Lord Lansdowne's Indian designs. Jeremy
Bentham (1748–1832), who was close to Lansdowne, thought that he 'did not much care about
Hastings; but knowing the part the king took, . . . he professed to take Hastings' part'.

prominent part in the Regency crisis occasioned by George III's illness in the winter of 1788–89.

My dear Lord,

I have little to say of importance, and nothing to say that is pleasant: But I do not choose to let my friend Mr Nevile[1] depart without taking with him some token of my constant Love and respect to your Lordship. Your friendship and partiality are things too honourable and too dear to me for me to suffer them to escape from my memory; or from yours, if I can help it. Indeed I want consolations; and these are consolations to me of a very powerful and cordial operation. We draw to the End of our Business in this strange Session.[2] I have taken no part whatsoever in the *latter* part, though in the *former* I exerted myself with all the activity in my power, and which I thought the Crisis called for.[3] Nature has made a decision[4] which no art or Skill of parties could have produced. When that was done, I had nothing further to do. My time of Life, the length of my Service, and the Temper of the publick, renderd it very unfit for me to exert myself in the common routine of opposition: Turpe senex Miles.[5] There is a time of Life, in which, if a man cannot arrive at a certain degree of authority, derived from a confidence from the Prince or the people, which may aid him in his operations, and make him compass useful Objects without a perpetual Struggle, it becomes him to remit much of his activity. Perpetual failure, even tho' nothing in that failure can be fixed on the improper choice of the Object or on the injudicious choice of means, will detract every day more and more from a mans Credit until he ends without Success and without reputation. In fact a constant pursuit even of the best Objects, without adequate instruments detracts something from the opinion of a mans Judgment. This I think may be in part the Cause of the inactivity of others of our friends, who are in the Vigour of Life, and in possession of a great degree of Lead and authority.[6] I do not blame them; tho' I lament that state of the publick mind, in which the people can consider the exclusion of such Talents and such Virtues from their Service as a point gained to them. The only point

[1] Probably Richard Neville (*c.* 1745–1822), M.P. for Wexford in the Irish Parliament.
[2] Parliament was prorogued on 11 August, after a session in which the King's illness had deferred the transaction of normal business until March.
[3] Burke had been active in the Regency debates, but apparently made no speeches in the House of Commons between 11 February and 8 May, except in defence of himself against a petition from Hastings; since then he had spoken at least seven times.
[4] The King's recovery.
[5] Shame when an old man is a soldier; see Ovid, *Amores*, I, ix, 4.
[6] Fox is certainly the chief person alluded to here.

in which I can find any thing to blame in those friends, is their not taking the effectual means, which they certainly had in their power, of making an honourable retreat from the prospect of power into the possession of reputation, by an effectual defence of themselves, and of the great person whose honour is involved in theirs.[7] There was an opportunity, which was not made use of, for that purpose, and which could scarcely have failed of turning the Tables effectually on their adversaries, but I ought to stop; because I find I am getting into the fault common with all those who lose at any play, that of blaming their partners—and indeed nothing has hastend, at all times, the ruin of declining parties so much as their mutual quarrels and their condemnation of each other.

My particular province has been the East Indies.[8] This Session has shewn the power and predominance of the Queen in this Province. Hastings is known to be under her protection.[9] Last year her influence, though considerable, was not so decided; and the Lords did not look up to her so fully as since the time when the leading cabal in that house had reason in the Regency Business, to attach themselves to her Majesty as the head of their faction. Lord Kenyon takes the lead in the protection of Hastings;[10] and as he is a violent, hotheaded vulgar man, without the least Tincture of Liberality, or generous erudition, and though of some low acuteness, is void of any thing like enlarged Sense; and has no regard whatsoever for reputation any further than as it may be the means of procuring money, he scruples nothing in the way to any Objects he has to gratifye on the part of passion or of interest. The Chancellour never, without him, would have ventured to take the Steps which he has taken.[11] The Judges have not been

---

[7] Burke had strongly supported the proposal that the Prince of Wales should present a memorial to the King in defence of his conduct during the Regency crisis.

[8] The second session of the Impeachment of Warren Hastings, which began on 21 April and ended on 8 July, had been a frustrating one for Burke. The Managers had opened the Presents Article (the 6th Article of Impeachment), but during the whole session they had not been able to get beyond the first allegation in the Article, in which Hastings was accused of accepting three and a half *lakhs* of rupees (about £35,000) as bribes for various appointments made in 1772 at the Court of the Nawab of Bengal (Mubarak-ud-daula; reigned 1770–93). Hastings's Counsel had objected to nearly every significant piece of evidence offered by the prosecution, and most of their objections had been upheld.

[9] As Fanny Burney's diaries and letters show, the Court was extremely sympathetic to Hastings. But whatever the Opposition may have thought, there is no evidence which suggests that either the King or the Queen ever tried to influence the course of the Trial.

[10] Lloyd Kenyon, 1st Baron Kenyon, (1732–1802), Lord Chief Justice since 1788, had quarrelled with Burke at a session of the Hastings Trial on 10 June, when Burke termed a decison by the Lord Chancellor 'preposterous'; Kenyon called this expression 'disrespectful to the house'.

[11] Edward Thurlow, 1st Baron Thurlow (1731–1806), the Lord Chancellor, presided over the Impeachment. He was Hastings's closest ally among leading politicians and was regarded with deep suspicion by the Managers.

ashamed to quit the dignity of their situation, and instead of being good Judges to become bad adovacates, and to plead the Cause of the base fellow before us, as if they had been his feed Counsel. Their method was to prevent the appearance of the recorded documents of the India House on their Minutes—because they knew that if they had once appeard there his Condemnation must have been the infallible result.[12] For this purpose, they not only abandond the great golden Rule of Evidence, which is founded in the Nature and Circumstances of the Object to be proved, but even the most ordinary Course in their own municipal Tribunals—The Lords were pleased to charge upon them the infamy they were so desirous of incurring; and accordingly they, under the direction of Kennyon, have in reality tried the Cause.[13] However tho' they have caused much delay and suppressed much Evidence, there is ground enough to find him guilty on this the first of the eight heads of direct Bribery. I do not see how they can resist the matter which is actually before them.[14] We have rest, or something like it, for the present[15]—but depend upon it, I shall persevere to the End—and shall not add myself to the Number of bad examples in which the audacity and corruption of delinquents have wearied out the constancy of their prosecutors. We may not go thro' all the charges[16]—I fear it will be out of our power to do this—But we shall give a specimen of each great head of criminality—and then call for Judgment. This man has the impudence to complain of the delays he

[12] The most important pieces of evidence on the first allegation in the Presents Article were the examination of Maharaja Nandakumar (c. 1720–75), substantiating his accusation that the Governor General had taken bribes (11th Report of the Select Committee, Appendix I, *Reports from Committees of the House of Commons*, VI, 705–7), and an admission by Munni Begam (d. 1813; widow of Nawab Mir Jafar, 1691–1765), supported with various accounts and depositions, that she had given Hastings one and a half *lakhs* of rupees (11th Report, Appendix E, *op. cit.* VI, 627–57). Although these documents appeared on the Company's records, Hastings's counsel objected that they had not been properly authenticated, either by being taken on oath or by being taken in the presence of the accused. The Court upheld counsel's objections.

[13] Burke believed an impeachment should follow precedents from earlier impeachments, embodying 'the law and usage of parliament' and allowing some latitude in rules of evidence and pleading ('Report . . . from the Committee of the House of Commons, appointed to inspect the Lords' Journals', 30 April 1794, *Works*, Bohn, VI, 428; Little, Brown, XI, 9). Most lawyers, on the other hand, considered that previous impeachments had been dominated by their political backgrounds and that precedents from them should be rejected where they conflicted with contemporary legal standards. In the session of the Trial which had just ended, the Court had referred three disputed points on the admissibility of evidence to the judges, who, clearly applying contemporary standards, had decided all three against the prosecution (*ibid.* Bohn, VI, 524–5; Little, Brown, XI, 142–4). Burke was later to assert that the judges' answers to questions put to them were 'not to be regarded as declaratory of the law of parliament, but are merely consultory responses . . .' (*ibid.* Bohn, VI, 427; Little, Brown, XI, 8).

[14] When judgement was given on 23 April 1795, the Lords were unanimous in finding Hastings 'not guilty' on this particular section of the Presents Article.

[15] The Trial had been adjourned on 8 July until the next session of Parliament.

[16] They did not.

has caused and the hardships he suffers.[17] God knows, we who prosecute him, betrayed by those who employ us,[18] and traversd by the corruption of the Judges before whom we plead, are those who really suffer. I believe you will think so. So far as to a general View of my sole share of Business. As to the Politicks of Ireland as I see nothing in them very pleasant in the contemplation I do not wish to revive in your Mind what your best Philosophy is required to make tolerable. Enjoy your Marino and your amiable and excellent Family. These are comfortable Sanctuaries when more extensive views of society are gloomy and unpleasant or unsafe. May I request that your lordship and Lady Charlemount will think of us in your retreats as of those who love and honour you not the least amidst the general good opinion in which it is your happiness to live. Ever My dear Lord

> Your Lordships
> most faithful
> and most obedient humble Servant
> EDM BURKE

Gerard Street July 10. 1789.

To HENRY DUNDAS—[*circa* 17 *March* 1796]

Corr. (1958), VIII, 437–42

This incomplete draft of a letter was written after the House of Lords had acquitted Hastings to protest a decision by the Board of Control, under Dundas, to give Hastings an annuity of £4000.

(Private)

My dear Sir,

You will, I am sure, have the goodness to attribute every feeling I entertain, and every Step I take in this matter, and in all matters, to any thing in the world, rather than to a want of most sincere respect, regard, and gratitude to yourself. After this most true and most solemn assurance you will have the goodness to suffer me to say a few words on my particular situation; then on the subject matter of your Letter.

---

[17] Hastings had done so most recently in his address to the Court on 8 July (*Speeches of the Managers and Counsel*, II, p. xxviii). He had also submitted a formal petition on the subject to the House of Lords on 9 February (*Journals of the House of Lords*, XXXVIII, 349–50).

[18] Burke is referring to the vote of the House of Commons on 4 May, that his allegation that Hastings had 'murdered' Nandakumar 'by the hands of Sir Elijah Impey . . . ought not to have been spoken'.

As to myself, I have been employd by the House of Commons, to charge Mr Hastings, not with this or with that Crime, but with every Crime, which can deform and degrade human Nature, and which can vex and destroy, a great people committed by an act of Parliament to his Charge as well as with several acts of fraud of the meanest kind upon Individuals.

In the Execution of this Duty; there is no mode of persecution that for many years I have not endured. Amongst these instances of persecution I reckon amongst the least four or five attempts upon my Life, direct attempts under pretence of honour but to intimidate me by persons whom I could name to you.[1] Besides the anonymous, but not idle threats of assassination that from day to day were made upon me.

The Libels which were wrote upon me, and which most assuredly were paid for, from the poor empty purse of Mr Hastings because they were many if not all of them circulated Gratis, would amount to a tolerable Library.[2] This systematick obloquy has been carried into effect, by the whole Indean Interest, which is a great part of the Kingdom, of all Ranks classes and descriptions, spiritual and temporal; and it has had a real effect on my reputation and has procured for me a number of Enemies greater than probably ever man had and that with a degree of rancour and bitterness hitherto unexampled. You know with what Temper I endured this ill Behaviour to the House of Commons in my poor person, at the Bar of the House of Lords where besides the contumelious treatment I daily met with from the Court and particularly from a person of the highest rank in the church, and I believe the third of any in the Kingdom, I mean the Archbishop of York[3] the fortune of whose family was derived from the Spoil, which made the first article of charge voted by the House of Commons.[4]

This My dear Sir, I endured not with any prospect that the Court would do adequate Justice. I knew it too well. But I thought that common decency would have made them find some part of the Clause, and particularly the low and swindling part so as to keep some Terms

[1] During the course of the prosecution of Hastings several attempts had been made to obtain redress from Burke by individuals who thought that he had slandered them. At least three people, Sir Samuel Hannay, 3rd Baronet (c. 1742–90), in vindication of his brother the late Colonel Alexander Hannay (c. 1742–82), General John Caillaud (c. 1724–1812), and Captain John Grey (1760–1837), appear to have contemplated challenging Burke.

[2] Hastings appears to have spent £6408 on publicizing his cause during the Impeachment, of which £2400 was spent on newspapers.

[3] The Archbishop openly abused Burke in 1793.

[4] The Archbishop's son, Wiliam Markham (1760–1815), had been Resident at Benares from 1781 to 1783.

with their own reputation and that of the House of Commons. In that I was disappointed. The judgment of the House of Lords is a ⟨ . . . ⟩ against any man.

You know, that responsibility is not diffusive.—You know, that the Character of a persevering false accuser for 14 years together is the vilest and basest that can be conceived. With that, I am charged. I am charged with deluding the House of Commons into that Crime and causing expence to the publick of not less than perhaps four score thousand pound first and last. My reputation, as I might naturally expect, [is] of no importance to you: but you will I am sure be generous enough, to allow, that it may appear of Some importance to myself.

This is too large a part of English History not to hand down the parties concernd in an unjust charge with merited glory or infamy to the latest posterity. If it were otherwise the Example would be yet more terrible. The House of Commons has virtually pleaded guilty by not publishing under its authority, for the first time, the whole of the Trial. If they think that too chargeable, they might be satisfied with ⟨ . . . ⟩. If the House did me the Justice to get the Evidence on the side of the prosecution under the inspection of the Speaker to be methodized together with the Evidence rejected with remarks to point out the Nature and quality of the Testimony and the arguments, I should be perfectly satisfied. The other party cannot complain of this. They [are] free to publish—their Evidence, as they please, with such remarks as they see fitting, and even the Orations of their Counsel if they think proper,[5] or let the House of Lords print it in their publications.[6] I do not see why I have not a right to this protection as well [as] others who have gone before me.

Now as to the subject of your Letter. The Money voted to Mr Hastings is on a supposition, either that he is guilty or that he is innocent. His innocence must be supposed not only in the Sense of the court in which he is tried, which has nothing to do, but to acquit him; but he must be innocent in the Sense of those who direct him a compensation. This Pension is given directly as you state it and as truly it [is] in consequence of the prosecution and to indemnifye him

[5] In 1797 Hastings published a single volume entitled *Debates of the House of Lords on the evidence delivered in the trial of Warren Hastings*. It contained the debates of the House of Lords on their verdict, those of the East India Company on his annuity, and testimonials in his favour from India, with a frontispiece of Lord Thurlow.

[6] The House of Lords published no part of the Trial, except for the official *Minutes of Evidence*.

for the money he has borrowd to support him under it. It is cost given directly against the publick, as it is given on the East India Revenues whose Estate has a publick charge and a very large one.

He is then supposed innocent by those who prosecuted him. If he is; though I never knew the publick pay costs and damages before, yet I do not quarrel with the making of a precedent which has a foundation in Equity. It is not fit, as you observe, though thro the vilainy of our contemptible and oppressive institutions it happens daily, that an innocent man should die in Jail [acquitted] of a Count which secures him against penal Effects leaving opinion where it was, but that the accuser still believes in his own justice—to him he is guilty—and then the Question will be whether the prosecutor is obligatus in fore[7] conscientiously to make good to the person formally but in his judgment not rightly all that he has suffered. I believe not as to Mr Stone [who] was acquitted the other day. I do not think you in conscience bound to pay his Debts nor do I believe you will though he had been arrested and for ought you know may die in Jail. Very few acquitted at the old Baily (though their Crimes are not to be mentiond with those of Mr Hastings) whose Circumstances are not infinitely worse, and yet they never receive a Shilling of indemnity. Mr Barring[ton][8] (not half so low a Cheat) received no indemnity when he was once acquitted at the old Baily.

But then he is poor; and the Indemnity is not only as a payment of damnum emergens[9] damages to an injured man but as Charity to one distressed. This sore leg of his Poverty is an old affair and was laugh'd to scorn in the House of Commons. It is against all probability and depends wholly on his own assertion; and that of his Tools. If it be no matter of notoriety, well. Though such a way of acting on a claim for pecuniary aid never has been before heard of, I will allow that it may be right to give him eighty or an hundred thousand pound on his word, if he passes with you for a man of simplicity Candour and Truth. But my dear Sir, Mr Anstruther your Counsel,[10] will tell you, that it has been our Business under the authority of the House of [Commons] to prove and that we have proved that this man has

[7] Publicly obliged.

[8] George Barrington (1755–1804), the celebrated pickpocket, was acquitted at the Old Bailey on three occasions, 1784, 1785, 1789.

[9] A factual loss, a loss which can be evaluated in money.

[10] John Anstruther, Counsel to the Board of Control, had been one of the Managers of Hastings's prosecution.

been in constant habit of concealment, fraud falshood, falsification and even forgery. Such I call putting the Companies seal to bonds to himself for money not due to him. Is the word of a man so convicted to be taken to entitle himself to money. I will put the whole on this one Issue; if there is one single word of Truth in the paper of Mr Hastingss expences deliverd by him in a Petition to the House of Lords,[11] I will admit he is to be taken at his word for this great Sum of money, and for as much more as he chooses to demand.

It is true that the fact of Poverty in some testimonials may be so probable, that even the word of a known and corrupted Liar may be taken for it. I shall acquiesce in this too if such is the probability. Mr H. received by regular honest salary, thirty thousand pound a year; or thereabouts for fourteen years, that is to say 420,000. Now if this be the secret for making a man a beggar, I do not know how a state can contrive to make a man rich? But this is not all we have proved, and he has admitted and justified it, that in one year the year 1772 or 1773—he received three Lack of Roupee's[12] thirty six thousand pound from the Munni Begum,[13] and six thousand pound from the Company as one of the Committee of Circuit for an excursion to Morshedabad,[14] which with his emolluments as president (equal to the new Salary) makes for this one year—seventy two thousand pound. Another year he cheated (as it is proved and not denied but which he contended he had a right to do) the Rajah Nobkissen of Calcutta of thirty seven thousand pound—so that his emollument in that year was sixty seven thousand pound, and having pretended to borrow this money at an Interest, he has the benefit of it, without until it amounts to a sum at this day of ninety thousand pound and upwards. These two extra Sums of 42000 and 37000 making, 79,000 besides (the Interest) over and above his Salary is more than he pretends to be worth in the

[11] Hastings did not submit a financial statement to the House of Lords. Burke is no doubt referring to his statement to the Chairman of the East India Company.

[12] A *lakh* is a hundred thousand, a rupee about two shillings.

[13] In one of the accusations of the Presents Article it was alleged that Hastings had received three and a half *lakhs* of rupees (about £35,000) from Munni Begam (d. 1813), widow of the Nawab Mir Jafar (1691–1765). Hastings admitted that he had received one and a half *lakhs*, but denied any knowledge of the rest of the money.

[14] Hastings and several members of his Council formed themselves into a Committee of Circuit to tour parts of Bengal from June to September 1772. They visited Murshidabad, the capital of the young Nawab Mubarak-ud-daula (reigned 1770–93), where Hastings received Munni Begam's one and a half *lakhs*. The Managers discovered that the Governor was paid £5080 for 'contingent expences' in 1773.

World.[15] I say nothing here of the sums of which there are irrefutable presumptions of his having received. I speak only of those which he directly acknowleges

To FRENCH LAURENCE—28 *July* 1796

Corr. (1958), IX, 62–4

Bath July 28. 1796.

My dear Laurence

I thank you for employing the short moment you were able to snatch from being useful, in being kind and compassionate. Here I am in the last retreat of hunted infirmity. I am indeed aux abois: But, as thro the whole of a various and long Life I have been more indebted than thankful to Providence, so I am now. Singularly so, in being dismissed, as hitherto I appear to be so gently from Life and sent to follow, those who in Course ought to have followd me, whom, I trust, I shall yet, in some inconceivable manner, see and know; and by whom I shall be seen and known. But enough of this. However as it is possible that my stay on this side of the Grave, may be yet shorter, than I compute it, let me now beg to call to your Recollection, the solemn charge and trust I gave you on my Departure from the publick Stage.[1] I fancy I must make you the sole operator, in a work, in which, even if I were enabled to undertake it you must have been ever the assistance on which alone I could rely. Let not this cruel, daring, unexampled act of publick corruption, guilt, and meanness go down—to a posterity, perhaps as careless as the present race, without its due animadversion, which will be best found in its own acts and monuments. Let my endeavours to save the Nation from that Shame and guilt, be my monument; The only one I ever will have. Let every thing I have done, said, or written be forgotten but this. I have struggled with the

---

[15] In his statement of 22 September 1795 Hastings said that his fortune on his return from India amounted to no more than £65,313. As Burke points out, in view of his immense official income, to say nothing of unofficial profits, this figure strains credulity. Yet it appears to be more or less accurate. Hastings's scale of living in India was such that it consumed the greater part of his salary, and his spending in England before and after his return had been on an equally lavish scale.

[1] Burke was anxious that a history of the Impeachment of Warren Hastings should be prepared and published.

great and the little on this point during the greater part of my active Life; and I wish after my death, to have my Defiance of the Judgments of those, who consider the dominion of the glorious Empire given by an incomprehensible dispensation of the Divine providence into our hands as nothing more than an opportunity of gratifying for the lowest of their purposes, the lowest of their passions—and that for such poor rewards, and for the most part, indirect and silly Bribes, as indicate even more the folly than the corruption of these infamous and contemptible wretches. I blame myself exceedingly for not having employd the last year in this work and beg forgiveness of God for such a Neglect. I had strength enough for it, if I had not wasted some of it in compromising Grief with drowsiness and forgetfulness; and employing some of the moments in which *I* have been rouzed to mental exertion, in feeble endeavours to rescue this dull and thoughtless people from the punishments which their neglect and stupidity will bring upon them for their Systematick iniquity and oppression: but you are made to continue all that is good of me; and to augment it with the various rescources of a mind fertile in Virtues, and cultivated with every sort of Talent, and of knowlege. Above all make out the cruelty of this pretended acquittal, but in reality this barbarous and inhuman condemnation of whole Tribes and nations, and of all the abuses they contain. If ever Europe recovers its civilization that work will be useful. Remember! Remember! Remember!

It is not that I want you to sacrifice yourself blindly and unfruitfully, at this Instant. But there will be a Season for the appearance of such a Record; and it ought to be in Store for that Season. Get every thing that Troward[2] has.

Your kindness will make you wish to hear more particulars of me. To compare my State with that of the three first days after my arrival, I feel on the whole less uneasiness—But my flesh is wasted in a manner which in so short a time no one could imagine. My limbs look about to find the Rags that cover them. My strength is declined in the full proportion; and at my time of life new flesh is never supplied; and lost strength is never recoverd. If God has any thing to do for me here—here he will keep me. If not, I am tolerably resigned to his Divine pleasure. I have not been yet more than a day in condition to drink the Waters—but they seem rather to compose than to disorder my Stomach. My illness has not sufferd Mrs Burke to profit as she ought of this situation. But she will bathe to Night. Give Woodford

[2] Richard Troward (d. 1815), one of the prosecution solicitors.

a thousand kind remembrances. Please God, I shall write to him tomorrow. Adieu. Your ever true friend

EDM BURKE

Mrs Burke never forgets you nor what remains of poor William.[3]

---

[3] William Burke.

IRELAND

BURKE'S CONSTANT CAUSE

B URKE WAS NEVER FAR from his concern for Ireland, "The Country in which I was born," as he says matter-of-factly (letter to Windham, 1794). He was also raised and educated there, and in his first political post as secretary to William Gerard Hamilton, he had returned to Dublin in 1761 and had observed Irish politics from the inside. At the same time, though his concern for Ireland was constant, Ireland never became his primary occupation. He was a promoter, but not— like Henry Grattan, for example—a champion of Irish reform. And to Burke, "Irish reform" meant that the Irish must be initiated into the prescribed liberties of the British constitution, thus escaping the oppressions of British rule but not forsaking the protection of British sovereignty. In Burke's works one can find several celebrated paeans to the British constitution, but neither his letters nor his published writings are loaded with yearning sentiment for Hibernia. In leaving Ireland to study law in London, and in remaining there to make his way in politics, Burke had made his choice.

One item of Irish reform, the lifting of restrictions on Irish trade, was accomplished during the American war, when the legislated patterns of trade among Britain, Ireland, and the colonies were disrupted. We must leave to the Irish "the use of the natural faculties which God has given to them," said Burke to the Bristol merchants he then represented in Parliament, even if they compete with Britain (letters to Samuel Span; Harford, Cowles & Co.; Garrett Nagle, 1778). Burke undertook to read his constituents a brief lesson in modern economics: "It is the interest of the commercial world that wealth should be found everywhere." And if that did not suffice, then he would also repeat a lesson in the duties of a representative: "I had much rather run the risk of displeasing [my constituents] than of injuring them."

In the 1790s Burke became alarmed (as did the British government) at the growing strength of French revolutionary ideas ("Jacobinism") in Ireland. He feared that Irish Catholics might join with Protestant dissenters to rise against British rule, perhaps in conjunction with a French invasion (such an invasion was actually attempted in late 1796). It was imperative, therefore, to relax the laws dating from the previous century that put civil penalties on Catholics, for example depriving them of the franchise and of the right to own landed property, the "penal laws." "Ireland will be a strong Digue [dike] to keep out Jacobinism; or a broken bank to let it in" (letter to Windham, 1794). Just as Burke argued for religious toleration but also defended the established Church, so here we find him proposing relief for Catholics from the penal laws but also opposing the desire for Irish independence. Irish Catholics have a grievance, Burke agreed, but since Britain provides protection, "what Grievance has Ireland, as Ireland, to complain of with regard to Great Britain?" (letter to the Rev. Thomas Hussey, 1795). Although Burke considered Catholic Relief to be just, he supported it insofar as it would promote "concord of the citizens" and would prevent hatred of the few by the many that is the hallmark of Jacobinism (letter to Sir Hercules Langrishe, 1795). Here we see an instance of Burke's prudence guiding, and tempering, his sense of justice in the service of reform.

To SAMUEL SPAN—23 April 1778

Corr. (1958), III, 431–36

At the beginning of April the critical state of the American war, and French intervention in it, prompted urgent debates in Parliament. Burke, at this time M.P. for Bristol, supported a proposal for relaxing restrictions on Irish trade. Bristol merchants, fearing Irish competition, protested; Burke writes to defend his action.

To Samuel Span, Esq., Master of the Society of Merchants Adventurers of Bristol.

Sir,

I am honoured with your letter of the 13th, in answer to mine, which accompanied the resolutions of the House relative to the trade of Ireland.

You will be so good as to present my best respects to the Society, and to assure them, that it was altogether unnecessary to remind me of the interest of the constituents. I have never regarded anything else since I had a seat in parliament. Having frequently and maturely considered that interest, and stated it to myself in almost every point of view, I am persuaded, that, under the present circumstances, I cannot more effectually pursue it, than by giving all the support in my power to the propositions which I lately transmitted to the hall.

The fault I find in the scheme is,—that it falls extremely short of that liberality in the commercial system, which, I trust, will one day be adopted. If I had not considered the present resolutions merely as preparatory to bigger things, and as a means of showing, experimentally, that justice to others is not always folly to ourselves, I should have contented myself with receiving them in a cold and silent acquiescence. Separately considered, they are matters of no very great importance. But they aim, however imperfectly, at a right principle. I submit to the restraint to appease prejudice: I accept the enlargement, so far as it goes, as the result of reason and of sound policy.

We cannot be insensible cf the calamities which have been brought upon this nation by an obstinate adherence to narrow and restrictive plans of government. I confess I cannot prevail on myself to take them up, precisely at a time, when the most decisive experience has taught the rest of the world to lay them down. The propositions in question did not originate from me, or from my particular friends. But when things are so right in themselves, I hold it my duty, not to inquire from what hands they come. I opposed the American measures upon the very same principle on which I support those that relate to Ireland. I was convinced, that the evils which have arisen from the adoption of the former, would be infinitely aggravated by the rejection of the latter.

Perhaps gentlemen are not yet fully aware of the situation of their country, and what its exigencies absolutely require. I find that we are still disposed to talk at our ease, and as if all things were to be regulated by our good pleasure. I should consider it as a fatal symptom, if, in our present distressed and adverse circumstances, we should persist in the errors which are natural only to prosperity. One cannot indeed sufficiently lament the continuance of that spirit of delusion, by which, for a long time past, we have thought fit to measure our necessities by our inclinations. Moderation, prudence, and equity, are far more suitable to our condition, than loftiness, and confidence, and rigour. We are threatened by enemies of no small magnitude, whom, if we think fit, we may despise, as we have despised others; but they are enemies who can only cease to be truly formidable, by our entertaining a due respect for their power. Our danger will not be lessened by our shutting our eyes to it; nor will our force abroad be increased by rendering ourselves feeble and divided at home.

There is a dreadful schism in the British nation. Since we are not able to re-unite the empire, it is our business to give all possible vigour and soundness to those parts of it which are still content to be governed by our councils. Sir, it is proper to inform you, that our measures *must be healing.* Such a degree of strength must be communicated to all the members of the state, as may enable them to defend themselves, and to co-operate in the defence of the whole. Their temper too must be managed, and their good affections cultivated. They may then be disposed to bear the load with cheerfulness, as a contribution towards what may be called with truth and propriety, and not by an empty form of words, *a common cause.* Too little dependence cannot be had, at this time of day, on names and prejudices. The eyes of mankind are opened; and communities must be held together by an evident and solid interest. God forbid, that our conduct should demonstrate to the world, that Great Britain can, in no instance whatsoever, be brought to a sense of rational and equitable policy, but by coercion and force of arms!

I wish you to recollect, with what powers of concession, relative to commerce, as well as to legislation, his Majesty's commissioners to the united colonies have sailed from England within this week.[1] Whether these powers are sufficient for their purposes, it is not now my business to examine. But we all know, that our resolutions in favour of Ireland are trifling and insignificant, when compared with the concessions to the Americans. At such a juncture, I would implore every man, who retains the least spark of regard to the yet remaining honour and security of this country, not to compel others to an imitation of their

---

[1] The commissioners were empowered to make virtually any concessions short of independence; and the abandonment of parliamentary regulation was so far assumed as to be attacked by the Opposition as unconstitutional.

conduct; or by passion and violence, to force them to seek, in the
territories of the separation, that freedom, and those advantages, which
they are not to look for whilst they remain under the wings of their
ancient government.

After all, what are the matters we dispute with so much warmth?
Do we in these resolutions *bestow* anything upon Ireland? Not a shilling. We only consent to *leave* to them, in two or three instances, the
use of the natural faculties which God has given to them, and to all
mankind. Is Ireland united to the crown of Great Britain for no other
purpose, than that we should counteract the bounty of Providence in
her favour? And in proportion as that bounty has been liberal, that
we are to regard it as an evil, which is to be met with in every sort
of corrective? To say that Ireland interferes with us, and therefore
must be checked, is, in my opinion, a very mistaken and very dangerous principle. I must beg leave to repeat, what I took the liberty
of suggesting to you in my last letter, that Ireland is a country, in the
same climate, and of the same natural qualities and productions, with
this; and has consequently no other means of growing wealthy in
herself, or, in other words, of being useful to us, but by doing the
very same things which we do, for the same purposes. I hope that in
Great Britain we shall always pursue, without exception, *every* means
of prosperity; and of course, that Ireland *will* interfere with us in
something or other; for either, in order to *limit* her, we *must restrain*
ourselves, or we must fall into that shocking conclusion, that we are
to keep our yet remaining dependency under a general and indiscriminate restraint, for the mere purpose of oppression. Indeed, Sir, England and Ireland may flourish together. The world is large enough
for us both. Let it be our care not to make ourselves too little for it.

I know it is said, that the people of Ireland do not pay the same
taxes, and therefore ought not in equity to enjoy the same benefits
with this. I had hopes, that the unhappy phantom of a compulsory
equal taxation had haunted us long enough. I do assure you, that until
it is entirely banished from our imaginations, (where alone it has, or
can have, any existence,) we shall never cease to do ourselves the most
substantial injuries. To that argument of equal taxation, I can only
say,—that Ireland pays as many taxes as those, who are the best judges
of her powers, are of opinion she can bear. To bear more, she must
have more ability, and, in the order of nature, the advantage must
precede the charge. This disposition of things being the law of God,
neither you nor I *can* alter it. So that if you will have more help from
Ireland, you must *previously* supply her with more means. I believe

it will be found, that if men are suffered freely to cultivate their natural advantages, a virtual equality of contribution will come in its own time, and will flow by an easy descent through its own proper and natural channels. An attempt to disturb that course, and to force nature, will only bring on universal discontent, distress, and confusion.

You tell me, Sir, that you prefer an union with Ireland to the little regulations which are proposed in parliament. This union is a great question of state, to which, when it comes properly before me in my parliamentary capacity, I shall give an honest and unprejudiced consideration. However, it is a settled rule with me, to make the most of my *actual situation;* and not to refuse to do a proper thing, because there is something else more proper, which I am not able to do. This union is a business of difficulty; and, on the principles of your letter, a business impracticable. Until it can be matured into a feasible and desirable scheme, I wish to have as close an union of interest and affection with Ireland as I can have; and that, I am sure, is a far better thing than any nominal union of government.

France, and indeed most extensive empires, which by various designs and fortunes have grown into one great mass, contain many provinces that are very different from each other in privileges and modes of government; and they raise their supplies in different ways, in different proportions, and under different authorities; yet none of them are for this reason curtailed of their natural rights; but they carry on trade and manufactures with perfect equality. In some way or other the true balance is found, and all of them are properly poised and harmonized. How much have you lost by the participation of Scotland in all your commerce?[2] The external trade of England has more than doubled since that period; and I believe your internal (which is the most advantageous) has been augmented at least fourfold. Such virtue there is in liberality of sentiment, that you have grown richer even by the partnership of poverty.

If you think that this participation was a loss, commercially considered, but that it has been compensated by the share which Scotland has taken in defraying the public charge—I believe you have not very carefully looked at the public accounts. Ireland, Sir, pays a great deal more than Scotland; and is perhaps as much and as effectually united to England as Scotland is. But if Scotland, instead of paying little, had paid nothing at all, we should be gainers, not losers, by acquiring the hearty co-operation of an active, intelligent people, towards the

[2] After the Parliamentary Union of 1707.

increase of the common stock; instead of our being employed in watching and counteracting them, and their being employed in watching and counteracting us, with the peevish and churlish jealousy of rivals and enemies on both sides.

I am sure, Sir, that the commercial experience of the merchants of Bristol will soon disabuse them of the prejudice, that they can trade no longer, if countries more lightly taxed are permitted to deal in the same commodities at the same markets. You know that, in fact, you trade very largely where you are met by the goods of all nations. You even pay high duties on the import of your goods, and afterwards undersell nations less taxed, at their own markets; and where goods of the same kind are not charged at all. If it were otherwise, you could trade very little. You know, that the price of all sorts of manufacture is not a great deal enhanced (except to the domestic consumer) by any taxes paid in this country. This I might very easily prove.

The same consideration will relieve you from the apprehension you express with relation to sugars, and the difference of the duties paid here and in Ireland. Those duties affect the interior consumer only; and for obvious reasons, relative to the interest of revenue itself, they must be proportioned to his ability of payment; but in all cases in which sugar can be an *object of commerce*, and therefore (in this view) of rivalship, you are sensible, that you are at least on a par with Ireland. As to your apprehensions concerning the more advantageous situation of Ireland for some branches of commerce, (for it is so but for some,) I trust you will not find them more serious. Milford Haven, which is at your door, may serve to show you, that the mere advantage of ports is not the thing which shifts the seat of commerce from one part of the world to the other. If I thought you inclined to take up this matter on local considerations, I should state to you, that I do not know any part of the kingdom so well situated for an advantageous commerce with Ireland as Bristol; and that none would be so likely to profit of its prosperity as our city. But your profit and theirs must concur. Beggary and bankruptcy are not the circumstances which invite to an intercourse with that or with any country; and I believe it will be found invariably true, that the superfluities of a rich nation furnish a better object of trade than the necessities of a poor one. It is the interest of the commercial world that wealth should be found everywhere.

The true ground of fear, in my opinion, is this: that Ireland, from the vicious system of its internal polity, will be a long time before it can derive any benefit from the liberty now granted, or from any thing else. But, as I do not vote advantages in hopes that they may not be enjoyed, I will not lay any stress upon this consideration. I rather wish, that the parliament of Ireland may, in its own wisdom, remove these impediments, and put their country in a condition to avail itself of its natural advantages. If they do not, the fault is with them, and not with us.

I have written this long letter, in order to give all possible satisfaction to my constituents, with regard to the part I have taken in this affair. It gave me inexpressible concern to find, that my conduct had been a cause of uneasiness to any of them. Next to my honor and conscience, I have nothing so near and dear to me as their approbation. However, I had much rather run the risk of displeasing than of injuring them;— if I am driven to make such an option. You obligingly lament, that you are not to have me for your advocate; but if I had been capable of acting as an advocate in opposition to a plan so perfectly consonant to my known principles, and to the opinions I had publicly declared on a hundred occasions, I should only disgrace myself, without supporting, with the smallest degree of credit or effect, the cause you wished me to undertake. I should have lost the only thing which can make such abilities as mine of any use to the world now or hereafter; I mean that authority which is derived from an opinion, that a member speaks the language of truth and sincerity; and that he is not ready to take up or lay down a great political system for the convenience of the hour; that he is in parliament to support his opinion of the public good, and does not form his opinion in order to get into parliament, or to continue in it. It is in a great measure for your sake, that I wish to preserve this character. Without it, I am sure, I should be ill able to discharge, by any service, the smallest part of that debt of gratitude and affection which I owe you for the great and honourable trust you have reposed in me.

> I am, with the highest regard and esteem,
> Sir,
> Your most obedient and humble Servant,
> E.B.

Beaconsfield, April 23, 1778.

To HARFORD, COWLES AND CO.—2 *May* 1778

Corr. (1958), III, 440–44

On 27 April Messrs Harford, Cowles and Company, iron merchants—the firm of Joseph Harford, one of Burke's chief supporters in Bristol—had written explaining that they might be adversely affected by the Bill favouring Irish trade, and mentioning the great alarm of merchants and manufacturers. 'It is considered a great Misfortune', they wrote, 'that one of their Members on whom they placed their chief dependance should at so critical a moment have taken so active and decided a part against his Constituents, and sorry we are, if they have given him any Just cause for so doing'.

Gentlemen

It gives me most sensible Concern to find, that my Vote on the Resolutions relative to the Trade of Ireland, has not been fortunate enough to meet with your approbation. I have explained at large the Grounds of my Conduct on that occasion in my Letters to the Merchants Hall. But my very sincere regard and Esteem for you will not permit me to let the matter pass without an explanation, which is particular to yourselves, and which I hope, will prove satisfactory to you.

You tell me, that the Conduct of your late Member,[1] is not much wonder'd at; but you seem to be at a loss to account for mine; and you lament, that I have taken so decided a part *against* my Constituents.

This is rather an heavy imputation. Does it then really appear to you, that the propositions, to which you refer, are on the face of them so manifestly wrong, and so certainly injurious to the Trade and Manufactures of Great Britain, and particularly to yours, that no Man could think of proposing, or supporting them, except from resentment to you, or from some other oblique Motive? If you suppose your late Member, or if you suppose me, to act upon other reasons than we choose to avow, to what do you attribute the Conduct of the *other* Members, who, in the beginning, almost unanimously adopted these Resolutions? To what do you attribute the strong part taken by the Ministers, and along with the Ministers, by several of their most declared opponents? This does not indicate a Ministerial Jobb; a party design; or a provincial or local purpose. It is therefore not so absolutely clear, that the Measure is wrong, or likely to be injurious to the true Interests of any place, or any person.

The reason, Gentlemen, for taking this step, at this time, is but too obvious, and too urgent. I cannot imagine, that you forget the great

---

[1] Robert Nugent, 1st Viscount Clare (1709–88), M.P. for Bristol until 1774.

War, which has been carried on with so little success (and as I thought with so little Policy) in America; or that you are not aware of the other great Wars, which are impending. Ireland has been called upon, to repel the attacks of Enemies of no small power, brought upon her by Councils, in which she has had no share.[2] The very purpose and declared object of that Original War, which has brought other Wars, and other Enemies on Ireland, was not very flattering to her dignity, her Interest, or to the very principle of her Liberty. Yet she submitted patiently to the Evils she suffered from an attempt, to *subdue* to your obedience, Countries, whose very Commerce was not open to her. America was to be conquered, in order that Ireland should *not* Trade thither; whilst the miserable Trade, which she is permitted to carry on to other places, has been torn to pieces in the struggle. In this situation, are we neither, to suffer her to have any real Interest in our quarrel; or to be flatter'd with the hope of any future means of bearing the Burthens, which she is to incurr in defending herself against Enemies which we have brought upon her?

I cannot set my face against such Arguments. Is it quite fair to suppose, that I have no other Motive for yielding to them, but a desire of acting *against* my Constituents? It is *for* you, and *for* your Interest, as a dear, cherished, and respected part, of a valuable whole, that I have taken my share in this question. You do not; you cannot suffer by it. If Honesty be true policy with regard to the transient Interest of Individuals; it is much more certainly so with regard to the permanent interests of communities. I know, that it is but too natural for us to see our own *certain* ruin, in the *possible* prosperity of other people. It is hard to persuade us, that every thing which is *got* by another is not *taken* from ourselves. But it is fit, that we should get the better of these Suggestions, which come from what is not the best and soundest part of our Nature; and that we should form to ourselves a way of thinking, more rational, more just, and more religious. Trade is not a limited thing; as if the objects of mutual demand and consumption, could not stretch beyond the bounds of our Jealousies. God has given the Earth to the Children of Man; and he has undoubtedly, in giving it to them, given them what is abundantly sufficient for all their Exigencies; not a scanty, but a most liberal provision for them all. The Author of our Nature has written it strongly in that Nature, and has promulgated the same Law in his written Word, that Man shall eat his Bread by his Labour; and I am persuaded, that no man,

[2] In April there was 'great alarm in Ireland on apprehensions of a French war and invasion, and great zeal thence' (Horace Walpole, *Journals*, II, 168).

and no combination of Men, for their own Ideas of their particular profit, can, without great impiety, undertake to say, that he *shall not* do so; that they have no sort of right, either to prevent the Labour, or to withhold the Bread. Ireland having received no *compensation*, directly or indirectly, for any restraints on their Trade, ought not, in Justice or common honesty, be made subject to such restraints. I do not mean to impeach the Right of the Parliament of Great Britain to make Laws for the Trade of Ireland. I only speak of what Laws it is right for Parliament to make.

It is nothing to an oppressed people, to say, that in part they are protected at our Charge. The Military force, which shall be kept up in order to cramp the natural faculties of a people, and to prevent their arrival to their utmost prosperity, is the instrument of their Servitude, not the means of their protection. To protect Men is to forward, and not to restrain, their improvement. Else what is it more than to avow to them and to the world, than that you guard them from others, only to make them a prey to yourself. This fundamental Nature of protection does not belong to free, but to all Governments; and is as valid in Turkey as in Great Britain. No Government ought to own it exists for the purpose of checking the prosperity of its people; or that there is such a principle involved in its policy.

Under the impression of these Sentiments, (and not as wanting every attention to my Constituents, which affection, and gratitude could inspire) I voted for these Bills which give you so much trouble. I voted for them, not as doing compleat Justice to Ireland; but as being something less unjust, than the general prohibition which has hitherto prevailed. I hear some discourse, as if, in one or two paltry duties on Materials, Ireland had a preference; and that those who set themselves against this Act of scanty Justice, assert that they are only contending for an *equality*. What Equality? Do they forget, that the whole Woollen Manufacture of Ireland, the most extensive and profitable of any, and the natural Staple of that Kingdom, has been in a manner so destroyed by restrictive Laws of *ours*, and (at our persuasion, and on our promises) by restrictive Laws of *their own*, that in a few years, it is probable, they will not be able to wear a Coat of their own Fabrick?[3] Is this Equality? Do Gentlemen forget, that the understood faith, upon which they were persuaded to such an unnatural Act, has not been kept; but a Linen Manufacture has been set up and highly encouraged against them? Is this Equality? Do they forget, the State of the Trade of

---

[3] The seventeenth-century prohibition of the export of Irish woollens had been explicitly retained in the new proposals.

Ireland in Beer,[4] so great an Article of consumption, and which now
stands in so mischievous a position with regard to their Revenue, their
Manufacture, and their Agriculture? Do they find any equality in all
this? Yet if the least step is taken towards doing the common justice
in the lightest Articles for the most limited Markets, a Cry is raised
as if we were going to be ruined by partiality to Ireland.

Gentlemen, I know, that the deficiency in these Arguments, is made
up (not by you but by others) by the usual resource on such occasions,
the confidence in Military force and superior powers. But that ground
of confidence, which at no time was perfectly just, or the avowal of
it tolerably decent, is at this time very unseasonable. Late experience
has shewn, that it cannot be altogether relied upon; and many if not
all our present difficulties have arisen from putting our Trust in what
may possibly fail; and if it should fail, leaves those who are hurt by
such a reliance, without Pity. Whereas Honesty, and justice, Reason
and equity, go a very great way in securing prosperity to those who
use them; and in case of failure, secure the best retreat and the most
honorable consolations.

It is very unfortunate, that we should consider those as Rivals, whom
we ought to regard as fellow labourers in a common Cause. Ireland
has never made a single step in its progress towards prosperity, in
which you have not had a share and perhaps the greatest Share in the
Benefit. That progress has been chiefly owing to her own natural
disadvantages, and her own Efforts; which, after a long time, and by
slow degrees, have prevailed in some measure over the Mischeivous
Systems, which have been adopted. Far enough she is still from having
arrived even at an ordinary state of perfection; and if our jealousies
were to be converted into Politicks as systematically as some would
have them, the Trade of Ireland would vanish out of the System of
Commerce. But believe me, if Ireland is beneficial to you, it is so, not
from the parts in which it is restrained; but from those in which it is
left free, though not unrivalled. The greater its freedom the greater
must be your advantage. If you should lose in one way, you will gain
in twenty.

Whilst I remain under this unalterable and powerful conviction,
you will not wonder at the *decided* part I take. It is my custom so to
do, when I see my way clearly before me; and when I know that I
am not misled by any passion or any personal Interest; which in this
Case, I am very sure, I am not. I find that disagreeable things are

---

[4] Irish trade in beer and salt was subject to severe restrictions.

circulated among my constituents; and I wish my Sentiments, which form my justification, may be equally general with the Circulation against me. I have the honour to be with the greatest regard and Esteem

Gentlemen
your most Obedient
and humble Servant

Westminster May 2d 1778   EDM BURKE

To GARRETT NAGLE—25 *August* 1778

Corr. (1958), IV, 18–9

Garrett Nagle (d. *c.* 1791) of Ballyduff, County Cork, and Killarney, County Kerry, was Burke's first cousin.

My dear Garrett,

Your Letter came upon me at the very instant that I was sitting down to write to you. I had deferred it, until I should be able to congratulate you on the success of the important Bill which had been for some time depending in the Parliament of Ireland. I now wish you joy of that success, with the most cordial satisfaction. Be assured, that no Event of my time has given me such pleasure. The plan of relief indeed is not quite so large and liberal as that adopted in England upon the same subject: But still it is a great acquisition.[1] It is highly beneficial in itself; and it contains a principle, which in time will extend further; and which cannot fail, by a judicious use of opportunities, of putting you upon as good a footing, as a people of a persuasion different from that of the State, can reasonably expect. You may now raise up your heads, and think yourselves men. The mark is taken off. You are now for the first time acknowleged as Subjects, and protected as such. Laws indeed cannot make men rich or happy. That they must do for themselves—But the Law now leaves their Natural faculties free. Whatever inheritance has come to them from their Ancestors is not made any longer the instrument of distracting the peace and destroying the Credit of their families. Those who have nothing but the *means* of acquiring Substance, their Industry, Skill, and good œconomy, have those *means* left free. When one considers the force of powerful and inveterate prejudice, which must naturally operate against

---

[1] Irish Catholics were to be allowed to take leases for 999 years. This was a modification of the original intention to allow them to acquire freehold property, a privilege conferred on English Catholics by the Acts which provided the precedent for the Irish Bill.

your relief, and the many Errours, to call them by no worse a name, into which some of those who had the conduct of this Business have fallen, it is rather to be wonderd how so much has been done, than how no more came to be obtaind. If some anger appears in many upon this occasion; remember, it is pleasanter to endure the rage of disappointment, than the insolence of Victory. There will be much arming, much blustering, and many pretended fears and apprehensions on this occasion. But I recommend it to you, and all you converse with, to bear all such things with good humour and humility. It will all speedily pass over. It is only the natural vent and purging off of an old distemper. It is your Interest at this time to shew, that the favour you have received has produced the best Effects imaginable; that you are truly attached to the constitution which has opend its doors to receive you; that you are modest and placable to those whose opinions have induced them to oppose your relief; and that you are thoroughly grateful to those whose humanity and enlarged Sentiments have made that opposition fruitless. . . .

To ANTHONY DERMOTT—17 *August* [1779]

Corr. (1958), IV, 120–21

Anthony Dermott (d. 1784) had sent a gift of three hundred guineas from the Catholic Committee in Dublin to Burke in appreciation of his work on behalf of the Catholic cause in Ireland. Burke writes to refuse.

Sir,

I am favourd with your Letter of the ninth of this Month. The Substance of it had been communicated to me a post or two ago by my friend Dr Curry.[1] I wrote my answer without a moments delay; but I am sorry to find that it could not get to his hands in time to prevent an Offer, of which I cannot possibly avail myself consistently with my manner of thinking and feeling, although it was I make no doubt very kindly intended on your part, and though it is very honourable to me, so far as it is a mark of your approbation. I therefore beg leave to return you the Bill as I receivd it, with my best acknowlegements to you and to the Gentlemen you act for, for your partial and obliging opinion of my Endeavours to serve you. If I am so happy as to have contributed in the smallest degree, to the relief of so large and respectable a part of my Countrymen, as the Roman Catholicks

[1] Dr. John Curry (*c.* 1702–80).

of Ireland, from oppressions, that I always thought not only very grievous to them, but very impolitick with regard to the State, I am more than enough rewarded. If I were to derive any advantage whatsoever, beyond what comes to my share in the general prosperity of the whole, from my Endeavours in this way, I should lose all the relish I find in them; and the whole Spirit which animates me on such occasions. My Principles make it my first, indeed almost my only earnest wish, to see every part of this Empire, and every denomination of men in it happy and contented, and united on one common bottom of equality and justice. If that Settlement were once made, I assure you, I should feel very indifferent about my particular portion, or my particular situation, in so well constituted a Community. It was my wish, that the Objects of such a settlement should be much more extensive, and gone, not only beyond the Irish Sea, but beyond the Atlantick Ocean. But since it has happend otherwise, I hope we shall be wise enough to make the most of what is left. Whenever things are ripe for any Judicious Steps to be taken in so salutary a Plan, you may be assured, that my Principles will always lead me to take a very active part in promoting your Ease and happiness and not the less active because I can never have any private Interest in it. I have the honour to be with great regard and Esteem

Sir
Your most obedient
and humble Servant
EDM BURKE.

Augst 17 Beaconsfield

To JOHN MERLOTT—4 April 1780

Corr. (1958), IV, 223–25

In April 1778 Burke had displeased his constituents by supporting the limited concessions then made to Ireland in commercial matters. In February 1779 he had again supported proposals to free Irish trade from restrictions imposed on it by British legislation. The Government's complete surrender to Ireland on this question had demonstrated Burke's foresight, but had not restored his reputation in Bristol. In this letter to John Merlott (d. 1785), one of his supporters, Burke restates his position. As a sugar refiner Merlott belonged to an economic interest especially hostile to the liberalization of Irish trade.

Dear Sir,

I am very unhappy to find that my conduct in the business of Ireland, on a former occasion, had made many to be cold and indifferent, who would otherwise have been warm, in my favour. I really thought that events would have produced a quite contrary effect; and would have proved to all the inhabitants of Bristol, that it was no desire of opposing myself to their wishes, but a certain knowledge of the necessity of their affairs, and a tender regard to their honour and interest, which induced me to take the part which I then took. They placed me in a situation which might enable me to discern what was fit to be done on a consideration of the relative circumstances of this country and all its neighbours. This was what you could not so well do yourselves; but you had a right to expect that I should avail myself of the advantage which I derived from your favour. Under the impression of this duty and this trust I had endeavoured to render, by preventive graces and concessions, every act of power at the same time an act of lenity;—the result of English bounty and not of English timidity and distress. I really flattered myself that the events which have proved beyond dispute the prudence of such a maxim would have obtained pardon for me, if not approbation. But if I have not been so fortunate, I do most sincerely regret my great loss; with this comfort, however, that, if I have disobeyed my constituents, it was not in pursuit of any sinister interest, or any party passion of my own, but in endeavouring to save them from disgrace, along with the whole community to which they and I belong. I shall be concerned for this, and very much so; but I should be more concerned if, in gratifying a present humour of theirs, I had rendered myself unworthy of their former or their future choice. I confess, that I could not bear to face my constituents at the next general election, if I had been a rival to Lord North in the glory of having refused some small, insignificant concessions, in favour of Ireland, to the arguments and supplications of English members of parliament; and in the very next session, on the demand of 40,000 Irish bayonets, of having made a speech of two hours long to prove that my former conduct was founded upon no one right principle either of policy, justice, or commerce. I never heard a more elaborate, more able, more convincing, and more shameful speech.[1] The debater obtained credit; but the statesman was disgraced

---

[1] Delivered on 13 December 1779 (*Parliamentary History*, XX, 1272–85).

for ever. Amends were made for having refused small but timely
concessions by an unlimited and untimely surrender, not only of every
one of the objects of former restraints, but virtually of the whole
legislative power itself, which had made them. For it is not necessary
to inform you that the unfortunate parliament of this kingdom did
not dare to qualify the very liberty she gave of trading with her *own*
plantations, by applying, of her *own* authority, any one of the commercial regulations to the new traffic of Ireland, which bind us here
under the several acts of navigation. We were obliged to refer them
to the parliament of Ireland, as conditions; just in the same manner
as if we were bestowing a privilege of the same sort on France and
Spain, or any other independent power, and, indeed, with more studied caution than we should have used, not to shock the principle of
their independence. How the minister reconciled the refusal to reason,
and the surrender to arms, raised in defiance of the prerogatives of
the Crown to his master, I know not; it has probably been settled, in
some way or other, between themselves. But however the king and
his ministers may settle the question of his dignity and his rights, I
thought it became me, by vigilance and foresight, to take care of yours;
I thought I ought rather to lighten the ship in time than expose it to
a total wreck. The conduct pursued seemed to me without weight or
judgment, and more fit for a member for Banbury than a member for
Bristol.[2] I stood therefore silent with grief and vexation on that day
of the signal shame and humiliation of this degraded king and country.
But it seems the pride of Ireland in the day of her power was equal
to ours, when we dreamt we were powerful too. I have been abused
there even for my silence, which was construed into a desire of exciting
discontent in England. But, thank God, my letter to Bristol was in
print;[3]—my sentiments on the policy of the measure were known and
determined, and such as no man could think me absurd enough to
contradict. When I am no longer a free agent, I am obliged in the
crowd to yield to necessity; it is surely enough that I silently submit
to power; it is enough that I do not foolishly affront the conqueror;
it is too hard to force me to sing his praises whilst I am led in triumph
before him; or to make the panegyric of our own minister, who would
put me neither in a condition to surrender with honour, nor to fight
with the smallest hope of victory. I was, I confess, sullen and silent
on that day; and shall continue so until I see some disposition to
inquire into this and other causes of the national disgrace. If I suffer

[2] Banbury elected one member: Lord North.
[3] The letter referred to is the official letter to Samuel Span as Master of Merchants' Hall.

in my reputation for it in Ireland, I am sorry; but it neither does nor can affect me so nearly as my suffering in Bristol, for having wished to unite the interests of the two nations in a manner that would secure the supremacy of this.

Will you have the goodness to excuse the length of this letter. My earnest desire of explaining myself in every point which may affect the mind of any worthy gentleman in Bristol is the cause of it. To yourself, and to your liberal and manly notions, I know it is not so necessary. Believe me,

My dear Sir,
Your most faithful and obedient humble servant,
EDMUND BURKE.

Beaconsfield, April 4th, 1780.
To John Merlott, Esq. Bristol.

To RICHARD BURKE, JR—[post 3 January 1792]

Corr. (1958), VII, 8–12

A letter to his son on the condition of Catholics in Ireland. Since 1760 they had been represented by a General Committee to obtain a further relaxation of the penal laws (laws that attached penalties to being Catholic), and in September 1791 it appointed Richard Burke, Jr. as its agent in England, being well aware that this was the best way to get Edmund Burke's active support. Pitt and Dundas were favorable to a relaxation of the penal laws because they feared that without it Irish Catholics might turn to the principles of the French Revolution. When they decided to accede to most of the Catholic proposals, Richard went to Ireland to consult with his principals, and to draw up a petition to the Irish House of Commons.

My ever Dear Richard, We are not to tell you, how thankful we were to you for your Letter from your fireside at Holyhead. It is true we had no anxiety about the Weather which with you was so tempestuous. It was here as quiet a Night with a fine gentle steady Easterly wind as possible. Thank God however you were on shore. I trust the same providence will return you to our prayers with Safety, health, and success.

I find what pains the Irish Government has taken to perplex itself. I rather wonder that before they took these Steps that they did not previously enquire into the Temper and opinions of those in Office here.[1] As to some Gentlemen amongst the Catholicks, I should be

---

[1] The Irish Government was in fact well aware that both Dundas and Pitt favoured the Catholic claims.

rather surprised if they did not act just as they have done upon any
signification from power. Those of any fortune, are persons of antient
and respectable families, though none of them have of late, and many
of them never, illustrated their Names. Their Education, connexions,
Habits and sole Views of preferment have been in France and Germany, where their Pedigrees alone afforded them any hope of distinction. They were therefore more proud of their quality of Gentlemen,
than any of those could be, who had hopes from any thing else. On
the other hand, the Majority of their own Communion, who remaind
in the Kingdom, being doomed to an Abject Servitude; and by the
Laws, (so far as laws could operate in that Case) sentencd to Beggary,
The distinction, between the old Gentlemen who still retaind their
religion and Estates, and the commonality of that Religion and the
middle sort, was without all comparison greater than between people
in the same ranks among Protestants. To my knowlege (at least in my
time) they perfectly despised their Brethren, and would have been
glad at any time, if any thing, without extremely wounding their
Conscience, or perhaps of rebounding on themselves, could have been
contrived to discriminate them from the rest of the description, even
at the expence of those from whom they were so seperated, they would
have desired nothing better. As a new race of Catholicks have risen
by their industry, their abilities, and their good fortune, to considerable opulence, and of Course to an independent Spirit, the old
Standard Gentlemen were still less disposed to them, (as rivals in
consideration and importance) than to the old Catholicks who were
only poor struggling Citizens, farmers, or Tradesmen. They despised
them less; but they hated them more. If this Spirit should continue,
I should not be at all amazed, tho' extremely concernd to find it so,
if they should choose of the two rather to remain under their present
disqualifications, than partake in the advantages of Freemen, with
those they ought to cherish, love, protect, and cooperate with in every
thing rationally proposed for their common benefit. If you happen to
fall in with any Gentleman, who is in the situation without acquiring
the Character I have described, try to get him to make the rest sensible
of the mischief which must arise to them from cherishing any longer
this mistaken Spirit so perfectly contrary to their dignity and their
Interest. By comparing themselves with the individuals of their Brethren they may indulge some sort of Pride; but if they compare themselves with the Protestants, either in Landed pro[per]ty,[2] in Titles, in

[2] Arthur Young estimated that in 1776 Catholics held only five per cent of the land in Ireland.

Rank, in Gentility illustrated by great Offices, and high command they are as *nothing;* and even by many Protestants they are equalled, and indeed much exceeded, in the Vain matter upon which they despise their Brethren. But by identifying themselves to the Corps to which they naturally belong, their properties will tell tenfold in consideration; then and then only, they become of real importance; and if they know how to use their situation may rank, as I wish them to do, with any men in the Kingdom. As to the Catholick Clergy, I am not all surprised at their Servility. The name of a Popish priest has so long been a matter of reproach, and of a mixed heterogeneous Sensation of fear, abhorrance, and contempt, that there was no charge, however absurd and ridiculous, which would not readily be credited against them. They were supposed to be possessd of an influence hardly possible to be obtaind by any set of men; but which, in them, had no existence in that degree, or (to my certain knowledge) almost in any degree at all so that every disorder amongst the common people was attributed either to their direction or connivance. As Catholick secular Clergy without any support from the State, it was impossible that their power should be considerable. Every part of the dogmas of that religion are so known, so fixed, so much in rule, and so unalterable that the Clergy had no scope in the wide field of metaphysical, theological or critical matters, which form such means of obtaining friends and partizans, and producing pleasing novelties to the audience, to exercise those modes of influence which are known to be so very powerfull. The Sacraments are in the same fame. The confession which is thought so much, is but a routine, and may be made to any; and the absolution on conditions of which the penitent himself must judge, is a thing of Course. The Masses are at a fixed Rate; and never are or can be refused, or delayed. Preaching, the most powerful arm of popular Priesthood, is sparingly used by them—and what there is of it is mostly in the hands of Friars, who have something more of influence than the Parish Clergy but not much. If the Catholick Clergy should [be] so unwise as to meddle in political matters and disgust their people, they may lose the little consideration they possess; they may lose their flocks, and they will have neither profit or Credit in return. But if they either wholly lie by, or fall in with their people in their civil pursuits, which the others understand better than the Clergy do, and which they will pursue, whether the Clergy like it or not, they will rise every day in the respect and influence which belongs to their Office. Let them not deceive themselves they *cannot* possess the Sources of influence and lead that are in the hands of dissenters of other descriptions. But if they do not counteract their own Interests, there is a decent field yet open to them.

As to Government,[3] by this you know what they mean to do. I see their scheme has been to divide the Catholicks a measure, which whether they mean to use them to oppose to other more dangerous factions, or merely to keep them aloof from those factions is equally ill judged and mischeivous. They may divide them indeed—but in the partition the weakest part will fall to their Share. The Strength of the Catholicks is not in their dozen or Score of old Gentlemen. Weak indeed they would be if this were the Case. Their force consists in two things; their numbers; and their growing property, which grows with the growth of the Country itself, and contributes to its encrease. If Government abstracts the old Gentlemen from that which is the natural Strength of the body they will leave the Gentlemen without Credit and themselves without the Service they might derive from their influence with the rest. They will lose the Substance and catch a Shadow indeed.

Perhaps the address of these misguided Gentlemen may require another from the General Committee. If so (a point of which I cannot judge) it ought to be full as expressive of Zeal and Loyalty as theirs— much Gratitude for what is past the most perfect attachment to his Majesty's Government and to the Constitution of the State; the most perfect acquiescence in that of the Church. With regard to religion to express an inviolable attachment to their own because its principles lead to make them good men and good Citizens; but that they are thoroughly satisfied with its present Condition—but as they find themselves worthy of the constitution, and know the Benefits of its Franchises they must not dissemble the uneasiness they feel, and the dangers they are continually exposed to from the total want of them and what they suffer from many other restraints which they are sure they have not deservd; hoping every thing from the Benignity of Government and of Parliament &c. Surely if Government was in its senses it would be glad to give these points to the R.C. tho' they were not enough in their Senses not to desire them. Thank God nothing new here. Our poor dear friend Sir Joshuas melancholy and obstinacy growing worse and worse.[4] Your Mothers ten thousand blessings. We expect your Uncle from Town tomorrow. He was very well last Night. I could not get the Letter for Langrish ready till Tuesday Night. It is gone;

---

[3] The Irish government in Dublin under the Lord Lieutenant John Fane, 10th Earl of Westmoreland (1759–1841).

[4] Sir Joshua Reynolds (1723–92).

imperfect and clumsy. But the Stuff is right. We shall be rather impatient to hear from you though we dont expect much. Your ever affectionate father Edm. Burke.

To HENRY GRATTAN—8 *March* 1793

Corr. (1958), VII, 360–62

Grattan (1746–1820) was M.P. in the Irish parliament and a leader of the Opposition.

My dear Sir,

I most sincerely congratulate you, and both these Countries, on the final Success in the House of Commons of the last and greatest Effort of your Genius. Your wonderful abilities were never more distinguishd, nor in a better Cause. You have restored three Millions of Citizens to their King and their Country.[1] In reality they had not the Benefit either of the one or of the other; indeed they were lost to themselves. There was even a circumstance in the melioration of their condition, which made it in some respects Worse; as it exposed them more to the Jealousy, and made them more the Object of the fears, of the ruling party, without any real Strength on their part to oppose to those passions.[2] I speak, you observe, as if, in obtaining thus much for the Catholicks, you had obtain'd every thing. I do so. When the Title is fully admitted, when an interlocutory decree, leading to a final judgment, is given, the Business, in effect, is done. You have brought things nearer this year to a compleat equality in favour of the Catholicks than last Session they were to the most parsimonious grant of the elective Franchise. If you can pass this Bill thro' the Lords with any tolerable good humour, I shall not only consider the great Object as substantially gained, but more usefully gained in this progressive mode, than in nominally more had been obtained with the grudging and ill will of the predominant party. Their exclusive Liberty, as they possessd it, was not freedom but dominion; and must naturally produce in them haughtiness by the habit of holding it, and rancour and indignation by the total and immediate loss of it. That description must, and perhaps ought, to possess the sole Patronage. Their satisfaction, of Course, is of moment. It would be no great Bargain for

---

[1] On 27 February the most important single clause in the Catholic Relief Bill, that which gave the franchise to Catholics, had been passed in committee by 144 votes to 72.

[2] Burke presumably means that the relaxing of the Penal Laws relating to the holding of property by Catholics in 1778 and 1782 had aroused the jealousy of Protestants.

the Catholicks to obtain a capacity for every thing with the enjoyment
of nothing at all.

The great Object now remaining is to make this Measure of concession on the one hand, and of reservation on the other, subservient to
the Tranquility of the Country, and the Strength of the Empire. The
Spirit of Jobbing, in the principal people; must some way or other be
abated, and kept within some degree of moderation—It will be then
more easy to get the better of the mutinous Spirit which is in the very
constitution of the lower part of our compatriots of every description,
and now begins to ferment with tenfold force by the leven of repub-
licanism, which always existed, though without much Noise in the
Northern parts of the Kingdom but now becomes more evident and
requires no small degree both of firm and of prudent management.[3]

I confess I tremble for the Conduct of the Chancellour, who seems
for a long time past desirous of putting himself at the head of whatever
discontents may arise from concession to the Catholicks.[4] When things
are on the very Edge of a precipice or indeed between two precipices
he appears resolved that they shall be tumbled headlong down one of
them. Surely, of all Virtues, Temper more eminently belongs than any
other to that *balancing* Office. Whatever other qualities or Talents
unite in that noble and learned person, who holds the great Seal,
Temper does not shine with any remarkable brilliancy.

All this depends upon having a Government. Government seems to
be a thing given up in Ireland. During the interregnum the vacant
place is filled by one man, who appears rather as a great and steady
Minister than a leader of opposition. Without his Virtue and constancy
all would have gone to ruin *Patriam tutore carentem, accepit.*[5] It is
unpleasant to be obliged to contrast his Conduct with that of a great
Leader of Party on this side of the Water.[6]

It gives me great consolation, among a thousand Vexatious Circumstances, to reflect, that my Son, who is much devoted to you, has
been perhaps of some use as Pioneer, to you, who, as a great General,
have conducted the operations of the Campain. In his two Journies
to Ireland he has done his best; and he has employd himself as a

---

[3] There was still widespread disorder in many parts of rural Ireland, usually attributed to
the Catholic 'Defender' movement. Evidence of open sympathy for France, the collection of
arms, and the drilling of men to use them in and around Belfast was given in a report of a
Secret Committee of the House of Lords of 7 March (*Journals of the House of Lords*, VII, 129).

[4] Lord Fitzgibbon had shown himself resolutely opposed to concessions to the Catholics in
the debate on the Speech from the Throne of 10 January.

[5] When his country had no guardian, he took her in charge; see Lucan, *Pharsalia*, IX,
24–5.

[6] Fox.

sollicitor, or rather as a *Dunn* with Ministers, both by verbal representation and Memorials on this Subject; and perhaps has been of some use in removing prejudices and obviating Objections.

Present Mrs Burkes and my most respectful Compliments to Mrs Grattan and believe me ever in the highest possible respect and regard

My dear Sir
Your most faithful
and obedient humble Servant

Duke Street   Edm Burke
March 8. 1793.

To WILLIAM WINDHAM—[16 *October* 1794]

Corr. (1958), VIII, 35–42

Windham (1750–1810), a friend and disciple of Burke's, had entered the cabinet as Secretary at War in July 1794 when the Portland Whigs finally split with Fox and formed a coalition with Pitt. Soon afterward, the coalition was endangered by the design of the new Lord Lieutenant for Ireland, Burke's friend Lord Fitzwilliam, to purge the Irish government of its antireform officials and to introduce further measures of Catholic Emancipation.

My dear Sir

My State of Mind was not the most enviable before the present unhappy misunderstanding. I cannot think without horrour on the effects of a breach in the Ministry, in this state of our affairs, and just before the meeting of Parliament.[1] It will compleat our Ruin. Every honest man in every Country in Europe will by this Event be cast into dismay and despair. It looks as if the hand of God was in this, as it is strongly marked in all the Rest. However, we must still use our poor human prudence and our feeble human efforts, as if things were not, what I greatly fear they are, predetermined. I am out of action, but not out of anxiety. I feel deeply for yourself—I feel for my other friends. I feel for the general Cause. Ireland, the Country in which I was born, is the immediate subject of the dispute. Lord Fitzwilliam, the man in the world I am the most obliged to, is the party chiefly concerned in it. To Mr Pitt the other party, I have strong and recent obligations. Before I had any such, I was clearly of the opinion, that his power, and all the chance we have for the Rescue of Europe were inseparably connected. You know, that, though I had no part in the

[1] Parliament had been prorogued until 4 November; it finally met on 30 December.

actual formation of the present System of a coalesced Ministry, that no pains were wanting on my part to produce the dispositions which led to it. You of all men, therefore are the best judge, how much I am in earnest, that this horrible breach should not be made. How to prevent it I know not. I cannot advise. I can only make statements; which I submit entirely to your Judgement. I do not write to any one else; because you alone have desired to hear my sentiments on this Subject.

I will trouble you with no other View of the matter, than as it concerns the Interest, the stability, perhaps the existence of Mr Pitt's power. I was one of those who were of opinion, that he could have stood merely on his own Basis. But this was my private Speculation— and hardly justified, I fear, by the experience of mankind in cases any way similar. But to have gone on without this new connexion, and to bear the loss of it are two very different things. The accession of a great Mass of reputation, taken out of a State of very perilous and critical Neutrality, and brought to the decided support of the Crown; and an actual participation in the responsibility of measures rendered questionable by very great misfortunes, were the advantages which Mr Pitt derived from a coalition with you, and your friends. I say nothing, just now, of your weight in the Country, and the abilities, which, in your several ways, you possess. I rest only on your Character, and reputation for Integrity, independence and dignity of Mind. This is every thing at a moment, when Opinion (never without it's effect) has obtained a greater dominion over human affairs than ever it possessed; and which must grow, just in proportion as the implicit reverence for old Institutions is found to decline. They who will say, that the very name, which you, and the Duke of Portland, and Lord Fitzwilliam and Lord Spenser, have, as men of unblemished honour and great publick Spirit, is of no use to the Crown at this time, talk like flatterers who despise the understandings of those whose favour they court. It is as much Mr Pitt's Interest as a faithful and zealous servant of the Crown (as I am sure he is) to hold high your honour and Estimation with the publick, as it is your own. Can it be preserved, if Lord Fitzwilliam continues in office after all that has happened, consistently with the Reputation he has obtained, and which, as a sacred Trust for the King and Country, he is bound to keep as well as for his own inward satisfaction?

I will not say, that Lord Fitzwilliam, has not in some respects acted with a degree of indiscretion. The Question is, whether Mr Pitt can or ought to take advantage of it to his own material prejudice? You are better acquainted than I am with the Terms, actual or understood, upon which the D. of Portland, acting for himself and others, has accepted Office. I know nothing of them, but by a single conversation with him. From thence I learned, that (whether authorised or not) he considered without a Doubt, that the administration of Ireland was left wholly to him, and without any other reserves, than what are supposed in every wise and sober servant of the Crown. Lord Fitzwilliam, I know, conceived things exactly in that manner, and proceeded as if there was no controversy whatsoever on the Subject. He hesitated a long time, whether he should take the Station—but when he agreed to it, he thought he had obliged Ministry, and done what was pleasant to the King, in going into an Office of great difficulty and heavy responsibility. He foresaw no other obstacles, than what were found in his own inclinations, the nature of the employment, and the circumstances in which Ireland stands. He therefore invited several persons to converse with him, in all the confidence, with which men ought to open themselves to a person of honour, who, though not actually, was virtually in Office.[2] Whether the D. of Portland and Lord F had reason for this entire security, you are better able to judge than I am. I am sure they conceived things in the Light I state them; though I really think, that they never can reconcile it to the rigid rules of prudence, with regard to their own safety, or to an entire Decorum with regard to the other Cabinet Ministers, to go so far into detail as has been done, until all the Circumstances of the appointment were settled in a more distinct and specifick manner than they had been. But I am sure that they thought, that a very large discretion was committed to them; and I am equally sure, that their general plans, (so far as I know them) were perfectly upright, and perfectly well understood for the King's service, and the good of his Empire. I admit, and lament the errour into which they have fallen. It must be very great, as it seems, Mr Pitt had no thoughts at all of a change in the Irish Government; or if he had, it was dependent on Lord Westmoreland's sense of the fitness of some other Office to accommodate him, on his resignation of the great place which for five or six years

---

[2] Towards the end of August Fitzwilliam had informed a number of the Irish Whigs that he was to be appointed Lord Lieutenant.

he has held.[3] This puts off the Business sine die.[4] These are some of the mischiefs which arise from a want of a clear explanation on the first digestion of any political System.

If an agreement is wished, criminations and recriminations, charges and defences, are not the way to it. If the communication hitherto has not been as full and as confidential as it ought to have been, Let it be so now. Let it be such as becomes men engaged in the same Cause, with the same Interest, and with the same sense of the arduous Trust, which in the most critical of all times, has been delivered over to them by their King and Country. In this dreadful situation of things, is it not clearly Mr Pitt's Interest, without considering whether he has a Case as against his Colleagues or not, to keep up the reputation of those, who came to his aid, under circumstances liable to misconstruction; liable to the exaggerated imputations of men able, dexterous, and eloquent; and who came to him, when the whole of the affairs under his administration bore the worst aspect that can be imagined?— I am well aware, that there is a sort of Politicians, who would tell Mr Pitt, that this disgracing his Colleagues, would be to him a signal Triumph; and that it would be to the publick a splendid mark of his power and superiority. But alas! it would be a Triumph over his own force. His paramount power is well understood. His power is an object rather of Envy and terrour than of contempt. I am no great dealer in General Maxims. I am sensible how much the best of them are controlled by Circumstances. But I am satisfied, that where the most real and solid power exists, there it is the most necessary, every now and then, to yield; not only from the real advantages of practicability, but from the advantages which attend the very appearance of it. What is given up by power is a mark of moderation; what is given up because it cannot be kept, is a mark of servility and meanness. What Coffee-house politician is so grossly ignorant, as not to know, that the real seat of power is in Mr Pitt; and in none of you, who by the Courtesy of England are called Ministers? Whatever *he* gives up will be manifestly for the King's Service; Whatever *they* yield will be thought to flow from a mean desire of Office to be held without respect or consideration. If he yields any point he will be sure to put out his concessions, to be repaid to him with Usury. All this unfortunate notion of

[3] When it was originally suggested that Fitzwilliam be appointed Lord Lieutenant, it had been agreed that the actual appointment must be postponed until Westmorland, who had been Lord Lieutenant since 1790, could be moved to another post. Westmorland ultimately left Dublin on 5 January 1795 and was apponted Master of the Horse. Later he was to hold Cabinet office for about twenty-five years.
[4] Indefinitely.

Triumph, on the one part and the other, arises from the Idea, that Ministry is not *one* thing, but composed of separate and independent parties; a ruinous Idea, which I have done every thing in my power to discourage—and with a growing success. I can say, almost with assurance, that if Mr Pitt can contrive (and it is worth his while to contrive it) to keep his new acquisition of friends in good humour for six months more, He will find them as much of his party, and in my opinion more surely to be depended upon, than any which he has hitherto considered as his own. It is of infinite importance to him to have it *thought*, that he is well connected with others besides those who are believed to depend on him.

If it is once laid down, that it is true policy in Mr Pitt to uphold the Credit of his Colleagues in Administration, even under some difference in opinion, the question will be, whether the present is not a case of too much importance to be included in that general Policy— and that Lord F. may very well give up the Lieutenancy, and yet hold his office,[5] without any disgrace. On that, I think, there can be Little difference in opinion. He must, to be sure, resign, and resign with every Sentiment of displeasure and discontent. This I have not advised him to do; for most certainly, I have had no conversation with him on the subject; and I am very glad I have not had any such discourse. But the thing speaks for itself. He has consulted with many people from Ireland, of all descriptions, as if he were virtually Lord Lieutenant. The D. of P. has acted upon that supposition as a fundamental part of his arrangement. Lord Fitzwilliam cannot shrink into his shell again, without being thought a light man, in whom no person can place any confidence. If on the other hand, he takes the sword, not only without power, but with a direct Negative put upon his power, he is a Lord Lieutenant disgraced and degraded—with infinite sorrow I say it—with sorrow inexpressible—he must resign. If he does the D. of Portland must resign too. In fact they will both consider themselves as turned out—and I know it will be represented to them, because I know it has been predicted to them, that their being brought into Office was no more than a stratagem, to make them break with their friends and original natural connexions, to make them lose all Credit with the independent part of the Country, and then to turn them out as objects of universal scorn and derision without party or adherents to resort to! I believe Lord F has in his Bureau one letter

---

[5] The Presidency of the Council.

to this effect;[6] (I well recollect that he was much affected by it and indeed doubtful of accepting) perhaps more than one. I am certain, that whether they stay in under a state of degradation, or are turned out, their situation will be terrible; and such as will be apt to fill men with rage and desperate resolutions. Both their coming in and their going out will be reviled: and they will be ridiculed and insulted on both by the Opposition. They will affect to pity them—They will even offer to pardon them. Amongst Mr Pitt's old adherents, as perhaps you know as well as I do, there were many who liked your coming in as little as Mr Fox or Mr Sheridan could do. They considered Mr Pitt's enlarging his Bottom as an interloping on their Monopoly. They will join the Halloo of the others. If they can persuade Mr Pitt that, that this is a Triumph—he will have it—But may God of his goodness avert the consequences from him and all of us!

But why, will some say, 'should not Lord F. take the Lord Lieutenancy and let the Chancellour[7] remain where he is—He will be good-humoured and subservient, and let the Lord Lieutenant do as he pleases'. But after what has passed the true question is, which of these two is to govern Ireland? I think I know what a Lord Lieutenant of Ireland is, or I know nothing. Without an hearty and effectual support of the Minister here, he is much worse than a mere Pageant. A man in the Pillory is in a post of honour in comparison of such a Lord Lieutenant. 'But Lord Westmoreland goes on very quietly'. He does so. He has no discussions with the Junto who have annihilated English Government. Be his abilities and his spirit what they may, he has no desire of Governing. He is a Basha of Ægypt, who is content to let the Beys act as they think proper. Lord F. is an high minded man. A man of very great parts; and a man of very quick feelings. He cannot be the instrument of the Junto with the name of the King's representative, if he would. If Lord F was to be sent to Ireland, to be exactly as Lord Westmoreland is, I undertake to affirm, that a worse choice for that purpose could not be made. If he has nothing to do but what Lord W. does, neither ought Lord W: to be removed, nor the Chancellour, no nor the Chancellour's Trainbearer. Lord F. has no business there at all. He has Fortune enough, He has Rank enough. Here he is infinitely more at his Ease, and he is of infinitely more use here than he can be there, where his desire of really doing Business, and

---

[6] Perhaps Burke refers to a letter of 7 July written to Fitzwilliam by Lady Rockingham, treating the idea of a coalition with Pitt as 'too hazardous . . . They will borrow your Zeal and uprightness; and will pay you back again *only* in *Honours* and *Compliments* . . .'

[7] John Fitzgibbon, 1st Baron Fitzgibbon, the Lord Chancellor of Ireland.

his desire of being the real Representative of the Crown, would only cause to him infinite trouble and distress. For it is, not to know Ireland, to say that what is called opposition is what will give trouble to a real Viceroy. His embarrassments are upon the part of those who ought to be the supports of English Government—but who have formed themselves into a Cabal to destroy the King's authority, and to divide the Country as a spoil amongst one another. *Non regnum sed magnum Latrocinium*[8]—The Motto which ought to be put under the Harp. This is not talk. I can put my hand on the Instances—and not a doubt would remain on your Mind of the fact: His Majesty has the Patronage to the Pashalick, as the Grand Seignor has to that of Ægypt—and that is all. Such is the State of things. I think matters recoverable in some degree: but the attempt is to be made.

If Ireland be well enough, and safe enough as it is—If the Chancellour and the Government of the Junto is good for the King, the Country, and the Empire, God forbid, that a stone in that Edifice should be picked out, to gratify Lord Fitzwilliam, or any body else. But if that Kingdom by the meditated and systematick corruption (private personal not politick corruption) of some; and the headlong violence and Tyrannical Spirit of others, totally destitute of Wisdom, and the more incurably so, as not being destitute of some flashy parts— is brought into a very perilous situation—then I say, at a time like this, there is no making questions about it mere discussions between one Branch and the other of Administration, either in England or Ireland. The State of Ireland is not like a thing without intrinsick merits; and on which it may be safe to make a Trial of Skill, or a Trial of Strength. It is no longer an obscure dependency of this Kingdom. What is done there vitally effects the whole System of Europe, whether you regard it offensively or defensively. Ireland is known in France; Communications have been opened and more will be opened.[9] Ireland will be a strong Digue to keep out Jacobinism; or a broken bank to let it in. The Junto have weakened the old European System of Government there, and brought it into utter discredit. I look in this affair, to Ireland; and in Ireland, to G. Britain; and in Great Britain to Europe. The little Clicks there are to me as nothing—They have never done me a favour nor an injury. But that Kingdom is of

---

[8] Not a government but a great robbery; see Cicero, *In Vatinium*, VIII.

[9] In April 1794 the Rev. William Jackson (*c.* 1737–95), a French agent who had been sent to Ireland and who had had interviews with leading Irish radicals, was arrested and charged with high treason. He was brought to trial in 1795 and on 30 April when sentence was about to be passed he committed suicide.

great· importance indeed. I regard in this point, all descriptions of men with great comparative indifference. I love Lord Fitzwilliam very well; but so convinced am I, on the maturest reflexion, of the perilous State, into which the present Junto have brought that Kingdom (on which, in reality, this Kingdom, at this Juncture is *dependent*) that if he were to go with a resolution to suport it, I would on my knees entreat him, not to have a share in the ruin of his Country under the poor pretence of governing a part of it. Oh! my dear friend, I write with a sick heart and a wearied hand. If you can pluck Ireland out of the unwise and corrupt hands that are destroying us! If they say, they will mend their manners, I tell you they cannot mend them; and if they could, this mode of doing and undoing; saying and unsaying; inflaming the people with voluntary violence, and appeasing them with forced concession, Their 'keeping the word of promise to their ear, and breaking it to their hope'[10]—Their wanton expences, and their fraudulent œconomy—all these and ten times more than these; but all of the same sort, are the very things which have brought Government in that Country to the State of contempt and incurable distrust under which it labours. It cannot have it's very distemper for it's Cure. You know me, I think enough to be quite sure, that in giving you an opinion concerning Mr Pitt's Interest and honour, I have not an oblique regard, at his Expence, to the honour and interest of others. No! I always thought advice the most sacred of all things; and that it always ought to be given for the Benefit of the advised. I am now endeavouring to make up all my accounts with my Creator. I am almost literally, a dying man. In several senses and to many purposes, I am dead. I speak with all the freedom and all the clearness of that situation. I speak as a man under a strong sense of obligation to Mr Pitt, when I assure him under the solemn sanction of that awful situation, that my firm opinion is, that by getting rid of the new accessions to his strength and especially upon the ground of protection to certain Irish politicians (at what distance of time I cannot say) but he is preparing his certain ruin, with all the consequence of that ruin, which I tremble to think on. God bless you all—and direct you for the best. Ever ever your affectionate and unhappy friend

EDMD BURKE

[10] See *Macbeth*, v, vii, 50–1.

To the REV. THOMAS HUSSEY—18 *May* 1795

Corr. (1958), VIII, 245–50

The Rev. Thomas Hussey (1741–1803) was a friend of Burke's and a Catholic leader who in 1797 was made a Bishop. Burke discusses with him the discouraging situation of Irish Catholics after Lord Fitzwilliam's brief, unhappy tenure as Lord Lieutenant of Ireland and the apparent dashing of hopes for further reform.

My dear Sir,

I dont know exactly why I am so unwilling to write by the Post. I have little to say that might not be known to the world. At the same time there is something unpleasant in talking the confidential Language of friendship in the publick Theatre. It is still worse to put into the power of any one to make unfaithful representations of it, or to make it the subject of malicious comments. I thank you for your Letter. It is full of that good sense, and good Temper, as well as of that fortitude, which are natural to you. Since persons of so much greater authority than I am, and of so much better judgment, are of opinion you ought to stay, it was clearly right for you to remain at all risques: Indeed if it could be done with tolerable safety, I wishd you to watch over the cradle of those Seminaries, on which the future weal or woe of Ireland essentially depend. For you I dreaded the Revolutionary Tribunal of Drogheda[1]—For the Country, if some proper mode of Education is not adopted, I tremble for the spread of Atheism amongst the Catholicks. I do not like the Style of the meeting in Francis Street.[2] The Tone was wholly jacobinical. In Parliament the Language of your friends (one only excepted)[3] was what it ought to be. But that one Speech, though full of fire and animation, was not warmed with the fire of heaven. I am sorry for it. I have seen that Gentleman but once. He is certainly a man of parts; but one who has dealt too much in the Philosophy of France. Justice, Prudence, Tenderness, moderation, and Christian Charity, ought to become the measures of tolerance, and not a cold apathy, or indeed rather a savage hatred, to all Religion, and an avowd contempt of all those points on which we differ, and on those about which we agree. If what was said

[1] Burke is referring to the trial at Drogheda, Ireland, of Catholic merchants who were charged with conspiring against the government.

[2] On 9 April a meeting of the Catholics of Dublin was held at the Catholic chapel in Francis Street to receive a report from the delegates who had been commissioned to present to the King the Address voted by the meeting held on 27 February. At the meeting on the 9th strongly radical and anti-English speeches were delivered.

[3] Arthur O'Connor (1763–1852), an Irish M.P. who later took up the cause of France and went to live there.

at Francis Street, was in the first heat, it might be excused. They were
given to understand, that a Change of administration, short only of a
revolution in Violence, was made, only on account of a disposition in
a Lord Lieutenant to favour Catholicks: Many provoking Circumstances attended the Business. Not the least of them was, that they
saw themselves deliverd over to their Enemies, on no other apparent
ground of merit, than that they were such. All this is very true: But
under every provocation, they ought not to be irritated by their Enemies out of their principles, and out of their senses. The Language
of the day went plainly to a seperation of the two Kingdoms. God
forbid, that anything like it should ever happen. They would both be
ruined by it; But Ireland would suffer most and first. The thing
however is impossible. Those who should attempt that impossibility
would be undone. If even the arms, which indirectly these orators
seem to menace, were to be taken up, surely the Threat of such a
measure is not wise, as it could add nothing to their strength; but
would give every possible advantage to their Enemies. It is a foolish
Language adopted from the united Irishmen, that their Grievances
originate from England. The direct contrary. It is an ascendancy, which
some of their own factions have obtain here; that has hurt the Catholicks with this Government. It is not as an English Government that
Ministers act in that manner, but as assisting a party in Ireland. When
they talk of dissolving themselves as a Catholick body, and mixing
their Grievances with those of their Country, all I have to say is, that
they lose their own importance as a body by this amalgamation; and
they sink real matters of complaint in those which are factious and
imaginary. For, in the name of God, what Grievance has Ireland, as
Ireland, to complain of with regard to Great Britain? Unless the protection of the most powerful Country upon Earth, giving all her priveleges without exception in common to Ireland, and reserving to her
self only the painful preeminence of tenfold Burthens be a matter of
complaint. The Subject, as a subject, is as free in Ireland as he is in
England—as a Member of the Empire, an Irishman has every privelege
of a natural born Englishman, in every part of it, in every occupation,
and in every branch of Commerce. No monopoly is establishd against
him any where—and the great Staple manufacture of Ireland[4] is not
only, not prohibited, not only not discouraged, but it is privelegd in
a manner that has no example. The provision Trade is the same—nor
does Ireland, on her part, take a single article from England but what

[4] Linen.

she has with more advantage than she could have it from any Nation upon Earth. I say nothing of the immense advantage she derives from the use of the English Capital. In what Country upon Earth is it, that a quantity of her Linnens, the moment they are lodged in the Warehouse, and before the sale, would intitle the Irish Merchant or manufacturer to draw Bills, on the Terms, and at the time, in which this is done by the Warehouse man in London? Ireland therefore, as Ireland, whether it be taken civilly, constitutionally, or commercially, suffers no Grievance. The Catholicks as Catholicks do; and what can be got by joining their real complaint, to a complaint which is fictitious, but to make the whole pass for fiction and groundless pretence? I am not a man for construing with too much rigour the expressions of men under a sense of ill usage. I know that much is to be given to passion; and I hope, I am more disposed to accuse the person who provokes another to anger, than the person who gives way to natural feelings in hot Language. If this be all, it is no great matter; but if anger only brings out a plan, that was before meditated, and laid up in the mind, the thing is more serious. The Tenour of the Speeches in Francis Street, attacking the Idea of an incorporating union between the two kingdoms, expressed principles that went the full length of a seperation; and of a dissolution of that union which arises from their being under the same Crown—That Ireland would, in that Case, come to make a figure amongst the nations, is an Idea which has more of the ambition of individuals in it, than of a sober regard to the happiness of an whole people: But if a people were to sacrifice solid quiet to empty glory, as on some occasions they have done, under the Circumstances of Ireland, *she*, most assuredly, never would obtain that independent glory, but would certainly lose all her Tranquility, all her prosperity, and even that degree of Lustre which she has by the very free and honourable connexion she enjoys with a Nation the most splendid and the most powerful upon Earth. Ireland *constitutionally* is independent—*Politically* she never can be so. It is a struggle against Nature. She must be protected; and there is no protection to be found for her, but either from France or England. France even, (if under any form she may assume) she were disposed to give the same Liberal and honourable protection to Ireland, has not the means of either serving or hurting her, that are in the hands of Great Britain. She might make Ireland, supposing that kind of independence could be maintaind (which for a year I am certain it could not) a dreadful Thorn in the side of this Kingdom; but Ireland would dearly buy that malignant and infernal satisfaction, by a dependence upon a power, either

despotick as formerly, or anarchical as at present. We see well enough
the kind of Liberty which she either enjoys herself, or is willing to
bestow on others. This I say with regard to the scheme of those who
call themselves united Irishmen,[5] that is to say of those, who, without
any regard to religion, clubb all kinds of discontents together in order
to produce all kinds of disorders. But to speak to Catholics as such,
it is plain that whatever security they enjoy for their religion, as well
as for the many solid advantages, which even under the present restrictions, they are intitled to, depends wholly upon their connexion
with this Kingdom. France is an Enemy to all religion; but eminently
and with a peculiar malignity an Enemy to the Catholick religion;
which they mean, if they can, to extirpate throughout the Globe. It
is something perverse, and even unnatural, for Catholics to hear even
the sound of a connexion with France; unless under the colour and
pretext of a religious description, they should, as some here have done
in this Country form themselves into a mischeivous political faction.
The Catholicks, as things now stand, have all the splendid abilities,
and much of the independent property in Parliament in their favour;
and every Protestant, (I believe with very few exceptions) who is really
a Christian. Should they alienate these men from their Cause, their
choice is amongst those, who indeed may have ability, but not wisdom
or Temper in proportion; and whose very ability is not equal either
in strength, or exercise, to that which they lose. They will have to
choose men of desperate property, or of no property; and men of no
religious and no moral principle. Without a Protestant connexion of
some kind or other they cannot go on;—and here are the two sorts of
descriptions of Protestants between whom they have an option to
make. In this state of things their situation I allow is difficult and
delicate. If the better part lies by in a sullen silence, they still cannot
hinder the more factious part both from speaking and from writing—
and the Sentiments of those who are silent will be judged by the
effusions of the people who do not wish to conceal thoughts that the
sober part of mankind will not approve.—On the other hand, if the
better and more temperate part come forward to disclaim the others
they instantly make a breach in their own party, of which a malignant
enemy will take advantage to crush them all. They will praise the
sober part; but they will grant them nothing they shall desire; nay

---

[5] In October 1791 a radical club calling itself the Society of United Irishmen was founded
in Belfast. In November 1791 a Dublin Society was constituted and later similar clubs in other
parts of the country were founded. The Dublin Society issued a number of manifestos, printed
in their *Transactions*, Dublin, 1794.

they will make use of their submission as a proof, that sober men are perfectly satisfied in remaining prostrate under their oppressive hands. These are dreadful dilemmas; and they are such as ever will arise, when men in power are possessd with a crafty malignant disposition without any real Wisdom or enlarged policy.

However as in every Case of difficulty, there is a better way of proceeding and a worse; and that some medium may be found between an abject, and for that reason an imprudent Submission, and a contumacious absurd resistance;—what I would humbly suggest is, that on occasion of the declamations in the Newspaper, they should make, not an apology (for that is dishonourable and dangerous) but a strong charge on their Enemies for defamation; disclaiming the Tenets, and practices, and designs impudently attributed to them; and asserting in cool, modest, and determined Language, their resolution to assert the priveleges to which as good Citizens and good Subjects they hold themselves intitled without being intimidated or weaned out by the opposition of the Monopolists of the Kingdom. In this there will be nothing mean or servile; or which can carry any appearance of the Effect of Fear; but the contrary—at the same time it will remove the prejudices, which on this side of the water as well as on yours, are propagated against you with so much systematick pains. I think the Committee would do well to do something of this kind in their own name. I trust those men of great ability in that Committee who encline to think, that the Catholicks ought to melt down their cause into the general Mass of uncertain discontents and unascertaind principles, will, I hope, for the sake of agreeing with those who I am sure they love and respect among their own Brethren, as well as for the sake of the Kingdom at large, waive that Idea, (which I do not deny to be greatly provoked,) of dissolving the Catholick body before the objects of its union are obtaind; and turning the Objects of their relief into a national quarrel. This I am satisfied on recollection they will think not irrational. The Course taken by the Enemy often becomes a fair Rule of action. You see by the whole turn of the Debate against them, that their adversaries endeavourd to give this Colour to the contest, and to make it hinge on this principle. The same policy cannot be good for you and your Enemies. Sir George Shee[6] who is so good to take this, waits, or I should say more on this point. I should say something too of the Colleges. I long much to hear how you go on. I have however said too much. If Grattan by whom I wish the Catholicks

[6] 1st Baronet (1754–1825).

to be wholly advised, thinks differently than me, I wish the whole unsaid—You see Lord Fitzwilliam sticks nobly to his Text and neither abandons his Cause or his friends though he has few indeed to support him. When you can pray let me hear from you. Mrs Burke and myself in this lonely and disconsolate House never cease to think of you as we ought to do. I send some Prints to Dublin; but as your House is not there I reserve a memorial of my dear Richard for your return. I am ever

My dear Sir
faithfully and affectionately,
Your miserable friend
EDM BURKE

Beconsfield May 18. 1795.

To SIR HERCULES LANGRISHE—26 *May* 1795

Corr. (1958), VIII, 253–57

Sir Hercules Langrishe, 1st Baronet (1731–1811), was a supporter of the Irish Administration and for many years had been an eloquent advocate of Catholic relief.

My dear Sir,

If I am not as early as I ought to be in my acknowledgments for your very kind letter, pray do me the justice to attribute my failure to its natural, and but too real, cause,—a want of the most ordinary power of exertion, owing to the impressions made upon an old and infirm constitution by private misfortune and by public calamity. It is true I make occasional efforts to rouse myself to something better, but I soon relapse into that state of languor, which must be the habit of my body and understanding to the end of my short and cheerless existence in this world.

I am sincerely grateful for your kindness in connecting the interest you take in the sentiments of an old friend with the able part you take in the service of your country. It is an instance among many of that happy temper which has always given a character of amenity to your virtues, and a good-natured direction to your talents.

Your speech on the Catholic Question[1] I read with much satisfaction. It is solid; it is convincing; it is eloquent; and it ought, on the spot, to have produced that effect which its reason, and that contained in

[1] In the debate of 4 May in the Irish Parliament.

the other excellent speeches on the same side of the question, cannot possibly fail (though with less pleasant consequences) to produce hereafter. What a sad thing it is that the grand instructor, Time, has not yet been able to teach the grand lesson of his own value; and that, in every question of moral and political prudence, it is the choice of the moment which renders the measure serviceable or useless, noxious or salutary.

In the Catholic Question I considered only one point. Was it at the time, and in the circumstances, a measure which tended to promote the concord of the citizens? I have no difficulty in saying it was; and as little in saying that the present concord of the citizens was worth buying, at a critical season, by granting a few *capacities*, which probably no one man now living is likely to be served or hurt by. When any man tells *you* and *me* that, if these places were left in the discretion of a Protestant Crown, and these memberships in the discretion of Protestant electors, or patrons, we should have a Popish official system, and a Popish representation, capable of overturning the establishment, he only insults our understandings. When any man tells this to *Catholics*, he insults their understandings and he galls their feelings. It is not the question of the places and seats; it is the real hostile disposition, and the *pretended* fears, that leave stings in the minds of the people. I really thought that in the total of the late circumstances, with regard to persons, to things, to principles, and to measures, was to be found a conjunction favourable to the introduction, and to the perpetuation, of a general harmony, producing a general strength which to that hour Ireland was never so happy as to enjoy. My sanguine hopes are blasted, and I must consign my feelings on that terrible disappointment to the same patience in which I have been obliged to bury the vexation I suffered on the defeat of the other great, just, and honourable causes in which I have had some share; and which have given more of dignity than of peace and advantage to a long, laborious life. Though, perhaps, a want of success might be urged as a reason for making me doubt of the justice of the part I have taken, yet, until I have other lights than one side of the debate has furnished me, I must see things, and feel them too, as I see and feel them. I think I can hardly overrate the malignity of the principles of Protestant ascendency, as they affect Ireland; or of Indianism, as they affect these countries, and as they affect Asia; or of Jacobinism, as they affect all Europe, and the state of human society itself. The last is the greatest evil. But it readily combines with the others, and flows from them. Whatever breeds discontent at this time will produce that great master-mischief most infallibly. Whatever tends to persuade the people that the *few*, called by whatever name you please, religious or political, are of opinion that their interest is not compatible with that of the *many*, is a great point gained to Jacobinism. Whatever tends to irritate the talents of a country, which have at all times, and at these particularly, a mighty influence on the public mind, is of infinite service to that formidable cause. Unless where Heaven has mingled uncommon ingredients, of virtue in the composition—*quos meliore luto finxit præcordia Titan*[2]—talents naturally gravitate to Jacobinism. Whatever ill humours are afloat in the state, they will be sure to discharge themselves in a mingled torrent in the *Cloacâ Maximâ*[3] of Jacobinism. Therefore people ought well to look about them. First, the physicians are to take care that they do nothing to irritate this epidemical distemper. It is a foolish thing to have the better of the patient in a dispute. The complaint, or its cause, ought to be removed, and wise and lenient arts ought to precede the measures of vigour. They ought to be the *ultima*, not the *prima*, not the *tota* ratio of a wise government. God forbid, that on a worthy occasion authority should want the means of force, or the disposition to use it. But where a prudent and enlarged policy does not precede it, and attend it too, where the hearts of the better sort of people do not go with the hands of the soldiery, you may call your constitution what you will, in effect it will consist of three parts, (orders, if you please,)—cavalry, infantry, and artillery,—and of nothing else or better.

I agree with you in your dislike of the discourses in Francis Street; but I like as little some of those in College Green.[4] I am even less pleased with the temper that predominated in the latter, as better things might have been expected in the regular family mansion of public discretion, than in a new and hasty assembly of unexperienced men, congregated under circumstances of no small irritation. After people have taken your tests, prescribed by yourselves as proofs of their allegiance, to be marked as enemies, traitors, or at best as suspected and dangerous persons, and that they are not to be believed on their oaths, we are not to be surprised if they fall into a passion, and talk, as men in a passion do, intemperately and idly.

The worst of the matter is this: you are partly leading, partly driving, into Jacobinism that description of your people whose religious principles—church polity, and habitual discipline—might make them an

---

[2] Whom Titan has fashioned with kindlier skill and of a finer clay; see Juvenal, *Satires*, XIV, 35.

[3] The main sewer in Rome.

[4] The Irish Parliament House stood in College Green.

invincible dyke against that inundation. This you have a thousand mattocks and pick-axes lifted up to demolish. You make a sad story of the pope!—*O seri studiorum!*[5]—It will not be difficult to get many called Catholics to laugh at this fundamental part of their religion. Never doubt it. You have succeeded in part; and you may succeed completely. But in the present state of men's minds and affairs do not flatter yourselves that they will piously look to the head of our church in the place of that pope whom you make them forswear; and out of all reverence to whom you bully, and rail, and buffoon them. Perhaps you may succeed in the same manner with all the other tenets of doctrine, and usages of discipline, amongst the Catholics. But what security have you that in the temper and on the principles on which they have made this change, they will stop at the exact sticking-places you have marked in *your* articles? You have no security for anything, but that they will become what are called *Franco-Jacobins*, and reject the whole together. No converts now will be made in a considerable number from one of our sects to the other upon a really religious principle. Controversy moves in another direction.

Next to religion, *property* is the great point of Jacobin attack. Here, many of the debaters in your majority, and their writers, have given the Jacobins all the assistance their hearts can wish. When the Catholics desire places and seats, you tell them that this is only a pretext (though Protestants might suppose it just *possible* for men to like good places and snug boroughs for their own merits); but that their real view is to strip Protestants of their property. To my certain knowledge, till those Jacobin lectures were opened in the House of Commons, they never dreamt of any such thing; but now the great professors may stimulate them to inquire (on the new principles) into the foundation of that property, and of all property. If you treat men as robbers, why, robbers sooner or later, they will become.

A third part of Jacobin attack is on *old traditionary constitutions*. You are apprehensive for yours, which leans from its perpendicular, and does not stand firm on its theory. I like parliamentary reforms as little as any man who has boroughs to sell for money, or for peerages, in Ireland. But it passes my comprehension, in what manner it is, that men can be reconciled to the *practical* merits of a constitution, the theory of which is in litigation, by being *practically* excluded from any of its advantages. Let us put ourselves in the place of these people, and try an experiment of the effects of such a procedure on our own

---

[5] O yet late learners; see Horace, *Satires*, I, x, 21.

minds. Unquestionably we should be perfectly satisfied when we were told that houses of parliament, instead of being places of refuge for popular liberty, were citadels for keeping us in order as a conquered people. These things play the Jacobin game to a nicety. Indeed, my dear Sir, there is not a single particular in the Francis Street declamations which has not, to your and to my certain knowledge, been taught by the jealous ascendants, sometimes by doctrine, sometimes by example, always by provocation. Remember the whole of 1781 and 1782[6]—in parliament and out of parliament; at this very day, and in the worst acts and designs, observe the tenor of the objections with which the College Green orators of the ascendency reproach the Catholics. You have observed, no doubt, how much they rely on the affair of Jackson.[7] It is not pleasant to hear Catholics reproached for a supposed connexion—with whom?—with Protestant clergymen! with Protestant gentlemen! with Mr Jackson!—with Mr Rowan,[8] &c. &c.! But *egomet mi ignosco*.[9] Conspiracies and treasons are privileged pleasures, not to be profaned by the impure and unhallowed touch of Papists. Indeed, all this will do, perhaps, well enough with detachments of dismounted cavalry and fencibles from England. But let us not say to Catholics by way of *argument*, that they are to be kept in a degraded state, because some of them are no better than many of us Protestants. The thing I most disliked in some of their speeches (those I mean of the Catholics) was what is called the spirit of liberality, so much and so diligently taught by the ascendants, by which they are made to abandon their own particular interests, and to merge them in the general discontents of the country. It gave me no pleasure to hear of the dissolution of the committee.[10] There were in it a majority, to my knowledge, of very sober, well-intentioned men; and there were none in it but such who, if not continually goaded and irritated, might be made useful to the tranquillity of the country. It is right always to have a few of every description, through whom you may quietly operate on the many, both for the interests of the description, and for the general interest. Excuse me, my dear friend, if I have a little tried your patience. You have brought this trouble on yourself, by your

---

[6] The struggle for Irish parliamentary independence.

[7] William Jackson, the French agent in Ireland. In the debate of 4 May, opponents of the Catholic Relief Bill emphasized the contacts between the United Irishmen and the Catholic leaders.

[8] Archibald Hamilton Rowan (1751–1834) had had meetings with Jackson, and on hearing of his arrest, Rowan fled to France.

[9] For myself I take no notice; see Horace, *Satires*, I, iii, 23.

[10] The Catholic Committee.

thinking of a man forgot, and who has no objection to be forgot, by the world. These things we discussed together four or five and thirty years ago.[11] We were then, and at bottom ever since, of the same opinion on the justice and policy of the whole, and of every part, of the penal system. You and I and everybody must now and then ply and bend to the occasion, and take what can be got. But very sure I am, that whilst there remains in the law any principle whatever which can furnish to certain politicians an excuse for raising an opinion of their own importance, as necessary to keep their fellow-subjects in order, the obnoxious people will be fretted, harassed, insulted, provoked to discontent and disorder, and practically excluded from the partial advantages from which the letter of the law does not exclude them.

Adieu! my dear Sir, and believe me very truly

Yours,

EDMUND BURKE.

Beaconsfield, May 26, 1795.

To the REV THOMAS HUSSEY—[post 9 December 1796]

Corr. (1958), IX, 161–72

A long blast of Burke's sarcasm against the Irish government for putting the danger to Protestantism in Ireland ahead of the danger from Jacobinism.

My dear Sir

This morning I received your Letter of the 30th of November from Maynooth. I dictate my answer from my Couch, on which I am obliged to lie for a good part of the Day. I cannot conceal from you, much less can I conceal from myself, that, in all probability I am not long for this world. Indeed things are in such a Situation independantly of the Domestic wound that I never could have less reason for regret in quitting the world than at this moment; and my End will be, by several, as little regretted.

I have no difficulty at all in communicating to you or, if it were of any use to mankind at large, my sentiments and feelings on the dismal state of things in Ireland; but I find it difficult indeed to give you the

---

[11] Burke was in Dublin for the 'Parliament winter' of 1761–2. Langrishe became a member of the Irish House of Commons in 1760.

advice you are pleased to ask, as to your own conduct in your very critical Situation.

You state, what has long been but too obvious, that it seems the unfortunate policy of the Hour, to put to the far largest portion of the Kings Subjects in Ireland, the desperate alternative, between a thankless acquiescence under grievous Oppression, or a refuge in Jacobinism with all its horrors and all its crimes. You prefer the former dismal part of the choice. There is no doubt but that you would have reasons if the election of one of these Evils was at all a security against the other. But they are things very alliable and as closely connected as cause and efect. That Jacobinism, which is Speculative in its Origin, and which arises from Wantonness and fullness of bread, may possibly be kept under by firmness and prudence. The very levity of character which produces it may extinguish it; but the Jacobinism which arises from Penury and irritation, from scorned loyalty, and rejected Allegiance, has much deeper roots. They take their nourishment from the bottom of human Nature and the unalterable constitution of things, and not from humour and caprice or the opinions of the Day about privileges and Liberties. These roots will be shot into the Depths of Hell, and will at last raise up their proud Tops to Heaven itself. This radical evil may baffle the attempts of Heads much wiser than those are, who in the petulance and riot of their drunken power are neither ashamed nor afraid to insult and provoke those whom it is their duty and ought to be their glory to cherish and protect.

So then the little wise men of the West, with every hazard of this Evil, are resolved to persevere in their manly and well timed resolution of a War, against Popery. In the principle and in all the proceedings it is perfectly suitable to their character. They begin this last series of their Offensive Operations by laying traps for the consciences of poor Foot-Soldiers. They call these wretches to their Church (empty of a Volunteer congregation) not by the Bell, but by the whip. This Ecclesiastic military discipline is happily taken up, in order to form an Army of well scourged Papists into a firm Phalanx for the support of the Protestant Religion. I wish them Joy of this their valuable discovery in Theology, Politicks and the Art military. Fashion governs the World; and it is the fashion in the great French Empire of Pure and perfect Protestantism, as well as in the little busy medling Province of servile imitators that apes, at an humble distance, the Tone of its Capital, to make a Crusade against you poor Catholicks. But whatever may be thought in Ireland of its share of a War against the Pope in that outlying part of Europe, the Zealous Protestant Buonoparté has given his late

Holiness far more deadly blows in the center of his own power and in the nearest seats of his influence,[1] than the Irish Directory can arrogate to itself within its own Jurisdiction from the utmost efforts of its political and military skill. I have my doubts, (they may perhaps arise from my ignorance) whether the Glories of the Night expeditions in surprizing the Cabin fortresses in Louth and Meathe[2] or whether the Slaughter and expulsion of the Catholic Weavers by another set of Zealots in Armagh, or even the proud trophies of the late potatoe Field in that County, are quite to be compared to the Protestant Victories on the Plains of Lombardy; or to the possession of the Fiat of Bologna,[3] or to the approaching Sack of Rome where even now the Protestant Commissaries give the Law. In all this Business great Britain, to us merely Secular politicians, makes no great figure; but let the glory of great Britain shift for itself as it may. All is well, provided Popery is crushed.

This War against Popery furnishes me with a Clue that leads me out of a *Maze* of perplexed politicks, which without it I could not in the least understand. I now can account for the whole. Lord Malmsbury is sent to prostrate the dignity of the English Monarchy at Paris, that an Irish Popish common Soldier may be whipt in to give an appearance of habitation to a deserted protestant Church in Ireland. Thus we balance the account. Defeat and dishonor abroad; Oppression at Home—We sneak to the Regicides, but we boldly trample upon our poor fellow Citizens. But all is for the Protestant Cause.

The same ruling principle explains the Rest. We have abdicated the Crown of Corsica, which had been newly soldered to the Crown of Great Britain and to the Crown of Ireland, lest the British Diadem should look too like the Popes triple Crown. We have ran away from the People of Corsica, and abandonned them without Capitulation of any kind; in favour of those of them who might be our friends. But then, it was for their having capitulated with us, for Popery, as a part of their Constitution. We make amends for our Sins by our Repentance, and for our Apostacy from Protestantism by a breach of faith with popery. We have fled, overspread with dirt and ashes but with hardly enough of Sack Cloath to cover our nakedness. We recollected that this Island, (together with its Yews and its other salubrious pro-

---

[1] The Pope had just been forced to make peace with France.

[2] Burke is probably referring to the methods used in repressing Defenderism.

[3] 'The Senate of Bologna has issued a proclamation by which it announces to the inhabitants of that new Republic, that the Constitution is completed, and that it has been sent to General *Buonoparte*, and the Commissioners of the Executive Directory, for their approbation' (*The Times*, 9 December).

ductions) had given birth to the illustrious Champion of the Protestant World Buonoparté—It was therefore not fit (to use the favorite Franch expression) that the Cradle of this religious Hero should be polluted by the feet of the British Renegade Slaves, who had stipulated to support Popery in that Island whilst his friends and fellow Missionaries are so gloriously employed in extirpating it in another—Our policy is growing every day into more and more consistency. We have shewed our broad back to the Mediterrenian. We have abandoned too the very hope of an alliance in Italy. We have relinquished the Levant to the Jacobins. We have considered our Trade as nothing—Our policy and our honor went along with it; but all these objects were well sacrificed to remove the very suspicion of giving any assistance to that Abomination, the Pope, in his insolent attempts to resist a truly prot-estant power resolved to humble the Papal Tiara, and to prevent his pardons and his dispensations from being any longer the standing terror of the wise and virtuous Directory of Ireland; who cannot sit down with any tolerable comfort to an innocent little Job, whilst his Bulls are thundering thro' the world. I ought to suppose that the arrival of General Hoche is eagerly expected in Ireland;[4] for He, too, is a most zealous Protestant; and he has given proof of it by the studied cruelties and insults by which He put to death the old Bishop of Dol;[5] whom, (but from the mortal fear I am in lest the suspicion of Popery should attach upon me) I should call a glorious martyr and should class him among the most venerable prelates that have appeared in this Century. It is to be feared however, that the Zealots will be disappointed in their pious hopes by the Season of the Year, and the bad condition of the Jacobin Navy, which may hinder him this Winter from giving his Brother Protestants in Ireland his kind assistance in accomplishing with you what the other friend of the cause, Buono-parté, is doing in Italy; and what the Masters of these two pious Men the Protestant Directory of France, have so thoroughly accomplished in that the most Popish, but unluckily whilst popish the [most] cul-tivated, the most populous and the most flourishing of all Countries the austrian Netherlands.

When I consider the narrowness of the views and the total want of human wisdom displayed in our Western Crusade against Popery, it is impossible to speak of it but with every mark of contempt and

---

[4] General Louis-Lazare Hoche (1768–97) was in charge of the French forces which had been assembled at Brest to invade Ireland.

[5] Urbain-René de Hercé (1726–95), the Bishop of Dol, had been executed on 28 July 1795 after Hoche's defeat of the royalists at Quiberon.

scorn—yet one cannot help shuddering with horror when one contemplates the terrible consequences that are frequently the results of craft united with Folly—placed in an unnatural elevation. Such ever will be the issue of things, when the mean vices attempt to mimick the grand passions.—Great men will never do great mischief but for some great End. For this they must be in a state of inflammation and in a manner out of themselves—Among the nobler Animals whose blood is hot, the bite is never poisonous, except when the Creature is mad; but in the cold blooded reptile race, whose poison is exalted by the Chemistry of their icy complexion, their venom is the result of their health, and of the perfection of their Nature—Woe to the Country in which such snakes, whose primum Mobile is their Belly, obtain wings and from Serpents become dragons. It is not that these people want natural Talents and even a good cultivation; on the contrary, they are the sharpest and most sagacious of mankind in the things to which they apply—But having wasted their faculties upon base and unworthy objects, in any thing of a higher order, they are far below the common rate of two legged animals.

I have nothing more to say, just now, upon the Directory in Ireland which indeed is alone worth any mention at all. As to the Half Dozen, (or half score as it may be) of Gentlemen, who, under various names of authority, are sent from hence to be the subordinate agents of that low order of beings, I consider them as wholly out of the question— Their virtues or their vices; their ability or their Weakness, are matters of no sort of consideration. You feel the thing very rightly—all the evils of Ireland originate within itself. That unwise body, the United Irishmen, have had the folly to represent those Evils as owing to this Country, when in truth its chief guilt is in its total neglect, its utter oblivion, its shameful indifference and its entire ignorance, of Ireland and of every thing that relates to it, and not in any oppressive disposition towards that unknown region. No such disposition exists. English Government has farmed out Ireland, without the reservation of a pepper Corn rent in Power or influence, publick or individual, to the little narrow Faction that Domineers there. Thro' that alone they see, feel, hear, or understand, any thing relative to that Kingdom; nor do they any way interfere that I know of, except in giving their countenance and the sanction of their Names to whatever is done by that *Junto*.

Ireland has derived some advantage from its independance on the Parliament of this Kingdom; or rather it did derive advantage from the arrangements that were made at the time of the establishment of that Independance. But human blessings are mixed; and I cannot but think, that even these great blessings were bought dearly enough, when along with the weight of the authority, they have totally lost all Benefit from the superintendancy of the British Parliament. Our Pride is succeded by fear. It is little less than a breach of Order, even to mention Ireland in the House of Commons of Great Britain. If the people of Ireland were to be flayed alive by the predominant faction it would be the most critical of all attempts so much as to discuss the Subject in any public Assembly upon this side of the Water. If such a faction should by its folly or iniquity or both, provoke disturbances in Ireland, the force paid by this Kingdom would infallibly be employed to repress them. This would be right enough, if our public Councils here at the same time possessed and employed the means of enquiry into the merits of that cause in which their blood and treasure were so laid out. By a strange inversion of the order of things not only the largest part of the Natives of Ireland are thus annihilated; but the Parliament of Great Britain itself is rendered no better than an instrument in the hands of an Irish faction—This is ascendancy with a Witness! In what all this will end it is not impossible to conjecture; tho' the exact time of the accomplishment cannot be ⟨fixed⟩ with the same certainty as you may calculate an Eclipse.

As to your particular conduct it has undoubtedly been that of a good and faithful Subject, and of a man of integrity and honor—You went to Ireland this last time,[6] as you did the first time, at the express desire of the English Minister of that Department, and at the request of the Lord Lieutenant himself. You were fully aware of the Difficulties that would attend your Mission; and I was equally sensible of them— Yet you consented, and I advised, that you should obey the voice of what we considered as indispensible duty. We regarded as the great Evil of the time the growth of Jacobinism, and we were very well assured that from a variety of causes no part of these Countries were more favorable to the growth and progress of that Evil than our unfortunate Country. I considered it as a tolerably good omen, that Government would do nothing further to foment and provoke the Jacobin malady, that they called upon you, a strenuous and steady Royalist, and an enlightened and exemplary Clergyman; A man of birth and respectable connexions in the Country; a man well informed and conversant in State Affairs, and in the general Politicks of the several Courts of Europe, and intimately and personally habituated

---

[6] Hussey had spent the summer of 1796 in England.

in some of those Courts. I regretted indeed that the Ministry which had my most earnest good wishes declined to make any sort of use of the reiterated information you had given them of the designs of their Enemies, and had taken no notice of the noble and disinterested Offers, which thro' me, were made for employing you to save Italy and Spain to the British Alliance. But this being past and Spain and Italy lost I was in hopes, that they were resolved to put themselves in the right at home by calling upon you that they would leave on their part no cause or pretext for Jacobinism except in the seditious disposition of Individuals; but I now see that instead of profiting by your advice and services, they will not so much as take the least notice of your written representations or permit you to have access to them on the part of those whom it was your Business to reconcile to Government as well as to conciliate Government towards them. Having rejected your services as a friend of Government, and in some sort in its employment, they will not even permit to you the natural expression of those sentiments which every man of sense and honesty must feel, and which every plain and sincere man must speak upon this vile plan of abusing Military discipline and perverting it into an instrument of religious persecution. You remember with what indignation I heard of the scourging of the Soldier at Carrick for adhering to his religious Opinions—It was at the time when Lord FitzWilliam went to take possession of a short lived Government in Ireland—Breves et infaustos populi Hiberni amores.[7] He could not live long in power because he was a true Patriot, a true friend of both Countries a steady resister of Jacobinism in every part of the World. On this occasion he was not of my Opinion. He thought, indeed, that the Sufferer ought to be relieved and discharged and I think he was so: But as to punishments to be inflicted on the Offender, he thought more lenient measures comprehended in a general plan to prevent such Evils in future, would be the better course. My Judgement, such as it was, had been, that punishment ought to attach so far as the Laws permitted, upon every evil action of subordinate power as it arose. That such acts ought at least to be marked with the displeasure of Government because general remedies are uncertain in their Operation when obtained, and that it is a matter of great uncertainty whether they can be obtained at all. For a time *his* appeared to be the better Opinion. Even after He was cruelly torn from the embraces of the people of Ireland, when the Militia and other Troops were encamped, (if I recollect rightly, at

---

[7] Brief and unblest the loves of the Irish people; see Tacitus, *Annals*, ii, 41.

Loughlinstown) you yourself with the knowledge and acquiescence of the suceeding Government publickly performed your function to the Catholicks then in Service. I believe too that all the Irish who had composed the foreign Corps taken into British pay had their regular Chaplains. But we see that things are returning fast to their old corrupted Channels. There they will continue to flow.

If any material Evil had been stated to have arisen from this Liberty that is, if Sedition Mutiny, or disobedience of any kind to Command, had been taught in their Chappels, there might have been a reason for not only forcing the Soldiers into Churches where better doctrines were taught, but for punishing the Teachers of disobedience and Sedition,—But I have never heard of any such Complaint. It is a part therefore of the Systematic illtreatment of Catholicks—This System never will be abandonned as long as it brings advantage to those who adopt it—If the Country enjoys a momentary quiet it is pleaded as an argument in favour of the good effect of wholesome rigours—If, on the Contrary, the Country ⟨grows⟩ more discontented; and if riots and disorders multiply, new Arguments are furnished for giving a vigorous support to the authority of the Directory on account of the rebellious disposition of the people. So long therefore as disorders in the Country become pretexts for adding to the power and emolument of an odious Junto, means will be found to keep one part of it or other in a perpetual state of confusion and disorder. This is the old traditionary policy of that sort of men. The discontents which under them break out among the people become tenure by which they hold their situation.

I do not deny, that in these Contests the people however oppressed are frequently much to blame, whether provoked to their excesses or not, undoubtedly the Law ought to look to nothing but the Offence and to punish it. The redress of grievances is not less necessary than the punishment of disorders; but it is of another resort. In punishing however, the Law ought to be the only rule—If it is not of sufficient force, a force, consistent with its general principles, ought to be added to it. The first duty of a State is to provide for its own conservation. Until that point is secured it can preserve and protect nothing else; but, if possible, it has a greater interest in acting according to strict Law, than even the Subject himself. For if the people see, that the Law is violated to crush them they will certainly despise the Law, They on their part will be easily Led to violate it whenever they can, by all the means in their power. Except in cases of direct War, whenever Government abandons Law, it proclaims Anarchy.

I am well aware, (if I cared one farthing for the few Days I have to live, whether the vain breath of men blow hot or cold about me) that they who censure any Oppressive proceeding of Government are exciting the people to Sedition and revolt. If there be no oppression it is very true or if there be nothing more than the lapses, which will happen to human infirmity at all times and in the exercise of all power, such complaints would be wicked indeed—These lapses are exceptions implied: an allowance for which is a part of the understood covenant by which Power is delegated by fallible men to other men that are not infallible; but whenever a hostile spirit on the part of Government is shewn the Question assumes another form.—This is no casual Errour, no lapse, no sudden surprise. Nor [is] it a question of civil or political Liberty. What contemptible stuff it is to say, that a Man who is lashed to Church against his conscience would not discover that the whip is painful, or that He had a conscience to be violated, unless I told him so? Would not a penitent Offender confessing his Offence, lamenting it, and expiating it by his blood, when denied the consolation of Religion at his last moments, feel it as no injury to himself or that the rest of the world would feel so horrible and impious an oppression with no indignation, unless I happened to say it ought to be reckoned amongst the most barbarous acts of our barbarous time. Would the people consider their being taken out of their beds and transported from their family and friends to be an equitable and legal and charitable proceeding, unless I should say that it was a violation of Justice, and a dissolution, 'pro tanto,' of the very compact of human Society? If a House of Parliament whose Essence it is to be the Guardian of the Laws, and a Simpathetic protector of the rights of the people (and eminently so of the most defenceless) should not only countenance but applaud this very violation of all Law, and refuse even to examine into the Grounds of the necessity upon the allegation of which Law was so violated, would this be taken for a tender Solicitude for the welfare of the poor, and a true proof of the representative Capacity of the House of Commons, unless I should happen to say (what I do say) that the House had not done its duty either in preserving the sacred rules of Law or in justifying the woeful and humiliating privilege of necessity. They may indemnify and reward others. They might contrive, if I was within their grasp, to punish me, or if they thought it worth while to stigmatize me by their censures; but who will indemnify them for the disgrace of such an Act? Who will save them from the censures of Posterity? What act of Oblivion will cover them from the wakeful memory, from the Notices and issues of the Grand remem-

brancer, the God *within?* Would it pass with the people, who suffer
from the abuse of lawful power when at the same time they suffer
from the use of lawless violence of Jacobins amongst themselves that
Government had done its duty and acted leniently in not animad-
verting on one of those Acts of violence? If I did not tell them, that
the lenity with which Government passes by the Crimes and oppressions of a favourite faction, was itself guilty of the most atrocious of
all Cruelties. If a Parliament should hear a declamation, attributing
the Sufferings of those who are destroyed by these riotous proceedings
to their misconduct and then to make them self-felonious, and should
en effet refuse an enquiry into the fact, is no inference to be drawn
from thence, unless I tell men in high places, that these proceedings
taken together form not only an encouragement to the abuse of Power,
but to riot, sedition, and a rebellious Spirit which sooner or later will
turn upon those that encourage it?

I say little of the business of the Potatoe field,[8] because I am not
yet acquainted with the particulars. If any persons were found in arms
against the King, whether in a field of Potatoes, or of Flax, or of
Turnips, they ought to be attacked by a military Power, and brought
to condign Punishment by course of Law—If the County in which
the Rebellion was raised, was not in a temper fit for the execution of
Justice, a Law ought to be made, such as was made with regard to
Scotland[9] on the Suppression of the rebellion of 45 to hang the Delinquents. There could be no difficulty in convicting men who were
found 'flagrante delicto'. But I hear nothing of all this. No Law, no
tryal, no punishment commensurate to Rebellion; nor of a known
proportion to any lesser delinquency, nor any discrimination of the
more or the less guilty. Shall you and I find fault with the proceedings
of France, and be totally indifferent to the proceedings of Directories
at home. You and I hate Jacobinism as we hate the Gates of Hell—
Why? Because it is a System of oppression. What can make us in love
with oppression because the Syllables Jacobin are not put before the
ism. When the very same things are done under the *ism* preceded by
any other Name in the Directory of Ireland.

I have told you, at a great length for a Letter, very shortly for the
Subject and for my feelings on it, my sentiments of the scene in which
you have been called to act,—on being consulted you advized Sufferers

---

[8] In the Fall of 1796 crowds had collected at farms in Northern Ireland and as a gesture of
sympathy had dug the potatoes for the owners, some of whom had been imprisoned.

[9] 'An Act for the more easy and speedy Trial of such Persons as have levied, or shall levy
War against His Majesty . . .' (19 Geo. II, c. 9), which was passed in 1746.

to quiet and submission; and giving Government full credit for an attention to its duties you held out, as an inducement to that submission, some sort of hope of redress. You tryed what your reasons and your credit could do to effect it. In consequence of this piece of Service to Government you have been excluded from all communication with the Castle;[10] and perhaps you may thank yourself that you are not in Newgate. You have done a little more than in your circumstances I should have done. You are indeed very excusable from your motive; but it is very dangerous to hold out to an irritated people Any hopes that we are not pretty sure of being able to realize. The Doctrine of Passive obedience, as a Doctrine, it is unquestionably right to teach; but to go beyond that, is a sort of deceit; and the people who are provoked by their Oppressors do not readily forgive their friends, if whilst the first persecutes and the others appear to deceive them. These friends lose all power of being serviceable to that Government in whose favor they have taken an illconsidered Step. Therefore my Opinion is, that untill the Castle shall shew a greater disposition to listen to its true friends than hitherto it has done, it would not be right in you any further to obtrude your services. In the mean time upon any new Application from the Catholics you ought to let them know simply and candidly how you stand.

The Duke of P——d[11] sent you to Ireland from a situation in this Country of advantage, and comfort to yourself and of no small utility to others. You explained to him in the clearest manner the conduct you were resolved to hold. I do not know that your writing to him will be of the least advantage—I rather think not; yet I am far from sure, that you do not Owe it to him, and to yourself to represent to his Grace the matters which, in substance, you have stated to me.

If any thing else should occur to me I shall, as you wish it, communicate my thoughts to you. In the mean time, I shall be happy to hear from you as often as you find it convenient. You never can neglect the great object of which you are so justly fond; and let me beg of you not to let slip out of your mind the Idea of the auxiliary studies and acquirements, which I recommended to you to add to the merely professional pursuits of your young Clergy; and above all, I hope that you will use the whole of your influence among the Catholics to persuade them to a greater indifference about the Political Objects which at present they have in view. It is not but that I am aware of their importance; or wish them to be abandond. But that they would follow

[10] The Castle in Dublin, the seat of government.
[11] The Duke of Portland.

opportunities and not to attempt to force any thing. I doubt whether the priveleges they now seek or have lately sought are compassable. The Struggle would, I am afraid only lead to some of Those very disorders which are made pretexts for further Oppression of the oppressed. I wish the leading people amongst them would give the most Systematic attention to prevent a frequent communication with their adversaries. There are a part of them proud, insulting, capricious, and tyrannical. These of Course will keep them at a distance. There are others of a seditious Temper who would make them at first the instruments and in the End the Victims of their factious Temper and purposes. Those that steer a middle course are truly respectable but they are very few. Your friends ought to avoid all imitation of the Vices of their proud Lords. To many of these they are themselves sufficiently disposed. I should therefore recommend to the middle ranks of that description in which I include not only all merchants but all farmers and tradesmen, that they would change as much as possible those expensive modes of living and that dissipation to which our Countrymen in general are so much addicted. It does not at all become men in a State of persecution. They ought to conform themselves to the circumstances of a people whom Government is resolved not to consider as upon a par with their fellow Subjects. Favour they will have none. They must aim at other rescources to make themselves independent in fact before they aim at a nominal independence. Depend upon it, that with half the privileges of the others, joined to a different System of manners they would grow to a degree of importance to which, without it, no privileges could raise them; much less any intrigues or factious practices. I know very well, that such a discipline among so numerous a people is not easily introduced; but I am sure it is not impossible—If I had youth and strength, I would go myself over to Ireland to work on that plan, so certain I am, that the well being of all descriptions in the Kingdom, as well as of themselves depends upon a reformation among the Catholicks. The work will be very slow in its operation but it is certain in its effect. There is nothing which will not yield to perseverance and method. Adieu! My dear Sir—you have full liberty to shew this Letter to all those (and they are but very few) who may be disposed to think well of my Opinions. I did not care, so far as regards myself, whether it was read on the change; but with regard to you more reserve may be proper—But that you will best judge.

CHAPTER TEN

PARTY

BURKE ON HIS OWN

"A LL ACTING in Corps tends to reduce the consideration of an
individual who is of any distinguished value," said Burke in
1779 (letter to Shackleton, Chapter 4). Though it would obviously
have been foolish to cite in his own case this potential exception to
his doctrine of party loyalty, it was in his mind, ready for use. Burke's
isolation began in the Regency Crisis, when after one visit to see Fox
in which he pressed an argument that did not find favor, he admits:
"Afterwards I was little consulted" (letter to Windham, 1789). But it
was of course the receptiveness of Fox and of the Whigs he influenced
to the French Revolution that led to the break between Burke and
his party.

A difference of opinion over the Revolution had become clear in
the debate on the Army Estates of February 9, 1790, but the famous
break occurred after the publication of Burke's *Reflections on the Revolution in France*, on May 6, 1791, when Fox attacked Burke personally
as well as politically. In a series of encounters Burke defended himself,
but he stood alone. This, he said in his account of the event, "I confess
. . . forms a presumption against my whole life" (letter to Lord Fitzwilliam, June 1791). But it was a presumption he was ready to rebut
with the charge that it was the party that had changed, not he. The
party had always been esteemed (or reproached) for being aristocratic;
now it had become democratic and gone on to "propagate the principles of French levelling and confusion" (letter to Lord Fitzwilliam,
November 1791).

"How can you aristocrates exist if you are not true to one another?" demanded Burke of the Duke of Devonshire (letter of March 1795). As defender of aristocrats, he said: 'I am an aristocrate in principle; in situation God knows nothing less." "New men" like himself should support aristocratic principles rather than the democratic ones that speculative upstarts promote. While Burke stands behind—and occasionally ahead of—his aristocrats, speculative thinkers such as the *philosophes* in France and the "French faction" of dissenters in England urged the people to overthrow the aristocracy. Such men are "sublime Metaphysicians." "They only ask whether the proposition be true? whether it produces good or evil is no part of their concern" (letter to William Weddell, 1792).

In letters to and on Lord John Cavendish we have Burke's estimate of the "English Nobleman of the Old Stamp," the perfect gentleman who because of his gentlemanly lack of decisiveness is an imperfect politician. Only a party can "make an excellent whole out of defective parts"; but such a party may also be imperfect at certain decisive moments. As Burke was dying, we learn, he refused an offer of reconciliation from his old friend Fox. Although in Burke's earlier years public friendship was the visible proof that partisanship was consistent and legitimate, now it was necessary that Burke be seen to have sacrificed his friendship in order to maintain his sincerity (letter of Jane Burke, 1797).

To WILLIAM WINDHAM—[*circa* 24 *January* 1789]

Corr. (1958), V, 436–45

The Regency Crisis of 1788–89 was caused by a period of insanity or delirium in King George III. The Prince of Wales, as heir apparent, would obviously serve as Regent for the King until he recovered, but the question was whether the Prince should have full powers while he was Regent, or limited powers. Opinions on this question were affected by the general anticipation that the Prince would replace Pitt's ministry with one led by Fox. Limitations to the Prince of Wales's powers as Regent proposed by Pitt were adopted by the House of Commons on 16 and 19 January and sent to the Lords. Burke took advantage of the intermission of Regency business in the Commons, while the Resolutions remained with the Lords, to spend a few days at Beaconsfield. He was becoming increasingly uneasy at what he considered to be the Opposition's lack of clear policy. He confided his doubts to Wiliam Windham, who had spoken strongly against Pitt's limitations in the debate of the 19th.

(Copy)

I staid at Brookes's on Tuesday Night, in hopes of seeing you, until after twelve. I had a good deal of discourse with Pelham,[1] who gave me leave to flatter myself that you and he might dine with me, and pass a night here, between this and Monday. We have means of feeding you, though without our Cook. But the dairy Maid is not a bad hand at a Pinch, and we have just killed a Sheep which though large and fat, is I believe full six years old, and very fine meat. I have already I think, received some small benefit to my health, by coming into the Country. But this view to health though far from unnecessary to me, was not the chief cause of my present retreat. I began to find, that I was grown rather too anxious; and had begun to discover to myself and to others, a solicitude relative to the present state of affairs, which though their strange condition might well warrant in others, is certainly less suitable to my time of life, in which all emotions are less allowed, and to which, most certainly all human concerns ought in reason to become more indifferent, than to those who have work to do, and a good deal of day and of inexhausted strength to do it in. I sincerely wish to withdraw myself from this scene for good and all, but unluckily the India Business binds me in point of honour, and whilst I am waiting for that, comes across another of a kind totally different from any that has hitherto been seen in this country, and which has been attended with consequences very different from those which ought to have been expected, in this Country or in any Country, from such an event. It is true, I had been taught by some late proceedings and by the character of the persons principally concerned, to look for something extraordinary. With a strong sense of this, my opinion was that the Prince ought to have *done* what has been *said* it was his right to do, and which might have been as safely done as was unsafely said.[2] He ought himself to have gone down to the House of Lords, and to *them* by himself, and to the House of Commons by *Message*, to have communicated the King's condition, and to have desired the advice and assistance of the two Houses.[3] His friends would then have been the *proposers*, and his enemies the *opposers* which would have been a great advantage. The proceedings in Council ought also

---

[1] Thomas Pelham (1756–1826), a supporter of the Opposition, had written of 'The Wickedness, Political Profligacy and immorality' of Pitt's plan to limit the powers of the Regent.

[2] By Fox in the House of Commons on 10 December 1788. Fox had said that 'In his firm opinion, his royal highness the Prince of Wales had as clear, as express a right to assume the reins of government, and exercise the power of sovereignty . . . as in the case of his Majesty's having undergone a natural and perfect demise' (*Parliamentary History*, XXVII, 706–7).

[3] The Prince himself had objected to this procedure.

to have originated from him. Whereas we admitted the *Official* Ministers as the Kings *confidential* Servants, when he had no confidence to give. The plans originated from them; We satisfied ourselves with the place of Objectors and Opposers, a weak post always; and we went out with the spirit (if it may be so called) of *inferiority,* and of a meer common Opposition with the Prince of Wales, Regent in designation, and future King at our head, he unable to support us and we unable to support him. Though I went to town strongly impressed with this Idea, which I stated to Fox when I saw him in his bed, and to others, it met so ill a reception from all to whom I mentioned it, and it seemed then a matter of course, that the men who remained in place (as Pitt and the Chancellor did) without character or efficiency in Law were under an exclusive obligation to take the lead; and some were of opinion that they ought to be called upon and stimulated to the production of their plans. I was really overborn with this, I may say almost universal conceit, so much so, that I gave over pressing my own and wrote to my Brother, then here, that I found it necessary to give it up, and even to change it; and on this he wrote me a strong remonstrance. Afterwards I was little consulted.[4] This Errour of ours (if such it was) is fundamental, and perhaps the cause of all our subsequent disasters. I don't trouble you with these remarks, as complaining of what was done, or as laying too much weight on my first opinions. In truth things have turned out so contrary to all my rational speculation in several instances, that I dare not be very positive in what appears to me most advisable, nor am I at all disposed very severely to censure the proceedings most adverse to my own Ideas. I throw out these things to you, and wish to put you in possession of my thoughts, that if they meet with a reception in your mind, you may urge them in time and place with a force, which for many reasons, (perhaps some of personal fault or defect or excess in myself but most certainly from a sort of habit of having what I suggest go for nothing) I can no more hope for. I look back to any thing that has been done or omitted, for no other purpose than to guide our proceedings in future. In the first place I observe, that though there have been a very few consultations upon particular measures, there have been none at

---

[4] There may have been another reason for Burke's isolation besides differences over policy. The party leaders were embarrassed by the problem of what position he was to occupy in the expected Regency Government. They did not approve of him for the post of Chancellor of the Exchequer and intended to re-instate him in his old place as Paymaster General. Nor were they willing to let him dominate East India policy. Fox, who was to be Foreign Secretary, placed his own name at the head of a list of the Board of Control, and as a Secretary of State he would have the right to take the chair of the Board, of which Burke would be an ordinary member.

all *de summa rerum*. It has never been discussed, whether, all things taken together, in our present situation, it would not be the best or the least evil course, for the publick and the Prince, and possibly in the end for the party that the Prince should surrender hmself to his enemies and ours. Of one thing I am quite certain; that if the two houses, animated by a number of addresses to the Prince and of instructions to the members, should be bold enough to reverse all their pretended principles (as in case of such addresses and instructions they certainly will do) and demand of the Prince Regent to keep in these Ministers, I believe it will be found very difficult, if not absolutely impossible to resist such a requisition. It has always hitherto been thought wise rather to foresee such an extremity, and to act in the foresight, than to submit to it when it happens; —to make peace, whilst there is some faint appearance of choice left on the subject, has hitherto been the policy. If that surrender should be thought necessary, then it will be for the consideration of our friends, how to do it in the manner most honorable to themselves, and the best fitted to make an impression on the publick and this I think would best be done in the way of a strong, well reasoned Memorial on the Subject advising the Prince for the sake of the publick tranquility, and to prevent further outrages on the Constitution to yield to the present exigence thanking him for the Justice he was willing to do to the King's subjects, and for his Equity in delaying so long to yield to so wicked a proscription as that projected.—This in my poor Judgment, ought to be signed by all the Lords and Commoners amongst us and possibly by other Notables in the Country and then, without a formal secession, to absent ourselves from Parliament until favourable circumstances should call us to it. I am far from being certain that this method (this of yielding) would not be the best, considering who the Prince is, and who and of what stuff, we are. But if we choose the other way, which is, at all events to fight it out against a majority in the two houses, and a very great, bold and active party without doors making, for aught I know, the majority of the nation, then I am sure we ought to prepare ourselves for such a combat in a different manner, and to act in it with a very different spirit from any thing which has ever yet appeared amongst us. In the first place we ought to change that tone of calm reasoning which certainly does not belong to great and affecting interests, and which has no effect, but to chill and discourage those upon whose active exertions we must depend much more than on their cold judgment. Our style of argument, so very different from that by which

Lord North was run down,[5] has another ill effect. I know it encreases the boldness of some of those who are thus bold less from the courage of their original temperament than from the air of inferiority, debasement, and dejection under which we have appeared for some years past. In daring every thing, they see they risque nothing. Far from apprehending any mischief from our future just resentment, they are not troubled with any degree of present disgrace, or even with an hard word or a reflexion on their character, two or three trifling instances excepted. I suppose a more excellent speech than Foxes last,[6] has never been delivered in any House of Parliament, full of weighty argument eloquently enforced, and richly though soberly decorated. But we must all be sensible that it was a speech which might be spoken upon an important difference between the best friends, and where the parties had the very best opinion of each others general intentions for the publick good. Mr Pitt commended as he had reason to do, the singular moderation of a speech Mr Fox had made before,[7] with an oblique reflexion on those who had debated in another manner.[8] If a foreseen coalition with Mr Pitt should make this style of debate advisable for Mr Fox, the word ought to be given to others—who may bring much mischief on themselves, when such a coalition shall be made, for having spoken of Mr Pitts conduct as highly corrupt, factious and criminal; and in the mean time they may be considerd as hot and intemperate Zealots of a party with the main springs of whose politicks they are not acquainted.[9] So far as to the general style of debate. I will trouble you on this point, with a word on the use we may make of the degree of strength we possess in both Houses. We are a minority: but then we are a very large minority; and I never knew an instance in which such numbers, did not keep a majority in considerable awe. This was the case in a parliament of recognised authority. But in the present case it is universally admitted that the acts of the two houses are not legal, but to be legalized hereafter, and that our proceedings are not founded on anything but necessity. The submission therefore of the smaller number to the greater is a mere voluntary act, and not an acquiescence in a legal decision. I see no sort of reason to hinder

[5] When as First Lord of the Treatury he was forced to resign in the spring of 1782.

[6] Fox's speech of 19 January in the Commons debate on Pitt's proposal to place control of the King's person and household in the Queen's hands.

[7] On 22 December.

[8] Pitt's 'oblique reflexion' was almost certainly directed at Burke, who had opened the debate on 22 December.

[9] The possibility of a coalition between Pitt and Fox had often been rumored since the beginning of the King's illness.

us from protesting on the Journals, or if they prevent us from that, from publishing strong manifestoes signed with our names. Our conduct cannot be more irregular than theirs. If it is objected that this principle might lead us a great deal further, I confess it; but then their principle would lead them further too, and they have in fact gone to ten times worse and more serious lengths against the substance, and the solid maxims of our Government, than we can be suspected of going, who, should we take the steps I suggest, only trespass against form and decorum. But whilst they neither attend to form or to substance, and we are the slaves of form, it is self evident, that we do not engage upon equal terms. I do not dwell upon this point so much for the sake of this measure (which I wish rather we did not think forbidden, than that I pressingly recommend) but for another and more serious reason. When I consider the change of Mr Pitts language I am convinced that an intention is entertained of addressing the Prince to keep him in power. To the last day's debate, he constantly spoke of himself as virtually out of place, and of Mr Fox as Minister in certain designation. That day he totally changed his note.[10] His friend Mr Rolle had arrived with his address from Devonshire.[11] Are any on our part to advise the Prince not to comply with that address? Or are we to consider ourselves as bound by the faith which Mr Sheridan has held on the part of the Prince, that he will comply with the requisition of the House of Commons? To what to attribute the two voluntary declarations made by Sheridan on that subject, especially the last, I am wholly at a loss.[12] If the Prince has authorised him to speak in this manner, all that I have said, or have to say on this side of the alternative, is vain and useless. We must submit, and there is an end of it. Even without this declaration, the difficulty in opposing such an address though from an House framed on principles directly contradictory to these addresses, would be very great. I should contend for as much as any one, perhaps more, the constitutional propriety of the King's submitting in every part of his executive Government to the advice of Parliament. But this like every other principle can bear

[10] i.e. on 19 January.

[11] John Rolle (1756–1842), later (1796) 1st Baron Rolle, M.P. for Devon, a loquacious backbench supporter of the Government.

[12] Richard Brinsley Sheridan (1751–1816) was thought to be in the Prince of Wales's confidence, and his speeches in the Commons were accordingly of particular importance during the Regency crisis. The two 'declarations' to which Burke refers appear to have been speeches on 22 December and 16 January in which Sheridan was understood to say that the Prince, as Regent, would respect the wishes of the House of Commons (*Parliamentary History*, xxvii, 852 and 966). In fact, Sheridan envisaged a dissolution of Parliament soon after the Prince became Regent.

a practical superstructure of only a certain Weight, if the two Houses, without any sort of reason, merely from faction and caprice should attempt to arrogate to themselves under the name of advice, the whole power and authority of the Crown, the Monarchy would be an useless incumbrance on the Country if it were not able to make a stand against such attempts. If then such a stand is to be made, my opinon is first, that the way ought to be prepaved for it by a previous strong re-monstrance to the House of Commons from Westminster against their whole proceedings. I am told we may depend upon Westminster.[13] If we may, then I think it, from its vicinity, and the habitation in it of so many people from all parts of the Kingdom, (which makes it a sort of general representative of the whole), of more importance than any other whatsoever, if properly used, and if the means are taken which were taken on the accession of the present Royal Family, by the Duke of Newcastle[14] and others, to keep up and direct a spirit capable of seconding their petitions and addresses. I am not in general very fond of these things, but on occasions they must be used, and I hope they are not yet among the *artes perditiæ*. They have the monied interest,[15] let us use the interest of those whose property is their freedom. Other places will probably follow. But so far as I can discern, no attempt has yet been made to do more than merely to prevent the corporations or people from appearing against us, at Bristol excepted, where my Brother and his friends in the Corporation attempted more, but did not succeed. I should recommend that the same should be attempted where it might be more likely to succeed—but what I contend for in all these attempts, is, that we should not at all hold ourselves on the *defensive;* a post which in such affairs as these has never failed to bring ruin on those who have chosen to occupy it. The people, to be ani-mated, must seem to have some motive to *action;* and accusation has more to engage their attention than apology, which always implies at least a possibility of guilt. It is something abject at best. In order to prevent where we can do no better, or to act where we can act I am

[13] The Opposition had decided to obtain an address from Fox's constituents at Westminster in support of the Prince of Wales. Fox's ill health made difficult the arrangement for a rally at which he could be present; and before it could take place he was forced on the 25th to go to Bath to recuperate. In the end, a meeting of Westminster electors was held in his absence at the Crown and Anchor in the Strand on 14 February, when it was resolved to prepare a petition to the House of Lords 'against the Regency Bill, which was stated as insulting to the Heir Apparent, and injurious to the spirit of the Constitution.' The King's recovery, known within a day or two of this meeting, made both the Bill and the petition unnecessary.

[14] Thomas Pelham (1693–1768), 1st Duke of Newcastle, had begun his public career by organizing support for the new dynasty at the time of George I's accession in 1714.

[15] The 'monied interest', centred in the City of London, almost always supported the gov-ernment of the day and was particularly favorable to Pitt.

clear, that none but a corps of Observation ought to attend Parliament. We ought to give over all thoughts of division and the Members who have any interest ought to be sent down to their several districts. It was the present King and the present Ministers who have made, and who continue this Parliament out of Doors. It is now fixed, and it is for us to take our advantage of the actual state of the Country which is to the best of their power employed against us, at least until we shall be furnished with the means of establishing the constitutional bodies of the Kingdom in the degree of sober independence and decent respect which they ought to enjoy. Whilst these and other obvious measures, are going on abroad, the great security for their success, or the great remedy for their failure, is in the Conduct of the Prince himself. On that, more depends than on all the rest. All his actions, and all his declarations ought to be regular and the consequence of a plan, and if he refuses to comply with the addresses, he ought, once for all, to give them an answer which should be as much reason'd as his situation will admit, and which will serve for a manifesto. All his written proceedings must be so many manifestoes; for he will not be in Government by being appointed Regent but only in a situation to contend for it. Dead, cold, formal pieces, containing no sentiment to interest the feelings, nor no animated argument to go to the understanding, may serve well enough when power is secure, and able to stand on its own foundations, and in this precarious shew of government a party must be made, and it must be made as parties are formed in other Cases. There is not one rule, principle, or maxim of a settled Government that would be useful to us, that of general good conduct excepted. That which I should chiefly rely upon, in all these manifestoes, is a sentiment of dignity and independence and an indifference to the object unless it can be held on those terms. If this indeed be not supported by a degree of courage, either natural or infused, and a *real* resolution, rather to forfeit every thing than his own honour, and the safety of those embarked with him on the same bottom, to be sure such a style of speaking would be unsuitable and mischievous. But if the conduct and declarations are of a piece, I think they can hardly fail of success in the End, I say in the *End*, for we deceive ourselves wofully if we are [not] at the very opening of a dreadful struggle. All these and every thing else, however depend upon that, which if nobody has spirit and integrity enough to inculcate into the Prince he is and we are ruined. He must marry into one of the Sovereign houses of Europe. Till then he will be liable to every suspicion and to daily insult. He will not be consider'd as one of the Corps of

Princes; nor aggregated to that Body, which people here, more even than in other countries, are made to look at with respect. There must be a queen for the Women, or a person to represent one, else this Queen will have them all. I say this independently of the suggestion concerning Mrs Fitzherbert,[16] which I know to have great weight, and much the greatest in the extremities of the Kingdom. No King in Europe who is not married, or has not been so: No Prince appears settled unless he puts himself into the situation of the Father of a Family. I began this with a notion, that I could bring all I had to say into a few short heads, but I have been drawn into a length which I did not expect. One thing or other has taken me off—so that I must deliver myself the letter which I thought was to bring you hither— Perhaps what I have thrown down is of little moment—at any rate it is in safe hands, it is in the hands of one who will pardon and will conceal my weakness. Adieu and believe me ever

Sincerely and affectionately uours
EDMD BURKE

To EARL FITZWILLIAM—5 June 1791

Corr. (1958), VI, 271–75

In the debate of 11 May Burke had spoken twice of his approaching retirement from the House of Commons (*Parliamentary History*, xxix, 403, 416). The following day the *Morning Chronicle* put its own interpretation upon his statements. 'The great and firm body of the Whigs of England', it said, 'have decided on the dispute between Mr Fox and Mr Burke; and the former is declared to have maintained the pure doctrines by which they are bound together, and upon which they have invariably acted. The consequence is, that Mr Burke retires from parliament'. Burke resolved to write a pamphelt to demonstrate his consistency, *An Appeal from the New to the Old Whigs*. In the meantime his relations with his political friends were bound to be awkward, since no one else in the party had broken with Fox.

My dear Lord
. . . The difference between me and the party turns upon no trivial Objects. I am persuaded, that the world is threatned with great changes: I say threatned, because I do not think them likely to be changes for the better. Whilst there is any chance for preventing them any where,

<hr>

[16] The Prince of Wales had secretly married Mrs. Maria Anne Fitzherbert (1756–1837), a Roman Catholic, in December 1785. The Prince's intention if he became Regent was, according to his own account, that 'Mrs Fitz[herbert] should be as happy as he could make her, but should have no rank'.

especially within the sphere of our nearest duties, I do not conceive, that any one can be much blamed for an endeavour to keep things in their old and safe Course. On that Ground, and on full deliberation, I wrote and publishd my late Reflexions; and I was persuaded, that in such a View of things my personal Interest, ease, and convenience ought not to hold too high a place in my consideration.

I wished that Book to be, in the first instance, of service to the publick, in the second, to the party, as a valuable part of that publick. I beleive the service of the party was only second in my thoughts; but perhaps it was the first. I am sure its Interests were important considerations with me in every step I have taken on this and on all occasions.

I was persuaded, that the succession was the moment, and probably the only moment, favourable to the power of your party; at the same time, that the moment favourable to your power, would of all others be the most critical to you, and to the whole State. I was convinced to a certainty, that whatever tended to unsettle the succession, and to disturb the recognized ranks and orders, and the fixed properties in the nation would be of all men the most fatal to your friends, I mean the Princes friends, and the chiefs of your party, Whether you are considerd as politicians; or as private men of weight in your Country. I found, that at one time, most of the party concurred with me in that opinion. I know to a certainty, that many persons, taking in the highest of all,[1] and descending very low, were much reconciled to the party by that writing. I was pleased with this, as it might be the means of saving, one nation at least, from what I must think a terrible contagion; and as a set of people, dear to me by all ties, would be served themselves by their share in this Service.

I soon found, that things were much changed. There were those in the party, who chose rather to injure themselves than to be so served. I found that great, and almost systematick pains were taken to discredit that work in the Party, to get its principles disclaimed; and of course (for medium there is none) to get the Principles of Paine, Priestley, Price, Rouse, Mackintosh, Christie[2] &ca &ca &ca magnified and extolled, and in a sort of obscure and undefined manner to be adopted as the Creed of the party. The supper at Brookes's was a sort of Academy for these Doctrines. Individuals, little courted before, were seperately talked over, and, as it were, canvassed. I found, that the Prince of Wales, to Whose very existence the principles of that Book

---

[1] The King.

[2] These are authors of replies to Burke's *Reflections on the Revolution in France*.

were necessary, was very early led to take, and to express, no small dislike to them; and to abstain even from expressions of common politeness on the Pamphlets being presented to him.[3] If I had not receivd very particular intelligence of all these manœuvres, to the moment of the explosion in Parliament, yet the face of things, and the extraordinary change in Persons, could have left no Doubt in my Mind upon the subject.

When it came to that point, and that I was perfectly apprised, that Mr Foxes publick declaration in Parliament in favour of the French Whiggism[4] was a condition of the support he was to meet with from the first abilities in this Kingdom,—and when accordingly these dangerous declarations (as I thought them) were growing daily, with the daily growth of the French mischief, both at home and abroad, I must be thought to abandon my principles, or I must speak out. I made my option.

Mr Fox took that opportunity, when nothing of my Book was in question, to declare strongly and vehemently against *all* the doctrines it contained, in the whole, and in every part.[5] He then brought out, in an elaborate review (which I had reason to beleive had been for some time compiling and digesting) every action and every expression almost of my whole Life, whether publick or private, whether in jest or in earnest, wresting and misrepresenting them, with little Logick and less candour, to make me pass for an Apostate from my Principles, and a deserter from my party, and thereby to countenance a base charge, that I could have no other motive for the part, which during near two years I had taken against the propagation of French principles in this Kingdom, than a secret Bribe which I had received from the Ministers, an impudent calumny, which he well knew his friends the Presbyterians had been active in publickly propagating.[6]

On this occasion, the Party, as to a man, applauded his general principles; and not one of them, either at that time, or at any time since, by speech or declaration of any kind, by any thing directly written or spoken, or even suggested, have given it to be understood that they differd from him either in his general principles on this

[3] Lord Inchiquin later said that when the *Reflections* was first published, the Prince asked him '*How the Devil could your friend Burke publish such a Farrago of Nonsense?.*'

[4] Fox's speech of 15 April 1791.

[5] On 6 May. Fox had said that their opinions on the Revolution 'were wide as the poles asunder' and that 'he differed upon that subject with his . . . friend *toto cælo*'; in his second speech that day, Fox also said that when the *Reflections* was published 'he condemned that book both in public and private, and every one of the doctrines it contained' (*Parliamentary History*, XXIX, 377, 380, 389).

[6] This was a charge frequently made by Burke's enemies.

Subject, or upon the particular Charge of apostacy, and implied corruption on myself.

Another day came.[7] The same subject was revived. If there were heats there was time to cool. No word of blame or recrimination had escaped me in the Debate. I had confined myself solely to my defence. On that second day when I stated the injury I had receivd from this labourd inquisition into all my Life, in order to draw from it matter to disgrace me at the close of it, Not one word came from Mr Fox tending to retract or to soften the words, or to give them a Sense less harsh than they seemd to bear. He spoke in a manner much more suitable to the real greatness of his situation in parliament than to the friendly partiality he was pleased to express for me on the preceding day. On the second day not one of the party spoke one conciliatory word. Perhaps I might be to blame in the discussion which brought on this affair. I think I was not; but be that as it may, it is when people fall into mistake that they stand in need of friends and apologists. It is in that Case, that old services are to be put up against new Errours.

It was an exhibition absolutely new, to see a man who had sat twenty six Years in Parliament, not to have one friend in the House.

I confess it forms a presumption against my whole Life. Though it has been said by a wise man, 'Turpem esse senectutem quae se *oratione* defenderet,'[8] yet I am reduced to that humiliating necessity without I hope that imputation. I hope I shall acquit myself of my defence with an attention to my own little dignity, and without asperity to others.[9]

After this, what is my situation? After the reiterated declarations of those, who are taken for the mouth of the Whigg party, and are understood both at home and abroad to speak its sentiments, and when the rest of the party do mostly speak the same language, and others fall in, by at least, a tacit acquiescence, the result is, that I have the misfortune totally and fundamentally to differ with that party in constitutional and publick points of such moment, that all those, on which I have hitherto ever differd from other men and other Parties, are, in comparison, mere toys and Triffles.

What is personal to me is of no consideration to others. To myself it is of some. Charged as I am in full Parliament with having, from corruption, or some motives not much more respectable, contradicted and disgraced the whole Tenour of my Life, I beg to appeal to your

[7] May 11.

[8] . . . miseram esse senectutem quae se oratione defenderet; old age is wretched which needs to defend itself with words. See Cicero, *De Senectute*, XVIII, 62.

[9] Burke was already at work on his *Appeal from the New to the Old Whigs*.

Equity and candour, whether I could receive any further Obligations of any kind out of a party whose publick principles are the very reverse of mine, and who have recorded an account of my publick and private Character, which if admitted must reflect on me and on all my posterity, as long as the History of this Country is read. If I did I must allow the fidelity of the Picture.

I only draw myself within my own Circle. I blame nobody. I have been one way or another obliged to almost all. To some of you I owe the highest Obligations and to you my affections are ten thousand times stronger than my Obligations. I desire nothing now but to depart quietly into such a retreat as Providence (he only knows what sort of retreat it is to be) shall allot for my declining hours. After all you lose nothing. I leave your party far richer in abilities than I found it.

To EARL FITZWILLIAM—21 *November* 1791

Corr. (1958), VI, 449–53

Burke explains further his break with Fox and with his party.

My dear Lord,

I have received with the proper Sentiments, though I can never match with the proper expressions, the new mark you have given me in your Letter of the fifteenth, of your persevering and unconquerable friendship. No heart can be more truly filled than mine is with an affectionate and grateful Sense of all that is past, and all that you desire to continue, between us. Believe me, My dear Lord, the day I had taken the resolution[1] which your unparralleld goodness wishes me to alter, I did not act from the smallest particle of Pique, Jealousy, or resentment. God forbid. I would have been absurd, unjust, unnatural.

In one thing I am obliged a Little to disagree with your Lordship. If political Views had been an ingredient in your original kindness, as you never had any political Views, which did not arise from so many Virtues as you had purposes, instead of derogating from your honour, it would, in my poor Judgment, have rather added to it. It could never make you look the less in your own Eyes, that in being solidly useful to a friend you added Strength to a service which you thought intimately connected with the publick Welfare. I, for my part, would not have felt myself lowerd in my own opinion, in being thought

[1] Burke's refusal in his letter of 5 June, to accept further financial assistance from Fitzwilliam.

a person willing to be serviceable to such a Cause and capable of being so. Bitter Enmities have arisen out of Politicks. It would be a reflexion upon mankind, if dear and Lasting Friendships were not sometimes to spring from the same source. I confess, I did believe, that my industrious zeal in the publick service was one motive, (not the sole motive, there are others more flattering to my heart) to the share I had in your Lordships regard and Esteem. If wearied, and wasted out in that service, overpowerd with years, and with a very near prospect of a rapid encrease of the infirmities of body and Mind which attend the close of Life, if in those Circumstances one of the wisest and worthiest of my fellow Labourers was willing to make my retreat easy to me, I should be as happy to owe the repose of my declining years to friendship as to fortune.

You see, my Lord, that in declining to profit of your partiality, I had not the smallest Idea, that in taking advantage of it I had formerly disgraced either your Lordship or myself. But it has pleased God, that things should take a very unexpected turn. Instead of being sufferd to retire with Credit, and with a kind acknowlegement of service, my retreat has been imperiously orderd.[2] An attempt has been made by that Party, (in which I had acted, I am sure with zeal, and I think with Judgment, to the hour of my publick condemnation) to affix an eternal Stigma on my good name so far as it was in their power to brand me. In that situation, I appeal to the Equity and Candour inseperable from your Nature, to judge, whether thus *publickly* condemned, I can continue with honour to receive *privately* a favour of any kind from one of the chiefs of the party, which has thought proper, uncontradicted by any one from that day to this, to describe me in the manner in which I have been described. I confess, I cannot bear to appear to myself, in the light of a pardond criminal, who receives something as an alleviation of his punishment and as a compensation for his disgrace. My ever dear and honourd friend, this sacrifice, great to me in every light, is not made to Pride or popular opinion. But they who give up their self Estimation give up every thing.

Let me say, (I have examined myself and I can say it with truth) that no consideration of personal reputation, feeling or Interest, affects me in any degree equally with the entire Revolution which has taken place in the party, by which it has wholly changed its Character, its principles, and the foundations on which it stood. That party had always had, from Fools and knaves, the reproach, from honest and

---

[2] Burke is referring to the article in the *Morning Chronicle* announcing his expulsion from the Party.

wise men, the Estimation, of being an Aristocratick party. Such I
always understood it to be, in the true Sense of the word; that is to
say, a party grave and moral, equally removed from popular giddiness
and profligacy on the one hand, and from servile Court compliances
on the other. This Aristocratick Character, I thought, formed for that
party, in and out of power, a Ground of confidence with all the thinking
part of the Nation; and my opinion was, that, as men of activity and
parts should be successively joined to the party, they were to adopt
that Spirit. These opinions I endeavord to maintain in my two obnoxious Books (the Reflexions and the Appeal) and in whatever else
I have written concerning the Grand Revolution in Human affairs
which has begun in France. I must add, that there were few indeed
of the Party from whom I had not received either a written or explicit
verbal declaration of their perfect satisfaction in the first of these
Books, and an assurance that they considerd the publication as highly
seasonable, and highly serviceable to the publick, but eminently honourable and useful to the Party—and this Tone they continued, until
the word was given them to change it.

The Leaders have ever since gone on, and are with all their might
going on, to propagate the principles of French Levelling and confusion, by which no house is safe from its Servants, and no Officer
from his Soldiers, and no State or constitution from conspiracy and
insurrection. I will not enter into the baseness and depravity of the
System they adopt; but one thing I will remark, that its great Object
is not, (as they pretend to delude worthy people to their Ruin) the
destruction of all absolute Monarchies, but totally to root out that
thing called an *Aristocrate* or Nobleman and Gentleman. This they do
not profess; but in France they profess it and do it; and the party
here spare no pains to magnifye all that is done there, and to propagate
its principles. They gain ground daily in the party, and thro' the party,
in the Nation. They have two agents of the national assembly[3] one at
Paris and one here whom the party pays, or has lately paid, whose
sole Business is, in a Paper to which the party has given Patronage
and an amazing Circulation,[4] to spread opinions from French publi-

---

[3] On 7 July an English informant in Paris had written to Grenville, 'Two *Deputies* are arrived
here from the Revolution Society of London, to the Jacobins of Paris, a *Mr Perry*, editor, and
I believe proprietor, of a London morning paper called the *Morning Chronicle*, and a Mr Christie,
conductor of the *General Review*'. Perry (see next note) is obviously one of the two agents
referred to in Burke's letter, but the other may not be Christie.

[4] In December 1790 the *Morning Chronicle* was bought by James Perry (1756–1821) and
James Gray (d. 1796). The new proprietors immediately announced that their paper was 'the
Organ of that honourable and temperate Body The Whigs . . .' (*ibid*. 13 December 1790).

cations (such as the dialogue from Volney &c &c) which can have no other Effect than to root out all principle from the Minds of the Common people, and to put a dagger into the hands of every Rustick to plunge into the heart of his Landlord.

I believe, that having obtaind one of their Objects, which, trivial as it is, they have had many years at heart, to drive me out of the publick Service under obloquy, they may, in future, be a little more cool and guarded: But I know they are not a jot more disposed to alter their opinions, or the Spirit of their proceedings, which latter, by being better measured, may become more dangerous—Who can resist their doctrines, when no man in the party of a different opinion can look for his justest Objects, from those, who countenance no other, than the disciples of that System; and that no power exists, which can save from the Ban of the Party any Member of it, who shall be, (as I have been) bold enough to set forth any thing, in speaking or writing, against what is done in France for a Pattern to the world; or against the Principles upon which that Transaction has proceeded?

Now my dear Lord judge me fairly. I will tell you simply what in this Situation I mean to do, unless I see great reason to change my Mind. The Business of Hastings's prosecution I cannot abandon. My Stay in Parliament will not be one hour after that Business is closed. The time to its conclusion, though I hope short, appears to me as long as it can do to Mr Fox, or Mr Fitzpatrick,[5] or Mr Sheridan, or Mr Windham, or Mr Church,[6] or Mr Pelham,[7] or Mr Francis, or whoever else is the most ardent admirer of the French System. My Intention, almost a resolution, is during that painful Interval not to intermeddle with any political matter, except it relates to some change in this constitution, or that by bringing on French Questions I am called upon not to fly from my Ground, as if the Success of that scheme had made me ashamed of the Ideas I had formed in relation to it. It is impossible to say, what changes may take place,—but, neither with the Ministers, nor with the newmodeld Whiggs, will I act, or take any employment whatsoever. My Sense of what I owe to myself prevents me from the first, as well my abhorrence from giving a moments disgust to the two best friends which ever any man has had the happiness to possess—My Principles, my honour, my conscience, my feelings, will I hope effectually guard me from having any

[5] Richard Fitzpatrick (1748–1813), brother of Lord Ossory and intimate friend of Fox; at this time M.P. for Tavistock.

[6] John Barker Church (c. 1746–1818), M.P. for Wendover.

[7] Thomas Pelham (1756–1826), later (1805) 2nd Earl of Chichester; M.P. for Sussex.

connexion with the latter. In this situation, surely your Lordship does not think it would become me, when before the Session is three days old I may be called to speak strong things against those whom you honour with your confidence, and regard, or when, from the Depth of my retreat, I may be again impelled to put my pen to Paper, in a manner not less disagreeable than any I have yet wrote in, that it would be proper or decent for me, to receive large pecuniary assistance from one of the most considerable and respectable individuals of that Party, whose Cause and Interests I was, at the same time, perhaps injuring in the most essential manner? To be sure, the fact is known, only to my own family, your Lordship, and the D. of Portland. But the operation of honour (as seperated from *conscience*, which is not as between man and man but as between man and God) is to suppose the world acquainted with the transaction, and then to consider in what light the wise and virtuous would regard it. I am sure such men would never justifye my Conduct.

You see, my dear Lord, that I do not go upon any difference concerning the best method of preventing the Growth of a System which I believe we dislike in common. I cannot differ with you, because I do not think *any* method can prevent it. The Evil has happend; the thing is done in principle and in example; and we must wait the good pleasure of an higher hand than ours for the time of its perfect accomplishment in practice in this Country and elsewhere. All I have done for some time past, and all I shall do hereafter, will only be to clear myself from having any hand, actively or passively, in this great change. My dear Lord continue your Goodness and partiality to me, and let me cultivate as long as I live your Society and friendship. I shall have infinite satisfaction in finding when I pay my respects to you in London, that you still continue your old partiality to me. Believe me there is one way in which I deserve it—that is the most sincere and zealous affection, the most perfect Esteem and the warmest Gratitude to you. These Sentiments will never alter in whatever way, or in whatever country, or under whatever Circumstances the remaining thread of my Life may be drawn out. I am with the most cordial attachment

My dear Lord
Your ever faithful and ever obliged
humble Servant
EDM BURKE

Beconsfield Novr 21. 1791.

Of course your Lordship will throw this Letter into the fire after you have perused it—except you wish first to shew it to the D. of Portland from whom I have hitherto conceald nothing, nor ever wish to keep any thing secret. Mrs Burke gives your Lordship and Lady Fitzwilliam a thousand thanks for your attention to her. Within these few days she is much better.

To WILLIAM WEDDELL—31 *January* 1792

Corr. (1958), VII, 50–63

On 27 August 1791 William Weddell (1736–92), Burke's colleague as M.P. for Malton, had written to thank him for the *Appeal from the New to the Old Whigs*. Burke had originally intended to write a more or less public reply to him in the autumn.

My dear Sir,

. . . As to the party, which has thought proper to proscribe me on account of a book[1] which I published on the Idea, that the principles of a new, republican, frenchified Whiggism was gaining ground in this Country, I cannot say it was written *solely* with a view to the Service of that Party. I hope its views were more general. But I am perfectly sure, this was *one* of the Objects in my contemplation; and I am hardly less sure, that, (bating the insufficiency of the execution) it was well calculated for that purpose; and that it had actually produced that effect upon the minds of all those, at whose sentiments it is not disrespectful to guess. Possibly it producd that Effect without that exception—Mr Montagu[2] knows, many know, what a softening towards our party it produced in the thoughts and opinions of many men in many places. It presented to them Sentiments of Liberty which were not at war with order, virtue, Religion and Good Government; and though, for reasons which I have cause to rejoice that I listend to, I disclaimd myself as the organ of any party,[3] it was the general opinion, that I had not wanderd very widely from the Sentiments of those with whom I was known to be so closely connected. It was indeed then, and it is much more so now, absolutely necessary, to seperate those, who cultivate a rational and sober Liberty upon the plan of our existing constitution, from those, who think they have no Liberty, if it does

---

[1] The *Reflections*.

[2] Frederick Montagu (1733–1800), M.P. for Higham Ferrers 1768–90.

[3] Burke declared in the first paragraph of the *Reflections* that he wrote '. . . neither for, nor from, any description of men . . . My errors, if any, are my own. My reputation alone is to answer for them'.

not comprehend a right in them of making to themselves new constitutions at their pleasure.

The party with which I acted had, by the malevolent and unthinking, been reproached, and by the wise and good always esteemd and confided in—as an aristocratick Party. Such I always understood it to be in the true Sense of the word. I understood it to be a Party, in its composition and in its principles, connected with the solid, permanent long possessd property of the Country; a party, which, by a Temper derived from that Species of Property, and affording a security to it, was attached to the antient tried usages of the Kingdom, a party therefore essentially constructed upon a Ground plot of stability and independence; a party therefore equally removed from servile court compliances, and from popular levity, presumption, and precipitation.

Such was the general opinion of the substance and original Stamina of that party. For one, I was fully persuaded, that the Spirit Genius and Character of that party *ought* to be adopted, and for a long time I thought *was* adopted, by all the *new* men who in the Course of time should be aggregated to that body—whether any of these new men should be a person possessd of a large fortune of his own creating; or whether the *new* man should be (though of a family long decorated with the honours and distinctions of the State) only a younger Brother,[4] who had an importance to acquire by his Industry and his Talents— or whether the *new* man should be (as was my Case) *wholly* new in the Country and aimed to illustrate himself and his family by the services he might have the fortune to render to the publick. All these descriptions of new Men, and more, if more there are, I conceived, without any formal engagement, by the very constitution of the Party to be bound, with all the activity and energy of Minds animated and awakend by great hopes and Views, to support those aristocratick principles, and the aristocratick Interests connected with them, as essential to the real Benefit of the Body of the people, to which all names of party, all Ranks and orders in the State, and even Government itself ought to be entirely subordinate. These principles and Interests I conceivd were to give the Bias to all their proceedings. Adhering to these Principles, the aspiring Minds, that exalt and vivifye a Party could not be held in too much honour and consideration: departing from them they lose more than they can gain. They lose the advantages which they might derive from *such* a party, and they cannot make it fit for the purposes for which they desire to employ

---

[4] e.g. Fox.

it. Such a party, pushd forward by a blind impulse, may for some time proceed without an exact knowlege of the point to which it is going. It may be deluded; and by being deluded it may be discredited and hurt; but it is too unwieldy, both from its numbers, and from its property, to perform the services expected from a Corps of light Horse.

Against the existence of any such description of men as our party is in a great measure composed of, against the existence of any mode of Government on such a Basis, we have seen a serious and systematick attack, attended with the most complete success, in another Country, but in a Country at our very door. It is an attack made against the thing and against the Name. If I were to produce an example of something diametrically opposite to the composition, to the Spirit, to the Temper, to the Character, and to all the Maxims of our old and unregenerated Party, something fitted to illustrate it by the strongest opposition, I would produce—what has been done in France. I would except nothing. I would bring forward the principles; I would bring forward the means; I would bring forward the ultimate Object. They, who cry up the French Revolution, cry down the Party which you and I had so long the honour and satisfaction to belong to.—'But that party was formed on a System of Liberty.' Without question it was; and God forbid that you and I should ever belong to any party that was not built upon that Foundation. But this French Dirt-pye, this its hateful contrast, is founded upon *Slavery;* and a slavery which is not the less slavery because it operates in an inverted order. It is a Slavery the more shameful, the more humiliating, the more galling, upon that account, to every Liberal and ingenuous Mind. It is on that account, ten thousand times the more destructive to the peace, the prosperity, and the welfare, in every instance, of that undone and degraded Country in which it prevails.

My Party principles, as well as my general politicks, and my natural Sentiments, must lead me to detest the French Revolution, in the act, in the Spirit, in the consequences, and most of all in the example. I saw the Sycophants of a Court, who had, by engrossing to themselves the favours of the Sovereign, added to his distress and to the odium of his Government, take advantage of that distress and odium to subvert his authority, and imprison his person; and passing, by a natural progression, from flatterers to Traitors, convert their ingratitude into a claim to Patriotism, and become active agents in the ruin of that order, from their belonging to which, they had derived all the opulence and power of their families. Under the auspices of these base Wretches, I had seen a senseless populace employd totally to annihilate the antient

Government of their Country, under which it had grown, in extent, compactness, population, and Riches to a greatness even formidable; a Government which discoverd the Vigour of its principle, even in the many Vices and Errours, both of its own and its peoples, which were not of force enough to hinder it from producing those Effects. They began its destruction by subverting, under pretext of rights of man, the foundation of civil society itself. They trampled upon the religion of their Country and upon all religion; They Systematically gave the rein to every Crime and every Vice. They destroyd the Trade, and manufactures of their Country; They rooted up its Finances; They caused the greatest accumulation of Coin, probably ever collected amongst any people, totally to disappear as by Magick; and they filled up the void by a fraudulent compulsory Paper currency, and a coinage of the Bells from their Churches. They possessd the fairest and the most flourishing Colonies which any Nation had perhaps ever planted. These they renderd a Scene of carnage and desolation, that would excite compassion and remorse in any hearts but theirs. They possessd a vast body of Nobility and Gentry *amongst* the first in the world for Splendour, and the *very* first for disinterested services to their Country, in which I include the most disinterested and incorrupt Judicature (even by the confession of its Enemies) that ever was—These they persecuted, they hunted down like wild beasts, they expelled them from their families and their houses, and dispersed them into every Country in Europe, obliging them either to pine in fear and misery at home, or to escape into want and exile in foreign Lands. Nay they went so far in the wantonness of their insolence, abrogated their very Name and their titular description, as something horrible and offensive to the Ears of mankind.

The means, by which all this was done leaves an example in Europe never to be effaced, and which no thinking man, I imagine, can present to his Mind without consternation—that is the bribing of an immense body of soldiers taken from the lowest of the people to an universal revolt against their Officers, who were the whole body of the Country Gentlemen and the landed Interest of the Nation, to set themselves up as a kind of Democratick Military, governd and directed by their own Clubbs and committees!

When I saw all this mingled Scene of Crime, of Vice, of disorder, of folly, and of madness, receivd by very many here, not with the Horrour and disgust, which it ought to have produced, but with rapture and exultation, as some almost supernatural Benefit showred down upon the Race of mankind; and when I saw, that arrangements were publickly made for communicating to these Islands their full share of these blessings, I thought myself bound to stand out and by every means in my power to distinguish the Ideas of a sober and virtuous Liberty, (such as I thought our party had ever cultivated) from that profligate, immoral, impious, and rebellious Licence, which, through the medium of every sort of disorder and calamity, conducts to some kind or other of Tyrannick domination.

At first I had no Idea, that this base contagion had gained any considerable Ground in the Party. Those who were the first and most active in spreading it, were their mortal and declared Enemies, I mean the leading dissenters. They had long shewn themselves wholly adverse to, and unalliable with the Party. They had shewn it, as you know, signally in 1784. At the time of the Regency,[5] (which, when Prices Sermon appeard,[6] was still green and raw) they had seized the opportunity of division amongst the great, to bring forward their democratick Notions; and the object against which they chiefly directed their seditious doctrines, and the passions of the Vulgar, was your Party; and I confess they were in the right in their Choice: For they knew very well, that, as long as you were true to your principles, no considerable innovations could be made in the Country; and that this independent embodied Aristocracy would form an impenetrable fence against all their attempts to break into the constitution. When I came to Town,[7] though I had heard of Dr Prices Sermon, I had not read it. I dined the day of my arrival with our friend Dr Walker King;[8] and there, in a large and mixed Company, partly composed of Dissenters, one of that description, a most worthy man, of Learning, sense, and ingenuity, one of the oldest and best friends I had in the world,[9] and no way indisposed to us, lamented that the dissenters never could be reconciled to us, or confide in us, or hear of our being possessed of the Government of the Country, as long as we were led by Fox; this was far from his own opinion; but he declared, that it was very general in that body, who regarded him, and spoke of him on all occasions, in a manner that one would not speak of some better sort of Highwayman. Of the rest of the Party, they had a good opinion; but thought them weak men, and dupes, and the mere instruments

---

[5] The crisis produced by the temporary illness of George III which lasted from November 1788 to March 1789.

[6] The sermon of Richard Price (1723–91), entitled *A Discourse on the Love of Our Country*, had been delivered on 4 November 1789.

[7] In January 1790.

[8] (1751–1827), later (1809) Bishop of Rochester; elder brother of John King.

[9] Perhaps Dr Richard Brocklesby (1722–97).

of the person of whom they had conceived such unfounded Ideas. I was warmd; and continued, with vehemence, in a conversation which lasted some hours, to do justice to Mr Fox, and in as ample and strenuous a manner, as I thought the Duties of Friendship, and a matter that touchd the publick Interest, required. It is unnecessary to enter into further details on the subject. I went home; and late as it was, before I went to bed, I read Dr Prices sermon, and *in that very sermon,* (in which were all the shocking Sentiments, and seditious principles, which I have endeavourd to expose) the leading feature was a personal invective against Mr Fox—very much in the Style and manner, (a triffle indeed less coarse) in which my worthy friend, had represented the general conversation of the Dissenters when Mr Fox was the Subject.[10]

It was, I think, but a day or two after that conversation and reading, that I met Mr Sheridan[11] at Lord Norths.[12] He was just come to Town; and, of himself, he spoke with great resentment of the Dissenters for their Treatment of Mr Fox in other parts of the Kingdom, which, from him I learned, was as bad, particularly at Birmingham, as in London. Concerning the French revolution not a word passed between us. I felt as Mr Sheridan did; and it does not rest on my single assertion; It is known to others, that some part of the asperity with which I expressed myself against these Gentlemen arose from my resentment for their incurable, and as I thought, treacherous animosity to Mr Fox; particularly when I knew that during the whole of the preceding Summer they were solliciting his friendship and connexion. However they knew Mr Fox better than I did. The several shots they fired, to bring him to, produced their Effect. I take it for granted, that publick principles, connected with magnanimity of Sentiment, made him equally regardless of their Enmity, and of my friendship; regardless of my friendship who was weak enough to adopt his Cause with a warmth which his Wisdom and Temper condemned.

What I had thrown down on the first reading of Prices declaration and correspondence with France, was only in a few Notes, (though

---

[10] The passage in Price's sermon to which Burke refers does not mention Fox by name. It concludes: 'Oh! that I could see in men who oppose tyranny in the state, a disdain of the tyranny of low passions in themselves . . . I cannot reconcile myself to the idea of an immoral patriot, or to that separation of private from public virtue, which some think to be possible. Is it to be expected that—But I must forbear. I am afraid of applications, which many are too ready to make, and for which I should be sorry to give any just occasion' (*A Discourse on the Love of Our Country,* 3rd ed., London, 1790, pp. 42–3).

[11] Richard Brinsley Sheridan (1751–1816), M.P. for Stafford.

[12] Frederick North (1732–92), styled Lord North from 1752 to 1790 when he became 2nd Earl of Guildford.

intended for publication) when Mr Fox, to my great astonishment and sorrow, chose for his theme of panegyrick on the French revolution, the Behaviour of the French Guards.[13] I said what occurred to me on that occasion. The day ended with sentiments not very widely divided, and with unbroken friendship. I do not think that at any period of my Life I have given stronger proofs of my attachment to that Gentleman, and to his party, than I had done after that explanation, during the whole of that Session, and the next, both within and without doors.

In the mean time the opinions, principles, and practices which I thought so very mischievous were gaining ground particularly in our party. The festival of the fourteenth of July was celebrated with great Splendour for the first time.[14] There Mr Sheridan made a strong declaration of his Sentiments, which was printed. All that could be got together of the party were convened at the Shakespeare the Night before, that as the expression was, they might go in force to that anniversary. Applications were made to some of the Prince of Wales's people, that it might appear to have his R. H.'s countenance. These things and many more convinced me, that the best service which could be done to the Party, and to the Prince, was to strike a strong blow at those opinions and practices which were carrying on for their Common destruction.

As to the Prince, I thought him deeply concernd that the Ideas of an elective Crown should not prevail. He had experienced, and you had all of you fully experienced, the Peril of these doctrines on the question of the Regency. You know, that I endeavourd, as well as I could, to supply the absence of Mr Fox, during that great controversy. You cannot forget, that I supported the Princes Title to the *Regency* upon the Principle of his Hereditary Right to the Crown: and I endeavourd to explode the false Notions, drawn from what had been Stated as the Revolution Maxims, by much the same arguments which I afterwards used in my printed reflexions. I endeavourd to shew, that the Hereditary succession could not be supported, whilst a person who had the chief Interest in it, was, during a virtual interregnum, excluded from the Government; and that the direct tendency of the measure, as well as the Grounds upon which it was argued, went to make the Crown itself elective contrary (as I contended) to the fundamental Settlement made after the Revolution. I meant to do service

[13] This was in the debate on the Army Estimates on 9 February 1790.
[14] In 1790.

to the Prince, when I took this Ground on the Regency; I meant to
do him service when I took the same Ground in my publication.

Here the Conduct of the party towards themselves, towards the
Prince, and (if with these names I could mix myself) towards me, has
been such, as to have no parralel. The Prince has been persuaded not
only to look with all possible coldness on myself; but to lose no opportunity of publickly declaring his disapprobation of a Book, written
to prove, that the Crown, to which (I hope) he is to succeed, is not
elective. For this, I am in disgrace at Carleton House. The Prince, I
am told, has expressed his displeasure, that I have not mentiond in
that Book his Right to the Regency. I never was so astonishd as when
I heard this. In the first place, the persons against whom I maintaind
that controversy, had said nothing at all upon the subject of the Regency. They went much deeper. I was weak enough, to think that the
Succession to the *Crown* was a matter of other importance to his Royal
Highness than his Right to the *Regency.* At a time when the King was
in perfect health, and no question existing of arrangements to be made
on a supposition of his falling into his former, or any other grievous
malady, it would have been an imprudence of the first magnitude, and
such as would have hurt the Prince most essentially, if it were to be
supposed he had given me the smallest encouragement, to have wantonly brought on that most critical discussion. Not one of the freinds,
whom his Royal Highness 'delighteth to honour,' have thought proper
to say one word upon the subject, in Parliament, or out of Parliament.
But the Silence, which, in them is respectful and prudent, in me is
disaffection. I shall say no more on this matter. The Prince must have
been strangely deceived. He is much more personally concerned, in
all questions of *succession,* than the King, who is in *possession.* Yet his
Majesty has receivd, with every mark of a gracious Protection, my
intended service to his family. The prince has been made to believe
it to be some sort of injury to himself. Those the most in his favour
and confidence are avowed admirers of the French democracy. Even
his attorney and his Sollicitor General,[15] who by their legal knowlege,
and their eloquence as advocates, ought to be the Pillars of his succession, are even Enthusiasts publick and declared for the French revolution and its principles. These, my dear Sir, are strange Symptoms
about a future Court; and they make no small part of that fear of
impending mischief to this constitution, which grows upon me every
hour. A Prince of Wales with democratick Law Servants, with de-

[15] Thomas Erskine and Arthur Leary Piggott (1749–1819), knighted in 1806.

mocratick political friends, with democratick personal favourites! If this be not ominous to the Crown, I know not what is.

As to the party and its Interests,—in endeavouring to support the legal Hereditary succession of the Prince of Wales, I considerd their power as included in the assertion of his Right. I could not say positively how soon the Ideas they entertaind might have recommended them to the favour of the reigning King. I did not however conceive that whatever their Notions might be, the probability of their being called to the Helm was not quite so great under his present Majesty as under a Successor; and that, therefore the maintenance of the Right of that successor, against those, who as one attakd the Settlement of the Crown, and were the known declared Enemies of the Party, was, in a *political light*, the greatest Service I could do to that Party, and more particularly to Mr Fox;—infinitely more so, than to the Duke of Portland or to Lord Fitzwilliam; Because for many reasons, I am satisfied, that these two noble persons are not so ill at St James as he is; and that they (or one of them at least)[16] are not near so well at Carlton House as Mr Fox and Mr Sheridan.

According to the common principles of vulgar politicks, this would be thought a service, not ill intended, and aimed at its mark with tolerable discretion and judgment. For this the Gentlemen have thought proper to render me, obnoxious to the party, odious to the Prince, (from whose future prerogative alone my family can hope for any thing) and at least suspected by the Body of my Country. That is they have endeavourd completely and fundamentally to ruin me and mine, in all the ways, in which it is in the power of man to destroy the Interests and objects of man, whether in his friendships his fortunes, or his reputation.

But I thought there was another and a more important point of View, in which, what I had done for the publick might eminently serve the party, and that in concerns of infinitely more importance to those who compose the Major part of the body than any share of power they might obtain. I considerd the Party as the particular mark of that anarchical faction; and that the principles of the French revolution, which they preached up, would have them for its first and most grateful Victims. It is against them, as a part of an Aristocracy, that the nefarious principles of that groveling Rebellion and Tyranny, strike, and not at Monarchy, further than as it is supposed to be built upon an Aristocratick Basis. They, who would cheat the Nobility and Gentry

---

[16] Presumably the Duke of Portland.

of this Nation to their ruin, talk of that Monster of Turpitude as nothing but the subversion of Monarchy. Far from it. The French pride themselves, on the Idea however absurd, that theirs is a *Democracie Royale*. The name of the Monarchy, and of the hereditary monarchy too, they preserve in France; and they feed the person whom they call King, with such a Revenue, given to mere luxury and extravagance, totally seperated from all provision for the State, as, I believe, no people ever before dreamed of granting for such purposes. But against the Nobility and Gentry they have waged inexpiable War. There are, at this day, no fewer than ten thousand heads of respectable families driven out of France;[17] and those who remain at home, remain in depression, penury, and continual alarm for their Lives. You and I know, that (in order as I conceive still to blind and delude the Gentlemen of England) the French faction here pretended, that the persecution of the Gentlemen of France could not last; that at the next election they would recover the consideration which belonged to them, and that we should see that Country represented by its best blood, and by all its considerable property. They knew at the time, that they were setting forward an imposture. The present Assembly the first born, the Child of the Strength of their constitution, demonstrates the value of their prediction. At the very instant in which they were making it, they knew, or they knew nothing, that the two hundred and fifty Clubbs; which govern that Country had settled their Lists. They must have known, that the Gentlemen of France were not degraded and branded in order to exalt them to greater consequence than ever they possessd. Such they would have had if they were to compose the whole or even the Major part of an Assembly which rules, in every thing Legislative and executive, without any sort of Balance or control. No such thing. The assembly has not fifty men in it, I beleive I am at the outside of the Number, who are possessd of an hundred pound a year in any description of property whatsoever. About six individuals of enormous wealth, and thereby sworn Enemies to the prejudice which affixes a dignity to virtuous well born poverty, are in the Number of the fifty. The rest are, what might be supposed, men whose names never were before heard of beyond their Market Town. About four hundred of the seven are Country practitioners of

[17] This is the lowest of the estimates of the number of 'nobility and gentry' who had emigrated from France which Burke was to give in little over a year. Modern research would suggest that even Burke's lowest figure is a considerable exaggeration. Emigration did not reach its peak until after 1792, and only a small proportion of the total could be classified as 'nobility and gentry'—about 17,000 as nobility and about 11,000 as upper bourgeoisie—out of a total of 129,000 for the whole period from 1789 to 1815.

the Law, several of them, the Stewards and men of Business who managed the affairs of Gentlemen, Bishops, or Convents, who for their merits towards their former employers are now made the disposers of their Lives and fortunes.[18] The rest, no one can give an account of, except of those, who have passed to this Temple of Honour thro' the Temple of Virtue called the House of correction. When the King asked the president who the Gentlemen were who attended him with a Message, The President answerd, that he did not know one of them even by Name. The Gentlemen of this faction here, I am well aware, attribute this to the perverseness of the Gentlemen themselves, who would not offer themselves as Candidates. That they did not offer themselves is very true—because they knew, that they could appear at the primary assemblies only to be insulted at best, perhaps even murderd, as some of them have been; and many more have been threatned with assassination. What are we to think of a constitution, as a pattern from which, the whole Gentry of a country, instead of courting a share in it with eagerness and assiduity, fly from, as from a place of infection? But the Gentlemen of France are all base, vitious, servile &c &c &c. Pray Let not the Gentlemen of England be flatterd to their destruction by railing at their Neighbours. They are as good as we are to the full. If they were thus base and corrupt in their Sentiments, there is nothing they would not submit to in order to have their share in this scramble for wealth and power. But they have declined it, from sentiments of honour, and virtue, and the purest Patriotism. One turns with pity and indignation from the View of what they suffer for those Sentiments; and, I must confess, my animosity is doubled against those amongst us, who, in that situation, can rail at persons who bear such things with fortitude; even supposing, that they sufferd for principles in which they were mistaken. But neither you, nor I, nor any fair man, can believe, that an whole Nation is free from honour and real Principle; or that if these things exist in it, they are not to be found in the men the best born, and the best bred, and in those possessd of rank which raises them in their own esteem, and in the Esteem of others, and possessd of hereditary settlement in the same place, which secures with an hereditary wealth, an hereditary inspection.—That these should be all Scoundrels; and that the Virtue, honour, and publick Spirit of a Nation should be only

[18] The Legislative Assembly, containing 745 representatives, had been elected in September 1791. Members of the Constituent Assembly, its predecessor, could not be elected to it. Burke's analysis of its composition is in general terms correct. He had taken some pains to inform himself on the matter.

found in its Attornies, Pettyfoggers, Stewards of Mannours, discarded
officers of Police, shop boys, Clerks of Counting houses, and rustics
from the Plough, is a paradox, not of false ingenuity, but of Envy and
Malignity. It is an Errour not of the head but of the heart. The whole
man is turned upside down before such an inversion of all Natural
Sentiment, and all natural reason, can take place. I do not wish to
you, no, nor to those who applaud such Scenes, angry as I am with
them, Masters of that description.

Visible as it was to the world, that not the despotism of a prince,
but the condition of a Gentleman was the grand Object of attack, I
thought I should do service to a Party of Gentlemen to caution the
publick against giving Countenance to a project, calculated for the
ruin of such a party.

When such an attempt was not excused, even as well intended,
there was but one way of accounting for the conduct of Gentlemen
towards me, it is, that from my hands they are resolved not to accept
any Service—Be it so. They are rid of an Incumbrance; and I retire
to repose of body and mind, with a repose of conscience too perfect,
with regard to the Party and the publick, however I may feel myself,
as I do, faulty and deficient in other respects. The only concern I feel,
is, that I am obliged to continue an hour longer in Parliament. Whilst
I am there, except on some deep constitutional Question, I shall take
no part. Lord Fitzwilliam and the Duke of Portland shall not be seen
voting one way in the House of Lords, whilst I vote another in the
House of Commons; and any Vote of mine, by which I may add even
my Mite of contribution, towards supporting the System, or advancing
the power of the New French Whiggs, I never will give. That corruption has cast deep Roots in that Party, and they vegetate in it
(however discredited amongst the people in general) every day, with
greater and greater force. The particular Gentlemen who are seized
with that Malady (such I must consider it) have, to my thinking, so
completely changed their Minds, that one knows no longer what to
depend upon, or upon what Ground we stand. Some of them (besides
the two Leaders)[19] are indeed so high in Character, and of such Great
abilities, that their Mistake, if such it be, must make a most mischievous impression.—I know they say, that they do not want to
introduce these things here &c &c. But this is a poor Business, while
they propagate all the abstract principles, and exalt to the Stars the
realization of them at our Door. They are sublime Metaphysicians;

[19] Fox and Sheridan.

and the horrible consequences produced by their Speculations affect them not at all. They only ask whether the proposition be true? whether it produces good or evil is no part of their concern.—This long Letter my dear friend is for you; but so for you, as that you may shew it to such of our friends, who, though they cannot, in prudence, support, will not, in Justice, condemn me. My dear Sir

most faithfully
Your most obliged
and obedient humble Servant

Beconsfield Jany 31. 1792.   EDM BURKE
   late at Night.

To the DUKE OF DEVONSHIRE—11 *March* 1795

Corr. (1958), VIII, 183–85

On 11 March William Cavendish, 5th Duke of Devonshire (1748–1811), called on Burke and showed him a copy of Fitzwilliam's justification of his conduct in Ireland, addressed to Frederick Howard, 5th Earl of Carlisle (1748–1825).

My dear Lord,

I return to your Grace, the clearest, the ablest, and in all respects, the most satisfactory political Memorial that I have ever read. It has no fault but one—that it gives any answer at all to the most foolish, the most futile, and the most malignant Objections, that ever have been made to a Servant of the Crown in high and arduous Situation. I dare say, that Lord Carlisle thought of them just as I do. But, such as they are, he was perfectly right in transmitting them to his friend. Let us see how the descendant of Lord Strafford,[1] with all his abilities, and none of his faults, will get out of this Scrape.

A complete and honourable support to Lord Fitzwilliam from us all, from those of your Graces rank and consequence to my insignificance and misery, is what is due, to him, to our King, to our Country, and to ourselves. In such Company I dont know how I should intrude such a crawling existence on Earth as I am; but having by weak and inconsiderate Counsels in some small degree contributed to involve such a man as Lord Fitzwilliam, and his respectable connexions, in the most dreadful perplexity in which men of honour can be involved,

---

[1] Fitzwilliam was the great-great-great-grandson of the daughter of Thomas Wentworth, 1st Earl of Strafford (1593–1641), Viceroy of Ireland 1632–41; attainted by the Long Parliament and executed in 1641.

I feel myself absolutely bound to take my full share in all the results. Since I began my political carreer, I have been ever attached to your family.[2] God forbid, that after all the experience I have had, I should, with my Eyes broad open help to betray You into the loss of all your personal honour, and of all your importance in your Country. Whose are you?

There is one way, and but one way, out of this cursed situation. Let Lord Fitzwilliam be prevailed on to go back to Ireland. Seat him there with the honour that becomes an honest Servant of the Crown. Crush the betrayers of English Government there; and Let those who have refused compensation for their Offices, know what it is to feel punishment for their Crimes. Let us hear no more of compromises and compensations, since, instead of peace, they have producd War. Then we, or rather you, may hope to see better days. There is some difficulty in what I recommend. True. But difficulties, and far Greater difficulties, have attended the ruin of the Kings Government in the person of yours, and the Duke of Portlands friend, and his Countrys friend. If anyone thinks, that the considerate opinions of so low, undone, and degraded a Creature as I am can be of any weight your Grace may tell them this. Perhaps I dote. Very likely. But if by accident, I should not, then these are the dictates of age and experience. How can you aristocrates exist if you are not true to one another? I am an aristocrate in principle; In situation, God knows nothing less. God bless and guide you all. I am ever

My dear Lord Duke
ever faithfully
your unhappy friend
EDM BURKE

March. 11. 1795.

To EARL FITZWILLIAM—2 *September* 1796

Corr. (1958), IX, 77–80

After Pitt's 'Regicide Peace', Burke is disgusted with both him and Fox.

---

[2] In a famous passage of his *Letter to the Sheriffs of Bristol* Burke referring to his political connexions declared: 'If I have wandered out of the paths of rectitude into those of interested faction, it was in company with the Saviles, the Dowdeswells, the Wentworths, the Bentincks; with the Lenoxes, the Manchesters, the Keppels, the Saunderses; with the temperate, permanent, hereditary virtue of the whole House of Cavendish' (*Works*, Bohn, II, 37–8; Little, Brown, II, 239).

Bath Septr 2.1796.

My dearest Lord,

I feel as I ought, but I never can express as I ought to do, my Sense of your astonishing, unexampled friendship to me; I was going to say unmerited too—but as friendship is merited rather by sentiments than services, I will not lower the value of what, I beleive, you are persuaded I feel for you.

I was, and am, clearly and uniformly of opinion, that you never ought to recommend a Member for any place in which you have an influence, who will not take your general Line, both as to persons and things—and mark a decided attachment to yourself—and this, not from honour and gratitude only, but from a Strong opinion, of the Wisdom of your Views, and the rectitude of your principles. I am so strongly of that opinion, that if I were myself in the vigour of my Life, and had as much desire, or indeed ten times more desire than I have ever had, of employing myself in the Service of the publick I should not hesitate to say, that you ought not to bring me into Parliament with an Obligation to Mr Pitt hanging about my Neck. It would never indeed induce me to go along with him in the Paths, in which, unguided by all moral and all political principle, he has lately walked—But I never could with decorum, join in that personal Hostility, in which you are so well justified in bearing to him, in every thing which does not wound those opinions and feelings, which have joined you to him, and seperated you from him. Thank you for Laurence. I should never have thought of him—God, God forbid! if I thought that he was capable of making use of your Patronage, as the means of his own private advancement; or that he could, for a moment, prevaricate and shuffle where your honour was concerned. No! I am well convinced, that if he finds, but an iota, in what you propose, to be such as he cannot promise absolutely to comply with, he would rather keep out of Parliament for ever than accept it. Such is my opinion of him; on which opinion (subject to human errour) I have ever recommended him; full as much at least for your sake as for his own. I love him and trust him—but I owe much more to your Lordship, and I love you much more.

I go with your Lordship in every word almost that you have said. I really do not know how I can directly dissent from *any* part of it: But it is exceedingly to be lamented, that the course of Events, and the proceedings of all descriptions of persons have brought things to that pass, that really there are but *two men in the Country;*[1] and that

[1] Pitt and Fox.

there appears a sort of necessity, of adopting the one or the other of them, without regard to any publick principle whatsoever. This extinguishes party, as party; and even the Nation as a Nation. Every thing is forced into the shape of a mere faction, and a contest for nothing short, in substance and effect, than the sovereign authority, for one or the other of the chieftains: I was in serious hopes that the party[2] which was at last rallied under its proper standards, a little time before I left Parliament, might, either in Ministry or out of Ministry, as the publick necessities required, become some sort of Asylum for principles moral and political, and might control that disposition to factious servitude, which could see nothing, in the constitution or the country, but the power of one or two individuals: But by some mistakes in the manner of your coming into Ministry, but much more, and more decisively, by the conduct pursued towards your Lordship, not one Stone is left upon the other, in that party—nor do I see the least possible chance for its reconstruction either from the same materials or from any other. I am of opinion that these two Leaders have done irreperable mischiefs to the Country, one in one way, the other in another, and very often both of them in the same way. I think I am the furthest in the world from a personal animosity to Mr Fox: but it appears to me evident beyond all doubt and discussion, that if he is not quite out of his senses, and has any drift or determined pursuit at all, that he founds his hopes upon something that is neither in his Native Country nor in its antient constitution. His Politicks are astray, and absurd; and he cultivates and studies nothing at all at home but whatever is most wicked, unprincipled, dark, dangerous, and traiterous. His Enthusiasm in favour of Regicide France, declared over and over again during the last Session, in defiance of all the Maxims of Prudence, his evident Triumph in seeing their Arms victorious over all nations—The part he had taken with every sort of conspirators, and assassins of every description in this Kingdom—His avowed adoption of one of the worst of their Leaders, publickly on the Hustings at the late Westminster election,[3] if there was nothing else would make all pretence of doubt concerning his principles, politicks, and connexions perfectly ridiculous. It is for this reason, that I should be far from recommending to your Lordship to make his establishment in power one of the Objects of your Life. Pitt takes the part he does in

[2] The Portland Whigs, or 'Old Whigs'.
[3] John Horne Tooke (1736–1812).

this French Business, thro' shabbiness, selfishness and a mean desire to linger for some time, under the sufferance of France, in name a British Minister; but Mr Fox has that connexion abroad, and all belonging to it at home, as an Object of preference, desire, and predilection. Between them we are undone—but with this last much more certainly, much more rapidly, and in a way beyond all cure. Whoever takes up Mr Pitt only enlists with a set of low Wretches who follow him backward and forward thro' all the windings and turnings of his unhappy politicks—They who inlist with Mr Fox, know the Terms of the service, their Cause, and their Company. The Cause is avowed; and the Band, both in the Officers in the first stage of subordination, and thro' all the degrees, is regular, Systematick, firm, and consistent. God almighty direct you! This is the only point of the Condition which, I wish you not to make with any Member You bring in but to leave that matter open. Indeed I would do so as to *both* the leaders—making it a point to connect with no leader but thro' you. I beg you to recollect that all the Evils which have befallen you have been owing to your distrust of yourself, and your putting too much confidence in some Leader. You have every capacity to be a Leader yourself, which Nature and experience can give, except the disposition to it. Mr Fox would never give you up, and sacrifice you thro' weakness. There is no danger of that; But under his Guidance you may be led, with sufficient fidelity and firmness to your person, into ways foreign both to your nature and your principles.

What I say on this head is merely as to yourself. To Laurence, I shall do nothing more than to lay your generous and noble offer before him for his consideration—which, whether he thinks it safe and honourable to accept, with the only thing which he may imagine a drawback on it,—(the Case of entering into Mr Foxes party. To his person he rather leans.) I am sure he will receive the honor intended for him with becoming, that is to say, with the greatest gratitude. If he should not, I wish you to have your Eye on some person on whom you may depend as wholly and exclusively yours. Except the man we talk of— I cannot point out one to you my acquaintance in the world is so poor and limited.

As to me, whose existence, nothing but your extreme partiality could make important, The bottom of my complaint always remains the same—but with far less of pain—with no dejection and with rather a recovery than any loss of strength. But as yet I am incapable of any application. Mrs Burke, thank God, is a little better—and joins in a thousand thanks and salutations to Lady Fitzwilliam. Ever My dear Lord the most Obliged of men. Yours truly

EDM BURKE

To LORD JOHN CAVENDISH—n.d.

Corr. (1958), IX, 447–49

It is impossible to assign this letter to any year. The probability is that the draft was written after Lord John Cavendish's defeat in 1784 and before the quarrel between Burke and Fox in 1791. There is no evidence that it was completed.

My Lord,

I address my thoughts upon a Subject which has long engaged my Mind and deeply affected it, to your Lordship; because I know you. I am sure that if I have conceivd an Esteem for your Character it is not because I have seen it at a distance, have seen you placed after long meditation in a single chosen light with spikes between you and the Crowd[1] enlarged by the deceptions of Art above the human form, and painted out for Theatrical shew and Vulgar admiration. I have walked all round you and have seen you at all hours and in all humours. And I who have brought my Mind so exclusively to veneration for the divine perfections, that I have no admiration left for those of men beyond my understanding of them; am yet very willing to recognize and honour Virtue so far as I am able [to] comprehend it. I should be ashamed to look for it in Statues and on Shelves and to neglect it in Life. But if I see the same great qualities in John or Charles[2] I trust that I am disposed to give them as much Credit, and to love them full as well, as when I read of them in a Cato or a Timoleon. The heart is pinched up and contracted by the very studies which ought to have enlarged it, if we keep all our praise for the Triumphant and Glorified Virtues and all ones uneasy suspicions, and doubts, and criticisms and exceptions for the companions of our Warfare. A mind that is temperd as it ought, or aims to come to the Temper it ought to have, will

[1] A common feature of eighteenth-century theatres, to protect the actors against rioters in the audience.
[2] Lord John or Charles Fox.

measure out its just proportion of Confidence and Esteem for a Man of invariable rectitude of Principle, steadiness in friendship, moderation in Temper, and a perfect freedom from all Ambition duplicity, and revenge, though they see the owners of these inestimable qualities in the Tavern and on the Pavement, as well as in the Senate, or with what appears more decency than solemnity even there; He will put his confidence in them though they should appear in a figure not lofty nor much imposing. Though his address should at first be cold dry and reserved and without any thing at all of advance or Courtship in it. Far from taking away his value every thing makes simple virtue accessible and familiar and companionable makes its use more frequent, and its reality a great deal less doubtful. Neither I apprehend is the value of great qualities taken away by the defects or errors that are most nearly related to them. And men of moderation will sometimes [be] defective in vigour. A simplicity and a Want of Ambition does something detract from the Splendour of great qualities. Minds (and these are the best minds) which are more fearful of reproach than passionate for glory, will want that extemporaneous promptitude and that decisive stroke which is often so absolutely necessary in great Affairs. And I have often thought that it is one of the main advantages in the social endeavours of publick men acting by joint principle, consent and council, that they produce opposite Virtues and faults whilst they honestly ⟨stick together⟩ and bear one anothers Burthens as men and Christians ought and temper one another, and make an excellent Whole out of defective parts.[3] It is fit that our social condition should be our best. The knowledge of the world will operate differently according to our Temper. Almost every body in the sanguine season of youth, looks for more perfection in the world than he is likely to find. But a good temperd man, that is to say a man of a wise constitution, will be pleased to find the Beneficial effects of human faults whereas the other grows peevish at finding what he will as certainly find the ill consequence attending the most undoubted Virtues. I believe we shall do every thing something the better for putting ourselves in as good a humour as possible when we set about it.

[3] In the margin at this point Burke has written: 'The Individual is to be sure the less perfect for this; and those who love to whine over human infirmity rather than to releive it will think it a subject of great lamentation; Yet many a thing which single is mischievous, in arrangement is useful. Let this man [act] with another, and his very defect will be of service. You know my opinions upon insulated morality and politicks'.

To DUDLEY LONG NORTH—28 *December* 1796

Corr. (1958), IX, 213–214

Dudley Long North (1748–1829), a Foxite Whig M.P. who had been one of the Managers of the Impeachment of Warren Hastings, was an old friend of Burke.

My dear Sir,

The late melancholy event of Lord John Cavendish's death, as soon as it came to my knowledge, made the trifling strain in which I wrote to you, appear to me as a sort of impiety, at the moment when one of the oldest and best friends I ever had, or that our common Country ever possess'd was perhaps in his last Agony—I was then totally ignorant of that Circumstance, and without the least apprehension of any thing like it: The truth is, that it affected me more than I thought I could be affected with any thing, long as I have been familiar with Death at home, and having reason daily to expect my own dissolution. Lord John appear'd so very well, and so very strong, far beyond what could be look'd to from his age, that his Departure came on me like a Thunderstroke; I am told, that it was to your goodnatur'd Visit to me, and to your having let him know, that I was in Town for a day or two, and broken and afflicted as I was, I should be happy to see my old friends, I owe the solid comfort I feel in having embrac'd him for the last time, and of finding in him, so near our last hours, marks of sympathy, of cordiality, and of confidence, at least equal to any I had receiv'd from him at any period since I first had the happiness of being acquainted with him.

There is lost to the world, in every thing but the example of his life the fairest mind that perhaps ever inform'd a human body. A mind totally free from every Vice, and fill'd with Virtues of all kinds, and in each kind of no common rank or form; benevolent, friendly, generous, disinterested, unambitious almost to a fault; Tho' cold in his exterior, he was inwardly quick and full of feeling, and tho' reserv'd from modesty, from dignity, from family temperament and not from design, he was an entire stranger to every thing false and counterfiet: so great an Enemy to all dissimulation active or passive, and indeed even to a fair and just ostentation, that some of his Virtues, obscur'd by his other Virtues, wanted something of that burnish and lustre which those who know how to assay the solidity and fineness of the metal wish'd them to have. It were to be wish'd that he had had more of that Vanity of which we who acted on the same stage had enough and to spare. I have known very few men of better natural Parts, and none more perfected by every species of elegant and usefull erudition. He served the publick often out of Office, sometimes in it, with Fidelity, and diligence, and when the occasion call'd for it, with a manly resolution. At length when he was overborne by the Torrent, he retir'd from a world that certainly was not worthy of him. He was of a character that seems as if it were peculiar to this Country. He was exactly what we conceive an English Nobleman of the old Stamp, and one born in better times, or what in our fond fancies we imagine such men to have been and in such times.

As to my connexion with him, I began my weak career of publick Business under his Auspices.[1] I was of too free a spirit not to have opinions of my own; and He was too generous to think the worse of me on that account. Differing with him sometimes about measures, I think we never had any material difference in principle, no not upon one point. As with him I began my Course, so with him most certainly I would have retir'd, If the Business in which you and I were so long engag'd had not appear'd to me to be a solemn and indispensible engagement[2] from which no human consideration could discharge me untill redress was obtain'd for a suffering people, or that in the judgement of all kinds nothing further could be done. When the latter happened I lost not one moment to execute my purpose. As to the Nation, God of his mercy grant they may not suffer the penalties of the greatest and most shamefull Crime, that ever was committed, by any people: Excuse me! talking of our departed friend, my Pen has run on—I now seldom write but dictate what I have to say to any absent friend. Be assur'd that the consolation you have procured me in the last interview with Lord John Cavendish is an obligation very near my heart, I owe you many; but this is the greatest. I am with very cordial regard

My dear Sir

your most faithfull

and obedient humble Servant

December 28 1796   E. BURKE

[1] It was Lord John Cavendish who first mentioned Burke's name to Lord Rockingham.

[2] Burke seriously considered retirement in 1782–3, but once he had begun his pursuit of 'Indian delinquency' felt obliged to remain in the House of Commons until the conclusion of his work on the Hastings Trial.

JANE BURKE *to* CHARLES JAMES FOX [*ante*—9 *July* 1797]

Corr. (1958), IX, 372–73

At some time close to Burke's death, Fox made an attempt to arrange a last reconciliatory meeting with him. Mrs Burke returned the following reply.

Mrs. Burke presents her compliments to Mr Fox, and thanks him for his obliging inquiries. Mrs Burke communicated his letter to Mr Burke, and, by his desire, has to inform Mr Fox that it has cost Mr Burke the most heart-felt pain to obey the stern voice of his duty in rending asunder a long friendship, but that he deemed this sacrifice necessary; that his principles remained the same; and that in whatever of life yet remained to him, he conceives that he must live for others and not for himself. Mr Burke is convinced that the principles which he has endeavoured to maintain are necessary to the welfare and dignity of his country, and that these principles can be enforced only by the general persuasion of his sincerity. For herself, Mrs Burke has again to express her gratitude to Mr Fox for his inquiries.

INDEX